Volume Two

JOHN 8:44

EXPOSING THE SONS OF SATAN

"YOU HAVE MADE MY HOUSE A DEN OF THEIVES"

Collected Essays of JOE CORTINA

VOLUME 1 OF 3

Ye are of your father the devil, and the lusts of your father ye will do. He was a murderer from the beginning, and abode not in the truth, because there is no truth in him. When he speaketh a lie, he speaketh of his own: for he is a liar, and the father of it. – **John 8:44**

Woe unto you, scribes and Pharisees, hypocrites! For ye travel sea and land to make one convert, and when he is made, ye make him twice as much a son of hell than yourselves. – **Matthew 23:15**

About the Author

Joe Cortina is a retired Florida businessman who has done substantial world traveling – some purely as a 'tourist'; and some in areas - shall we say - 'nothing to do with vacationing'. He has served as a Green Beret, Special Operations Officer, Intelligence Investigator, IBM representative and Honeywell scientist.

Cortina's intelligence work covers a span of 15 years, some of it overseas in Central America, and also in the Middle-East. In later years he worked as President of his own manufacturing company. Cortina describes his political posture is 'conservative' and his religious values as Christian.

Exposing lies and revealing the truth was what he did professionally for a long time. Cortina hunted REAL terrorists in jungles with Salvadorian Rangers and Marines – so he is no stranger to dangerous environments and is familiar with basic protocols of civilized conduct regarding civilians and the military – something which Cortina insists that the Israelis do not consider applicable to them.

Says Cortina of his experience in Israel:

"I was invited to Israel by a former military comrade who attained a substantial rank and subsequently ended up as the ranking military attaché' from our govt., to the Israeli military (IDF). I went places and saw things only a hand full of 'private sector' Americans will EVER experience. My 'specially authorized' trips included Gaza City, Hebron and areas of militarily protected Israeli 'settlements'. I can't stress this enough. What I write about Israel and the Jewish influence over America and Europe is but a tear in a sea of misery that I have witnessed."

Posing with Arab friends in the Upper Nile / Pools of blood of dead Palestinian children – witnessed firsthand!

As to his motivation for collecting his essays and putting them in book form, Cortina adds:

"I have two sons and 2 granddaughters who are the reason for my dedication to expose the threats to the freedoms I hope to see them enjoy as I did many decades ago when America was still a Christian-based sovereign nation free of Zionist influence."

To paraphrase a well-known beer commercial, Cortina is - if not "the most interesting man alive" – certainly a man who has seen and accomplished much. Cortina's "in-your-face" style may come as a shock to some – but it's a much need shock. Dismiss his warnings at your own peril; but do understand that he knows of what he speaks.

Green Beret Days / the unit which Cortina commanded / Retired and enjoying his Harley!

The handsome young Lt. Cortina / Checking the oil on his crash-landed plane / Carrying his good friend Peron the Black Panther on his back

FOREWORD

By Mark Glenn

A NOT SO AVERAGE JOE

Any fan of American history--and particularly that period dealing with America's revolution against Great Britain--can appreciate the very powerful 'ambush' scene appearing in the 2000 blockbuster film *The Patriot* starring Mel Gibson. Gibson, playing the role of Benjamin Martin (whose fictional character was based on the real-life historical figure Francis Marion, known as the 'Swamp Fox' for the guerilla tactics he employed against the British) has just had one son killed by the British and another taken away to be hanged as a spy. Having just suffered one tragedy and about to suffer another, he wastes no time, but rather gathers up muskets, powder and ball, and along with his two young sons, runs out to greet the British with the military skills he acquired while fighting during the previous French and Indian War.

Finding a good spot to lay in wait for the British, he hands a musket to each of his two young sons and instructs them what they are to do--*'Start with the officers and work your way down'*. Then, reminding them about the importance of not wasting precious time and ammo as a result sloppy shooting, asks them *'What did I tell you fellas about shooting?'* to which both boys respond in near-unison--*'aim small, miss small'*.

Despite the fact that *Patriot* was the product of Hollywood--in effect a sewer cranking out mental garbage 25 out of 24 hours in a day--nevertheless there are important lessons to be be taken from this particular scene, and especially for those beginning to see that the fruits of 1776--whereby America became a free nation--have in effect been erased from history. True, for a time--a very brief time--Americans did free themselves from the shackles of a hostile, foreign power, but in truth this was to be but a brief honeymoon, for shortly thereafter, these same Americans whose forefathers sacrificed blood, sweat and tears in winning their liberation from a far-away parasite dedicated to their destruction then willingly surrendered themselves to something infinitely more wicked and deadly to life, liberty, and the pursuit of happiness, not the British this time, but rather the Yiddish.

The notion that America is owned lock, stock and barrel by organized Jewish interests is as much a wild-eyed conspiracy theory as saying that rice is served in Chinese restaurants. So much has America become the plaything of La Kosher Nostra that even war criminals such as Ariel Sharon can now boast openly--indeed, as he did years ago--that *'We, the Jews, control America'*. So pervasive and overwhelmingly present is this control that it no longer functions as just some inconsequential spice flavoring the stew of American politics and culture, but rather has become the stew itself. It is in the air we breathe, the water we drink, even in our toothpaste.

The real tragedy of it all however is that so few Americans are aware of it even in the least. Like 'drugged cockroaches' (the derogatory term used by former Israeli intelligence operative Rafael Eitan in describing those Arabs whose lives have now been completely overtaken by Palestine's Jewish invaders/marauders) Americans today flit from senseless thought to senseless thought, engaging and entertaining themselves with meaningless mental meanderings all the while the vampire continues draining the life-sustaining blood of the nation to perilously low levels.

Tragically, this condition afflicting the average American, whereby playthings--mental as well as material--have become the nucleus around which all attention orbits while criminals ransack the national home is not something limited to just the average Joe even those who at least make the pretenses of awareness concerning the existence of this parasite have now been bitten and infected to a large extent. Understanding the importance of decapitation and of leaving nothing to chance and having taken control of the American mind through the mainstream media, now organized Jewish interests have as well wormed their way into 'the movement', introducing and installing various ideological viruses onto the group's mental hard drive so as to make any kind of coherent, rational counterattack against them virtually impossible. Rather than focusing on the target and employing the skills discussed at the beginning of this essay, i.e. '*starting with the officers*' and of *'aiming small, missing small'*, the presumptive forces making up 'the movement' prefer instead to expend their energies and scant resources on all sorts of wasteful, counterproductive activities that at day's end produce only defeat after defeat, after which time it all becomes the topic of snickering, sneering ridicule by the enemy as he begins plotting his next moves and then the cycle begins anew.

Probably the most counterproductive behavior in this regard is the 'good Jew' meme that is mindlessly elevated and promoted in discussion after discussion and at every opportunity. In this fashion, Jews--being both the products and proponents of the violent, rapacious cult-mentality known as Judaism--are differentiated between 'good' and 'bad' based solely on what their position viz a viz Israel happens to be. "Good' Jews like those from the group Neturei Karta, clad in black with their long, unsightly, unkempt beards holding up signs protesting against 'the Jewish State' and weeping buckets of crocodile-tears over Zionism's victims are praised while 'bad Jews' such as Benjamin Netanyahu are excoriated.

What gets lost in the discussion of course is the root cause of the problem itself, which is Judaism, a universally toxic force incapable of producing anything good and as evidenced by 6,000 years of written history. Those whose interests lie in relegating all discussion to the modern day phenomenon of 'Zionism' fail to mention that 'the Jewish problem' did not begin in 1948, the year that Israel celebrates her re-conquest of the Holy Land. Every ancient civilization, whether it is Egypt, Greece, Rome, Persia, etc, has faced the exact same problems mankind is facing now as a result of the toxic, radioactive element --poetically referred to as *Jtonium 666*--in the affairs of Gentile peoples, the only difference being that in the case of those aforementioned ancient civilizations, the carriers of this deadly disease did not have nuclear weapons with which to annihilate all life on earth.

And it is in this context then why it is of vital importance--now more than at any other time in human history--that accurate focus and attention be paid to these affairs. For those making up 'the movement', wasting time on circular, profitless, meaningless mental meanderings that feature so prominently in public discussions these days, whether it be chemtrails, fluoride, vaccines or--more importantly, the infamous *'Zionism is bad but Judaism is good'* theme, must be made to understand that every shot wasted is a wasted shot never to be replaced, that time is running out, and soon, if the tide of battle is not turned, truly everything will be lost--irretrievably.

That is why strong, competent leadership is not just some mere luxury. Just as battles are neither won nor lost because of bad armies but rather because of bad generals, likewise victory begins at the top and works its way downward. Great men with great ideas arise during times of great desperation; and now is no different. During the time of America's fight to free herself from the shackles of a parasitic British Empire, the fighting spirit of the average Joe was certainly there but severely wanting in terms of discipline and focus. The American militia--too haphazard in its methods to effectively engage with well-trained British regulars--racked up loss after loss, leading to weakened morale which in itself threatened the disintegration of what could at that time be referred to as 'the movement'.

It was not mere chance nor a bolt out of the blue that turned the tide for the great experiment in American independence, but rather the influence of a Prussian drill sergeant--Baron Von Steuben. Imposing upon American irregulars the same discipline and training that made the British the superior force that they were resulted in what became the Continental Army and which later produced the surrender of Lord Cornwallis to General George Washington at Yorktown in October, 1781.

By the grace of God, America has its Von Steubens today, men who understand the need for discipline & focus and who have no patience for bad habits within the ranks...Men who grasp that this present struggle is not just some game, pastime, or distraction, but rather a fight to the death where '2nd place' equals defeat and the only consolation prize awarded to the loser is enslavement, war, and the death of the nation. It is just such men--oftentimes your 'average Joe'--who step forward during desperate times such as now and who make it their personal mission to use the skills and talents God gave them in the service of their fellow man, and oftentimes by rooting out the sloppy shooting and shoddy soldiery that in the end only aids the enemy.

The following book features the thoughts and writings of just such a man. A former officer in one of America's most elite fighting forces--the Green Berets--who then went on to act in both diplomatic and intelligence capacities in various hotspots *(including the Middle East)* Joe Cortina became one of my personal heroes many years ago after hearing him for the first time being interviewed on a radio program. Tasting with my ears and digesting with my mind what he had to say with the authority that comes both from his time as an officer in the Green Berets and from his personal time spent in the belly of the beast--Israel--I knew in an instant that I was not listening to just some 'average Joe' who imagines himself more important and knowledgeable than he really is *(and which seems to predominate in this 'movement' today)* but rather to a warrior from another time, a better time, when good was good, evil was evil, and never the twain did meet.

Some will undoubtedly be shocked back into reality because of what they're about to read. Yes, hearing first-hand stories about little Palestinian children living in bombed out homes, being deliberately gunned down like dogs by vicious carnivores wearing the uniform of the IDF can and indeed will be unsettling. Hearing first-hand accounts of Brooklyn-born Jews moving to Israel and donning the uniform of a foreign country while mocking the notion of ever wearing the uniform of the country of their birth, America, can and indeed will be hard on the eyes and on the mind.

But it is something that needs to take place if any chance exists of saving America and the world from a certain fate that is so horrible in its implications that even the creative genius of horror novelist Stephen King would have a difficult time envisioning it.

The main weapon our enemy utilizes with devastating success against us is his ability to deceive and distort, a fact made clear in the very words now enshrined in the motto of Israel's assassination agency Mossad--*'By way of deception, we shall make war'.*

And the only antidote for deception and distortion is truth and clarity, and for those calling themselves Christians who doubt that this is indeed the case, perhaps they should consider the words of their Commander-in-Chief, Jesus Christ, who truly 'walked the walk' and 'paid his dues' when it came to doing battle against the Jewish mafia of His own day--

'You shall know the truth, and the truth shall at you free.'

Equally important however were the marching orders Christ issued to His troops before sending them out onto the battlefield against this Judaic enemy--*'Speak plainly...Let your yes be yes and your no be no, for everything else is of the devil'.*

Indeed, between the front and back covers of this very book is some very salty, stringent truth, and exactly as the doctor ordered. Not artificially sweetened--like so much in this world today, so as to take out the necessarily-bitter medicine contained therein. Joe Cortina, a not-so-average Joe who long ago decided that his yes would be yes and his no would be no, understands the nature and severity of the war for survival taking place right now and understands that the battle for the hearts and minds of man will be won not by luck but rather by skilled intellectual combat and that indeed, if man stands a snowball's chance in hell of victory, all those on the battlefield must train their sights on the truth, the whole truth, and nothing but the truth so help them God. He understands that rather than making noise simply for the sake of making noise, instead this people's army of citizen soldiers must not simply be mere trigger-pullers, but sharpshooters, engaging the enemy in a systematic, methodical manner by employing the same shooting skills which the character Benjamin Martin famously passed along to his sons in the film *The Patriot*--

'...Aim small, miss small...'

Mark Glenn

TABLE OF CONTENTS

INTRODUCTION 15

DECEMBER 2009

KNOW THE DOMESTIC ENEMIES OF AMERICA 20

THE REAL JESUS, ACCORDING TO 'DEMONICUS 24

ZIONISTS BAD – JEWS GOOD? WRONG! WRONG! WRONG! 27

AN OPEN LETTER TO WAR CRIMINAL, COL. SAM WHITEHURST 29

AMERIKAN WAR CRIMES WEEKLY –AMERIKA'S NEWEST DIGEST 32

FEBRUARY, 2010

ISRAEL – MY EXPERIENCES THERE IN THE SUMMER OF 1989 38

MIKE HUCKABEE – THE USEFUL IDIOT HYPOCRITE HUCKSTER 45

MARCH, 2010

NATIONAL JEWISH HISTORY MONTH 50

IGNORANCE IN AMERICA – A DISGRACEFUL EPIDEMIC 54

AN OPEN LETTER TO THE MILITARY KILLERS OF LITTLE CHILDREN 60

APRIL, 2010

SILENCE OF THE LAMBS AND THE BOVINE STUPIDITY OF THE GOY 63

THE NATIONAL CONSTITUTION CENTER – PATRIOTIC SHRINE? OR MORE ZIONIST MOCKERY 67

MAY, 2010

COMMUNISM DEAD IN THE USSR BUT ALIVE AND WELL IN THE USA 75

"ARMY STRONG"? OR A STRONG ARMY OF CRIMINALS 78

"BLESSED ARE THE PEACEMAKERS - THE CHILDREN OF GOD" 80

AN EX-GREEN BERET REMEMBERS MEMORIAL DAY 2010 **85**

JUNE, 2010

IT WASN'T THE ARABS, STUPID! IT WAS THE JEWS! (PART 1) **88**

IT WASN'T THE ARABS, STUPID! IT WAS THE JEWS! (PART 2) **91**

IT WASN'T THE ARABS, STUPID! IT WAS THE JEWS! (PART 3) **97**

NEWSFLASH! ISRAEL HAS BEEN WIPED OFF THE FACE OF THE EARTH **100**

WHY JEWS ARE DANGEROUS TO THE WELL-BEING OF NON-JEWS (PART 1) **103**

WHY JEWS ARE DANGEROUS TO THE WELL-BEING OF NON-JEWS (PART 2) **107**

WHY JEWS ARE DANGEROUS TO THE WELL-BEING OF NON-JEWS (PART 3) **112**

AN OPEN LETTER TO JEW LIAR, FRAUD – JEFF GREENE **115**

AN OPEN LETTER OF ALL MEN OF GOOD WILL OF ALL NATIONS **118**

WHY ARE AMERICAN CHRISTIANS ASHAMED TO SPEAK THE WORD OF GOD REGARDING THE JEWS? **120**

JULY, 2010

OFFENSIVE AMERICAN TV ADS **127**

OPEN LETTER TO RACIST HATE/WAR MONGER – DEVVY KIDD **130**

I AM ISRAHELL **132**

WALT DISNEY vs THE JEWS- FROM THE CDL REPORT, 1999 **136**

OPEN LETTER TO PATRIOTS RESISTING JEW WAR EVIL **149**

'THE 4th OF JULY' – A MEANINGLESS AND SHALLOW HYPOCRISY **150**

A NEW MORE GODLY WAY TO CELEBRATE INDEPENDENCE DAY **152**

AUGUST, 2010

AMERICAN BAPT-DUH ZIONISTS – THE OTHER "SONS OF THE DEVIL" **154**

THE MATRIX CRUCIBLE – REDUX OR – WHAT THE DEMOCRATS BELIEVE, DON'TBELIEVE, AND SUPPORT (by a former Democrat) *157*

"YE ARE OF YOUR FATHER, THE DEVIL"–JESUS TO THE JEWS JOHN-8-44 (PART 1) *165*

"YE ARE OF YOUR FATHER, THE DEVIL"– JOHN-8-44 (PART 2) *166*

SEPTEMBER, 2010

9-11 — LEST WE FORGET! *168*

DECEMBER, 2010

"IT'S NOT A 'HOLIDAY' – STUPID – IT'S A HOLY DAY!" OR – HOW THE JEWS STOLE CHRISTMAS – PART 1 *170*

"IT'S NOT A 'HOLIDAY' – STUPID – IT'S A HOLY DAY!" OR – HOW THE JEWS STOLE CHRISTMAS – PART 2 *173*

JANUARY, 2011

THE DIFFERENCE BETWEEN DEMOCRATS AND HUMANS *178*

WHY CELEBRATE MARTIN LUCIFER KING JR. DAY? AN ENDLESS DISGRACE TO ALL DECENT AMERICANS - LOSE IT! *180*

FEBRUARY, 2011

BRENDON LEE O'CONNELL - AUSTRALIAN CHRISTIAN HERO *187*

OCTOBER, 2011

THE BEST PLAN TO TAKE BACK OUR COUNTRY *197*

JANUARY, 2012

THE WORLD 100 YEARS AFTER JEWS - 'FINAL EPISODE' - A NEW AMERICA *206*

IN DEFENSE OF MEL GIBSON *212*

OPEN LETTER TO WAR CRIMINAL, CAPTAIN BRUCE H. LINDSEY *213*

THE 'JEWISH GOD'- CRUEL MEAN SADISTIC-MORE LIKE THE DEVIL THAN JESUS *218*

THE US ARMY TODAY-THE ULTIMATE EVIL-ONE NATION UNDER ISRAHELL! *225*

FEBRUARY, 2012

'LARRY – THE ASSHOLE GUY' –RANCID PIECE OF HUMAN GARBAGE *229*

MARCH, 2012

AMERIKA THE GREEDY–AMERIKA THE NEEDY–AMERIKA THE CORRUPT–AMERIKA THE CRUDE *231*

DEPLETED URANIUM WEAPONS (DU) – THE REAL 'DIRTY BOMBS' *235*

POP QUIZ ON JEW BEAUTY QUEENS *240*

OPEN LETTER TO AMERICANS–HOWEVER FEW IN NUMBER–WHO CAN STILL HANDLE THE TRUTH *241*

APRIL, 2012

A JEW IS A JEW IS A JEW AND CAN ALWAYS BE TRUSTED TO BE UNTRUSTWORTHY – JOHN -8-44 *245*

OUR GODLESS MILITARY – SINKING EVEN LOWER INTO THE ABYSS OF THE DAMNED *248*

JULY, 2012

OPEN LETTER TO ALL TRUE FREEDOM FIGHTERS AGAINST THE EVIL WICKED JEWS *252*

A QUIZ FOR EVERY TRUE AMERICAN PATRIOT *257*

YOU MIGHT BE A TRUE, INFORMED 'WALK THE WALK' AMERICAN FATHER – VETERAN – PATRIOT IF… *262*

AUGUST, 2012

A JEW WALKS INTO A BARBER SHOP AND SAYS… *265*

KNOWLEDGE IS A COLLECTION OF FACTS- WISDOM IS THE MORAL USE OF KNOWLEDGE 268

WHY DO AMERICANS, ONCE CHRISTIAN, WORSHIP WAR CRIMINALS LIKE CHRIS KYLE 271

OPEN LETTER TO WAR CRIMINAL CHRIS KYLE –WORLD'S WORST HUMAN BEING 281

OPEN LETTER TO LIFE SITE NEW – CULTURE OF DEATH 284

SEPTEMBER, 2012

DEMOCRAT PARTY: TODAY'S SCUM MAGNET FOR THE DREGS OF SOCIETY 287

USA: LAND OF FALSE PROPHETS, JEW LOVERS, CHRIST-MOCKERS, LIARS AND WARMONGERS 296

OBAMA: A REAL LIFE DEMONIC MONSTER 299

LOOK INSIDE THE DEPRAVED MINDS OF THE VILEST, MOST EVIL AND WICKED CREATURES ON EARTH 301

FULL TEXT: BIN LADEN'S 'LETTER TO AMERICA' 303

A LETTER TO AMERICA – BY AN AMERICAN – CENSORED BY AMERICAN NEWS MEDIA – WHOSE JEW MASTERS FEAR THE TRUTH 315

IGNORANCE BREEDS FEAR – FEAR BREEDS HATE – HATE BREEDS VIOLENCE. EDUCATION BREEDS CONFIDENCE – CONFIDENCE BREEDS HOPE – HOPE BREEDS PEACE 319

OCTOBER, 2012

WHAT IS TERRORISM? WHO ARE TERRORISTS? 324

THE ACLU: TROJAN HORSE OF THE JEW 333

A JEW DENYING HIS LIES IS LIKE A SKUNK USING 'BAN' 349

WHERE I STAND ON TRUTH 351

AND TO THE REPUBLIC FOR WHICH IT ONCE STOOD 359

REQUIEM FOR A DEGENERATE NATION – THE FINAL MORAL ROTING AND DEMISE OF THE STUPID WEST 366

IMAGINE THE USA WITHOUT JEWS TO CAUSE US BLUES 374

SELF DAMNATION FROM THE MOUTHS OF JEWS THEMSELVES 384

IDF JEWS – TERRORISTS, BULLIES, PERVERTS AND COWARDS 388

SATANIC GODLESS JEWS BRUTALIZE CHRISTIANS IN THE HOLY LAND 394

CUNNING JEWS DEMONIZE THEIR VICTIMS AND ABSOLVE THEMSELVES 397

JOHN HAGEE – ONE OF THE MOST EVIL PEOPLE IN AMERICA 403

NOVEMBER, 2012

AMC MAKES TRASH FOR YOU – CREATED BY THE GREEDY JEW 407

JEW BUCKS / STARBUCKS SUPPORTS THE KILLING OF INNOCENT CHILDREN 410

INTRODUCTION

First of all – if you are reading this – it means that you are interested enough in the TRUTH to try to find it. That is a good step in the right direction. If you take the time to read what I have spent the last several years of my life attempting to do – and that is – to expose by irrefutable well documented TRUTHS – both historic and current – of the greatest evil on earth since the beginning of recorded history. My work is a compendium of events and facts exposing the demon beings we have come to know as the Jews. If the reader is an atheist or a person who believes that our Lord was either non-existent - then the painstakingly assembled facts based upon my personal travels and life experiences as well as universally accepted facts will fall on deaf ears and blind eyes. However – if the reader is an intellectually honest person with an open mind – a good heart and a thirst for TRUTH – I promise that you will find the wisdom contained here one of the most valuable REWARDING collection of documents you have ever read.

Unless you are an absolute fool – you are aware at least to some degree of that fact our country is on the verge of total economic and moral collapse as we RACE to our destiny on the trash heap of history! The situation we find ourselves in was entirely preventable and we have the map-handbook – guide to guide us on the right path of goodness righteousness decency honor wisdom peace and the reputation envisioned by our Founding Fathers which would have made us a 'light Among Nations' – loved and respected by the rest of the world. To those of you who are Christian - you have the Christian Bible for your moral compass. I speak of the New Testament only – and NOT the horrid jew Torah of Moses – filled with hate murder deceit slavery pedophilia and other horrors. No innocent young child should ever have to be exposed to the sanguinary jew mentality of this antipathy of the teachings of Christ.

Instead – we have so involved with our own petty lusts for self- gratification – material and carnal pleasure and shallow diversions that we are now neither 'sovereign' nor 'free' - but simply a puppet owned and servile to a race of demons whose legacy has been the moral and economic destruction of nation after nation. I speak of creatures so universally evil that they have been damned by our Lord – 'God the Son – and God the Father – in the Christian Bible that we know as the NEW Testament – many, many times over. Jews have also been exposed as universally evil by hundreds of the world most prominent figures from Popes to Presidents to playwrights. The list would fill a book.

All you need do is to spend just ONE evening watching our Jew-owned financed operated staffed 'Talmud-Vision' video entertainment and observe the current level of filth - degeneracy homosexual glorification – mockery of the Sacrament of Marriage – promotion of graphic violence – elevation of the dregs of society to be accepted as 'equals' - legitimacy of the murder of children – the acceptance of pornography as normal American entertainment – the constant portrayal of Christians as losers – the depiction of war and WAR CRIMINALS as our children's newest role models – the carefully promoted racist hatred of entire races of people - the denigration of ALL Christian holy days as secular shallow carnival mentality party and playtime themes - the constant exposure of our innocent children to vile profane language – children's shows that have lost all decorum as we see our daughters portrayed looking like whores and our sons looking like thugs and gang bangers - the promotion of serial wars against innocent nations as fabricated enemies and dozens more pure evil agendas – ALL created by jews to destroy any remaining qualities of decency and compassion we might have had.

Twenty centuries ago the Roman Senate kept the people placated and ignorant of the rot and decay in their own government by offering free violent spectacular 'entertainment' in the Coliseum. The fools bought the trick and lost their Roman empire because of apathy ignorance and indifference. Today it is the same ploy. Our street mob mentality population literally WORSHIPS the thug idiot morons of the NFL and know every detail of every game – but of course know NOTHING of our own history or what freedoms our jew run government destroy – one by one. Same game – only the names have changed. Our totally and PURPOSEFULLY failed jew-run public educational system has guaranteed a new generation of idiots imbeciles and morons to insure our collective failure by CRIMINAL ignorance.

Over twenty five years ago I had the opportunity to be exposed to the TRUE nature of the jews in IsraHELL as an 'insider' and witness these demons without their 'masks'. I saw things and went to places where NO tourist is ever allowed. As a soldier I was no stranger to certain aspects of death and destruction and as a seasoned world traveler with visits to over thirty nations – I was also familiar with many different cultures. My experience with the CIA inside Gaza (Palestine) changed my life forever. A book that used to be required reading for Special Forces officers was THE ART OF WAR by Sun Tzu. One of the BASIC premises was simply to KNOW who the enemy was. I will give you a hint. The Arab people are NOT the enemy.

However – NOTHING could have prepared me for the 'in your face' education I experienced in this horrid place. IsraHELL was not only the most 'unholy' environment I have ever observed – but As I came to realize – it was the home of the 'children of Satan' - LITERALLY! Before I had traveled to the Mid-East – I had a preconceived notion of jews that was less than good (from years and years of experiences with their sleaze and deceit at universities – in business and social events) but I do remember that in my mind I expected Israelis to be different from the slime I experienced in the States. They were different than the disgusting jews I knew at home. They were WORSE - to a level that I could not imagine had I not witnessed so many horrid putrid shocking filthy acts of terrorism - blasphemy – crime – sadism and pure demonic evil – like nothing I had seen or heard with my experiences with terrorists in Nicaragua and El Salvador.

The jew is the master of deceit – a creature with NO compassion – NO morals – NO ethics. He lies with the ease of a criminal. His capacity for cruelty rivals the horrors of the crimes committed by the Soviet Union against the Christians – but then of course – virtually ALL of the Communist leadership were jews and the Marxism/Communism they so embraced was their 'religion'! The jew leads the world in the dark evils of pornography – Infanticide – treason – war crimes – mass murder of civilians – homosexual perversions – pedophilia - organ theft – white slavery and every other major evil known to man.

I WANT MY COUNTRY BACK! It may already be too late but I feel that those of us who still care and ever really loved our country. My books WILL give you all the information you will ever need to know about the lies we have been spoon fed for over a century. We are a nation virtually built upon layers and layers of lies. All the major lies of the twentieth Century have been fabricated by jew treason within our own government. Here are but a few lies deceptions and false flag operations which have finally reduced us to the whimpering servile obedient attack dog for IsraHELL which we are today. Many of these disgraceful mendacities are detailed in the books. Most of these lies were to promote wars or weaken our Constitution. The USS Maine sinking – the Lusitania sinking – The USS Liberty massacre - Pearl Harbor – Gulf of Tonkin attacks – 9-11 - Sandy Hook - and countless more lies promoted by the jew-run 'mainstream media' run Press!

The key word to prevent these unconscionable mistakes (like TWO world wars that we had NO business being involved with) is KNOWLEDGE and the WISDOM that comes with the ability to assimilate knowledge. We are without any doubt - the most poorly educated nation on EARTH! The collective jews are the mortal enemies of not just Christianity – but ALL man of good will on EARTH! If you retain just one fact from my book remember this Quote from the book of John -8-44. In the virtually NEVER read quote – Christ condemns the jews as being the sons of Satan and that the jews WILL continue to LIE and COMMIT MURDER in the name of their 'god' – Satan. READ IT FOR YOURSELF!

I dedicate this work to the memories of all the beautiful defenseless helpless but brave Arab children of Palestine – both Christian and Muslim – who were butchered by cowardly demonic jew monsters on their own land out of pure hatred and sadistic evil. I know few if ANY professing Christians who use such words of respect and love when referring to our lord as do the Muslims here and in other Arab nations. Conversely - I can't even repeat the putrid rancid hate filled rhetoric referring to Christ that would hear in public from jews in IsraHELL.

I also dedicate it to the surviving daily suffering orphans and widows who are left with no hope – no help – no food or shelter and a life of living hell thanks to the shameful cruel and uncompassionate spineless worms I must exist within my own country who will EAGERLY spend $HUNDREDS on a 50 yard line 'ticket' to a meaningless Stupid Bowl game – but too cruel and too cheap to give so much as a kind word of compassion to a suffering starving child in the world's largest outdoor prison camp – run by the jews and financed with US dollars. May God serve you with the TRUE justice you so richly deserve.

To those of you still members of the human race – may God bless you for caring enough to learn the TRUTH and DOING something MEANINGFUL about it.

Scripture (the - CHRISTIAN BIBLE - about the life and teachings between good and evil – as given by Christ in the NT and NOT the horrid Satanic worship of Moses and his jew demons from hell) tells us of at least three bad traits of man that He personally despised.

(1) The people with the "itchy ears". Those were the morally weak cowards who wanted to listen ONLY to things that made them 'feel good' regardless of how morally degenerate they were. The classic example is of course the putrid arrogant Christ mocker Joel Osteen – whose HUGE OPPULANT 'syanagogues of Satan' were always filled to the brim with people who were anything but followers of Christ. These puppet people were 'spoon fed' the Devil's sermons of how much Jesus wanted us ALL to be filthy rich and that we should all be more "greedy" if we to be 'good' Christians. Osteen is but one of a laundry list of super wealthy Christ mocking jet-setter super stars who live like Hollywood icons.

(2) The Hypocrites – those fraud fake people who never practiced what they preached. Those who you see making their appearance 'pious' in Church on Sunday – in their finery and jewelry and fancy cars and trophy wives – but on MONDAY MORNING , were back to their TRUE nature of cheating their business partners and screwing their wives in secret. These are the rich who give ONLY to causes that their CPAs tell them are good 'tax shelter' benefits to them personally. I have NEVER EVER met or even heard of one wealthy businessman who openly gave to ease the suffering of the orphans and widows we have caused in Palestine. These worms are ALWAYS more concerned with pleasing everyone and being popular – than actually doing good deeds.

(3) And of course the third category of moral weaklings are the 'fence straddlers.' We all know their ilk. These are the cowards who believe that by not taking a stand AGAINST EVIL or a stand FOR righteousness – that they will appear to be neutral. They DO not wish to appear to purposefully mock the teachings of Christ – but are even more reluctant regarding offending Satan's children, lest such moral righteous anger should make them too "controversial". Virtually all of our high elected officials are like that. Ron Paul had the opportunity of a lifetime to speak to the nation of the TRUE evil that has strangled our nation – but did not!. The ONLY Congressman I knew of in my lifetime that had the integrity and moral courage to speak the truth regarding these demonic slime was Paul Findley and the jews destroyed his career for his love of his country. The only President in my lifetime to take a moral stand against this murderous filth was JFK. And of course – it cost him his life!

For those of you who know little or know nothing of what our Lord thought of these moral cowards. Here are His exact words on the matter: Christ to the apostate corrupt church – Revelations 3-15-16. *"I KNOW thy works – that thou are neither cold nor hot:.... I would that thou were cold OR hot 'So because you are lukewarm, and neither hot nor cold,* I will spit you out of my mouth. ...

Not exactly a compliment – is it?

Now tell me who and where ALL of these morally degenerate people sound are and come from today! Truthfully – how many of your current neighbors do NOT fall into at least one of those?

DEAR reader – What you will see and learn in my work is the result of a lifetime of personal experiences – extensive travel – thousands of hours of exhaustive research and a quest for TRUTH that could not be extinguished despite endless sets backs disappointments and barrages of lies to cover and obscure the TRUTH.

I would like to remind you of the infinitely more tedious complex and demanding aspects of writing TRUE historic FACTS – compared with pulp fiction. The people involved with these narrations of actual historic events – both current and those of more distant history are faced with an enormous task of being historically correct - accurate and TRUTHFUL in their chronicles. This demand for provenance requires proof readings as many times as necessary to 'GET IT RIGHT'.

The unforgiving public will long remember a single mistake while they over look or take for granted - a WEALTH of priceless wisdom and information served up to the reader on a 'silver platter' – so that he or she may gain the knowledge and hopefully – the associated wisdom with which to defeat these age old forces of pure demonic evil which seek to destroy and bury us all – with OUR OWN SHOVELS! ALL of my fellow 'truthers' suffer the same obstacles the 'evil ones' place in our paths. Truth and justice are the armor of the righteous and must be restored to the American people if they ever expect to be free again.

The pulp fiction writer need ONLY be imaginative- is under no stress for his mistakes – as there are NO 'mistakes' in fiction stories. If J R R Tolkien preferred his hobbits to be 7 feet tall warrior like creatures – then that is the TRUTH for his creations – as far as the reader is concerned. If James Cameron preferred his fictitious beings of 'Avatar' to be green short furry footed and meek in nature – then THAT would be 'his truth'. If Ian Fleming preferred his super-spy to be an Israeli with curly hair – a big nose and a mustache who carried an Uzi as his trademark – than THAT is what it would be – PERIOD.

That is why you NEVER EVER see ANY fiction writer 'crucified' in public and discredited or censured for his literary creations – ESPECIALLY if the masses AND their children are totally distracted from truly important issues that are destroying our freedoms our goodness and our identity as a people – day by day. Hollywood wants ALL Americans to think like they do. They dictate what pour children should look and dress and act like. They have replaced traditional parental role model figures with more and more violent fictional 'super-heroes' – ALL created by ONE entity – MARVEL HEROES/MOVIES.

These fictional figures are today actually worshiped by our children. The enemies of ALL of these super-heroes – are oddly enough – also totally IMAGINARY fictional and have absolutely nothing whatsoever to do with the reality of REAL LIFE genocidal mega-criminals. IMAGINARY heroes battling IMAGINARY enemies for children who live in an IMAGINARY world - while the REAL world is FILLED with REAL monsters which are of course downplayed or even nonexistent in the mush minds of kids with parents who are as ignorant as they are.

BTW – I'm not talking about 1st graders here. The vast majority of these 'super-hero' fans are teenagers. Guess who has created ALL of these 'classic' all American heroes? I will give you some clues. They are NOT the Arabs – and they are NOT traditional Anglo Saxon patriotic loyal ancestral Americans whom you would associate with our once proud wholesome pioneer heritage like Henry Ford or The Wright Bros or Thomas Edison or Eli Whitney – or Lewis &Clark or Admiral Perry or Charles Lindbergh or any such TRUE American icon pioneers. I will let you figure out who these treasonous deceitful Godless aliens were.

ALL fiction writers work under an umbrella where ALL they create is proprietary and is neither right nor wrong. Their ONLY concern is whether or not their make believe fantasies will be entertaining enough to be "critically acclaimed" (a Hollywood term that means= Jew approved) in a positive light.

Speaking the TRUTH is a VERY dangerous endeavor – especially today. Throughout history - more people have murdered for speaking TRUTHS than for speaking LIES. That is another ugly truth. Many of the murdered were famous figures – ranging from Socrates – to John F Kennedy. OH – and lest we forget the most famous of all victims who paid for speaking TRUTHS with His life – Jesus of Nazareth.

We have gone form a nation which respected loved honored esteemed praised hallowed glorified and even worshiped TRUTH – to a degenerate people who have made TRUTH just another 'dirty word'! TRUTH – however cannot ever be destroyed. It is immutable holy and righteous. It is one of the virtues most favored by God. The evil entities I expose in my books will stop at nothing to cover hide obscure pervert twist conceal and bury TRUTHS – but they will ALWAYS be revealed – sooner or later. This writer intends to at least TRY to change all that. If you read my books – perhaps the TRUTH may come back to its original venerable lofty and righteous place in your life.

DECEMBER, 2009
KNOW THE DOMESTIC ENEMIES OF AMERICA

One of the basic premises of the 'Rules Of War' as taught at the US Special Warfare School at Ft Bragg – which also incorporated many rules of Sun Tzu's 'Art Of War' – was to FIRST OF ALL know who the hell your 'ENEMY' was. Now – as well all know (SHOULD know) – all nations potentially have TWO types of enemies – both FOREIGN AND DOMESTIC – as in the oath that all of us who served in uniform swore to protect our nation against.

Well folks – we ARE in the PUREST sense of the definition – an occupied nation today. AND those 'enemies' of our freedoms values blessings and Christian heritage ARE DOMESTIC and as deadly as those of any foreign power.

There are two types of DOMESTIC ENEMIES in America today – EXACTLY as there were in pre-Communist Russia. There they had the communists themselves – headed almost exclusively by Jews – AND – equally deadly – the 'useful idiots' or "poleznye idioty" as the Jew mass murderer Lenin called them. . A "useful idiot" is one who is ignorant of the facts to the extent that they end up unwittingly advancing an adverse cause that they might not otherwise support. Most of the street mobs incited by the Marxist Jew hierarchy were these useful idiots.

Today – in our new improved AmeriKa – we have the exact same scenario. There the Jews who now dominate our banks – our entertainment – our news media, from the printed news to the TV – our government from the President to the Congress to the Supreme court – AND our Christian churches from Catholic to Protestant. BUT – since there over three hundred million 'goy' (Gentiles) and only less than 3 million Jews – they must have a large number of domestic allies to support their treasonous agendas.

AND indeed they DO have a huge number of witless allies in their demonic quest to dominate and destroy us. These are the AmeriKan useful idiots – a combination of mostly robotic imbeciles such as the 50 million Southern Baptist – so-called Christian-Zionists (an oxymoron definition for Christian-morons) – AND – those Gentiles who are simply greedy and evil to begin with and have sold their souls to the Jew – and in return- sell their country FOR THE JEWS. Classic examples are war criminal mass murderers George Bush – Colin Powell – Cheney – Rumsfeld and Rice and more currently the puppet Obama and all of his Godless Gentile useful idiot cabinet – replete with scores of Jews of course.

Speaking of war criminals – useful idiot, George Bush – who added his rancid mockery of Christ to his national treason – genocide, and long list of other crimes – here is a PARTIAL listing of his virtually ALL Jew (domestic enemies) cabinet and advisers:

Richard Pearle – Paul Wolfowitz – Douglas Feit – Edward Lottwak – Henry Kissinger – Dov Zakheim – Lewis Libby – Ken Adleman – Robert Satloff – Elliot Abrahams – Mark Grossman - Richard Haass – Robert Zoellich – Ari Fleisscher – James Schlesinger – Daid Frum – Joshua Bolton – John Bolton – David Wormer – Eliot Cohen – Michael Chertoff and a laundy list more of other 'Chosenite' neocon country-selling ENEMY bastards. Oh Vey – Such a deal!

Our current traitorous Israeli-first Obamanation lying Godless imposter (who STILL has NOT proven his own citizenship) President – also has an ALL Jew/useful idiot cabinet and advisers who are loyal 'troops' of the DOMESTIC ENEMY of The United States Of America!

Are you beginning to get the picture of this disgraceful treasonous TRUTH, FOLK? OUR MORTAL ENEMIES – THE JEWS – OWN THIS NATION LOCK STOCK AND BARREL – simply because we were TOO stupid to recognize what the enemy has done to us – and TOO cowardly to do anything to defend OUR OWN NATION!

More examples of the latter useful idiot criminal scum who sell us out 24-7 for BIG BIG money are Hannity – Colmes – O'-Reilly – Limbaugh – Coulter and – Beck. These are just some of the 'whores' who work for the greater glory of IsraHELL. Money and fame are the driving force of these 'shabbus goy' scumbags. For example – the 'prince' of the whores is Bill O-Reilly. This useful idiot's Jew boss – (Sumner Redstone – whose REAL name is Sumner Murray Rothstein) pays his racist sock puppet more in ONE DAY than I earned as a company commander training young Paratroopers during a REAL enemy threat to the US – FOR AN ENTIRE YEAR! Why not ask Mr. O'Reilly if he ever served his country – that is – when he wasn't SELLING IT OUT!

There are literally HUNDREDS of 'cultural' and ethnic think tanks' in AmeriKa – all run by our mortal JEW ENEMIES. Some 90% of political councils, institutes, and centers are controlled by our mortal ENEMY – the JEWS

The internet is controlled almost exclusively by our Christian hating enemies – the Jews. Google – E bay – Facebook – Yahoo – My Space – and Wikipedia are just some of their domains. Check it out for yourself.

Remember – ALL of these people are domestic enemies. I would venture to guess that there is not a Jew in one THOUSAND in the USA today who has not contributed in some way to our moral rot – our economic collapse – our religious degeneration and the massive acts of war criminal genocide by our Government – either actively or passively. Anyone who still thinks that only 'card carrying' Zionist Jews are evil, are, either hopelessly ignorant or deaf-dumb -and blind.

The Jew News media both printed and televised is 100% controlled by the JEW ENEMY. Here are some of the most well known : ESPN – ABC- NBC – CBS – FOX – Time – Newsweek – New York Times – Washington Post – Atlantic Monthly – Daily News – US News & World Report and hundreds more – ALL in the hands of THE ENEMY!

Entertainment. EVERYTHING that you AND your CHILDREN see hear and learn – including homosexual perversions and other unimaginable filth is ONE HUNDRED PERCENT controlled by the JEW ENEMY. Here are but a few examples: Paramount – Disney (Dreamworks, Touchstone, Buena Vista, Miramax) – 20 th Century Fox –CNN – Blockbuster – Time Warner(Castle Rock, New Line Cinema, HBO) – NAT-GEO Channel – Science Channel – History Channel – Discovery Channel – Military Channel – LOGO Channel [homosexual perversions]

Folks – we are AT WAR with the Jews – a mortal deadly combat to the death – literally. Here is just one of COUNTLESS examples of their in-your-face filth to express their demonic hatred of ANYTHING – decent – wholesome – innocent and Godly. Although this filth is a Comedy Central type cartoon example of what the Jew wants your children to watch and consider 'funny' Do not watch this with young children present! One of those greedy evil variety of useful idiots is Ted Turner! Surprised? Turner Broadcasting made this hateful blasphemy possible and it may be seen by your child. The Jew has made this site one of the most popular with young America.

Every American who ever even considered themselves Christian MUST SEE THIS JEW HATRED – made possible by one of the above 'Jew entertainment' Channels! This one of hundreds that promote hatred of Christ, mockery of our Christian faith, graphic violence, disrespect of parents – teachers and social order, mockery of the Islamic faith, mockery of The Founding Fathers mockery of Christmas, Mockery of Easter and promotion of lurid sex and homosexual filth.

The biggest acts of treason against America have been by our DOMESTIC Jew enemies The Rosenbergs and Jonathan Pollard were just two examples of a laundry list of Jew ENEMY

The greatest thefts have been by our Domestic Jew enemies (an example is gangster fraud Bernard Madoff who stole $65.000.000.000) That is more than the entire net worth of most small nations on the planet! That is BILLION -not million. It was never really accounted for - supposedly siphoned to IsraHELL.

The lists of these categorically undeniable truths are – sadly – endless. The reason for that is our own greed – ignorance – moral cowardice and criminally irresponsible attitudes.

The IS a REAL and MORTAL enemy in our midst. That MORTAL DEADLY and REMORSELESS ENEMY is the JEW. The Jew has CREATED strife misery suffering despair violence moral degradation and DEATH wherever he is found on the planet. He is evil incarnate and the harbinger of death to all who welcome him into their midst.

Communism is but ONE of his many demonic creations which has claimed the lives of over TWO HUNDRED MILLION INNOCENT CIVILIAN HUMAN BEINGS and over a BILLION ruined lives. He is the enemy of all men of good will and has been since Christ condemned him – collectively – as being of a DEMONIC FATHERHOOD.

Greed – cruelty – malice – lies – deception – cunning – perversion and hatred are his hallmarks and codes of life. His malicious venomous hostile nature have made him a pariah to all nations for all recorded history. His 'celebrations' and commemorations are ALWAYS involved with death destruction and the suffering of other innocent people. There is no Jew celebration that has its roots in hope – good will – kindness – charity or love – only hatred violence and hostility so emblematic of an inbred and predisposition of a criminal psychopath.

He perverts his young from the day they are born with hatred distrust and greed as I have witnessed by the sickeningly perverse typical acts of Jewish children in IsraHELL. The Jew is genetically wired to love anything that is by its nature – evil – perverse – vile – base – abominable – offensive – obnoxious and repulsive. Conversely – he hates all that is beautiful wholesome – noble- chaste – benevolent – wise – true – honorable – and virtuous. His consistency in these behaviors is remarkably predictable.

Heis a master at twisting the truth – robbing his neighbor – victimizing the victimizer – cheating the honest – murdering the innocent – starving the hungry – ridiculing the faithful – attacking the defenseless – elevating hypocrisy – exalting opportunism – glorifying homosexual perversions – praising deception – mocking the pure of heart , and the Jew could teach a thing or two concerning the art of being a parasitic vampire – to leaches and vampire bats.

The Jew has traditionally profited from the misery and misfortune of others since the time of Christ. Jew bankers have historically funded most major wars – not for patriotic reasons – but for sheer greed – as they customarily fund both adversaries. The only 'winners' in any major or global conflict have been JEWS! Their true god WAS – IS – and always WILL BE MONEY.

You -the reader – assuming that we as a people – will continue our 'don't give a rat's ass' attitude about our dying nation – do realize you will witness the LAST 'Christmas' celebrated in America – THIS year 2009. Because of our cowardice – we WILL see the that gigantic ugly hideous demonic Hanukkah menorah on the White House lawn – PERMANENTLY replace our centuries old traditional Christian Christmas in mockery of our obviously too outdated to defend anymore Christmas

So enjoy 'the holidays' (READ: Happy Hanukkah) because the Negro/Jew Gestapo WILL come next year if you DARE to try to show homage to our Lord Christ in any place but your backyard! The Name of Christ and using the word Christmas has ALREADY been outlawed in many places in AmeriKa. The cruel irony is the FACT that while we send tens of thousands more thugs to murder millions more Muslim Arab civilians and lift not even so much as an EYEBROW of disapproval when Jew TV curses – mocks – defiles – slander Jesus as – a BASTARD- and His Blessed Mother – a WHORE -as if they were mangy dogs in the street –

REMEMBER THIS FACT AND REMEMBER IT WELL – SHOULD WE LOSE OUR NATION COMPLETELY.

The VERY SAME innocent civilian Arab Muslims – mostly women and children – who you CHEER for our paid assassins to murder in cold blood – ALWAYS refer to Jesus and Mary IN THE HIGHEST RESPECT AND REVERENENCE. ANY reference to them is ALWAYS made with the following veneration = "MAY PEACE BE UPON HIM (or HER)" Been there – KNOW that.

STOP THE IGNORANCE! STOP THE HATRED! SAVE OUR COUNTRY! STOP THEJEWS!

Have a 'Merry and peace filled Christmas' — while you still can.

DECEMBER, 2009
THE REAL JESUS, ACCORDING TO 'DEMONICUS'

Here is what I learned about the Lord Christ on the 'Nat-Geo' Jew Tube last night. I am so grateful to the Jews for revealing the 'truth' to this poor superstitious ignorant illiterate Christian. The show was called 'THE REAL JESUS'. Obviously my 65year formal religious Christian training has been telling me lies about an 'UNTRUE' or FALSE Jesus – otherwise why the title – "The REAL Jesus"

Here are a few 'Jew Truths' from the all Jew Jesus 'experts'. I mean – after all – they must know SOMETHING about my Lord – since they were the ones who had Him murdered for exposing their false faith. You remember that big ruckus during the Passover in Jerusalem when Jesus discovered that the Jews were conducting loan-shark business in the Temple? You know how the Jews are – anytime there is a buck to be made. Its a Jew thing. The worshipers were charging a fee to enter the temple – but some enterprising Jew high priests decided that it would look better if the people used these walk through banking facilities' to also buy 'sacrifices' on the spot – so it also looked like a barnyard as well as a bank – but then after all – we should be more tolerant. Business is ALWAYS FIRST for the Jews.

The Lord lost His cool and proceeded to 'clean house' saying to them, "It is written, 'AND MY HOUSE SHALL BE A HOUSE OF PRAYER,' but you have made it a ROBBERS' DEN.-Take these things away; stop making My Father's house a place of business." This condemnation of the sleazy conduct of the Jews really pissed them off and the high priests – especially the wealthy influential Pharisee of the Sanhedrin – high priest Caiphus – who decided that Christ had to be done away with.

The presentation was replete with lots and lots of comments by learned Jews – kinda like a modern day Caiphus. One of them – an especially big nosed gentleman with a rather disgusting New York Jew accent showed his unveiled mockery for Christ by explaining in his best contemptuous voice, why the high priests "simply had to get rid of this guy". Oh vey!– I never really thought of the Lord – as " this guy" – how naive of me.

Here are some other interesting 'facts' about the 'REAL JESUS' that I had been totally ignorant of all these years. I am eternally grateful to these learned Pharisee scholars and Rabbis for setting it straight.

Did you know that Mary had other children and Jesus had brothers and sisters?

Did you know that Jesus of Nazareth was a JEW?

Did you know that Jesus sought out the approval Of John The Baptist who was a nut case wandering around aimlessly in the desert eating locusts?

Did you know that Jesus was not really Jesus – the anointed one – until he was baptized by John?

Did you know that Mary Magdalene – a woman of highly questionable reputation – was the one who actually started Christianity?

Did you know that the Sermon On the Mount was fake? (through the incomparable wisdom of the Jews who presented this program – I learned that it was physically impossible for the people to have even heard Jesus – that must have been embarrassing for Him)

Did you know that the people who listened to his Sermon On the Mount would have gotten bored with it – because according to one the learned Jew panel experts [Marcus Borg] – ("it (the sermon) just doesn't make any sense to me.")

Did you know that the Romans were ALWAYS the bad guys in Judea and Jerusalem but NEVER the Pharisees?

Did you know that the fisherman – now, 'fishers of men', followed Jesus ONLY because they were "poor and bored and had nothing else to do"?

Did you know that Jesus' ministry was nothing more than a "road show"? We know this true because one of those big nosed Jew panel experts [Marcus Borg] said so!

Did you know that Jesus was an idiot for having said: "blessed are the poor"? We know this is also true because the learned and wise Rabbi Borg sarcastically commented: "Oh – REALLY! – what is so blessed about being poor?"

Did you know that Jesus was an exorcist?

Did you know that Jesus really didn't perform any 'healing miracles'? The people simply healed themselves by positive thinking that they would be healed.

Did you know that Mary Magdalene was a brazen hussy for using her hair to wash the feet of Jesus with oils? Another 'learned' Rabbi HARSHLY condemns Jesus for even allowing such an un-Jewish thing.

Did you know that Mary Magdalene was one of THE Disciples?

Did you know that The DaVinci Code was true?

Did you know that "Jesus loved her more than ALL of the Disciples"?

Did you know that Jesus was intimate with Mary Magdalene and more than likely had sex with her? – according to learned Rabbis like Shiffman

Did you know that the philosophy of Jesus was "radical"? According to sarcastic Rabbi Shiffman

Did you know that Judas (a Jew) did NOT betray Jesus – "he had no choice but was COMMANDED by Jesus to do so"? We know this the REAL truth, as learned Jew Rabbis say so.

Did you know that Jesus said that the Romans condemned Him to death -not the Jews?

At the point of the crucifixion in the 'special' – I felt I had learned enough 'truths' from these people

I found the detailed description of the crucifixion to be rather morbid. These 'learned' Jews seemed to delight themselves in their detailed autopsy in bloody morbid details of how many bones were broken and how much flesh was torn and how many sinews were shredded – exactly where the nails were driven in every possible scenario – as if that were of great importance. The blood and gore was shown and described with a clinical coldness one might expect in a slaughterhouse . The atmosphere created by these Jews was a macabre scene out of a horror movie or the autopsy of a mad dog shot in the street – not the Son of God.

Had this blasphemous outrage been presented by Arab people instead of Jews – I would be reading of our invasion of Iran AFTER nuclear devastation. And of course this presentation would be all the rave of Hollywood 'critics' and not ONE 'Christian house of worship' would utter so much as a whimper of outrage. If this mortal insult to true followers of Christ and all that Christians used to hold sacred had been committed in my youth – every filthy Synagogue Of Satan existing on our hallowed shores would have been laid waste and the earth there salted as a reminder.

TODAY – in our occupied land of spineless worms where once there walked MORAL BRAVE MEN – we would simply say – "Oh that's interesting Joe – but I'm late for a tailgate party to the Bucs game – see ya!"

DECEMBER, 2009
ZIONISTS BAD – JEWS GOOD? WRONG! WRONG! WRONG!

This has been a topic that SCREAMS for clarification. I can't tell you how many times I have been in discussions with people whom I gave credit for being well educated – who parroted that tired overused mantra of: "Zionists are the real enemy but there are a LOTS of GOOD Jews". OH REALLY? I would sincerely like to meet "lots of GOOD JEWS". Give me a BREAK!

Now let me clarify that. When I call a person "GOOD (moral)" – it encompasses several qualifications. They SHOULD be, – generous – affable – friendly – agreeable – hospitable and fun to be with. HOWEVER – NONE of these qualities really make a 'GOOD' person. However – he MUST be – at least for the most part – GODLY – HONEST – TRUTHFUL – COMPASSIONATE – MODEST – LOYAL – PATRIOTIC – SINCERE – MORALLY RESOLUTE – WISE – EDUCATED and RIGHTEOUS.

THAT – folks – even with benefit of doubt – just disqualified about 99+% of ALL Jews that I have known – read about – heard about or will EVER MEET – PERIOD! It is therefore safe and accurate to say that Jews – collectively – as a race (and they are a RACE – and NOT a religion) are 'bad' people – to put it politely. There is not another ethnicity on planet earth which can be honestly and truthfully so identifiable as consistently and universally evil.

If – your 'ethic brother' sees you committing an evil act – and he – even if not involved – approves – he too is evil.

I have NEVER EVER IN MY ENTIRE LIFE witnessed or even been made aware of ANY high profile prominent Jew 'leader'– especially an American, who has EVER put himself in harm's way even from public or peer ridicule or condemnation by taking a stand for any major issue concerning goodness – wholesomeness- sanctity of life – patriotism – compassion – sanctity – Godliness – morality – honesty – virtue – truthfulness – benevolence – or similar qualities universally considered essential components of a society of 'GOOD PEOPLE'. Notice I indicated that I had also never even been made AWARE of such – and odds are – neither have any of you!.

You want to hear the CLASSIC typical quintessential position of the typical prominent – high profile American Jew? How about this one? "When only Jews are present we admit that Satan is our god." (Harold Rosenthal, former administrative aide to Sen. Jacob Javits, in a recorded interview) … I could truthfully quote HUNDREDS more – as bad or worse – but you should 'get it' by now.

BTW – for those of you still sharing brains – the ostensibly 'good' organizations formulated by Jews – like the NAACP – for the REAL purpose of inciting racial strife and consolidating the Negro voting block for purposes of political power to enhance the traditionally immoral Jew agendas of infanticide – homosexual perversions – subjugation of the Constitution – destruction of Christian principles – promotion of violence – moral degeneration of our youth – organized crime – gambling – drugs – prostitution – legislation of phony 'hate crimes' – suspension and abrogation of Constitutionally guaranteed freedoms- and a hundred more Jew crimes – are NOT acts of goodness – but cunning perverse calculated acts of EVIL – to deceive us goy.

Now lets address this Zionist – non- Zionist nonsense. Zionism is simply the formal politically stated manifestation of the Jew wet dream which has been the Jew agenda since the Jews looted Egypt under the guidance of their hero – Moses . This Eretz Israel agenda was formulated in 1897 by a Jew bastard named Theodor Herzl. It was a political movement having nothing to do with religion. Herzl and the other demonic Godless scum arrogantly demanded that these Jews should STEAL land belonging the Arab people (Palestinians) for the past fifteen hundred years . After much deceit and other dishonest influence – these Jew demons finally succeeded in extorting the British into legitimizing the document that would seal the fate of millions of innocent non-Jews in the years to come with terrorism and wars upon wars. It was called ; The Balfour Declaration – a license to steal – AND to murder. Read it for yourself.

Of interest is that these Jew scum eventually formed the backbone of the first Socialist International. Sound familiar? It should since these demons were the genesis of what would later become the most murderous gangsters of all recorded history. Hardly any American family today has not suffered the loss or injury of a loved one due to Communists (the beloved created demons of the Jews). Next time you visit a grave of a loved one lost in Vietnam or Korea – thank a Jew! As a matter of fact many of the Jews making their Aliya to IsraHELL were dedicated Godless criminal Communists. These murdering scum whose whole existence was to bring death destruction and misery to their captive victims, were actually given special treatment upon their arrival to the unholy land of the"SONS OF THE DEVIL" (John 8-44)

Lets clear the air about Bad Zionists and Good Jews. Zionism has only been around for a little more than a hundred years. BUT – Jews have been murdering – stealing – lying – cheating – committing atrocities – blasphemy – usury – homosexual perversions – pedophilia and every other evil imaginable to man for over TWO THOUSAND YEARS. Think about it. IF all these Jew parasites here – in government – in Hollywood – in TV – with their seduction of our children – creation of ALL the filth we see and hear on TV – who have looted almost the entire nation as of recent – who have been the biggest purveyors of prostitution, pornography, white slavery, organized crime – the destruction of ALL Christian practice – prayer in school – celebration of the TRUE spirit of Christmas (reduced to a gaudy spectacle of sex infused secular commercialism) – serial wars against innocent people (where not a drop of precious Jew blood has been shed) – and – the murder of more unborn children than ALL of the lives lost in ALL the wars since we became a nation – just to mention a few Jew crimes – ——are still here – then WHY?

Think about it. If all of these filthy psychopathic Jew criminals were 'card carrying ZIONISTS' – then – why in hell are they not ALL not aboard flights to their precious IsraHELL to make their special little Zionist Aliya in Jew-ville. WHY? Because -simply – virtually none of these lying cheating criminal demonic scum really call or consider themselves 'Zionists'. If they REALLY were 'Zionists' – they would be there with their fellow Christ hating arrogant superior than thou Jew scum Zionists in IsraHELL. Stealing and murdering to get a 'homeland' is only a tiny part of the demonic Jew mindset. They have been damned as "SONS OF THE DEVIL" by

God the Son for their universally sinful conduct almost two thousand years before there even EXISTED any such thing as Zionists. Get it?

So lets STOP this: "Zionists – BAD = but– Jews – Good", crap! Oh sure – to quote one of the better known moron goyem mantras: " You don't have to be a Jew to be a Zionist scumbag" Well – with that little profound statement of lemming logic – how about this? " You don't have to be a Zionist to be a Jew scumbag" – either!. This nonsense about Jews good – Zionists bad, was simply another Jew ploy to divert righteous and justifiable anger from universally evil Jews in general. They knew that most Americans (goyem) were so stupid ,that they would buy this nonsense. Jews are natural born LIARS. Christ SAID SO! Are they ever described as "clever" or "wise" ? NO – they are ALWAYS termed "CUNNING" – as in 'serpents are cunning' Read: (Oxford American Dictionary – 'CUNNING' adj. 'skilled at deceiving people')

Even the OFFICIAL Jew military motto reveals their treacherous nature: " By DECEPTION – We Wage War". So -class – do we finally get it? Lung cancer bad – brain cancer bad. Jews bad – Zionists bad . Now go out and do something good for your country – expose a Jew and the sock puppet brain dead useful idiot scum who support his evil. It is the RIGHT Thing to do for God and country!

DECEMBER, 2009
AN OPEN LETTER TO WAR CRIMINAL, COL. SAM WHITEHURST

What in God's holy name has happened to decency character honor -wisdom- compassion and TRUTH since I left the military? This filthy lying animal is more concerned with his paycheck and status with his Jew puppet masters than he is for common decency. You just had to go there and kill innocent people – and disgrace the uniform – didn't you

You – my young Col. Are a disgrace to God country and the honor of the uniform that you have soiled like so much used toilet paper with your slavish fealty to your Jew masters. You are nothing more than a filthy animal – a war criminal – a sniveling ass- kissing sycophant and a total sadistic piece of human shit! I believe – were he alive today – a real man I once knew – Col. Dave Hackworth – would concur.

First you allow yourself AND the honor of the uniform – the same uniform incidentally that I wore – to be mocked – pissed on- shit on and mocked by the Jews in the Jew newspaper you so eagerly prostituted yourself to. I couldn't believe an American officer could sink that low as to ALLOW YOURSLF AND YOUR UNIFORM to be so transparently used by filthy Jews to promote their propaganda hate campaigns. That Sir – is unconscionable! Did you get your thirty pieces of silver? Have you considered hanging yourself for your cruel mockery of Christ?

I PRAY That some decent moral ethical REAL man in your cabal of child murderers will finally have had enough and serve TRUE justice by blowing your brain out! Now THAT JUSTICE would be an occasion for celebration by MILLIONS of decent moral people all over the world –

ESPECIALLY the widows and orphans whose civilian family members you and your murdering psychopaths have put in graves.

There are no words there is no known syntax to adequately describe the intense hatred I bear you and all filthy war criminals of your ilk! You have no honor – no moral courage – no soul and are as evil as ANY Godless Chi-com or Soviet butcher commissar of my generation.

Perhaps the 'straw' was your brutally cruel lie that your murdering rampage against defenseless human beings – the endless rapes – cold blooded murders of innocent civilian human beings (I believe the twisted propagandized Jew term is "detainees" – or "insurgents") – "And there are people in this country that are alive today because of the sacrifices made by those soldiers. I do think it was worth it. I can look back, and I think all of us can hold our heads very high."

You filthy Jew puppet animal – what sacrifices? Their incessant rapes and murders? Their looting stealing and destruction of the infrastructure of their country? Shooting detainee "sand niggers – "camel jockeys" – and "towel-heads" in the back of the head and dumping their corpses in canals? I was going to do a paper on these cold-blooded psychopaths – but the problem is that thee are SO MANY of these documented crimes and SO MANY uniformed criminals – it is difficult to decide which are the most sadistic. During the six years or so I served in uniform – I don't remember hearing of more than a couple of war crimes by US soldiers. Today – I get at least one or two a WEEK!

"Was it Worth it?" – worth WHAT – you arrogant murdering bastard? Worth the MILLION FIVE HUNDRED THOUSAND COLD – BLOODED CIVILIAN MURDERS – MOSTLY CHILDREN!? "WORTH" creating tens of millions of TOTALLY innocent civilian refugees? "WORTH" millions of homes destroyed by your roving thug gangster mercenary killers? Even the life of one American boy whose father will eventually realize that his precious son died for the stinking State of IsraHELL and the Godless Jews who sent him to his death to serve monsters like you in the first place?

The TRUTH is that THERE WOULD BE OVER A MILLION PEOPLE that WOULD be alive today –let me repeat that TRUTH – " that WOULD BE ALIVE TODAY" – why? – because of the murderous conduct of you and your precious uniformed killers. You twisted sick bastard – have you no sense of decency at all? You think you are so superior don't you? YOUR children are worth a THOUSAND 'sand-niggers' — isn't that so – isn't that what your Jew masters have told you – Mr. baby-killer hypocrite?

Your shallow twisted values are an embarrassment to me and my family and a disgrace to this country. I will spend the rest of my life exposing garbage like you – and you can take that to the bank.

" all of us can hold our heads up high" – US WHO? – you putrid child murdering criminal. Are you saying to the American people that they can be proud of the fact that we have MURDERED over a MILLION INNOCENT HUMAN BEINGS – for the security of the stinking Jews? Is THAT what you suggest – you Jew loving scumbag?

OH excuse me – mea culpa – mea maxima culpa – I almost forgot that you Christ mocking Jew worshipers consider Arab children OR ANY – non- kike children – for that matter – as "animals" – according to their host highly esteemed demonic books!

Apparently the best part of you was flushed down the toilet the night you were conceived because you have no character – no ethics – no morals – no humility – no compassion – no truthfulness and no goodness. Your conduct has proved that disgusting fact to me clearly. . I know you don't understand – because some fifteen years before the unfortunate event of your birth – I had already trained well over a thousand young men to defend this nation against a REAL Enemy – not defenseless innocent people – something you have never and will never experience in your worthless life.

You took the same oath that I did as an officer – only I honored MY oath whereas you have committed no less that high treason against America – of course, in addition to your war crimes. You see – I do NOT want you to run over an IOD. That would be too good for the likes of you. I can only pray that you are captured and handed over to one of the countless family survivors of the people you and your gang of thugs have murdered . I would pay a handsome reward for the opportunity to be there to watch you beg for your worthless life and be torn to pieces by the widows and orphans of the murdered and fed to the dogs. NOW THAT – would be biblical justice!

I pray that your black soul will spend a thousand years of endless torture for every innocent child who has died a horrible death at your hands. Your violent death will be a source of great joy for me personally and I'm sure to those men who served me so long ago and are no longer with us. Why them? Because they were – unlike the sadistic psychopathic mercenary scum losers who serve you – these were decent men with souls compassion and a conscience. Your murderous rampages "protected" NOBODY here. You did it because you love killing kids.

Your mockery of the Lord and His teachings may be unseen by the ones who surround you but I believe that why goes around comes around. You WILL get yours – baby killer – and I pray NIGHTLY that it is in THIS Life. I am thankful that I never had to serve lying sadistic murdering scum like you. Thanks to sadistic treasonous butchers like you, my country is now nothing more than a morally rotted corpse – occupied by the criminal Jew demons you and your cabal of useful idiot gangsters are paid to murder for. Get it yet? You have stolen the goodness and honor I once knew as a younger man here.

Watch your back baby killer – justice does not 'sleep' nor take holidays. I will be reading to see when you make my day. Know this fact – baby killer – your death will be celebrated by MORE people than those who mourn you – and you can take that to the bank too. Have a nice day – while you still can.

DECEMBER, 2009
AMERIKAN WAR CRIMES WEEKLY –AMERIKA'S NEWEST DIGEST

Folks – Isn't it just so special? There are now so many war crimes committed by AmeriKan criminals in Iraq and Iran – and with such frequency that there should be a weekly journal just to keep up with the ones that are exposed. By that I mean – that according to military intelligence – the public only learns of about ten percent of these horrible cowardly sadistic jew incited crimes against defenseless innocent civilian citizens of the lands that we have invaded occupied and raped to appease the Jew.

Those of you who don't spend your entire life in front of the Jew-tube, worshiping the gods of the NFL may remember that in the 80s, Reader's Digest featured dozens of stories which chronicled Soviet war crimes in Afghanistan. That was a good thing as it kept our intellectually challenged public informed of the predictable abominable criminal conduct of the Godless Soviets. At that time we were still not an entirely kike occupied nation and we were still a reasonably good and decent people. Our public was outraged and demanded that we aid these courageous people in defending themselves.

A committee to aid the poor Afghans was established (in which I was active) -our Congress pressured to aid these besieged unfortunates, and soon Stinger missiles were bringing down those fearsome flying tanks – the Hind helicopters, and evened the playing table for these valiant people defending their families and country. That was when we were still a good people with hearts and souls. A gang of pasty faced fat moronic imbeciles known as 'Southern Baptists' under the tutelage of Christ hating Jew trained sock puppets like John Hagee, soon changed the American soul from good to garbage.

These demonic mindless scum – know as 'the enablers' – gave the middle finger to Christ by the unholy marriage of Christianity – the belief system in Christ and goodness – with ZIONISM – the belief system of the sons of the Devil – as SO CLEARLY EXPOSED by Christ. These ultra scumbag morons had created the greatest blasphemy against Christianity in history! They had joined the demonic Jew in supporting the most evil cabal of criminals ever assembled in the 'HOAR HOUSE' to pursue endless serial wars against innocent people who had never done us any harm. We had now become clones of the 'Evil Empire'. The rest is history.

The irony was that – not only had NONE of these nations EVER committed and act of war against the body of the United States – BUT that the Jew who incited these horrible crimes in the first place – had IN FACT – committed an act of war against America on 8 June 1967. Had it of course been an attack by 'sand niggers' or 'camel jockeys' – or 'towel heads' – as our crude imbecile useful idiot field commanders address Arab people – we would have wiped Egypt off the map.

Since it was in FACT IsraHELL who's PM Ordered that cowardly murderous attack – we did what all ass-kissing cowards do. We put our collective tails between our collective legs and turned the other way even as the decks of the Liberty ran red with the life blood of our sons fathers and brothers. To the EVERLASTING disgrace of The United States Of America –

NOTHING has EVER been done to serve justice and avenge our national reputation. NOTHING!

ALL Americans – ESPECIALLY the young – should have that date – June 8 1967 – burned in their souls, as it was the turning point of American sovereignty. Want proof? Just try to get ANY patriotic article containing irrefutable proof and truth – published in ANY major newspaper in AmeriKa today – exposing our mortal Jew enemies and see what happens. It was the watershed of cowardice in the American spirit which has since imprisoned us as a people, transformed us into a morally rotted corpse – now totally occupied by the demonic Jew – LOCK STOCK AND BARREL! But I digress.

Back to the topic du-jour – our new status as international war criminals and servants of the Jew. There are many well documented horror stories of the most sadistic conduct imaginable – but I will touch lightly on only a few.

1st Lt. Michael Behenna is charged with premeditated murder, but during trial testimony Thursday at Fort Campbell ..Behenna said he made several mistakes while he was interrogating the detainee in a secluded railroad culvert near Beiji, Iraq. He said he should not have stripped the detainee and pointed his weapon at him, but that he was trying to scare him into giving information about insurgents. Behenna said he looked away and then saw Mohammed moving his hands toward the gun. Behenna said he shot the detainee twice.

Ed comment: = So tell me Mike – did it feel GOOD to blow away an unarmed civilian in a country that YOU DON'T BELONG IN? When people worldwide finally get tired of our raping their women – murdering their fathers and children – looting their homes and warmongering their beloved country – and perhaps end up at the doorstep of YOUR FAMILY – parade your father our of HIS home – identify him not as a father or citizen or MR. Behenna – but as a TERRORIST – or an INSURGENT – or a DETAINEE – strip him naked and humiliate him in every way possible – terrorize and threaten his life and finally blow his brains out in cold- blood – I want you to understand that he was only 'doing his patriotic duty for his country' – Is THAT OK – scumbag? OH and BTW – how many OTHER Innocent civilians did you murder before you got caught?

Here was another story on CNN (thanks for telling the truth) about some of the most cowardly sadistic criminals I have ever seen. I saw the entire official Army tapes on TV.

The three sergeants who killed the detainees were convicted of premeditated murder and conspiracy in a military courtroom in Germany earlier this year. All three are serving their sentences at the U.S. military prison at Fort Leavenworth, Kansas.

Hatley received a life sentence that was later reduced to 40 years; Sgt. 1st Class Joseph Mayo, who had pleaded guilty to the charges, and Sgt. Michael Leahy, a medic, are serving 20-year terms. Hatley and Leahy are appealing their convictions, while Mayo is seeking a lighter sentence. Hatley and Leahy were found not guilty of killing an injured Iraqi in a prior incident. (gee – wonder who did murder the Iraqi then?) Note that a cold blooded murder of a helpless injured civilian is a:"killing "and not a murder and this horrible sadistic capitol crime is relegated down to a mere = "incident" So here is yet ANOTHER apparent war crime.

Ed Comment; = Read the whole thing in detail on the CNN site. These filthy murdering psychopathic scum are what our 'new improved mercenary Army' is all about. You need to see the faces and tattooed bodies of this raunchy scum. One look at Hatley's face is enough to tell you this is a twisted sick anti-social killer – and I DO NOT mean – a 'good soldier'. You needed to hear his Godless hateful racist comments to understand why NO decent commander would want such filth in his command – at least when I was in uniform before the Jew occupation. Were REAL justice to be served – ringleader – monster – racist – Jew incited sadist – Hatley – WOULD have been HUNG!

They murdered four innocent helpless Iraq civilians. Stripped bound and shot in the back of the head just for sadistic meanness. PUT IN PERSPECTIVE – Just imagine if we were invaded by a powerful foreign army at the insistence of a demonic country who controlled that army and the 'enemy' rounded up your family by force at gunpoint. You are now demeaned and slandered as "terrorists – detainees – insurgents – and other insults .Your brothers – your father – your uncle are then murdered in cold blood and their bullet riddled corpses unceremoniously dumped in a nearby drainage canal .

If that horror of the murders and dehumanization were not enough sorrow – THEN your surviving family reads that the citizens of the nation who invaded you – raped your daughters, destroyed your homes, schools, hospitals and infrastructure – actually calls the murderers HEROES! How would you honestly feel about that country?

I'll tell you how you would 'feel'. You would want justice and revenge for the murders of your loved ones – the destruction of your country – and the years of endless humiliations you and loved ones suffered. Anyone who says otherwise is a hypocrite and liar. We have collectively become as evil and Godless a people as ever existed in recorded history. NO honest man can refute that FACT! IF – there was ANY substantial number of good and decent people left here – we simply would not be like this. Think about that truth for a moment – because it should scare the crap out of you!

Do you want to see just how sick we as judiazed Godless AmeriKans have become since we have been under Jew control and occupation? Go to the CNN site type in 'Killings At The Canal' and read the racist filth 'comments' that your 'neighbors' are actually PROUD of! It is a good litmus test for your level of decency. It should make you sick to your stomach to see what putrid sadistic Godless filth we have become as a people since we sold our souls to the Jew.

This ugly prevailing sickness was probably said best by one mindless arrogant supremest Jew sock -puppet punk (usa civilian) who spewed out this diatribe of racism and moronic ignorance as only an AmeriKan useful idiot for the jews, can.

—– "Mark989, you have no future. These men should be freed and given a slap on the hand AT MOST. They did the job they were sent to do. A little late, but….better late then never. No one here should even know about this so called unfortunate event. . [It wasn't unfortunate, it was productive]. However, where are the laws that prevent the media from releasing this information to the public? It's ridiculous, like the rest of this post, and all posts from posters who agree with the sentence given to these soldiers. "

"Oh and as far as the difference between this war and other wars is that this war doesn't involve humans of the same caliber. Iraq is a wasteland. They're second from the bottom on the evolutionary totem pole. They've been at war with anyone and everyone throughout the entire course of human history"

" THEY WERE JUST DOING THE JOB THEY WERE SENT TO DO".? REALLY? How would you like to have THIS SCUM for a neighbor – OR see him in uniform with a GUN? I guess if his superior 'ordered' him to murder an entire defenseless American family not named Jones or Smith – he would be eager to oblige. We have some serious problems her folks. In the REAL America that I grew up in – this sicko sadistic filth monster would have been clubbed by a Cub Scout unit! His message is that ANY society – no matter how intelligent or or innocent that doesn't measure up to his racist standards- should ALL be murdered.

Pretty sick don't you think?

Now here is one last true horror story-perhaps the worst – that we KNOW OF! I decided that the reader should have all of the grizzly details so I included almost the whole report.

23-year-old Steven Green is accused of bragging 'that was awesome' after the premeditated killing of Abeer Qasim Hamza al-Janabi and her family. It was called one of the most horrific crimes by U.S. troops against Iraqi civilians: In March 2006, a group of whiskey-fueled soldiers, their faces concealed and wearing black long underwear, descended upon a farmhouse some 20 miles south of Baghdad, gang-raped a teenage girl and shot her in the head, killing her along with her younger sister and their parents. The soldiers then tried to burn the bodies, setting fire to the house.

The grisly crime was initially blamed on insurgents — "This is what happens when you harbor terrorists," a military translator told a relative after the bodies were found — but three months later, the truth was revealed, when a fellow soldier from the unit told combat-stress counselors about what had happened.

Initial reports claimed that the girl, Abeer Qasim Hamza al-Janabi, was in her 20s. But her Iraqi ID card, obtained by Reuters, showed her date of birth is confirmed to be August 19, 1991, making her 14 years old at the time of her death

.News reports of the incident describe it as a "premeditated" act — and indeed it was. A federal affidavidt tells the story of how the soldiers, stationed at a traffic checkpoint near the town of Mahmoudiya some 1,000 feet from Abeer's home, would often stop by the house just to stare at her.

According to a 2006 article in TIME magazine, "Her mother, who grew concerned enough to make plans for Abeer to move in with a cousin, told relatives that whenever she caught the

Americans ogling her daughter, they would give her the thumbs-up sign, point to the girl and say, 'Very good, very good.'"

Abeer's brother Mohammed, 13, told TIME he once watched his sister, frozen in fear, as a U.S. soldier ran his index finger down her cheek. Mohammed has since learned that soldier's name: Steven Green."

Today, Steven D. Green, 23, stands trial for planning and leading the assault and massacre of Abeer and her family. A former Private First Class from the 101st Airborne Division who was honorably discharged with a "personality disorder" soon after the killings, Green became the first person identified as one of the perpetrators of the grisly crime, which has been compared to the notorious Haditha massacre in 2005. His trial began this week, at a U.S. District Court in Paducah, Kentucky.

Green was arrested in North Carolina in June 2006, days after the real story came to light, Because his role in the massacre was uncovered following his discharge, he is being prosecuted in federal, rather than military court. (Four other soldiers involved in the massacre have already been court-martialed, sentenced to five to 100 years in prison.)

Green, who, despite having told an Army investigator "I did that; I killed them," is pleading not guilty to the charges against him, which include conspiracy, rape, murder, unlawful use of a weapon and obstruction of justice. He is reportedly the first former soldier to face trial in a civilian court for conduct during war. He faces the death penalty.

In his opening statement on Monday, attorney Patrick Bouldin, a public defender, tried to contextualize the killings as the horrible consequences of a hellish situation. "You have to understand the background that leads up to this perfect storm of insanity," he told the jury, according to Reuters.

"They couldn't tell the village people and the farmers from the insurgents and the terrorists," he said.

But federal prosecutor Brian Skaret described how Green bragged about the murders afterward, telling people "that was awesome" at a celebratory barbeque afterward.

Meanwhile, Abu Firas Janabi, the cousin of Abeer's mother, was the first to find the bodies. "Never in my mind could I have imagined such a gruesome sight, "he recalled, describing how he found Abeer with her head smashed in "by a concrete block or a piece of iron."

"There were burns from the bottom of her stomach to the end of her body, except for her feet," he said.

"I did not believe what I was seeing. I tried to fool myself into believing I was in a dream. But the problem was that we were not dreaming. We put a piece of cloth over her body. Then I left the house together with my wife."

Ed. Comment; = Well there you have it. The now daily typical conduct of the US Army soldier. These animals were not only child rapists and murderers – but were such sick bastards that they felt compelled to celebrate their unparalleled grizzly deeds with a FORMAL celebration – a PARTY – as if it were a demonic cult killing. I noticed that two of the names of the killers were typically Jewish – Green and .Spielman and the ONLY ethnicity in history to ever celebrate such crimes of lust and hatred are the Jews with their 'blood libel'. The entire murder ritual smells to high heaven of Jew influence. The whole truth will come out sooner or later but the crime was so horrible that It really doesn't matter if it was Jew inspired or done by former 'St Andrew's choir boys – their crimes scream for the death penalty

As of the writing of this post – there has STILL been no justice served for one of the most horrible murder crimes EVER committed ANYWHERE!

It has been three and half years since his arrest and still no justice served.

This is a national disgrace as there was never ANY question of the quilt of the accused. They should have ALL been hung the same day and hour their guilt was unquestionably established. THAT IS JUSTICE!

No DECENT GODLY American who abides by the laws of God and State concerning this kind of crime can Ever again honestly feel pride in 'being an American'. I VOLUNTEERED to serve my nation in uniform performing hazardous duty but I can feel no pride any longer for that. But after all – mockery of true justice in our new occupied judiazed AmeriKa has been a disgusting farce for a long, long time.

The creatures who oversee our current justice system are of the same ilk as that 'thing' who considered that poor murdered raped humiliated and burned Iraqi child "subhuman trash on the evolutionary totem pole – living in a wasteland "So all you NFL fans out there who wouldn't stoop so low as to even try to save your own country – enjoy your drunken tailgate parties! Responsible conduct just isn't fun – is it fans?

War crimes will escalate and will be predictably overlooked again and again as we race to the ash heap of history -, with the parasitic Jews – like grinning vampires on the tree limbs above their victims looking forward to feasting on the collective prostrate body of an America, long metastasized into a Godless cancerous rotted corpse devoid of any courage or goodness or wisdom.

So -like I hear ALL Americans say – even to terminal patients in hospitals – and I kid you not ==

HAVE A NICE DAY!

FEBRUARY, 2010
ISRAEL – MY EXPERIENCES THERE IN THE SUMMER OF 1989

My name is Joe Cortina. I am a retired Florida businessman who has done substantial world traveling – some purely as a 'tourist' and some in areas – shall I say – that have 'nothing to do with vacationing'.

I am a former airborne special operations commander and have done intelligence investigator work for over 15years – some of it overseas – mostly in Central America – but also in the Mid-East. My political posture is "conservative" and my religious values are Christian.

Exposing lies and revealing the truth was what I did professionally for a long time. I have hunted REAL terrorists in jungles with Salvadorian Rangers and Marines – so I am not a stranger to dangerous environments and am familiar with basic protocols of civilized conduct regarding civilians and the military – something that the Israelis do not consider applicable to them.

For anyone wishing to challenge my credibility – I am willing to show credentials. I have a flawless civic record, an honorable military record and have never committed a crime nor ever been accused of such. I am mentioned as my father's son in the registry – 'PIONEER FLORIDA'. My grandfather was a pioneer in Florida in the most literal sense, and my father was a respected businessman and foreign diplomat.

I was invited to Israel by a former military comrade who attained a substantial rank and subsequently ended up as the ranking military attache' from our govt., to the Israeli military (IDF). I went places and saw things only a hand full of 'private sector' Americans will EVER experience. My 'specially authorized' trips included Gaza City, Hebron and areas of militarily protected Israeli 'settlements'. I will touch on only a few of what I considered the most revealing experiences. I can't stress this enough.

What I write here is but a tear in a sea of misery that I witnessed.

Treason to the United States:

While there I witnessed MANY signs and graffiti showing enthusiastic and shameless support by Israelis for the convicted American traitor Jonathon Pollard – a Jewish – Zionist Soviet spy. Intelligence experts in America have termed Pollard's treasonous acts second only to the Rosenbergs in the level of betrayal and endangerment to every American man woman and child.

According to officials in Tel Aviv, Pollard was AND STILL IS considered a hero – literally – to the Israelis.

I have personally witnessed COUNTLESS examples of pro-Traitor anti-American grafitti throughout many Israeli cities and towns. The casual "Fallwellian" putty brained robotic moron – on his pilgrimage to worship the "hometown of Satan" will probably never see these offensive TRUE feelings of the Israeli Jew – as few voyage beyond the safety and comfort of Tel Aviv – the carefully sanitized Jew showplace for their goy victims.

Make NO mistake – the neo-con Jew traitor Pollard was – and STILL IS a NATIONAL HERO in IsraHell – an urban legend. Mockery of traditional America and the TRUE Christian values most of us were raised with is a national pastime in IsraHELL. I have ventured well over the world and the only REAL threat to our beloved freedoms and blessings comes from the Jew in America and IsraHELL. PERIOD!

So much for any laughable notion of the Israeli 'love and concern' for American families.

There is no more mortal enemy to what is left of Godly decent patriotic families in "Israeli occupied AmeriKa, than the Zionist " be he an ethnic Jew or those who have sold our country out to the Jew – such as our IsraHELL Zionist loyal Treasonous Satan worshiping, blasphemous war-criminal, mega-murder Traitor President and his murderous ilk "advisors".

Israeli destruction of civilian homes and businesses:

The road blocks as one neared Gaza strip became increasingly secure and formidable. The absence of any civilian traffic was conspicuous. Once in either a suburb of Gaza or another city in the 'Strip' – I don't remember the exact name – a ride down the main street looked like a scene from some WWII movie. Windows shattered, charred rubble and destroyed vehicles littered the area. (I saw one still burning).

Then I noticed something a little strange. There was no building with any floor above the first. ALL buildings had any additional floors blasted into rubble – much of the jagged former construction black and charred. This was a city street not much different from any American small town. Shops, restaurants, services, apartment etc. – blown to bits and vacant as a tomb.

I learned quickly why the upper parts of the buildings (peoples homes and businesses, incidentally) – were blown away. This was to reduce any cover for potential snipers who might threaten Israeli patrols. Kind of like the mentality and rationale if it had been your hometown – after being occupied by the Soviets or Chinese communists. Just blow it all up! It is of no consequence if these were homes and businesses of the Palestinians — it was occupied by the Israelis now!

Mockery of America:

At one of the many roadblocks – usually manned by a small IDF military unit, we stopped our armored vehicle just long enough for the CIA to 'inspect' the situation.

I got outside and overheard 2 of these young soldiers speaking. Much to my surprise, they had Brooklyn accents! I asked them where they were from and they answered New York. Apparently they had left the States to serve a foreign power – remember – these were American citizens (who just happened to be Jews).

Puzzled at this bizarre reply, I decided to give benefit of doubt and responded with something like: "Boy, you guys are really something – having served the military of our country (remember – they were AMERICAN citizens) and then investing your time in a 'feeling for duty' to Israel".

They answered proudly and without hesitation: " Oh no – we haven't served in the United States military – there's no way". Then they both broke out in a cynical mocking laughter. So if there is any doubt where their loyalties lie – consider their unabashed answer of contemptuous scorn for the notion of patriotically serving in uniform for America.

I can't think of ANY male American CITIZEN who would sneer at serving the United States but willingly owed their loyalties to say Italy, or Greece or Ireland, or France or Germany just because his ancestors were of that ethnic group. AND – if one such person voiced such an opinion – you can imagine what people would think of him. But of course – apparently if you are Jewish – such odious and OPENLY PROUD mockery of love of this country is acceptable conduct. So much for the loyalty of the average American Jew to America.

Israeli sanctioned creation of 'incidents':

I witnessed 'settlers' vehicles driving around and around the homeland of the Palestinians (JUST LIKE YOUR HOMETOWN – NEVER FORGET THAT FACT!) whose purpose was only to taunt and humiliate the local inhabitants.

One of these cars had a sun roof through which protruded an Israeli flag (just like a Red Chinese flag from a car driving around in your American 'occupied' neighborhood) AND an M-16 automatic rifle to insure their torment of the helpless Palestinians was 'enforced'. ANY resistance to the dreaded 'settlers', and the UNITED STATES supplied IDF rolls in and just blows them away.

After all – remember – the Palestinians are considered no more than animals to the Israelis. Do you see some sort of hypocrisy here?

Regarding the horrendous brutality to the Palestinian civilians, more than one conscientious Israeli journalist has concluded that "the Palestinians are now the Jews and the Israelis are now the NAZIS".

This is a COMMON reference in Israel today. Ever see that analogy in an American Newspaper, magazine or TV presentation? Ever wonder why not?

There are dozens of such stories involving brutality and inhumane treatment of the Palestinians by the Israelis which must be put in historic perspective. This is the ancestral heritage and home of these Palestinians for over TWELVE HUNDRED YEARS! An entire MILLENNIA longer than the United States has been in existence! Just imagine a FOREIGN power GIVING AWAY some 85% of the entire United States to an invading foreign Colonizer!

This land has been the home for generations and generation of Palestinians, and 'Israelis' are the intruders and occupying force here NOT the other way around.

Cold-blooded murders, torture, shelling of schools and hospitals, bulldozing of homes with civilians buried alive, PURPOSEFUL destruction of ambulances full of wounded children and nearly every type of war crime imaginable including torture of eight out of ten Palestinians brought in for "questioning"!

The Jew terrorist Gestapo – the so-called IDF – have routinely committed the worst imaginable acts of sacrilege and blasphemy against religious believers in Palestine.

To FULLY appreciate the Barbaric, inhuman conduct of the Jew terrorists and their TRUE criminal sadistic nature I must reiterate my analogy of a "WHAT IF" scenario:

In YOUR home town, in your places of worship – a freedom which has been secured throughout history ONLY at the cost of life and limb – freedoms for which many a freedom loving American has sacrificed – and in my case – only risked his life to defend.

You walk into your church and to your horror witness soldiers of a Godless imperialist occupation army (the Red Chinese for example) defecating and urinating on the most sacred of the texts of your faith – the Holy Bible for instance. Grinning, soulless animals laughing and mocking our lord Jesus, and should lift even-so-much as a finger, you and your children and your priest or minister would be murdered on the spot.

Think on that ugly filthy scenario for just a few seconds – and should you even DARE to believe that such is a horrid nightmare fantasy of the mind – you had better come to the REALITY that this is NOT a hypothetical scenario for millions of enslaved Muslims and Christians (who are some 20% of the Palestinains) but an EVERYDAY HORROR THAT YOU HAVE MADE POSSIBLE by our cowardice, ignorance and hypocrisy.

Are you beginning to get the picture folks! A substantial number of the murdered civilians, murdered by the US financed terrorist IDF AND approved/enabled and supported by so-called American Christian churches (ESPECIALLY the Baptists) THESE PALESTINIAN VICTIMS ARE CHRISTIANS – living for centuries in peace with Islam!

I suggest that ALL of you that are not well educated read from the Quoran. Pick a translation and or source that satisfies your level of truth and conviction and READ THE TRUTH! Of all the religions other than Christian that I have had any opportunity to be acquainted with, the tenets of Islam come nearest to reflecting the TRADITIONAL Christian family values that I, as a Christian, learned from childhood!

TWO religions – ONE GOD! Jesus and mother Mary of the Christian NT are ALWAYS spoken about in the highest of regard and true reverence. LEARN THIS TRUTH for yourself.

THEN I ask you to learn the TRUTH from the books of law and protocol for Jew "religious" dogma. Our lord is OPENLY AND CLEARLY termed in the most contemptible of terms – A BASTARD! His blessed Mother Mary is OPENLY called a WHORE – a PROSTITUTE!

Or should you require a more contemporary, in your face source for Jew blasphemy of our Lord, His mother and our religious beliefs, simply go to the Jew controlled, Jew Produced and Jew directed "COMEDY CENTRAL". There you will find the TRUE face of the Jew and his vile blasphemous contempt for our Christian faith. But I digress. Back to IsraHELL and their concentration camps of death, starvation, murder and every horror imaginable to civilized man.

Remember I was in a unique position, rubbing elbows with CIA /Mossad and other Israeli officials who assumed that I was an "ally" or "colleague". I will remember the cruelty I witnessed there till the day I die! I had witnessed substantial horrors in other countries but never such criminal conduct bought and paid for by my own countrymen!

Many of these incidents were shared with me – although several from UNQUESTIONABLY reputable sources – many with established intelligence associates, I cannot PERSONALLY attest to but have absolutely NO REASON whatsoever to doubt their authenticity. Most of what I have told the reader and will tell – are incidents and conduct I witnessed FIRST HAND. Truths that I would unhesitatingly speak to the face of God if need be!

Brutality against children:

I will share one more incident (one I will not forget) which classically characterized the Israeli attitude to people which they OPENLY refer to as "animals".

While in another area of Gaza, we were following our IDF Para escort. It was an open jeep with heavily armed Paratroops. Suddenly it screeched to a halt not 10 yards in front of us and out jumped the men, one of whom immediately dropped to one knee and took careful aim at his victim to our immediate right.

The 'enemy', some 30-40 feet away, hands above his little head, brandished his weapon of defense (an egg size pebble) in the face of his tormentors – the 5th largest military in the world. Hardly sophisticated or dangerous – but there he stood – proud, defiant and fearless – a 10 year old child. This was HIS neighborhood and HIS country and HIS land and he was a prisoner in this Israeli 'concentration camp' for "animals". Think of it as a 'role change' for David and Goliath.

Children like this young lad, routinely 'disappear' in occupied territories. They are just never seen or heard of again. I have children and grandchildren whom I would defend with my life. I would like you to imagine for just a moment that you are not an American. Just close your eyes and visualize finding your beloved 10 year old child with half his head blown away, the flies feasting on his scattered brains. The unimaginable accident? NO – a war crime- and it is YOUR child! The 'sin' of your child? He was throwing egg sized rocks at an Israeli tank, BOUGHT and PAID FOR by AMERICAN citizens.

Could you just forget it as if were only the family cat or would you swear revenge/ justice against the monsters that made it happen? Could you possibly be so arrogant as to believe that this Palestinian mother and father loved their child any less than you would, or that 'his' life is 'worth' less in the eyes of God?

I had a Canon 35mm camera (official CIA issue at the time) and immediately jumped out of our vehicle and zeroed in on the would-be murderer – locked and loaded – not 10 paces in front of me. Apparently he saw what I was doing and muttered something I couldn't hear and angrily stood down as he withdrew back to his jeep. I never saw the child again and was grateful that I had been able to save his life by my 'intimidation' with a camera.

Upon returning to the embassy vehicle one of the people from Langley commented that I had undoubtedly saved the child's life. Another "intel passenger" in our group wryly stated that even so that same child probably would not live to see the end of the following week, much less his next birthday!

God only knows how many children that same jeep full of soldiers had murdered before or after I was there. It is a common practice by the Israeli govt. military to murder children for even the slightest provocation – or just for "sport". Just another dead "goy" animal to the Israelis. These were just some of the experiences of terror by the IDF that I had personally experienced. The stories I was told by other intelligence personnel there, would make your skin crawl. Depravities – rapes, murder, humiliation, beatings, desecrations and every manner of inhumane horrors.

The most accurate description of the IDF that I had heard was that they were in FACT " the largest institutionalized terrorist organization in the world". The conduct of these sadistic animals – more recently in Lebanon – as they mercilessly shelled fleeing civilians with 155mm white phosphorous (well documented war crimes!) – bear even more undeniable witness to the truth of that assessment. The documented lists of their terrorist acts as war criminals are now legion!

These are the events that occur daily in the 'concentration camps' of the Israelis – and MUCH MUCH worse! You will NEVER EVER see these horrors in the 'news' and rarely if ever even hear of them. Virtually ALL of these brutal activities are 'filtered' from the American public. You are ONLY ALLOWED to see what the 'entities' which control the media see fit for you to see.

ONLY relatively recently – with the wider offerings of 'chat rooms' 'web sites' and other similar internet facilities, do we begin to gain access to the truth without thousands of miles of travel, years of seasoned intelligence experience or personal perils. Look for the Jew to use his wealth to close down the internet as a "hate vehicle" while all the time he is the most hateful creature on the earth!

If you are disgusted with the mega-lies and misleading propaganda then educate yourself as to what is REALLY going on in the world. You will NOT find the complete truth in the newspaper – or Time – or Newsweek – Or Rush – or our Govt. – or TV or even our hypocrite evangelical pseudo-Christian church 'leaders'. These daily atrocities committed by the Israelis AND funded by YOU and ME, are carefully 'filtered' by our Israeli controlled press. Despite the one-sided propaganda, disinformation, distortions, and outright lies that we have been fed for years, you may now find and know the truth. The REAL truth, as in "so help me God".

We, the American people, with the help of the Godless blasphemous pseudo-Christian fundamentalist evangelist moronic scum who grovel at the feet of our Jew President, have now ALL been accomplices in the murders of over one million innocent civilian men women and children in Iraq and Afghanistan, ALL in the name of the Prince of Peace.

Perhaps our thinking has now been poisoned by the Jew so as to imitate the mentality of one of the most bloody monsters of all recorded time, Josef Stalin who, when he responded to the criticism of some of the more sane Russians at he time regarding his sadistic bloody purges of Christians said, "History will judge the unjust death of one human being as a tragedy but the murder of millions of innocents will remain nothing more than a statistic".

The cruel irony is that the same Jew mentality still permeates today as echoed in the acrid cruel comment of Jew Madeline Albright when questioned about the huge numbers of innocent civilians "ESPECIALLY CHILDREN" murdered in the process of warfare. In typical Jew fashion she called this enormous crime against the most helpless of God's creatures as "necessary collateral damage".

We have become what we used to despise the most – racist killers – soulless murderers of helpless children, thieves, imperialists and mindless mobs screaming for the endless blood of innocents, all in the name of Jesus. My mind cannot conjure a more revolting reality , except perhaps the mindless, Godless Jew Marxist mobs in the streets of Moscow screaming for the blood of the Christians some 80 years ago.

We American have been responsible for the deaths of WAY too many innocent human beings throughout the world recently. Sooner or later the truth will come to light – as it always does.

Do YOU have innocent blood 'on your hands'? ESPECIALLY encouraged by the blasphemous hatred sponsored by your supposedly "Christian" church? A LOT of Americans do – and a 'higher' Judge WILL hold them accountable for these crimes against humanity – even if not in this life.

Keep your eternal soul. Keep you conscience clean. The truth IS available. World War III is in the 'making' folks. The "model" revelation for "Armageddon" as described by Nostrodamus centuries ago, is now, at the beginning of the second millennium, becoming frighteningly clear. It is a no-brainer if you just open your eyes and your ears.

Thank you for taking time to learn this. I am willing to speak personally with any moral American who still possesses a conscience and wants to know the truth.

May God grant you the conscience to care about the good and the evil.

May God grant you the wisdom to distinguish the good from the evil.

May God grant you the courage to defend the good and expose the evil.

May YOU open your eyes and your ears AND your heart so God may be able to grant you these priceless gifts.

FEBRUARY, 2010
MIKE HUCKABEE – THE USEFUL IDIOT HYPOCRITE HUCKSTER

Just when you thought it was safe to go back to 'church' – here is one of the most hateful Christ mockers in Jew occupied AmeriKa. (Yes Dorothy – we ARE an occupied nation which has lost her sovereignty many years ago)

When I first saw this creep with his OWN TV show on the JEW/Fox channel – I smelled a rat. I asked myself: 'Joe – how is it possible in our Jew occupied nation today – for a supposedly professing 'Christian minister' to have his own Mega-glitzy TV show – AND – have the blessings of his Jew master boss – the Zionist Christ hating – Rupert Murdoch?'

You will NOT see even ONE truth speaking Christian personality on ANY major network show today.

The answer of course – is that it IS impossible – just as it is impossible for for Jew gangsters like Viacom's Sumner Redstone to allow any truth or decency or Christian values to be shared from his networks. In case you the reader has forgotten – ALL major TV and radio and printed news media in occupied Amerika are owned lock stock and barrel by the Jews. These Jews allow ONLY those sock puppets like Bill O-Reilly to spew their racist hatred and pseudo-Christian hypocrisy to their racist zombie brain-dead listeners. ANYONE who DARES to speak the truth of what the Jews do – will be destroyed – PERIOD! Show me even ONE man (or woman) who will speak out against the evil destruction of this nation's morals and economy by the Jew on a popular network for any length of time and have a job to come to the following day. We are a near 100% Jew censured nation today.

For those of you fools who still proclaim loyalty to frauds like Huckabee – here are some facts about your 'role model Christian'- NOT.' Here is some of the UNDENIABLE truth about the man who you wanted to become the 'CONSCIENCE OF THE NATION' – role model for your children – a man of impeccable morals who would defend the Christian based Constitution of The United States Of America.

Lets learn the TRUTH about this seedy greedy Godless IsraHELL loyal war mongering fraud

HUCKABEE THE HUCKSTER – is a greedy materialist. The Holy Bible tells us that it is better to give than to receive. Apparently Mr. Huckster believes otherwise. He and his equally greedy wife have accepted hundreds of thousands of dollars of bribes n the form of jewelry – exotic vacations – luxurious wardrobes. Just for a few examples – a $3700 pair of boots -a $500 belt – $20,000 in clothing – $70,000 in furniture – $43,000 in misuse of airplane and personal uses of campaign funds. He received over $120,000 of these bribe gifts in one year alone when Gov of Arkansas. Ordained preacher – MY ASS!

HUCKABEE THE HUCKSTER – His first loyalties are NOT To THIS country- but to IsraHELL. 'Huckster' claims to be an ordained (by who- SATAN?) Baptist minister yet his mockery of Christ and His holy Mother are as cruel as those of his good friends – the Talmudic Jews. To refresh your memory – the single most responsible evil entity for the cold-blooded murder of over one and a half MILLION innocent defenseless civilians in Iraq and Afghanistan – the total destruction of their nations – their economy – their schools – places of worship – sanitation facilities – hospitals – schools – cultural centers – are the fat pasty brain-dead Baptist scum of this nation.

Remember – these people have NEVER – done us any harm or ever been a threat to America's well being in any way whatsoever! Neither one of these unfortunate sovereign nations has ever attacked America – yet ' evangelist Christian minister' Huckabee – along with his demonic mentor – Hagee – SCREAM for the blood of these innocent human beings to be murdered to the last woman and child!

Here is but one of the Huckster's arrogant displays of loyalty of his murderous Baptist scum: " There ought to be one city. It ought to be a Jewish State and it ought to be secure. So maybe one of the hard things is to convince some of our Jewish friends that Evangelicals are the best friends they've got— because I think generally, that's the case."

Proof enough? But like the TV salesman says : BUT WAIT – THERE'S MORE!

HUCKABEE THE HUCKSTER – also mocks God by cheap 'Elmer Gantry' mentality carnival stunts like staging a personal cell phone conversation with God – Who tells him that GOD wanted mega murderer war criminal drug addict alcoholic George Bush to be elected President. Huckabee ALSO tells people that Jesus also wants HIM to be elected. Talk about a BLASPHEMOUS piece of crap! I just can't make this stuff up folks. Check it out for your self. Not even the POPE has ever been so audaciously brazen, impious and arrogant as the HUCKSTER! In his Presidential campaigns he does his Jesus thing to the max – as long as he is in 'friendly territory'. BUT – once he is out of his Bible belt environment – he 'leaves the cross at home'. Ask anyone who has followed his campaign. How brave! What a spineless hypocrite.

Peter denied Jesus three times – a cowardly act – BUT he later repented and became a great leader of the Church. Apparently the HUCKSTER is STILL too busy and STILL too cowardly counting his 30 pieces of Jew silver to repent his denial of Jesus committed during his political campaigns. Doubt that as the TRUTH? Check it out for yourself.

HUCKABEE THE HUCKSTER – publicly mocks Mary, the virgin mother of Jesus as if she was a 2 bit street whore. He calls the virgin birth of Christ a "COMPLETER DISASTER". Now isn't that special Next time you readers who are TRUE Christians – perhaps Catholic – as I was raised, before the Pope sold out to the Pharisees – and are visited by some Hagee Baptist creep – just keep this sick rancid Jew menality attitude of theirs in mind.

I invite you to listen to the HUCKSTERS ridicule and contempt of the Blessed Virgin Mary. Here are just a few of his rancid Jew mentality comments of mockery. [Huckabee in interview]: "Silent Night, Holy Night? Are you kidding me! She was probably screaming – OH MY what's going on here. She's gotta be saying to herself – IF THIS IS REALLY GOD'S CHILD – where are all those angels that are supposed to be around. The sanitized church version is what we imagine Mary looking up at heaven and saying oh my baby!" This is the way that the Jews like to ridicule the Mother of Jesus – NEVER ANY TRUE CHRISTIAN- OR far that matter NEVER EVER any TRUE Islamic

HUCKABEE THE HUCKSTER – On knowledge of our Government and the Founding Fathers. Remember – this asshole wanted to be our PRESIDENT! Read what this uneducated arrogant moron has to say about all those poor ignorant camel jockeys and sand-niggers : "Although we cannot export democracy (gee Mr. huckster – I always thought that we had a REPUBLIC – as the Founding Fathers warned us about the evils of [MOB RULE] Democracy) as if it were Coca-Cola or KFC, we can nurture moderate forces in places where AL- Qaeda is seeking to replace modern evil with medieval evil. Such moderation may not look or function like our system–it may be a benevolent oligarchy or more tribal than individualistic–but both for us and for the peoples of those countries, it will be better than the dictatorships they have now or the theocracy they would have under radical Islamists." (WOW – brilliant foreign policy idea huckster – as you can see – our "moderate forces" have MURDERED IN COLD-BLOOD over 1,500,000 innocent civilians so far and destroyed 10,000,000 homes – totally destroyed their civilian infrastructure schools government hospitals all electric power water and sanitation industry businesses – with OUR version of 'MODERN EVIL' – so let's see if I understand your 'Zio/Christian' mentality. By murdering and making homeless tens of millions of citizens in THEIR OWN sovereign nation – it will be better for them AND us?)

HUCKABEE THE HUCKSTER – on foreign policy. OH – Here is a GOOD ONE! Protect U.S. sovereignty, but earn respect abroad I don't want to ever give up one ounce of US sovereignty. Our soldiers would never march to the orders of somebody else's generals. (Gee wiz Huckster – is that why you give total loyalty to IsraHELL and use your Godless Christian hating Baptist buddies to take us into endless serial wars against nations that IsraHELL doesn't like and has not shed a drop of Jew blood there themselves?) I wouldn't give up our territory. I wouldn't give up our rights. I wouldn't give up our strength.
In fact, I'd want to strengthen this country. I think the greatest way to export democracy is not to force it, but rather to build the best possible version of it right here so people are attracted to it.

There is an important role that the United States has as the most powerful nation on earth militarily and economically, to act in such a way that people respect us and that people also realize that we are a great nation, not one that wants to push ourselves on others. ("NOT FORCE IT" – "NOT ONE THAT WANTS TO PUSH OURSELVES ON OTHERS" – I'm confused huckster. You want to help IsraHELL by destroying nation after nation after nation and murder millions of innocent women and children – and also want to send 300,000 MORE of someone elses sons to murder even more innocent people and destroy even more innocent lives?)

HUCKABEE THE HUCKSTER – on Attack Iran's nukes even if Congress says no
Q: If you were president, would you need to go to Congress to get authorization to take military

action against Iran's nuclear facilities?
: A president has to do whatever is necessary to protect the American people. If we think Iran is building nuclear capacity that could be used against us in any way, including selling some of the nuclear capacity to some other terrorist group, then yes, we have a right to do it. And I would do it in a heartbeat. (WOW – Mr. Huckster what balls you have! Just where did you get all that military experience know how – more personal cell phone calls from God? I am so impressed. Why – I was training thousands of young warriors before you had learned your ABCs – LITERALLY! – and I would shudder at such a responsibility to have to murder so many millions of innocent people since I was only a lowly Captain.

Speaking of nuclear capability – there IS – in fact – one country in that part of the world who DOES have WMDs. HUCKSTER – Did you know that this country has threatened to use these WMDs against us? Did you know that this rogue country is considered by the rest of the educated free world to be the biggest threat to world peace? Did you know that this country is the only nation on earth to have COMMITTED an ACT OF WAR – by technical definition – against the sovereignty of the United States in the past 69 years? Did you know that this war mongering country harbors the world's largest institutionalized TERRORIST organization? Do you know ANYTHING – Mr. Huckster? as 'foreign policy' means OUTSIDE OF LITTLE ROCK)
Q: Without going to Congress?
A: Well, if it's necessary to get it done because it's actionable right now, yes. If you have the time and the luxury of going to Congress, that's always better. (So HUCKSTER – you WILL trash the Constitution AND the will of the people and start WWIII just to please your Jew friends -correct?)
Q: And if Congress says no, what do you do? A: You do what's best for the American people, (But Huckster – since when is loyalty FIRST to another foreign power " BEST FOR THE AMERICAN PEOPLE" – as you so often state?) and you suffer the consequences. What you never do is let the American people one day get hit with a nuclear device because you had politics going on in Washington instead of the protection of the American people first. (SO – when are you going to protect OUR nation form this rogue lunatic cabal of gangsters that have ALREADY attacked us by ORDERS FROM THEIR LEADER – AND threatened to nuke us this time?)

HUCHABEE THE HUCKSTER – on 'winning the war in Iraq at all costs' Q: Why not withdraw the troops from Iraq?

A: Because we are winning. Civilian deaths are down 76% since the surge. Even the military deaths are down over 60%. And that's not the only way we know we're winning. (Just what is IT that we are WINNING Mr. huckster? Is it the hearts and minds of the people by our kindness in murdering them? Is the safety we now enjoy in our homes not having the army of these invaders and occupiers in our cities and towns anymore? Are we winning back for what terrible things these armies did by bombing and burning our towns and cities – raping our women – murdering our children by the hundreds of thousands – and torturing and humiliating our townsfolk?) We're winning because we see in the spirit of our own soldiers a sense of duty and honor that they are being able to carry out a mission that they were sent there to do. (let me see if I have this straight – you see that "our soldiers have a sense of duty and honor" – DUTY and HONOR to do exactly WHAT MR. warmonger? To murder another MILLION WOMEN AND CHILDREN? The maim and disfigure and make homeless refugees out of another TEN MILLION INNOCENT HUMAN BEINGS – MR. WAR MONGER? I know where I got my notion of duty and honor huckster – but WHERE IN HELL DID YOUR GET YOURS? – from your years of military service? – OH I forgot – you were such an obese glutenous 300# pig – you could barely walk up stairs – while other young men served – sorry I asked) To take them out of it not only means we lose, but it means we totally destroy their sense of morale, and it may take a generation to get it back. But there's more at stake than just their morale. It's the safety and the security of the Middle East and the rest of the world. This is about every one of us being able to be free, to have a future, and to be able to know that we're not going to allow a vacuum there, which happens if we lose–and we lose when we walk away–to create an opening so that terrorists (By TERRORISTS – you obviously mean the every day families – mostly civilian women and children who comprised the bulk of the ONE MILLION FIVE HUNDRED THOUSAND graves we left behind as our legacy to them) can build even greater cells of training there. That's why we have to stay. And it's why we have to win. (READ: MURDER MORE INOCENT PEOPLE) HUCKABEE THE HUCKSTRER – on his phony hypocrite pro-life bullshit. This one I personally watched. I happen to be a defender of innocent life and have been since I was old enough to know right from wrong. I love most animals – but I am speaking of HUMAN LIVES HERE. Here is the extent of what Huckabee the hypocrite views as a 'LIFE' worthy of protecting from murder. He had a woman who ostensible had worked FOR an abortion clinic – but apparently had this marvelous 'epiphany' one day as she observed an ultrasound of an infant being murdered in the mother's womb by the assassin (a paid killer). She made no effort to stop the murder but said she was emotionally affected by it. She referred to the infant not as a child - or a baby or infant – but "IT". In one ten second segment of her description she referred to the doomed child – as "IT" over and over : "Then the Dr. (the serial child murdering abortionist) inserted the probe and I could see "IT" trying to escape, then the probe was pushed into "IT" and "IT" died before my eyes.

I thought silently to myself – what in name of God was this woman thinking? This was a CHILD – a HUMAN LIFE – a creation of GOD – to be a son or daughter and all she could describe was an "IT" – the same demeaning term used by abortionists to dehumanize a human life. I fully expected Huckabee to tactfully correct her crude identity or at least wince – but he only applauded and smiled with approval. Out of curiosity I looked in my Oxford Thesaurus. "IT means a "THING". Have you ever heard a father or mother call their infant son or daughter – A THING – or- IT?

But the real hypocrisy of this Jew sock puppet is that – while – he spouts his staunch uncompromising pro-life posture like a holy grail – he has ABSOLUTELY no problem with our murderous psychopath 'troops' murdering HUNDREDS OF THOUSANDS OF INNOCENT CHILDREN AND PREGNANT MOTHERS IN IRAQ AND AFGHANISTAN – AND of course as he so bravely spouted – he would bypass our Congress and our nation's laws AND the law of GOD to murder millions of more innocent human beings! I have only scratched the surface of the TRUE character of this rancid Christ mocking goy puppet – but you get the picture. 'LIFE' is important to him ONLY if the 'LIFE' is white Anglo-Saxon Protestant Zio/Christian. The Huckster's 'Jew-Jesus' apparently doesn't love "Rag-head – camel-jockey – sand nigger" children. So much for the HUCKSTER's 'SELECTIVE' pro-life mentality.

For ANY American who freely voted for this piece of greedy lying hypocrite impious crap – go to your room for a 'time out'!

MARCH, 2010
NATIONAL JEWISH HISTORY MONTH – GIFTS TO AMERICAN LIFE BY OUR JEWISH FRIENDS

Well here we are once again – just a few weeks away from another annual celebration of all those wonderful things that the 'chosenites' have seen fit to bequeath to us ignorant goy to enrich our history.

The person who created this wonderful taxpayer funded official recognition day to honor Jews is no other than the Jew – Fl. Rep Debbie Wasserman Schultz. If after learning of the extent of these wonderful 'enriching contributions' to Christian America – perhaps you may wish to contact Rep. Debbie Wasserman Schultz your self and express your 'gratitude' and 'pleasure' for her efforts. You may contact her at any of these various numbers : In DC @202-2262052 in Fl @ 954-4374776 or @ 305 -9365724

Debbie has an agenda and here is part of her PERSONAL contributions to Jew history in America. Her policies which are in predictably concert with all Jew legislators are as follows: She is 100% for confiscation of your private firearms. She is pushing legislation to make freedom of speech and expression a crime punishable by prison (the Jews call it hate crime legislation) She is 100% in support of homosexual perverts – pedophiles etc. She is 100% in support of the continued mass murder of unborn children and is presently pushing legislation to make sure we stupid goy Christians must use our personal earnings to fund these murders. Keep in mind that she is considered a 'rising star' in Democrat circles and may very well become the next Democrat speaker of the House – GOD FORBID!

"The Jewish people have enriched our culture and contributed to a more compassionate and hopeful America. I call upon all Americans to observe this month [May] with appropriate programs and activities that honor the significant Jewish contributions Jewish American have made to our nation" (statement by war criminal George Bush – when he signed this Jew proposed bill into law)

The list of Jew contributors is so sumptuous and rich that it is difficult to express the awe and gratitude with which we Americans should feel for the enrichment to our lives freedoms and blessings which the Jewish people have so selflessly bestowed upon us and all mankind. It is hard to know where to start when it involves such a generous compassionate wise truthful trustworthy loyal wholesome sincere honest kind and noble race as the JEWS! I will do my best to try and remember ALL of the 'special gifts' from 'god's chosen people'.

Perhaps one of the best examples of my gratitude is 'Operation Cast Lead'. In my initial ignorance I mistakenly placed my sentiments with the suffering and dying children of Gaza –

slaughtered by the thousands – mutilated and burned to death by weapons outlawed by the Geneva Convention – all 100% supported by powerful influential American Jews. After listening to the wisdom and logic of prominent Zionist leaders like Joe Biden and Joe LIEberman – I came to realize that these children were in actuality not really human or valuable like Jewish children in IsraHELL and had to be eliminated like 'cockroaches' – as the Jews mock them. After all, these kids might come to attack America and take over our proud nation and steal our freedoms – so it is better to kill them all now – just in case. Thank you Jews for protecting our nation.

At first I was against that Medical care Reform Bill because it was obvious that most of America was too and that so much was done behind closed doors and that the costs would be passed on to my grandchildren and beyond. Another issue that bothered my very soul was the use of my tax dollars to murder unborn children. You see – I'm one of those superstitious Christians who believe that it is against the will of God to murder a helpless innocent child. However – I'm glad that the wisdom of people like President Obama and his chief of Staff Rohm Emanuel and Jews in general has prevailed to remind me that it is a woman's right to murder her own child and as Zionist Nancy Pelosi stated – it is unfair to many Americans to penalize a woman for having a "pre-existing condition" such as being pregnant and not having Christians fund the murder. I know this was the right thing to do because I watched the hearings and final arguments and a Jew would never lie to us.

Like all parents – we love our children and worry when they are placed in harm's way. My youngest son recently joined the Army and proudly showed me how in basic training he was taught how to smash down the doors in someone's home and arrest or kill all the civilians inside. Being against immoral wars you can understand my concerns with the safety of my child's life AND of the effect of his murdering civilians on his conscience and soul – but what do I know. If the President and the Congress with all those wise Jews like Debbie advising and watching over every thing they do don't know what is right for AmeriKa – who does? Since we are waging these wars solely to protect our good friend and ally – IsraHELL – even though we have murdered over TWO MILLION INNOCENT CIVILIANS – and lost tens of thousands of our sons in the process – it must be the wise thing to to since you Jews tell us so, and your Rabbis tell us that the "Jews will always take the moral high ground".

I noticed that there are some TV adds that I found disturbing in their sexual nature to be watched by my innocent granddaughters. One asked me recently "Gramps – what does it mean when the lady says that "a mans member gets longer and harder and makes sex more fun'? " Oh and Grandpa – what is an erection? And why is an erection dangerous if it lasts too long". At first I was angry that such things would be said in front of innocent children and arouse their curiosity. But later – I found out that all of these companies that sold these sex aids were owned by Jews. Boy was I relieved! I figured that if JEWS thought it was Ok for young children to be exposed to this – it had to be OK. Thanks Jews – for your wisdom.

I keep seeing our Lord Christ and His mother Mary being called "BASTARDS" and "WHORES" on your Jew History Channel. I was angered at first – but when a whole bunch of those Jew 'religious' men – I believe they are called Rabbis – were quoted as proof that it was so – I didn't feel any better about it – but at least I wasn't angry any more. After all – a wise Jewish Religious man wouldn't purposely tell lies about such a good person – now would they. Once again Jews – thanks for setting me and my family straight about the TRUE history of 'illegitimacy of Jesus and his 'prostitute' mother – and a SPECIAL thanks from my family to you- Debbie.

This last Christmas I saw something disturbing at the White House. They always since I was a child – celebrated the Birth of baby Jesus with those beautiful nativity manger scenes and lots of Christmas carols about joy and hope and peace and brotherhood. This year it was different. A Jew hate group called Chabad Labavitch put up a huge 3 story thing that looked like a giant fish gig – called a Menorah. I don't remember ever seeing this thing associated with the celebration of the birth of Jesus. I looked it up and instead of celebrating hope and joy and love and brotherhood like Jesus preached – these people celebrated a bloody massacre of thousands of innocent Greek People.

It seems like whenever you Jews have a formal celebration of some sort – it is always about violence, bloodshed hatred and murder. But once again – logic must prevail. Would the President of my own Christian founded and led America – allow such a horrid thing – a cruel and blasphemous mockery of all that Jesus stands for – allowed on the LAWN OF THE WHITE HOUSE NO LESS? Of course not. That would be total insanity and a slanderous insult to the nearly 200 million professing Christians here. Unthinkable! SO -the only obvious answer would be that this strange message of the Jews is of more historical and moral and patriotic importance than silly Christmas trees and childish Nativity scenes. Thanks again Jews for your superior wisdom and guidance in teaching us your history.

(7) I used to think that traitors like the Jews Julius and Ethyl Rosenberg who sold the plans to the atom bomb to the Communists and the Jew Jonathan Pollard sold submarine technology to the Israelis and Red Chinese were terrible people for selling out our country to mortal enemies. I remember seeing in Jew cities outside of Tel Aviv in Israel – that the people all supported these spies, and that Pollard was especially loved as a national hero for his betrayal of America. The Graffiti was everywhere. Well – I guess I must admit I was wrong – because if President Bush is so convinced that "The Jewish people have enriched our culture and contributed to a more compassionate and hopeful America" – I and tens of millions of other patriots and veterans must simply not understand that these and dozens of other mostly Jew spies did what they did out of "compassion" and a desire to "enrich" our lives. Thanks, Debbie- for clearing this up for us inferior stupid cattle.

(8) I remember being taught in school that without the Second Amendment – all the others would literally have no real protection if our Government decided to take these rights away – like our two Presidents past and seated have done against the will of the people. Here are a few statements of that wisdom from the Founding Fathers that I remembered "No free man shall ever be de-barred the use of arms. The strongest reason for the people to retain their right to keep and bear arms is as a last resort to protect themselves against tyranny in government."- Thomas Jefferson ——and :"The said constitution shall never be construed to authorize congress to prevent the people of the United States who are peaceable citizens from keeping their own arms."- Samuel Adams —- and: "The great object is that every man be armed. Everyone who is able may have a gun." – Patrick Henry —— also: "Americans need never fear their government because of the advantage of being armed, which the Americans possess over the people of almost

every other nation."- James Madison. But I guess that these old men were just not 'progressive' (Debbie likes that word) enough for today's America and should be disregarded as suggested by Debbie and most other prominent American Jews. Thanks Jews!

(9) I was always taught that human life was precious and that the purposeful taking of an innocent life was MURDER – the greatest of sins. But since I learned that from my CHRISTIAN Bible – it must be wrong because most Jews hate Christ and what he taught and stood for. Debbie the Jew makes no apologies for her agenda to kill more unborn children and make us Christians pay for the murders!

And After all – if a wise contributing 'chosen' Jew like Debbie – flat out refused to take her oath in Congress on our "anti-Semitic" Christian Bible – this unquestionably being a nation founded upon Christian principles – there must be something terribly wrong with it – OTHERWISE she would NOT have been allowed to mock our holiest Book – now would she? AND since she showed open contempt and mockery towards her Christian opponent in a fairly recent election – for his use of the 'Cross' in his campaign – He must have been wrong. If it is Ok for the 'chosenites' to promote child murder – it certainly must be OK for us inferior gentiles. I mean – since there isn't even a National CHRISTIAN History Month – and a professing Christian President decrees a National JEWISH History Month – and the White House now only celebrates a JEW festival celebrating violence and murder on Christmas day -the Jews and their beliefs MUST be more important than ours – right? Thanks once again Jews- for bringing us out of our ignorance with our foolish superstitions.

(10) To those who have pioneered in the area of finance – we are eternally grateful. The Jew has always been the master of economics and without his manifold contributions to our economy – who knows where we night be today without their guidance and intervention. Fiscal giants who name are household words today have led the way. Greenspan – Bernake – Boesky -Milken – Grubman – Fastow – Winnick- Frankel – Richs – Finklestein – Wachsals – Fagan – Driers – Belsky- Israel – Nadal- Madoff – Merkin and Stein. The total 'contribution' to the economic well being of the average American citizen may never be fully realized. I'm sure that our recent total economic collapse was not due to criminal mismanagement of the banks or the Fed by Jews. It must all be some sort of misunderstanding as people as noble as JEWS would NEVER do anything that greedy selfish cunning and criminal – RIGHT – Debbie?

And finally – we owe thanks for the American Jew contributions to all the Jew directors and producers of all those really exciting gory violent sex filled movies. I used to be worried about the innocence of my children – and then my grandchildren, regarding what they saw on TV and in movie theatres and even in children's entertainment parks like the now Jew run Disneyworld. Years ago my wife had friends that worked there and we were shocked to learn that there was a HUGE percentage of homosexual perverts in M. Eisner's employ. I remember he even bragged about it.

The Jew TV teaches our children that violence is good and I'm sure that Debbie agrees 100%. Jews have been pioneers in the entertainment industry and of course 'own' Hollywood. By the time your son or daughter in in high school – he or she has witnesses well over a HUNDRED THOUSAND VIOLENT MURDERS rapes beatings mutilations shootings crashes and every kind of terror imaginable on your Jew dominated TV. Many prominent physicians analysts social workers and clinical researchers have testified that the main cause of teen crime, suicide, pregnancies, assaults and now endless war crimes unparalleled in American military history – are a result of the desensitization of our children due to the 1500+ hours /yr that our youth is exposed to in Jew produced sex violence and endless demonic perversions on TV and hyper violent sadistic bloody 'war game' videos.

Once again – I must resign myself to the fact that these Jews with their superior intellects somehow know what is best for our children and that it is not just done because it is immensely profit table. Since we have voluntarily afforded Jews total control of everything our children see and do and believe from 1st grade on – I must assume that it is for the best as they are much more wise than we cattle. AND since they ALSO control ALL of our government from the executive to the legislative to the Judicial – from Federal to urban level – it has been the will of the people.

How do I know that for fact? Well – aside from the fact that the Jews themselves – like Rep. Debbie and their puppets – excuse me – I meant associates – have told us that they know what is best for us – there is another good reason. I know that I am right because of the following truism of wisdom so stated by a famous patriot: "In America – a free Republic – the values and morals of our elected officials – from the President down to the city councilman are a mirror image of those values and morals of the electorate". Therefore our leaders are EXACTLY what we wished for and EXACTLY reflect our own values. Unfortunately this speaks disgracefully of our OWN character as a people today.

My undying gratitude to all of these Jews in America – for their "contributions – enrichment – and hope" – they have so selflessly bestowed upon our occupied nation of 'Christian cattle'.

MARCH, 2010
IGNORANCE IN AMERICA – A DISGRACEFUL EPIDEMIC

Human beings are scientifically identified from all other life-forms by nine classifications. Those are Kingdom – Phylum- Subphylum -Class-Subclass- Order – Family – Genus- and Species

The complete classification description reads ; ANIMALIA- CHORDATA- VERTEBRATA-MAMMALIA- THERIA- PRIMATE- HOMINIDAE- HOMO-SAPIENS The most prominent difference between homo-sapiens and lower animals – WAS – our large highly developed brain.

What is sadly apparent is that American Homo-Sapiens has apparently degraded over generations into something more like the early 'Hominids -or human like creatures. A logical explanation might be that our brains simply began to atrophy from disuse – much like what happens to muscles not being used for an extended period of time as when in a '.cast'. They simply waste away and if in disuse for long enough they simply become useless. Sitting on a couch with a cold six-pack and pizza in front of your TV for thousands and thousands of hours

For instance – here are some interesting if not downright disturbing (assuming that the reader is not one of the newly designated idiots) facts about what Americans most cherish and or allow their children to. You can verify any or all of this yourself on your computer with most search engines.

Your younger children watch the Jew Tube (Yes Dorothy virtually ALL American TV networks are run by financed by and directed by the self-chosen) for an average of FOUR hours a day. Adults watch 30-35 hours of brain numbing mush a week. In the average American home the TV set is turned on an average of almost SEVEN HOURS A DAY! The percentage of Americans who watch TV while eating dinner (Remember when we were kids – that was a time for family to get together and talk.) is 66%. The number of HOURS Americans watch the Jew Tube annually – 250,000,000,000! Number of library books checked out by our kids daily in the US = 3,000,000. The number of video rented daily in America = 6,000,000. But wait there's MORE – and it only gets WORSE!

Ever wonder why your kids are strangers in their own home – why your daughters are pregnant at 13 – why your sons have a police drug record at 15? Consider this disgraceful American fact! While your kids spend almost TWENTY EIGHT HOURS a week watching Jew violence sex profanity blasphemy perversions adultery and a laundry list of lies — The average time per WEEK – that parents spend meaningful conversation with their children is = LESS THAN 4 MINUTES TOTAL! The average hours per year your kids spend in school – ostensibly to keep from becoming idiots? = 900. AND the average hours per year that your kids are getting dumbed-down and becoming emotionally desensitized by violence and killing and perversions on the Jew Tube 'learning' how to hate and kill and cheat and lie? = ONE THOUSAND FIVE HUNDRED!

Oh and here is a really EXTRA special 'side benefit' of the Jew dominated filth and violence on TV. Your own kids prefer the 'exciting' Jew way of life than that boring old fashioned home life I loved as a kid . When asked which they would prefer – the MAJORITY of your innocent impressionable 4-6 year old children actually preferred watching the neat – dazzling crap on the JewTube -rather than spend time with THEIR OWN FATHERS! More Jew incited horrors to come.

The number of gruesome murders your child will see on the Jew Tube by the time he has finished ELEMENTARY school (6 years) ? = EIGHT THOUSAND! That is TEN TIMES more than the number of real murders investigated by the head of a homicide division of a major metropolitan city like Chicago in an entire lifetime (25 years) By the time your son is out of high school – he has witnessed almost a QUARTER MILLION acts of violence on the Jew Tube. The Jews REALLY love violence you know!

And for you adult Jew Tube addicts – here is more bad news. For every hour of news you watch – you are forced to watch 20 minutes of commercials. AND – well over half of the time of news stories on your Jew owned and operated 'news' facilities – are devoted to war crime disaster and other violence. Remember when there was 'news' that included ordinary GOOD people doing GOOD deeds? That was when Christians like Walt Disney had a hand in what we and our children saw. The Jews took care of that sentimental nonsense and insured that we became dumbed-down with what THEY want us to see. Why – today you can't find more than15% of adult Americans who can name 3 supreme court justices – BUT 60% can name the Three Stooges. Are you getting the message yet?

But back to the reclassifying of 'dumbed down' American citizens. A body builder is an example of the zenith of muscular perfection through excessive musculature training. A genius does the same thing to his brain – and both examples must 'stay in training' if they wish to maintain a certain high level of development. When I was growing up in America – most people maintained a moderate condition of both mental and physical condition for reasons which were apparent. One helped our appearance and health and the other allowed us to make good decisions- stay out of trouble – make a living and know when we were being fooled or lied to or compromising our freedoms and morals. This necessity to remain free was not just an option in the minds of the wisest of the elect – it was a MANDATE. It has been voiced a hundred times by a hundred of the world's wisest men over hundreds of years – but always the same message. A stupid people will ALWAYS eventually lose whatever freedoms their wiser forbearers bequeathed to them so as to ultimately become slaves.

"If a nation expects to be ignorant and free, in a state of civilization, it expects what never was and never will be."

– Thomas Jefferson

After a lifetime of observing what can only be described as the dumbest creatures on the planet – it seemed logical that most Americans – aside from becoming globular and spherical in shape – had evolved into creatures so devoid of rational thinking that we now needed a new biological classification – perhaps THIS more typifies the average American today:. Animalia – Chordata – Invertebrata – Mammalia – Americanus – Vulgaris – Homo -Moronicus – Illigitimus – stupidicus. OR – more easily abbreviated as : Americanus – Vulgaris – Timorous – Moronicus. Spineless common American morons. The proof of this phenomenon is legion! Here are a few classic examples.

The bogus medical reform bill is coming up for a vote as I write this. It is one of the most corrupt larcenous boondoggles in American legislative history – yet it will probably pass against the will of the sheeple. Last night it was revealed that former scumbag – coward – draft dodger – druggie – murderer – whore monger – liar – adulterer – traitor– in- chief Bill the Klintonista, Clinton was selected by the Demoncrap Party as their revered poster boy hero, to convince 'undecided' Demoncrap legislators to support the Obamanation's world-class disaster 'for a change' – death Bill!

Just the FACT that HALF of voting America – has of their own free will – decided to even associate themselves with the biggest consortium of thieves, political whores, Zionists, liars and country-sellers is a per-se validation of my suggestion for a re-classification of the mentally ossified 'hominids' who make up the 'power base' of that cabal of fools and idiots.

For at least the past half century the Demoncrap Party has been a human garbage magnet for virtually all of the brain-dead detritus in this country. Virtually ALL of the lowlife rap-trap crap gang banger mentality Negros and low life red-neck 'wiggers' comprise the backbone of the Party. 95% of the Jews in this country (100% of which are loyal to IsraHELL) are Demoncraps. Near 100% of the pedophiles- sex deviates – baby killers – porn kings and organized crime tzars call it home. Aside from the Jews – who are not in the stupid category – but are just plain demonically evil – the majority of the rest are of the brain sharing 'new genus/species'. More proof?

The innocence of our children is bombarded 24-7 – 12 hours a day by 'Jew Tube' filth of every kind imaginable, from non-stop mockery of Jesus and His mother as well as All things truly Christian – to endless graphic ultra-violence and lurid sex/porn – to in your face descriptions of how to make your cock bigger and sex more fun – to the glorification of every sin on the 'Tablets' with some to boot. Do you morons do ANYTHING about these serious attacks on the virtue and souls of your OWN children?

NA! – too busy with really important intellectual stuff like NFL foooot-ball 'games' and tailgate parties. Ever take time to teach your kids about REAL heroes like the Founding Fathers or people who sacrifice their lives daily to secure your freedoms – or what America is REALLY all about? NA! – don't bother me kid – can't you see I'm watching the 'Stupid Bowl' and my beer is getting warm wasting time with your nonsense? I have watched exactly that scenario in my own neighborhood for years! Need more proof of our moronic transformation?

I Had my service flag (was a former Special Forces airborne commander) flying upside down in my front yard for THREE YEARS to protest the insanity of the needless Jew inspired and mandated serial wars in which over TWO MILLION INNOCENT CIVILIANS HAD BEEN MURDERED IN COLD BLOOD and over 50,000 American sons returned home in pine boxes (Yes Dorothy – we HAVE been lied to about the TRUE casualties – among OTHER LIES!) Keep in mind that it was seen thousands of time by thousands of people and most neighbors knew I was a former Green Beret. In all of that exposure only ONE person even bothered to ask what would have upset a veteran neighbor enough to display the 'flag' in the universal sign of distress. This one sole mental midget said; – "Duhh – did somebody die?" Here's your sign! Convinced yet? NO? Here's more.

I can't begin to tell you how many ADULT American citizens have voiced their anger that "then damned MOOSELIMS" caused the 911 incident – or the obscene price of gas – or the triple digit inflation – or our collapsing economy – or the main threat to American freedoms – or the way we are now treated as cattle at airports – or how they plan to take over AmeriKa – or how they threaten our way of life – or how "we need to fight them (the 2,000,000 civilians -mostly defenseless children we have murdered) 'there' so we won't have to fight then here" moron mentality – or how offended some red-neck was because an American woman of Arab descent had her face covered (I'm SURE that this troglodyte brain-sharing 'hominid' wouldn't have been offended if the modest girl had half her tits and ass exposed for every mother' son to ogle at – like our exhibitionist home grown sluts find so cool. Most of these idiots have never been outside their own State! Ask them about the USS Liberty massacre by the Jews in the Med and they will say something like this one idiot did = "Duh – was that one of them old British wood boats?" Still not convinced? I got plenty more – folks – so read on.

Some creative TV show people in urban LA decided to see just how dumb we really are. A few months ago -a guy went around shopping centers and boardwalks displaying a Canadian 'maple leaf' one ounce gold coin – a real one. He told the people he spoke with that IF they could tell him the value of the coin within 30% they would own it – no tricks no joke. I can't imagine ANY adult American in a metropolitan area in the USA not realizing that gold – the monetary value standard for all civilization for thousands of years! (which at the time was in the news – TV everywhere) was then over $1100/ounce. He interviewed at least a dozen adult men and women – all well dressed and Caucasian. The guesses ranged (and I'm NOT kidding!) from $25 to $200 – not remotely close! Here's your sign! But it gets better!

As I was leaving my physician's office a few months ago at an upscale medical center – I noticed an elderly well dressed Negro patient with pleasant smiling face – using a cane and limping her way to the elevator. I held the door for her and noticed that as she got in – she was wearing a colorful quality fashionable Obama sweatshirt. As we were the only ones there and the elevator moved at about a foot per month – I decided to ask her a question. I said: "Excuse me -and I know it is really none of my business – but I am curious – may I presume you voted for President Obama?" She smiled and said "yes". I then told her I did political analysis (which was true) and asked her what was the main reason she used for her decision. She looked pensive for a moment and then somewhat sheepishly but honestly admitted that it was he was "black" (which of course was exactly what I expected).

Now I was ready for the REAL 'test'. I said that I presumed that she had children and perhaps grandchildren – to which she proudly responded she had several grandchildren (which I also expected) I stated that I bet she love these children and that I would also bet that she supported the sanctity of life for all children (this was the part of which I was only guessing – so I braced for an answer) Without hesitation – she responded that she was Christian and very pro-life. Then I gave her the 'punch line' which was the purpose of my 'experiment' in the first place. I said – OH! So – how could you vote for a man who is Godless and hates children so much as to legislate a law to have them killed'! She looked shocked and before another word was spoken I clarified the true shocking claim.

I informed her that Obama had actually spearheaded a gruesome legislation that mandated that if a child should be so fortunate as to have SURVIVED being murdered by an abortionist – that child was to be murdered on the spot! She looked very uneasy and I proceeded to gently suggest that in the future perhaps she should have learned more about the TRUE nature of the people who were empowered by her – since that information and truth was available to ANYBODY who cared enough to seek it. Hopefully she then realized that her terrible mistake – repeated a million time over by other ignorant Negros was what is destroying the very heart and soul of America. Inexcusable – criminal – ignorance.

What is really frightening about this epidemic of idiocy is that apparently on the rise with no end in sight. When I was growing up – NOBODY wanted to be thought of as stupid or even ignorant – although the latter is curable simply by the will to learn of important issues. Today – this nation is actually having a love affair with stupidity. The evidence is also on the Jew Tube.. We have become a WILLFULLY Stupid people and have in effect elevated the status of stupidity as a VIRTUE!. There are popular JEW TUBE shows based on stupid characters. There are 'funny' shows based of people doing stupid things. Half a dozen 'popular' (not necessarily with me) entertainers/comedians base their entire careers on acting stupid and I don't mean the old Red Skelton or Jerry Lewis classic acts.

When is the last time you saw a Negro comedian male or female who didn't totally trash the English language WITH A VENGANCE! Heaven forbid, that knowledge and wisdom become popular and encouraged among blacks today – or even white entertainers for that matter. Frankly – I am not amused by American stupidity any more . For one thing- it may get my son killed in the very ner future.

STUPIDITY AND IT'S FIRST COUSIN IGNORANCE – KILLS! It WILL be out ultimate undoing. It is the plan of the Jew to use our own stupidity to affect our own destruction. These endless serial wars we wage for the Jews gives these vampires the blood they must have to destroy even more innocent people. The evil Jew is a master butcher – but he must have the American sheeple dumbed-down and stupid – as his goy slaves to accomplish his demonic agenda. We have been warned about the consequences of ignorance by the world's best minds – and we had best start taking it seriously. Let us encourage knowledge wisdom logic and education. Let us decry ignorance and encourage the disregarding of those cretins who lionize and worship it and bring society down..

Stupidity has already killed thousands of American sons and millions of innocent civilians in foreign lands. Wisdom and knowledge WILL set us free from our Jew masters. I know the Jew mind well -and he fears TRUTH and above all an educated public – as the entire collective Jew apparatus is based on greed deception and lies. Remove the veil of lies and smash the ignorance that suffocates us like a poison gas and the Jew and his bought sock puppets can no longer keep his control of us no matter how much of our hard earned wealth he steals for his evil agendas. Do it for your children and their children

How much more bloodshed? How many more innocent lives ? How many more murdered children? How many more dead American sons – all in the name of lies upon lies upon lies. And WHO is – after all the father of ALL lies? AND who have been exposed as his children? Who is the enemy of ALL mankind. That TRUTH is NOT from my 'word'. It is a TRUTH from the mouth of the Lord Christ and NOTHING – no amount of Jew lies and slander and blasphemies will EVER CHANGE IT! READ IT!

MARCH, 2010
AN OPEN LETTER TO THE MILITARY KILLERS OF LITTLE CHILDREN - AND THEIR CIVIIAN ENABLERS

I am finally convinced that a huge percentage of the American people are the worst hypocrites imaginable – considering the fact that some 80% of us claim to be "Christians". The AVAILABLE facts that our barbarian young sons have murdered many thousands of COMPLETELY innocent women and children in Iraq and ten times that many in Afghanistan tell me a great deal about our present day character. The number of innocents dying or dead from disease, starvation, suicide, and deformed mutated newborn (thanks to our "safe" DU weapons) are now over SIX figures.

But – that's OK – because these are Arab peoples and are only "animals" as we are taught by our criminal Zionist leadership – and as I was advised while in the Occupied Territories' at GAZA in the Summer of 89. There – I witnessed the world's largest institutionalized terrorist organization – the IDF – commit sadistic war crimes against helpless defenseless children – mock America – blaspheme Christ and commit the cruelest vicious crimes against unarmed civilians imaginable. I have been a lot of places and seen a lot of 'bad' things – but I have never experienced a more demonically evil devious lying treacherous people on earth than these "sons of Satan" in IsraHELL. For that matter – I never met a more generous hospitable warm people than the Arabs – that is – before our Zionist occupiers 'taught' our sheeple that they were our 'enemies' – and that we had a mandate to murder ALL of them to satiate the blood lust of IsraHELL!

The Talmudic Jews call all non-Jews 'golem' (cattle), and our own 'intellectually challenged' people – especially high ranking Zionists and bovine mentality useful idiots slander TRUE Christians with terms the most debasing of terms. The tens of millions of American evangelical 'Judeo-Christians' who have been weaned on the blasphemous Oxford University Press's 'New and Improved' Schofield Bible don't consider Arab/Muslim people worth being respected as fellow humans – and these 'sub-humans' are ALL considered to be "cursed" by God. But of course you are just doing "God's will". Foregoing the fact of course that the Arab people are the ONLY ancient culture that in modern times can trace their unbroken genealogy far back enough to Biblical times to truly be called Semites. I doubt if there is a living 'Jew' that can do that – even white collar ADL terrorist monster – Foxman.

I suggest that all this, will – in the very near future – lead us into more and more pre-emptive serial wars concluding logically in a real Armageddon. I believe that this madness will ignite consequences of unimaginable proportions and will ultimately lead us into a 'dark age' in America's history the likes of which will eventually destroy ALL semblance of any goodness left in this country. A country that has endeared itself to me – in uniform and civilian life for over 70 years. As the venerable French philosopher, writer and statesman, Alexis De Tocqueville so ominously stated over 170 years ago: "America is great because America is good, and when America ceases to be good, America will cease to be great". Remember that – remember it WELL – because it might very well be the 'epitaph' on our nation's tombstone when we end up on the trash heap of history .

So, – for those Americans who feel so arrogant and proud of the unspeakable horrors we have committed against these innocents – including Palestinian women and children – murdered by the thousands with equipment WE have DISGRACEFULLY supplied – in the name of "just cause" – "honor" – "liberation" etc. – I have decided to do something different.

Instead of endlessly trying to make the "deaf" hear or the "blind" see – I will give you something to remember, a 'tool' which should ease you collective consciences – should you ever come to the future realization – that the Godless horrors you now so proudly boast about – just might in fact be a hypocritical abomination in the 'eyes of God.

If the time for soul searching comes – and the nightmares of unspeakable horrors that YOU and your mindless cruelty made possible -creep into your peaceful sleep – just repeat this mantra, over and over and over again until you believe it. That pesky conscience will eventually 'go-away' and your conversion into a Zionist robot will be complete – so not to worry. Keep your self occupied with inane trivia – send lots of cute jokes and trivia on the net – watch a lot of NFL and keep focused on the REALLY important things in life – faster cars – bigger homes – longer boats – better jobs and above all – being popular and wealthy!.

Try NOT to REMEMBER the FACT – that these dead, mutilate and dying people were NOT your enemies – they were CREATED 'enemies'. Created by our Jew dominated press – our leaders – and ESPECIALLY by our CRIMINAL IGNORANCE!

HERE THEN, IS THE 'BLUEPRINT' WITH WHICH TO 'CREATE' AN 'ENEMY' – KILL HIM – BEAT HIM – RAPE HIM – TORTURE HIM – MUTILATE HIM – STARVE HIM – IMPOVERISH HIM – HUMILIATE HIM, AND NOT HAVE THE SLIGHTEST REMORSE FOR YOUR MINDLESS BARBARIC CRIMINAL CONDUCT.

This is how to ignore the cold-blooded MURDER of almost TWO MILLION innocent human beings – MOST of then HELPLESS INNOCENT CHILDREN – NO different – NO less loved than YOUR children or MY grandchildren – all brutally slaughtered by our imperialist Jew controlled Jew loyal government by an Army of psychopathic sick animals in Iraq ALONE. I trained your GRANDFATHERS year ago – to DEFEND this nation against REAL enemies – BUT NOT – to be child murderers for the greater glory of IsraHELL – as we have become ========.

Start in your mind with an 'empty canvass' – then sketch, in broad outline, the forms of the men, women and children- ESPECIALLY the children – beautiful alive happy little children.

Dip into the unconscious inkwell of your own disowned darkness, and with a WIDE brush – stain these strangers with the sinister hue of the shadow. Now you are getting it!

Trace onto the faces of 'the enemy', the greed, hatred, and cruelty – you dare NOT claim as your own. Strip them of all dignity and humanity – ease your collective consciences in knowing that they are nothing more than "rag-heads" or camel jockeys" or "sand- niggers" as they are so cruelly termed by our brave field commanders.

Obscure the sweet individuality of each and every face – ESPECIALLY the children! Then erase all hints of the myriad of the loves, hopes, and fears that play through the kaleidoscope of every finite little heart.

Twist the smile on every face – ESPECIALLY the children – until it forms the downward arc of cruelty. Strip the flesh from bones until only the abstract skeleton of death remains. However you accomplish this as long as they are reduced to soulless sub-humans – inferior to our precious Western children.

Exaggerate each feature until a man is morphed into a beast – or vermin – or insect. Fill in the background with malignant figures from ancient nightmares – devils, demons, and other specters of evil. Envision ALL of them regardless of innocence and age as 'terrorists' that must be exterminated like roaches as the Israelis prefer to call them.

When your icon of the enemy is complete, you will be able to KILL without GUILT – and SLAUGHTER without shame or conscience. The thing you destroy will have become merely 'an enemy of God' – an impediment to the sacred dialectic of history!

Now – that wasn't so hard was it?

Envision this morbid panorama over and over until you are comfortable with it and rendered whatever conscience remains as childish and impotent. Then – in your mind-you will have made the truth into lies – evil into righteousness – horror into duty and feel at ease with having sold your soul to the devil. It worked in Afghanistan – it worked in Iraq – and even worked here in Waco – AND will work in every relatively defenseless country we allow the Jews to decide must be destroyed.

It works every time – but ONLY with a dull witted ignorant criminally irresponsible racist hateful people – the type we see worshipping material riches in their oxymoronic prosperity based Christian-Zionist Synagogues Of Satan complete with false prophets galore!. But of course we were SPECIFICALLY warned about this. Scholars of Scripture know the book, verse and lines by heart.

Death will become a merciful escape for most of the poor peoples of the next country we decide to destroy for the greater glory of IsraHELL . If we can find no more enemies to torment – be assured that Israel will identify them for us until their last enemy is murdered. THEN there will be only one last enemy – the Christians. The Jews murdered some 20,000,000 Christians in Russia and then worldwide the Jew created Marxist genocide topped two hundred million! WACO was just a 'test'. The forced removal of the Laws of God from Chief Justice Moore's courthouse was just another 'small' test.

THREE HUNDRED MILLION PEOPLE – most of whom profess to be 'Christians' – and essentially – NOBODY offered to protect the children from being burned alive or the sacred tablets from being stolen. We will witness more and bolder actions against our own people and our most sacred traditions in the very near future. Not to worry – even if we run out of people around the world to destroy for our amusement – we will be provided with lots of "religious cults" to incinerate as "threats to society" and children to kill "for their own protection" right here at home. There is today – no place on earth that TRUE Christianity is more persecuted than right here in what USED to be America OR – where Christians will do less to defend their own faith.

And for those who begin to question these grizzly murders, there will always be and lots of 'gladiators', NFL tailgate parties and 'chariot races' and other perversions in our 'Coliseums' around the country, to keep our minds off of those 'unpleasant' issues like defending our Christian faith or our Christian based Constitution, or even defending our OWN neighbors! We can ALWAYS buy God's favor with catchy bumper sticker slogans like – 'Proud To Be An American' – or ' Have A Nice Day' – or 'My God's More Awesome Than Your God' Our new-age preachers tell us that we can sin all we like as long as we are sorry and we 'believe'. Oh and I almost forgot the important part. Our MOST prominent and wealthy preachers (Hinn – Parsley – Graham – Hagee et al) also tell us that it is God's Will to kill these children (as long as we send in plenty of 'love gifts'= READ: $dollars$).

May God forgive you for your cruelty to the most helpless and innocent of God's creations and your arrogance and ignorance – because I DAMN sure won't!

APRIL, 2010
SILENCE OF THE LAMBS (Cowardice) AND BOVINE STUPIDITY OF THE GOY (Ignorance) – THIS IS WHAT HAS DESTROYED AMERICA

Just when I thought it was 'safe' to go back 'online' and see what Americans think and place value on after the overwhelming evidence of mass corruption – a totally irrevocably 'broken' government – a 100% Jew owned deceitful lying News media – the same exact unconscionable insults to our heritage and Christian foundations in our faces day after day 24-7 – endless acts of high treason from Comrade Obama's Zionist Flying Circus – Endless senseless killings of innocent civilians in endless trillion dollar serial wars for IsraHELL – triple digit inflation – spiraling unemployment – our treasonous 'Fed' counterfeiting worthless fiat currency as fast as they can – our Christian traditions TOTALLY replaced by Talmudic filth celebrating murder violence and destruction – an unpopular Socialist 'death care' nightmare forced on the public – promises of total disarming of the American public and invalidating the 2nd Amendment – and on TV = promotion of violence, gluttony, obesity, adultery, homosexual perversion, gratuitous sex, abortion, mockery of traditional marriage – human evolution from amoebas and apes – blaspheming of Christ and His Mother – war mongering – genocide – heavy metal satanic garbage and rap trap crap ugly noise promoted as our 'music' – and general – VALIDATION – of very type of what was universally unacceptable indecent and profane conduct imaginable.

What I see is – that even with all of these horrors of economic and moral degradation – we still don't 'get it' – AND for those very few souls who actually realize that all these unconscionable events which have twisted our land into a collective moral garbage dump – are too spineless to stand up to protect their families – their freedoms and the goodness we once considered what America was all about. Their silence is deafening. The other half of the coin is that the majority are too stupid to even be aware that we have been used – morally raped – robbed – mocked – made fools of – and essentially become slaves of the Zionists who now own even our souls. For those still sharing brains to function at levels requiring more intelligence that organizing a tailgate party for the Stupid Bowl spectacle – here is a news flash for your overtaxed underdeveloped walnut size brains.

There is a reason that the Jews mock us a "goy" or cattle. Cattle are cared for – fed -watered and fattened up for one reason and one reason ONLY. That reason is to be led to the slaughterhouse to be used for FOOD – to serve man – in the most literal sense. Cattle are too stupid to fight back or defend themselves and are easily fooled into being docile – as long as they are well fed. Jews are reputed as notorious liars and deceivers of course. Even the IsraHELL government's motto is a statement of deceit – "BY DECEIT -WE WAGE WAR" (war against ALL non-Jew cattle). In The New Testament – in the Book of John (NEVER EVER read today, in our Jew – re-educated faux Christian churches) you will see that Jesus condemned the Jews as "SONS OF THE DEVIL" – and that their 'father' Satan – is the "father of ALL LIES". But – as it is said – even the Devil must have his due.

In this instance – they spoke the truth. They could not have uttered a more disgraceful TRUTH in their classic depiction of the nature of American non-Jews. We are indeed as stupid as cattle – as we cheerfully witlessly march in lockstep to the slaughterhouse.

Which brings me to the classic example of our salivating knee-jerk Pavlovian predictable bovine reaction to events which the average high school student of my time would have seen through as immoral and outrageously insulting to their intelligence. *(that was however before a steady diet of Jew instigated sex- drugs – rock and roll – materialism – Godlessness and the resultant irrational disrespect for our parents.)*

You may have seen or heard about the incident in which a funeral was picketed by a Baptist Church. The deceased was a young Marine corporal who lost his life while participating in the military goal of destroying homes and killing civilians in Iraq – to "make them free" of course. When I first saw the article I was encouraged and impressed that a Church had finally had the guts to confront these cold-blooded psychopathic killers who had disgraced the uniform I wore when I was training that young Marine's grandfather to defend this land from a REAL enemy of freedom loving people – the Soviet Communists. I TOTALLY despise these mindless killers who use their 'license to kill' to murder innocent people – mostly children – all for the greater glory of the filthiest most cruel barbaric Godless sadistic animals on the planet – the Jews in IsraHELL. These are cowardly scum who murder helpless defenseless 3 year old children for sport and target practice. BEEN THERE – SEEN THAT!

As I read into the article further I realized that this church was apparently not concerned about the cruel barbaric murderous nature of American killer in uniform – BUT They might be homosexuals! Now – for the record – I abhor homosexual perverts and they have NO Place in the American military. The reasons are legion and range from moral to practical – but for a church to disrupt a funeral service (I have no idea whether the fallen soldier in question was a pervert or not) based upon the fact that there simply were homosexuals in the military seemed absurd and on the face of it – way out of line.

NOW – if the demonstration was because this guy who was being honored as a hero – had participated in the most disgraceful murderous barbaric unthinkable mega-crime in the history of my nation – the cold-blooded- pre-mediated murder of nearly TWO MILLION INNOCENT CIVILIANS – I would have been delighted to be there with them. I would gladly inform their equally guilty parents, that their son AND themselves by their support – had disgraced the uniform of millions of DECENT HONORABLE MORAL GODLY COMPASSIONATE men – myself included- who had gone before him. THAT is a different story.

I contacted the church and wrote a lengthy letter explaining my concern with their motives – and indicated that I wished to know why the homosexual issue was even addressed. That would be very much like a cop catching a mad witnessed committing multiple first degree murders of totally innocent people – but being handcuffed and thrown in prison without bond for being charged only with an expired driver's license. It would be criminally irrational. They refused to even answer – but that act in itself gave me the answer I wanted. For all I knew they were the same ilk of sick hypocrites who screamed for the murders of these innocent people. These are those cruel animals we know as Christian/ Zionists (with a 'small c')

But the plot thickens. That article first appeared some time ago. This week it re-surfaced in the news to the extent that that a law suit had transpired. The greedy hypocrite father of that young Marine decided it was an opportunity to become an instant millionaire – so he sued the church for "damages" whatever the hell that means – as the protesters were out of sight and three football fields away! I wonder if that greedy immoral brain-dead moron had any concern of what kind of"DAMAGES" killers like his son's comrades had inflicted on families in Iraq. How much 'damages' money is it worth to see your 13 year old daughter gang raped and murder and before your eyes – your youngest – a 5 year old girl murdered on the spot and your home sacked and burned – and then learn that the animals who committed these unspeakable crimes went back to their barracks got drunk partied and celebrated the rape murders! OH and by the way – these criminals were ALSO young Marines – comrades in arms of his son. How much would the parent's " damages" be worth – compared to his feelings being 'bruised' .

What was really disgusting were the support blogs from their Ziobot apologists who were lauding his son "a real hero for protecting our country". I wanted to vomit. In the States – some little girl disappears and there is a media crisis. We hear about every tiny detail with lots of shots of the mother husband or boyfriend the next door neighbor. It isn't that American media moguls care a rat's ass about the life of one little girl (which it should in a compassionate nation – which we are definitely NOT)– but that it sells – like a soap opera for bored middle age housewives.

In the Mid- East where we have RAPED BEATEN ROBBED MURDERED – IN COLD BLOOD nearly TWO MILLION INNCENT CIVILIAN human beings- the best we can expect is a 'ho-hum' and zero chance of it becoming in the MNM at all . That is like an entirely NEW level of hypocrisy and I REALLY despise hypocrites. One soldier gets killed (because he is somewhere he doesn't belong- in the first place – trying to kill innocent people of that country in their own homes) and his father is in an uproar that some little church group demonstrates at the funeral. Being a greedy opportunist sees an chance to get rich quick and sues the church for over ten million dollars – gets awarded 5 million but the decision is reversed and now 'Mr. greedy' has to pay 16K in court costs and does the hearts and flowers routine to get more stupid people to pay his 'American Greed' bill on a special site.

This greedy dad wants his aggressor Army son to be buried with "dignity". Gee – wonder if he feels that the millions of dead by the hands of his son's comrades have been complaining about their sons or daughters or father or mothers or brothers or sisters being buried with 'DIGNITY"- like the entire family that was raped murdered mutilated and burned in their home by marines like young Snyder. Doesn't sound like a "dignified" burial to me. These thoughtless church demonstrators had a sign that read " Thank God For Dead Soldiers". Snyder say he still sees that sign when he lays in bed. OOHH – that must be painful – wonder if the thousands of orphans created by his Marine son's Marine criminal comrades as they lay shivering in muddy streets (their homes and beds are all destroyed by our military) are still seeing those signs that the Marines have that say: "Thank God for dead sand-niggers"

Snyder is all upset about the " invasion of his privacy".(from church demonstrators almost a quarter mile away behind a hill) Well – Mr Snyder – have you ever thought about what kind of 'invasion' of privacy has been forced upon millions of innocent civilians of a sovereign nation whose people have never done us any harm. Their "invasion of privacy by people like your son was of course a REAL armed shooting kicking doors down invasion. I'm talking an entire country that has been LITERALLY INVADED and destroyed by rockets bombs and artillery. Do THESE people have any cause to complain about the "RIGHT TO THEIR PRIVACY"? How about the RIGHT TO THEIR OWN LIVES MR. SNYDER – DENIED BY MARINES JUST LIKE YOUR SON?

Snyder's hypocrisy just keeps getting uglier and uglier. He said "American military personnel are in Iraq fighting for freedom of speech "they're not fighting for hate speech." Fighting for freedom of speech? Are you totally insane Mr. or on drugs?. We MURDER hundreds of thousands of totally innocent civilians because our corrupt Godless Zionist occupied government – with the help of morons like him to encourage more wars and more killing – and that is somehow " fighting for freedom of speech".

I have lost MY freedom of speech in my own country Mr. Snyder – a freedom that I risked my life to protect – now lost anyway thanks to imbeciles like you – right here in our OWN country. Will you lift your little finger to defend MY right to freedom of speech in AMERICA? "They are not fighting for hate speech" Really Mr. Snyder? And what would you call the countless displays written and verbally used by even our highest field commanders of slanderous hateful mocking derisive terms like 'sand niggers" – "camel – jockeys" – "rag- heads" and WORSE!

You say that "your God is a loving God" – so why do you support endless killing and brutal occupation and untold suffering and misery of a people who have done you no harm. YOU ARROGANT HYPOCRITE! " I don't look for hatred in the Bible" Oh isn't that just Zio-special. Tell me Mr. Snyder – What is the most damning condemnation of an entire race in the entire Bible. Who said it and where is it to be found. Do you 'not look for it' because it might embarrass your Zionist masters. Are you ASHAMED OF THE WORDS OF CHRIST? Do you not fear your mockery of the teachings of Christ? Screaming for the death of innocent children is the work of Satan – and YOU sir promote it

Oh and by the way Snyder – since Jew owned Fox News, sock-puppet country seller war-monger Bill O-Reilly has ALREADY (as of this writing) agreed to foot 100% of your court costs bill – why are you continuing to advertise for donations? Is it the greed or public exposure? I can feel some compassion for your son despite what he did – because of his age and un-sophistication. He probably didn't deserve to die-but he certainly deserved a 'lesson' in life. He might have turned out to be a decent person once he learned the TRUTH – in spite of having an ignorant greedy hypocrite for a father. YOU are the one who deserves to be severely punished. You foolish man – how many more brain-dead parents will have to come to grips with the FACT that their child died ONLY for the security and blood lusts of a people so horribly evil – that the Lord Christ condemned them as the "SONS OF SATAN"? You KNOW I have spoken the truth – albeit an ugly one. Now DO the right thing before it is YOU son that gets you a 'free flag' for your mantle piece!

APRIL, 2010
THE NATIONAL CONSTITUTION CENTER – PATRIOTIC SHRINE? OR MORE ZIONIST MOCKERY

Here is their description of 'The National Constitution Center' on their site–

"The National Constitution Center is an independent, non-partisan, and non-profit organization dedicated to increasing public understanding of, and appreciation for, the Constitution, its history, and its contemporary relevance, through an interactive, interpretive facility within Independence National Historic Park and a program of national outreach, so that "We the People" may better secure the Blessings of Liberty to ourselves and our Posterity."

"The National Constitution Center in historic Philadelphia is America's most interactive history museum. Located just two blocks from the Liberty Bell and Independence Hall, it is the only museum devoted to the U.S. Constitution and the story of we, the people."

AND – Here – is the lineup of the creatures that run this Zionist abomination of lies deception hatred and hypocrisy on a scale that would have embarrassed the Pharisees condemned by Christ.

CHAIRMAN: William Jefferson Clinton – the biggest piece of human crap to ever disgrace the Presidency and the dignity of the White House. A certified WHORE MONGER – ADULTERER – LIAR – BLASPHEMER – MURDERER – ABORTIONIST – friend of all HOMOSEXUAL PERVERTS – DRUG USER – DRUNKARD – CONSTITUTION BASHER – TRAITOR and WORLD-CLASS HYPOCRITE!

CHAIR EMERITUS : George W Bush – A war criminal formally charged in July 2006 with war crimes during the first Gulf war. Over a million Iraqi civilians mostly children under 5 years OF age died of starvation and disease associated with sanctions placed on the civilian populace by Bush Sr. HELLO! Have we already forgotten that 'the father' as ALSO a war criminal?

PRESIDENT: and Chief Executive Officer David Eisner – a bona fide 100% JEW

BOARD OF TRUSTEES: Reads like a who's who of Jews (over 30%) and Jew wanna-be Christian hating 'Israeli firsters'.

DISTINGUISHED SCHOLARS AND ADVISORY PANEL: Another laundry list of the self-chosen (almost half) and 'shabbus goy' liberals.

Hillary Clinton and Barky Obama have been highly honored guest speakers there – but then after all – if you look at the morals and values of the Chairman- and the chairs – why should I be surprised.

The highest award the institution bestows on those they admire is their 'LIBERTY MEDAL'

"The Liberty Medal is awarded annually by the National Constitution Center to men and women of courage and conviction who have striven to secure the blessings of liberty to people the world over. The Liberty Medal was established by We the People 2000 celebration of the bicentennial of the U.S. Constitution to heighten recognition of the principles that founded this nation and to serve as a lasting legacy to the Constitution."

"A global initiative of the Constitution Center, the Liberty Medal reflects the values of the U.S. Constitution — a belief in justice, fairness, self-governance, and a balance between individual rights and communal responsibility; in the power of people to effectuate change; and in resolving issues through deliberation, compromise, and respect for diverse viewpoints."

Past Liberty Medal winners include Mikhail Gorbachev, Nelson Mandela, Shimon Perez, Kofi Annan, George W Bush – Bill Clinton, and Sandra Day O'Connor. The latest winner is Zionist filmmaker Steven Spielberg. Since this is the highest honor that Eisner and his Jew pals could bestow. Lets see who these people REALLY are and what they REALLY did and REALLY believed and if THEIR values do in fact reflect the values of our Founding Fathers

Mikhail Gorbachev = Marxist ideologue – former Secretary General of the Communist Party Soviet Union (CPSU). Directed the mass genocides in Afghanistan which earned his country the title of 'EVIL EMPIRE' from then President Ronald Reagan.

Nelson Mandela = Marxist – President of African terrorist group called African National Congress – listed as terrorists in the US Dept. of State publication = "Terrorist Group Profiles" Responsible for murder of thousands of innocent non- Communist Africans by a horrible act called necklacing – where the victim is burned alive.

Shimon Perez = Former President of IsraHELL Zionist – sadistic war criminal – mass murderer of defenseless civilians mostly children in Gaza. He openly mocks God by 'praying' with his IDF (world's largest institutionalized terrorist organization) to murder all the children in Gaza. This liar and hypocrite never EVER loses an opportunity to publicly mock God.

Kofi Annan = Marxist Secretary General of the Communist inspired UN and friend and admirer of terrorist Nelson Mandela – 'one-worlder'

George W Bush = Former US President – drunken alcoholic traitorous Zionist – 9-11 co-conspirator – Constitutional rights trasher – mass murderer war criminal responsible for the murders of over a million innocent civilians in Iraq and Afghanistan – Constitutional rights trasher – and Christian basher.

Bill Clinton = TOTALLY AMORAL Former US President – drug addict – alcoholic – Christian mocker – adulterer – whore monger – homosexual pervert supporter – baby killer – pathogenic liar – anti – Constitutional rights advocate etc etc etc ad nauseam. There just isn't enough time to list all of his endless disgraceful embarrassing putrid conduct.

Sandra Day O'Connor = Closet Zionist – voted WITH the Jews Ginsberg and Souter, Stevens, and Breyer to remove the Ten commandments from courthouses and to legalize the murder of unborn children by the horrors of Partial Birth Abortion just for openers. She also voted with the Jews on promoting the racist abomination of 'affirmative action' – actually an insult to ALL decent responsible black people.

STEVEN SPIELBERG = Oh and of course the latest Liberty Medal winner is the Zionist Jew film maker Steven Spielberg. His award is for his tireless efforts for the preservation of human rights (of course – as long as those "humans' happen to be JEWS!) Spielberg has created countless films regarding the Hollowhoax so that we inferior guilt ridden ignorant 'goy' may be reminded daily about the ethnic superiority of the 'self-chosen'.

"Spielberg has captured the stories of courageous people in this nation and abroad who have worked, fought, and sacrificed for the gift of freedom." (only for Jews of course). "Survivors of the Shoah -the collection – the largest archive of its kind in the world – now stands at 52,000 videos with 105,000 hours of testimony in 32 languages, representing 56 countries." Additionally, the Foundation now intends to collect testimony from the survivors and witnesses of other genocides."

Of course – as long as these genocides were NOT committed by the self-chosen themselves – as that might prove embarrassing to the world to realize that the most horrible FULLY DOCUMENTED genocides in history were committed by JEWS – AGAINST CHRISTIANS! How about the TWENTY MILLION + CHRISTIANS MURDERED BY YOUR 'TRIBE' IN RUSSIA? Or – how about the TEN MILLION+ CHRISTIANS MURDERED (some of my relations by marriage) BY YOUR JEW FRIENDS in Ukraine – Mr. Spielberg? Oh so thoughtless of me. I forgot that you superior Jews consider us non-Jews as mere goy (cattle) – put here to be your slaves – so their lives were meaningless – unlike Jew lives!

Oh yes Mr. Spielberg – just one more thing. Do you think that of all those 52,000 videos with 105,000 hours of testimony in 32 languages, representing 56 countries – that you might just find it morally mandated by the God who created ALL human beings – that you devote just a couple of those videos and few of those hours – in just one language – say English. – for just ONE country – say the US – to the documentation of those poor thousands of innocent helpless defenseless children murdered in cold-blood by you Jews in Gaza? Would that be asking too much from "God's chosen people" – "a light among nations" – who are "mandated to take the high moral ground"? To quote your own self description terms.

Do we see some sort of pattern developing here? Terrorists – Marxists – Zionists – Jews – war criminals – mega hypocrites and world-class- liars – but not a single person of high moral character – not a single real Christian honored with the coveted LIBERTY MEDAL. Certainly NOBODY that ANY founding Father would REMOTELY consider to be anything but evil Godless trash and the antithesis of American ideals and values and conduct.

Certainly the heroic decorated Captain of the USS Liberty massacre would have been a good choice – OOPS- sorry Mr. Eisner – that would have been rather embarrassing wouldn't it. A 'goy' American military officer of unquestionable courage and character risking his life to protect his men from an act of war by a foreign military power – a power who virtually ALL of the officers of the National Constitution Center – from the President to the Chair to the Advisory Board to the trustees – SUPPORT – NOT The USA who was attacked – but the stolen Godless murderous rogue state of IsraHELL – who was the ATTACKER!. Isn't that so – Mr. Eisner?

I'll bet my pink slip that your organization has never spent time on any national special event to protest that disgraceful incident. I think the Founders of our Constitution would wholeheartedly agree that you SHOULD honor the Liberty Captain with the Liberty Medal.

OH and so not to forget two of Eisner's most honored most admired guest speakers. Barack Obama and Hillary Clinton. Kind of makes one wonder just what these two God mocking Zionist/Marxist country selling scum would have to say about our blessed Constitution and it's writers and founders.

OBAMA= Zionist Marxist Ideologue seated President of the US who has yet to even prove his own citizenship. A Jew sock puppet whose cabinet is almost entirely dual citizenship treasonous Israelis. He is a Christian mocker so sadistically cruel that he forged legislation to INSURE that any child who miraculously survived the horror of a partial birth abortion – would be instantly killed by the abortionist anyway. A man who has committed high treason against the United States and has trashed the Constitution. A war monger who has escalated the killing murders and destruction and human misery in Afghanistan and Iraq by sending tens of thousands more of our young psychopathic killers into an already impoverished destroyed nation to inflict even more pain and misery. A spineless worm – a talking head loyal to the State of IsraHELL who has just condemned our grandchildren with a financial burden that staggers imagination. A tax and spend criminal who cheerfully breaks the backs of honest working class people to finance yet another TRILLION DOLLAR SLAUGHTER of innocent people to please his masters in IsraHELL. What a slap in the faces of all of the Founding Fathers to honor this piece of putrid criminal garbage in their names!

HILLARY CLINTON = Current US Secretary Of State. A lesbian atheist Zionist who hates children supports all manner of sexual perverts When confronted by a reporter from The Washington Week after she had told Hillary that it was against God's law to kill babies – an enraged Hillary screamed back; "It IS God's law to kill babies!" She is a confirmed Marxist and that fact has been observed by countless dignitaries – one for instance being TX. Rep Dick Armey who commented that Hillary's thoughts are Marxist -her friends are all Marxist and she hangs out with all Marxists. She is the quintessential New Age feminist/goddess who has often opined he desire to do away with 'God' and overthrow Christianity. Her new world embraces lesbianism – murder of the unborn and homosexual marriage. She is the emblematic 'feminazi' who openly scorns patriotism an marriage. Her role model was Communist feminist lesbian pervert Eleanor Roosevelt. Her personally approved cabinet of Lesbians Marxists whores perverts and all around scummy trash were All females (If you could call these creatures women) who set a new level of decadence evil and filth unparalleled in the history of the United States. You may recognize some of these appointee names. Roberta Actenberg – Madeline Albright – Jane Alexander – Maya Angelou – Carl Bellamy – Joycelen Elders – Janet Reno – Laura Tyson – Ruth Bader Ginsberg and Donna Shalala. Our forefather founders must be rolling in their graves at such an insult by these scum.

"What is Constitution Day?"

The "signing of the U.S. Constitution on September 17, 1787, by the Founding Fathers is one of the most important and influential events in American history, establishing the many rights and freedoms "We the People" enjoy today."

Interesting that a Zionist Jew should be heading an organization which honors war criminals – murderers- drug dealers – Marxists – terrorists – child murderers – racists and people who in general have done everything humanly possible to trash our Constitution and the good names of our Founding Fathers in their daily mockery of the teachings of Christ.

WARNING! The next fact about the Jew run National Constitution may make you physically sick to read – as it is incomprehensible that ANY American would sink to such depraved immorality AND announce it PROUDLY to your children as they do.

"Induction of Harvey Milk to the American National Tree"

Wednesday, September 17, 2009, 1:00 p.m.

"The Constitution Center, in partnership with the Alliance for Young Artists and Writers and the M.R. Robinson Fund, selected high school student Sammi Massey to author the biography of Harvey Milk as an addition to the American National Tree exhibit, which tells the stories of over 100 Americans whose actions have helped write the story of the Constitution. Milk was best known for his courageous fight for equal treatment for homosexuals as the first openly gay man elected to political office in California"

Harvey Milk was a filthy Jew animal -a sexual predator of children whose entire purpose in life was to promote legislation in his sick State of Sodom (Californication) so as to teach our children how to perform unthinkable perverse acts on same sex playmates, and filthy old perverts like him. He was the very personification of everything evil sordid and filthy.

I wonder what our Christian Founding Fathers would think of a Zionist Jew who founds an organization whose purpose is to mock them and their beliefs and the words of our Lord by presenting an unrepentant practicing filthy pedophile sex pervert fellow Jew as being on the same moral plane with our Founding Fathers?

YET Eisner's National Constitution Center did exactly that . They promoted his filthy unconscionable pervert agenda so as to elevate this piece of human feces to the heroism of the Founding Fathers. READ Eisner's glowing homily again! What insulting demonic arrogance! But wait – it gets worse!

Articles of Confederation to the Constitution Demonstration

September 17, 2009, at 10 a.m., 12 p.m., and 2 p.m.

Join in this interesting demonstration about the journey our country took from the Revolution to the Constitution. Find out more about this rocky road to a Democracy.

The lies just don't stop ! Our blessed nation was founded as a REPUBLIC – a nation of LAWS – not a democracy (MOB RULE) That was made abundantly clear by the first Continental Congress and the wishes of the founders. Coming out of Constitution Hall in Pennsylvania a lady asked: "Dr. Franklin – what kind of government do we have?" And he said – We have a Republic – if you can keep it" When I was growing up in the NON-OCCUPIED – NON-DUMBED DOWN – REAL UNITED STATES OF AMERICA – there wasn't a school child who could read and write who didn't know that historic encounter by heart!

I wore the uniform and risked my life to defend a REPUBLIC – NOT a Mob-ocracy – you know – a REPUBLIC – like in " I pledge allegiance to the United States Of America and the R-E-P-U-B-L-I-C for which STANDS – PERIOD! What part of REPUBLIC don't you understand Mr. EISNER?

I recently watched a totally disgusting presentation hosted by this so-called NATIONAL CONSTITUTION CENTER. I wanted to vomit! What in hell is wrong with us? Is all we can do today – is to scream for more and more and more killing – more destruction – more violence – more murders of innocent children. This wasn't a legitimate discussion – it was a HATE FEST hosted by Jews and their sock-puppets – with a few badly intimidated brow beaten carefully selected Jew apologist young journalists in the audience with one possible exception – who of course got the run around. I'm a seasoned mature educated well traveled journalist – AND have a son who is now in danger of coming home in a pine box to satisfy the blood lusts of the Jews. Why wasn't I invited so I could ask some pointed pertinent honest questions to these uniformed puppet whore criminals of our Israeli masters?

Isn't TWO MILLION MURDERED INNOCENT CIVILIANS ENOUGH? FOR WHAT? TO DEFEND WHAT? Certainly not MY country! ISRAHELL? Those Godless Christian -hating lying sadistic immoral murdering bastards can take care of themselves. If Jews started acting like HUMAN BEINGS for a change and stop murdering everyone else's children – they wouldn't have enemies. Been there – seen that!

HERE THEN is the Godless war mongering SCUM that these so-called Constitution lovers and promoters and protectors invited to mock all that for which we are supposed to stand.

Bruce Ackerman – Zionist Jew Marxist on panel of war-mongers. A man who has been on record as desiring to trash our present Constitution by suspending all constitutional rights of citizens in event of war or disaster. That has a term – Mr. Zionist. It is called TREASON! What qualifies YOU to send my son to his death or to murder children for your 'tribe'. Did you serve this nation in uniform at risk of your life – Mr. Ackerman? I did!

General H.R. McMaster =[Mc – WARMONGER] – an American Army general on the panel of warmongers. Spoke of what we owed the American public as revenge for the "mass murder on Sept 11". He never mentioned the FACT that well known respected public figures from America and all over the world including Dr. Alan Sobrosky, former Director Of Studies at the US Army War College – have spoken up regarding the unquestionable involvement of Israeli Mossad in the 9-11 disaster.

What make YOU GOD – Mr. war-monger. Is another 'star' bought with the blood of countless innocent human beings, the extent of your moral character? And no lectures please! I was training young warriors how to defend us against a REAL enemy – before you ever took your first breath of air on earth!

General Jack Keane (Ret.) = On the panel of war-mongers. As bloodthirsty as they come. No compassion for the TWO MILLION INNOCENT CIVILIANS our military has already murdered. When asked by journalist in audience about our torture of prisoners – he evaded the question and spoke of how how honorable the American soldier was and how moral our Army was. Apparently he didn't take time to read hundreds and perhaps thousands of reports of rapes tortures thefts beatings and countless cold-blooded murders of helpless innocent defenseless civilian " detainees" – unparalleled in the history of modern warfare.

The best this sadist could come up with regarding the torture of mostly innocent people simply trying to DEFEND THEIR OWN COUNTRY – as that ; "The torture was obviously ineffective" How about if you are thrown in prison for trying to DEFEND YOUR FAMILY AND HOME from invading thugs and we see just what kind of torture to YOU – that the invaders find "EFFECTIVE". You are a WAR CRIMINAL – Get IT?

What's the matter General – haven't caused enough human suffering and misery yet? What the hell is it with you bastards? You sell your souls to the Jews ?– or are you just mean and cruel by nature? You know DAMN WELL that NONE of those people over 'there' have EVER done anything bad to you or me or our families. I was in Pershing Rifles in college also. I was training basics when we were in peril of going to war with the Soviets and you were just about to graduate high school. I was at Bragg too – also part of 18th Abn.Corps. Jim Gavin pinned my wings on my chest at Benning.

Now – I didn't have 'stars' on my tabs but I too, served my country as an officer – and UNLIKE YOU – I did NOT disgrace the uniform by committing treason to my Constitution and war crimes against innocent people. God doesn't like that and neither do I! How in the name of all that is good, can a man like you live with yourself? I don't believe ANY adult can be that stupid. So – what did those Jew scum pay you to become a criminal – a murderer and a traitor – 30 pieces of silver? Thanks to thugs like you – I'm ashamed to even admit I'm an American anymore. You are not a 'man' – you are a REAL LIFE monster!

I want the reader to simply think on what facts I have revealed. I discovered this disgrace by accident. All I wanted was an evening of peace and relaxation until these criminals just HAD to prove once again what kind of horrible ignorant shallow cruel mindless people we have turned into. Go to their site and see these disgusting facts for yourself. God only know how many of our most cherished institutions have been 'kidnapped' by Zionists and twisted into hateful Godless filth right under our noses. You should be outraged!

Stop this madness and the lies upon lies upon lies. Do you even understand the filthy paradox I have described? A bunch of mostly Godless Zionist Jews who have gone to great effort to deceive the American people by using the hopes and dreams of the people whose selfless sacrifices gave painful bloody birth to a struggling young Republic.

Have you even bothered to read about their lives and dreams – the legacy they hoped would endure for all generations – the hard built foundations crafted of love courage – honor – truth – wisdom – compassion – so as to be able to keep the freedoms they envisioned for all generations to come. This bastardization of the purpose and meaning of those sacred documents by these indecent perverse anti-patriots is as cruel and malevolent as may be imagined. REAL Americans would not DREAM of doing these horrible hateful things.

They have twisted and mocked the goodness and wisdom of our beloved Constitution until it has been metastasized into an ugly cancerous malignancy indistinguishable from it's intended design and purpose. These are learned but evil people – and it is not by accident – but by design.. I implore you. Read the original papers – learn of the TRUTH the great colonial Founding Fathers spoke and lived by – and then see for yourselves what lies deceit and perversions these horrible people whose Talmudic ranks are filled with homosexual perverts – Marxists – Christian haters – war criminals – adulterers – baby killers – deceivers – and every stripe of Godless conduct – presented to you as Godly – truthful – wise – moral and Christ-like.

As Americans – and those few left who are TRUE Christians – voice your outrage to these bad people and let them know what they have done is unconscionably evil. Do what you KNOW is right for God and country. Phone these 2 faced imposters and tell what you think of their unconscionable deceptions – praise for some of the most putrid Godless criminal demonic murderous filth on earth – and dishonorable mockery of our Constitution and the gallant men who forged it. JUST DO IT!

MAY, 2010
COMMUNISM MAY BE DEAD IN THE USSR BUT IT IS ALIVE AND WELL IN THE USA

Just when you thought 'Red Rallies' and 'May Day' celebrations and 'clenched fists' and all those catchy 'commie clichés' – had ended up on the ash heap of history – they are back with a vengeance! No – I'm not taking about a new movie or TV series or a revitalized craze for 'Che' T-shirts.

I'm talking about the REAL thing coming from the City where Communism was classically supported in the 60s before it was discredited for the demonic Godless ideology which ultimately caused more civilian murders that all of the wars -plagues and natural disasters of the 20th Century COMBINED.

It would also be prudent to remember that FACT that this global nightmare was a 'gift' from the Jews of course. You remember the 'tribe' don't you? The self-chosenites who got America into two world wars and and have succeeded in turning out once Christian based nation into a cesspool – a morally rotted corpse and a financially decimated occupied nation of subservient sheeple.

Well anyway – Like in 'The Shining' – they're back! This time – no waffling around with drugged up – dropped out – 'love children' at Woodstock orgies. THIS time its POWERFUL Congressmen – union thug leaders – and other people with respectable sounding titles – albeit the fact they are pure unadulterated scum.

The straw-man issue – their whipping post, their facade – for all this self- sanctimonious show of 'righteous indignation' and hate-mongering? The newest legislation in Arizona enacted to stem the invasion of illegal criminals from Mexico. I could fill BOOKS with documented FACTS regarding organized gangs – high rates of crime – rapes – robberies – hard drug smuggling – freeloading and stealing citizens benefits bought and paid for LITERALLY – from the sweat and tears of the American working family – but the unemployment lines and lost homes and jobs crowded hospitals and many other problems resulting from the recent economic collapse and of course uncontrolled invasion of illegal freeloaders and irresponsible undesirables speak for themselves.

Next time you are in an emergency room with a life threatening condition and observe it if FILLED with vagrants migrant workers and an assortment of people who cannot even speak our language – who are not even citizens and who have never had to pay a dollar of medical insurance – and must wait for hours and hours for care YOU HAVE PAID FOR – let me know how you feel about these Communists who are so eager to see our system in shambles and place these illegal freeloaders' welfare AHEAD of yours!

I sent the following letter to the Governor of Arizona. Everything contained therein is verifiable and true. I believe it should be read by EVERY literate man woman and child who are citizens of this country – and are struggling to maintain their families basic needs – so you will understand the TRUTHS that are shielded from you with layers upon layers of outright lies by some of the most pernicious greedy lying lowlife criminal thug mentality evil scum ever spawned in this country!

Dear Governor Brewer; Tampa – May 7 2010

I am a Hispanic. I am also a Former Green Beret airborne commander of the 60s. I was also a former Vice-Consul to Costa Rica (obviously multilingual). I was also the past president of a company (many years ago) I built with my own hands during the worst recession of the past 50 years. I was also an aerospace engineer who helped solve high-tech problems for NASA. I am well educated – well traveled – well informed and am a journalist to boot. I supported the Democrat Party for 23 years as a moral but naive ignorant young man. As I gained wisdom and truth, I was repulsed. I then sustained the Republican Party for almost as long – till it became a cabal of Godless war-mongering hypocrites. The stench of innocent death and the appalling hypocrisy were unconscionable – so I am now a 'homeless political orphan'. I am a Christian – a Catholic as you may suspect.

Having said these things – I wish to inform you of my approval of your legislation to combat illegal immigration. Your actions are responsible moral and WAY overdue. Hopefully the rest of our population who are not gangsters or are NOT sharing brains – will follow your example. American citizenship is NOT a right. It is a privilege! I learned that at the knee of my father whose parents came here to find a better life over a hundred years ago. They were poor in material wealth – but rich in spirit – Godly – moral – decent – responsible – educated pioneer mentality CONTRIBUTORS.

I have read the entire HP 1070 – including the revisions. From what I can see it is not only 'fair' – but MANDATORY to the security of a safe, drug free, violence free community that is geographically juxtaposed to a foreign country unquestionably reputed for its violence -crime and drug influence – not to mention a level of corruption which even surpasses our current administration – a fact of which I am painfully aware. I have spent enough time and experience there to know what I am talking about.

I applaud ANY foreign visitor who wished to share our blessings – BUT ONLY if he or she 'obey the rules of the house' – as I would expect to do were I the 'guest'. Life is tough enough here economically as of recent – without unnecessary added burdens of more guests – especially larcenous immoral and nefarious ones. IF – I were 'king' – learning to speak OUR language would be MANDATORY. It is no less arrogant of them, to pre-suppose that we 'Gringos' must expend extra effort and funding to accommodate their laziness to learn OUR language – than for an American – as a permanent guest in another nation – perhaps theirs – to expect THAT nation to accommodate Our language.

Something you might not know. The Bishop of Phoenix who so condescendingly suggests to censure you and your entire State is NOT the holy man of God he would have you believe. As matter of fact – Bishop Kicanas is no more a 'Vicar of Christ' than was that- dyed in the wool African Marxist 'Bishop Desmond Tutu'. He is a high ranking official in the USCCB – which in itself is blasphemy! He should more correctly be referred to as 'Comrade Bishop Kicanas' for his apostasy in supporting the totally discredited 100% Marxist ideology of Liberation Theology embraced by the USCCB. The USCCB is RIDDLED with corruption hypocrisy and rot, as a thorough examination will reveal!

I was educated from day one by the nuns and then the Jesuits – so I know true Christian based Catholicism. As a Christian who had risked his life in defense of my Christian heritage against communism and all the other evil 'isms' – I RESENT his hypocrisy. He is a false 'priest' and should have been excommunicated long ago for embracing the maxims of Christianity's greatest modern enemy! He and needs to be exposed. Compassion and Communism are not moral equivalents.

On a closing note – I suggest that if you and or your advisers have not done so – that you acquire a full transcript of a TV special – The May Day – Migrant Workers and Rights Rally – in New York City – presented by C-SPAN-3. I saw it on May 5. It was one of if not THE most disgraceful consortium of thugs, social slime, union gangsters and Marxists I have witnessed in this country. Many of the communist there openly and shrilly spouted their mantras of ; ' Workers of the world unite!"

A half dozen United States Congressmen (and women) contributed to this disgusting leftist hate fest. ALL of these Reps were either Negro or Hispanic. ALL emphasized their pride of being a Cuban or Puerto-Rican or Mexican etc. – but NONE stated pride of being an AMERICAN! ALL were Democrats. ALL suggested that the mob they were addressing should go to Arizona and demonstrate against the people and the State. ALL kept reinforcing the lie that these criminals somehow had American citizen's rights AND were somehow entitled to ALL citizens' benefits.

NONE spoke of or even suggested that these law breakers assume responsibility for their OWN actions. NONE spoke of the privilege of citizenship or ANYTHING remotely moral. None condemned the violence – gangs – crime – illegality – financial burden on-working Americans or anti-American nature of this invasion of our sovereignty. NO mention was made suggesting that these illegal immigrants should leave or that they should be trying to address THEIR problems with THEIR OWN country. It was a hate fest of lies for export to useful idiots. The Devil would have blushed.

It was ALL choreographed and ALL right out of the 'Little Red Book. The crowd was of course too ignorant to understand that the greedy immoral union thugs and the mobsters and the disgraceful Congressional Hispanics and Negros would benefit greatly from an all out open door of amnesty and uncontrolled invasion. More hundreds of thousands of uneducated masses needing social benefits medical benefits – unemployment benefits – food stamp benefits – public housing benefits and a laundry list of more 'entitlements' of a universal Pandora's box.

Consequently, of course – this huge potential power base voting bloc of all these jobless hungry homeless 'huddled masses' would of course logically consider these thugs and criminals on the podium to be their benefactors – and become the obligatory electorate for whatever THESE Socialist union mentality thugs supported. Bingo! – instant mega-welfare State – soon to be a financially and morally bankrupt third world country. THAT – Governor Brewer – IS the agenda of our Democrat Party.

That is EXACTLY how it happens – and EXACTLY what WILL happen. That's how I see it

Good luck. Stand firm. Remember those scum on that Marxist podium are still not who represent what America is really about – God willing. Responsible traditional value moral informed people like myself and millions of others like me – contributors – not takers – who have PAID our dues in blood sweat and tears – ARE America – NOT the mobsters!

Sincerely,

Joe Cortina – father – veteran – scientist – writer – investigator – diplomat and patriot

MAY, 2010
"ARMY STRONG"? OR A STRONG ARMY OF CRIMINALS

I am the father of an 18 year old son who recently decided (against my better judgment) to involve himself with our terrorist criminal mercenary 'army'. He was, as of May of 2010 probably in AIT but I am not sure. My older son has half grown children and did not have the experience of serving in the military- although I'm sure if called he would have risen rise to the occasion in a spirit of duty to 'God and country' that prevailed when I was young and America came first and we had not yet sold our beloved nation to IsraHELL.

Forty eight years ago I trained young men at the USATC (US Army Training Center) during a 'cold-war' crisis few young people even remember. We were on 24 hour mobility test alert status and in real anticipation of a real shooting war with the Soviets. It was known as the Berlin Crisis and all leaves had been cancelled indefinitely. I worked 12 hour 6 day weeks on training committees and later given my own training company – E-5-2 – to receive special discipline as they were to be designated for airborne units. I was told that I was the youngest officer on record to have been given a a company. Times were tough and we were short on personnel and time – but we all did our best.

NO – I did not make a mistake. I am a 71 year old father with an 18 year old son. Years ago – before our occupation (yes Dorothy – America has been under total Jew occupation by the Jews for many years now) – I would have been proud to have a son in uniform, and even perhaps be a paratrooper like his dad. We were all pretty much 'gung ho' young lions and proud of our opportunity to serve to defend the nation in times of danger. Our code was HONOR – NOT blind obedience to murder children.

After my second broken ankle from parachute mishaps – a military Dr. advised me that I injured the same ankle one more time I risked being crippled the rest of my life. I just told him thanks for the advice but I had a job to do. It was just the way we were – all of us.

That was BEFORE our military became IsraHELL's slavish obedient attack dog and transformed into a mercenary sadistic mob of mostly mindless Godless bloodthirsty civilian murdering criminal psychopaths and losers who couldn't make it in competitive real life. AND its good money! My son makes nearly TEN times more as a basic trainee than I did as a basic training company commander!

Today's occupation forces are nothing less than criminals – thieves – rapists – sadists. They are the world's largest terrorist organization – bringing death and destruction and misery to millions of totally innocent people who have never harmed America or American citizens. Remember – they are ALL mercenaries, and were NOT FORCED to be murdering other people in their homes schools hospitals and places of worship.

We have murdered – in cold-blood- over TWO MILLION INNOCENT CIVILIAN HUMAN BEINGS – all for the greater glory of the most evil lying murdering cheating deceiving scum on the face of the earth – the IsraHELL Jews. The DOCUMENTED war crimes committed by our forces now fill volumes and are as bad or worse than any committed in military annals and it as even young school children today know – it has ALL been based on Jew LIES UPON LIES UPON LIES.

Every decent Godly man woman and child in this once decent Christian nation SHOULD despise what our Godless killers stand for today. They defend NOTHING that is sacred or dear to America in ANY way WHATSOEVER!.

EVERY MAN IN UNIFORM NEEDS TO REMEMBER HIS PURPOSE. It IS to DEFEND this nation – NOT To occupy and destroy innocent people's nations and murder their citizens. The Jews and their treasonous whore consorts like Obama and Bush have betrayed us – the non – Jews. War criminals like Bush and his IsraHELL gangsters have led us into endless serial wars based on lies.

Every son of every mother who came back in a bag – died for the greater glory of ISRAHELL – PERIOD! They ALL died for NOTHING! They defended NOTHING of America. Their legacy is murder torture rape destruction misery and terrorism. There is not ONE country of decent peace- loving people one Earth who does not despise and fear us. If my OWN son comes back a vegetable or a rotted corpse – the God's TRUTH is that he would have died in vain – only to satisfy the blood lusts of the Jews who now control EVERY ASPECT of our daily lives.

For those of you who see the TRUTH and understand what has happened to us – you need to fight for goodness and decency. Do NOT allow your beloved sons to become cannon fodder for the demonic sadistic lying Jews. At EVERY opportunity stand against these recruiting scum who lure your sons to their deaths for the most EVIL of causes. THESE SCUM are the ENEMY – not some poor destitute starving Palestinians or Afghanis or Iraqis.

I implore you to support REAL patriots like Brother Nathanael at RZN (bronathanael@yahoo.com) = and make a generous donation to your nation's future. His site is a REAL source for TRUTH that is not controlled by the Jews as is ALL mainstream media – and I mean ALL! This country today , under Jew occupation – is as censured as Castro's Cuba – or Red China or the 'former Soviet Union'.

I defy ANY American to be able to have an article such as the truths contained here – published in ANY major newspaper. The Jews and their useful idiots will simply not allow it. Think I exaggerate? Just try it yourself.

YOU pick the article exposing the Jews that you deem the most important to our futures and freedoms – and see what happens!

Just remember this – you sheeple out there who parrot the mantra of "BUT- They were just following orders". When our Godless Jew indoctrinated psychopath gangster military comes "kicking in YOUR door to YOUR home" – and they WILL – because our spineless Jew loyal leaders are telling them to do so – just like they taught my own son – and they beat up your parents- rape your daughters – murder your sons in front of your eyes – then loot and burn your home – as YOUR sons are NOW doing in Iraq and Afghanistan – and soon Iran – please don't complain, because – WE ARE NEXT ON THE JEW AGENDA – and remember – that-"THEY ARE JUST FOLLOWING ORDERS"!

My name is Joe Cortina. I was a 60s Green Beret commander and a representative for IBM as well as a scientist for Honeywell Aerospace in Florida. I later became President of my own manufacturing company. I have two sons and 2 granddaughters who are the reason for my dedication to expose the threats to the freedoms I hope to see them enjoy as I did many decades ago when America was still a Christian-based sovereign nation free of Zionist influence.

MAY, 2010
"BLESSED ARE THE PEACEMAKERS, FOR THEY WILL BE CALLED THE CHILDREN OF GOD"

...And – they damn sure will NOT be Americans – ESPECIALLY Baptist Americans (are you listening hypocrite monster Hagee?) – for WE ARE

PROUD TO BE WARMONGERS – destroyers – murderers – criminals – REAL terrorists! Can you connect the dots? Can you figure out WHOSE 'children' we have of our OWN free will elected to be today? I'll give you a hint. Read John 8-44.

Well – folks – there you have it from the 'highest authority' – straight from the Sermon on the Mount. So – what does that mean to the very few authentic Christians left in this secular Godless Jew dominated land? We have rejected Christ and His teachings. We are 'on our own'!

Our military is now the most hated and feared terrorist complex on earth. Under the demonic tutelage of war criminals like Bush and Obama and their war criminal puppets like Betrayus – I GUARANTEE you that we have FAR more to fear from our own Government than ANY 'foreign enemy'. I DEFY you to produce even ONE prominent influential American leader in the land today – who will actually walk the walk for peace and stand up to our useful idiot war-mongering puppets and their Jew masters.

Here is how it will start. At some point many of the decent thinking moral Godly patriotic brave people left in America – will finally have had enough of the outright criminals like the Obamanoids and the Bushwhackers and the best Congress that Jew money can buy. These REAL Americans will then be labeled with the usual Jew and Jew useful idiot (shabbus goy) mantras – -racists anti-Semitics – un-patriotic and the usual worn-out clichés.

IF – ANY true American patriot should resist becoming slaves of the Jews – they will cry foul and have their then treasonous puppet President declare martial law. Habeas corpus will be suspended and of course the military will be called upon to suppress any dissenters – as our neighborhood police by the grace of God just may STILL be loyal to the Constitution and their own neighbors. He Jews are very cunning and have already thought of this.

They have a hugely powerful military that has ALRADY been brain- washed to kill on order. We know this fact from our disgraceful record of human rights violations in Afghanistan and Iraq – ranging from outright murders to rapes beatings robberies and all forms of desecrations – unparallel in American military history!

Suicides by gulf-war veterans have reached such alarming proportions that they have now exceeded combat fatalities! Let that ugly fact sink in for a moment. American veterans are so filled with guilt from the vast magnitude and enormity of war crime atrocities they have committed – according to VA studies – that they are taking their own lives at home in greater numbers than actual combat casualties! That is how abysmally morally degenerate we have become.

We also know that Marines have been so brain-washed as killers – that in a study years ago at the 29 Palms Naval/Marine base in California – it was proved that a significant percentage of them would murder civilians – THEIR OWN NEIGHBORS – is ordered to.

Combine that terrifying disgusting loathsome FACT with the actuality of our own children being currently trained and conditioned – AT THE VERY SAME TRAINING BASES I ONCE TRAINED RECRUITS MYSELF – only NOW they are taught to smash in civilian homes and kill anybody who dares to protect their family or home. My OWN son just went through basic and shared that disgusting reality with me!

Yes – these sick depraved psychopathic Jew trained Obamanoids WILL kill you and your children and your husband and your neighbors. The transition from murdering civilians in Faluja Iraq -to murdering civilians in Fredericksburg USA – is just a matter of logistics to these sadistic Godless psychopathic trained killers.

Our youth has already been conditioned to ENJOY watching suffering death sand horror from DECADES of watching and participating in the most ultra-violent Jew created WAR 'games' on earth!

The examples of the results of this sicko mentality conditioning are common. The remorseless killers at Columbine were ardent WAR GAME video fans – just for one example. Prominent clinical researchers have proven conclusively that the PRIMARY cause of violence and aggression in our children in the last decade plus – is directly attributable to their constant diet of ultra-violent WAR GAME videos!

Here is are occurring common observations of returning Gulf-War veterans: "Video games that allow players to murder REAL HUMAN BEINGS are desensitizing generations of American society!"

Here is another similar conclusion: "Kids get in the Army and get to live out their aggressive fantasies of violence and killing". Yet another Vet's chilling observation: " The Army gives you the ultimate license to KILL!"

That one says it ALL!

For God sake – listen to the FACTS – SEE the TRUTH – embrace REALITY – gain WISDOM. Our current mercenary military has accomplished 4 Jew goals.

Maiming and killing of thousands of our sons and fathers – especially Christians Impoverishing our economy with war debts our grandchildren cannot pay. Making NEW enemies of people who once liked and respected us Endangering the entire planet with the prospect of nuclear global conflict. The only people who will benefit from more death and violence and endless war?

Look at history. WHO has prospered at the expense of mankind from virtually all wars?

The JEWS ! THE JEWS! THE JEWS THE JEWS THE JEWS – AND- THE JEWS!

LOOK at the TRUTH of WHO are the one who scream in shrill voices for WAR and MORE WAR AND KILLING – AND YET MORE WAR AND KILLING OF INNOCENTS. It is the Jews and their evil demonic treasonous country selling Zionist useful idiots.

For those of you who still try to conduct your lives in the spirit of the TRUE word of Christ. – remember that IsraHELL and 99% of ALL Jews do NOT want peace. They want what they have shown to love for all of recorded history – BLOOD KILLING VIOLENCE and the endless suffering of their victims. Did IsraHELL loyal Bush ask for an end to these insane immoral demonic WARS – and be a 'PEACEMAKER'? NO! ANYONE who worked in his Jew infested administration who so much as DARED to stand for peace justice sanity truth and righteousness – like decorated 4 star Admiral – US CENTCOM Commander – William Fallen was simply 'thrown under the bus'. Has IsraHELL loyal Obama – with his Zionist Jew dominate cabinet strived in ANY Way to end this madness and insanity and be a peacemaker

NO!

Has his shifty beady eyed monstrously evil Zionist IsraHELL loyal VP done ANYTHING other than PURE TREASON TO AMERICA – and 100% devotion to Jew war-mongering causes? NO!

Has our criminal IsraHELL loyal Congress made their wishes to be peacemakers manifest to the American people – EVER – NO!

Has ANY of the Jew owned MNM or their useful idiot puppet show hosts – Hannity – Colmes – O* Reilly -Limbaugh – or ANY major news personality voiced ANY sincere wish to end this immoral slaughter of innocent people – NO!

Have any of our all powerful super influential multi- billionaires like Buffet or Gates used their vast resources to implement an anti-war peace movement to bring an end to these senseless barbaric genocides of innocent civilians – NO!

Have any of the major churches of the 50 million or so Hagee inflamed Zionist Baptist churches who so ardently support the Jews who tirelessly work 24-7 for the destruction of Christ – Christianity -and everything Christian in America ever voiced their loathing at these brutal genocidal demonic wars for the greater glory of IsraHELL NO!

Are you listening yet – Hagee – you devious lying evil hypocrite bloody child killing warmongering Christ- mocking Godless monster?

Are our own children taught anything today that is good – wholesome – Godly – charitable – compassionate and Christ like today in our 100% Jew controlled public schools – or on the 100% controlled JEW TV – or our 100% Jew controlled 'entertainmant1 industry – NO!

50 years go – as a young man – nothing that I have said would have been pertinent – simply because it wouldn't have been necessary – as we still had decent people who knew right from wrong – and the putrid demonic incredibly evil conduct of ALL the afore- mentioned mega-criminal greedy self-serving parasite anti American scum would have NEVER been tolerated for a day!

BUT TODAY – in our occupied serfdom of Godless 'IsraHELL West – I will assuredly be persecuted for even DARING to be so insolent as to defend and put America first and honor the teachings of our Lord that are now so unopposed and boldly mocked by the powers that be and their spineless 'news' shills who do their evil bidding.

Our modern 'improved' Zionist loyal military are the world's largest cabal of criminal gangsters – virtually no different from the Chi-Coms or the former Soviet military. For ANYBODY who thinks that is ANYTHING but the absolute Gospel truth – I challenge you to study your modem history. Look at the dozens and dozens of articles in the Reader's digest alone which chronicle the sadistic brutal criminal conduct of the Soviet military in their mid-late 80s military occupation of Afghanistan – which rightfully earned them the title of THE EVIL EMPIRE!

The only difference is that we have now committed more brutal atrocities to those poor people than they did. READ THE TRUTH FOR YOURSELF. We are even MORE guilty than the Communists – simple because WE – as a free people in a Christian based Republic – UNLIKE the subverted closed society ignorant Soviet masses – HAD A CHOICE – and we CHOSE TO BE EVIL .

That is the unvarnished ugly immutable TRUTH – like it or not THIS is what WE – of our own free will have allowed ourselves to become – the NEW EVIL EMPIRE – with a murderous Godless out of control psychopath military that WILL murder ANYONE they are ordered to. That is NOT just 'my opinion'. THAT is a historically proven documented ten times over frightening disgusting proven FACT!

DO NOT ALLOW YOUR SONS TO TAKE PART IN OUR GODLESS MURDEROUS ZIONIST MILITARY!

My name is Joe Cortina. I was a 60s Green Beret commander and a representative for IBM as well as a scientist for Honeywell Aerospace in

Florida. I later became President of my own manufacturing company. I have two sons and 2 granddaughters who are the reason for my dedication to expose the threats to the freedoms I hope to see them enjoy as I did many decades ago when America was still a Christian-based sovereign nation free of Zionist influence.

Book Of John Chapter 8 – as Christ damns the Jews (and NOT JUST THE HIGH PRIESTS AND Pharisees – see notes below)

"Ye do the deeds of your father (the devil). If God were your father. ye would love me; for I proceed forth and came from God: neither came I

of myself, but He sent me."

"Ye are of your father the devil and the lusts of your father ye will do. He was a murderer from the beginning and abode not in the truth,

Because there is no truth in him. When he speaketh a lie – he speaketh of his own; (the Jews) for he is a liar, and the father of it"

"That this SATANIC FATHERHOOD cannot be limited to the Pharisees is MADE CLEAR in 1 John 3;8-10″

Matthew 23:15″ Woe to you, teachers of the law and Pharisees, you hypocrites! You travel over land and sea to win a single convert, and when

he becomes one, you make him twice as much a son of hell as you are.

"You serpents, you generation of vipers, how can you escape the damnation of hell?" (Jesus – to the Jews; in Matthew 23:33)

MAY, 2010
AN EX-GREEN BERET REMEMBERS MEMORIAL DAY 2010

Do I 'remember' Memorial day? You bet your sweet buns I do! I also remember how it started and how it was celebrated in REAL AMERICAN LIFE, and the total hypocrisy it is today!

This is how it got started. A Union General named John A Logan who was the Union Vets assoc leader decided to see if he could inflict even more pain and insult to still grieving widows and crying orphans of those terrible "rebels". Notice the callus use of language that could ONLY be interpreted as demeaning to ALL of the CSA dead who fought in defense of THEIR land and THEIR families and THEIR freedom. Remember – all you witless brainwashed history experts – the civil war was NOT fought for freeing the slaves bullshit! IT WAS FOUGHT FOR STATES RIGHTS. Yes Dorothy – the North had slaves too

Here is the text of what our 'thoughtful tactful' General Logan stated that we should do to remember the fallen dead: …"for the purpose of strewing with flowers, or otherwise decorating the graves of comrades who died in defense of their country during the late rebellion, and whose bodies now lie in almost every city, village, and hamlet churchyard in the land"

Rebellion? as if men like Lee were criminal scoundrels? THEIR COUNTRY!? – as in belonging to the victors and Jew carpetbaggers as in SPOILS OF WAR? What malicious lying divisive hate speech – REAL HATE SPEECH! Rot in hell John Logan! FACT: even Union Generals Sherman and Grant – as hard-nosed as they were – tried their best to kick the wretched Jews parasites out of the defeated South and allow healing to begin.

And as for Abraham Lincoln – Certainly not MY idea of what a Godly American president should be. My opinion? His Gettysburg address did nothing more than fuel the fires of hatred between brother and brother – lionized the Union soldiers and demonized the Confederates. More than a million fighting men have given the last full measure of devotion. Their valor and sacrifices have made possible our freedoms our values our very existence" What a crock of shit! Do you have ANY idea of how many young American men suffered torture and starvation and deprivation in Union prisons for their sincere loyalties to their families and traditions IN AMERICA?

Does ANYBODY remember the pure hell that was imposed on every man woman and and child in the South? Whose freedoms? – Whose values? Whose existence?. I was born in the 'North' but I am NOT ASHAMED to admit that I AM ashamed of what the North did to a defeated impoverished American people after the war. The cruelty and hardships imposed on innocent women and children was unparalleled with the exception of our treatment of aboriginal people here – certainly nothing to be proud of. We are MASTERS of war crimes and atrocities – even to our OWN people! Don't even get me started on Wounded knee Ruby Ridge and Waco.

That NEEDED to be said – I have paid my dues – and so agree or not – I said it because I believe it.

Anyway – later on it became apparent that MY simple observation today – had been shared by MILLIONS of offended Americans and rightfully so! After WWI it was renamed to the present designation of 'Memorial Day' – so apparently a lot of other learned sincere people felt the same way.

Yes – I will remember the men I knew – some well and some only slightly – like Bo Gritz and David Hackworth – who were REAL heroes who risked life and limb against REAL ENEMIES – not old men, children, and pregnant mothers like our brave sociopathic trash today whose fathers were not even born when I trained their grandfathers. I will mourn the REAL MEN – Godly men – like the ones I trained nearly 50 years ago – not the putrid child murdering scum criminals I see today!

Memorial Day was meant to be a period of solemn reflection of the sacrifices Americans in uniform made to preserve our most sacrosanct values and human ideals – family – God – country – through selfless sacrifice – of duty – commitment – honor, and valor. Those were lofty ideals – to be sure – but NONE of those values or traits even exists anymore in today's mercenary dumbed down paid killers sadists psychopaths and human garbage – who mostly have total approval of their brain-dead equally immoral parents. I have encountered that disgrace more times than I can recall.

Just look at the putrid leadership we have – starting with a Negro Marxist /Zionist sock-puppet 'President' – who can't even prove his citizenship – a 100% Jew cabinet – and pure 100% ass-kissing ambitious war criminal military leaders with ABSOLUTELY no MORALS – NO compassion – no souls, and KNOWING FULL WELL – that their heinous crimes protected NO American in ANY Way – and whose greed and lust for power are loyal ONLY to the Jews and Jew puppets who they so eagerly grovel to.

General 'BETRAY-US' and General 'McWARMONGER' are two examples of criminal thugs. I would RELISH to see these 'IsraHELL first' – Godless hypocrites, HUNG for their sadistic grizzly crimes! These criminals are the EXACT type who would command military troops to murder civilians in our own neighborhoods if commanded to. A Marine base called 29 Palms has already proven that disgraceful terrifying FACT! I have known their evil ilk my whole life! I have witnessed this type of Jew brutality in Palestine. It is a killing field more brutal and sadistic than even the mass murders of Cambodia.

Remember the Genocide in Cambodia under Pol Pot ? (a Marxist who learned his killing art form the Jew Commissars of the USSR) It was considered one of the world's most horrible mass killings – YET the genocide our brave young killers have committed in Iraq – FACTUALLY EXCEEDS CAMBODIA (1.7 million) IN NUMBER OF MURDERS! That is a truth you will NEVER Learn form our Jew controlled MSM. Have you ever bothered to ask your local church – or newspaper – or TV station – WHY you were never told – or do you even give a damn any more as long as you have your fancy SUV – your credit cards and cold beer?

And after all – YOUR son is a 'GOOD' boy and would NEVER do such horrid things – right? Most of those two million civilians must have slipped on camel dung and hit their heads – right?

NONE – not ONE of these killers in desert camo's today are ANYTHING but cold-blooded murdering bastards. Do your own net searches and see the horrible crimes they commit 24-7 against defenseless civilians in their OWN homes in their OWN country. Next time you see of of these bastards home on leave – remember – he is a CRIMINAL – a monster and should be treated as such.

The rapes – cold-blooded execution murders – and beatings of innocent terrified innocent human beings go on 24 hours a day. Only a VERY VERY small percentage of the TRUE number of crimes will EVER be shown or filmed. Even so, the factual evidence of these atrocities are LEGION! Helicopter gunships murdering dozens of helpless children and elderly in the streets – young girls being raped beaten to death and burned – an old man on HIS OWN STREET gunned down by a dozen brave armed US killers – fathers dragged our of their homes – bound & gagged shot in the head and thrown in drainage ditches like dogs. Their terrible crimes? Trying to defend their OWN wives and children!

See these atrocities for yourself. In quantity savage sadistic cruelty and frequency they are unparalleled in modern warfare! In just the 24 hours of the Memorial day it self – these scum we are supposed to honor for "keeping us free" or other cute little lying Jew clichés to keep us dumbed down and continue our endless serial wars and genocides against people who have NEVER DONE ANYBODY HERE ANY HARM OR HAVE NEVER EVER BEEN ANY REMOTE THREAT IN ANY WAY – will murder in cold-blood a lot more innocent souls for the greater glory of the Jew.

Do you know how many more women and children must be raped – beaten to death shot – blown to pieces by bombs and heavy artillery – incinerated by white phosphorous – and other horrible deaths? Care to guess? We have already slaughtered a MINIMUM of TWO MILLION CIVILIANS. Take that figure times the months and years we have been MURDERING these poor people – there will be ONE THOUSAND MORE DEAD BABIES WOMEN AND CHILDREN in that 24 hour period while we BRAVE American party animals get drunk and party and stuff our fat faces as we pat our respects to the murderers our Godless Jew dominate society has created to protect IsraHELL!

These poor souls do not get a 3 day 'holiday' – so there will be more like THREE THOUSAND MORE corpses that we can gloat over having murdered by Tuesday morning. Have a great orgy – party animals – your Jew masters will be proud. I have spoken ONLY the truth – a dirty word in 2010 AmeriKa. I can practically guarantee that by this time next year – we WILL be a police state and anyone who DARES to speak out against evil as I have – will have the Jew Gestapo at his door and will disappear – legally of course from the then totally Jew controlled Federal Judicial System.

We are only a HEART BEAT away from that EXACT scenario at this moment in time – for those of you who can tear yourselves away from your cold-Bud and tailgate parties long enough to see what is before your very eyes . Like it or not – what I said is the truth and you had damn well better give it thought before the 'though police' come to your home. May God forgive you for doing nothing to save our own country from Jew greed and goy stupidity. Now go out and party – or be an AMERICAN!

My name is Joe Cortina. I was a 60s Green Beret commander and a representative for IBM as well as a scientist for Honeywell Aerospace in Florida. I later became President of my own manufacturing company. I have two sons and 2 granddaughters who are the reason for my dedication to expose the threats to the freedoms I hope to see them enjoy as I did many decades ago when America was still a Christian-based sovereign nation free of Zionist influence.

JUNE, 2010
IT WASN'T THE ARABS, STUPID! IT WAS THE JEWS! (PART 1)

I wrote this for the education of my unfortunately poorly educated 'fellow Americans' – and ESPECIALLY for all of those brain-dead pasty faced Pavlovian drooling Zionist Baptists who by your own FREE WILL – KNOWINGLY and PURPOSEFULLY mock the teachings of our Lord with your racist hatred and unconscionable demonic war-mongering. What kind of sadistic filth would scream an endless blood lust for the lives of innocent women and children who have done you no harm?

You have already been the prime enabling cause of the murders of over TWO MILLION innocent human beings – mostly CHILDREN – and yet – FULL WELL knowing this – you STILL cannot satisfy you lust for even MORE killing, destruction, rapes, tortures, and dehumanization of innocent souls! That is the TRUTH and no amount of protest can change it.

For the immense human misery and suffering you have caused by your evil and criminal ignorance – may you ALL spend eternity in the most inconsolable place in HELL! It is YOUR ILK who have been more responsible for the destruction of true Christianity in America than all of our enemies combined. History will not soon forget nor forgive the apostasy of you demonic creatures – for your role in the destruction of our beloved America and its premature death sentence to the ash-heap of history.

It wasn't the Arabs who called the mother of Jesus a "WHORE" – it was the jews

It wasn't the Arabs who wrote the largest assemblage of anti-Christ/Christian hate literature (TALMUD) in history – it was the jews

It wasn't the Arabs who mocked the early death of our Lord – it was the jews

It wasn't the Arabs who declared that our Lord's fate was to be boiled alive in a pit of excrement (shit) – it was the jews

It wasn't the Arabs who said that Jesus "seduced, corrupted and destroyed Israel" – it was the jews.

It wasn't the Arabs who called Jesus an "Idolator" and "seducer" – it was the jews

It wasn't the Arabs who said Christians "were idolaters, the worst kind of people, much worse than the Turks, murderers, fornicators, impure animals, like dirt, unworthy to be called men, beasts in human form, worthy of the name of beasts, cows, asses pigs, dogs and worse than dogs; that they propagate after the manner of beasts, that they have a diabolic origin, that their souls came from the devil in hell after death; and that even the body of a dead Christian is nothing different from that of an animal" – it was the jews.

It wasn't the Arabs who said " A Nazarine is one who follows the false teachings of Christ.." it was the jews

It wasn't the Arabs who called Christians "Goy" – an insulting and demeaning term – lower than an animal, it was the jews

It wasn't the Arabs who said that the sexual intercourse between Christians is like that of a beast – it was the jews.

It wasn't the Arabs who said that " They (Christians) give birth to sucklings the same as dogs" – it was the jews.

It wasn't Arabs that said "The send of a 'Goy' (Christian) is the same as that of a beast" – it was the jews.

It wasn't the Arabs who called Christians the "children of the Devil – it was the jews.

It wasn't the Arabs whose laws demanded that a Christian's greeting must not be returned – it was the jews.

It wasn't the Arabs whose law states that they cannot go before a Christian Judge – it was the jews.

It wasn't the Arabs whose laws state that a Christian – because he is considered lower than an animal – cannot be used as a witness – it was the jews.

It was not the Arabs who refused to associate with Christians because they were considered unworthy and "unclean" – it was the jews.

It is not the Arabs who must refuse to be attended by a Goy Christian physician – it is the jews

It is not the Arabs who teach that whenever possible they must murder Christians and do so without mercy – it was the jews

It is not the Arabs who call Mary, the mother of Jesus – "chairia" – shit, dung , it is the jews

It is not the Arabs who call Christian Saints perverts an homosexuals. It is the jews.

It is not the Arabs who call Christian Churches a house of evil – it is the jews.

It is not the Arabs who teach that Christians honor 'their' God (Jesus) by shitting before Him – it is the jews.

It is not the Arabs whose law says that Christians must NOT be told if they are paying too much – it is the jews.

It is not the Arabs who teach that the rightful property of Christians must NOT be returned to them – it is the jews.

It is not the Arabs who teachings state that it is allowed to cheat/defraud Christians – it s the jews.

It is not the Arabs whose written laws encourage 'usury' against Christian 'Goy' – it is the jews.

It is not Arab law that teaches that they may lie and perjure themselves to condemn a Christian – it is the jews.

It is not the Arabs who teach that an injured Christian must NOT be aided – it is the jews.

It is not the Arabs who teach that a Christian must ALWAYS be deceived whenever possible – it is the jews.

It is not the Arabs that teach a Christian woman in childbirth or that ANY Christian in danger of DEATH must NOT be helped – it is the jews

It is not the Arabs who teach that all of the Christians – even the best of them are to be killed (as were 20,000,000 Christians in Russia!) – it was the jews

It is not the Arabs who teach their ilk that no festival – no matter how solemn must prevent the murder of a Christian – it was the jews

It is not the Arabs whose leader teach that it is OK for them to do evil if they do it in a city where they are not known – it is the jews.

It is not the Arabs who teach that hitting one of them is the SAME as hitting God – it is the jews.

It is not the Arabs who are taught that if they are hit by a Christian, it is permissible to murder that Christian – it is the jews.

It is not the Arabs who teach that they need not pay a just debt to a Christian – it is the jews.

It is not the Arabs who are taught it is good to rob, cheat or kill a Christian – it is the jews.

It is not the Arabs who consider all Christian children as "animals' – it is the jews.

It is not the Arabs who taught that the disciples of Jesus practiced sorcery and black magic – it was the jews.

It is not the Arabs who were taught that the very name of Jesus was an abomination – it was the jews.

It is not the Arabs who were taught that agriculture is the lowest form of occupations – it was the jews.

It is not the Arabs who are taught that it is "nothing" for an adult male to have sex with a child (sound very much like the USA jew originated NAMBLA perverts?) – it is the jew.

AND – of course it was NOT the Arab mobs who screamed for the death of Jesus and openly declared that His murder should be upon their blood and that of their children – it was the JEWS!

It is important to know that even TODAY – Jews in Israhell STILL continue to blaspheme mock and curse the Lord in ways I cannot even repeat. They are unrepentant as they have been for two thousand years. They STILL shrilly scream that they would crucify Him AGAIN and AGAIN – and are arrogantly boastful about it!. It is an evil and insane hatred in the nature of the demonic Jew that has transcended millennia and all sense of decency. Go to IsraHELL – as I did – BUT – as an insider – and you will see and hear the hatred for the Lord alive and well. What you will see and hear there today is nothing less than the fulfillment of the self imposed curse upon themselves and their children for all times . "His blood be upon us and our children" Matthew 27-25

JUNE, 2010
IT WASN'T THE ARABS, STUPID! IT WAS THE JEWS! (PART 2)

Here is yet more wisdom for the hungry for knowledge and truth. The most prolific liars of all time as proven by their own conduct for the past two thousand years and of course by the word of the Son of God – Jesus of Nazareth – the Christ – as written in the Gospel of John – are of course THE JEWS!

In fairness – not 'ALL' Jews are liars. And of course — Not all large sharks are man-eathers. Not all Vipers are deadly. Not all Grizzly bears are man-killers. Not all gypsies are cheats. Not all scorpions are poisonous. Not all home invadors are going to kill the family. Not all homosexual perverts are pedophiles. Not all cancers are deadly. Not all drug addicts ruin their lives. Not all poisons are fatal. Not all psychopaths are killers. Not all black widdow bites aere fatal. Not all AIDS viruses are contagious. Not all gunshots to the head are fatal. Not all plane crashes are fatal. Not all Russian Roulette players die.

BUT – the odds are very much against you if want to flirt 100 -1 or 1000 – 1 odds. I have not EVER witnessed a single substantial truth about the conduct of the Israelis or criminal Jews in America for that matter – come from ANY Jew Congressman – Rabbi – Hollywood personality

– TV news spokesman – White House official – wealthy businessman or any other prominent Jew – PERIOD!

Note – that every one of these following facts are based upon LIES spoken by the Jews. There are and have been no greater liars than the Jew. The entire collective history and life of the Jews is one gigantic lie.

The Israhell press is constantly parroting the monstrous lie that "their army is the most moral in the world". The IN – YOUR – FACE from endless irrefutable evidence truth IS – that the Jew military is the most sadistic – cruel – cowardly – blasphemous – terrorist – murderous – child-murdering gang of thugs on earth! How can you top that lie!

How about this one? "We Jews are a light among nations – a people who improves all countries we touch". What overbearing stiff-necked arrogance! These are demonic creatures exposed as the "Sons of Satan" by the Son of God – a people so evil and corrupt that they have been kicked out of over a hundred nations and city States over the past 1500 years for their rancid criminal conduct.

No Jew has ever been 'persecuted'. Look up the meaning of the word PERSECUTED for yourself. The Jews have been 'punished' for THEIR criminal CONDUCT – CONDUCT – CONDUCT! It has been the JEWS who have persecuted OTHER innocent people – NOT the other way around. The Jew and his lies have made him the master of reverse discrimination. The shrewd cunning Jew makes HIMSELF the victim – while HIS victims become the victimizers.

The perfect example of this demonic art of the Devil is how the poor people of Gaza – inprisoned beaten starved tortured humiliated and murdered for over SIXTY YEARS – by these horrible Jews – wealthy beyond any wildest imagination – have somehow been the perpetrators and the Jews with one of the largest armies on earth are the poor victims.

Such are the magnitude of the lies of these demonic "SONS OF SATAN" with their "SYNAGOGUES OF SATAN".

ALL of these TRUTHS below are to counter and expose lies promoted by the Jews!

It wasn't Arabs who sent our military into Afghanistan and Iraq to murder innocent women and children by the HUNDREDS of thousands – it was jews (Bush's neocons).

It isn't Arabs who refuse to serve in the US Military in numbers proportionate to their population percentage – it is jews (1/10 of 1%, vs. 5%). (I trained a LOT of combat troops during the Vietnam and Berlin Crisis era, and I KNOW this for a fact FIRSTHAND!)

It wasn't Arabs who sued to remove "under God" from the Pledge of Allegiance – it was jews.

It wasn't Arabs who sued to remove the Ten Commandments from that Alabama courthouse, had Judge Moore removed from the bench and now seek to disbar him – it is jews.

It isn't Arabs who sue to remove nativity scenes from public venues – it is jews.

It isn't Arabs who erect menorahs in public venues in place of crosses – it is jews.

It wasn't Arabs who sued to remove group prayer from public schools – it was jews.

It wasn't Arabs suing to remove decorative lights from schools at Christmas – it was jews.

It isn't Arabs who refuse to allow children to say grace over their school lunches – it is jews.

It isn't Arabs who continue to impose affirmative action upon us in all walks of life – it is jews.

It isn't Arabs who began and continue to expand militant feminism – it is jews.

It isn't Arabs who buy off all our legislators with our own tax dollars – it is jews.

It wasn't Arabs who tried to sink the USS Liberty and killed and maimed so many of its crewmembers during an extended attack – it was jews.

It isn't Arabs enacting hate crime laws designed to outlaw criticism of themselves – it is jews.

It isn't Arabs who run NAMBLA (North American Man-Boy Love Association) – it is jews.

It isn't Arabs suing to force us to allow homosexuals to lead boy scout troops – it is jews.

It wasn't Arabs who started and ran so many black militant organizations like the NAACP – it was jews.

It isn't Arabs importing huge numbers of Somalians and Bantu into American cities – it is jews.

It wasn't Arabs who formulated American legislation providing pensions to Russian jewish immigrants for doing nothing – it was jews.

It isn't Arabs who run organized crime throughout America – it is jews.

It isn't Arabs who import tons of drugs into America every day – it is jews.

It isn't Arabs who literally own and run all of Hollywood's moviemaking filth enterprise – it is jews.

It isn't Arabs who literally own and run all of America's mainstream media – it is jews.

It isn't Arabs spewing obscenity and race-mixing propaganda from the TV and movie screens – it is jews.

It isn't Arabs trying mightily to block release of the Mel Gibson movie, "The Passion" – it is jews.

It isn't Arabs lying about and guilt tripping us with "the holocaust" – it is jews.

It isn't Arabs stealing American tax dollars to fund all their holocaust monuments throughout America – it is jews.

It wasn't Arabs who forged the Anne Frank "diary" – it was jews.

It wasn't Arabs who lied about gas chambers at Dachau and Auschwitz – it was jews.

It wasn't Arabs who lied about mass graves at Treblinka – it was jews.

It wasn't Arabs who lied about jews being made into lamp shades and soap during WWII – it was jews.

It wasn't Arabs who doctored WWII prison camp photos to appear to be belching smoke from crematoria – it was jews.

It wasn't Arabs who used WWII pictures of dead non jews, claiming they were jews – it was jews.

It wasn't Arabs who made anti-semitical talk punishable by death in Russia after they took power – it was jews.

It wasn't Arabs who killed over 20 million Russian Christians – it was jews.

It wasn't Arabs who looted and destroyed the Russian economy with their usury and greed – it was jews.

It isn't Arabs who have amassed an illegal arsenal of over 300 nuclear weapons in the Middle East – it is the jews.

It isn't Arabs who brag about controlling America – it is jews.

It isn't Arabs who advocate the use of torture by and on Americans – it is jews.

It isn't Arabs who twist American laws to punish anti-semitical speech – it is jews.

It isn't Arabs endeavoring to get America to outlaw anti-semitical speech – it is jews.

It isn't Arabs who sell goods that it is illegal in America to boycott – it is Israeli jews.

It isn't Arabs who extort "fees" for allowing their kosher label on goods – it is jews.

It isn't Arabs who retaliate against rock-throwing children by shooting them in the head – it is jews. (I HAVE PERSONALLY WITNESSED THIS SADISTIC ISREALI PASSTIME)

It isn't Arabs stealing land in Palestine – it is jews.

It wasn't Arabs who ran down Rachel Corrie with a bulldozer – it was a jew.

It isn't Arabs who have caused America to spend $2.5 trillion ($31,250 per American family) in the Middle East – it is jews.

It isn't Arabs who send teams of trained assassins into foreign countries, including America, to kill people with whom Israel disagrees – it is jews.

It isn't Arabs who run the ADL, which maintains dossiers on thousands of law-abiding American citizens, for the purpose of punishing those with whom they disagree – it is jews.

It isn't Arabs who break into and enter the offices and homes of law-abiding American citizens, to procure evidence both for their database and in the hopes of getting evidence they can pass to the FBI for prosecution – it is jews.

It isn't Arabs who have caused America to go from being the most-loved country in the world to the most hated – it is jews.

It wasn't the Arabs who produced the biggest traitors to America in all history (Rosenbergs – Pollard & more!) it was the jews

It isn't the Arabs who participate in – support and or participate in EVERY MAJOR HOMOSEXUAL organization in America – it is the jews

It wasn't the Arabs who treatened the lives of Christian Actor /director MelGibson and his father for honoring God in his movie about the Passion of Christ – it was the jews!

It wasn't an Arab Congressman that made the following disgusting blasphemy and open hatred of Christians on the floor of Congress "Do not let the forces of evil [Christians] take over to make this a Christian America."(Senator Howard Metzenbaum, 11/6/86) – it WAS A JEW!

It isn't the Arabs who constitute an overwhelming majority of the treasonous Communist Party in OUR America – IT IS THE JEWS!

It isn't the Arabs that want to take our guns away in America – it is the jews

It isn't the Arabs who dominate the psychiatric quacks in America that keep our children drugged up 24/7 on Ritalin – it is the jews. ONE of these stinking jew pseudophysicians has ruined my own teenage son's life! It is a story EVERY AMERICAN PARENT NEEDS TO HEAR!!

It wasn't the Arabs who murdered several of my ex wife's family in cold blood because they were Christians – it was the jews! (My ex wife's grandmother witnessed the horror of having her husband and sons murdered right before her very eyes by the sadistic jew CHEKA in the predominately Christian Ukraine!)

It wasn't an Arab Mayor that turned the quaint Latin quarter of my grandparents into a rotted hellhole of porn/ sleaze – and a haven for homo-pervert bars – it was a jewess.

It is not the Arabs who dominate America's virtually Marxist 'Democrat Party' of sleaze and filth – it is the jews (over 90% of American jews are Democrats)

It is not the Arabs who have turned my once proud and wholesome America into a morally rotted corpse – it is the jews.

It is not the Arabs who percentage-wise dominate the militant in- you-face Christian hating – boy scout hating homosexual filth in America – it is the jews

It is not Arab representation in America that has turned virtually all of the former 'educational channels' on TV into vehicles for promoting atheism – it is the jews.

It was not the Arabs who have rotted/ruined perverted an entire generation of our youth with their filth, violence, vile language, perversions, gratuitous sex on cinema and TV- it has been the work of the jews

It wasn't the Arabs who have worked tirelessly to insure never ending hatred between the races – it IS the jews (eg. NAACP)

It isn't Arabs who regularly phony up "hate crimes" against themselves – it is jews.

It wasn't Arabs who caused the Great Depression – it was jews.

It wasn't Arabs who dragged American Christian sons into WWI – it was jews.

It wasn't Arabs who dragged American Christian sons into WWII – it was jews.

It wasn't Arabs who had JFK killed – it was jews.

It wasn't Arabs who demolished the World Trade Center – it was jews.

AND —- It isn't Arabs bent upon destroying Christianity – it is jews.

And lest we forget: It wasn't Arabs who had Jesus Christ crucified – it was jews.

JUNE, 2010
IT WASN'T THE ARABS, STUPID! IT WAS THE JEWS! (PART 3)

Here are yet more factual truths concerning the endless lies perpetrated against the Arab people by the masters of lying, deceit, fraud, crime, duplicity, betrayal, and treason.

To all those of you who in your hearts do NOT – hate nor cruelly mock Christ as do those Baptist demons whose only 'love' is the stench of death – the wailing of grieving parents of hundreds of thousands of murdered innocent children – and joy in the human suffering of millions upon millions of innocent civilians, who these witless bovine mentality uneducated redneck morons consider only as "sand-niggers" – "camel-jockeys" and " towel – heads" — I dedicate this third part of a wakeup call to reestablish decency and humanity – compassion and wisdom – in a nation I scarcely recognize today.

You Baptists and other so-called Christian-Zionist scum are the antithesis of true Christian conduct. I thought that I had witnessed the ultimate in the hatred of Christ and what He stands for and has taught – when I was in IsraHELL. Your mockery and cruelty of his truths surpass even the profane openly voiced desire to crucify Him again that I witnessed there. You people ARE the collective anti-Christ!

The Baptists are not the only guilty parties to these mass genocidal murders – just the largest and most criminally minded morons of the lot. Congratulations – you have all qualified for an unlimited vacation in that place we commonly call Hell. However it was a 'pricy' ticket. You traded your immortal souls for doing what was obvious to a ten year old child as demonically evil.

You Baptists want not only endless wars – but the violent deaths of countless millions of innocent people – as ordained by your Jew and Jew – wanna-be useful idiot masters. For that you will have earned the undying enmity of every decent informed principled compassionate Godly man woman and child on earth.

I will do everything within my ability to make sure that my children and grandchildren and their children hold EVERY ONE OF YOU SADISTIC demons responsible for all of the carnage you have caused so far and that yet to come – should you get your Third World War for the greater glory of IsraHELL and the physical destruction of America – since you have ALREADY guaranteed it's total moral and economic destruction. The deaths and destruction and mass suffering of humanity that YOU BAPTISTS WILL CAUSE – will make the pogroms of the 20th century Communists look like child's play.

Your arrogance and 'world-class' criminal stupidity will cause our destruction should you continue with your insane diabolic madness. The survivors of the Armageddon you are so eager to create will seek their justice for what you have done to their loved ones – and whatever happens to you and your evil ilk would NEVER be enough to pay for the magnitude of your crimes. Remember that – as you shrilly scream for more innocent blood.

There will be no hole dark enough nor rock large enough for you to hide from the wrath of a parent who has lost his only son on the altar of your demonic insanity!

It wasn't the Arabs that sadistically murdered countless innocent civilian refugees in Lebanon – It was the JEWS!

It wasn't the Arabs who have dragged us into needless serial wars with people who have done us no harm – it was the JEWS!

It wasn't the Arabs who use horrible demonic weapons like white phosphorous and cluster bombs against helpless civilians – it was the JEWS!

It wasn't the Arabs who have murdered thousands of civilians in Palestine – many women and children many of whom are Christians – it is the JEWS!

It wasn't the Arabs who constantly carry out 'false flag' operations to blame their heinous crimes innocent parties – it is the JEWS!

It Wasn't the Arabs that murder helpless children in the streets – for 'sport' – it is the JEWS!

(Yes – it is TRUE – yes – I have witnessed this – Yes – I have been in these prison camps)

It wasn't the Arabs whose sick twisted society condones and promotes prostitution and white slavery – it is the JEWS!

It wasn't the Arabs who are the 'undisputed kings' of international pornography – it is the JEWS!

It isn't the Arabs who now control our government for their own benefits – it is the JEWS!

It isn't the Arabs who are pushing night and day to destroy our constitutionally granted right to defend our families – it IS the JEWS!

It isn't the Arabs who are legislating laws to rescind our Constitutional right to free speech – it is the JEWS!

It isn't the Arabs who have through criminal organizations like the Federal Reserve, have all but destroyed any real value of our currency – it is the JEWS!

It isn't the Arabs who have nearly succeeded in the complete destruction of the recognition of the birth of our Lord – it is the JEWS!

It isn't the Arabs who are responsible for the REAL 'holocaust' of the cold-blooded murder of more than twenty million Christians in Russia – it was the JEWS!

It wasn't the Arabs who have made speaking the TRUTH a serious crime punishable by prison – it was the JEWS!

It wasn't the Arabs who have promoted the filthy plague of homosexual perversion in America– it is the JEWS!

It wasn't the Arabs who strive endlessly to destroy the sanctity of the sacrament of holy matrimony – it is the JEWS!

It isn't the Arabs who promote AND DEFEND pedophilia in America – it is the JEWS!

It isn't the Arabs who CONSTANTLY mock traditional Christian family values – it is the JEWS!

It isn't the Arabs who use the vehicle of cinema to promote violence – pre-marital sex-perversions – disrespect for parents – and general mockery of ANYTHING wholesome – it is the JEWS!

It isn't the Arabs who called our Lord Jesus a "bastard" and His mother a WHORE – it was the JEWS!

It wasn't the Arabs who use the vehicle of TV 'educational channels' to promote the mockery of Holy Scripture with evolution and other blasphemies – it is the JEWS!

It wasn't the Arabs who teach their children that it is proper to cheat, lie and betray Christians – it is the JEWS!

It wasn't the Arabs that created the treasonous – ACLU – the legal arm of the Communist Party – it was the JEWS!

It wasn't the Arabs that promoted so much inane and irrational hatred for Blacks against Whites that race relations will never be attainable – it was the JEWS!

It wasn't the Arabs that sold out America to the Soviets – It was the JEWS!

It wasn't the Arabs who have historically the greatest number of their ilk – commit treason against our country – it was the JEWS!

It wasn't the Arabs who caused gas prices to soar out of sight – it was the JEWS!

It wasn't the Arabs who had unduly large proportions of their people supporting the Communist Party – it was the JEWS!

It wasn't the Arabs who were responsible for the thousands of children forced to take dangerous narcotics for a non-existent 'disease' – many of whose lives were irrevocably damaged – it was the JEWS!

It wasn't the Arabs who have the world's largest and most powerful institutionalized terrorist organization on earth – The IDF – it was the JEWS!

It wasn't the Arabs who organized – financed and promoted the most deadly political organization in history – whose terror murdered over 200,000.000 innocent civilians since 1914 – it was of course – the JEWS!

JUNE, 2010
NEWSFLASH! ISRAEL HAS BEEN WIPED OFF THE FACE OF THE EARTH

UPI – Reuters – AP – BBC and dozens of other news agencies reported that as of 0500 hours GMT yesterday – Israel no longer exists. Apparently a combined unilateral attack of over a dozen allied nations using high tech mini-nuke clean bombs leveled every city in Israel after a massive bomb destroyed the Dimona nuclear complex. The surgical precision with which the ordnance was delivered prevented any major damage to neighboring Palestinian cities. A further warning was issued to American Zionist supporters that should there be any further hostilities perpetrated by Imperialist America – there would be a heavy price to pay.

A pipe dream of wishful thinking by every decent peace-loving moral person on earth? Of course.

BUT – let's take a REALISTIC look at what would be the most probable results – short term and long term for the world – AND especially the United States – which has been occupied by the Jews for decades and has been in the truest sense of the word – IsraHELL's whore – and her spineless treasonous leadership – IsraHEll's lap dogs. We have IN FACT been nothing more than an extension of the will of the DEVIL!

Every well-informed, educated, well-traveled, thinking person will have his or her own version – but since this is MY site and since I have been involved with these matters for many years and have had substantive experience at all levels with the Jew mentality and their strengths and weaknesses – I will give you MY prognostications. You can envision your own.

Keep in mind – that ALL of the evils we see today in what was once America – regardless of the fact that these evils flourished due to the ignorance and cowardice of millions of useful idiots – they were still undeniably the 'products' of the influence of Godless evil JEWS – PERIOD!

I predict a resurgence of traditional values not experienced for decades!

I see Christian churches returning to being what they used to be – formal visible vehicles for the promulgation of the word of Christ and not twisted demonic Synagogues of Satan – spewing hate, lies, racism, and Zionist ambitions of world domination.

I see all denominations of evil doers – ESPECIALLY the Baptists – whose hands are dripping with the blood of innocent children – exposed for the non-repentant, pernicious, evil, demonic, Godless hypocrites they are – and become ostracized from the company of decent men – as they should have been YEARS AGO! They KNEW the truth and still screamed for innocent blood!

I see homosexual perverts – mostly Jews – in high places of entertainment and politics being expelled from their evil influence on our children and recognized as the filth of society and abominations they have been to all decent people of all nations of all times.

I see treasonous mega-war criminals like George Bush and Obama brought to justice by a righteously outraged America – tried, prosecuted and sentenced!

I see the laws for the integrity and sovereignty of our nation enforced to the letter and EVERY SINGLE gang member, criminal drug dealer, freeloading illegal parasite alien INSTANTLY deported with a boot in their ass!

I see our schools once again as places of LEARNING and not platforms to create good little Jew-influenced, Godless, Democrat, Socialist parasites.

I see a collective surge of compassion for the poor Palestinians who have endured torture, murder, rapes, destruction, and dehumanization longer than ANY innocent people in history.

I see a LOT of Jews who have NEVER EVER put in an honest hard day's work in their entire greedy lives – out of a 'job' – of stealing money.

I see a return of our News media to traditional moral Christian ownership and management.

I see our entire Congress of cowards – greedy apostates – country sellers – opportunistic parasites – and criminal frauds running for their very lives from a hundred million angry honest Americans whom they have abused for so long.

I see lying, soulless, mega- hypocrite, greedy, fat cats like Rush Limbaugh – Sean Hannity – Bill O'Reilly – Jon Stewart – Holmes and a dozens more Jew puppets who sold their country out for popularity and money – being beaten in the streets by mothers of dead sons lost in the Jew wars.

I see Disney World being returned once more to its original wholesome, decent, Christian heritage as envisioned by Walt Disney, and it's current Jew landlords kicked out of this country.

I see filthy Jew-controlled TV confiscated and re-licensed to REAL Christian businessmen and women so that your parents and your grandchildren can ALL watch TV at home together without fear of Jew filth.

I see Hollywood's Jew multibillionaires given 24 hours to leave America with their lives and shirts on their backs and their immense stolen wealth donated to cancer and heart and diabetes and other worthy research.

I see – TRUE – Christian-tradition returned to our Christian nation and all symbols of murder and killing and violence like their putrid menorah banned from the White House FOREVER!

I see virtually all Jew parasites getting one way tickets to someplace other than THE UNITED STATES OF AMERICA!

I see our educational system having a mandatory history of the Jews and their Godless crimes against mankind in every schoolhouse in America.

I see our corrupt Jew instigated IRS reduced to near zero and our 1040 will be the SAME 1 page FORM used in the USA when our grandfathers earned a living!

I see our corrupt Jew run 'FED' dissolved and ALL Jew criminals starting with scum like Greenspan put away for LIFE!

I see The BATF disbanded and reduced to a modest admin office of clerks who process no-cost carry permits for law abiding citizens.

I see ALL former active Zionists – whether Jews or not – charged arrested and prosecuted for high treason and imprisoned or given 24 hr mass extradition – AND their trillions of stolen dollars and properties confiscated – liquidated and used to pay war reparations to the families of the murdered civilians in Iraq and Afghanistan.

I see Democrats who openly supported the illegal Negro Zionist sock puppet Obama – or Republicans who openly supported Zionist IsraHELL first war criminal George Bush – being ostracized by every decent American man woman and child.

I see MASS reforms in our corrupt FBI and other law enforcement agencies. ALL current members WILL be thoroughly investigated and the crooks, sadists and any other unacceptable types weeded out, charged, fined or imprisoned and ALL new agents and officers undergoing a stringent moral and intelligence aptitude test.

I see mega-monster criminals like Bernie Madoff doing hard time in high security prisons and NOT Jew VIP country clubs.

I see NOBODY in their right mind EVER again entertaining the possibility of a Jew in Congress or in ANY position of public office – or gaining entrance to law school or Med school or the military or the education system.

I see a better informed, more moral America where the mere mention of supporting a Synagogue Of Satan (the oxymoronic Christian Zionist church) would elicit such righteous anger within the community that it would be unthinkable!

I see a renewed people in whom the spirit of righteous outrage is NOT DEAD – a people who would NEVER EVER consider NFL football 'scores' more important than 'scores' of dead sons and fathers bodies on the deck of an American ship – butchered by terrorist Jews – as we disgracefully did before.

I see an America that now places VALUES on VALUABLE things – like wisdom- knowledge – truth – compassion – justice – goodness – self-sacrifice – hard work – responsibility and all those qualities that made us good people long ago. THESE were the virtues that made us great – NOT tailgate parties – NFL games – shiny toys – sex – alcohol – porn and drugs

I see a people renewed in their spirit and priorities and responsibilities to their children – parents who TEACH THEIR CHILDREN WELL – and TEACH THEM THE TRUTH.

I see a new breed of people who will NEVER again allow themselves to become as evil as the Jews themselves – as well as enslaved by them.

AND – I see an America where flying our flag and a bumper sticker that says: PROUD TO BE AN AMERICAN – is not some act of repulsive hypocrisy that sticks in your throat like warm vomit – as it MOST CERTAINLY has been! I see an America that is OURS again! I see an America that has kept faith with the original observation of one of our greatest foreign admirers – and proven that we are still worthy of God's grace and the respect – NOT FEAR – of all men of good will on earth. It is my dream that we are 'good' again.

"America is great because she is GOOD – and if America ever ceases to be good – America will cease to be great. "

Alexis DeTocqueville – French philosopher and historian – 1805 – 1859

JUNE, 2010
WHY JEWS ARE DANGEROUS TO THE WELL-BEING OF ALL NON-JEWS (PART 1)

I wrote this for the education of my unfortunately poorly educated 'fellow Americans' – and ESPECIALLY for all of those brain-dead pasty faced Pavlovian drooling Zionist Baptists who by your own FREE WILL – KNOWINGLY and PURPOSEFULLY mock the teachings of our Lord with your racist hatred and unconscionable demonic war-mongering. What kind of sadistic filth would scream an endless blood lust for the lives of innocent women and children who have done you no harm?

You have already been the prime enabling cause of the murders of over TWO MILLION innocent human beings – mostly CHILDREN – and yet – FULL WELL knowing this – you STILL cannot satisfy you lust for even MORE killing, destruction, rapes, tortures, and dehumanization of innocent souls! That is the TRUTH and no amount of protest can change it.

For the immense human misery and suffering you have caused by your evil and criminal ignorance – may you ALL spend eternity in the most inconsolable place in HELL! It is YOUR ILK who have been more responsible for the destruction of true Christianity in America than all of our enemies combined. History will not soon forget nor forgive the apostasy of you demonic creatures – for your role in the destruction of our beloved America and it's premature death sentence to the ash-heap of history.

It wasn't the Arabs who called the mother of Jesus a "WHORE" – it was the jews

It wasn't the Arabs who wrote the largest assemblage of anti-Christ/Christian hate literature (TALMUD) in history – it was the jews

It wasn't the Arabs who mocked the early death of our Lord – it was the jews

It wasn't the Arabs who declared that our Lord's fate was to be boiled alive in a pit of excrement (shit) – it was the jews

It wasn't the Arabs who said that Jesus "seduced, corrupted and destroyed Israel" – it was the jews.

It wasn't the Arabs who called Jesus an "Idolator" and "seducer" – it was the jews

It wasn't the Arabs who said Christians "were idolaters, the worst kind of people, much worse than the Turks, murderers, fornicators, impure animals, like dirt, unworthy to be called men, beasts in human form, worthy of the name of beasts, cows, asses pigs, dogs and worse than dogs; that they propagate after the manner of beasts, that they have a diabolic origin, that their souls came from the devil in hell after death; and that even the body of a dead Christian is nothing different from that of an animal" – it was the jews

It wasn't the Arabs who said " A Nazarine is one who follows the false teachings of Christ.." it was the jews

It wasn't the Arabs who called Christians "Goy" – an insulting and demeaning term – lower than an animal, it was the jews

It wasn't the Arabs who said that the sexual intercourse between Christians is like that of a beast – it was the jews.

It wasn't the Arabs who said that " They (Christians) give birth to sucklings the same as dogs" – it was the jews.

It wasn't Arabs that said "The send of a 'Goy' (Christian) is the same as that of a beast" – it was the jews

It wasn't the Arabs who called Christians the "children of the Devil – it was the jews

It wasn't the Arabs whose laws demanded that a Christian's greeting must not be returned – it was the jews.

It wasn't the Arabs whose law states that they cannot go before a Christian Judge – it was the jews.

It wasn't the Arabs whose laws state that a Christian – because he is considered lower than an animal – cannot be used as a witness – it was the jews.

It was not the Arabs who refused to associate with Christians because they were considered unworthy and "unclean" – it was the jews.

It is not the Arabs who must refuse to be attended by a Goy Christian physician – it is the jews

It is not the Arabs who teach that whenever possible they must murder Christians and do so without mercy – it was the jews

It is not the Arabs who call Mary, the mother of Jesus – "chairia" – shit, dung , it is the jews

It is not the Arabs who call Christian Saints perverts an homosexuals. It is the jews.

It is not the Arabs who call Christian Churches a house of evil – it is the jews.

It is not the Arabs who teach that Christians honor 'their' God (Jesus) by shitting before Him – it is the jews.

It is not the Arabs whose law says that Christians must NOT be told if they are paying too much – it is the jews.

It is not the Arabs who teach that the rightful propertyof Christians must NOT be returned to them – it is the jews.

It is not the Arabs who teachings state that it is allowed to cheat/defraud Christians – it s the jews.

It is not the Arabs whose written laws encourage 'usury' against Christian 'Goy' – it is the jews.

It is not Arab law that teaches that they may lie and perjure themselves to condemn a Christian – it is the jews.

It is not the Arabs who teach that an injured Christian must NOT be aided – it is the jews.

It is not the Arabs who teach that a Christian must ALWAYS be deceived whenever possible – it is the jews.

It is not the Arabs that teach a Christian woman in childbirth or that ANY Christian in danger of DEATH must NOT be helped – it is the jews

It is not the Arabs who teach that all of the Christians – even the best of them are to be killed (as were 20,000,000 Christians in Russia!) – it was the jews

It is not the Arabs who teach their ilk that no festival – no mater how solemn must prevent the murder of a Christian – it was the jews

It is not the Arabs whose leader teach that it is OK for them to do evil if they do it in a city where they are not known – it is the jews.

It is not the Arabs who teach that hitting one of them is the SAME as hitting God – it is the jews.

It is not the Arabs who are taught that if they are hit by a Christian, it is permissible to murder that Christian – it is the jews.

It is not the Arabs who teach that they need not pay a just debt to a Christian – it is the jews.

It is not the Arabs who are taught it is good to rob, cheat or kill a Christian – it is the jews.

It is not the Arabs who consider all Christian children as "animals' – it is the jews.

It is not the Arabs who taught that the disciples of Jesus practiced sorcery and black magic – it was the jews.

It is not the Arabs who were taught that the very name of Jesus was an abomination – it was the jews.

It is not the Arabs who were taught that agriculture is the lowest form of occupations – it was the jews.

It is not the Arabs who are taught that it is "nothing" for an adult male to have sex with a child (sound very much like the USA jew originated NAMBLA perverts?) – it is the jew.

AND – of course it was NOT the Arab mobs who screamed for the death of Jesus and openly declared that His murder should be upon their blood and that of their children – it was the JEWS!

It is important to know that even TODAY – Jews in Israhell STILL continue to blaspheme mock and curse the Lord in ways I cannot even repeat. They are unrepentant as they have been for two thousand years. They STILL shrilly scream that they would crucify Him AGAIN and AGAIN – and are arrogantly boastful about it!. It is an evil and insane hatred in the nature of the demonic Jew that has transcended millennia and all sense of decency. Go to IsraHELL – as I did – BUT – as an insider – and you will see and hear the hatred for the Lord alive and well. What you will see and hear there today is nothing less than the fulfillment of the self imposed curse upon themselves and their children for all times . “His blood be upon us and our children” Matthew 27-25

JUNE, 2010
WHY JEWS ARE DANGEROUS TO THE WELL-BEING OF ALL NON-JEWS (PART 2)

Here is yet more wisdom for the hungry for knowledge and truth. The most prolific liars of all time as proven by their own conduct for the past two thousand years and of course by the word of the Son of God – Jesus of Nazareth – the Christ – as written in the Gospel of John – are of course THE JEWS!

In fairness – not ‘ALL’ Jews are liars. And of course — Not all large sharks are man-eaters. Not all Vipers are deadly. Not all Grizzly bears are man-killers. Not all gypsies are cheats. Not all scorpions are poisonous. Not all home invaders are going to kill the family. Not all homosexual perverts are pedophiles. Not all cancers are deadly. Not all drug addicts ruin their lives. Not all poisons are fatal. Not all psychopaths are killers. Not all black widow bites are fatal. Not all AIDS viruses are contagious. Not all gunshots to the head are fatal. Not all plane crashes are fatal. Not all Russian Roulette players die.

BUT – the odds are very much against you if want to flirt 100 -1 or 1000 – 1 odds. I have not EVER witnessed a single substantial truth about the conduct of the Israelis or criminal Jews in America for that matter – come from ANY Jew Congressman – Rabbi – Hollywood personality – TV news spokesman – White House official – wealthy businessman or any other prominent Jew – PERIOD!

Note – that every one of these following facts are based upon LIES spoken by the Jews. There are and have been no greater liars than the Jew. The entire collective history and life of the Jews is one gigantic lie.

The Israhell press is constantly parroting the monstrous lie that “their army is the most moral in the world”. The IN – YOUR – FACE from endless irrefutable evidence truth IS – that the Jew military is the most sadistic – cruel – cowardly – blasphemous – terrorist – murderous – child-murdering gang of thugs on earth! How can you top that lie!

How about this one? “We Jews are a light among nations – a people who improves all countries we touch”. What overbearing stiff-necked arrogance! These are demonic creatures exposed as the “Sons of Satan” by the Son of God – a people so evil and corrupt that they have been kicked out of over a hundred nations and city States over the past 1500 years for their rancid criminal conduct.

No Jew has ever been ‘persecuted’. Look up the meaning of the word PERSECUTED for yourself. The Jews have been ‘punished’ for THEIR criminal CONDUCT – CONDUCT – CONDUCT! It has been the JEWS who have persecuted OTHER innocent people – NOT the other way around. The Jew and his lies have made him the master of reverse discrimination. The shrewd cunning Jew makes HIMSELF the victim – while HIS victims become the victimizers.

The perfect example of this demonic art of the Devil is how the poor people of Gaza – imprisoned beaten starved tortured humiliated and murdered for over SIXTY YEARS – by these horrible Jews – wealthy beyond any wildest imagination – have somehow been the perpetrators and the Jews with one of the largest armies on earth are the poor victims.

Such are the magnitude of the lies of these demonic "SONS OF SATAN" with their "SYNAGOGUES OF SATAN".

ALL of these TRUTHS below are to counter and expose lies promoted by the Jews!

It wasn't Arabs who sent our military into Afghanistan and Iraq to murder innocent women and children by the HUNDREDS of thousands – it was jews (Bush's neocons).

It isn't Arabs who refuse to serve in the US Military in numbers proportionate to their population percentage – it is jews (1/10 of 1%, vs. 5%). (I trained a LOT of combat troops during the Vietnam and Berlin Crisis era, and I KNOW this for a fact FIRSTHAND!)

It wasn't Arabs who sued to remove "under God" from the Pledge of Allegiance – it was jews.

It wasn't Arabs who sued to remove the Ten Commandments from that Alabama courthouse, had Judge Moore removed from the bench and now seek to disbar him – it is jews.

It isn't Arabs who sue to remove nativity scenes from public venues – it is jews.

It isn't Arabs who erect menorahs in public venues in place of crosses – it is jews.

It wasn't Arabs who sued to remove group prayer from public schools – it was jews.

It wasn't Arabs suing to remove decorative lights from schools at Christmas – it was jews.

It isn't Arabs who refuse to allow children to say grace over their school lunches – it is jews.

It isn't Arabs who continue to impose affirmative action upon us in all walks of life – it is jews.

It isn't Arabs who began and continue to expand militant feminism – it is jews.

It isn't Arabs who buy off all our legislators with our own tax dollars – it is jews.

It wasn't Arabs who tried to sink the USS Liberty and killed and maimed so many of its crewmembers during an extended attack – it was jews.

It isn't Arabs enacting hate crime laws designed to outlaw criticism of themselves – it is jews.

It isn't Arabs who run NAMBLA (North American Man-Boy Love Association) – it is jews.

It isn't Arabs suing to force us to allow homosexuals to lead Boy Scout troops – it is jews.

It wasn't Arabs who started and ran so many black militant organizations like the NAACP – it was jews.

It isn't Arabs importing huge numbers of Somalians and Bantu into American cities – it is jews.

It wasn't Arabs who formulated American legislation providing pensions to Russian jewish immigrants for doing nothing – it was jews.

It isn't Arabs who run organized crime throughout America – it is jews.

It isn't Arabs who import tons of drugs into America every day – it is jews.

It isn't Arabs who literally own and run all of Hollywood's moviemaking filth enterprise – it is jews.

It isn't Arabs who literally own and run all of America's mainstream media – it is jews.

It isn't Arabs spewing obscenity and race-mixing propaganda from the TV and movie screens – it is jews.

It isn't Arabs trying mightily to block release of the Mel Gibson movie, "The Passion" – it is jews.

It isn't Arabs lying about and guilt tripping us with "the holocaust" – it is jews.

It isn't Arabs stealing American tax dollars to fund all their holocaust monuments throughout America – it is jews.

It wasn't Arabs who forged the Anne Frank "diary" – it was jews.

It wasn't Arabs who lied about gas chambers at Dachau and Auschwitz – it was jews.

It wasn't Arabs who lied about mass graves at Treblinka – it was jews.

It wasn't Arabs who lied about jews being made into lamp shades and soap during WWII – it was jews.

It wasn't Arabs who doctored WWII prison camp photos to appear to be belching smoke from crematoria – it was jews.

It wasn't Arabs who used WWII pictures of dead non jews, claiming they were jews – it was jews.

It wasn't Arabs who made anti-semitic talk punishable by death in Russia after they took power – it was jews.

It wasn't Arabs who killed over 20 million Russian Christians – it was jews.

It wasn't Arabs who looted and destroyed the Russian economy with their usury and greed – it was jews.

It isn't Arabs who have amassed an illegal arsenal of over 300 nuclear weapons in the Middle East – it is the jews.

It isn't Arabs who brag about controlling America – it is jews.

It isn't Arabs who advocate the use of torture by and on Americans – it is jews.

It isn't Arabs who twist American laws to punish anti-semitic speech – it is jews.

It isn't Arabs endeavoring to get America to outlaw anti-semitic speech – it is jews.

It isn't Arabs who sell goods that it is illegal in America to boycott – it is Israeli jews.

It isn't Arabs who extort "fees" for allowing their kosher label on goods – it is jews.

It isn't Arabs who retaliate against rock-throwing children by shooting them in the head – it is jews. (I HAVE PERSONALLY WITNESSED THIS SADISTIC ISREALI PASSTIME)

It isn't Arabs stealing land in Palestine – it is jews.

It wasn't Arabs who ran down Rachel Corrie with a bulldozer – it was a jew.

It isn't Arabs who have caused America to spend \$2.5 trillion (\$31,250 per American family) in the Middle East – it is jews.

It isn't Arabs who send teams of trained assassins into foreign countries, including America, to kill people with whom Israel disagrees – it is jews.

It isn't Arabs who run the ADL, which maintains dossiers on thousands of law-abiding American citizens, for the purpose of punishing those with whom they disagree – it is jews.

It isn't Arabs who break into and enter the offices and homes of law-abiding American citizens, to procure evidence both for their database and in the hopes of getting evidence they can pass to the FBI for prosecution – it is jews.

It isn't Arabs who have caused America to go from being the most-loved country in the world to the most hated – it is jews.

It wasn't the Arabs who produced the biggest traitors to America in all history (Rosenbergs – Pollard & more!) it was the jews

It isn't the Arabs who participate in – support and or participate in EVERY MAJOR HOMOSEXUAL organization in America – it is the jews

It wasn't the Arabs who threatened the lives of Christian Actor /director Mel Gibson and his father for honoring God in his movie about the Passion of Christ – it was the jews!

It wasn't an Arab Congressman that made the following disgusting blasphemy and open hatred of Christians on the floor of Congress "Do not let the forces of evil [Christians] take over to make this a Christian America." (Senator Howard Metzenbaum, 11/6/86) – it WAS A JEW!

It isn't the Arabs who constitute an overwhelming majority of the treasonous Communist Party in OUR America – IT IS THE JEWS!

It isn't the Arabs that want to take our guns away in America – it is the jews

It isn't the Arabs who dominate the psychiatric quacks in America that keep our children drugged up 24/7 on Ritalin – it is the jews. ONE of these stinking jew pseudo physicians has ruined my own teenage son's life! It is a story EVERY AMERICAN PARENT NEEDS TO HEAR!!

It wasn't the Arabs who murdered several of my ex wife's family in cold blood because they were Christians – it was the jews! (My ex-wife's grandmother witnessed the horror of having her husband and sons murdered right before her very eyes by the sadistic jew CHEKA in the predominately Christian Ukraine!)

It wasn't an Arab Mayor that turned the quaint Latin quarter of my grandparents into a rotted hellhole of porn/ sleaze – and a haven for homo-pervert bars – it was a jewess.

It is not the Arabs who dominate America's virtually Marxist 'Democrat Party' of sleaze and filth – it is the jews (over 90% of American jews are Democrats)

It is not the Arabs who have turned my once proud and wholesome America into a morally rotted corpse – it is the jews.

It is not the Arabs who percentage-wise dominate the militant in- you-face Christian hating – boy scout hating homosexual filth in America – it is the jews

It is not Arab representation in America that has turned virtually all of the former 'educational channels' on TV into vehicles for promoting atheism – it is the jews.

It was not the Arabs who have rotted/ruined perverted an entire generation of our youth with their filth, violence, vile language, perversions, gratuitous sex on cinema and TV- it has been the work of the jews

It wasn't the Arabs who have worked tirelessly to insure never ending hatred between the races – it IS the jews (eg. NAACP)

It isn't Arabs who regularly phony up "hate crimes" against themselves – it is jews.

It wasn't Arabs who caused the Great Depression – it was jews.

It wasn't Arabs who dragged American Christian sons into WWI – it was jews.

It wasn't Arabs who dragged American Christian sons into WWII – it was jews.

It wasn't Arabs who had JFK killed – it was jews.

It wasn't Arabs who demolished the World Trade Center – it was jews.

AND —- It isn't Arabs bent upon destroying Christianity – it is jews.

And lest we forget: It wasn't Arabs who had Jesus Christ crucified – it was jews.

JUNE, 2010
WHY JEWS ARE DANGEROUS TO THE WELL-BEING OF ALL NON-JEWS (PART 3)

Here are yet more factual truths concerning the endless lies perpetrated against the Arab people by the masters of lying, deceit, fraud, crime, duplicity, betrayal, and treason.

To all those of you who in your hearts do NOT – hate nor cruelly mock Christ as do those Baptist demons whose only 'love' is the stench of death – the wailing of grieving parents of hundreds of thousands of murdered innocent children – and joy in the human suffering of millions upon millions of innocent civilians, who these witless bovine mentality uneducated redneck morons consider only as "sand-niggers" – "camel-jockeys" and " towel – heads" — I dedicate this third part of a wake up call to reestablish decency and humanity – compassion and wisdom – in a nation I scarcely recognize today.

You Baptists and other so-called Christian-Zionist scum are the antithesis of true Christian conduct. I thought that I had witnessed the ultimate in the hatred of Christ and what He stands for and has taught – when I was in IsraHELL. Your mockery and cruelty of his truths surpass even the profane openly voiced desire to crucify Him again that I witnessed there. You people ARE the collective anti-Christ!

The Baptists are not the only guilty parties to these mass genocidal murders – just the largest and most criminally minded morons of the lot. Congratulations – you have all qualified for an unlimited vacation in that place we commonly call Hell. However it was a 'pricy' ticket. You traded your immortal souls for doing what was obvious to a ten year old child as demonically evil.

You Baptists want not only endless wars – but the violent deaths of countless millions of innocent people – as ordained by your Jew and Jew – wanna-be useful idiot masters. For that you will have earned the undying enmity of every decent informed principled compassionate Godly man woman and child on earth.

I will do everything within my ability to make sure that my children and grandchildren and their children hold EVERY ONE OF YOU SADISTIC demons responsible for all of the carnage you have caused so far and that yet to come – should you get your Third World War for the greater glory of IsraHELL and the physical destruction of America – since you have ALREADY guaranteed it's total moral and economic destruction. The deaths and destruction and mass suffering of humanity that YOU BAPTISTS WILL CAUSE – will make the pogroms of the 20th century Communists look like child's play.

Your arrogance and 'world-class' criminal stupidity will cause our destruction should you continue with your insane diabolic madness. The survivors of the Armageddon you are so eager to create will seek their justice for what you have done to their loved ones – and whatever happens to you and your evil ilk would NEVER be enough to pay for the magnitude of your crimes. Remember that – as you shrilly scream for more innocent blood.

There will be no hole dark enough nor rock large enough for you to hide from the wrath of a parent who has lost his only son on the altar of your demonic insanity!

It wasn't the Arabs that sadistically murdered countless innocent civilian refugees in Lebanon – It was the JEWS!

It wasn't the Arabs who have dragged us into needless serial wars with people who have done us no harm – it was the JEWS!

It wasn't the Arabs who use horrible demonic weapons like white phosphorous and cluster bombs against helpless civilians – it was the JEWS!

It wasn't the Arabs who have murdered thousands of civilians in Palestine – many women and children many of whom are Christians – it is the JEWS!

It wasn't the Arabs who constantly carry out 'false flag' operations to blame their heinous crimes innocent parties – it is the JEWS!

It Wasn't the Arabs that murder helpless children in the streets – for 'sport' – it is the JEWS!

(Yes – it is TRUE – yes – I have witnessed this – Yes – I have been in these prison camps)

It wasn't the Arabs whose sick twisted society condones and promotes prostitution and white slavery – it is the JEWS!

It wasn't the Arabs who are the 'undisputed kings' of international pornography – it is the JEWS!

It isn't the Arabs who now control our government for their own benefits – it is the JEWS!

It isn't the Arabs who are pushing night and day to destroy our constitutionally-granted right to defend our families – it IS the JEWS!

It isn't the Arabs who are legislating laws to rescind our Constitutional right to free speech – it is the JEWS!

It isn't the Arabs who have through criminal organizations like the Federal Reserve, have all but destroyed any real value of our currency – it is the JEWS!

It isn't the Arabs who have nearly succeeded in the complete destruction of the recognition of the birth of our Lord – it is the JEWS!

It isn't the Arabs who are responsible for the REAL 'holocaust' of the cold-blooded murder of more than twenty million Christians in Russia – it was the JEWS!

It wasn't the Arabs who have made speaking the TRUTH a serious crime punishable by prison – it was the JEWS!

It wasn't the Arabs who have promoted the filthy plague of homosexual perversion in America– it is the JEWS!

It wasn't the Arabs who strive endlessly to destroy the sanctity of the sacrament of holy matrimony – it is the JEWS!

It isn't the Arabs who promote AND DEFEND pedophilia in America – it is the JEWS!

It isn't the Arabs who CONSTANTLY mock traditional Christian family values – it is the JEWS!

It isn't the Arabs who use the vehicle of cinema to promote violence – pre-marital sex-perversions – disrespect for parents – and general mockery of ANYTHING wholesome – it is the JEWS!

It isn't the Arabs who called our Lord Jesus a "bastard" and His mother a WHORE – it was the JEWS!

It wasn't the Arabs who use the vehicle of TV 'educational channels' to promote the mockery of Holy Scripture with evolution and other blasphemies – it is the JEWS!

It wasn't the Arabs who teach their children that it is proper to cheat, lie and betray Christians – it is the JEWS!

It wasn't the Arabs that created the treasonous – ACLU – the legal arm of the Communist Party – it was the JEWS!

It wasn't the Arabs that promoted so much inane and irrational hatred for Blacks against Whites that race relations will never be attainable – it was the JEWS!

It wasn't the Arabs that sold out America to the Soviets – It was the JEWS!

It wasn't the Arabs who have historically the greatest number of their ilk – commit treason against our country – it was the JEWS!

It wasn't the Arabs who caused gas prices to soar out of sight – it was the JEWS!

It wasn't the Arabs who had unduly large proportions of their people supporting the Communist Party – it was the JEWS!

It wasn't the Arabs who were responsible for the thousands of children forced to take dangerous narcotics for a non-existent 'disease' – many of whose lives were irrevocably damaged – it was the JEWS!

It wasn't the Arabs who have the world's largest and most powerful institutionalized terrorist organization on earth – The IDF – it was the JEWS!

It wasn't the Arabs who organized – financed and promoted the most deadly political organization in history – whose terror murdered over 200,000.000 innocent civilians since 1914 – it was of course – the JEWS!

JUNE, 2010
AN OPEN LETTER TO JEW LIAR, FRAUD – JEFF GREENE

Hear the name Jeff Greene lately? NO? Not to worry – as you will see his evil face and beady shifty eyes EVERY DAY on TV – very soon. He wants to be another IsraHELL loyal US Senator , and has the bucks to buy the seat – Jew style – with money and lies. As if we didn't have enough death destruction misery moral rot economic chaos and hopelessness due to Jew occupation – here is yet another ULTRA greedy ULTRA immoral ULTRA lying ULTRA deceiving Jew parasite who wants 'to be our landlord – owner ruler and god.'. A billionaire whose fortunes were so OBVIOUSLY gained – NOT Through hard labor – honesty – character – self-sacrifice and sweat – buy by typical Jew conniving and parasitic opportunism.(AKA – Oh veh! Such a deal – in tribe talk)

Mr. Greene – is your capacity for deceit lying fraud cunning and cruelty the new benchmark for your 'tribe' – or is it just the way all of your Jews treat decent people. Isn't the fact that you have already amassed a huge fortune – billions of dollars at the expense and grief and misfortune of the stupid 'goy' you feed upon – enough? Is there ANY limit to Jew greed or are you the emblematic Jew who's most sacred aspiration in life – as with all Jews – is the old Jew mantra of "He who dies with the most toys wins"?

BTW- Greene – in what branch did you serve your country? Like most of my (non Jew) peers I served my country with honor. Did you feel your precious arrogant Jew hide was too 'above' us common goy to risk in the procurement of the freedoms and blessings that your tribe so cruelly mocks? I presume with all that effort in gaining what cannot be spent in a hundred lifetimes by a thousand of our stupid goy fathers left you with SOME feeling of 'giving back' to the country who made you immeasurably wealthy. Oh I know – I don't understand the fine points of how a Jew can twist fraud and deceit into just plain smart business practice. I'm just an honest dumb goy – here for your amusement – right?

Tell me Greene – have you given so much as a dollar to the orphans or widows created by your filthy 'tribe'? I may only presume that the undeniable sinister cruelty I see etched in your features is an inbred genetic hatred of all things tender loving wholesome and sentimental.

I have witnessed cruelty and callousness in men that can only be termed 'monster' – in my life. People so filled with hatred of goodness that their only real happiness comes from the agony of God's most defenseless and vulnerable creatures. Supposed humans whose cruel natures demand a new word to replace the now obsolesced term of sadist.. That description would be a flawless description of your classic bestial Jew black soul.

Here is what you so proudly stated about your love for the filthy murdering Jews from which you were spawned. You obviously learned this hatred of goodness form the monsters who parented you.

You live a lie – you live in hatred and lies and you pass on that hatred and the lies to the monsters you breed to assure there will always be rabid mad dogs to kill the innocent.

First of all in typical Jew style you use endless lies and deceptions to hide one of the most heinous acts of barbarism and piracy in recent history. It is NOT ANY American's duty to lie to the American people to protect cold-blooded murders – scumbag! Second of all IsraHELL is not and have NEVER been is the most remote sense a "DEMOCRACY". It is a racist apartheid State and has been since day one you lying scumbag! Israhell in FACT broke ALL rules of International law – you lying scumbag! Third of all, EVERYONE including your war criminal PM Netanyahu KNEW before hand that the ship contained only peace activists – some of whom were world dignitaries and even Nobel Peace prize laureates – and even so, he authorized 'Shyatet 13′ a gang especially trained professional gangsters – who are part the world's largest institutionalized terrorist organization (IDF). These are murderers I know quite well from professional experience – SCUMBAG!

Fourthly – you indecent Jew lying scumbag – your precious IsraHELL to whom you obviously TREASONOUSLY owe your FIRST allegiance – is the mortal enemy of all Americans. In case you had another selective Jew amnesia episode – you stinking treasonous murdering Jews butchered over two hundred American sons brothers father and friends aboard the USS LIBERTY – in COLD- BLOOD in BROAD DAYLIGHT. Treacherous treasonous Jew – I

SERVED in my nations elite military – so who in hell are you to lecture ME – a patriot and veteran about "protecting our country" Murdering innocent defenseless civilian men women and children on a mercy ship does NOT "PROTECT MY COUNTRY" – you filthy animal lying sadistic scumbag! I laid it on the line and did my time – long before you were even potty trained – scumbag – so don't you EVER DARE INSULT me with your spineless hypocrite Jew bullshit again!

Let's review the TRUE nature of the cargo of that ship of brave decent caring humanitarian people murdered by your filthy Jew friends. Wheelchairs – medicine – books – food & water (for the innocent children your kikes had been starving for years – YES ASSHOLE – I HAVE BEEN THERE!) and countless other everyday items of basic substance.

And fifthly – the IDF terrorists MURDERED – cowardly shot several times in the back of the head – several young boys whose only goal was to help the dying and starving children. People who gave their lives simply to defend defenseless – to help the helpless – to clothe the naked – to feed the hungry – to tend to the injured and ill and to give hope to the hopeless. These were the most Godly kindest people imaginable – yet YOU – a filthy soulless demonic Jew – simply MUST show your unparalleled sadistic evil with your foul lying nasty mouth!

I PRAY that the one true God – not the 'god' of sex perversion wealth fame and glamour you Jews 'created' – put you in the most forlorn part of hell for all eternity – so that you may be with your TRUE 'father' – as proclaimed by the Christ you people so demonically hate!

NO- I'm not through with you yet scumbag. What the hell is it with you Jews in your hatred for Christ? READ YOUR OWN FILTH -JEW! You mock the sanctity of life with your Jew double speak. You – like all Jews and all Democrats – demean the value of human life to nothing but garbage – literally! You are so incredibly evil that you BOAST of your dedication to the murder of even more innocent children. You even have the audacity to BOAST of those Demoncrap values taught to you by your demonic parents. DEMOCRATS HAVE NO VALUES – SCUMBAG!

I have a LOT more experience than you with Democrats – so no lectures from the peanut gallery about what they 'stand for'. There is not a living man who knows more about what these Godless filth stand for. That is why after I became a mature man and realized what these degenerates stood for and hold today – I got out! I could no longer stand the stench of evil! BUT YOU! – it is not for the money. You have already stolen enough for a hundred lifetimes. It is simply this – YOU are an EVIL MONSTER and you are at home with other evil monsters..

The rest of your sleazy 'goals' and Godless lying agendas are enough to make a maggot convulse. I'l bet you don't even cast an image in a mirror.

You and filth of your ilk are an embarrassment and enemy to EVERY decent man woman and child in America. You are the antithesis of ALL that is good and wholesome and decent and kind and brave and noble in the America off my youth. People like you are a disease to this land. I do not have your billions or your millions – but I do have something you will NEVER have and will

NEVER be for sale – the righteous outrage against evil and the conviction to defend truth and the right from liars like you.

JUNE, 2010
AN OPEN LETTER OF ALL MEN OF GOOD WILL OF ALL NATIONS OF THE WORLD

I am personally beyond my limits of faith in my fellow man – at least here in what USED to be the United States of America, and is now as evil as any empire – soon to be police State – as ever recorded in history .

I have served my nation well and with honor and voluntarily placement of myself in harm's way – I have tried to be a good father – a good husband – a good neighbor – a good friend, and a fair honest moral businessman.

I have placed knowledge and wisdom above ignorance and foolishness as I grew to mature manhood. When I traveled as I frequently did – I strived to show to other peoples and other cultures that Americans were generous respectful courteous Godly people who were a model for the world to respect and hopefully even love. I have witnessed ignorance destroy an entire country abroad. Now I see it will destroy my own.

TRUE respect has NEVER been engendered from FEAR – be it your child or wife or neighbor or foreign host at the time. A man – can and should learn grow and gain wisdom from a lifetime of involved selfless meaningful living – not just shallow existence. One of those life's lessons is that FEAR ONLY BREEDS HATRED.

I was as a young man – once a Captain of paratroopers – hospitalized twice on peacetime operations and certainly not a heroic personality – but I neither am- nor was I ever a coward. My sense of 'DUTY' my LOVE of country and my code of HONOR – have now become so much nonsense to our youth.

DUTY – HONOR and LOVE are now dirty words in the lexicon of the average secular beer-guzzling greedy American. They have been replaced by DERELICTION – DISHONOR – AND HATRED. This is NOW the American way.

The straw that broke my 'faith' in this dying nation was the recent murderous sadistic attack upon defenseless people who had dedicated their lives – and in this case FORFEITED their lives to defend the defenseless to feed the hungry to clothe the naked – to minister to the sick and to give hope to the hopeless.

Pure goodness love charity hope and kindness – against Pure Godless Jew evil greed malice deception and of course the hallmark of the Jew – remorseless cold-blooded murder

The incident was a massacre upon a civilian ship loaded with hope and life and emergency vitals for a besieged helpless people trapped by the Jews in the world's largest outdoor concentration camp called Gaza. I know the Gazans – many are fellow Christians and some of the most resilient affable peace loving people on earth. I had the opportunity to be in IsraHELL with some of the world's ranking intelligence community and witness some of the most brutal sadistic animalistic horrors cruelties perversions sacrileges tortures and genocidal murders committed on earth in modern times. IsraHELL is the most Godless cruel den of devious lying vipers on earth. Every man woman and child on earth needs to know what I saw and heard there.

These crimes were committed with the same abandon glee and barbaric ferocity which you might imagine a mad dog ripping the flesh from the face of a helpless 2 year old child. I witnessed horrors in IsraHELL that could not be shown in the most grizzly horror movie of modern times.

Children as young as infants are murdered in cold-blood – AND I MEAN TARGETED FOR SPORT by the Jew every day of every week of every month of the year for decade after decade after decade – and my OWN country – once officially a Christian nation, STILL turns it collective head as the worldwide killing continues with FULL approval of Presidents Bush and Obama – using the Jews own preposterous lies of "self-defense".

I am fully convinced that the Jew can murder as many people where ever and whenever he chooses with impunity. By corruption and cunning lies – the Jew has already seduced 50 million Baptists to mock Christ's TRUE teachings and enable our putty-brained sons to murder over TWO MILLION INNOCENT MEN WOMEN AND (mostly) CHILDREN. Keep in mind that as our killing continues at the rate of a THOUSAND INNOCENT HUMAN LIVES A DAY – to satisfy the Jew lust for endless bloodshed – as well as the deaths of our not so innocent own sons – hardly a drop of Jew blood has been shed.

The Jew has been using this worn out lie for THOUSANDS of years and gets away with mass murder ANY TIME HE WISHES. To give you a CLASSIC example of how these filthy animals think – consider this horrific murder of a 3 year old Christian child by a Jew Rabbi. This Jew animal raped murdered a three you old little girl and got caught (these Jew Rabbi sex crimes are LEGION all over the world).

His Defense attorney (a Jew of course) argued that the poor Rabbi was not guilty because he was "taunted" by the baby who "inflamed his passions when she raised he little dress". This is CLASSIC Jew mentality at it's emblematic best. To the Jew – his VICTIM becomes criminal – get it? It was the little girl's fault – not the poor 'victimized' Jew Rabbi. This twisted sick depraved Jew only logic permeates their entire lives!

A JEW terrorist IDF soldier blows the brains out of a 5 year old Palestinian child because the child threatened his 50 ton Merkava II tank with a pebble sized rock (which was killing civilians in HIS city) and then destroys the kid's school with a 105mm cannon shell – because other children there might also have pebbles. Been there – seen that.

VERY brave soldiers these Jews. It take a LOT of guts to stand up to a pregnant mother or white haired old man or a crying terrified child who has just witnessed his entire family murdered by Jews – just for meanness and sadism – like they did to Rachel Corrie.

Jews are SO brave and So patriotic that while I was training young men to become paratroop warriors by the hundreds and thousands in 1962 – guess what. I will swear on all I hold holy that there was not ONE Greenberg or Fishfinkle or Lieberman in the lot – NONE!

Do you understand this FACT? International mass murder and piracy at sea – children murdered indiscriminately 24-7 in Gaza – helpless civilians murdered by Jew criminals for their body parts – American NAVY sons and father and brothers slaughtered on the high seas by the Jews and NOTHING is ever done – no arrests no real criminal investigations – nothing – as they continue to murder at will like mad dogs. NOBODY – NO INNOCENT person on this plant is safe from being murdered by the Jew or their thugs – NONE!

I want to make a deal with any foreign country – since freedom of speech has been stifled by our Jew masters here for a long time and I am no longer allowed to speak the TRUTH to MY OWN PEOPLE as I did a generation ago. Here's the deal. You give me the venue and the news coverage that MY OWN COUNTRY DENIES ME and I will promise to deliver ALL of the truths I know to your people before it is too late.

This is NOT a joke or publicity stunt. People who know me well – know I do not say anything I do not mean – and that I mean what I say. I full well know the murderous Jews might have me killed – for that is what they do best – murder innocent human beings to protect their life of lies– but I would rather have my children and other people who STILL believe in truth and goodness will remember me as that man who tried to save us and died on his feet instead of on his knees. I may be old – but I'm not dead-yet. If it be God's will – I will do it with your help. Someone must at least try – and I see few else with my knowledge that will stand up and be counted. I have already lost everything of real value to the Jews

It is too late for this country and yours may be next.

JUNE, 2010
WHY ARE AMERICAN CHRISTIANS ASHAMED TO SPEAK THE WORD OF GOD REGARDING THE JEWS?

Today – in this 'collective morally rotted corpse' of what USED to be Christian America, about 99% of ALL American so-called Christian churches from Baptist to Catholic are ashamed of Jesus and embarrassed to speak it aloud from the pulpits.

The NT (the Christian Bible) is legion with damnation of the evil of the Jews – yet I defy ANY reader to be able to recall the last time he heard even ONE of the quotations of the Disciples or the prophets or even the Lord Himself strongly condemning the Jews for who they really are.

Have truth honor wisdom and knowledge become dirty words in America?

It is not complicated and I will tell you what you at least SHOULD already know about this disgraceful mockery and denial of our faith. There is also a grave penalty for that kind of hypocrisy.

It was best said in Matthew 10:33.. "But whosoever shall deny me before men, him will I also deny before my Father which is in heaven." Are you paying CLOSE attention – ALL of you treacherous demonic false preachers who have come to serve the "sons of the Devil" – first – even before our lord? You know who you are!

Just in case you phony baloney false Christians believe that your mockery has gone unnoticed – FOOLS! You would rather mock the Lord than chance offending those who had Him murdered. You are too ashamed to even READ HIS WORDS TO YOUR FLOCK. On your death beds – how will you tell the Lord that you chose Satan's sons over Him – because you were ASHAMED to speak HIS truths – yet, half the world has been witness to that fact!

Ever hear this one? : Romans 1:16 "For I am not ashamed of the gospel of Christ: for it is the power of God unto salvation to everyone that believeth; to the Jew first, and also to the Greek." So why are you ashamed – Baptists

Perhaps the most virulent condemnation of all is in John 8- and most clearly stated in vs 44 where God- the Son accuses the Jews (and Scripture tells us that He is NOT speaking exclusively to the high priests but Jews in general) of being "SONS OF THE DEVIL". I 'sign' ALL of my blogs with it. Ever hear that Quote by Christ in your phony Synagogue Of Satan? Of course not – as it might offend Satan.

Was there an organized Jewish conspiracy against the life and ministry of our Savior – the Lord Jesus Christ? Let the Scriptures speak for themselves!

How about this one: "Speaking of the Jews: Who both killed the Lord Jesus, and their own prophets, and have persecuted us; and they please not God, and are contrary to all men: Forbidding us to speak to the Gentiles that they might be saved, to fill up their sin away: For the wrath is come upon them to the uttermost." I Thessalonians 2:14-16 Ever hear that read in your false 'church' – you Baptists? Of course not – the demon Hagee would NOT approve!

In the earthly life and ministry of our Lord, He encountered much opposition as He traveled throughout the ancient land of Palestine in doing

The work that His Father sent Him to do. During the first century the land of Palestine where Jesus lived and ministered was divided into three Roman provinces. They were Galilee to the north where Jesus lived as a child and began His ministry; Samaria located in central Palestine where He ministered to the woman at the well in John chapter 4; and Judea to the south where He encountered most of His opposition from the leadership of the Jewish nation and was eventually illegally tried, falsely convicted and crucified as a result of the scheming efforts of the Jews and their manipulation of the Roman civil authorities.

In the Gospel of John the Apostle records the masterful discourse of Jesus that He gave concerning His equality with God and His manifestation as being the living bread sent down from heaven (chapters 5-6). After giving this discourse and seeing the open anger of the Jews in response to His message, He left Judea where Jewish Pharisee-ism was in total control, and returned to Galilee which offered Him more personal safety. John records:

"After these things Jesus walked in Galilee: For He would not walk in Jewry, because the Jews sought to kill Him." (7:1, 11:53-54)

In the earthly life and ministry of our Lord, He encountered much opposition as He traveled. The Jewish leadership, which included Scribes, Pharisees, Sadducees, Chief Priests and the Sanhedrin heckled and taunted the Lord Jesus as He conducted His teaching and healing ministry among the people. Their purpose was to catch Him in heresy and blasphemy and eventually use it as evidence against Him at His trial (Luke 20:19-26). Are you paying attention 'pastor' (barf) Hagee?

Reasons Why the Jews (NOT the Romans – NOT the Arabs) Crucified Jesus: Read up on it Robertson – before you join your demon friend in HELL!

He claimed Kingship – John 18:33-37; John 19:12-22

Telling the truth – Luke 4:21-29, John 8:40

Healing on the Sabbath – Matthew 12:9-14, John 5:16

Envy – Matthew 27:18, Mark 15:10

Blasphemy –

(A) Forgiving sins – Matthew 9:1-3, Mark 2:1-7

(B) Claiming equality with God – Matthew 26:59-66, Mark 14:61-64, John 10:25-33; 19:7

Jewish (NOT ARAB- NOT ROMAN) Accusations Against Jesus Christ:

Ever read these to your brain-dead Ziobot imbeciles Falwell? Have a nice eternity in HELL – take the time to read the lying filth you worshiped.

. Keeper of bad company – Matthew 9:10-11

Of poor, common-stock – Mark 6:3

Laborer – Mark 6:3

Possessed of Beelzebub – Mark 3:22

From the wrong neighborhood – John 7:41, 52

A deceiver and hypocrite – John 7:10-13

Unlearned – John 7:14-15

Had a persecution complex – John 7:20

Demon possessed–full of the devil – John 7:20, 10:20, 8:48, 52

Provoker to anger – John 7:23

A divider of the people – John 7:43

Unpopular, not recommended by rulers, unrecognized by leaders – John 7:45-49 (v. 48)

False prophet – John 7:50-52

Liar, falsifier – John 8:13

A bastard – John 8:19

Had suicidal tendencies – John 8:22

A half-breed – John 8:48

Dishonorable – John 8:49

Boaster, false representative of God, impostor, self-made man – John 8:53

Ungodly, or cometh not from God – John 9:13-16

A sinner – John 9:13-16

Crazy, insane – John 10:20

Perplexing, causing doubt – John 10:22-24

A blasphemer – John 10:31-33

JEWISH (NOT ARAB – NOT ROMAN) Hatred and Murder Attempts on the Life of Jesus Christ. Did you bother to tell your moron friends about this as you spewed hate and death for innocent Arab children – monster Franklin Graham and your perfidious demonic father?

Matthew 2:16 – As a child Herod tried to kill Him.

Matthew 12:14, Mark 3:6 – Pharisees held a council with the Herodians to discuss destroying Jesus because He healed a man on the Sabbath day.

Luke 4:28-30 – Attempted to throw Him off the hill because of His sermon.

John 5:16 – The Jews persecuted Jesus and sought to kill Him for healing the impotent man on the Sabbath day.

John 5:18 – Jews sought to kill Jesus because He claimed equality with God.

John 7:30-32 – The Jewish plot to arrest Jesus with intent to kill Him for claiming He was from God.

John 7:25 – It was common knowledge that the Jews sought to kill Jesus.

John 7:40-44 – Some people desired to arrest Jesus with intent to kill Him.

John 8:59 – Jews attempted to kill Jesus by stoning Him for claiming that He was God.

John 10:31 – The Jews again attempt to kill Jesus by stoning for claiming His Deity.

John 10:39 – The Jews sought to take Jesus for proving His Deity.

John 11:47 – The chief priests and Pharisees plot against Jesus.

John 11:53-54 – The Jews make a determined effort to kill Jesus.

John 11:55-57 – The Jews sought Jesus even at the Passover Feast.

John 12:9-11 – The Jews even desire to kill Lazarus because of their hatred for Jesus.

John 18:3, 10, 12 – Jesus was arrested by Jewish soldiers.

John 18:13-14 – Jesus was tried by Jewish leaders who had already decided on his guilt.

John 18:36 – Jesus acknowledges that it was the Jews who would kill Him.

John 18:38-40, 19:1-7, 12-15 – The Jews are adamant in their desire to kill Jesus.

John 19:11 – Jesus acknowledges a lesser and a greater sin in those who condemned Him to death.

John 19:16-18 – The Jews led Jesus away to be crucified.

NOW – we get into the REAL filth of Jew hatred for and blasphemy against Jesus – THE TALMUD!

The Talmud is a vast literary work written by Jewish Rabbis that contains civil and religious law. It is not a part of the inspired sacred Scripture. The Palestinian Talmud was written in the 3rd century AD, while the Babylonian Talmud was written around 500 AD. It contains discussions concerning every aspect of Jewish life and thought. The Talmud was written by Jewish Rabbis who were men of 'perverse minds and destitute of the truth'.

Concerning the names of Jesus, the Talmud (NOT THE KORAN) refers to Him as: Did you even know these facts? – hate monger Gary Bauer?

Immach Schemo Vezikro which means, "May His name and memory be blotted out."

Otho Isch = "That man"

Peloni = "A certain one"

Naggar Bar Naggar = "The carpenter son of a carpenter"

Ben Charsch etaim = "The son of a wood worker"

Talui = "The one who was hanged"

Talmud (NOT THE KORAN) accuses and slanders Christ as being: Do your 'useful idiots' know of these blasphemous lies ?– Hal Lindsey

Illegitimate Possessed by the soul of Esau and being Esau himself.

A fool and insane

A conjurer and a magician

An idolater

A seducer

Crucified His crimes

Buried in Hell

Wrongfully worshiped

An idol

The Talmud (NOT THE QUORAN) condemns the teaching of Christ as follows: More slanderous lies with your demonic approval Pastor LaHaye?

Falsehood

Heresy

Impossible to observe

Illegitimate

Possessed by the soul of Esau and being Esau himself.

A fool and insane

A conjurer and a magician

An idolater

A seducer

Crucified For His crimes

Buried in Hell

Wrongfully worshiped

An idol

The Talmud (NOT THE QUORAN) condemns the teaching of Christ as follows: So – you teach your false Christian fools that Jesus was an irrational liar and heretic – fake preacher Van Der Hoven?

Falsehood

Heresy

Impossible to observe

Jesus was of course innocent – and there WAS historic testimony from many figures. The Jews of course have been unrepentant and are still in the business of lies deceit fraud murder and the endless hatred of Christ and Christianity. The innocence of Christ was declared by these historic figures:

Pilate's wife – Matthew 27:19

Judas Iscariot – Matthew 27:4

Pilate – Matthew 27:24; Luke 23:22; John 19:6

Thief on the cross – Luke 23:41

Roman soldiers – Mark 15:39

And as an added insult to Christ Christianity and all those who truly Love Him (NO demonic hypocrite brain dead oxymoronic Christian-

Zionist need apply) Here is a Talmudic description of the birth and death of our Lord (AGAIN – it wasn't the ARABS who committed these foul crimes of blasphemy – it was (drum roll) THE JEWS – AND THE JEWS – AND AGAIN THE JEWS! GET IT YET?" J-E-W-S!!!

Jesus is referred to as: "the son of Pandira, a soldier. Illegitimate and conceived during menstruation. Hanged on the eve of Passover, seduced, corrupted and destroyed Israel. Died like a beast and buried in animal's dirt heap." Taken from Defender's Magazine October 1957, which quoted Freedman's "Facts are Facts".

Next time you encounter one of these Christ mocking scum who have now nearly totally destroyed true Christianity (I speak of the Goy scum who mock the Lord mercilessly in their own churches (Synagogues of Satan) – be sure and tell them how you feel about their cruel perversions and betrayal of Jesus.

Remember – without the 100% support of these evil people – over 50 million of these ignorant scum – the Jew would NEVER have been able to bring down America – morally – economically and spiritually – by himself.

I can guarantee it. That IF Christ came back to this country in the form of a man again and reasserted the evil nature of the Jew – as He did TWO THOUSAND YEARS AGO – He would be crucified AGAIN – this time Hagee's Baptists will do the job – while their Jew masters wring their hands with delight as they continue to occupy America.

I have only uncovered the tip of this black iceberg of evil – but only a fool or an imbecile who purposefully WILL NOT SEE THE TRUTH and WILL NOT HEAR THE TRUTH – will remain in denial of this cruel revilement and insult to Christ. Ignorance is no longer an excuse! How much longer will you false Christians continue this monstrous hypocrisy against the Lord?

JULY, 2010
OFFENSIVE AMERICAN TV ADS

I see more and more patently insulting offensive TV adds every time I watch Television. There is a truism of wisdom I learned many years ago, and is just as valid today, as it was when I learned it. Simply this: One of the ways to identify a total imbecile moron? A person who doesn't even realize that he or his values – usually moral in nature – are being openly mocked. We have all witnessed this at some time.

It happens in America more than any place I have been. Recent TV adds in particular – tell us that those who created them consider the average American to be witless – immoral – and simply brain-dead stupid. They offend me – and hopefully you as well.

Here are but a few of the more recent insults. Ford Motor company: Their add depicting General George Washington as a NASCAR type redneck as he races into battle the Redcoat British. It is demeaning and and insult to the honor dignity and memory of this great man – the 'Father' of our nation. You STILL bought a Ford? "HERE'S YOUR SIGN"

Here is another especially odious and disgusting add by the US ARMY which insults the memory of the Godly Christian Father of our country. It shows Washington as he leads his outnumbered poorly equipped demoralized men across the icy Delaware river in December 1776 in a daring move to capture a garrison at Trenton. It was undoubtedly the most critical battle of the entire Revolutionary war and decided the future fate for America to be or not to be – a free new nation, based on Christian principles.

It was the epitamy of exemplified noble valor honor and sacrifice to defend America against a REAL enemy. If it had failed – the war would have undoubtedly been lost. It was in fact a do – or – die – against all odds – situation for America against a powerful occupying ruthles agressor. It was the only time in our military history that our entire future and freedoms were at mortal risk on 'one roll of the dice'!

It then shows progressively later commemorative moments of America's military history ending with portraying our new GODLESS mercenary Jew controlled murderous psychopath civilian murderers raping Iraq and Afghanistan – as if that our modern war crimes mentality filth, was on par with Washington's noble cause of saving our nation and gaining our liberty.

That was the ULTIMATE insult to the man and the memory – of George Washington – a man of honor – courage – principles – and his Army of REAL MEN – of courage and honor – to be compared to the filthy rapist thieves child murdering animals and their Godless war-monger leaders the Jews and their useful idiot Zionist Bapt-duhs have sent to destroy and plunder innocent defenseless third word sovereign nations for the greater glory of demonic Godless IsraHELL! . It may as well have compared the birth of Jesus to a degenerate debauched sex orgy at a sodomite festival! How stupid and morally bankrupt can an AmeriKan be – to even tolerate that insulting garbage on TV?

Encouraged your precious son to go to one of those war-criminal enlistment places? "HERE'S YOUR SIGN"

To ridicule and mock the Founding Fathers has been a goal of the 'chosenites' since the beginning. Obviously the reason to smear our finest sons is that they exposed the TRUTH of the evil nature of the self-chosen. Read the TRUTH of comments exposing Jew evil by iconic American leaders such as Washington Franklin and Jefferson for yourself.

I served with honor in my nation's military and wore the uniform with pride and respect. After what we have done to MURDER – 2,000,000 innocent people in the past nine years – under the disgraceful banner of our flag– and in the blasphemous mockery of the name of Christ – I would rather wear used toilet paper – than that shameful filthy rag we now call the US ARMY uniform of baby murdering war criminal scum! We are not just stupid – we are IMMORALLY stupid! Now we need 'TWO signs.'

Last Christmas – there were so many major US companies who mocked the holy event of the birth of our Lord – by demeaning it into some shallow materialistic shopping frenzy and calling this – the holiest day of Christian tradition – by its commercial secular Jew name of the "HOLIDAYS" – that I simply lost count. Virtually every major auto manufacturer – major restaurant chain – retail shopping mall – insurance company – bank – service company and fast food place has decided of their own free will to mock Christian tradition.

A short list would include Kmart, Sears, Koh'ls, Home Depot, Target, Cosco, Walgreens, JC Penny, Best Buy and Walmart – but the list would fill a book! Remember – EVERY one of these places where YOU so-called Christians spend your discretionary dollars – has insulted you TO THE CORE OF YOUR MOST SACRED BELIEFS – and MOST OF YOU – are too stupid to even realize it. "HERE'S YOUR SIGN"

Also last Christmas – Fox and virtually all the rest of our 'media whores' – boasted of a gigantic devil's fork looking 'Menorah' (another Jew festival symbol celebrating death destruction of other people) Instead of it being reported as an outrageous affront to Christian tradition at Christmas in OUR OWN CHRISTIAN NATION'S CAPITOL – it was promoted by the Christ hating Jew owned mega- media as replacing our traditional Nativity. The 3 % Jews in OUR country – with the approval of our Negro Marxist traitorous Jew puppet President – just gave the mostly remaining 300 million mostly Christians the 'finger'. Were Christians outraged at the blasphemous insult by the "sons of Satan"? NA – To stupid to even realize the insult "HERE'S YOUR SIGN"

You NASCAR fans with children that you SUPPOSEDLY love and protect – have you so much as written even ONE angry letter to the Jew producers who allow those filthy 'EXTENZE' – "make your cock bigger" commercials using redneck NASCAR celebrities? NA – of course not. Did you even REALIZE that scum who produce this swill are Jews? Yes 'Dorothy' – those obscene smutty shameless Jew produced commercials are aimed at brainless witless Gentile morons who they know will not even realize the scornful ridiculing offending nature of the add.

Are YOU so stupid – you don't even realize the depth of these insults? Then – Like Jeff F. and Bill E. say: – "HERE'S YOUR SIGN"

For those of you informed moral readers still 'keeping the faith' – and in agreement – by all means – please share similar typical adds that are insulting to the wisdom morals and values of decent Americans – that you have seen or heard recently. The deeply insulting lying/add comments from useful idiot Bapt-duhs 'handlers' like the Satanic war-mongering demon – Hagee, are legion and in a category of evil all by themselves. I only scratched the surface. Go for it!

JULY, 2010
OPEN LETTER TO RACIST HATE/WAR MONGER – DEVVY KIDD

Madam – I 'deal with' Jews and their useful idiot scumbags 24-7 in an effort to expose them to decent Godly people so they can defend our nation against REAL enemies and I know a HELL of a lot more about that than you do.! You promptly wrapped your self in the flag and reminded the readers that you had a First Amendment right to act like an asshole.

Although you never did ANYTHING to defend or secure that right – as I have – I will concede it to you. AND – since I DID PAY MY DUES – I will also exercise that right and expose you for the putrid 'cancerous ooze' that YOU ARE to this country and any semblance of goodness decorum and decency we may have left!

After reading your – 'A Cancer Oozing Across America' – slanderous diatribe of lies, racism, mockery of God (you insolent moron redneck – they worship the SAME 'God' Christians do) and Jew mentality hatred – in Rense.com – I wanted to vomit! I thought that Jeff had more class than that. Perhaps my TRUTHS were too 'truthful' for many of his Jew friends – but I never resorted to slanderous lies and will stand by everything I said.

How much did the Jews pay you to write this filth, lady? The obligatory 30 pieces of silver? How much time have you physically spent in the Mid-East? In IsraHELL? In the occupied territories of Palestine? Ever witness a 'brave' Jew soldier murder a terrified half naked, half starved crying 5 year old Arab Palestinian child whose mortal crime was simply NOT being a self-chosen? I didn't think so.

Since you HATE Arab people so much – you'll love this! I'll bet in your sick twisted mind – I'll bet you especially hate 'sand-nigger' kids – right? Tell you what I'll do for you. Let me know – and I will send you dozens of cool shots of 'rag-head' kids – some just babies – with their brains blown out by Jew snipers – or charred little bodies burnt beyond recognition by Jew white phosphorous complete with grieving 'camel-jockey' parents. Isn't that the kind of violence hate porn that women like you 'get off' on?

OH – I almost forgot – as an added bonus – many of these Arabs you would love to see die agonizing deaths because they don't measure up to your pompous egotistical WASP Western expectations – are Christians.

Deceivers like you are a disgrace to ALL decent educated informed Americans. What's the matter – butcher lady – 2 MILLION INNOCENT CIVILIANS MURDERED by our filthy psychopath loser mercenary criminal gangsters not enough blood and suffering for your mindless irrational racist hatred of Arab people? And until you have been where I have been – seen what I have seen – no sophomoric condescending lectures please.

Will it make you happy to know that your Jew lies and Jew propaganda will undoubtedly cause even more deaths of innocents? HOW DARE you call yourself a Christian! You are NO Christian – you are a miserable arrogant Godless war-mongering 2-faced deceiving hypocrite – and THAT is being compassionately reserved!

IF – you WERE a Godly informed wise woman – you would fall on your knees and thank THE – God – that these Arab people you consider less than dirt – as do your Jew friends – are IN FACT – the ONLY people on the planet who now have the guts to stand against the Jews who have destroyed EVERYTHING. Including everything I ever loved cherished and worked for —— – my country – my children – my people – my living – our goodness – our freedoms – the uniform of a Special Forces Abn. commander – honor truth compassion and goodness – ALL now destroyed by the Jews who have made my once beloved country a morally rotted corpse.

And NOT just 'Zionists' – but most JEWS as well! Only amoeba-brained witless bovine useful idiots still believe that good Jew bad Jew bullshit. The imbecilic notion that ONLY 'card carrying' Zionist Jews are evil Godless greedy child murdering lying demonic violence and sex worshiping scum – is a third world joke to well traveled well educated people.

The JEWS most holy books cruelly mock Jesus as a "BASTARD" and His holy Mother as a "WHORE" – or – if you don't have a Talmud – just watch Jew TV . This was done some nineteen hundred years BEFORE the WORD 'ZIONIST' even came into being as you MUST know. How come you didn't mention THAT FACT after boasting of your extensive studies.

Conversely – the holy book of Islam – which you claim to know so much about – ALWAYS – not just sometimes – but ALWAYS speaks of Christ and His blessed Mother Mary in the absolute most reverent and loving of terms. That – you insolent ignorant woman – is a FACT!

Interesting to see the FACT that one can openly bash slander demean libel smear and defame the religious beliefs of the TRULY Semitic Arab people on Rense, but are censured should you DARE too speak the GOSPEL TRUTH about what JEWS – NOT THE NEO-ZIONISTS – but just plain JEWS – have openly bragged about for two thousand years! I wonder what the 'non-Zionist good Jews' threatened Jeff with to make him 'look the other way.'

You are an embarrassment to everything and everyone decent in America. Have you no shame? You do not honor the teachings of Christ – you MOCK THEM! Do you REALLY think what you wrote was a sterling example of "Truth and Patriotism" as your site boasts? How about Islamophobic lies, IsraHELL first-ism and a malicious wagging tongue .

Do America and the world a favor – stay at home and take care of the 'hearth' – the evil lies you spread make you very ugly as a woman.

A man who served his nation long before 'HONOR' and 'TRUTH' became dirty words

JULY, 2010
I AM ISRAHELL

I recently read what has to be one of the most offensive pack of lies deceit hypocrisy and putrid Jew filth I have yet to experience. If any educated person still has the SLIGHTEST doubt as to why Jews have been condemned – and or hated – mistrusted – loathed – despised and considered social pariahs for the past two thousand years – you need to check out the comments about their incomparable evil by the world's most arguably famous people – from Jesus of Nazareth to George Washington – from Martin Luther to Mark Twain – from Cicero to Seneca – from Henry Ford to Charles Lindberg – and from Shakespeare to Napoleon.

The sick twisted Zionist Jew who wrote this disgusting diatribe of mega-mendacities is Howard Galganov. The Jew was – is – and always will tend to be an arrogant sociopath and a pathogenic liar. It seems to be in their genes. My sources? Right from the 'top! Christ's credentials impeccable enough for you?

Then how about this: The Gospel of John -chapter 8 vs 44 " Ye are of your father – the DEVIL and the lusts of your father you will do. He was a murder from the beginning and abode not in the truth, because there is NO TRUTH IN HIM. When He speaketh a lie – he speaketh of his his own (the Jews) for he is a liar and the father of it". Any of you "children of Satan" Jew lawyers like to cross examine my 'client'? I didn't think so.

I spent some 'insider' time in IsraHELL during the first intifada. I have been a foreign diplomat and have traveled abroad for over forty years to over two dozen nations. During that period I had some harrowing experiences and witnessed some 'bad' things – but NEVER EVER anything like the evil I encountered in IsraHELL. The place and the people are evil beyond all description. Helpless children murdered in cold blood – Christian Palestinian home-owners lives threatened by ugly violent Jew mobs screaming blasphemies and obscenities Against Christ too filthy to even be repeated here.

Mega traitor Jew Jonathan Pollard heralded as a folk hero by the Jews. Open mockery of America by dual citizenship American Jews openly loyal to IsraHELL. Armed Jew thugs racing around in Palestinian neighborhoods trying to provoke violence. Jew children OPENLY taught by their parents to hate and wish death to other nation's children. The most cruel sadistic military I had ever experienced as a former Spec-Ops para commander – desecration of Palestinian Mosques and churches by the Jew occupation military – the Jew IDF would urinate and defecate on holy books. The list of Jew filth would gag a maggot. If there is one place on earth I have experienced where the Devil would feel welcome – it must be IsraHELL. If you are actually stupid enough to ask why you haven't read that in your local Jew newspaper or TV – just go back to your 'Bud' sponsored NFL games or your redneck 'EXTENZE' sponsored NASCAR follies – otherwise keep reading -cause you have never seen arrogance and lies like this in your LIFE!.

Here then is the most disgusting and by far the largest diatribe of serial lies regarding IsraHELL I have ever read. The Jew's comments are in italics. My 'truth proofed' rendition follows each of his lies.

"I was RE-BORN after an exile of 2,000 years, because I am Israel."

–I was re-born from the Devil after 2,000 years of making life miserable for mankind, because I am IsraHELL!

"I rose from the ashes of Hell on Earth we call the Holocaust, because I am Israel."

–I AM – a hell on earth, because I AM IsraHELL

"I clung to the earth of my promised land with flesh-torn-hands to reclaim what for thousands of years was always mine, because I am Israel."

–I cling to the lifeblood of my victims in THEIR land with innocent blood on my hands to steal what for a thousand years has been other people's land – like a parasite, because I am IsraHELL

"I opened my Jewish doors to Christians, Muslims and all others who yearned to live in religious FREEDOM, because I am Israel."

–I slammed the doors of my racist Jewish arrogance in the face of Christians and Muslims who yearned to live in peace, because I am IsraHELL

"I ask for nothing other than to be allowed to live in peace and security, so that my children can also grow and prosper under the Sun and Stars like all others, because I am Israel."

–I ask for my neighbor's blood so that he can never live in peace and security – but inconstant terror so that my demonic spawn can also grow up to be murderous children of Satan, because I am IsraHELL

"I stand with but a few friends, who stand by me in a hostile world with whom I will stand forever, because I am Israel."

–I stand with but a few evil friends – all sons of the Devil like me who help our hostility towards the world and our goal of eternal evil, because I am IsraHELL

"But I also know that in the end, I will be standing alone, because I've always stood alone, because I am Israel."

–But I also know that in the end, I will stand alone because of the endless crimes my ilk have committed against mankind. No other people on earth have conducted themselves with such criminal conduct, Because I am IsraHELL

"I live by the tenets of thousands of years of Biblical Covenant to do what is right, regardless of the cost and risk, not just because of the word of God, but more so because without a moral compass there is no direction, because I am Israel."

–I live by the tenets of a thousand years of pure evil in my Satanic covenant with the Devil to always do what is evil – regardless of the condemnation of Christ and the prophets as well as worldwide condemnation – and not just because of the words of Satan, but more so because I have no moral compass – no ethics – no goodness – just evil, because I am IsraHELL

"I pray every night to be accepted by those who wish me ill, even though I know my prayers will go unanswered, because I am Israel."

–I pray every night to my god, Satan – to destroy those who seek justice against my abominable crimes – even though I know I am wrong, I have no conscience – no compassion – no sense of decency, because I am IsraHELL.

"I've begged to be accepted. I've surrendered territory won in bloody battles to be accepted. To be accepted, I've forcibly removed my own people from their homes as they cried with despair, because I am Israel."

–I've begged to be accepted by the people I have sadistically brutalized in my usual deceitful fashion by portraying myself as the victim. I've surrendered NO stolen territory to my hapless victims. I have forcibly removed innocent people who have lived on land they have tilled for over a thousand years so that my demonic mad-dog insane ilk may prosper on that stolen land, because I am IsraHELL

"I rush to give aid in times of need during a Tsunami or a massive Earthquake, even to those who wish I did not exist, or wouldn't lift a finger to help me in my hour of need, because I am Israel."

–I rush to give aid in times of need – but of course only to our superior tribe of Jews. To those who wish I did not exist because of our endless rapes tortures murders desecrations humiliations and theft – I simply kill their children to satisfy the dual Jew NEED of inflicting misery pain and terror and of stealing the wealth of other nations, because I am a sick psychopath. I am IsraHELL

"I warn the families of those who are trying to murder my family, when and where we will attack, so as not to harm those who are not directly engaged in our destruction, because I am Israel."

–I warn the families of those who would DARE to defend their lives – that we will exterminate them all with the most horrible barbaric weapons prohibited by the Geneva Convention– so as to inflict the MAXIMUM harm to those most vulnerable and defenseless and innocent – their children, because I am IsraHELL

"I share with the world magnificent technologies, medical discoveries, and ways to feed those who without my help could not feed themselves, because I am Israel."

–I share with the world – all of the filth – garbage – hate – corruption- lies – porn – white slavery – abortion – homosexual perversion – racism – and other Jew 'gifts' to insure we pervert the innocent. We also find ways to corrupt those who without our 'help' might not corrupt themselves, because I am IsraHELL.

"BUT I AM NOT JUST A PLACE: I am not just defined as a piece of barren unproductive geography brought to life by the dreams and resilience of a people who reach far beyond their grasp."

–BUT I AM NOT JUST A PLACE: I am the incarnation of the Devil here on earth – brought to life by the "sons of the Devil" with all of their nightmares and cunning treachery and their innate greed to reach out and grasp anther's livelihood.

ISRAEL IS AN IDEAL: All of us who reach beyond our grasp, who live by a moral code that cannot be shaken, who wake every day in the hopes of waking to a better world are Israel.

–ISRAHELL IS AN IDEA: A people who live outside of ANY moral code – who have been damned by the Lord Himself, who wake up every day with new evil ideas with which to destroy all goodness in the world

All of us who stand against evil while defending the essence of truth, justice and FREEDOM are Israel."

–All of us who stand with EVIL while mocking the essence of TRUTH JUSTICE and FREEDOM are IsraHELL

"Christians who care about their soul are no less Israel. Jewish believers and non-believers who do right by mankind are Israel. And people who believe only in the heart of mankind to do the right thing are also Israel."

–Christians who care NOTHING about their soul ARE IsraHELL. But people who believe only in the heart of mankind to do the right thing realize that the greatest evil on earth is IsraHELL

"People who will not bend a knee or surrender to those who cast upon them terrible aspersions, lies and hatred are Israel."

–People who will not bend a knee or surrender to those Jews who cast upon them terrible aspersions lies and hatred as they have for thousands of years ALL yearn for the destruction of IsraHELL

"Those of us willing to share our good fortune with others, not through coercion, but through compassion are Israel."

–Those of us willing to share our good fortunes with others who have lost their to the evil greedy lying Jews should all stand against the house of the Devil – IsraHELL

"Those who will defend those who cannot defend themselves are Israel."

–Those who will defend those innocent Palestinians who cannot defend themselves are the enemies of Satan and the enemies of IsraHELL.

"And all those who stand and fight against all who wish to force themselves upon humanity to take what is not theirs are Israel."

–And those who stand and fight against all who wish to force themselves upon humanity to take what is not theirs – mainly – the JEWS who now occupy and rape our America must stand AGAINST IsraHELL

"Israel can never be defeated without first defeating decency in humanity, because in the final truth, those of us who really care about doing what is right are Israel. Even to the last person. Because of the ideals of Israel, and as long as one decent person who is willing to stand-up and be counted continues to take breath, Israel will survive to the end of time."

–IsraHELL can never be defeated without first defeating Satan – since the Jews are His children and IsraHELL will NEVER EVER do what is right because they are an evil Godless racist people – mass murderers who murder not only their helpless neighbors but an alarming percentage of their OWN unborn children! IsraHELL also leads the world in prostitution and white slavery organ theft and harboring of world-class criminals.

Because of the inherent demonic evil nature of IsraHELL and its Satanic ilk – unless ALL decent people stand up to be counted and oppose this demonic threat to world peace and all mankind – the Devil's children will continue poison the earth with their criminal filth and insure the greater glory of Satan.

May that demonic hexagram of Satan along with that cabal of criminal demons be forever extinguished from the face of the earth so that peace and goodness and freedom among men of good will may once again flourish in brotherhood. DEATH TO ISRAHELL AND ALL WHO SUSTAIN SATANIC EVIL!

JULY, 2010
WALT DISNEY vs THE JEWS- FROM THE CDL REPORT, 1999

I usually do not use another person's article word for word in it's entirety in my articles – but this was simply too powerful to be diluted in any way. I grew up with Disney and his wonderful contribution to family and children – decency and wholesomeness – American-Christian patriotism and his dedication to honor trust decency and virtually everything we ever held sacred in a more innocent time when we were still a CHRISTIAN REPUBLIC!

I will not deny – a flood of wonderful memories swept through my consciousness as I read it. I also shed more than a tear when the full realization of what the filthy Jew had done to my country and a TRUE American icon of decency who was hounded, threatened, mocked, cheated, defrauded and destroyed by the most evil sadistic greedy hate filled Godless filth to ever disgrace

American shores. Only those of you who are peers and were raised by decent Godly parents will remember the nostalgia that I felt when I first read this. Younger readers – I pray you still have the wisdom to 'connect the dots' and comprehend the tremendous evil forces at work .

Walt Disney will always be my hero. If you ever had the slightest doubt about actors like John Wayne – Ward Bond – Robert Taylor Charles Coburn – and Gary Cooper being REAL PATRIOTS – read the entire story. And if you ever made the mistake of thinking Woody Allen was just a pathetic Jew nerd type – but never a treasonous Marxist piece of crap -READ ON!

I wasted my time so many years ago thinking our mortal enemy was some wretched oriental in black pajamas with his half cooked rice in his belt hiding in a jungle. The only REAL MORTAL enemy of EVERY DECENT MAN WOMAN AND CHILD in America is a JEW!

The next time I hear ANYTHING about "good Jews" from anybody – I think I'm going to kick him in the teeth! Next time you hear some Jew apologist bullshit from an evil Christ mocking ppasty faced brain dead 'Bapt-duh' whose main goal in life is to destroy America – destroy Christianity and destroy EVERYTHING that was EVER good and decent here – ALL for the greater glory of the Devil – IsraHELL and the Jew scum in this story who have turned America into HIS toilet – REMEMBER WELL – WHAT YOU READ HERE TODAY!-

Unknown to most Americans is the fact that the first motion picture camera was invented by Thomas Alva Edison in East Orange, New Jersey. A lifelong inventor, Mr. Edison had over 1,000 inventions patented when he died in 1931. Inventing a motion picture camera that worked properly was the easy part for Edison. Keeping Jews from using the camera without paying him royalties for his invention was the hard part.

As soon as the German born Jew, Carl Laemmle found out about motion pictures, he started figuring ways to exploit the new invention. Efforts by Laemmle and other Jews to deprive Edison of his fees for using his cameras forced Edison and other movie makers like Dickson, Casler, Koopman, Long, Smith, Klein and Marion to form a protective association called the TRUST. As fast as these Jews could get their hands on Edison's equipment and started using it, the Trust would file lawsuits against them to stop their illegally using his patented equipment.

Not to be outdone, Laemmle and some other New York Jews, rushed around Europe in their efforts to circumvent the long arm of the Trust. Cameras based on Edison's invention were smuggled into the United States by Jews as well as raw film. Edison and the Trust had made arrangements with the Eastman Kodak Company to exclusively produce film for it and those who had been sanctioned to use the equipment by the Trust.

Laemmle and his Jewish co-racialists found film manufacturers in Europe to supply them with Kodak-like film which was also smuggled into the United States.

When the courts moved at a snail's pace or refused to stop these Jews from using Edison's invention, the Trust would send out it's own enforcement 'police' which would seize and smash the illegal equipment. As one author noted, this forced them to set up an elaborate warning system. Jewish lookouts would keep watch while they were filming and when they observed the

Trust 'police' on their way, they would quickly pack up their cameras and flee as fast as possible to another 'filming' location.

However, Laemmle knew that while the Trust controlled most of the movie cameras, they could not get their films into circulation without 'movie houses.' Edison and other non-Jewish movie makers distributed their movies through numerous non-Jewish independent 'movie house' owners across America. However, those owning the movie houses were completely independent and had no central distribution center or movie house chains.

Before Edison perfected his camera other individuals had developed a system of rapidly moving cards which depicted short scenes. The 'pictograph' system as it was called, was quickly seized upon by Jews as a means of making a fast buck by developing a series of cards depicting 'movies' of naked women or sex acts by couples. To exploit the 'pictograph' market Jews used their homes and buildings in New York to set up 'Nickelodeons,' which turned useless real estate into a means of making a fast buck—on this early form of pornography.

The Jewish 'Nickelodeon' system spread from New York and Carl Laemmle used the 'Nickelodeons' as a framework for organizing his own distribution system among his more than willing co-racialists nationwide. To fight the Trust they formed the Distributing and Sales Company.

To get the 'goyim's' support, Laemmle allowed some non Jews to become involved and bring their movie houses and money into the venture. The non-Jews Robert Cochrane and Pat Powers merged their holdings with Laemmle. However, most of the funding for the DSC came from Jewish investors Laemmle had managed to get control over distribution facilities and over 300 theaters nationwide. In his drive for power over the Trust and his competitors, Laemmle formed Universal Movie Distributors with Cochrane and Powers.

After destroying his competitors at Mutual Film Distributors, Laemmle then proceeded to use his investors to push Cochrane and Powers out of Universal, and before long he was in total control and was nicknamed the 'King of the Film Renters' At this point the control of the movie industry went from the non-Jewish hands of the Trust into the hands of Laemmle, Fox and other Jews. They had won the fight for the control to the thinking of the American public.

The movie producers aligned with the Trust felt they were producing quality movies and wouldn't distribute any 'less than perfect' films. Laemmle didn't have that problem, and to keep the films flowing into his theaters and going through his distributors, he used every piece of junk film he could get his hands on. His motto was 'the more the better.' The Trust simply couldn't keep up, because they could not understand the Jewish mentality.

The Trust still kept fighting back so these Jews decided to pull up roots in the East and head West to Hollywood, California where there would be over 3,000 miles distance between the Trust, the courts and the Trust's 'police.'

From that time on Hollywood became the motion picture capital of America. Edison and the members of the Trust felt that by producing wholesome movies they were helping to preserve the nation's morals.

However, these Jews were not governed by moral standards. In the book Walt Disney Hollywood's Evil Prince, Marc Eliot says: "Unlike their early East Coast counterparts, the heads of Hollywood's studios were less interested in artistic experimentation than profit. They put on the screen what sold the most. The public was willing to pay to see films with sex and violence, and Hollywood was more than happy to make them.

"By the early twenties, all that remained of Edison's Trust was the issue it had raised regarding the moral content of motion pictures. The federal government kept a close watch on Hollywood, the new capital of the film industry, to make sure the movies it produced remained 'socially acceptable.' However, Hollywood's moguls had no idea of what was meant by 'socially acceptable.' They didn't know if their movies were moral or immoral and couldn't have cared less... The more a film made, the better it was...Whenever the industry came under attack for being morally corrupt, none of Hollywood's owners believed the problem had anything really to do with morality."

The members of the Trust couldn't understand that Jews wanted control of the movies so they could promote their own social and religious agenda. In An Empire of Their Own: How Jews Invented Hollywood, the Jewish author, Neal Gabler says: "...But one major reason Edison and his cohorts lost their hegemony was that they misinterpreted what was at stake. They never seemed to understand that they were engaged in much more than an economic battle to determine who would control the profits of the nascent film industry; their battle was also generational, cultural, philosophical, even, in some ways, religious. The Trust's members were primarily older white Anglo-Saxon Protestants who had entered the film industry in its infancy by inventing, bankrolling, or tinkering with movie hardware: cameras and projectors. For them, the movies themselves would always be novelties. The Independents, on the other hand were largely ethnics, Jews and Catholics, who had entered the industry by opening and operating its theaters."

Trying to stop Jews from controlling the distribution of movies had cost the Trust $300,000 in legal fees. The Hollywood Jews had been hit with 289 lawsuits. Undaunted by the action taken by Edison and the Trust, they kept using his equipment. In a last ditch effort to stop them, Edison and his friends organized the General Film Company as a film exchange. However, by now it was too late: they had gobbled up half the market and had formed a monopoly that would thumb its noses at the 'goyim' from the Trust.

After Jews achieved complete control over the distribution of movies, they kept lowering the standards regarding morality and sex to the point where some members of Congress felt that film censorship was necessary and they introduced legislation to create a board of film censorship.

To get around this censorship board Hollywood Jews rapidly moved to form a 'self regulating' organization called the Motion Picture Producers and Distributors of America. (MPPDA) A non-Jew was picked to head the MPPDA, and this was former Postmaster General Will Hays who had been national chairman of the Republican Party. In his book Marc Eliot says: "The Jewish power faction in Hollywood hoped choosing a Christian to regulate the moral content of their films would improve the overall image of its industry."

Some members of Congress considered Hollywood not only to be immoral but also subversive. In 1929, U. S. Senator Smith Brookhart summed up the deteriorating situation in Hollywood as a battle between competing studios led by 'bunches of Jews.'

By the late 1920s most of the move theaters in America were Jewish controlled and the means of distributing movies. With Jewish control of the movie industry from A to Z it was almost impossible for a non-Jew to get a break. One of those who fought the system was Walt Disney.

Disney was born in the Midwest and learned cartoon animating on his own. His attempts to get his short subjects and cartoons marketed ran into constant roadblocks from the 'chosen' elite who ran Hollywood. Disney was able to sell a number of animated cartoons he produced for small stipends. At that time one of the most popular cartoons was 'Felix the Cat.' Trying to produce a cartoon that would equal 'Felix the Cat,' Disney came up with a character called 'Oswald the Rabbit.'

In an effort to get his work recognized, he contacted a New York distributor by the name of Margaret Winkler. Disney also produced a series of cartoons based on Alice in Wonderland, which Ms. Winkler contracted with him to produce. At this time a Hollywood Jew who had worked for Warner Brothers, Charles Mintz, was courting Ms. Winkler and upon seeing the 'Oswald the Rabbit' samples, could sense that 'Oswald the Rabbit' was every bit as good as 'Felix the Cat' and could make him rich. In order to get on Walt's good side and get to 'Oswald the Rabbit,' Mintz agreed to advance Walt $1,800 and to pay him for another eighteen cartoons in the 'Alice' series.

Jubilant, the Disney brothers took the deal and promptly set about purchasing a studio on Hyperion Avenue in Hollywood. Mintz had set the stage. After the Disney brothers had completed the construction of their modest studio, Mintz dropped the bomb on them. He told them that due to 'lack of interest' the 'Alice' series would have to be dropped and his contact with them would have to be cancelled. All this time Mintz had been traveling between Hollywood and New York making secret deals with his fellow co-racialist, Carl Laemmle. Laemmle wanted a cartoon character based on the 'Felix the Cat' to compete with 'Felix the Cat.' Mintz knew Disney had already created such a character, a rabbit named 'Oswald.'

Disney, not paying much attention to the contacts that Mintz had negotiated with him, had in fact, signed away all rights to 'Oswald the Rabbit' and to all goods sold through the promotion of the cartoon.

Keeping his side of the bargain, Disney produced Trolley Troubles featuring Oswald and faithfully gave Mintz new cartoons in the series every two weeks at $2,500 a cartoon and "part of the box office" gross. Walt learned by accident that without his knowledge, known consent or participation, Mintz had made a secret deal with Laemmle to market merchandise based on 'Oswald.' When Walt complained, his brother Roy calmed him down by telling him that the sales of the merchandise would help promote the 'Oswald' series and make him money when customers came to see the movies.

Then in 1928 he and his wife went to New York to negotiate a new contact with Mintz. When they met Mintz, in a typically arrogant fashion, told Disney that his advance per cartoon had been cut to $1,800. He went onto tell Disney that if "he didn't like it" the cartoon production would be taken over by a Mintz front called 'Snappy Inc.' and Walt's own employees would be hired to produce the cartoons, in spite of him. Walt called his brother Roy and told him what had happened and Roy told him that Mintz, according to the contract that Walt had signed, owned all the rights to 'Oswald' including the name! Roy then informed Walt that the animators Walt had hired in Hollywood to help produce 'Oswald' had suddenly quit. The Hollywood Jews went straight to work for Mintz and the non-Jews that Disney had brought with him from the Midwest stayed loyal.

In desperation Disney appealed to Laemmle about his rights and he told Disney that he couldn't help and that he would only deal with the series distributor, who was Mintz, also Jewish. Cut out by this Jewish group, Disney returned to Hollywood and created what was later to be known as 'Mickey Mouse.' After Mickey Mouse proved to be successful Carl Laemmle came to Disney in an effort to distribute the film. He offered to distribute Mickey Mouse if Disney would give him the copyright to it. It was now Disney's turn, he turned him down flat.

Laemmle and his fellow Jewish distributors of films were known as the 'Majors,' and after he gave the cold shoulder to Laemmle, none of them would distribute his Mickey Mouse series. Being a gentile, Disney could not penetrate what Eliot describes as the 'old world brotherhood.' Disney then turned to another man who had, had a falling out with Laemmle and the 'brotherhood,' Pat Powers. Powers made a deal to distribute the series on a 'states rights' basis, to as many independent theaters as possible. Irregularities in the amount of earnings and the amount the Disney's received brought about an end to the Disney/Powers alliance. However, as much as Disney searched he could not find a gentile distributor for his productions. Finally, he made a deal with Harry Cohen the head of Columbia Pictures. Sensing the profits to be made from Disney productions, Cohen fought off the other 'chosen' wolves in behalf of Disney.

The next problem faced by Disney as the popularity of his productions increased was organized crime and its efforts to form and control all movie based unions. The mob infiltrated the International Alliance of Theatrical Stage Employees (IATSE) in their effort to control Hollywood. Behind the effort to control the Hollywood unions were Bugsy Siegel and Meyer Lansky, both Jewish. The third man in the troika of mobsters was Charles 'Lucky' Luciano, the 'Sicilian' gangster who was responsible for massacring his fellow Sicilians in the 1920s when they had to be eliminated in order for him to make an alliance with Jews.

Even when Disney had found distributors he was always in need of money to cover production costs and expansion. Disney severed his dealings with Columbia Pictures and United Artists took over distribution of Disney productions. One of Disney's most successful cartoons was the Three Little Pigs. In the original Three Little Pigs, there was a scene where the Big Bad Wolf disguised himself as a Jewish peddler to trick one of the pigs into opening the door. As soon as word leaked out about this scene, representatives of a number of Jewish organizations beat a path to Disney to get the 'offensive' scene removed.

Disney removed the scene and told the Hollywood Jews that the scene was a spoof depicting Carl Laemmle's continuous efforts to "blow down the house of Disney." Julius Schenck of United Artists, which was distributing Disney productions, had carefully set a trap for Disney. Schenck recommended that Disney seek funding from the Bank of America, and personally contact UA's financial advisor at the bank, Joseph Rosenberg. He gladly opened a line of credit for Disney, but never gave him enough so he could be effective and later helped bring down the Disney empire. Disney constantly found himself the victim of walkouts by Jews he had hired or by Marxist agitators who were constantly forming unions in Hollywood.

Through the unions Hollywood Jews constantly used unions to curb the growth of Disney productions. An effort to break the control of the Majors over Hollywood was made when several independent film makers formed The Society of Independent Motion Picture Producers (SIMPP). SIMPP was formed to challenge the majors' domination of production, exhibition and distribution. The leading non-Jews in SIMPP were William Cagney, Walt Disney, Mary Pickford, Edward Small, Orson Wells and Walter Wagner. A few Jewish studio moguls who had found themselves cut out of the action by the insiders of the 'old world elite' supported SIMPP and these were: David O. Selznick, Sol Lesser and Sam Goldwyn. The dictatorial control of the Jewish 'Majors' is described in Walt Disney Hollywood's Dark Prince: "For the most part, the Majors were still controlled by the same group of men who had first broken the iron grip of the old Edison Trust. Ironically, a quarter of a century later, their success had led them to create an even more anti-competitive environment than the one from which they had desperately fled. So much so that no independent film could gain national distribution unless the filmmaker or studio dealt with one of the Majors, who not only controlled all the distribution networks but owned virtually every first run theater in the country...." Disney raised the ire of the Majors when he publicly attended America First meetings and had even stood beside Charles Lindbergh at one rally.

To retaliate the red dominated unions kept strife going at the Disney studios. In the early 1930s it was a well known fact that the sympathies of the majority of Jews in Hollywood was in favor of Socialism and Communism. In An Empire of Their Own, Neal Gabler talks about communist influence in Hollywood. He says: "Jews had first forged ties to the parties of the Left, and to the Communist party specifically, back in Europe...one leading Communist estimated that 50 percent of the Party's members were Jewish during its heyday in the thirties and forties, and a large minority—sometimes a majority—of the Party leadership was Jewish...What was true of the national Party was even truer in Hollywood, where they already formed a large part of the left leaning artistic community...One member complained that nearly 90 percent of the Party in Los Angeles was Jewish...Ring Lardner, Jr., himself a Party member had the "impression that it was well over 50 percent, somewhat like, maybe, two thirds."

As it became apparent that the Communist movement in the United States was mainly Jewish led, congressman Samuel Dickstein of New York, who was an Eastern European born Jew, took steps to protect his co-racialists. He moved to have a special committee set up in Congress to investigate those who were pouring forth documents proving that Jewish Bolsheviks were running the Soviet Union and had killed almost thirty million Russians and Ukrainians and were the leaders of the Communist movement in Europe.

By calling all those who dared to criticize Jewish groups as 'Nazi' Dickstein felt that he could bully loyal Americans into silence. In January of 1934 Congress voted to establish a House Committee on Un-American Activities (HUAC) to investigate German activities in the United States. The bias of Dickstein was so apparent that by 1937 his anti-German and anti-Gentile rantings and ravings in congress were drawing attention to other Jews. When he tried to get the HUAC mandate renewed, it measure failed.

The Hollywood Jews then backed Congressman Martin Dies, a non-Jew, in setting up a committee with the same name under his chairmanship. Dies voiced their concern in An Empire of Their Own, when he said: Many of our Jewish citizens wanted Dickstein eliminated because they felt he was furnishing ammunition to the Nazis and other anti-Semitic movements." By 1939 Die's investigation of subversion in America had opened his eyes to the fact that facts uncovered by the Committee substantiated the claim that Hollywood was, indeed, pro-Communist as many so-called 'anti-Semites' had claimed. Gabler quotes Dies as telling key figures in Hollywood: I told the producers that we had reliable information that a number of film actors and screenwriters and a few producers either were members of the Communist Party, followed the Communist line, or were used as dupes, and that there was evidence that the Hollywood Anti-Nazi League was under the control of the Communists."

Dies retired from Congress in 1944 and a fiery Congressman named John Rankin of Mississippi used his influence to get the HUAC made a permanent committee of Congress. Rankin's investigations further opened his eyes to the fact that Hollywood Jews were behind the anti-moral assault on America. Rankin told the press that: "...the information we get is that (Hollywood) is the greatest hotbed of subversive activities in the United States. We're on the trail of the tarantula now, and we're going to follow through...We are not trying to hound legitimate writers, but we are out to expose those elements that are insidiously trying to spread subversive propaganda, poison the minds of your children, distort the history of our country, and discredit Christianity...alien minded communistic enemies of Christianity, and their stooges are trying to take control over the radio. Listen to their lying broadcasts in broken English and you can almost smell them...They are now trying take over the motion picture industry, and how to high heaven when our Committee on un-American Activities propose to investigate them. They want to spread their un-American propaganda, as well as their ...immoral, anti-Christian...before the eyes of your children in every community in America."

Jews founded the HUAC in an effort stifle legitimate criticism of their activities in America, and by 1945 it had gone full circle and was being used as a legitimate vehicle for patriots to go after those who were influenced by Communism and trying to change the thinking of America. This gave Walt Disney and other non-Jews who had been discriminated against by the 'Majors' a chance to try to bring an end to the Jewish domination of Hollywood, and the HUAC hearings went on well into the mid 1960s. Disney and his Motion Picture Alliance for the Preservation of American Ideals tried to break the Jewish Communist stranglehold on Hollywood. As the MIAPIA and the HUAC fought the red/Jewish influence in Hollywood, the reds kept striking back by fomenting one strike after the other against Disney and others who opposed them.

Walt openly vowed to keep the commies out of his studio and told the press that the strikes at his studio were fomented by the Communist Conspiracy. Again Eliot says: "Ever since Sinclair's gubernatorial campaign helped unify Hollywood's left, the Communist Party of the United States of America (CPUSA) had made its presence felt by championing the rights of the film industry's workers. The CPUSA played a vital role in the Screen Writers Guild's long battle to exist, thus helping to make legitimate the industry's burgeoning union movement."

In 1941 the CPUSA backed strikers at Disney Studios who were fomenting trouble through the Screen Writer's Guild. Most of the Disney staff walked out 'on strike.' Pressure was brought on Disney to settle the strike by Bank of America representative, Rosenberg, who told him that the effects of the strike would "damage his relationship with the Bank of America." The Jewish tentacles through the Bank of America were brought to bear on Disney. A further attack was launched on Disney by King Features when Jewish groups accused Disney of being a 'Nazi' because they claimed that there was a swastika drawn in a Mickey Mouse cartoon in a panel in a cartoon on June 19th, 1940. The swastika was "in the form of two crossed musical notes."

Efforts to get Disney to support Roosevelt and his 'get us into war' effort failed as long as Walt Disney kept tight control over his studio. In an effort to get Disney away from the studio Roosevelt instructed Nelson Rockefeller to make Disney a part of a tour to South America by actors allegedly sent to "counter Nazi propaganda in South America." Rockefeller had been named the 'Official Coordinator' of the State Department's Inter-American Affairs group. Roosevelt was particularly concerned because of Disney's appearances at America First rallies alongside Charles Lindbergh. From all indications, Roy Disney was a part of the plot to get Walt away from the Disney studio so the "strike could be settled" and so Walt could 'clear' himself of the charges leveled against him of being a 'Nazi' sympathizer. Walt and his entourage left for South America on August 17th, and on the 9th of September, Roy Disney met with James F. Dewy and agreed to 'arbitration' to settle the strike. When Walt received news of the sell out by Roy, he vowed to close down the studio forever rather then have the red dominated Cartoonists Guild run his studio. It seems that Roosevelt and the Hollywood Jews had made plans well in advance to shut down Disney studios.

On December 8th, 1941 the Army seized Disney studios claiming that they had to use it as a 'defense station' to protect Lockheed which was nearby. Disney's studio was the only one seized by the government. His studio and production facilities sequestered by the government, Disney was now without a job. The next step in the plot against Disney was when the Naval Bureau of Aeronautics contacted him and offered him $80,000 to make twenty animated training films. The anti-Disney move was evidently orchestrated by Secretary of the Treasury Henry Morgenthau.

According to Disney he had been forced to 'accept that Jew' Morgenthau, and was being forced by circumstances to be used by Morgenthau "...to deliver political propaganda films that cashed in on the popularity of that all American Mouse, Mickey..." Disney referred to his cartoon characters as captives who were forced to perform for the Stromboli-like Morgenthau."

The 'crowning achievement' of Morgenthau was to have Disney produce a cartoon featuring Donald Duck which openly mocked Hitler, with the title Der Fuhrer's Face. According to Eliot, this move by Morgenthau produced 'more animosity' between Disney and Morgenthau, as

Disney made the movie under protest. However, Morgenthau made it look like Disney approved of the project and had him given awards by Hollywood and moved more business his way. The studio was returned to Disney eight months after it was closed.

Trying to ad insult to injury, the National Council of Christians and Jews contacted Disney in an effort to get him to make a cartoon to promote 'unity' in America. They told him that the move would 'depict human prejudices.' Disney rejected the proposal outright and said it was a disguised attempt by the National Council of Christians and Jews to promote communism in America.

This attempt to recruit him by the 'Brotherhood' gang confirmed Disney's view that Hollywood was being consumed by communism. In response he set out to make 'battle plans' to counter their moves and to recruit 'soldiers' for the fight against the reds in Hollywood. One of the first moves he made was to help found the Motion Picture Alliance for the Preservation of American Ideals in 1944. He was a co-chairman of the organization and among its members were: Robert Taylor, John Wayne, Gary Cooper, Ward Bond, Charles Coburn, Adolphe Menju, Hedda Hopper and sixty five other key Hollywood personalities.

As vice-president of the MPA, Disney wrote to Senator Robert R. Reynolds and called on the House Committee on Un-American Activities to investigate red influence in Hollywood. In his open letter of March 7, 1944 Disney said that Hollywood had been "coddling Communists…and those with un-American beliefs."

Having been denied access to the power and profits of Hollywood by the Jews and Communists, Disney felt it was time to strike back. Both Disney and the Jew Samuel Goldwyn had been cut off from full market access by the 'big five' who controlled most of the theaters in America: Paramount, Loews, Warner's, Twentieth Century Fox and RKO. When the Fox owned T & D theaters insulted Goldwyn when he wanted to exhibit his movie Up In Arms, Disney joined with Goldwyn in trying to break the hold of the 'big five' over film distribution. They rented the El Patio nightclub to review the movie and then all hell broke loose.

The power of the 'big five' was evident when the Reno county commissioners issued multiple violations for the El Patio and the fire department said it would prevent the showing. To appease the 'big five' the proceeds of the showing had to be contributed to the Red Cross. Legal action was taken to break up the 'big five' monopoly by SIMPP and in the case of the United States of America vs. Paramount the supreme court ruled that the 'big five' were prohibited from expanding their holdings and control over the production, distribution and exhibition of movies. A small victory for Disney, but a victory, nonetheless.

The actions of Disney, SIMPP and the handful of patriots in Hollywood led to the House Committee on Un-American Activities investigating hundreds of reds in Hollywood, mostly Jewish. A number of the most notorious reds were blacklisted by Hollywood movie makers because of fear that the HUAC would also investigate them. The ban on outright reds in Hollywood lasted until around 1965. After that many of those 'blacklisted' by the HUAC were back in Hollywood making movies 'exposing' their 'persecution.' One of the first efforts by the reds to show their rehabilitation and power over Hollywood was the movie the Front, by Woody

Allen. From screenwriters to producers to actors those involved in the movie the Front, were Hollywood reds who had been investigated by the HUAC and had been fired from their jobs by Jewish studio owners and producers who were afraid not to fire them.

The Jewish owners of the major studios knew that to allow those named as Communists by the HUAC to keep working would provoke the HUAC to investigate them as well. To circumvent this, the Jewish studio owners put a number of them on the 'blacklist' which kept them from working. However, as depicted in The Front, most of them kept working by hiring front men to use their names on their manuscripts. It seems that Americans have short memories and by the time Walt Disney died in 1966, the Jewish reds were back in Hollywood thumbing their noses at those who had fought so hard to bring Hollywood back under American control.

Always short of funds, Disney found a temporary ally in billionaire Howard Hughes. Hughes had purchased RKO studios and distribution and was also wary of the Jewish control of not only Hollywood but America. Hughes loaned Disney millions of dollars—interest free, which Disney paid back in full. While a good businessman, Hughes was a poor movie studio manager. Perhaps, when he took RKO over from Jewish control; the Jews who stayed on found it in their interest to break Hughes by producing flop after flop for him, as they have recently done to Columbia Pictures.

In any case, Disney wanted his own means of distribution and founded Buena Vista. Hughes offered to give Disney RKO for free and also give him a $10 million credit line with no interest rate. However, Disney's advisors soured him on the deal and he turned it down. Again, was it Rosenberg of the Bank of America who advised him to turn down the deal, fearing that in charge of RKO he would become a major challenge to the Jewish domination of Hollywood? After fighting the Jewish powers that control Hollywood, Disney became fascinated by the idea of forming theme parks. He eventually turned over control of Disney studios to his brother Roy and devoted full time to fulfilling his theme park dream. Disneyland opened in 1955 and Walt Disney died December 5, 1966 after a long bout with cancer. Then the battle for the 'Magic Kingdom' began.

One of the major drawbacks to Disney was the fact that his older brother Roy, was an accountant who turned manager. Roy had no vision and no courage to stand up for his convictions. When things got tough, Roy would always cave in to the opposition and even go against Walt's wishes, as happened during WW II when he moved to settle the red strike against the Disney studios when Walt was out of the country.

Walt's venture into the 'new' TV phenomena in the 1950s with the 'Musketeers' was successful beyond his dreams. However, Walt spared nothing in developing, directing and producing the 'Musketeers' and after the expense of production, the show lost money for Disney. He kept it going because it promoted Disney products, brought the Disney concept to national TV and he felt it would be a key vehicle for promoting his new Disneyland concept. Walt's first choice for Disneylandia, as he first called it, was Burbank. However, the attempt to build it there ran into constant trouble from the city council, which Walt felt was being influenced against him by Universal Studios. He then built Disneyland in Anaheim.

With the Mickey Mouse Club, ABC and the Jew Leonard Goldenson made their mark as a competing network. The Disney shows on ABC made it into a real competitor with the CBS and NBC. Around 1960 Disney complained to Goldenson that there were too many commercials on the shows. As other Jews had done to Disney, Goldenson cancelled the two Disney shows. ABC had now made so much money off Disney that they could produce their own shows and, again Disney was cut out of his fair share of Hollywood profits by the Jewish 'Brotherhood.' To keep his shows on national TV Disney approached NBC. However, Goldenson refused to let Disney out of his contract and Disney took ABC to court. In the end ABC turned over all rights to Disney productions and products to Walt and cut all ties with him. As Disney became more absorbed in his theme park he started shifting more responsibility to his son in law Ron Miller. This caused animosity from his brother Roy who felt that his son Roy E. Disney should be the future 'King' of the Disney Empire.

The problem was that neither Ron, Roy or Roy E. were really able to handle the Disney conglomerate and future events would prove this out. When Walt died the bulk of his estate went to the his wife and the female members of the family. His brothers Roy and Raymond were left out of the will as Walt believed that men should make their own livings and didn't need his help. In 1967 Ron Miller and Roy E. Disney were elected to the studio's board of directors. Since both were antagonistic to each other, two 'committees' were formed to run the Disney Empire.

Roy senior died in 1971, opening Disney up to challenges from all sides. Some Walt Disney loyalists were appointed to key positions in the studio and this didn't fit well with Roy E. Loyalist Card Walker became the president of Walt Disney Productions and Roy E. resigned from the board. However, the stock his father had given him made him the largest single stockholder. Ron Miller and his associates at Disney then proceeded to make a series of movie 'flops' and this prompted Roy E. to make moves he believed would keep the studio from going under. Advising Roy E. in his moves was attorney Stanley Gold, another Hollywood insider.

Gold urged Roy E. to hire his former law partner Frank Wells. Wells had been a vice-president at Warner Brothers. Roy felt he was in 'good hands' with what studio employees called the 'Troika.' As soon as he was in place, Frank Wells, who was Jewish, recommended that the studio hire Michael Eisner to replace Ron Miller. Eisner had been the president of Paramount Pictures, and had been recommended for the job by Barry Diller, Jewish, who was chairman of Warner Brothers. Seeing discontent at Disney, Saul Steinberg, also Jewish, felt that Disney was ripe for a corporate takeover. Using rumors of discontent, they drove Disney stock down almost 50% causing a near panic at the studio. Roy E's stock fell from $80 million to $50.

Roy was advised that a corporate takeover could be fought and that junk bond king Michael Milken was the man to 'save'Disney. He was hired by Roy E., Gold and Wells without the knowledge of the other board members.

Roy E. had wanted to purchase back most of the Disney stock to stop the proposed junk bond takeover. However, Jews at the Bank of America advised him that Steinberg could raise so much funny money that Disney would not be able to do so. At this point corporate raider Ivan Boesky entered the fray and made millions on the stock based on inside information he had received from Jewish insiders at Disney.

The Hollywood Jews were now in a position to completely take over Disney. The Jews at Disney convinced the board to pay what is called 'greenmail' to Steinberg and he was given a $31 million dollar pay off to call off his fight to take over Disney. Roy E's Jewish advisors came out on top taking control of Disney while Roy E. was 'paid off' by being made Chairman of Walt Disney Feature Animation at a yearly salary of $850,000. Gold convinced Roy E. that Ron Miller was responsible for the decline at Disney and that he should be replaced. Miller was asked by the board to step down and on August 17, 1984 the board asked Miller for his resignation. He resigned and his seat was taken over by the Stanley Gold – Jewish. They had effectively eliminated Disney heir apparent Ron Miller and now they started moving more Jews into Disney.

On September 22, 1984 the board of directors appointed Michael Eisner and Frank Wells to head Disney Productions. Eisner then brought Jeffrey Katzenberg, also Jewish, over to Disney from Paramount. Katzenberg's job was to 'revamp' Disney studios. Old Disney loyalists were considered by the self 'chosen' to be 'dead weight' and over 400 were fired and replaced by a hand picked Jewish team from Paramount. Former Morris Agency employee David Hoberman was put in charge of Disney subsidiary Touchstone Pictures. Richard Frank was recruited from Paramount to 'revitalize' Disney's television interests.

Jews had now taken over control of Disney. They used the Touchstone and Miramax to make racy and anti-Christian movies that Walt Disney would never have allowed at his studio.

Although gays were prohibited from any activities at Disneyland while Walt was alive, after the Jewish takeover, Eisner openly invited and courted homosexual groups to hold 'dances' and events at the theme parks. As we go to press a number of magazines have carried news articles gloating over how "Disney would be turning in his grave" if he knew what had now happened to his theme parks and movie productions. From the very beginning Disney was considered a 'goy' outsider by Jews who stole from Thomas Edison. They had defied the 'goy' Edison and by their tenacity had beaten him. They blocked out Disney because he wasn't one of the self 'chosen' and Disney had to fight his whole life to break into the closed Jewish society called Hollywood. Disney didn't like Jews and used every means at his disposal to counter them.

According to Eliot, Disney at an early age had been informed by his father about the self 'chosen' and how they operated. For awhile Disney was able through the HUAC to root out those Jews and non-Jews in Hollywood who had supported Communist causes. At least for fifteen or twenty years, he had his revenge. While Disney was alive the 'Magic Kingdom' remained in good hands in spite of his spineless brother Roy. His self chosen heir, Ron Miller proved to be no match for Ray and the ruthless Jews who became his close advisors.

Disney who was the descendant of Crusaders who left their village of Isgny in 1066 to fight the good fight, fought the good fight all his life. While alive he manned the ramparts and like his Crusader ancestors fought off the anti-Christ Hollywood Jews. However, despite his efforts he could not defeat the forces who made up the anti-Christ kingdom called Hollywood. They may gloat while they savor their victory in storming and taking the last Christian stronghold in Hollywood. However, he who laughs last, laughs best, and the time will come when Walt Disney will have his victory over the self 'chosen.'

MAY THE LORD SAVE US WHO HAVE REMAINED FAITHFUL – FROM THESE DEMONIC JEWS!

JULY, 2010
OPEN LETTER TO PATRIOTS WHO ARE ACTIVELY RESISTING JEW WAR EVIL

I was heartened to learn of the sabotage of the factory of war criminals – EDO MBM- in Brighton England. It is the first good feeling of camaraderie I have had for the British since I can remember. Even though this courageous moral deed took place some 18 months ago (16 Jan 2009) I feel compelled to acknowledge this wonderful act of humanity Godliness and patriotism. Since these weapons were to be used by the world's largest institutionalized terrorist organization –(the IsraHELL IDF) to murder and main innocent civilians especially children – in Palestine I applaud these REAL heroes with my greatest of sincerity and admiration.

There are no heroes wearing uniforms in Iraq or Afghanistan – only war criminals. The only heroes in uniform are those brave and moral REAL MEN that REFUSED to be pawns and lap dog puppets of the Jews in their murderous agendas of serial wars against civilians. I swear by God in heaven that if called upon to serve my nation to defend its shores – ONCE AGAIN – TODAY- from REAL enemies – like the JEWS and their Zionist useful idiots – I would render my last ounce of energy and life in her defense. HOWEVER – There is no force on EARTH who can compel me by intimidation or any other extortion to brutalize and murder innocent civilians – MOST ESPECIALLY – HELPLESS CHILDREN – as do the Jews – in Palestine or our own military 7 days a week – in whatever sovereign nation the Jews decide to destroy next – using American youth 'goy' as cannon fodder of course .

My salute goes out as well to those members of UK Govt. and court justices who supported the Godly actions of these heroes who aptly term themselves the 'decommissioners'. Special recognition goes to Brighton Pavillian PM , Caroline Lucas as well as Judge George Bathurst-Norman and defendants lawyer – Lydia Dagostino. To all of those men and women who participated in that act of heroism – I salute you with the deepest of respect and admiration. May the owners of that demonic factory of human misery and death ROT IN HELL!

Additionally – I strongly urge ALL TRUE Christian Americans to follow the Godly example of those Britishers of conscience and take action in the Jew occupied former USA to prevent the demonic greedy money grubbing filthy Jews here from making more weapons of death and destruction known to be specifically used by the Jew terrorists in IsraHELL to murder and butcher children in Gaza and other Palestinian cities. Be a patriot and a Christian – stop the manufacture of demonic weapons that Jews use to murder children.

I have been inside these giant outdoor Jew concentration camps and witnessed the very worst of the evil side of human nature as only the demonic Jew can exhibit. Until you have witnessed the terror in the eyes of a 5 year old child who has witnessed his sisters raped – his parents murdered and his home and orchards destroyed by these sadistic Jew demons – you cannot understand the level of malevolence and cruelty to the most helpless and defenseless of God's children that only the Jew can commit without ANY remorse or pity or compassion. Been there seen that – and I WILL NEVER FORGET IT! The JEWS ARE LIARS Christ said so! I say so!

IF – by trying to save these children from further brutality torture agony and death – I am some kind of criminal in this sick twisted morally degenerate perverse nation which I once loved passionately – SO BE IT! If our Jew/shabbus goy dominated FBI see fit to demonize me – intimidate me – threaten me – a half crippled old man in my own home – for what EVERY DECENT MORAL AMERICAN would have done when I was a young man – so be it.

I will compare my military and civic record with ANY FBI person regardless of age or position. I have never committed a crime nor been accused of such. I was training young warriors to defend this nation from REAL enemies – those historically supported and created by the Jews themselves – long before the Gestapo-like FBI agents selected to pound on my door in reference to 'complaints' by the Jews who hate me as a Christian – were even BORN! But that is what we have come to – in Jew occupied AmeriKa. A nation of moral cowards hypocrites and sociopaths – mockers of Christ and love – and lovers of war, racism and hate. IF – my love of justice – and Christian principles – and my longing to have MY country back the way we were before the Jew occupation – makes me a 'CRIMINAL' to my own government. I will wear it as a 'badge' – PROUDLY – in my home – or in a prison.

JULY, 2010
'THE 4th OF JULY' – IS TODAY – A MEANINGLESS – SHALLOW – HYPOCRISY

Can you 4th of July party animals tell your children what great American issued this grave warning against the evil Jews. He foresaw the ultimate destruction of our nation by this demonic scum. He predicted EXACTLY what you have witnessed come to pass today. Even as they suck out the last drop of our life blood – we race to our deaths – not with the name of our Lord on our lips – but of the Jews who have by their greed – lust – evil and demonic nature – have transformed us into nothing less than a morally rotted corpse – drained dry of every last drop of goodness – compassion – love – wisdom – honor – and Godliness.

Like you – your children do not even know his name – yet they can parrot the names of ALL of our 'AmeriKan Idols' and know every detail of every 'star' NFL millionaire and the names of every scumbag hard metal rock band.

Once again the less than meaningless 'celebration' of our independence on yet another less than meaningless 4th of July is at hand. To our witless spoiled children it means lots of firecrackers to set off (an act for which they haven't a remote clue as to its true meaning) and a mini-vacation . To our adult sheeple – the brain-sharing imbecile parents of these imbecile children – it is an opportunity to get drunk on Bud beer (the 'PROUD' sponsors of every major homosexual pervert group) – pig-out on lots of greasy fried food and worship NASCAR rednecks and millionaire thugs brawlers drug addicts rapists murderers on the TV – with screaming and yelling along with their brain-dead neighbors .

This enthusiasm is of course not for remembrance of our independence but – for the greater glory of thugs who get more money in a month than my honest hard working father earned in his LIFETIME taking care of his family – defending his country against REAL enemies and teaching his children meaningful wisdom – the REAL meaning of events like the 4th of July!

Oh – and of course the grand finale – the eye candy spectacle of all those fireworks displays which somehow engender feelings of 'patriotism' for our brave troops as they continue to murder a thousand innocent civilian men women and of course – mostly children -every day. These crimes are committed in nations we occupy as imperialist war-mongering killers – just as the British who occupied us and brutalized us for wanting to be a free people. Today – we have forgotten our heritage COMPLETELY. We are now murdering innocent civilian human beings in their OWN nation – at the rate of 1,000 – EVERY 24 HOURS OF EVERY DAY.

As a moral educated responsible veteran – you cannot imagine how painful it is to witness stupid irresponsible insensitive people making a farce of one of the most solemn and meaningful commemorations of our quest and subsequent victory for freedom from cruel occupying imperialist aggressors as a fledgling Christian nation which would later be the envy of all freedom loving men of good will. Today we ARE THE KILLERS AND OPPRESSORS. Do you know what the motto-creed of the Green Berets is – or more accurately – USED TO BE? 'DE OPPRESSO LIBER' Today that is nothing more than an unconscionable monstrous hypocrisy! It means 'to liberate from the oppressor. Today we ARE – THE OPPRESSORS – THE TERRORISTS

A great American wrote these words below. He was not some punk rock star – or shallow brain-dead NFL stud – or talk -show imbecile – or talking 'head' lying lap-dog news puppet. He was an American ICON – an intellectual giant – a 24 ct solid gold patriot – a man of God – a REAL MAN!

"There is a great danger for the United States of America, this great danger is the Jew. Gentlemen, in every land which the Jews have settled, they have depressed the moral level and lowered the degree of commercial honesty. They have remained apart and unassimilated. . .They have created a state within a state, and when they are opposed they attempt to strangle the nation financially as in the case of Portugal and Spain. For more than 1700 years, they have lamented their sorrowful fate.. namely, that they were driven out of their motherland, but gentlemen, if the civilized world today should give them back Palestine and their property, they would immediately find pressing reasons for not returning there. Why? Because they are vampires.. .they cannot live among themselves; they must live among Christians and others who do not belong to their race.

"If they are not excluded from the United States by the Constitution, within less than 100 years, they will stream into this country in such numbers they will rule and destroy us and change our form of government for which Americans shed our blood and sacrificed our life, property and personal safety. If the Jews are not excluded, within 200 years our children will be working in the fields to feed the Jews while they remain in the Counting House gleefully rubbing their hands.

"I warn you, gentlemen, if you do not exclude the Jews forever, your children's children will curse you in your graves. Their ideals are not those of Americans even though they have lived among us for ten generations. The leopard cannot change his spots. The Jews are a danger to this land and if they are allowed to enter they will imperil our institutions... they should be excluded by the Constitution."

(Found in the Library of Congress.)

JULY, 2010
A NEW MORE GODLY WAY TO CELEBRATE INDEPENDENCE DAY

Since we as Americans have become world class exponents of foot-in-mouth disease – perhaps we should try a different approach to the remembrance of an historic event which has LONG LONG since been twisted bastardized and perverted into something scarcely recognizable in its original sacred intent – an orgy of parties.

For those of you who can take your beer soaked eyes off your NASCAR Billy Bob Bad Ass redneck hero for 5 minutes – here is a revelation. If it is too profoundly deep for you to understand – by all means go back to your couch and continue guzzling your cold Bud and stuffing your pie-hole with dips and chips – hot dawgs – burgers and fries.

This may be a culture shock for many of you couch warriors – but on the fourth of July in 1776 a group of REAL patriots decided that they had suffered enough at the hands of their occupiers and FREEDOM and INDEPENDENCE were worth great sacrifice suffering and even death at the hands of their tyrannical masters.

They were to be the Founding Fathers of this then fledgling nation – who were to face the world's greatest super-power in a life and death struggle for freedom to assert their own destiny and their rightful place in the world as a sovereign nation free from foreign aggression. They would be called "rebels" – "Terrorists" and face brutal sadistic retribution from the oppressors of imperialist England

Here's a pop quiz for the 'fatson' family glued to your Zionist TV entertainment. What was the only nation in history to have murdered Americans on their own soil? How about you Billy Bob? Duhh it were them Arab rag heads on 9-11 – he proudly spouts. WRONG – Billy Bob – it was the British. Next question: Who was the only nation to commit an act of war against America since 1941? How about you – 'cable guy' redneck father ?

Duhh – dats an easy one – it were dem A'rabs on 9-11! WRONG AGAIN my bovine brained friend! It was the Jews from IsraHELL as they attacked and butchered over two hundred unarmed Navy American sons fathers and brothers on the USS Liberty on June 8 1967. Don't you know ANYTHING about your own country? I guess not. So go back to your party and pop-bottle rockets and your shallow meaningless affront to the memory of great freedom loving men who decided to die on their feet rather than live in servitude on their knees.

Fast forward to the year 2010 – July 4 . What are we celebrating? The murders of some TWO MILLION INNOCENT CIVILIANS – mostly children – people of sovereign nations who have never done America or Americans ANY HARM – in ANY WAY? What in God's holy name have we come to as a people – hypocrites who rail about our love of independence out of one side of our mouths – yet – with the other – we trash and crush freedom and independence of other people – and demean and slander and dehumanize them as insurgents – detainees – terrorists – rag-heads – camel jockeys – sand- niggers – all to please our Jew masters!

During this 4 day orgy of shallow meaningless gluttony and drunkenness – we the American people will have been guilty of the murders of over three thousand MORE innocent civilian human beings – all for the greater glory of the demonic Godless Christ hating people of IsraHELL! Do the math yourself. Have we all become MADMEN – incapable of decency or rational goodness? Have we no shame?

I suggest that we – as a nation -fall to our collective knees and BEG the Lord – Christ for forgiveness for our unconscionable crimes against the helpless and innocent in the name of the children of the Devil – as HE the Lord God PLAINLY – and CLEARLY professed in the book Of John twenty centuries ago!

For Americans to celebrate the event of our independence – won by bloody sacrifice by TRUE Christian men of good will – while at the same time – wreaking – murder rape – torture – starvation – terror – and endless agony of millions of children – is a demonic Godless unconscionable crime of incomparable proportions in the annals of recorded history! It is a gigantic hypocrisy and cruel mockery of the teachings of Christ unparallelled in our history. Can you no longer understand the truth?

THIS and ONLY this – might show some genuine repentance for the monstrous evil blasphemy we have committed and perhaps 'invite' Christ and His blessings once again to this modern Godless Sodom Gomorrah that WE by OUR FREE WILLS have created. Otherwise we are a nation – eternally damned by our unspeakable crimes – to be relegated to the trash heap of history is inevitable. I speak the truth.

Continue with our haughty stiff-necked arrogance and we WILL be damned!

AUGUST, 2010
AMERICAN BAPT-DUH ZIONISTS – THE OTHER "SONS OF THE DEVIL"

I believe it is high time I cleared the air on the issue of what the Bapt-duhs have done to my country. They are not the only one who mock the teachings of Jesus – but they are by far the largest and the worst. I believe that they are the most evil entity in America today – as they virtually alone have enabled our Jew occupied nation to wage unlimited serial wars of totally innocent people for the SOLE purpose of the greater glory of the greatest eternal enemy of all decent mankind – THE JEWS!

All that ANY American would need to do to understand how rancid and putrid the Bapt-duhs are is to listen to the demonic fat pig who is their leader and Satanic inspiration. He is of course hate-meister John Hagee – a disgustingly obese glutton whose claim to fame is war mongering for the Jews and getting as many of the 50 million of these bovine red-necks as possible to sell their souls to Satan and cruelly mock the teachings of Jesus. In that respect – Jew hit-man – racist – bigot – demon – mass child killer Hagee has found fertile ground for hate peddling with the pasty-faced putty-brained red-neck, feeble minded, retarded, comatose, phlegmatic Bapt-duhs!

Anti-Christ wanna-be Hagee constantly harps on his 'Stand For IsraHELL' rallies – BUT – I have yet to hear him mandate a 'Stand For What Christ Stands For' rally. He not only insults our Lord but insults the people who ostensibly stand for Christ by leading them into committing murderous horrors totally offensive to what Christ would do. It has been proposed that a litmus test for human stupidity is a person or group so stupid that they do not even realize they have been mocked.

Their idiocy is, and always has been unrivaled! I can still remember from some 60 years past that as a Catholic Christian I was actually asked if Priests had cloven hooves and did we really 'worship idols'. These abusive affronts were not done as friendly jests – but were actually believed by these witless morons! Today – that SAME insufferable evil level of doltishness – if not stopped – will foment the inevitable destruction of America by their Jew masters. Ignorance kills!

Bapt-duhs have already caused more innocent civilian human suffering destruction terror and evil by their criminal ignorance – than ALL lives lost and shattered in Vietnam and Korea COMBINED! REMEMBER – war criminal mass murderer George Bush could NOT have been able to wage wars against Afghanistan and Iraq – resulting in the cold-blooded murder of over two million innocent civilians – MOSTLY CHILDREN – and the destruction of tens of millions of homes schools hospitals and utilities – and the creation of millions of terrified civilian refugees – without THE APPROVAL OF THE DAMNED IGNORANT EVIL BAPT-DUHS!

This criminally ignorant breed of bovine scum is, in at least one aspect, even more evil than the Jew. The Jew at least makes no bones about his hatred for Christ. The graphic proofs of this truth are so legion I could write a lengthy essay on the topic.

The Jew in his most 'UN-holy books slanders our Lord as a "BASTARD" – a sorcerer and worse. The Jew cruelly mocks His blessed Mother as a common "WHORE". I have both read and heard (on their History Channel) both these putrid Jew blasphemies. The Jew terrorists –(their so-called IDF) routinely shit and piss on Christian Bibles as well as Islam holy books in Palestine. These barbaric acts of hate are common place and can easily documented – EVEN ON VIDEO!

The Jew so hates ANYTHING Christian that he will go to ANY end to blaspheme Christ – Christmas – Christianity and all things associated. Who do you think has been behind the removal of school prayer – or Nativity scenes- or even using the word Christmas at Christmastime? This – was only an ice cube from the tip of a 'Jew iceberg' of blasphemies and constant attacks against Christ in our Christian nation – enthusiastically approved by JEWS and not JUST Zionists.

BUT – all that TRUTH having been revealed about the conduct of Jews – one must then fully realize that the level of HYPOCRISY of the Bapt-duhs is BIBLICAL in scope and FAR surpasses even that of the Jews.

Just spend some time as a fly on the wall in a Bapt-duh 'church' – if you can call this evil place a house of worship. Worship of the DEVIL perhaps – but certainly not Christ – or Jaysus! As they call him. You will hear their head demon (pastor) pontificate on the evils of drugs and alcohol – of the evil of killing babies – or the sins of adultery – or the evils of theft – or the vileness of lying – or even the wickedness of homosexuality as "an abomination in the eyes of God". BUT STAY TUNED as the worst is yet to come.

Then the diatribes on the evil of the Islamics will spew forth with a vitriolic hatred seldom heard in mixed society. There will shrill pleas to support the Jews in IsraHELL – and even louder rhetoric mandating the murders of millions of Arab people (who have incidentally never done us any harm) The vehemence and fury of the contemptuous screed for war and killing and destruction these hateful people have is classic demonic evil. Their capacity for hypocrisy is dazzling!

They worship the very people (Jews) who so cruelly and openly and relentlessly mock our Lord and His blessed Mother in their filthy Talmud– yet they damn the innocent people (Arabs) whose holy book speaks in highest regard, love and praise For Christ –Mary and Christians in general. These are NOT opinions. They are verifiable truths known to ALL honest educated persons on earth! BUT – just present these truths to one of these imbecile Bapt-duhs in his 'Synagogue Of Satan' and you will suffer a hail of insults threats and profanities seldom heard even in a biker bar!

Think I exaggerate? Why don't you contact Phoenix minister Chuck Carlson of operation 'Straight Gate/We Hold These Truths'. His associates have continually been insulted threatened mocked and attacked outside these Satanic Bapt-duh false churches. Their crimes? Providing FACTUAL evidence – SPEAKING GOD'S TRUTH – and promoting peace – not war – PERIOD! To add insult to injury – a local rag newspaper – the Phoenix New Times – apparently leftist and Jewish – did an article on Chuck Carlson that was slanderous and libelous. He is one of the finest decent truthful moral educated people I have known in many years – and only scumbags would bash a man of his unquestionable character and courage.

Stupidity! I have never encountered a more abysmally and criminally ignorant – frighteningly ignorant people than the Bapt-duhs – hence their new given name. There is NOTHING 'Christian' about these scurrilous trash. Their association of the name our Lord next to that filthy profane term of Zionist – as in "Christian/Zionist" – is not only the ultimate oxymoron – it is pure blasphemy.

The instant they allowed the Demonic Jews to infiltrate and demonize their church with the filth of Zionism – they abandoned Christ forever! They have become soulless cruel vicious sadistic murderous hateful slanderous lying reprobate Godless hypocrite Pharisees no less damned by God than those who had Christ murdered.

The Jews they worship as 'God's chosen' routinely break every Commandment in the Holy Book. You name the evil – I'll show you where the Jews are. Jews as a race are a despicable people. They are world class liars. They are ALWAYS at the head of ALL Abortion movements. They are ALWAYS leaders in ALL homosexual/ pedophile activities. The Jew is always profane and blasphemes God at EVERY opportunity (ALL of the filthy dialogue and ALL of the damning of God you hear in movies is created and by and approved by JEWS!) Usury and cheating are Jew traits since the time Jesus kicked over the gambling tables in the Temple and are identified as Jew stigmas even today.

Murdering people for body organs – white slavery – pornography – drug dealing – money laundering – fraud schemes- real estate swindles and a hundred more sins are ALL associated with Jews since and before the time of Christ. There is not a school child above the age of twelve world wide who does not know this fact! Good Jews? BULLSHIT! DOUBLE BULLSHIT! ALL of the truly 'good' Jews – truthful – compassionate – brave – selfless – moral – kind – responsible – Godly – that I have know in my LIFE – here and abroad – would comfortably fit in one SUV.

YET – the code of life for the Arab specifically prohibits ALL of the above evils and true Islamics adhere to that code, whereas Jews violate it with a VENGEANCE here in America and in IsraHELL! There are literally hundreds of whore houses in Tel Aviv alone. There are none in Gaza. I witnessed Jews especially teens CONSTANTLY drunk in public in Hebron – in Bathsheba – in Eilat –Tel Aviv – all over – screaming horrible hate blasphemies against Christ and lionizing mega-traitor Jonathon Pollard. You don't see this disgrace in Palestine. IsraHELL has one of the highest abortion rates in the Mid East. The Palestinians don't even have a word for abortion in their language. I can do these comparisons point by point but you get the idea. Remember – I have BEEN THERE – SEEN THAT.

Jew parents teach their children to hate – to cheat – to lie –to Gentiles or Arabs- that money is their god – that being wealthy is their goal in life – that ONLY Jew life is precious – that there are TWO moral standards – one for Jews and another for everyone else. REMEMBER – BEEN THERE – SEEN THAT – HEARD THAT – EXPERIENCED THAT.

The Bapt-duhs are the MORTAL enemies of every TRUE Christian in America and on EARTH – for that matter. These brain-dead ignorant scum are responsible for the murders of over TWO MILLION TOTALLY INNOCENT CIVILIAN HUMAN BEINGS – SO FAR! They can NOT

Be reasoned with as they have no brains and no souls no integrity and no honor. They are total hypocrite moron scum and will eventually cause the destruction of our entire nation as they lead us headlong into another inane meaningless WORLD WAR! The BEST case scenario will be that we may escape total nuclear destruction by an angry world that has had enough AmeriKan aggression – but end up with an even more totally destroyed economy and martial law.

Remember this if you have Bapt-duh moron for a neighbor. Be he White or Negro – He is your MORTAL ENEMY! He is a partner of Satan and is the MORTAL ENEMY of your children. He is the Harbinger of Death and destruction. He is the dupe, shill, puppet, ally of the anti-Christ. DON'T ever forget that fact or it WILL cost you EVERYTHING!

He – the Satanic worshiping Bapt-duh fool – is an army for Satan that is 50 million strong and when he has outlived his usefulness as the useful idiot army for the Jew's endless serial wars – and betrayed ALL of America and the rest of the free world into Jew hands – he will be liquidated along with the last remaining TRUE Christian as has been the goal of the Jew since day one. He IS your MORTAL enemy and if left to his evil agendas – he WILL be the cause of your DEATH or ENSLAVEMENT.

The ONLY winner of this next global war – unless they are exterminated – will be IsraHELL and the Jews. ANYONE not understanding that CRYSTAL CLEAR FACT by THIS LATE DATE – is your mortal enemy by default. I wish to God it were not so – but you KNOW I am right!

If you don't have the courage to stop the Jews – stop their useful idiot imbecile brain-dead Bapt-duh allies – NOW – before they lead us into an insane war ONLY for the benefit of Jews that will be the spiritual economic moral and Constitutional end of our Republic forever! Let them know your disgust anger and revulsion at their insane conduct.

Short of violence – attack them any way you can – boycott them socially as the immoral pariahs they are. Treat them worse than like street filth. These rancid pukes are the one who will get your sons killed in these for Jews only wars – and eventually the whole family – when they finally cause the big one!

It is 'in your face' CLEAR ! Can anyone today possibly be so stupid as not to see?

AUGUST, 2010
THE MATRIX CRUCIBLE – REDUX OR – WHAT THE DEMOCRATS BELIEVE, DON'T BELIEVE, AND SUPPORT (by a former Democrat)

PROLOGUE: This was written about 8 years ago when there still was somewhat of a true 'Republican Party', and the putrid scum known as Bill Clinton had recently been the 'Coward-In-Chief' for the preceding disgraceful 8 years. The Jew had not yet gained total domination and total occupation of America and the Democrap Party seemed as if it could not possibly get any more immoral treasonous and Godless. But be of good cheer – and do not despair – as things WILL get worse.

Today there IS NO Republican Party and Barack Obama is simply a 'third term Bush Presidency. As impossible as it seems – the Demoncrap Party has sunk even lower morally – what is left of REAL American patriots is now what I term – the 'indigenous American political Diaspora , leaderless, Party-less, clueless and unorganized – Christianity has been virtually totally destroyed from within (the Bapt-duhs being the primary contributory element).

We as an occupied nation of collective 'goy' detainees are well on our way towards the trash heap of history – thanks to a mass cataclysmic epidemic know as 'Stupidiculosis Gravis Terminus'. This is 100% fatal – not to be confused with the more benign 'Ignoranticulosis Vulgaris' – which if is what you have, and you read my stuff regularly and let your brain absorb its healing qualities daily as a prophylaxis – you CAN be cured of 'IV' and inoculated against the fatal 'SGT'.

STOP smiling! This isn't funny – this is some serious shit!

"God help us" ! Really? God WHO? The TRUE Christ we allowed the Jews to throw out of our schools – our Congress – our courts – our entertainment – and now our churches? (READ: Jew infused Synagogues of Satan)

If I added the evils of the Demoncrap party SINCE the original writing – it would (A) fill a ten gig disc and (B) the toxic fumes of the additional evil would probably be a serious health hazard just to read!. Just add what has happened in the past 8 years prior to this mega list of evil and you will have a fairly accurate picture of what was the refuse dump of America for at least the past 40-50 years IS – in reality.

The war criminal Bush era is a whole different set of revolting evils of the Godless hypocrite totally Jew dominated totally destroyed Republican Party – as evil or worse than the Dems.

I spent a LONG time as a Democrat and there is not a living man who knows their TRUE EVIL NATURE better than I. It is the only organization I had been involved with at that time of my life – that I felt disgusted about being associated with as time went on.

I challenge any person to substantially invalidate ANY of the following facts – and – since I wrote this expose' – that foul organization has become SUBSTANTIALLY more evil. LOOK!

FACT: Virtually EVERY homosexual child molesting pervert organization in the US supports the Democrats. (there are literally hundreds of these organizations)

FACT: Virtually every leftist [Marxist, socialist, communist, Maoist] group in the USA supports Democrat 'values' – as well as THE Communist Party itself!.

FACT: The Communist Party has officially endorsed Democrat political candidates for decades.

FACT: Virtually every pervert, criminal, drug dealer, porn king, atheist, Marxist, baby murderer and traitor supports the Democrat Party.

FACT: The Democrats booed and humiliated our American Boy Scouts as they carried our nation's flag at the recent Democrat National Convention.

FACT: Virtually every Communist and homosexual organization in America had a delegate at the recent DNC

FACT: Virtually ALL the homoerotic filth, graphic violence, foul language and mockery of God and Christian principles from Hollywood, is a product of supporters of the Democrat Party

FACT: Destruction of the family unit and tireless mockery of family values and patriotic symbols such as our flag and our National Anthem is a major project of the Democrat Party.

FACT: Al Gore – who would be 'king' – was a close friend [as was his pro-Communist Senator father] of America's most notorious communist traitor and country seller – Armand Hammer

FACT: William Jefferson Clinton is a traitor (by definition), a liar of dazzling proportions, an adulterer, a blasphemer, a coward and a murderer of such large numbers of innocent human beings as to exceed Hitler's victims by hundreds and hundreds of percent.

FACT: Janet Reno – our Democrat Atty. General, is a notorious sex pervert, child hater and God mocker. This proven deviate signed the death warrants for 69 innocent people shot and burned alive in their own church. Twenty-six of those murder victims were innocent children and infants! Her venomous hatred for Christian principles was legendary -ESPECIALLY HER HATRED FOR CHILDREN – as this sex deviate pervert is childless. Her vicious deportation of a helpless innocent Cuban child BACK to a Marxist hellhole – against his DYING father's wishes is completely typical of immoral Godless Democrat mentality.

FACT: The Democrat administration committed high treason [trading nuclear secrets for campaign donations] and has endangered the lives of virtually every man woman and child in America. In case you have forgotten – the PLA of the Peoples Republic of China has reminded us that they not only have the ability to destroy us – but the desire to do so as well. These friends of Clinton are the remorseless animals who murdered over 60,000,000 of their own civilian population – and murdered 1,000 students in Tiananmen Square, for their 'treasonous' expression to want democracy in their communist hellhole.

FACT: The Democrat VP candidate – the Jew, Joseph Lieberman – was officially ex-communicated from his Synagogue by a formal rabbinical court of elders. Why? Because Lieberman has consistently mocked God and sacred Jewish law – for one reason – approval and support of the infanticide of millions of innocent children.

FACT: The reason most people don't know most of these outrages by the Democrat/Marxists is because the news media in America is now controlled almost 100% by Democrat /Marxists/Jews.

This fact has been PROVEN a hundred times over – again and again. These vital damning absolutely true facts will never be seen in any major newspaper. Democrats hate the truth.

FACT: The Marxist/Democrats have worked tirelessly to divide this country by creating class envy and encouraging welfare for the lazy and violent minorities that support the handout welfare mentality of their Marxist/Democrat Party. This technique is E-X-A-C-T-L-Y what the Russian street trash under Lenin was encouraged to believe and therefore revolt against anyone who had worked for and earned more than they did. It in fact did succeed in 1917 and continued to grow like a cancer, killing all in the way, subverting entire countries to slavery with the aid of traitors like Gore's friend Armand Hammer. Check ANY reputable history book.

FACT: Some 53 members of our Congress – ALL DEMOCRATS! – are card carrying Marxists/Socialists. This is classic as you can get for an act of treason! Any one who has a computer and can access the Web can see this.

FACT: There were 45 Communist goals that appeared in our congressional records (Jan10-1963). Today, all but 2 or possibly 3 of those subversive goals have been accomplished. EVERY SINGLE ONE OF THESE TREASONOUS aims were by and large, legislated, supported, endorsed and made possible by the Democrat Party. I will personally award $100 to anyone who can accurately disprove my statement!

FACT: One of those 45 treasonous goals to destroy America (#15) was: "To capture one or both of the political parties in the US". Just in case any reader really still thinks that all this is coincidence!

FACT: The ACLU is in fact the 'legal arm of the Communist Party. Their goal has been and still is – victory of Communism in America [as stated by it's founder- Roger Baldwin] – is always supportive of the leftist Democrat Party.

FACT: Destruction of our Constitution has been a long time goal of Democratic administrations. The Marxist country seller, Clinton (literally) – has stated he wants to "re-invent" our Constitution. Confiscation of private firearms has been the historical prelude to virtually EVERY SINGLE instance of a free people being enslaved. Russia, Germany, Cuba and China are but a few victims. Yet – the Democrats work tirelessly to put decent law abiding Americans (that is over 98% of us) in that same mortal danger.

FACT: Only the Democrats have had a House Speaker that OPENLY supported Marxist terrorist organizations. Actually – not just one – but TWO! (Tip O'Neil and Jim Wright)

FACT: According to the liberal Newsweek – and US News & World Report – Democrats were found to be far less moral than their Republican counterparts on issues of traditional family values and ethics. (Can you imagine any better reason not to associate with a Democrat?)

FACT: Four other major late 60's Communist goals of the CPUSA were achieved in the late sixties by Democrat legislators

FACT: In 1987, four more of the Communist Party's major goals were accomplished by aid from Democrat legislators! [stop SDI – stop all nuclear testing – stop aid to anti-Communist freedom fighters in Nicaragua – and ratify 'SALT II' treaty with the USSR]

FACT: In the 80's, the Chairman of the Communist Party here announced for the first time in decades that the Communists would not run their own candidate for President. Reason? Simply because of the similar agenda of the Democrat Party. (more details listed later) Since that time, the Communist Party has not only run no candidate of their own – but has vigorously thrown their weight behind the Democrat Presidential candidate! Talk about TREASON!

FACT: The Democrat Party is home to several PRACTICING homosexual perverts – Members of Congress!

FACT: Their hatred of God and Christian values is so strong that the Democrats have initiated EVERY legislation to force Christian Americans to pay for the murder of innocent children. [Check the voting records of the past dozen 'Congresses']

FACT: A Democrat President is the only one in our once proud history to have demonstrated AND organized a Marxist demonstration for the DEFEAT of Americans in battle against a real enemy. Clinton HIMSELF called for the defeat of the servicemen of the United States – but after all – remember his comment: " I loathe the military". REMEMBER – DEMOCRATS ELECTED this reprobate coward who never served in uniform!

FACT: The IPS (Institute for Policy Studies – America's most powerful think tank) sends advisers ONLY to Democrat legislators.

FACT: Democrat legislators are the only open supporters of homosexual pervert 'rights' [read; the 'right' to seduce our innocent children and promote their filthy lifestyle to our youth]

FACT: Democrats ALWAYS side with the Marxists in 'revolutions'

FACT: DEMOCRATS are ALWAYS the ones to mock and criminalize traditional family values.

FACT: The appointed Democrat Cabinet is predictably almost always comprised of Marxists, homosexuals, lesbians and atheists.

FACT: Democrats OPENLY support – and are OPENLY supported by Hollywood trash.

FACT: ALL leftist, foul-mouthed, lesbian, homo radio/TV personalities are Democrats.

FACT: MOST ALL Democrat sponsored 'think tanks' and 'foundations' are leftist.

FACT: Democrat legislators have taxed the American middle class almost out of existence.

FACT: Democrats strongly support the anti-God filth of the Marxist dominated NEA. They have controlled our public education system with their anti-God – anti-Christian – anti-family values – anti Constitution amoral decadence for almost four decades. An ENTIRE generation of America's youth – or possibly two – have for the most part, been 'dumbed down' – violent – disrespectful – druggies – leftist revisionist indoctrinated and taught to hate everything that our forefathers held sacred. These 'academically challenged' morons will never be productive decent citizens.

FACT: Democrats are responsible for making God and His law illegal in our schools and other public places.

FACT: Democrats appointed ACLU MARXIST Ruth Bader Ginsberg to the Supreme Court where she is empowered to mock Christianity, enforce the seduction of our children and destroy our Constitutional rights

FACT: Democrats have appointed the enemies of all that is decent and good in America as powerful cabinet heads. Carol Browner – brutal Marxist EPA 'land grabber head. Madeline Albright – leftist UN ambassador. Donna Shalala – Head of HHS with her Nazi style openly anti-Christian policies. Council of Economics advisor, Stalinist Laura Tyson. Just to name a few

FACT: Democrats control the anti-God, anti-Constitution, pro-homosexual/lesbian perverts NEA. If you want to read something to really make you sick – take a look at a few issues of the NEA's leftist 'Goals 200'

FACT: Democrats refuse to prosecute the criminal – Hillary Clinton for crimes too numerous to mention. Among them is support for Congressionally identified Latin-American terrorist groups. Direct violation of HB 1710 (S.390) Jan 1995. Title 3- section 301 – subsection 'D' paragraph '2'

FACT: Democrats are so greedy and immoral that they have legislated recent laws to prevent parents from leaving what they have worked for their whole lives to their children after their death.

FACT: Democrats are SO SIMILAR in their treasonous goals to the objectives of the Communist Party (the over-throw of our Constitution by any means) – that Party HEAD Avro Kusta Halberg, (AKA-Gus Hall), when asked by the national press as to why the Communists declined to run candidates for President/VP for the first time in decades – answered with this chilling and sobering statement: " Since the goals of the Democratic party are now so progressive, we feel that for us to field a candidate would be redundant". ["progressive" is a Marxist 'buzzword' indicating being in accord and conformity with Communist objectives and ideology]

Democrats are so close in their goals and beliefs to the Communists that the last dying wish of the Chairman of the Communist Party (CPUSA) was that the Democrats defeat the Republicans in this past critical Presidential struggle. It should be noted that this treasonous reprobate admirer of 'Comrade Klinton', – 'Secretary General' Hall was in fact a convicted felon – a treasonous criminal – having spent 8 years in federal prison for high treason and sabotage. Many Democrat Congressmen OPENLY mourned his passing.

FACT: Finally – the Democrats are 'world class' murderers! The accurate definition of murder is to take an innocent human life with malice and forethought. ABORTION IS LEGALIZED MURDER BY DEFINITION – PERIOD! To put the evil of these monsters in understandable perspective – consider these facts: In the war of independence, there were 2,500 Americans killed. In our civil war, there were 498,000 Americans killed. In WWI, 116,000 Americans lost their lives. In WWII, 407,000 of our countrymen were killed. In Korea, we lost 54,000 sons. In Vietnam, There was a loss of life that was over 58,000 souls. All together, a total of a little more than 1.1 million Americans were killed. That is a total death count for ALL major wars in the USA since our birth over 225 years ago!

In the Democrat/ACLU sponsored 'War Against Children' since 1973 – there have been over THIRTY EIGHT MILLION AMERICAN BABIES MURDERED! At LEAST 15,000,000 (FIFTEEN MILLION) of these cold-blooded pre-meditated murders was authorized and approved by our very own 'coward-in chief' William Jefferson Clinton – truly a world-class murderer. Historically this American butcher outranks Hitler's deeds by over ONE THOUSAND PERCENT – and is close to the horrific record by Mao and Stalin. The enormity of the horror and mass murders committed by the Marxist Democrats in this country has seldom been paralleled in history.

This disgraceful list could go on and on almost endlessly.

HERE is a list of ideals principles Democrats do NOT believe in.

Democrats DO NOT TRULY believe (obey) in God –

they do not believe in Family values –

they do not believe in a wholesome atmosphere for our children –

they do not believe in the sanctity of human life –

they do not believe in self-determination and responsibility for one's own actions –

they do not believe in the validity of our Constitution –

They do not hold any value for integrity, truth or honesty –

They do not believe there are any moral absolutes –

They do not believe in American culture and tradition –

They do not believe in patriotism and most every other

principle which decent Americans have honored since our country was founded — OR they wouldn't be so loyally supporting

the kind of filth that was so typified by the Klintonista administration.

HERE is a list of concepts ideas that Democrats DO believe IN

Democrats DO believe in promoting homosexual perversions –

They do believe that the Holy Bible is a fairy tale.

They do believe that the Ten Commandments are at best 'The Ten Suggestions' – They do believe that character or integrity is archaic idealism –

They do believe that "CHARACTER DOESN'T COUNT" – as nationally televised at their last national convention.

They do believe that our Constitution is vague, ambiguous, outdated and invalid –

They do believe that the 'end justifies the means' –

they do believe that 'it's OK if you don't get caught' –

They do believe in a big government that suckles them from cradle to grave – they do believe that the people are here to serve the government, and not vice versa.

Additionally, they do believe that frogs, tadpoles and owls etc. are more valuable than human life –

They do believe that our Boy Scouts are bigoted because they will not accept the ungodly nasty, filthy conduct of homosexual perverts in their ranks –

They do believe that honesty, reverence, respect and humility are signs of weakness – they do believe that society has a RIGHT to murder their own children BUT that to take the life of a cold-blooded murderer is illegal.

Not surprisingly – they do believe that they have a 'RIGHT' to a nice home (at some working person's expense) –

They do believe they have a 'RIGHT' to take money they haven't earned –

They do believe they have a right a RIGHT to have preferential treatment if black, Hispanic or homosexual –

They do believe that Communism [AKA Socialism] is an acceptable alternative for Americans –

They do believe that they have a 'RIGHT' to steal a man's income to use for grossly immoral purposes – regardless of how offensive it is to Christians.

I haven't covered it all – but you get the idea. The Democrat Party is a garbage dump for half the scum in America. It is a 'clearing house' for our national 'detritus'.

AUGUST, 2010
"YE ARE OF YOUR FATHER, THE DEVIL"–JESUS TO THE JEWS JOHN-8-44 (PART 1)

No truer words have ever been spoken by any man in any time in history. Jews are the essence of hatred cruelty malice and evil – like no other creature on the planet. Theirs is the kingdom of hell on earth – an evil so putrid – as only the Jew can be.

I have warned and pleaded with my 'neighbors' to heed the truths I witnessed in that God forsaken land of demons thieves liars cheats fornicators murderers and sadists. If any of my readers still respect my truth and passion for justice to give a voice to the voiceless – to defend the defenseless – to stand for the right against the greatest evil on earth – then promise me this:

You WILL without fail -pass this ugly horrific cruel event onto as many people as you can – each and every one of you. I have been inside this damned stolen lair of filth and depravity they call IsraHELL and there is no goodness in it -only evil upon evil upon evil. What you will witness here is the True face of the Jew.

The incomparable sadistic remorseless cruelty of the Jew -here for all to see is his TRUE and eternal nature – from his evil demonic children to his highest leaders – demons ALL! What barbaric soulless cruelty you see here is played out a hundred times a day in that filthy place. I have witnessed worse with my own eyes.

I swear on the altar of God that I will fight these filthy animals till my dying day with the only weapon the Jew fears the most TRUTH! OVER AND OVER AND OVER – no matter how many times it takes until these ugly truths light up their filthy lies for the whole world to see. And when I am gone – there will be more warriors of truth to take my place until mankind is finally rid of these filthy scum Jews!

Let me clearly state what you will see here. A young family desperate for water took some water for their survival from IsraHELL. These greedy selfish Jews decided to punish the parents and took then away – more than likely to never be seen again – beaten starved and tortured in some stinking Jew dungeon as was commonly done to Palestinians when I was there. An entire family separated and destroyed because they were thirsty and 'stole' drink of water – PLAIN WATER.

I saw plenty of 'settler' (read: LAND THIEVES) water used for watering entertainment purposes and even swimming pools – ALL on STOLEN land. The Jew is so filthy nasty greedy stingy

Godless evil that he will murder a family dying of thirst just for sadistic meanness. The terrified child you see will become an orphan – as his parents will undoubtedly be murdered. The terrified helpless orphaned child as I witness so many times in IsraHELL will without doubt be shot in the street like an animal as these Jew scum routinely do – BELIEVE ME! BEEN THERE in ISRAHELL – SEEN THAT!

I implore you – pass the evidence of this horrible daily crime on to EVERYONE YOU KNOW. You will be doing God's work against the Devil and his children. There is NO crime so brutal and Godless and NO criminal so evil and sadistic as a man who will terrify and brutalize a innocent child as you see here. That poor unfortunate waif KNOWS he will probably never see his family again.

These Jews are the ONLY culture on EARTH who do these demonic deeds to helpless people. In the name of He who loves and protects children – EXPOSE THESE JEW DEMONS TO THE WORLD – SO THAT JUSTICE WILL BE DONE AND THEY WILL FEEL THE WRATH OF GOD!!

REMEMBER What you see here well – as the Jew will do this to YOUR family and YOUR children once he gains total control of America and stamps out TRUE Christianity with the help of the useful idiot Bapt-duhs. How much more suffering and evil and lies and insanity do you need to see? I know them well They ARE – THE SONS OF SATAN!

HERE IS THE TRUE FACE OF THE CRUEL GODLES JEWS UNMASKED:

To anyone who has the SLIGHTEST reservation that virtually ALL Jews (collectively) are not the spawn of the Devil and are the most sadistic evil heartless soulless filth to ever inhabit Planet Earth – OPEN THE FOLLOWING!

AUGUST, 2010
"YE ARE OF YOUR FATHER, THE DEVIL"–JESUS TO THE JEWS JOHN-8-44 (PART 2)

Here is the second part of the exposure of the well documented incomparable war crimes of the filthy Godless sadistic remorseless demonic Jews – and there will be MORE – MUCH MORE. There are now so many well documented chronicles of Jew atrocities and cruelty and sadism that I can do this every week for a year and not scratch the surface.

It is interesting to note that using only Goggle – a Jew source, incidentally – AND searching ONLY for YouTube films of these atrocities – I was able to find over three thousand pieces of video evidence. IF – one considers that fact that the Jew will censor the worst

Additionally – the reader must understand that only a tiny fraction of these crimes will ever be filmed to begin with – perhaps 3-5% at the most, according to human rights groups and my own experiences inside Palestine. Keeping those facts in mind – it is only logical to assume that the vicious cruelty and sadism you may witness here – revealed only by the grace of God – is but a drop in a bucket of a sea of tears of suffering and misery caused by he most horrible remorseless filthy demonic subhuman animals I have ever witnessed or even heard about in my entire life. They are in fact the world's 2nd largest largest institutionalized terrorist gang of savage criminals – second only to the US ARMY.

Here are but a few of the crimes committed by these soulless demonic creatures. Some of these types of war crimes – although not the exact ones – I have personally witnessed when in IsraHELL during 1989.

You will witness the TRUE cowardly face of the Jew – who always attacks and terrorizes the helpless – the defenseless – the elderly -the child – the infant – the injured – the hospitalized – and the civilian. The Jew military is very brave when confronting a terrified crying 5 year old – or an old woman – or unarmed farmers as you will witness.

The Children of these "sons of the Devil" are as evil cruel and sadistic as their parents. As a world traveler and foreign diplomat I have experienced dozens of ethnicities. ONLY the Jew teaches their children to hate non Jews from the cradle to the grave. The Jew child is a cruel and inhumane and sadistic as the worst German or Soviet or Japanese prison guard ever documented. I have seen this putrid conduct – emblematic ONLY of Jew children – and you will see it here.

The Jew by nature is a filthy animal unlike ANY other human on earth! "The IDF the most moral army in the world" to quote IsraHELL Defense Minister Ehud Barak. REALLY? Well then lets take a look at what JEWS consider acts of morality. When I identify the Jew as filthy – I MEAN FILTHY! Jew soldiers regularly defaecate (SHIT) on property in places they have vandalized like dirty little hoodlums. These "MORAL" animals committed these unthinkable acts while I was in Gaza. They actually shit on holy books and vessels in Christian and Muslim places of worship. These desecations were common then and continue to this day -obviously with FULL approval of their "MORAL" commanders.

Why don't you ask Jew filth like Charlie Rose and Larry King and Sarah Silverman and 'KISS' and Eisner the dozens of other Jew 'entertainment' why they never speak of these outages committed by their 'chosen' people on their shows?

You will see the cowardly Jew shot a blindfolded handcuffed child for the crime of carrying the flag of his country INSIDE HIS COUNTRY. You will witness weapons long outlawed by the Geneva convention used to murder unarmed civilians I their own cities. You will see Jew TV making fun of the civilian peace activists they had just murdered in cold blood on a mercy ship with medical supplies. You will see Jew children joyously excited at the prospect of butchering and burning alive- Lebanese Christian children. You will see truths about the TRUE nature of the Jew that will literally churn your stomach.

Share these truths – tell everyone you know meet and speak with the TRUTH about the Jews. What you see here is wake up call to what the Jew has in store for you and remember that a significant percentage of these victims of Jew sadism are TRUE Christians – not this rancid dispensationalist Bapt-duh garbage who cruelly mock or Lord 24-7 under the tutelage of Godless hypocrite monsters like Hagee and Evans.

And remember – do NOT buy this 'good Jew – bad Jew crap'. I met lots of Jew in IsraHELL – in homes – on buses – in coffee chops – at tourist sites – in stores – at social gatherings – military and civilian. They were ALL supportive of their 'moral IDF'. 'GOOD' and 'JEW' are oxymorons. A TRULY good Jew is an enigma. I have had the good fortune to know a handful in my lifetime and treasure their friendship. ALL the 'good' Jews in America probably wouldn't fill the average high school football stadium. You will NEVER find a truly good and brave Jew who is NOT persecuted by 'his own' when he takes a stand for goodness justice and truth. Heaven forbid should he decide become a TRUE Christian!

The 'problem' is NOT primarily ZIONISM – it is Judaism. Jews against Zionism are still virtually ALL in support of IsraHELL – BAD JEWS!. 'Jews for Jesus'? The biggest Jew fraud yet – BAD JEWS – I know them well and so it goes. Remember the truths you have learned here. When you take a course in school and fail to learn and get an 'F' – you must take the course again. If you fail to learn these lessons about the Jews – the consequences are much more severe – you lose your freedoms – your country and your souls!

IsraHELL – JEWS – the Devil – evil – death – destruction – misery – suffering – hopelessness – anguish – fear – Godlessness – filth – depravity = all one and the same. THIS is what the JEW is all about and has been since day one.

Learn well and teach your children well – or be one of the victims you see here.

If you have not seen enough after this – I have about three thousand MORE!

SEPTEMBER, 2010
9-11 — LEST WE FORGET!

Yup – it's here with us again – the date we reserve to blame Arab people for a Jew crime. But heck – so what. We have been doing that for close to a decade now. It is just another opportunity to show AmeriKan stupidity and kiss Jew asses! Think you know STUPID? Just go to one of those New York hate rally sites and SEE the mobs of troglodyte Neanderthal creatures there that make the Geiko cave-man look like the Greek god Apollo! Talk about scummy looking street trash human garbage! Remember the movie 'I AM LEGEND' with Will Smith? Remember the horrid creatures? THAT is what these 'Nu Yoker' thugs look like – not like anyone I hang with.

These mobs come complete with their Jew inspired racist hate signs about some 'mythical holy' place where an atomic bomb was detonated by backwards Arab people. And since the term 'GROUND ZERO' is reserved only for the detonation site of an nuclear weapon (a true WMD) – it must have been an atomic bomb and not an airplane crash. But after all – to the amoeba brained thugs you see in these Jew inspired hate films – facts are not important – so – here's YOUR SIGNS – MORONS! Terrorists? I know what REAL terrorists are – first hand – and they are here – many in 'Nu Yok' – many in the White House – many in Washington – a lot in the Bapt-duh 'Synagogues' and a WHOLE LOT in uniform. WE are the terrorists!

As incredible as it seems – even after YEARS of irrefutable evidence and testimony and corroboration from demolition experts – scientists – chemists – eyewitness – historians – forensic experts – nano-contamination specialists – law enforcement officials as well as highly self-incriminating testimony of suspects and IsraHELL leaders – Mossad agents and other pertinent sources – we have fools who persist in believing the 'third world joke' deceptions of discredited leaders of two of the world's most corrupt and most criminal regimes.

The internet is BLOATED to overflowing with videos of contradicting testimony from some of the worst war criminals frauds liars and country sellers in American history! These lying putrid war criminal murdering scum include George Bush – Colin Powell – Dick Cheney – D. Rumsfeld – and C. Rice – have been caught RED HANDED LYING. Until these rancid mega-war-criminal treasonous lying greedy scum are brought to justice and HUNG – there will never be peace. Are you also listening – Obama – Jew puppet imposter? See this 'MUST SEE' – and listen to the chimp face's very last comment. Very revealing of his TRUE lying demonic nature.

These lies have already needlessly cost almost FORTY ONE THOUSAND killed or seriously injured American sons (Iraq/Afgh. Aug. 2010) – SO FAR! Hardly mentioned are the THREE HUNDRED AND TWENTY THOUSAND U.S. BRAIN INJURIES. Even more alarming and revealing are the 18 vet suicides a DAY! That is almost ONE AMERICAN SON per DAY feeling such guilt and remorse for their barbaric crimes against defenseless helpless mostly children civilians – that they simply could not cope with the horror any more! Multiply that by 365 times 7 years and you realize what the GUILT of their psychopathic criminal conduct has done to our children – not just alcohol or drugs.

Why shouldn't they feel terrible guilt. After all – their rapes thefts looting and murders were based on baseless LIES told by our Godless soulless war criminal leaders. TWO MILLION TOTALLY INNOCENT IRAQI AND AFGHAN CIVILIAN LIVES – MOSTLY DEFENSELESS CHILDREN have been murdered in cold blood! WHY? – all for the greater glory and security of the Jews in IsraHELL of course. NONE Of these people were ever ANY kind of mortal threat to ANY American. Myself and ALL decent informed responsible Americans knew that fact since day one! The Jews have been committing false flag deceptions since I was a child. Its a Jew thing. The motto of their country is: "BY DECEPTION WE WAGE WAR". Even the Lord condemned them as demonic liars in the Gospel of John.

REMEMBER – Christ did NOT condemn the Arab people – he condemned the JEWISH people!

Any part of that truth you don't understand – Hagee – you demonic lying fat slob!

But the horrors don't stop there. The injured are conservatively estimated at EIGHT to TEN million! The homeless created by our insanity and evil – at least twenty to thirty million! Remember – these were ALL civilians – mothers – fathers – sons – daughters – grandfathers grandmothers – aunts – uncles – babies. ALL human beings who dreamed loved hoped worked and wanted only to be free and ALIVE – no different from ANY American family – other than probably being more moral and more willing to put their lives on the line for THEIR country! Hell – Americans won't even turn off our Jew-tubes for a hour to learn protect and defend.

NOW – we are on the verge of yet ANOTHER Jew inspired war based on lies and criminal stupidity – all for the the glory of the evil people who have been busy destroying our nation morally and economically since the first day these evil scum set foot on this blessed land. THIS war WILL be different. It will without doubt involve several other nations and the ONLY winner – like vampire vultures be waiting to reap the spoils of the carnage – are the JEWS! We KNOW they are evil, since Christ condemned them as the 'SONS OF THE DEVIL" they are!

It will without doubt – be the end of the America my generation knew and loved. There will be REAL 'ground zeroes' and death unlike anything in your worst nightmares – and the Jew and his useful idiot puppets – BOTH Democrat AND Republican will have been the harbingers of death. REMEMBER THAT WELL when the bombs begin to fall – ON US!

Forget 9-11? HELL no. NEVER FORGET what the Jews did to America on that day. These evil demons have lied and cheated and stolen their way at our expense ever since they created their filthy demonic worship of Satan. Next time you see a Jew on the street – in your school – in your business – anywhere – I want you to REMEMBER this day and what the Jews and the scum that sold their souls to them – did to us – this day – before they do a false flag disaster again! Do something responsible to make us TRULY proud to be Americans again.

DECEMBER, 2010
"IT'S NOT A 'HOLIDAY' – STUPID – IT'S A HOLY DAY!" OR – HOW THE JEWS STOLE CHRISTMAS – PART 1

Well here we are once again – rapidly approaching the Jew's favorite time of the year. Is it because of sleigh bells and Christmas bells and the sound of laughter and joy in the air?

NA – it's because of the sound of cash registers opening and closing – the sweetest sound to the ear of the Jew, is heralding in another year of a goy buying frenzy to satisfy the Jew's hottest sales period of the year. I used to believe that the Jew hated Christmas time and Christian tradition. He still hates Christian tradition and his arch enemy Jesus – but since he worships only money – he has discovered how to get rich off we stupid goy, AND destroy the true spirit of Christmas at the same time.

When I was a child – Christmas was ALWAYS referred to as – what it was – the highest holy day for all Christendom – a time for family to join together – a time for reconciliation and forgiveness – a time for hope and joy and peace – good will and rebirth of the Spirit of Christmas as celebrated by Christians worldwide. People greeted people in the street – in stores – in ALL environments – even strangers with "MERRY CHRISTMAS" or "a joyous Christmas be unto you".

It was NEVER – EVER identified as a secular holiday or with the now almost obligatory Jew secular greeting of "HAPPY HOLIDAY". This sinister transformation did NOT happen by chance. It has long been part of the Jew agenda of gradual but eventual total destruction of ANYTHING and EVERYTHING related in ANY WAY to Jesus Christ. The ultimate Jew wet dream is a CHRISTLESS CHRISTMAS! The Jew has been the driving force in the removal of prayer from our schools – the removal of the laws of God from our courthouses – the removal of the traditional nativity scenes from ANY and ALL public view.

Did you see a Nativity at the White House last year? No ?– but you DID see that awful demonic Jewish devil's pitchfork – a gigantic menorah two stories high – tended to by some of the most evil Christ hating Jews on earth – the Chabad Lubavitch – invited by Obama's Chief of Staff – mega evil Jew, and son of a murdering terrorist – Rahm Emanuel.

These Chabad Jew creatures – racist and religious bigots, lump non-Jews together with "pigs, snakes and worms, and all other 'creatures' that are unclean and unfit for consumption". THIS FILTH is what the Jews think of Christ.

I'll wager that you haven't even heard of these Jew cultists before – YET – they have now brazenly stolen the Christmas spirit from we cowering ignorant Christian 'sheep' and now totally dominate OUR LAND with Jew cult symbols of violence hatred and killing. To have a Jew cult symbol (Hanukkah) displayed at the home of the American 'First Family' – and celebrating the Jews killing non – Jews is the ultimate slap in the face to Christ and Christians. The Jew has finally succeeded in totally trashing OUR heritage and perverting our most high holy day into a secular Jew money making scheme. Is NOTHING sacred to us today?

If one looks for the meaning of Christmas in the Jew owned 'Google' – you will find more negative feedback than goodness – virtually nothing about hope peace and good will with the birth of the Lord at the centerpiece. You will see a LOT about the 'fat man in the red suit' and flying reindeer and how discredited Christmas actually was.

It is for the most part, identified as a secular "HOLIDAY" of man – in true Jew style – and not a Holy DAY of God. Here is the exact title of the site as it appears: 'Christ, Claus and the evolution of our most popular holiday.' In other words, to the Jews who run this site – the most important meaning of Christmas should be 'Santa' and HOLIDAYS – and the money it brings in.

Now the plot thickens as the Jew closes in for the kill. I can confidently defy the average American to experience the traditional greetings of "MERRY CHRISTMAS" outside of his own family circle once he steps into the 'outside world'. Virtually every place one goes this time of year but especially towards the end of December – as Christmas draws near – you will hear and see only the Jew instigated and mandated "HAPPY HOLIDAYS".

Why? Because the Jew wants us sheeple to conform to his secular Godless mentality – by transforming Christmas into a collective drunken secular material shopping orgy achieves his goal of relegating the true spirit of the event, in the mind of the Christian – to be accepted as less spiritual and more material so that the TRUE meaning – helping the poor – reinforcing our faith – giving our ourselves and our time to the less fortunate – will fade from our memories and blend into this Jew vision of a 'Christ-less Christmas'.

This will of course have as much sex and violent entertainment as possible with the timely release of the latest blockbuster mindless meaningless shallow entertainment – endless parties – sports events and glamour vacation 'HOLIDAY SPECIALS' – HOLIDAY this and HOLIDAY that!

There is a 'cartoon' version of the Nativity created by the all Jew 'Adult Swim' channel that defies human decency in its level of blasphemous hatred for Jesus and His mother. Only a Jew could create such vile rancid filth knowing that his Jewish audience would fully approve. It is an example of the same kind of hatred by the Jew for Christ and Christmas

http://www.milkandcookies.com/link/83383/detail/

This nation was founded upon Christian principles – PERIOD! That is NOT an 'opinion' – conjecture – sentiment – theory – notion or impression. IT IS A FACT and the WELL documented uncontroversial arguable evidence is LEGION!!

IF – you in fact DO want your traditional Christmas values – those STOLEN by cunning JEWS – back – I will show you how.

You see – the Jews don't just want children to believe that Christmas is really all about flying reindeer – or a gluttonously obese jolly toy maker or what I'M going to get as presents(the spirit of GETTING) or bright lights and glittering shiny stuff or endless parties and fairy tales. He wants us ALL to play in a make believe world of self – indulgence and ironically also forget about one child in particular. The one in the manger some two thousand years ago who was to change the world forever!

This article is being done in two parts. In part one I have outlined the Jew goals of the total destruction of Christmas or what I call OPERATION CHRISTLESS CHRISTMAS.

It is amazing how these immoral bad people are so willing to support cultist purveyors of hate and violence like Hanukkah or modern tribal multicultural racist nonsense like Kwanzaa or Gaia earth goddess new age mythology – yet they are eager to trash Christ and Christmas – to please the Jews.

In part two – I will have compiled a substantive file of the offending merchants – TV adds – magazine adds – shopping malls – restaurant chains etc., who have collectively agreed in joining the Devil and his Jew allies for the de-Christianization of Christmas. You will soon know them all by NAME – so that you may admonish rebuke expose and 'take to task' these Jew and Jew supportive Christ haters.

After catching a major greeting card maker using the same rancid mentality – I got him to admit that the reason was that he saved a few pennies by not differentiating Thanksgiving or Kwanzaa or Hanukkah from Christmas. 'HAPPY HOLIDAY' covered it all. What a cheap shallow hypocrite scumbag. Is THIS then, what America and Americans are setting as moral example for their children?

This is a REAL war folks – with REAL enemies – the outcome of which will decide the future of your children and their children and perhaps beyond. These creatures do NOT understand civility or decorum – morals or honor. They never have – they never will. When I was growing up in a more moral America – these rancid social degenerates were where they belonged – where they could not corrupt our children – UNDER ROCKS!
I'm sure you have your own ideas but I will supply some time honored field-proven methods short of violence that WILL get their attention. See you in a couple more weeks with the list of offenders. If you wish to contribute to the effort – please send in your own observations of the Jew 'HAPPY HOLIDAY' offenses. I will use them.

The propitious event – the auspicious occasion – the felicitous happening – is CHRISTMAS! It is NOT a 'holiday' to fatten your wallets – it IS a holy day! The more you Jews mock the sanctity of this blessed day – the more you will seal your ultimate fate. You have no idea of the magnitude of the hostility you are creating upon yourselves by your conduct. You WILL murder Christ over and over as there is only hatred and arrogance and greed in your hearts.

DECEMBER, 2010
"IT'S NOT A 'HOLIDAY' – STUPID – IT'S A HOLY DAY!" OR – HOW THE JEWS STOLE CHRISTMAS – PART 2

Here it is – the part two of the Jew hate fest of Christmas. Read ALL of it – please! Here is where we take names and expose the filth whose goal it is to make Christmas nothing less than lengthy sex booze and drug Hedonistic secular irreligious orgy for our shallow materialistic secular Christ hating Jew occupied country. And all this time you believed it was a GRINCH that stole Christmas!

AND – if you would rather celebrate the MOCKERY of Christmas with the Jews in Hollywood – here is an actual add by Universal Studios where YOU – MR. Judized American -can indeed take you whole Godless family to a special bastardized pagan substitute for a true Christian Christmas – here is a grand opportunity.

CELEBRATE GRINCHMAS with the JEWS! (their actual add)

"Grinchmas" time is coming to Universal Studios Hollywood as The Entertainment Capital of L.A. prepares for a lively holiday season with the Grinch, his faithful dog Max, tons of fresh snow and a "Whoville Whobilation" at the original movie sets where the classic "Dr. Seuss' How the Grinch Stole Christmas was filmed."

Be sure to also celebrate the new age nonsense of Quanza – then go the White House and continue the mockery of Christ with a celebration of Jew Hate at the now annual Hanukah (which has now replaced the the two century old tradition of a Nativity) – be sure to attend one of Zionist hate- meister Hagee's Synagogues Of Satan (Bapt-DUHS 'church) IsraHELL first presentations – then top it all off with 'GRINCHMAS' in Hollywood – party on till you drop – BUT be sure and avoid ANY involvement with traditional Christmas foolishness lest your children be mocked at school as being backwards – or retarded – or not cool, or "DISRESPECTFUL OF ATHEISTS AND JEWS" (as CNN Prime News anchor declared this week.) as the general mood swing appears to be going.

Ask ANYONE my age if they EVER heard the cheesy shallow demeaning disrespectful Jew term "HAPPY HOLIDAY" substituted for MERRY CHRISTMAS when they were children.

"AH – so what's the big deal they say". Well people -let me TELL YOU WHAT THE BIG DEAL IS! The Jews who occupy and control EVERY ASPECT of EVERYONE'S Life in this nation today have the collective unified composite agenda of achieving two goals for their tribe of murderous vampires.

#1 It is the Jew's by FAR biggest opportunity to make themselves even richer than they are. I been told that Americans spent over four hundred BILLION dollars on Christmas related items in 2009. Christmas expenditures are traditionally counted starting in December. Since over 90% of ALL advertisers in America today – from restaurants to car dealerships to Jewelry to posh travel vacations sponsor adds that TOTALLY and AGGRESSIVELY negate Christ and Christianity from 'Christmas shopping' we can safely say that these are either Jew owned or Jew mentality owned businesses.

#2 This Jew dominated 'HOLIDAY SEASON' is also the catalyst which numbs the naive American public into at least passively being accomplices in the rancid act of transforming the true TRADITIONAL Christian spirit of Christmas – as the celebration of the birth of our Savior – into an orgy of buying and partying and jamboree saturnalia which has absolutely nothing to do with the Birth of Christ. The emphasis is NOW on make believe fat men in red suits (national Santa contests) – make believe flying reindeer (new popular blockbuster movies) – make believe singing rodents (the Seville Chipmunks) – make believe elves (more blockbuster movies) – dressing up ' HOLIDAY' trees – endless rock and roll songs which emphasize everything imaginable BUT Christ – 'Holiday parties – which are 100% social events of gluttony and excess which emphasize fun fun fun – but NEVER ever the slightest regard to Christ (imagine a birthday party where there is NO honored 'birthday' guest – this is EXACTLY what we now do in Jew occupied AmeriKa).

Mistletoe– stockings – bright lights – sleighs on roofs – snowflake and tinsel – cookies for Santa – Boats loaded with lights (in water front communities) – modern 'carols' which NEVER have the name Jesus in the script and TV extravaganzas with sensuous women displaying ALL of their ASSets in the most TITulating manner for every mother's son to 'admire'.

ALL of these are greatly welcome in the new improved Jew occupied America – since all are secular and nothing to do with the celebration of the birth of our Lord. AND- of course Nativity scenes are totally illegal and not PC – unless of course they are Comedy Central Jew approved like the following 100% Jew created and Jew produced piece of work: Place courser on text then press 'Ctrl' and left click to open site. A MUST SEE!!!!!

http://mcooki.es/83383.com

What you will see here is what Jews think is humorous. Remember – this filth is rated #1 in popularity with your Jew TV watching teens. I suggest that you show this popular Jew cartoon to your youngest children. If it does NOT traumatize them – and ESPECIALLY if they ALSO think it is 'funny' – it is too late – and their souls already belong to Satan and his children- the Jews. I'm dead serious – It is the PERFECT litmus test for just how far gone our children are AND how close the Jews are to achieving their goal of the total destruction of Christmas in America.

Speaking of children – just how old are 'children' supposed to be today before they are told that Santa is a make believe children's myth – and WAS a band aid for parents to deal with the TRUTH they feel a 5 or 6 year old may not be able to intellectually grasp.

I understand that – BUT when I was a child NO adults continued this nonsense long INTO ADULTHOOD – with Santa contests – Santa themes at every ADULT Christmas party – show girls dressed like strippers in female Santa costumes. Once we kids were of age of reason and beyond Easter bunnies and tooth fairies we were old the TRUTH It was to celebrate the birth of baby Jesus – and the beginning of our spiritual lives. NOBODY beyond 8-10 years old still begged to "sit on Santa's Christmas lap at a department store.

If YOU STILL DO NOT BELIEVE THE EVIL THE JEWS ARE CAPABLE OF – GO BACK AND SEE AGAIN – THAT MOCKERY OF CHRIST AND MARY IN THE COMEDY CENTRAL CARTOON – SEE IT UNTIL IT SINKS IN EXACTLY WHAT THEY REALLY THINK OF US AND OUR CHRISTIAN BELIEFS. MAKE SURE THAT YOUR CHILDREN SEE IT! They WILL remember it the rest of their lives. Remember – it was Jew produced financed and scripted by the Jew Comedy Central channel to corrupt YOUR children!

These are THE SAME Jews who have sent YOUR sons – not theirs – to murder over TWO MILLION INNOCENT CIVILIANS – MOSTLY CHILDREN – all for the greater glory of IsraHELL

These are the SAME JEWS who murder in cold blood – thousands of innocent helpless children – many who are also Christian – at the same time we celebrate Christmas – the Jew celebrates the slaughter of innocents! I didn't just READ or HEAR about these demonic sadistic barbaric horrors against children – I WAS THERE as a WITNESS!

Look for the American supported IsreaHELL Jew to be supported by virtually ALL Jews here – as they slaughter even more civilians during Christmas week just to show their hatred of Christ and Christians!

TODAY – the 'Nu Yok' Jew Madison Avenue Add men teach us that Jesus was a bunch of childish make-believe crap and that Santa is for real – and he helps sell everything from Cokes to shiny Cadillacs! TODAY – we have reverted into the Jew mindset that Christmas is nothing more than a 'HOLIDAY SEASON' to party – get drunk – act like children – BUY – BUY – BUY – all the latest electronic gadgets – and did I mention PARTY PARTY PARTY!

(I CLEARLY remember the disgraceful conduct of President George Bush drooling at these high kicking Vegas style 'Santa helpers' at a nationally televised 'Christmas at the White House' special for the 'first family'. There was some bizarre clown freak with 'Ronald McDonald' red hair howling a rock-n-roll version of Jingle bells as the heart pounding beat incited the show girls to display as much T&A as the law would allow to our foot stomping drunk drooling coward -in Chief – 'Conscience Of the Nation' REMEMBER THAT ONE?)

Today – in our 100% JudAized 'Tel Aviv West' – one RARELY sees ANY Christmas advertisement on TV or billboards or magazines that does NOT does FEATURE – LOTS Of flying fat men in red suits – elves – flying reindeer – colored balls – LOTS of Jew produced violent Horror films (just in time for XMAS) psychedelic snow flakes – tinsel – bright high tech lights and ANYTHING but the MENTION or SIGHT or ACKNOWLEDGEMENT of Jesus. – GET IT YET?

Here is something I found on the net that I thought clever and insightful for wayward Christians – especially for our Jew influenced children AND adults STILL ACTING like children!. Thank you Cindy!

Why Jesus Is Better Than Santa Claus

* Santa lives at the North Pole – JESUS is everywhere.
* Santa rides in a sleigh – JESUS rides on the wind and walks on the water.
* Santa comes but once a year – JESUS is an ever present help.
* Santa fills your stockings with goodies – JESUS supplies all your needs.
* Santa comes down your chimney uninvited .... JESUS stands at your door and knocks, and then enters your heart.
* You have to wait in line to see Santa ... JESUS is as close as the mention of His name.
* Santa lets you sit on his lap – JESUS lets you rest in His arms.
* Santa has a belly like a bowl full of jelly – JESUS has a heart full of love.
* All Santa can offer is HO HO HO – JESUS offers health, help and hope.
* Santa says "You better not cry" – JESUS says "Cast all your cares on me for I care for you."
* Santa's little helpers make toys ... JESUS makes new life, mends wounded hearts, repairs broken homes and builds mansions.
* Santa may make you chuckle but – JESUS gives you joy! That is your strength.
* While Santa puts gifts under your tree – JESUS became our gift and died on the tree.

So then – here is but a smattering of the merchants who are Christ hating Jew mentality worshipers or their useful idiots. I had to do the work all myself so the list is far from complete. Remember – these putrid Christ haters are fervent Comedy Central fans – who think it is cool to replace the over two century tradition of honoring the Christ Child (whom they call a BASTARD) and His Holy mother (who they call a WHORE) with that horrid Jew Devil's pitchfork (the filthy Chabad Lubavitch menorah) that now dominates and replaces the Nativity on the White house lawn. Check it out yourself!

What you do is your business – but for ANY TRUE Christian that still has the backbone to defend the faith of our fathers and forefathers – Below are some suggestions – but if you are too ashamed and spineless to call yourselves Christians – don't even bother – as it will make the Jews happy to see your noses rubbed in Jew shit – because THAT IS EXACTLY WHAT THEY WANT TO SEE YOU DO – be so cowardly that you are too afraid stand with the Lord against those who He CLEARLY accused of being the CHILDREN OF THE DEVIL.

DO THIS: I would notify them in the most UNPLEASANT -AND VOCIFEROUS of terms that they have mocked and blasphemed your most sacred personal convictions and that you will NOT ONLY never spend one dollar of your budges with them – BUT – that you will ALSO make it a PERSONAL RIGHTEOUS MORAL VENDETTA by informing every family member friend associate club member co-worker – AND CO-RELIGIONIST of their putrid insulting treatment of your beliefs.

AND – if you are really serious about taking your country and values back from these scum – that you WILL take notes of ALL advertisers who make such filth possible – AND that you will do the SAME with ALL of the advertisers – ONE BY ONE – LOUD AND CLEAR. If you did just a fraction of what I suggested – you WILL get your respect and dignity back from these low life Godless scum – and THAT IS EXACTLY WHAT THEY ARE!

ALL of the following services, retail stores, dealers, restaurants entertainment, news, media and more – went out of their way to let us goy KNOW that they thought Christmas is a bunch of crap – and Christians were easy targets to slander mock and insult – by demeaning our most sacred HOLY DAY – into a less than wholesome lustful 'pleasure of the flesh' (drunkenness – sex – spending sprees – gluttony) filled HOLIDAY.

There are shamefully – HUNDREDS of these rancid people who have given Christ the 'finger' – and you can make your own list from every day experiences – If you can stomach it.

I'm one guy. I have done what I can. What I have suggested has HISTORICALLY worked everywhere in the free world where people UNITE – and COLLECTIVELY stand up for themselves and their families and their honor had the guts and integrity to NOT have their noses collectively rubbed in Jew shit any more.

The rest is up to you. Live on your FEET – with dignity and conviction and honor -or live like spineless worms on your knees – servants of the Godless Jews for the rest of your shallow lives.

To those who still believe and still keep and defend the faith which has sustained this nation since its infancy – and who still have the courage honor and integrity to take back what has been rightfully inherited from our Founding Fathers -AND cruelly and cunningly stolen by the Jews and their 'shabbus goy' (useful idiots) allies —-

I wish you and your loved ones a Merry and JOYOUS and PEACE filled Christmas in honor of the remembrance of His birth and life and wisdom.

JANUARY, 2011
THE DIFFERENCE BETWEEN DEMOCRATS AND HUMANS

At the recent shooting in Phoenix – A Jew Congresswoman named Gabrielle Giffords was critically injured. One of her homosexual pervert aides assisted her (among her many typical rancid Jew blasphemous Christian hating policies – she vigorously supports special consideration for Homosexual perverts).

He – the pervert- traveled with her in the ambulance to the hospital and held her hand. He later stated that even in critical condition – she responded by squeezing his hand – presumably in gratitude -since she could not speak.

How very sweet and touching. A Jew who has been responsible for the murders of countless innocent babies who had no voice in the death sentence imposed upon them by Giffords – who ALSO supports the worlds largest institutionalized terrorist organization – the IDF child killers of IsraHELL – who ALSO supports the filthy lifestyles homosexual perverts like pedophiles such as her aide – reaches out to show her appreciation to this unrepentant practicing sodomite anal sex deviate by the only way she can communicate at that critical moment – by squeezing his fingers.

He – the pervert – supports his Godless baby murdering benefactor – because SHE legislatively and personally supports his openly Godless unrepentant filthy lifestyle – GET IT?

I'm touched to tears. An immoral God mocking woman with the blood of countless innocent babies and civilians on her hands – who has ALSO sold her fellow countrymen out to her nation of 1st loyalty – our mortal enemy- IsraHELL – in a silent unspoken bond of mutual acceptance with her anal sex loving pervert employee in their mutual support of each others horrible filthy Godless conduct.

Got the picture? This is the Demoncrap wet dream of ideological Godless Marxist sentiment at its very best.

Hold that image of mutual adoration of two people whose rancid and criminal and treasonous conduct is universally despised by ALL decent people of the world.

Now picture this: A different act of one human being squeezing the hand of anther – even though no words are spoken – ostensibly the purpose of which – the act – in both cases – was to communicate 'humanity'.

The scenario is a surgical theater in a hospital where a unique event is about to unfold. A surgeon is finishing a delicate in vitro surgical procedure on a 21 week old human baby (who is – by the way – alive and well today).

He has just successfully completed a spinal bifida correction on the child and is about to close the sedated mother's uterus as this incredible event is captured on film. The child reaches his tiny perfectly formed hand through the incision and grasps the surgeons finger as if in recognition of merciful service he has performed.

Never seen before – this amazing event is frozen in time by USA Today photographer for all posterity to bear witness to the miracle of human life – a tiny miniature human hand in all the perfection in every detail as granted by God reaches out to squeeze the finger of the physician– unable to speak – as if to acknowledge that he is indeed a human being – grateful for the gift OF LIFE – instead of the cruel knife OF DEATH – of the abortionist.

Two examples – both with similarities – but only one – a thing of beauty wonder and mystery. Only ONE – that could inspire the irrefutable presence of God – of tenderness – of goodness – of something clean wholesome and inspiring – a reason for hope, in a world gone mad – filled with hate evil and violence and hateful evil and violent PEOPLE.

The other example was a drama enacted by a pair of reprobate filthy animals – both unrepentant – both VOLUNTARILY leading horribly sinful self-ingratiating lifestyles.

Both of these evil people placated each other for the simple reason that their only common ground was the mutually accepted evil and wickedness their daily conduct entailed. Nothing more. Birds of a feather. Evil loves the company of evil.

To see this inspirational marvel – open the site below. If you are a human being – you will be inspired touched and reinforced in the righteousness of your faith.

http://www.theroadtoemmaus.org/RdLb/21PbAr/LifHlth/Abrt/Newborn.htm

If – on the other hand – you are Demoncrap – like Obama – you will NOT see a human hand – you will NOT even see a human being – you will NOT see the creation and majesty of God – you will see only sentimental rubbish – as a people whose heart will remain as hard and black as it has always been and incapable of seeing beauty and purpose in the universe – living a lie to it's fullest – less than useless – soul-mate to your Jew masters.

That is because you have aligned yourself with the Devil and his ilk. He has many names and many appearances. In this place we once knew as America, one of his disguises are known as the DEMONCRAPS — puppets of the Jews – who are "sons of the Devil".

They are soulless creatures who have renounced humanity Godliness goodness virtue wisdom and truth and refuse to become human beings.

We were ALL born with a 'blank slate' – ignorant and clueless. The difference between Demoncraps and humans is that Demoncraps are satisfied with living stupid AND dying stupid on their knees. Humans are willing to make ALL the sacrifices to live FREE on their own two feet – to stand tall in the light of truth wisdom honor and righteousness – as MOST OF US – once did!

JANUARY, 2011
WHY CELEBRATE MARTIN LUCIFER KING JR. DAY? AN ENDLESS DISGRACE TO ALL DECENT AMERICANS - LOSE IT!

Well here we are once again – on the verge of disgracing everything this nation once stood for – by actually honoring one of the biggest pieces of crap to ever disgrace it. We do NOT have a holiday for the FATHER OF OUR OWN COUNTRY – YET – the alien Jews who occupy our sacred land, have managed to FORCE their 2% – with their Godless Christian hating lying Marxist Godless filth and endless wealth – on the three hundred million REAL Americans – to celebrate the treasonous sinful blasphemous lust filled life of total puke (its a Jew thing).

WHY? Simple – the Negro voting bloc is the largest and therefore the most potentially powerful entity for promoting any and ALL evil Godless pro-Marxist treasonous destructive legislation of which sole purpose is the empowerment of the Jew agenda of the MORAL and ECONOMIC destruction of America. This has been accomplished for the most part through the total Jew control of the Democrat Party. Over 90% of all Jews in this country support the Democrat agenda. Over 90% of the least intelligent and least responsible and least moral Americans ALSO support the Democrat Party. These are the low-life imbecile Negros – low-life imbecile Hispanics and the low-life imbecile rednecks *(no – I didn't say good country folks)*.

This collective mob of lazy non-productive brain-dead 'eaters' – are ALSO VOTERS! The Jew utilizes them to follow their bidding as easily as a gang leader controls his thugs – by promising ANYTHING they want to hear. Not surprisingly – these social detritus morons are the backbone of all labor unions as well. They are incapable of independent thought – or of reason – or of wisdom or rational conduct – just intimidation and violence! I'm not just talking about things I have read or heard. I was talking about PERSONAL REAL LIFE EXPERIENCES! Jews are smart – we 'goy' are stupid.

King and his ilk are of that mentality. I remember it QUITE WELL! There was much talk about non-violence – while IN FACT – His entire LIFE was dedicated to violence hatred divisiveness and antagonism. The violence associated with his Marxist agendas ended ONLY after his death!

Sometimes he would 'talk a good talk' – BUT – he NEVER EVER – 'WALKED THE WALK'

His wife was DEEPLY involved with terrorist organizations – and I mean REAL TERRORISTS – almost exclusively MARXIST ones – as identified by our own State Dept. publications (I have the names and pages)

His own son MLK Jr 111 – in an interview with the ultra-liberal Rolling Stone – CLEARLY and OPENLY admitted that he believed that his father was killed because of his open support of COMMUNISM – America's mortal enemy! Hey – give the kid credit. At least he was honest. (Yup = got that issue as well – wanna see it too?)

King never held a real 'job' in his life, like us poor fools struggling to support and raise families

King was a thief – a liar – an adulterer – a whore monger – a drunkard – a draft dodging coward – a blasphemer – a traitor and a fraud! 'Dr.' King INDEED! He was an illiterate Ebonics speaking dullard who STOLE his Doctorate because he was too stupid and too dishonest to EARN IT! He was no more an 'ordained' representative for Christ than his Godless Christian hating idols – like Ho-Chi-Minh. He CRUELLY mocked and twisted the teachings of Christ.

Every American has seen that sound bite on TV where King shows his inability to even speak basic English properly. Remember this one:" WE BE ON DA MOOB NOW!" that low-life guttural street babble was supposed to mean; "WE ARE ON THE MOVE NOW!" 'DR.' king MY ASS! Give me a break! Even 5th grade inner city black children speak better than that!

This man was a total disgrace – ESPECIALLY – to every decent black man woman and child. To name a street or building or civic center in honor of this piece of crap was an OUTRAGE to decency civility and honor! A George Washington Carver Plaza or school? I support that 100%!

He was given a rare opportunity to shine in greatness modesty truth justice courage and honor and trashed it by living a lie – and a life filled with lust lies deception Godlessness dishonor and hypocrisy. He singularly did more damage to race relations – created more hatred and distrust for blacks – more divisiveness in his lifetime by his rancid conduct than if he had purposefully planned to do so. King was a BAD EVIL man NOT because he was a Negro – but because his heart and soul and conduct were EVIL!

For the very fact that he WAS a Negro – whether a fair or unfair observation – he should have if ANYTHING – striven to set an example of his daily conduct that was not of a perfect person but simply above reproach. That basic exemplary life was not only easily achievable as has been exhibited so many times by other Negro personalities – but mandatory for such a leadership AND religious position as King had ensconced himself. I had the opportunity to spend 3 days in close contact with his #1 Lt. of earlier campaigning days – The Rev. Joseph Lowery. I will say only that I could not have been less impressed with the sincerity and wisdom of that man.

THE FOLLOWING ARE FACTS REGARDING THE MARXIST GODLESS CRIMINAL TREASONOUS AFFILIATIONS OF THE JEW CREATED SUPPORTED FINANCED 'DR.' MARTIN LUTHER KING JR, HIS WIFE, CORETTA SCOTT KING, AND THE MARTIN LUTHER KING CENTER

(1) FACT- King's wife, as head of the King Center is on the advisory board to CISPES – an FBI identified subversive Marxist terrorist support group

(2) FACT – King has a huge and complete file made by several agencies, including the FBI. These records are to be kept secret from the public till the year 2027

(3) FACT – King had associated with great numbers of KNOWN communist party workers. time after time, with FULL KNOWLEDGE of who he was dealing with and after being advised by numerous people, even within his own ranks, to disassociate himself.

(4) FACT – King had Hunter Pitts (Jack) O'Dell, an identified member of the Communist Party Central Committee, on his staff.

(5) FACT – King publicly supported communist front organizations such as the W.E.B. DuBois Clubs, the Draft Resistance Union, the Communist Party USA,and the Revolutionary Action Movement.

(6) FACT – King openly supported the draft card burners whose cowardly actions undermined and betrayed our fighting sons in Vietnam. REMEMBER – this was NOT the insane madness in Iraq waged against innocent civilians on behalf of our Jew masters in IsraHELL. There were REAL COMMUNISTS. Communism in all of its 'isms' were – are – and always WILL Be the immoral soulless MORTAL enemies of free men. I know their ilk better than most men – up close and personal – FROM REAL LIFE.

(7) FACT – King, an ordained Baptist minister, had routinely consorted with prostitutes in extended drinking bouts.

(8) FACT – The 30 million Negroes in the USA today, are the most important racial target of the Communist Party USA, and infiltration, exploitation, and control of this large group ranks as one of the _party's_ top goals.

(9) FACT – A known close friend of King's was James A. Dombrowski, a known Communist active as early as 1935 when he helped launch a joint Socialist-Communist united front movement in the South.

(10) FACT – King sent members of his staff to attend a dinner sponsored by the National Committee to abolish the House Un-American Activities Committee.

(11) FACT – King's SCLC (Southern Christian Leadership Conference) did in fact support the Marxist Sandinistas in Communist Nicaragua.

(12) FACT – ALL of King's living lieutenants now command important positions, and ALL of them support Marxist ideology in one way or another.

(13) FACT – Virtually all the racially associated rioting and bloodshed ended with King's death. – Just a coincidence?

(14) FACT – King was a lecturer at a notorious communist training center – The Highlander Folk School- and more importantly – King KNEW THIS WAS A COMMUNIST CENTER.

(15) FACT – A leftist organization supported till this day, by the King Center has advocated unilateral disarmament by the USA – This is of course the ultimate Soviet dream.

(16) FACT – This same organization (IPS), so fervently supported by King's current movement, have recommended that the USA end aid to the anti-communist forces in Nicaragua, end all military aid to the anti-communist forces in El Salvador, withdraw all military presence in Honduras, deny any military support to Democratic Costa Rica, and normalize relations with Communist Cuba.

(17) FACT – The Martin Luther King Center has praised those terrorists who murdered six Americans in El Salvador,(June 85), murdered two helpless and wounded American servicemen (Jan 91), and publicaly _rejoiced_ at the death of our Challenger Astronauts.

(18) FACT – King's writings have received great praise from communist party leaders in Moscow.

(19) FACT – King supported the Viet Cong, and was a great admirer of Ho Chi Minh.

(20) FACT – King denigrated our country by calling us _the greatest purveyor of violence in the world_ – almost the exact words used against us by Cuba's Castro, Nicaragua's Ortega, Libya's Khadafy, PLO's Arafat etc,etc.

(21) FACT – The official US communist newspaper, the _DAILY WORLD_, on April 4, 1970, announced that King's radical anti-American book would be made available for distribution in every part of the Soviet Union.

(22) FACT – The preface of this book was written by Henry Winston, a chairman of the Communist Party USA.

(23) FACT – In a speech, shortly before his death, King ACTUALLY CRITICIZED ANTI-COMMUNISM_ (Dr. Edward L. Nitoberg; Academy of Science – USSR)

(24) FACT – On the second anniversary of his death, the USSR published at least two biographies, identifying King as a dedicated and highly respected supporter of the international communist _party line_.

(25) FACT – The infamous 1983 King _march on Washington_ was comprised mostly of Communist party fronts, Moscow leaning groups, anti-defense lobbies, Marxist oriented coalitions and terrorist support groups,to numerous to list.

(26) FACT – Even liberal presidents Kennedy and Johnson distrusted King so much that Attys.Gen. Robert Kennedy, N. Katzenbach, and R. Clark ordered FBI chief Hoover to keep close tabs on him because they knew of King's communist conspiracy activities.

(27) FACT – Former President Kennedy personally told King (regarding King's close association with communists O'Dell and Levison) personally; _They're Communists. You've got to get rid of them_. King made NO moves to sever his ties with these two known subversive agents, even at the president's request_

(28) FACT – King's own son stated: _...he talked about redistributing the wealth and resources of this land. That's what he was killed about._ In other words, Soviet style Marxist/Leninism

(29) FACT – Entire VOLUMES of King's secret files are labeled _OBSCENE__

(30) FACT – These files are so immense, that the inventory list is over 800 PAGES LONG_

(31) FACT – Andrew Young said of Communist Party Executive Committee member, Stanley Levison; _Stan Levison was on of the closest friends Martin Luther King ever had_.

(32) FACT – FBI bureau files from the extensive _SOLO_ operation quote King as telling comrade Levison; _I am a Marxist_.

(33) FACT – King's friend, Rev. James Bevel, was quoted in the New York Times (during violence of 63) _We need an army of captains and sergeants and privates to fight the white man this summer. I want captains to march whole schools to jail after graduation._ This close King aide went on to say; _We must move to destroy Western Civilization__

(34) FACT -During the Vietnam era, King had actually compared the United States with Nazi Germany with remarks so scurrilous, that Life magazine called them _a demagogic slander that sounded like a script for Radio Hanoi._

(35) FACT – A Johnson aide compared King's files to _an erotic book_, and FBI director Hoover said _King is a `tom cat' with obsessive degenerate sexual urges._

(36) FACT – the King biography by Stephen Oates, LET THE TRUMPET SOUND, revealed that the FBI had several editions of a monograph, with still more stories about sex, Communism and embezzlement.._

(37) FACT – FBI files show what was called a _two day drunken sex orgy_ at the Willard Hotel, involving King, SCLC colleagues, and two women from the Philadelphia Naval Yard.

(38) FACT – There was an episode at a Los Angeles Hyatt House where King made filthy, explicitly sexual references to the then assassinated President Kennedy, to Mrs. Kennedy, and to JFK's funeral.

(39) FACT – A Las Vegas prostitute complained in an official report about the violence to which she had been personally subjected by the Reverend Dr. King.

(40) Fact – Assistant FBI director Sullivan indicated King was under investigation for _embezzlement, employing prostitutes, alienating wives affection from their husbands, and violation of the Mann Act_. A typical memo at the Bureau spoke of exposing _King for the clerical fraud and Marxist he is, at the first opportunity_

SOURCES

The Martin Luther King Story

The Revolution Lobby (pp. 16-26 Brownfield/Waller)

Tampa Tribune – various commentary and feature stories

CISPES literature (a Marxist terrorist support group for the FMLN)

The Columbus Dispatch (April 88)

Let the Trumpet Sound (S.Oates)

The Manateean Newspaper (Jan 84)

Communist front literature from DC (summer 86)

Rolling Stone Magazine (April, 88)

Spotlight newspaper (Oct. 83,July 84, Jan 88)

Prophets or Useful Idiots? (James L. Tyson)

Florida Sentinel (various Fall 88)

Congressional records (98th Congress, Oct.83)

Bradenton Herald (Jan.17.88)

Conservative Digest (Jan 87)

Inside FBI Files on the Rev. M.L. King (William P. Hoar)

Personal interviews with Rev.Ralph Abernathy and others

Research of 172 files on communist front groups that I keep current

THE ABOVE FACTS, ABSOLUTELY VERIFIABLE, ARE ONLY THE TIP OF THE _ICEBERG_ OF THE REVEREND DR. KING'S CAREER OF SMUT AND SEDITIOUS TREASON. AFTER GAINING KNOWLEDGE OF THE ABOVE FACTS, WITH VERIFICATION IF NECESSARY, I WOULD CONSIDER ANY INTELLIGENT AMERICAN WHO WOULD STILL INSIST UPON SUPPORTING MARTIN KING, TO BE AS UNPATRIOTICALLY MORALLY DEGENERATE AS HE WAS. HOWEVER, I WOULD HARSHLY ADMONISH ANY PERSON WHO WOULD IMPUGN DR. KING SOLELY BECAUSE OF HIS RACE, AND WILL ACCEPT NO SUPPORT OF ANY KIND FROM ANY SUCH PERSON. I HAVE SUPPORTED RACIAL EQUALITY IN THIS COUNTRY AND RENOUNCED RACISTS AND BIGOTS SINCE I WAS OLD ENOUGH TO KNOW RIGHT FROM WRONG. FORCED SEGREGATION IS, AND ALWAYS WILL BE IDEOLOGICALLY IMMORAL. ANYONE WHO HAS KNOWN ME WELL FOR ANY LENGTH OF TIME, KNOWS THAT I WILL NOT TOLERATE RACISM AND BIGOTRY IN MY PRESENCE OR IN MY CIRCLE OF FRIENDS PUBLICLY OR PRIVATELY, PERIOD_ I ALSO HOLD EQUAL DISDAIN FOR _COUNTRY-SELLING_ MARXIST SYMPATHIZERS, BLACK, RED, BROWN, YELLOW OR WHITE. THE SEVERE CRITICISM I EXHIBIT FOR DR. KING IS ONLY BECAUSE HE WAS FACTUALLY, AND IRREFUTABLY PROVEN TO BE ONE OF THE MOST ODIOUS UN-AMERICAN LEFTIST PUBLIC FIGURES OF MY GENERATION. TO FORMALLY HONOR A MAN OF SUCH INCREDIBLE IMMORALITY AND TREASON IS A SLAP IN THE FACE TO EVERY MORAL AND PATRIOTIC AMERICAN – ESPECIALLY BLACK AMERICANS. THERE ARE EMPHATICALLY AND UNEQUIVOCALLY NO RACIST INDICATIONS INVOLVED IN THE RESEARCH OF THESE FACTS, AND I WILL CHALLENGE ANY LIVING PERSON, IN A COURT OF LAW OR OTHERWISE TO SUBSTANTIALLY REFUTE THE VIABILITY, VERACITY, AND OBJECTIVITY OF THESE FACTS OR MY HONORABLE INTENTIONS, WHICH ARE SOLELY TO BRING THE TRUTH TO THE MIS-INFORMED OR UNINFORMED.

This outrage of a Dr Martin Luther King Jr. day is an abomination and MUST BE ABOLISHED if the American Negro ever expects to be held in full and equal respect by American Whites. As long as that putrid treasonous Marxist fraud is honored – the animosity will NEVER GO AWAY! MARK MY WORDS!

FEBRUARY, 2011
BRENDON LEE O'CONNELL - AUSTRALIAN CHRISTIAN HERO

I don't tag many people with the term hero because they simply don't qualify. An act of heroism entails substantial personal risk in the performance of an act which would be considered gallant selfless and noble – such as the fireman who saves the child at this own peril – or people like Brendon Lee O-Connell.

We have NO military heroes in the past decade of Jew occupation – just sick demented twisted psychopathic killers who defend only IsraHELL and NOTHING Here at home. I trained their fathers and grandfathers – when you could still thank a man in uniform for service to his country without the hypocrisy of the words sticking in your throat like rancid vomit!

Mr. O-Connell is – as you read this – just beginning the start of a THREE YEAR prison sentence for doing something which not a handful of human beings on the planet would be willing to sacrifice themselves for.

He spoke for thousands of innocent defenseless helpless children who are tortured beaten humiliated and murdered daily in Gaza by Jew terrorists. I know these Jews well and have lived among them. They are called the IDF – and by purest technical definition are the world's largest institutionalized terrorist organization.

They target helpless defenseless civilians elected officials – Doctors schools hospitals homes farms medical workers – civil servants – religious figures – humanitarians and just about anybody who can't defend themselves. They are sniveling cowards by nature as I inescapably concluded when I was training American sons to defend this land from Communist aggression during the very real Berlin Crisis of 1962. Of the companies that I served as executive offer and eventually commanding officer – and the months I spent on training committees as an instructor of basic combat skills – I personally encountered several thousand young warrior trainees.

I will tell you in all honesty that I encountered not ONE Jew. OH there were PLENTY of Jews to be found at home – bedding down our wives daughters and sweethearts – or dabbling in the 'art' of Jew 'social engineering' that has turned our nation into amorally rotted corpse. These were cowards whose family connections kept them safe at home doing what Jews do best – making money and satisfying their sexual lusts.

But I MUST digress – as you the reader must understand certain FACTS about the nature of the homicidal maniacs we know as Jews. You see -Mr. O-Connell confronted a pair of Jew sayanims – professional troublemakers – whose demonic conduct – taught to them since childhood – was hate racism and how to very skillfully appear to be the victim as you victimized innocent decent godly people. In other words – TYPICAL Jews.

These two pieces of human slime were caught red handed in lies as they attempted to spy on pro-Palestinian humanitarian groups. The filthy ugly rancid objectives of these young children of Satan will be revealed in all their ugly putrid detail later in my report. You will be shocked to learn just how low Jews in Your communities DO sink in their endless hatred of Christians and Christ and Islam and Muslims.

Here is an example of the evil that is the Jew. Notice I did NOT say ZIONIST. I'm speaking of 'everyday' Jews who infest YOUR neighborhoods. Mr. Greenberg the pawn shop owner – Dr. Mensch the Dentist – Mr. Finklestein the banker – Ms. Lipshitz the social worker – or Mr. Ekstein the Jeweler. They are all the same. Remember Operation Cast Lead – a mass civilian murder committed by the Jews on Christmas 2008?

Thousands of defenseless civilians – including hundreds of Christians -MOSTLY CHILDREN were butchered in a three week slaughter by the terrorist Jew IDF monsters using weapons long outlawed by the Geneva Convention as inhumane and barbaric – such as white phosphorous – which burns through clothing skin – and bone and has permanently disfigured thousands of helpless children in Palestine. Remember – I have witnessed the sadistic barbarity of the IDF terrorists.

In Boston – at a large civic center gathering of ALL Jews – just like your neighbors – the Greenbergs – these Christian hating monsters were actually having a rally in Jan of 2009 for their beloved IDF terrorists and to counter an outraged Gentile public. The auditorium was reportedly JAMMED TO OVER CAPACITY WITH 'ORDINARY ' JEWS – SCREAMING IN SOLIDARITY FOR EVEN MORE BLOOD OF THE CHILDREN! I remember it WELL! Shamefully disgusting! So where is the outrage against mindless sadistic brutality and pain inflicted upon helpless defenseless terrified imprisoned systematically starved children?

THAT my friends – is the TRUE nature of the Jew – hateful racist – cruel – sadistic – compassionless demons! Hell will freeze over before you will see a sizable group of 'ORDINARY" Jews convene to condemn these diabolical mass murders committed against totally defenseless starving terrified children. The Jewish people have NEVER EVER shown the slightest sincere compassion for human suffering of non-Jews – NEVER!

I have traveled to over two dozen nations over the past fifty years as a tourist as well as a foreign diplomat executing Consular duties. Of all the ethnicities and nations I experienced – none were so totally evil rancid and demonically putrid as IsraHELL and her racist Christian hating Jews.

Our lord CLEARLY exposed them over two thousand years ago as the Sons of SATAN in the Gospel of John. Two millennia and millions of innocent murdered souls later – nothing has changed – not even the names! It was the JEWS who brought mankind COMMUNISM in all of its hideous forms and the TWO HUNDRED MILLIONS DEAD. Some of my own distant relatives by marriage were among the murdered SEVEN MILLION – yet our Jew run schools never mention that REAL holocaust of innocent Christians by Jews.

I have educated the reader on some important and universally acknowledged historic facts about the uniquely evil conduct of the Jewish people for many a good reason – one being a better understanding of the persecution and false imprisonment of Brendon Less O-Connell.

They are over 99% criminals pathogenic liars racists egomaniacs and criminals in one form or another – best known for their mass murder programs – their moral decadence – their putrid business larcenous business practices and their treasonous conduct towards their host nations. The historic proofs of their endless crimes against mankind are LEGION and IRREFUTABLY TRUE!

Because of thousands of years of predictable evil conduct – and hundreds of millions of innocent human beings caused immeasurable suffering and or their graves I would rather trust a rattlesnake not to do me harm than a Jew! Wisdom and logic dictates that ALL gentiles are potential victims and would be wise to heed this learned and prudent warning.

Jews from birth are taught every evil skill known to man – deceit – fraud – larceny – usury – lying – emotional blackmail – greed – terror – extortion – racketeering – perjury – witness intimidation – corruption – sexual depravities – intimidation – desecration – treason – war crimes – blasphemies and of course mass murder. Perhaps their best honed skill is one they use 24-7 from childhood to old age – is the 'advanced' hate course they teach their children in the art of whining and and wearing a persecution complex on their sleeves as if it were a badge of honor. This is their audacity to demonize their victims and simultaneously afflict themselves (the perpetrators of the crime) as poor victims.

The Jews are the ONLY creature on earth who practice this monstrous demonic mockery of justice. Their 'inferior' Gentile victim is the evil doer and the persons who commit the crime (the Jews) magically become the persecuted ones. PRESTO-CHANGO! – like the mystery of what goes on under the magicians cloak – all realities moral values decency proprieties matters of justice are trashed in an instant in the sick twisted demonic mind of the Jews.

Here is a particularly loathsome classic example I have seen. The Jew IDF thug terrorist murders a poor pregnant Palestinian woman in cold-blood – perhaps a Christian or perhaps a Muslim. He bravely boasts to his fellow Jew terrorists – "ONE SHOT – TWO KILLS" . He has just murdered an unborn child AND his pregnant mother with one bullet. Get the picture? These godless demonic baby murdering Jew animals are so impressed with themselves and their Jew notion that it is a manly brave act to murder a helpless defenseless pregnant mother that they were actually issued T-shirts showing a screen-print of a pregnant woman with a snipers riflescope crosshair over her stomach with the caption: ONE SHOT- TWO KILLS. This obscene Jew outrage was in the news and never denied by the Terrorist IDF!

The Jew's rationalization is that the woman was his enemy – BTW – (the Jew is taught by his Rabbi that EVERYONE who is not a Jew to be a potential enemy) The innocent baby he also blew into raw meat? Well – to the Jew that was just another potential enemy. He HAD to murder them – don't you understand? They were his enemy and potential enemy. It was SELF DEFENSE AFTER ALL! They were causing him and his tribe worry and stress and anxiety by being alive! Non Jews have NO right to live near Jews. Get it?

The poor innocent defenseless helpless victims – the mother AND child were INSTANTLY transformed into the ENEMY! The poor soldier had no choice but to defend himself as the victim. Too twisted – too sick – only a psychopathic lunatic rabid mad dog could 'reason' like that! It happens EVERY DAY OF EVERY WEEK OR EVERY MONTH OF EVERY YEAR – FOLKS.

BUT WAIT – it gets even more insane. Here is an example in the United States of the same kind of sick twisted Jew only thinking – so that you understand – ALL OF THE 99+% of JEWS think this way! It is a wicked evil demonic Talmudic racist supremacist mindset that has been taught to these evil people for millennia. It is what CLEARLY and ARGUABLY sets them apart from the human race!

A Rabbi – a Jewish 'holy man' was arrested for the torture rape murder of a 5 year old child in Florida some years ago. This monster hired himself a 'good Jewish lawyer' of course. This sick depraved filthy animal rape murdered an innocent helpless child – cuts her open in a ritualistic demonic act – disembowels her and strangles her with her own guts and threw her lifeless mutilated little body over a highway viaduct.

NOW here comes that sick Jew mentality of demonizing the victim and victimizing the poor Jew. The Jew atty actually pleaded that his client wasn't completely responsible for what he was doing – WHY?– because 'the little girl had taunted him sexually by lifting her little skirt'. If the rapist had been an Arab man – he would have been lynched by an angry mob of rednecks – but if you are a JEW – I guess it's OK. Do you get it YET? This IS the way that Jews think! There is not a race or ethnicity on EARTH that could suggest such putrid rancid filth – only a JEW. GET IT?

Hold those ugly facts in mind – because you will need to realize that the filthy little racist Marxist Godless scumbag psychopathic punks who so loyally support the mass murdering IDF terrorists in their beloved IsraHELL were the ones who brought charges against Christian patriot Brendon O-Connell recently in Perth Australia. This ugly farce and mockery of justice was under the aegis of a Jew bought and paid for kangaroo court complete with a Jew bought and paid for Judge.

Keep in mind that these vile reprobate scum of the earth 'youths' – in addition to lying their Jew asses off in court – were professional trained and coached agent provocateurs. They were dedicated – sayanims – troublemakers whose goal was to destroy the credibility of ANY and ALL who dared to expose the truth of their evil agendas of making thousands of murders of innocent defenseless children in Palestine – as acceptable.

These putrid little Jew punks were associated with organizations SO vile and So racist and So treasonous and so anti-Christian to the sensibilities of ANY decent civilized freedom loving men – that the TRUE nature of their 'school youth groups' would make the most jaded skinhead blush with embarrassment!

If you or I or OUR Gentile children had been involved with such abysmally filthy treason racist hate (for Jews ONLY) organizations we would have been ostracized from the company of our neighbors – or more than likely just asked by the community to "leave town". When you see the list of filth they supported you will understand. But of course if a JEW – conducts himself in this manner – its OK – because the Jews have designated themselves as above and superior to all of us lower Gentile animal creatures.

Australia is now totally dominated by Jews. Just like here in the USA – they dominate the entertainment – the MNM (news) – the legal system – our Congress – our Federal Judicial – the Presidency – Churches – the military – in other words – they control you entire life!

Mr. O-Connell is a citizen of the Commonwealth of Australia who lived in Perth and a TRUE practicing Christian – not to be confused with what America has turned into with the vast majority of our hypocrite phony 'Sunday Christians'. Australia is demographically over 60% Christian although I am led to believe that in reality, they have become as much of a decadent morally rotted corpse as we have.

Their legal system is so convoluted and complex even few citizens understand its structure with 8 separate State /territorial systems and one federal system – 9 separate systems – apparently all under Jew control today.

Mr. Brendon O-Connell is a well educated learned Australian patriot who like my self and many well informed responsible Americans – care about our freedoms and our sovereignty as we watch everyone from the Congress to our President commit high treason by endangering our nation's security – our economy and our moral well being by placing the criminal agendas of the rogue State of IsraHELL FAR FAR Ahead of those interests of our own nation. That is by PUREST DEFINITION – HIGH TREASON!

Brendon was some few months ago filming the infiltration of a Freedom for Palestinians group at a supermarket chain where Produce (oranges) from murderous terrorist IsraHELL has being sold. The peace activists were of course promoting a boycott of these literally 'blood soaked' oranges were being sold. In the crowd were two Jews who were there solely to make trouble for the humanitarians. There is nothing new about that – as Jew agents ALWAYS act as an irritant to spread lies about their murderous tribe and whitewash the countless murders and war crimes committed by the terrorist IDF – the Jew military.

It is important to FULLY be educated as to why the IDF is in the purest intellectual sense – the World's largest Institutionalized TERRORIST organization. It is often argued that one man's terrorist is another man's freedom fighter I have experienced the horror of terrorists up close and personal and I reject that often misused analogy TOTALLY!

The differences are clearly and intrinsically morally different. "Terrorists deliberately target noncombatants for their own cynical purposes. They kill and maim defenseless men women and children. They murder judges reporters newspaper men elected officials priests and other civic and religious leaders who defend the values of civilized societies." In other words the EXACT indisputable crimes committed endlessly by the Jew IDF. One of a lengthy list of war crimes by the IDF – was Operation Cast Lead which PURPOSELY targeted and slaughtered thousands of defenseless innocent men women and children – priests Drs. nurses school teachers and humanitarian workers.

Incidentally – that description of terrorists came DIRECT – verbatim from a 1988 official US Dept of State publication booklet entitled "TERRORIST GROUP PROFILES" and the statement itself in quote above -was made by then VP George W Bush(Sr of course)) Interesting?

I have worked with factions of democratically elected governments – both seated and in exhale as an adviser on how to handle terrorist propaganda and terrorist infiltration. For example – in 1988 – El Salvador – I have hunted and interrogated terrorists in their own language in Latin American nations and also been an adviser to local police as well as lecturing on Caribbean Basin terrorism to local universities and civic institutes many years ago. I have witnessed enough terrorist activities both in Central American and IsraHELL and their 'open air concentration camp' – to know what I am talking about. You don't get that kind of experience solely from books or behind a desk. Been there -seen that – done that. This matter of IsraHELL's terrorist IDF is important to understand the level of callous cruelty and inhumane cynicism exhibited by these Jew spies posing as simple benign innocent tourists on holiday ANYTHING BUT!

You see – these 'college tourists' – ALSO just happened to be Jews – who ALSO just happened to be ardent supporters of Jew IDF terrorism. Quite a coincidence considering that Jews in Australia consist of less than one half of one percent of the population. That their SWORN testimony also stressed that they had printed prepared propaganda leaflets to whitewash the LEGION NUMBER OF DOCUMENTED war crimes of their tribe in IsraHELL (is estimated that only about 5-10% of the IDF war crimes are ever reported – since most witnesses are routinely murdered!) I'm sure the presence of these agent provocateurs was mere coincidence – of course.

I have a complete transcript of the trial and the complete videos taken by Brendon of the infiltrators. It is a total sham and disgrace. It was as close to the classic 'kangaroo court trial" as I have ever seen. A Kangaroo court of course being a trial where the verdict was predetermined by a corrupt judge and a corrupt bought system. Remember – he had to face the Jews who had already 'fixed' the trial by himself – a frightening experience for ANY decent citizen of ANY nation to find himself in.

The whole thing was designed to sabotage any chance Brendon might have had for any justice. His atty was a loser and obviously had NO intention of defending him properly from the beginning. Brendon was left to defend himself from the beginning. I have seen And PERSONALLY experienced really rotten lawyers. Believe ME- It is better to trust your own abilities that be betrayed by someone who has NO intention of rendering you Any real help.

The Jew bough Judge was as DIRTY as I have seen in my life! His animosity towards Christians was unveiled as he CONSTANTLY interrupted and harassed and mocked and intimidated and even PERSONALLY INSULTED Christian defendant O-Connell as revealed by the transcript. It was the one place that wicked Jew Judge could NOT hide from the truth !

He assisted the seedy Jews who persecuted him so many times – especially by objection to pertinent questions that I lost count! The second that a question posed by the defendant was posed that was potentially obviously going to cause these Jew scum to perjure themselves – the Jew judge immediately jumped in to protect his Jew friends and censured him!

The Jew bought Judge even denied him a cup of coffee as he had not been able to eat a real meal in prison the night before. What personal hatred that Jew must have had for him. I am NOT entirely ignorant of court room jurisprudence – and this was as bad as it gets. It was the Godless amoral JUDGE who should be in prison! WHAT A DISGRACE

These two young punk scumbags were proven to be professional agitators over and over time after time to where it was like a Laurel and Hardy slapstick film. They contradicted themselves time after time after time – lie after lie after lie.

Here is the ultimate travesty of justice! The Jew bought Judge also denied ALL testimony – even expert testimony which I had painstakingly provided on video – as well as other expert testimony by Chuck Carlson – another eyewitness to Jew IDF terrorism war crimes and expert eyewitness testimony by Phil Tourney crewman of USS Liberty and witness of more war crimes mass murders of Crewmen of the USS Liberty. There was more – but you get the picture – dirty Judge bought of by Jews – who won't allow testimony that was ORIGINALLY PROMISED TO BE ADMITTED.

The vile evil wicked treasonous character of these two professional agitators – or sayanim as they are more properly exposed in the intelligence community – were as foul as could be imagined. Apparently these Jews spend their lives in subversive for Jew benefit only organizations.

For example – they were both members or had been members of treasonous Marxist racist organizations such as 'HABONIM DROR': from: Israel & Judaism = "Baron Cohen (the profane blasphemous nasty filthy Jew actor who played Borat) was a member of the Jewish Socialist Zionist youth movement Habonim Dror" ELEI WEISEL – the most discredited Jew liar hate monger and racist hollow-hoax fraud "is the honorary chair of the Habonim Dror Camp Miriam Campership and Building Fund". But there is more!

These Jew troublemakers were going to write their hate articles for a racist IsraHELL IDF terrorist supportive Jew newspaper 'The Maccabean'. They both were active with the AUSTRALIAN UNION OF JEWISH STUDENTS – (AUJS) – which is affiliate with the MARXIST RACIST HABONIM DROR – AND – the ultra racist 'AUSTRALIAN ZIONIST YOUTH COUNCIL' Also included under the 'AUJS' umbrella are the following putrid filthy Godless seditious anti-Christian Jew only organizations:

'BETAR' – a revisionist Zionist Jew youth group

'HINENI' – A Zionist Talmudic Jew study group

'HAS HOMER HATZAIR' – a Socialist Zionist Jew youth movement

'NETZER' – a Zionist World Union for progressive Judaism

'UIA Youth Leadership' – a UNITED ISRAEL APPEAL fund raiser for Dimona (the Jew atomic weapons site)

'CHABAD LUBAVITCH ' – Even worse – these professional agitators were also HEAVILY involved with a Jew cult so foul – so putrid – that even some Jewish groups will not even acknowledge them! That group name CHABAD LUBAVITCH is so evil that even a Jew site has this to say: Chabad-Lubavitch is a religious cult and a criminal organization. Chabad-Lubavitch is destroying the Jewish people from within. Chabad-Lubavitch is bad for the Jews.
www.chabad-mafia.com – Cached

This is what their OWN cult says- that Christians are 1. evil, Satanic creatures from birth (making all Gentile babies"little demons"); 2. no better than worms;3. not really living beings at all, but already "dead;"

AND- too many more to list – all exclusively Jewish and all monstrously evil.

There was a laundry list of AUJS connected services promoting Jewish culture – Jewish philosophy – Jewish living – Jewish businesses – Jewish websites – Jewish rallies – Jewish support for their terrorist IDF. In short – Jewish EVERYTHING. No goy are important and ONLY Jew interest are stressed.

In my entire life and extensive travel I have never experienced a more RACIST people than the Jews. They are the most egocentric arrogant hypocrites ON EARTH! Keep in mind that both of these poor sensitive abused mistreated student PUNKS were either active with or approved of all of these racist seditious Jew campus organizations.

I attended 4 separate universities during my studies and NONE of them offered these racist exclusive Marxist "youth" and "study "movement /group/organizations for any specific ethnicity – such as Italians – or French – or Germans – or Cubans – or Russians or Greeks or Canadians etc etc. ONLY The racist Jews offer racist educations for Jews exclusively! Note that virtually ALL Jew student organizations were in Hebrew – NOT ENGLISH – as if to say – Gentile cattle need not apply! JEWS ONLY!

Their played stupid (LYING) when being questioned by Brendon, was allowed over and over again. When Brendon finally cornered one of the little lying punks with something particularly damning- the Jew bought Judge would IMMEDIATELY jump in with either " DON'T ANSWER THAT!" – or " YOU DON'T NEED TO SAY ANYTHING" These outrages are all in the transcript for the world to see!

When one of these rancid pukes slandered ALL Arab people by identifying the 'Friends Of Palestine protestors as all terrorists . " Yeah – your know those scarves – its a checkered scarf that -uh you know – that the terrorists wear"

Decency would have dictated that a moral Judge would severely reprimand that Jew slime ball on the spot for such slanderous speech! The head scarf he spoke of – the keffeyeh – has been traditional with Arab peoples of many lands for centuries. For that little Jew racist punk to slander hundreds of millions of people should have been exposed as an outrage – but of course – The Christian – Brendon – must be made an example of since the trial was so transparently fixed by the Jews anyway.

The Jew bought Judge kept referring to the "JEWISH COMMUNITY" (.04%) – but NEVER even mentioned the truly offended 'CHRISTIAN COMMUNITY' Is that because he felt Christians in Australia were in actuality – such a minority – that they no longer mattered? How sad.

One of the Jew pals of these two Jew cry babies had actually infiltrated the pro-Palestinian group – humanitarians trying to save the lives of innocent children – but that putrid heinous act of betrayal apparently didn't matter to the Jew bought Judge.

Speaking of crying – the putrid Jew troublemaker Hate monger named Stan Keyser – in predictable Jew fashion had to play the Jew sympathy card and state that his mother and grandmother were in tears that their little Jew demon tribe member got caught for trying to mock the HONEST compassion of the Friends of Palestine for the countless thousands of Christian and Arab children these demonic Jews had beaten tortured terrified and murdered and the endless misery caused by the Jews in Palestine for over sixty five years. OH -VEY OH-VEY boo-hoo boo- hoo little Stanley vas poisikuted by der goyim!

The on video face of this punk coward showed his embarrassment of being caught by Brendon's intellectual exposure of his lies, and fraud as he perjured himself.

Keep in mind. The corrupt Jew Judge KNEW of these truths regarding the character of the plaintiffs and STILL sided with them to insure that a Christian – speaking the ARGUABLE ABSOLUTE GOD'S truth about their evil lying natures – would be the one to suffer in prison.

See the irony yet? The Christian defendant is charged with racism – yet the plaintiff are FOAMING AT THE MOUTH racists – associated with some of the most racist treasonous communist hate organizations on earth. I would rather my own son would come home and tell me had joined the CPUSA rather than any one of these putrid rancid filthy Godless seditious racist treasonous Christ hating popular Jew 'youth' groups

Do you understand NOW why Jew educational youth groups turn out total 100% treasonous Christ hating Christian hating scum?

So- the true Christian is thrown in the dungeon and the TRUE racist Jews who endlessly perjured themselves are free and celebrate another victory over their hated Christian adversaries. Te Jew perpetrators whine their Oh-Veys as being persecuted – as they simultaneously victimize their VICTIM! GET IT?

They have had two thousand years to perfect this endless deceit and mockery of justice.

Here are 5 three things anyone can do that collectively I believe will bring national if not international attention to the level of evil to which Australia has allowed itself to sink. I will do that and MORE – I do so swear on the altar of God. With your help – we will NOT fail him.

(1) Let the new catch phrase for Australia be " PUT ANOTHER CHRISTIAN ON THE BARBIE MATE"Use it often – on cards letters – Emails – ESPECIALLY to your church group

(2) Contact the Australian embassy. THIS is the time to show RIGHTEOUS ANGER. Let the bastards know how – as a moral freedom and truth loving human being – YOU ARE PISSED

(3) Contact your travel agency and let them know that as a Christian- you WILL NOT Be spending your vacation dollars in their anti-Christian Godless Jew controlled shithole country. Tell them why! NO – do NOT be POLITE

(4) Call your local OUTBACK STEAKHOUSE and tell them the story briefly and that they can take their Jew attitude of " put another Christian on a barbie" mentality and shove it up their arse.

(5) Insist that your local church pastor or priest include this outrage against Christians by Jews, in his next sermon

Remember – what you are witnessing is a brutal modern day version of IN YOUR FACE Christian persecution. A good man – a caring man – a BRAVE man – a righteous man – who stood up alone for the terrified little children of Palestine – whether Christian or Muslim – did THE RIGHT THING.

Brendon spoke no falsehood – he committed no sin – He sacrificed himself for these wretched poor little children who are daily tortured beaten and murdered by the Jews (as I HAVE BEEN WITNESS TO) ; Remember : "Whatsoever you do to the least of my brothers; That you do unto me. When I was weary, you helped me find rest.

When I was anxious, you calmed all my fears."

LET BRENDON LEE O-CONNELL KNOW HE IS NOT ALONE!

OCTOBER, 2011
THE BEST PLAN TO TAKE BACK OUR COUNTRY

"HE WHO IS THE ENEMY OF MY ENEMIES IS MY FRIEND"

"HE WHO IS THE FRIEND OF MY ENEMIES IS MY ENEMY"

No truer or more rational words have ever been spoken in the annals of recorded history war and conflict. In that respect the United States have been incredibly ignorant – or more accurately defined – treacherous!

If you are a grown individual who is still clinging to inane deceptions about the Bilderbergs or the Illuminati or the UN or giant corporations or chemtrails or shape shifting giant human lizards or Muslims or Al-qaeda or Al Jolson or other nonsense regarding the cause of our moral and economic demise – don't waste your time reading this – as you are stupid beyond help.

We have ONE MORTAL ENEMY – the jews – GOT IT? JEWS! Intelligent informed Americans already know this fact. The rest will die stupid.

What I am suggesting here is a sure fire – no nonsense – foolproof – 100% positive way out of the mess we have allowed to destroy us.

They are an evil people in a THOUSAND WAYS! Just look at what they have chosen for their national symbol – an occult symbol – the hexagram of Satan! Their national hero – king David – a whore monger and adulterer who like most jews couldn't keep his cock in his robes. David was such a rancid puke that he had his most trusted general – HIS VERY BEST FREIND – MURDERED – so he could screw his friend's wife, Bathsheba It's in the Bible -check it out!

David later said he was sorry. Oh – isn't that so special. I have my BEST friend murdered for a piece of ass – my friend's WIFE – but it's OK if you are a self-chosenite – commit as much murder and adultery as you want if you are a jew – because jews have a 'special privilege' direct from Satan that no other people on earth do. They recite some demonic gibberish nonsense (Kol Nidre) on one of their Satanic rituals called Yom Kippur and voila! – an automatic license to LIE! READ IT FOR YOURSELF!

But of course lying is an inseparable part of the soulless jew mentality. OH – and if you even THINK about calling me something inanely knee jerk stupid – like the obligatory jew mantra of 'anti-Semite' – you better damn well include the Lord Christ as well.

He CLEARLY PLAINLY stated that: (A) Satan is the father of ALL lies – and (B) the jews are his children. The JEWS – NOT the Arabs – got it? READ IT IN SCRIPTURE – John 8-44

The jew's national motto? HONOR? – COURAGE? – TRUST IN THE ALMIGHTY? – NATION OF PEACE? – TRUTH AND INTEGRITY?

NO! They BRAG about dealing with their neighbors by DECEIT! They use that exact WORD! Check it out for yourself. True to their evil – that is all I saw when I stayed in that wretched demonic place – IsraHELL – deceit upon deceit – lies upon lies!

You see – we still have a basic problem discerning the good guys from the bad guys. Primo important lesson at Ft Bragg Spec Ops Warfare school. First order of business according to the venerable 'Sun Tzu' in his classic 'ART OF WAR' – was to IDENTIFY THE ENEMY! However – we just can't seem to get it right!

I submit to you that our government has essentially betrayed most every TRUE ally we ever had and embraced those whose actions character morals and codes are anything but 'friend' – as our 'friends'. .

Let's Look at 3 nations who we have called friends and allies in the past as well as one MAJOR present enemy deceitfully masquerading as a "friend".

The FRENCH?

Are you kidding? They still despise Americans. Spend some time there and you will how much they love us! Been there twice – 2 bad experiences – American nationals are not even allowed to tour certain war memorials – but still the least sinister of the three.

The British?

Worse! Aside from the FACT That the vast majority of putrid rancid Godless jew-managed and promoted 'heavy metal' – 'hard rock' – satanic drug culture mentality filth which has already ruined an entire generation – totally transformed into useless garbage – was a 'gift' from the British – they also committed some of worst war crimes in history against American sons and daughters – not to mention serious war crimes in the Mid-East.

Ask you school children this question and see what you get. " Which is the ONLY nation on earth which has bombarded American soil – murdered American patriots and tortured beaten and starved thousands of our countrymen in a manner so cruel and brutal that it rivals ANYTHING the Soviets have done! "

The answers you will get will be the obligatory jew promoted lies about 9-11 – and of course these "horrible evil" people will be identified as the Arabs. Today – only the most EVIL and sinister of jew associated anti-Americans will parrot the tired worn out third world joke – that the Arabs or like our home spun amoeba brained hillbilly rednecks say – "A'- rabs"

And of course – the former Soviet Union – the 'evil empire'.

Even our most famous WWII field commander OPENLY despised these people for the godless barbarian butchers they were. They were the cradle of jew invented inspired supported and financed COMMUNISM!

I spent nearly an entire year training young warriors to DEFEND this land against our former Soviet "FRIENDS and ALLIES" – as we are about to go to war with them – FOR REAL – in 1962 . Most of you are too young to remember the frightening peak of the cold-war turned into a VERY realistic Armageddon scenario. Patton was spot on. He understood the evil of the jews and would have exposed them if he became President.

He AND JFK were BOTH – undoubtedly murdered by jews, who feared both of them had the guts and integrity to expose them and their criminal enterprises (Eg – the Fed) for the evil demonic murderous scum they are.

THESE were the people our treasonous President – self acknowledged Marxist jew traitor – FDR – chose to all our blood brothers – friends and allies! IF – by this late date – you are still incapable of understanding that historically and logically we fought the wrong people in Europe – then you are simply too stupid to understand the planned dynamics which have enslaved us morally and economically – especially in the last few decades.

Our nation is DYING – laying prostate immobilized and impotent as our jew enemies suck the last life from our collective – now dying morally rotted corpse! This jew toilet of frightened sheep and cattle we live in today does not remotely resemble the USA of my youth. Just ask my peers.

IF you REALLY are serious about taking back our nation – to some self- imagined 'restore point' – when we were parasite free – economically healthy morally healthy and respected by the world community – as a world leader – a light among nations – I will show you the way – not only the BEST – but THE ONLY WAY OUT – short of the horrors of another civil war – or the inevitable total endless occupation by the demonic godless criminal jews!.

I have examined the alternatives long and hard – every possibility from every angle and NOTHING else will work. I am so convince that what I propose is so completely doable – without the horrors of millions of American lives lost – I am willing to gamble ALL the cards I have left in my hand – my home my fortune – my freedoms – my life if necessary.

Today – there is virtually NO ASPECT of American life not controlled legislated and or influenced by the jews.

OUR PRESIDENTS = GONE! – both current past AND whoever the next puppet that IsraHELL decides will best serve Godless jewish interests = all totally immoral spineless frauds and criminal puppets of IsraHELL.

OUR CONGRESS = GONE! – 100% slavishly loyal FIRST To the Godless stolen State of IsraHELL. For any of you 'doubting Thomas' still in denial just watch this gut grinding horrible disgraceful conduct of our treasonous Congress as they pledged their undying loyalty to – the USA? NO – It was TO ISRAHELL. Open video to see how we have become slaves of the jew.

I will award a $20 to anyone who can unquestionably show me that so much as ONE Congressman – even Ron Paul – did not show their cowardly fealty – with tails between their legs – to war criminal – mass baby killer – terrorist racist Netanyahu as he played our entire Congress like a cheap guitar! Open video above to see how we have become slaves of the jew.

OUR JUDICUARY = GONE! The jews now control whatever they want in the Supreme Farce. Either jews or useful idiot puppets who do their bidding now call the shots.

OUR 'FREE PRESS' NEWS MEDIA – GONE! The jew controls ALL major media newspapers – TV – magazines. IF this is 'news' to ANY American reading this – YOU are part of the problem – just another useful idiot.

OUR ONCE WHOLESOME ENTERTAINMENT = GONE! – ALL jew-controlled. The jew decides why you AND your children will and NOT SEE. One evening of surfing the TV content should been enough to see what filth violence blasphemies Christ bashing Founding Father bashing promotion and or glamorizing of drugs homosexual perversions adultery casual sex gluttony greed evolution and sadism which DOMINATES our jew controlled culture.

OUR DECENT MORAL LAW ENFORCEMENT = GONE! – police brutality is encouraged and more common than ever – corruption is at an all time high thanks to jew control of the courts. In my OWN state of Florida – the jew has done away with our necessary consumer protection agencies at State level.

OUR EDUCATIONAL SYSTEM = GONE! We have forced integration forcing talented responsible children forced to take EXTREMELY dangerous psychotropic drugs and or forcefully taught anti-Christian Godless jew rhetoric. Classes are routinely interrupted by violent rancid drug gang mentality black 'yuts'. Spend a day in one of our jew supervised schools and be prepared for a horror show right out of 'Blackboard Jungle'.

OUR ONCE EFFICIENT HEALTH CARE SYSTEM = GONE! – just look at Obama care – and the worst is yet to come.

THE AMERICAN DOLLAR = GONE! Raped by jew bankers for decades. We are playing with Monopoly Money – and our own 100% jew owned and managed Fed Reserve has raped our wealth. It is in fact the world's largest counterfeit – printing near worthless fiat currency that is no longer respected in the world marketplace.

THE AMERICAN CHRISTIAN CHURCHES = GONE! 50 million brain dead hypocrite morons known as BaptDUHS – have made a total blasphemy our of Christianity. Their hillbilly imbecile stupidity made them easy targets for the jews to achieve their 2000 year old goal of discrediting and or destroying the TRUE Christian faith here. Even the presumably better educated Catholics have been corrupted. Christ has been told to take a hike. There is no moral cohesiveness in our fake 'churches' any more.

OUR ONCE HONORABLE MILITARY = GONE! We are now a mercenary army of overpaid losers – sick twisted psychopaths whose TRUE rationale for entering our now paid for hire assassins. In Afghanistan and Iraq alone – our paid killers for hire have committed more war crimes that in ALL previous conflicts! RAPES – MURDERS – LOOTING – THEIVERY – DRUNKENNES – SADISM are so common in the American military today – that we have surpassed the crimes committed by the barbarians of the USSR in Afghanistan.

Our treasonous military will not lift a finger to defend America from our true Mortal enemy. They are NOW in fact – THE enemy. Radical statement? REALLY? Look up

'29 Palms Naval base – Marines say they will kill their neighbors if ordered to in survey'.

I am WELL familiar with BOTH aspects – having been active with the 'Committee For a Free Afghanistan' in the 70s. I have substantive records of war crimes by BOTH the Soviets AND the Americans there. We have matched them for sadistic cruelties in every aspect!

I was myself an infantry basic training company commander during the Berlin Crisis so I am authority at what 'basic combat training' is all about – as well as highly advanced training I also received as a Special Operations paratroop commander.

Now get this! My son recently went through basic and was taught to terrorize civilians! Kick in doors to THEIR HOMES beat them up tie them up and kill them if necessary – just EXACTLY The IDF (jew military) trains their defenseless civilian killers to do. Been there and seen that TOO! The IDF cowards are the most Godless brutal sadistic bloodthirsty monsters ever spawned – and I have seen some bad folks.

Point is – our own jew run military is NOW training YOUR sons to be murdering monsters like the filth in their gangster military and I was in a position to KNOW. Just look at the HUGE surge of reported war crimes since Vietnam – AND keep in mind that everything possible has been done by our jew controlled media to suppress the real truth. Surveys indicate that less than 15% of these brutal senseless atrocities will ever see the light of day!

I'm talking green 18 year old kids – not seasoned paratroopers I had in my command years later! If that disgraceful state of our modern improved desensitized warriors does not upset the parents of military aged sons – then YOU are as sick as the jew bastards who created that sick perverted criminal filth in 'basic'.

My point of all this detailed disqualifying of ALL major aspects of American society? Simply this: to show that we have ALREADY sold our nation and our souls to the jews.

The ONLY 'group' left – the largest one – is 'Joe six-pack' and 'Bill the plumber'. Grass roots America is ALL we have left – MAYBE – as they are also poorly informed.

ALL of you remaining people who are NOT owned like cattle with a ring through your nose (that is what the jews call us 'GOY' Hebrew for cattle) – need to take what I am going to tell you dead serious – as it is our ONLY hope to EVER see your children live in a free decent America once more.

We have a common ally of people who simply want to live in peace and freedom just like many of us still do. I know them and they are a brave long suffering honorable 'people of the book '.

They are our ONLY hope! They are MY brothers in this battle to the death against Satan's children – and YOURS AS WELL. You just don't know it yet.

They have been lied about, slandered, ridiculed, mocked, and made into villains by jew deceit. REMEMBER – the ONLY news we have today is jew news. To forget that fact is a fatal mistake.

We have a common MORTAL enemy – the jews. There are some 6 billion Muslims mostly 'Arab' people worldwide who are brave enough to stand up to these demonic animals and DIE for their families and values.

Through pure lying meanness or plain stupidity our militray and our news media insist on slandering brave heroic patriotic (yes Virginia – Arab people love THEIR country and families as much as we arrogant AmeriKans love our own so 'superior' nation) men women and children with propaganda filth like: "detainees" – or " insurgents" – or "terrorists".

Oh – and of course the 'Larry the cable moron' hillbilly slurs like "sand-niggers – or camel jockeys – or rag-heads" etc. It's ok to call these poor persecuted people demeaning racist names – but better not call our so holier than thou hypocrite Merkans 'mean' names! WHAT GODLES UNCONSCIONABLE HYPOCRSISY!

Faux so called 'Christians' in my country are such spineless yellow bellied cowards that they are afraid to even suggest that their two hundred or so year old tradition of honoring Christ with a Natvity scene at the White House during the holy days of Christmas has been trashed for years – the Nativity thrown out – and a demonic 3 story high filthy 'pitchfork of Satan' substituded! SICK! DISGUSTING!

The brave Arab people of the world have proven their courage and have suffered unbelieveable hardship torture abuse beatings theft rapes and millions of cold blooded murders to protect what HOLD DEAR AND BELIEVE IN.

What the hell do we believe is worth protecting anymore?

Our Religion? Are you kidding ME. We have no religion. We smile as our spoiled brats laught at e jews mocking Christ as a monkey and worse – and His Blessed mother as a whore on jew TV.

Our Constitution? Trashed by the jews and their useful idiots in our now 100% controlled Congress. The video I attached proves that beyond ANYdoubt.

Our freedoms? Also trashed more and more by jew legislation – insane immigartion laws – tax laws and our money stolen to bail out the jew bank criminals who stole it in the first place – in case you have forgotten. One jew alone stole SIXTY FIVE BILLION DOLLARS – his justice? Living in a fancy semi luxury country club 'jail'.

OK – since it is obvious that we as Americans today are too cowardly selfish stupid and or apathetic to defend ANYTHING that decent normal people hold sacred – lets get the Arabs – since they have the GUTS to fight even superpowers for non material ideals that THEY hold dear – to do the job for us.

All we have to do (after we regain our sanity) is to give them moral support – stop murdering their families and destroying their homes – denounce our mortal enemy IsraHELL – AND all of their 'agents' in this country – meaning essentially ALL israHELL loyal jews.

The Arabs will take care of the demonic enemy of ALL mankind – IsraHELLand the jews – and we will have our country – our Congress – our Supreme Court – our Presidency – or entertainment – our military – our educational system – our fiscal system – our news media AND our Christian faith – ALL back under our control once more . It IS doable and the ONLY caveat that could possibly destroy our 'everyman's dream of freedom – is continued criminal ignorance.

THAT horrible contingency WILL send us right back on the fast track to the trash heap of history. The choice is yours. Enbrace what is brave noble Godly sober decent and honorable – or continue to sleep with the Devil and his filthy nasty putrid rancid cunning lying cheating greedy devious treasonous demonic scum THE JEWS!

If you EVER want to see your country free again – DECENT again – GODLY again – embrace them like your brothers in arms. They are a sober honest brave moral Godly freedom loving people – unbowed and untainted by the filth of the jews like the current generation of materialistic sensationalistic secular Godless filth they have created here in my beloved but occupied country. I will stake my life that I am right.

If you EVER want to see your children happy and free and your grandchildren grow up in the land we USED To be – free of these satanic filthy monsters – you had better be thinking about giving your FULL SUPPORT to these brave people.

The Arab people are the ONLY friends we have left – and we have mistreated them through stupidity and arrogance – TERRIBLY! Their moral values and family values are virtually identical to what decent moral Americans hold dear. Don't ever forget that FACT as you scream for their blood like mindless soulless insane street mobs.

I have been here – seen that – done that – with both cultures. While the jews call our Lord every filthy name in the book – blasphemer – sorcerer- bastard – mock Him 24-7 on their jew controlled TV in YOUR LIVING ROOMS EVERY NIGHT OF THE WEEK – in case you hypocrite 'sunshine Christians' haven't noticed.

The true Muslim ALWAYS refers to Christ with the MOST reverent of terms – as they do with His blessed mother Mary. While the filthy jews in their demonic nasty filthy UNHOLY books of the Devil like the Talmud – OFICIALLY curse our Lord in the cruelest of ways (I have witnessed jews doing this will FULL approval of all of their depraved jew ilk) the reverent Arab opens his comment about Jesus with these words; "PEACE BE UNTO HIM".

THAT IS TRUTH – not an opinion. learn it for yourself – or die an ignorant slave. An opinion is worth perhaps a cup of coffee. The TRUTH is inviolate and priceless.

The Christians have lived in peace with the Muslims in Palestine for centuries – yet the jew there murder ALL of them – shits and pisses on their churches and mosques – murders the priests and burns them to the ground. You will never EVER see or hear of THAT FACT in your jew owned newspapers and TV news. Been there – seen that.

The jew military – the IDF – is considered in the intelligence community to be the world's largest institutionalized terrorist organization! These satanic cowards target helpless children the elderly and women. Been there – seen that.

Let the good Arab people (REAL Semites incidentally) take the fight to israHELL – a STOLEN land based on ethnic cleansing by terrorist jews.

Just think of it. ALL of the bad things about this country – which have been supported and promoted by jews – will gradually be just bad memories.

In the past I have offered a HUNDRED Dollars for EACH wicked Godless sinful evil activity identified to not have ANYTHING To do with jew support legislation endorsement practice.

NO ONE has EVER collected simply because they ALL are pet projects of these Christ murderers! Pornography – infanticide – hard drugs – gambling – aids – homosexual perversions – pedophilia – PUBLIC blasphemies – extortion – usury and using the misery and bad fortune of their non jew fellow human beings to make them rich (one of their favorites) .

Jesus Himself exposed these monsters by revealing their TRUE identities in Scripture (John 8-44) as He accused the jews of being the sons of the Devil – LITERALLY! It was NOT spoken as a parable – but as a FACT!

We have one final opportunity to gain our freedom – not with violence – not with risk of military duty – not with tremendous personal expenses – not with lengthy time consuming obligations – buy by simply showing written and verbal support for the ONLY brave folks on earth with the balls to stand up to these disgusting filthy greedy Godless 2 faced liars and cheat blood sucking parasites from hell!

My experiences and conclusions are based on a lifetime of travel – personal experiences – MONUMENTAL research – and a clear sharp mind.

Learn the TRUTH – and it WILL set you free or die ignorant as a slave of the jew who considers you nothing more than an inferior animal placed here for his welfare.

Jews are consummate liars! Everything in their wicked live is based lies. READ John 8-44 and learn the TRUE nature of the jews. Scripture makes It abundantly CLEAR – He was addressing the jews as a people – and NOT just the Pharisee scribe and high priests.

The jews are the ONLY ethnicity in Scripture who are so damned by the Lord. Not the Greeks not the Romans not the Arabs – ONLY THE JEWS

Join with me in taking back my country – YOUR country. Don't let it become another jew sewer/toilet for their perversion.

I will trust my life and my families life with good Arab people ANY DAY. Their values ARE virtually like my Christian values and always have been.

The ONLY people on earth who can AND ARE WILLING TO SACRAFICE THEIR LIVES to live fear free from the jews are the Arab people.

DON'T EVER FORGET THAT FACT

SHOW THEM YOUR SUPPORT – write supportive articles – speak at your church – IF it is not too late and is now under Satan's control.

Show NO support to our child murdering military. They do NOTHING to defend my country and I should know better than most. As matter of fact our military is the biggest threat to world peace since the USSR!

I served with HONOR long before most of you were born.

Today's military disgrace everything good noble and decent left of our military.

Remember – any soldier who went to Afghanistan or Iraq to murder, rape, humiliate, terrorize and make homeless tens of millions of civilians went there for the money and thrills and above all – to commit treason against the United States by giving aid and comfort to our mortal enemy THE JEWS went there of his own free will! That is SICK!

They are putrid rancid psychopathic murdering sadistic heartless scum . GODLESS MURDERING THRILL SEEKING BULLIES WHO HAVE PLAYED TOO MANY JEW PRODUCED CD WAR GAMES.

I trained their GRANDFATHERS!! Honest decent real men with morals and compassion. This is one former Green Beret with a flawless civic and military record that openly warns ANY young man who has concern for his immortal soul – to steer clear of our wicked Godless jew run military.

To the handful of young warriors who are moral and brave enough to tell our murderous jew controlled military to "GO TO HELL – WE WILL NOT BE YOUR SICK TWISTED COLD – BLOODED MURDERERS AGAINST INNOCENT CIVILIANS WHO HAVE DONE US NO HARM" – I salute you! I take you into my heart as 'my true brothers in arms' – the TRUE spirit of the Green Beret.

To the rest of you scum who have disgraced the uniform – ESPECIALLY the Green Berets – look down at the inscription on your crest – and read our Special Forces motto – the one you have cruelly mocked and trashed =

DE – OPPRESSO – LIBER "FROM THE OPPRERSSOR WE LIBERATE YOU"

You ignorant redneck morons! You have VIOLATED YOUR OWN SACRED CODE! You have 'SHIT' on the very principles I risked my life to uphold for the security of this nation before most of your fathers were even BORN!.

You have become THE oppressors themselves, and serve ONLY the demonic Godless racist murderous criminal filth in IsraHELL. Have you no shame in your crimes?

You are without honor. You are Godless barbarian filth. Damn you to hell!

Educate yourself to the TRUTH. I would swear to the face of God on the souls of my grandchildren – that all I have said here is TRUE and from my heart. I just want my country back as it was when I was a young man.

Decent – honorable – informed – free – moral – Christian -compassionate and free of the suffocating stifling putrid stanch of death and hopelessness brought by the Godless lying jews.

I am willing to confirm anything I stated as fact here. Few Americans I know can handle ugly truths – which is why we have lost everything.

JANUARY, 2012
THE WORLD 100 YEARS AFTER JEWS - 'FINAL EPISODE' - A NEW AMERICA

Since the 'History' channel Jew Tube did a last 'WORLD – AFTER MAN' – FINAL EPISODE, a while back – you know – the everything all back to normal with nature in harmony without nasty people to interfere after all traces of 'man' had crumbled into oblivion scenario. – I thought I would follow suit with a parting-shot prognostication of my own. In my version, however – the only creature which has totally vanished from the face of the earth is the toxic Jew – the greatest threat to world peace in the history of mankind! I get goose bumps just thinking about the wonderful results for America alone!

It is hard to know exactly where to start but here goes. Remember – ALL of these conclusions are based on history – cause and effect type logic. They are really not too hard to conclude. For example – if there had been no Communism – there would be no 'Red' China and so on and so forth. The year is now 3000 and the world is pretty much at peace. The Mid-East is now back on the popular tourist list and the US has been at peace with all of its neighbors for almost a century. There are NO JEWS in America. They have been exiled for life – for decades.

America has once again established herself as a world leader – no longer a Jew occupied imperialist aggressor. The Gold standard has once again been established – gas is 25 cents a gallon and we are energy independent as we have discovered thousand year vast reserves of gas and oil and efficient ways to retrieve them. And most foreign nations–especially Arab ones–have outgrown their well-justified hatred of us. Being an American citizen is once again something to be proud of and citizenship is EARNED by respectable people, as it was 200 years before. We are once again recognized as a REPUBLIC – a nation of laws – and NOT MOB RULE. We are a market-based economy no longer with trade deficits at the mercy of powerful criminal Jew robber bank barons. The gigantic Jew Federal Reserve fraud has long since been disbanded and the perpetrators punished.

Israhell – the worlds' largest terrorist State will have been confronted by ALL of the world's powers with a VERY SHORT FUSED ultimatum. Dismantle your nuclear arsenal or suffer total annihilation. Every last dollar goes to your mass prison victims in Palestine. You criminals have 24 hours to vacate the land and relinquish it to its original owners or we will annihilate you anyway. Since you are such consummate liars perhaps you can still find some nation fool enough to take your miserable sorry asses in as guests so you can ruin their nation as the only thing you do well -BLOOD SUCKING PARASITES.

Churches are full on Sundays – The horrid Christian Zionist Baptists have need thoroughly discredited and shamed into the oblivion they so richly deserved. The corrupted infiltrated Roman Catholic church joined with the Eastern Orthodox church which KEPT THE Faith and now carefully monitors the background of ANY and All Papal aspirants lest they are betrayed again by the like of the abominable apostate Jew Pope Ratsinger who has reserved a SPECIAL place for himself in HELL!. Christians are once again acting like Christians. The shameless whore carnival mentality TV millionaire false prophets like Pat Robertson and his hate filled ilk have all been run out of town to become used car salesmen under different names.

Homelessness has been all but eradicated. Education has become as honored as it was to the ancient Greeks – unemployment is less than 1% – – medical care is affordable to all – as greed and corruption in that field have been sternly dealt with. Cures have been found for all of man's worst diseases and as education continues to be desired and sought by all – lawyers have only a narrow area of practice in highly specialized areas. There is a current saying regarding the civil court system –"Only a FOOL would hire a lawyer to do that which can be solved with truth and common sense".

Street gangs are virtually non-existent and are simply not TOLERATED by the public. Gangsters of any stripe are reviled so strongly by the general public that they must operate in total secrecy for fear of their lives. Racial conflict so frequently stirred up by the opportunistic Jews are a thing of the past. Blacks finally wise up to the fact that they were puppets of the Jews and would now like to become just plain good 'un-hyphenated' American citizens that must EARN respect like every one else and stop pissing off everyone else with their tribal Ebonics bullshit. Niggers gang bangers and rap trap crap filth are given one way tickets to third world countries. Today – any decent informed black American citizen would be insulted to be called the insulting obligatory 'Afro-American'.

Decent Negroes enjoy all the rights everyone does – just like they ALWAYS DID – as long as they follow the rules! Obama – arrested tried and convicted of high treason – will have just become a forgotten embarrassing third world joke by now to all educated blacks. Putrid treasonous scum like MLK are now described in history books as the degenerate he actually was. We now once again celebrate a LONG OVERDUE holiday for the father of our country – George Washington.

Oh and of course other unresolved matters of injustice have been dealt with. Bush, Cheney, Rice and Rumsfeld have all bee arrested tried and convicted of high treason and war crimes with non found guilty of treason and are serving lengthy prison sentences or an appointment with the hangman.

After the entire economy imploded due to mass corruption and Socialist heavy handedness under the Obama Zionist Socialist regime disaster – he was reported to have been assassinated by his own 'people' shortly after his trial. His all Jew cabal of illegally appointed 'tsars' will long be remembered as the treasonous criminals they were.

The USS LIBERTY massacre – an act of WAR against American by IsraHELL – was finally properly investigated in 2013 and a blockbuster movie was made to honor the crew and the worst case of a national treason cover up in our history. All the IsraHELL Jew criminals responsible were of course now gone and the names of mega-traitors President Johnson and Secretary of Defense McNamara will forever be disgraced in the history books of our schools as traitors and war criminals.

The 9-11 'truthers' finally had their day and the truth of the greatest crime against the American people ever committed. All of the Jews responsible were of course –'no longer' – but the names were burned into the memory of all American school children to be reviled for all generations to come as the ultimate enemies of ALL mankind. Also changed in schools are the lies taught making heroes out of monsters. FDR and Churchill will be exposed for the degenerate treasonous bastards they actually were.

Harry Truman will be reviled in history books as a war criminal for the needless murder of a million Japanese civilians – as well as the traitor who made all the evil of the jews possible by his treasonous recognition of terrorist IsraHELL as a legitimate new State rather than the rogue terrorist State it actually was. Woodrow Wilson will now be remembered for he ACTUALLY WAS – a cowardly spineless traitor to America. Scum like draft dodger Bill Clinton and his demonic wife will enjoy eternity knowing that they were considered the most degenerate abysmal filth to ever disgrace the White House. In other words – the TRUTH -both beautiful and ugly will be taught to our children so that we will never again be occupied slaves of the Devil.

Confidence in elected officials has risen to the way it was in the beginning. A special civil board has been empowered to deal swiftly with ANY and ALL corruption. ‘Public servants’ are EXACTLY that, and corrupt ones disappear overnight! Sexual improprieties will not be tolerated. ANY public display of homosexual perversion will be punishable by severe prison terms. With no Jew troublemakers to keep the race cards and hate cards going – educated citizens (something new in America after 50 years of being dumbed-down) are all in wise concordance with the new reforms.

With no more REAL enemies – our military has been greatly diminished and membership is ONLY after thorough selection based upon integrity of the highest standard as in my day – before the influence of the Jews. Being exposed as a sycophant in the military is now not only a disgrace but a crime today and especially serious when committed by a member of the judiciary. A lifetime of dishonor as an outcast would be the minimum consequence.

Since it has in fact always been considered a PRIVILEGE and not simply a right – like freedom - ONLY educated property owners may vote – but are now in the VAST majority today anyway. Wanna live here? Learn the language – learn the laws – or leave! Illegals have 24 hours to leave or end up in prison making license plates or building roads. The ambitious of all races embrace opportunities on equal playing fields. ‘Affirmative action’ is now a dirty word and insult to decent hard working achievers of all backgrounds. This is America like it was supposed to be. – all possible now with the absence of the devious greedy corrosive Jew.

Income taxes are EXTREMELY restricted with no special interest groups. The IRS was abolished decades ago as illegal and disbanded. The elderly – incapacitated – widows – orphans and honorable veterans (of non jew instigated wars) are treated with respect and consideration. ‘Veterans’ of the Gulf war era who murdered over two million innocent civilians were later rightfully branded as vicious war criminals – disgraced in public and given retroactive DDs and no benefits.

Those who did not commit suicide are mostly alcoholics and bums – held in deep contempt by all decent citizens. Even so – this was a token punishment for the untold misery terror and destruction and disgrace to our country they willfully caused. Many General grade officers like Petrayus and McChrystal were tried by military tribunals and hung for war crimes against humanity too numerous to chronicle here.

Entertainment which is filthy salacious blasphemous vulgar homoerotic or otherwise universally repugnant by nature (the way the Jews loved it) is not allowed on ANY public venue anyplace anytime and proven violations are severely fined and punished immediately. Corruption of our youth is dealt with swiftly and strongly. Religious freedoms are to be respected. The death penalty stands. Police brutality of any kind or other such abuse of power will be dealt with SEVERELY and SWIFTLY! Corrupt judges? Their fate is too horrible to contemplate.

You want to remove the laws of God from a courthouse in this nation today? Consider it a death wish in this revitalized and perhaps reborn moral nation.

There will be no more Communist Party –no more ACLU –any more ADL – Lambda or any other Godless anti- Christian, anti-American or pervert support groups tolerated. This was decided by public plebiscite. It was amazing how quickly morality, decency and propriety were restored once the daily poison of the Jew had disappeared!

The slightest infringement of any innocent citizen's 2nd Amendment rights will ALL bring prison sentences. An educated armed society is a polite society. Violent crime will become uncommon and remarkable. All so- called hollow-hoax museum business will have long since been confiscated and the proceeds diverted to victims of Jew crimes – here and abroad. History books will carry in detail – for all time in all schools the TRUTH of the Jews – who they were and what they did to mankind. The great wealth of the Rothschilds will have long since been confiscated as those of ALL Jew gangsters and given to charities to benefit their victims. The unrepentant jew mega-criminal Bernard Maddoff was reportedly beaten to death in his country club prison.

The willful cold-blooded murder of the unborn human child will carry the same penalty as the murder on any other innocent human DEATH! The sponsors of ALL Planned Parenthood (AKA MURDER INCORPORATED) abortion mills have long since been arrested tried and convicted for serial murder charges. Today in 'Jewless' America no serial child killer would dare show his face in public. Today's educated moral people simply would not tolerate ANY conduct that would corrupt their children. Our Faith will have been reestablished – strong – pure noble and just – freed by the TRUTH – we the people will never ever become the slaves of other evil ones again.

ANY violation of voluntary oaths sworn on the Bible – "I do solemnly swear to uphold and defend the Constitution of the United States of America against all enemies, both foreign and domestic – so help me God" – from a mayor to the President – from a private to a general officer will be dealt with in the most severe manner.

By this time the once 90% Jew supported Democrat Party will HAVE to change or cease to exist since there has been no Jew to keep it corrupt and Godless. Since there is no more (or WAS no more Republican Party) I can only guess. What WILL be a given – is that BOTH parties will be infinitely more moral. I have always believed that in a TRULY moral nation there is no need or reason for multiple parties – as true morality does NOT make concessions. Think about it. ANY person living here who has a problem with our original bill of rights or our Christian based guide for government can take a hike.

To wit – infanticide is murder – of the vilest kind. It always has been – and always will be in any society in any culture for all time – period! Homosexual perversions are and always have been "an abomination in the eyes of God". God has NEVER said that it is OK for Democrats to murder children. Infanticide was also FACTUALLY a 'Jew thing'. I can remember QUITE CLEARLY as a young man – the attitude of the American public towards the murder of the unborn child BEFORE – and AFTER the growing influence of the damned Jew and his blood soaked money!

By all reason – we should be enjoying moral mono-partisanship – and it would have a snappy name – like: THE AMERICAN PARTY! If basic Ten Commandment Christ mandated American morality becomes a problem to anyone – you don't need a different party with jew ideas – you need a different COUNTRY to call home!

By this time there will probably be real estate deals made for plots on Mars. Reminding me – that all a man earns in his life for his family friends or charities will NOT be taxed or encumbered in any way. Flying is once more affordable and enjoyable. There would be NO REASON to hijack an airline in the Jew-less future and the dreaded Gestapo Jew created Homeland security will have de-funded and remembered with disgust by American citizens as an affront to our freedoms dignity and values.

With no Jews to ruin Hollywood – entertainment will be like it was in olden times – fit for the whole family. Heavy metal 'music' – acid rock satanic rock AND the DRUG CULTURE THEY SPAWNED were ALL Jew creations and will have long since died out. This will be America's renaissance and the vast majority of the filth that once infected our nation will have been 'washed away' – like flushing the toilet.

Everything that was evil about man – greed – power- avarice – pride – hate – lies – filth – lust drugs – deception – fraud – violence – profanity – homosexual perversion – crime and especially murder – was perfected – nurtured – promoted – worshiped and loved by the Jew – who was at last – NO MORE! How the world must have rejoiced at the total disappearance of the "SONS OF THE DEVIL" forever from our shores.

America – 100 years after Jews no longer exist – hopefully a paradise – or close to it – tranquility – not only at home – but perhaps most of the world – with two generations of monstrous filth – gone forever and their legacy of greed hate and lies and the stench of death that followed anything and everything the Jew ever did or supported. Imagine if you will – his evil reign on earth – now replaced with peace and goodness – wisdom and compassion – hope and love –at last – a real chance at a future for mankind – the world – 100 years after Jews.

FINALLY! – after so many years of occupation –we can finally sing out with pride – " America the beautiful – home of the brave and land of the FREE – without the words sticking in or throats like warm vomit of blatant hypocrisy. At last – a "GOD BLESS AMERICA" sticker on a car will ONCE AGAIN – have some real meaning. We have returned the stewardship our own nation to its RIGHTFUL owners once again!

The 'story' – albeit speculation based on logic and historic fact – is still just a story. Our current occupation by the Jew is however – 100% REAL! Are we to become free men – or slaves in a colony of 'greater' Zionist IsraHELL – to be used up, and sucked dry of our lifeblood? Let us not wait 100 years! I want my country back – DO YOU?

JANUARY, 2012
IN DEFENSE OF MEL GIBSON

Regarding Mel Gibson's ACCURATE comment regarding how the jews have trashed the WORLD with evil and endless wars by which they have become wealthy with blood money – I will give a ONE HUNDRED DOLLAR reward to ANYONE who can produce undeniable evidence that jews have had absolutely nothing to do with America's worst moral and economic problems. GOT IT?

AND that means a hundred dollars for EACH AND EVERY rotted putrid filthy Godless demonic condition that we did NOT Have to any serious extent when I was a child long before we were a jew occupied nation run from IsraHELL.

Gambling – Alcoholism – mass Pornography – demon worship rock stars – trashing of our Constitution – open public mockery of Christ – open public mockery of His Sacred Mother – perversion of Christmas into a 'HOLIDAY' or orgasmic shopping and drunken partying instead of a HOLY DAY – serial wars against innocent people – mass murders of innocent people – removal of prayer from our schools – a now totally IsraHELL loyal corrupt Congress – mass drugging out of our children in schools with addictive deadly psychotropic drugs – a near 100% Godless jew-controlled media – a jew-controlled godless insane murderous military who teaches our sons to be terrorists and abortion facilities which have murdered more children than have been lost in all the wars of the past century – near 100% trashy garbage on TV to corrupt our children and the glamorizing of the lowest elements of society – bikers- gang bangers and homosexual perverts just for openers.

MAKE MY DAY!

God bless Brave men like Mel Gibson for having the courage albeit when intoxicated – to speak the GOD"S TRUTH ABOUT THE WICKED EVIL JEWS. I pray God grant him the moral courage to do the same when sober and overcome his drinking excesses.

And BTW – should the moderators decide to censure (as jews usually do when they are exposed) I will post this challenge on SEVERAL TRUE LARGE POPULAR PATRIOTIC WEBSITES – just in case it suddenly disappears.

AND – if it IS censured – for simply speaking the TRUTH about the evil of the jew – don't EVER EVER FORGET THIS: the words of God Himself. IF – YOU TRASH THIS – YOU WILL HAVE TRASHED THE WORD OF GOD. I am only the messenger.

HERE IS THE MESSAGE. It is directly from the New Testament – and was spoken in the simplest and clearest of words possible by Christ Himself – some two thousand years ago – to the most evil wicked non-repentant cruel sadistic lying murderous stealing cheating filthy Godless creatures to ever infect mankind.

Christ, to the Jews (NOT just to the Pharisees and high priests): from the Gospel of John Chapter 8 Vs 44 "YE ARE OF YOUR FATHER – DEVIL, AND THE LUSTS OF YOUR FATHER YE WILL DO. HE WAS A MURDERER FROM THE BEGINNING, AND ABODE NOT IN THE TRUTH, BECAUSE THERE IS NO TRUTH IN HIM. WHEN HE SPEAKETH A LIE -HE SPEAKETH OF HIS OWN (the jews); FOR HE IS A LIAR AND THE FATHER OF IT"

He CLEARLY COMPREHENSIVELY WITH AUTHORITY DAMNS THE ARROGANT HAUGHTY JEWS AS BEING THE CHILDREN OF THE DEVIL! GET IT?!

SO – WHAT will you do now – you wicked jews? Will you slander the Lord with your obligatory predictable worn out third world joke of a mantra- as an "ANTI-SEMITE"

JANUARY, 2012
OPEN LETTER TO ASS-KISSING WAR CRIMINAL, CAPTAIN BRUCE H. LINDSEY

Since this a condemnation of a madman – namely YOU – who are about to provoke WORLD WAR III with that harbinger of death and destruction warship USS Carl Vinson – and since you are there to WILLINGLY drag the entire world into the abyss of nuclear conflict – I will dispense with the formalities I would normally render a decent, honest man of honor and character of your rank. I learned in the military to 'SAY WHAT YOU MEAN – and 'MEAN WHAT YOU SAY' – a trait I have practiced my entire adult life.

What you are doing of your OWN FREE WILL (and I will NOT accept that" I was merely following orders" bullshit) – is the conduct of the insane! You are PURPOSEFULLY, with FULL KNOWLEDGE and with MALICE AFORETHOUGHT following orders given by a lying, treasonous, child-murdering, bastard who has sold our nation out from under us to a foreign, hostile nation for '30 pieces of silver' – or whatever the CURRENT 'hyperinflation' rate is for selling ones nation to the Devil.

Judging the tree by its fruit, a moral world can do no more than honestly acknowledge that Obama is a monster without morals, character or conscience who worships Satan and obeys Satan's children. You know this to be true – AND YET, TO SATISFY YOUR OWN LUST FOR APPROVAL AND POWER you are willing to be the catalyst for the murder of countless millions of totally innocent civilians – people who have neither done YOU or I nor this country any harm whatsoever…

And the worst part is that YOU KNOW this to be the truth.

That fact alone makes you a world class criminal along the lines of any we have been taught about throughout history. Your name will be remembered by DECENT humanity as a war criminal for as long as history is TRUTHFULLY told. Have you ever thought about how you will feel – knowing that MILLIONS of Godly, decent, freedom-loving human beings here and abroad will cry for justice against heartless mindless monsters like yourself? They hate our guts – and with good reason. We have become IsraHELL's vicious, remorseless attack dog – murdering, torturing, destroying, looting and desecrating any and all nations that the demonic Jews DEMAND. People like YOU have made us the most hated and feared nation on earth, 2nd only to Israel herself. As an American patriot I find your slavish fealty to the DEMONIC Jews beyond disgusting.

YES – DEMONIC. D-E-M-O-N-I-C.

No doubt, you think this is an "inappropriate" and–lest we forget– 'anti-Semitic'–term to describe the nature of your masters – the demons who had Jesus murdered. Well since warmongers, terrorists and war criminals like you OBVIOUSLY do NOT respect or love the Lord – let me educate you "Captain". Find a Bible somewhere and go to the New Testament – book of John – Chap 8 vs. 44. If you are too ashamed to read it aloud in the presence of your masters – lest you embarrass them – read it to yourself. It CLEARLY and COMPREHENSIVELY states the EXACT identity of who you serve. You got a problem with that? I would hate to be in your shoes come judgment day.

Make no mistake – I am one of MILLIONS of Americans who loathe what our military has become. You and your foul ilk are the worst war criminals in recorded history. Even Genghis Khan was left at the starting gate years ago. General McWarmonger and ass-kisser General BetrayUS are two glaring examples of the putrid IsraHELL-first scum who get rich from the misery of their helpless innocent civilian victims – over 2,000,000 so far and still counting. Too bad you don't have the moral courage of Admiral Bill Fallon – to tell war criminals like imbecile George Bush, a drunken, treasonous, drugged-out, Christ-mocking Constitution trasher – to SHOVE IT! All YOU had to do – was to say "NO WAY!"

Or does the FACT that a then-seated US President stated the following when cautioned about his treasonous conduct — "Stop throwing the Constitution in my face – it's just a Goddamned piece of paper"? Of course not. As long as you get your fat blood money assassins paycheck and your plush retirement – you could give a flying rat's ass about the corrupt Godless filth who use you as a pawn.

It may have cost Fallon his career – but at least he was a MAN – not a weakling spineless moral coward like yourself. You are a disgrace to the uniform and to every DECENT INFORMED GODLY vet and civilian in America. All you had to say was "HELL NO – my honor and country are NOT for sale at ANY price". You are either a spineless wimp or a greedy Godless SOB traitor who gives not a rats ass for anybody but himself.

You took an oath on the Bible – presumably the same oath I took – LONG after I did – when we became armed forces officers – to uphold and defend the Constitution against ALL enemies – BOTH foreign and DOMESTIC. The difference between you and me is a matter of truth and honor. I spoke the TRUTH and KEPT MY HONOR. YOU LIED – YOU BROKE YOUR OATH – just like ALL of the traitorous scum you work for – all the way up to the 'traitor-in-chief'. Was selling your country and fellow countrymen out to those Jesus referred to as 'children of the devil" really worth it? You are a hypocrite – a liar- a deceiver – a moral coward – and a war criminal.

Does the treasonous, Draconian, anti-American NDAA 2012 bill leave ANY doubt in your sick twisted mind as to WHO the ENEMIES of our country are – you hypocrite? NO – of course not – since it was sponsored by your Jew pals.

Monsters like you do not have hearts or souls like normal decent compassionate people – so the screams and agony of hundreds of thousands of innocent mutilated children – the probable and INTENDED result of your terrorist unfounded aggressor provocation – will never reach your ears. You see – I HAVE had that experience, one that–if you were to see that kind of suffering you would never feel the same nor ever forgive the monsters who caused it. In this case the monsters are YOU and your murderous mercenary crew of useful idiots. I pray their screams and agony haunt your dreams for the rest of your hypocrite life.

I still remember having to step outside the hospital ward to compose myself as the tears blurred my vision and shook me to my core to realize that wicked human beings – terrorists NOT UNLIKE you – could commit such horrid crimes against defenseless innocent human beings. But after all they were Marxists – you know – the Godless useful idiot scum created by the Jews to serve their causes. So you see – you both have much in common – you both are terrorists – you both serve the Jews and their agendas – and you both are Godless heartless remorseless monsters.

Many years ago – I was asked to be an advisor to a foreign nation for counterterrorist methods, a nation that had suffered horrible terrorist activities – much of it targeted towards its poor children. So no lectures from the peanut gallery about terrorists. I know some terrorist organizations inside and out – Middle East terrorists, like the largest institutionalized terrorist organization on earth – the so called Jew IDF – and the Caribbean variety like the FMLN.

Actually there is a new 'worst terrorist' title holder. That ULTRA terrorist group is the collective AmeriKan military – and YOU – YOU BASTARD – are as much a REAL terrorist as any on earth. Yes, Captain – the military I once served has now been perverted and supported by 'ambitious', soulless, Godless, cowardly worms like you – from defenders of our nation to oppressors of other sovereign nations.

Do you know what the official motto of the Special Operations command is? "DE OPPRESSO LIBER" – literally 'From the oppressor we will liberate'. I still keep an insignia at my desk that I wore – from almost 50 years ago- as a reminder of what putrid, lying, hypocrisy our Jew-occupied DOD has become.

The Green Berets in which I served long ago – and the Navy you serve today – their ONLY purpose – TODAY?

You don't 'LIBERATE oppressed people' – You OPPRESS FREE people that Jews hate – that simple!

You serve and protect – NOT AMERICA – but THE STINKING GODLESS JEWS AND THEIR STOLEN SHIT TERRORIST RACIST GARBAGE COUNTRY! I spent time in IsraHELL as an insider some thirty years ago, and they are the most putrid, evil, wicked, treacherous, lying, 2-faced bastards I have experienced in my life. Most people SEE shit on a television screen, but I WAS THERE and smelled it first-hand. Jesus spoke the truth about these vermin – so have I. So if the obligatory name calling starts – I will be in good company.

Here is a little historic reminder of the sound advice and wisdom from the 'Father of our country' as to your loyalty FIRST to IsraHELL instead of America, and in the event that the subtleties of his message are lost on you I have provided you some training wheels to help things out.

...A passionate attachment of one Nation (AMERICA) for another (ISRAEL) produces a variety of evils.—Sympathy for the favorite nation,(ISRAEL) facilitating the illusion of an imaginary common interest in cases where no real common interest exists, and infusing into one (ALL ISRAEL'S ENEMIES) the enmities of the other, betrays the former (AMERICA) into a participation in the quarrels and wars of the latter (ISRAEL), without adequate inducement or justification. It leads also to concessions to the favorite Nation (ISRAEL) of privileges denied to others, which is apt doubly to injure the Nation (AMERICA) making the concessions; by unnecessarily parting with what ought to have been retained; and by exciting jealousy, (TERRORISM) ill-will, (TERRORISM) and a disposition to retaliate, (TERRORISM) in the parties (ISRAEL'S ENEMIES) from whom equal privileges are withheld; and it gives to ambitious, corrupted, or deluded citizens, (NEOCONS, SPIES, SABATEURS, POLLARDS, JOHN HAGEE, RUSH LIMBAUGH, SEAN HANNITY, MITT ROMNEY, RICK SANTORUM, NEWT GINGRICH, AND TOO MANY OTHER ISRAEL-FIRSTERS TO LIST) who devote themselves to the favorite Nation (ISRAEL) facility to betray or sacrifice the interests of their own country (AMERICA) without odium, sometimes even with popularity:—gilding, with the appearances of a virtuous sense of obligation, a commendable deference for public opinion, or a laudable zeal for public good, and the base or foolish compliances of ambition, corruption, or infatuation.

As avenues to foreign influence in innumerable ways, such attachments are particularly alarming to the truly enlightened and independent Patriot.—How many opportunities do they afford to tamper with domestic factions, to practice the arts of seduction, to mislead public opinion, to influence or awe the public councils! Such an attachment of a small or weak, towards a great and powerful nation, dooms the former to be the satellite of the latter.

Against the insidious wiles of foreign influence, I conjure you to believe me, fellow-citizens, the jealousy of a free people ought to be constantly awake; since history and experience prove that foreign influence is one of the most baneful foes of republican Government.—But that jealousy, to be useful, must be impartial; else it becomes the instrument of the very influence to be avoided, instead of a defense against it.—Excessive partiality for one foreign nation, and excessive dislike of another, cause those whom they actuate to see danger only on one side, and serve to veil and even second the arts of influence on the other. Real Patriots, who may resist the intrigues of the favorite, are liable to become suspected and odious; while its tools and dupes usurp the applause and confidence of the people, to surrender their interests.

The great rule of conduct for us, in regard to foreign Nations, is, in extending our commercial relations, to have with them as little Political connection as possible.—So far as we have already formed engagements, let them be fulfilled with perfect good faith.—Here let us stop...

IF you cause a worldwide nuclear conflict by your insane criminal baseless provocations – thus endangering the safety of my country and my loved ones – I PRAY that you and your crew of WILLFUL MERCENARY accomplice murderers are sent to the bottom of the sea and all 5500 of you perish in hell. THAT will be SOME true justice for your unspeakable crimes against innocents.

You and the CVN 7 you command are symbols of AmeriKan aggression and DO NOT BELONG THERE! Your SOLE evil purpose for wasting MY TAX DOLLARS is to intimidate, terrorize, and push innocent people into a state of fear and desperation so that they will do what ANY honorable patriotic people on earth will do – DEFEND THEIR HOMES AND FAMILIES FROM AGGRESSORS and give you an excuse to follow the bidding of your Jew masters.

No respectable experienced analyst – including myself believes the Iranian people are a threat to the safety and freedoms of America. You cannot POSSIBLY be so stupid as to believe the lies of a people who's ENTIRE HERITAGE HAS BEEN BASED ON LIES FOR THOUSANDS OF YEARS – so the ONLY logical explanation for your treasonous conduct is ambitiousness, greed and criminal conduct.

Listen carefully, you ass kissing SOB. The ONLY people who want you to start WWIII are the demonic Jews who would have had our Founding Fathers rounded up and thrown in jail as terrorists had they been around in large numbers during the American Revolution. EVERYBODY ELSE ON THIS PLANET – including educated, informed, honorable veterans like me – HATE YOUR GUTS! You were–at best–a child when I was preparing American sons to be warriors to DEFEND this nation against a REAL enemy. Unlike today's Jew-occupied AmeriKa – we were still a decent people who were trained to DEFEND, not to rape, murder, terrorize, loot, sodomize, blaspheme, mock, and humiliate innocent defenseless civilians. Basic training today is an abomination run by criminals, sadists, psychopaths, and other social detritus approved by our Jew masters and their mindless useful idiot robots. I would rather see my sons in prison rather than do the bidding of the Devil.

Every day there are new war crimes committed by Jew worshipping monsters like you – MOSTLY by our Marines. Like the ones I saw today- so putridly evil and sadistic that they cannot be discussed in family groups. I saw no Marines. I saw grinning, sick, putrid punks pissing on the men they has just murdered – each of them somebody's husband, brother, father, or friend whose 'crimes' were to defend their homes, families, and freedoms. These psychopathic scum are not the Marines I trained in Special Forces airborne drop techniques and LZ prep a half century ago. ALL of this sadism and cruelty and Godlessness is a gift from the Jews and YOU are as guilty as they are.

I experienced this TRUE face of the Jew from their criminal IDF – child murdering scum of the earth. They actually shoot Palestinian children for sport. Been there – seen that. You know, the poor people you and your racist crew slander as "rag-heads" – or "Sand -niggers" – or "Camel

Jockeys" – and don't tell me any different because I have heard it a thousand times from 'uniforms' all over this country from two strips to two stars.

Every thing the Jew touches turns to evil or into money. Every wholesome or innocent thing the Jew touches turns to shit – and THAT includes our sons! STOP corrupting their innocence with your war mongering insane maniacal madness.

I have spoken ONLY the truth of my sentiments and truth of facts. I am one man – not influential – not wealthy – not for sale and getting old and crippled but still VERY sound of mind. I may not have had a multimillion dollar warship to protect me (just 30 lbs of silk and nylon) – but I have the power of righteousness and TRUTH on my side and I fear no one. I will back up ANY statement I have made anytime any place – with Capt. Lindsay – face to face – in public venue with honest non -Jew press present – THE OLD FASHIONED AMERICAN WAY. Honor is not a dirty word in my home – but a code I live by.

If you initiate or take part in the murder of these innocent people, may you burn in HELL, as well as all those who stood with you in this wickedness?

JANUARY, 2012
THE 'JEWISH GOD'- CRUEL MEAN SADISTIC-MORE LIKE THE DEVIL THAN JESUS

After years of honest intellectual introspection and sincere soul searching – I have come to a crossroads where I must choose one of 2 paths if I am to move forward.

As such, using the same mental faculties afforded me by the same creator responsible for all the laws of science, reason, physics, and decency, I cannot conclude anything other than that the Jewish Old Testament is indeed part and parcel of the same twisted mentality responsible for so much suffering and evil today, and is in effect a mere extension of the same Jewish mindset that created–carved if you will–a tin god out of the basest inclinations attributable to mankind that serves as a facilitator/enabler of a depraved, arrogant, self-serving evil, and greedy agenda.

If it were not for the fact that I still find it—the Old Testament–useful for research purposes, I would put it where it belongs – in the garbage.

If this Jew god described within the pages of this 'book' is in fact authentic – I could NEVER in good conscience 'worship' an entity so vicious, mean, cruel, sadistic, uncompassionate, unforgiving, and hypocritical. What the Jew god teaches me within the pages of this depraved book is the exact antithesis of what I have learned about the nature of Jesus Christ.

Having accepted and embraced the version of God the father taught by Jesus Christ I cannot but reject the Jewish god of the OT and therefore view him/her/it as a total fraud created by the sick, psychopathic, twisted, wicked nature of the Jews themselves. Karl Marx – the most wicked of all Jew demons openly admitted that "he who serves MAMMON pleases god" – because- of course – the REAL 'god' of the Jew IS Mammon – the monster we see created by the Jews of the OT.

The Jewish 'religion' is the most evil of all street gutter trash. 'By their fruits you shall know them' as Jesus taught, and in judging the bitter fruit of Judaism and its Old Testament one cannot conclude anything other than that it is nothing more than the 'wrapping up' of sharp business practices in a religious garment! Everything holy to Christians is UNHOLY to the precepts of Judaism and its followers. Their written religious practices are simply manuals for deeds considered deadly sins against Christ.

If you have the stomach for it – read in its entirety the Book of Leviticus. It is a cross between endless plots for horror movies unsuitable for ANY child and most adults and a compendium of morbidly disgusting, demoralizing, cruel, bloody minutiae totally VOID of ANY teachings of anything REMOTELY moral, wise, insightful, loving, kind or meaningful to anyone but a psychopath trapped in an insane asylum. It is FILLED with EXACTLY the kind of hypocrisy and sickening ritualistic barbarisms that had NOTHING WHATSOEVER to do with goodness or love of God, the same senseless garbage that incited Christ to violent anger against the disgusting conduct of Jews in the Temple.

Jesus taught that we should be kind, forgiving, truthful, and compassionate, self-sacrificing, and respectful of life (I have yet to meet even ONE person who is cruel to dumb animals who was not a bully). Feeding the hungry, clothing the naked, defending the defenseless and giving hope to those amongst us who have lost all hope—these are the qualities Jesus embodied which I strive to imitate with my finite abilities.

Lest you think to accuse me of blasphemy – take a LONG HARD CLOSE LOOK at the 'Yahweh of the Jewish Old Testament for yourself and tell me that you cannot see what a HORRID, SADISTIC, HATE-FILLED figure who is total anathema to the image of Christ. I will NOT LIVE A LIE! I am NOT a JEW nor do I embrace Jew 'values'! I AM A CHRISTIAN AND UNDERSTAND THAT NO ONE CAN SERVE 2 MASTERS.

In his book of laws of the OT – the Jew-created god 'Yahweh' mandates his people to COMMIT GENOCIDE (1-Samuel 15;-3) — then to COMMIT FRATRICIDE (Exodus 32: 27-28) — then suggests CANNIBALISM (Leviticus 26: 29) — ROBBERY AND THEFT (Exodus 3:22) — to KEEP SLAVES of neighboring nations (Leviticus 25: 44-46).

It only gets worse…

The God of the Jews teaches us to DISCRIMINATE AGAINST WOMEN and DESPISE CHILDREN (Leviticus 27: 2-8) —- He demands ALL GOLD BE DELIVERED COVETOUSLY TO HIMSELF (Exodus 25:3 33: 5) —-TORTURE OF ANIMALS (Exodus: 29:20 29:36)— Yahweh admits his JEALOUSY (Exodus 20:-5)

AND EVEN MORE WICKED VIOLENT SICK AND TWISTED!

God caused sibling rivalry by favoring Abel over Cain, with absolutely no attempt at justification. This act of favoritism led to Abel's death–Genesis 4:3-5

Genesis 7:23 He intentionally kills every man, woman, and child on the planet save eight of them.

God commands Hagar to return to servanthood and bear children for her master though she does not want to. Genesis 16:7-9

Genesis 19:23-25 God burns down a whole city (women and children included) simply because they were supposedly homosexual.

Er, Judah's firstborn, was "wicked in the sight of the Lord" and the Lord slew him. How was Er wicked? The Bible doesn't give us this bit of information, only that Er was wicked in the sight of the Lord. Genesis 38:7

Genesis 38:10 God murders Onan for refusing to commit incest with his sister in law.

Exodus 12:29–Yahweh repeatedly tells Moses exactly what calamity he will next visit upon the Egyptians if the Pharaoh does not allow the Israelites to be set free from slavery. He then tells Moses (repeatedly) that he will 'harden' Pharaoh's heart, so that he—Pharaoh–will refuse to allow the Israelites to go, thus bringing a calamity upon his own people, as well as showing him the awesome power of the Jewish God. This occurs over and over, bringing calamity upon calamity upon the Egyptian people. What is troubling about this verse is that when god "hardens the pharaoh's heart" he is interfering with the Pharaoh's free will and ultimately brings punishment on the Egyptians for something they are not responsible for. As a final punishment god decides to kill the entire first born of Egypt. The lord reduced himself to murdering innocent kids when he could have simply freed the Israelites himself with his "omnipotent" power.

God punishes children for the sins of their fathers, unto the third and fourth generations. Exodus 20:5&34:7

God endorses slavery. He even set up laws as to how slavery was to be carried out, and goes as far as Okaying beating them. Exodus 21:2-6

God sanctions the selling of one's daughter. (Exodus 21:7) How can any being tell another to literally sell their child into slavery?

Exodus 22:18–God orders the death of witches, sorceresses and anyone who practices magic. Sadly enough, this verse was justification for the Inquisition and countless innocent deaths.

Exodus 32:27 God ordered to be killed, 3,000 Israelites for no greater crime than worshipping a golden calf. (Not to mention that Yahweh obviously KNEW that his precious Jews had STOLEN the gold. Stealing OK – but don't injure my pride.

Leviticus 20:9-10 God commands death for cursing out one's parents and death for adultery. Gee, with these types of laws the population should be almost nil by now.

Handicapped people must not approach the altar. Leviticus 21:16-23 (great show of compassion Yahweh!)

Leviticus 27:28-29 God ordered and allowed human sacrifices.

Numbers 16:27 God buries alive Korah and his family.

Numbers 16:35 God killed 250 Levite princes who disagreed with Moses' leadership. He was so bloodthirsty that he wanted to slay more until he was talked out of it. Later he put a plague upon 14,700 Jews who thought there was something wrong in killing 250 princes. (HATE good! Compassion – BAD!)

Numbers 21:1-3 God utterly destroyed the Canaanites at Hormah as a favor to the Jews.

Numbers 21:27-35 God abetted Moses in utterly destroying the Amorites at Heshbon – "...the men, the women, and the little ones." (Can't let all those innocent little kids live!)

Numbers 31:17-18 God commands Moses to kill all the Medianite people including children and women. To top it off he commands that the virgins be saved for later raping by Moses' soldiers. (Convinced this is a monster created by the sick mind of the sociopathic Jew yet?)

Deuteronomy 3:3-7 God ordered Moses' army to "utterly destroy" 60 cities, killing all the women and children within!

Deuteronomy 7:12 God ordered the Israelites to kill all the people of seven nations. He even adds, "show no mercy unto them". (WAR WAR WAR KILLING KILLING KILLING – BLESSED ARE THE WAR MONGERS?)

Deuteronomy 20:16 God orders that the Jews kill everything that breathes in the cities that he gives them for an inheritance

Deuteronomy 23:2–A bastard can't attend church "even to his tenth generation." As if denying an innocent child rights to worship isn't cruel.

Deuteronomy 7:16-24 "You must destroy all the nations the LORD your God hands over to you. Show them no mercy and do not worship their gods. If you do, they will trap you. Perhaps you will think to yourselves, 'How can we ever conquer these nations that are so much more powerful than we are?' But don't be afraid of them! Just remember what the LORD your God did to Pharaoh and to all the land of Egypt. Remember the great terrors the LORD your God sent against them. You saw it all with your own eyes! And remember the miraculous signs and wonders, and the amazing power he used when he brought you out of Egypt. The LORD your God will use this same power against the people you fear. And then the LORD your God will send hornets to drive out the few survivors still hiding from you! "No, do not be afraid of those nations, for the LORD your God is among you, and he is a great and awesome God. The LORD your God will drive those nations out ahead of you little by little. You will not clear them away all at once, for if you did, the wild animals would multiply too quickly for you. But the LORD your God will hand them over to you. He will throw them into complete confusion until they are destroyed. He will put their kings in your power, and you will erase their names from the face of the earth. No one will be able to stand against you, and you will destroy them all." (PERFECT SCENARIO FOR WHAT THE JEWS HAVE DONE TO AMERICA)

Nahum 2:2-10 For the land of Israel lies empty and broken after your attacks, but the LORD will restore its honor and power again. Shields flash red in the sunlight! The attack begins! See their scarlet uniforms! Watch as their glittering chariots move into position, with a forest of spears waving above them. The chariots race recklessly along the streets and through the squares, swift as lightning, flickering like torches. The king shouts to his officers; they stumble in their haste, rushing to the walls to set up their defenses. But too late! The river gates are open! The enemy has entered! The palace is about to collapse! Nineveh's exile has been decreed, and all the servant girls mourn its capture. Listen to them moan like doves; watch them beat their breasts in sorrow. Nineveh is like a leaking water reservoir! The people are slipping away. "Stop, stop!" someone shouts, but the people just keep on running. Loot the silver! Plunder the gold! There seems no end to Nineveh's many treasures – its vast, uncounted wealth. Soon the city is an empty shambles, stripped of its wealth. Hearts melt in horror, and knees shake. The people stand aghast, their faces pale and trembling.

Numbers 31:7-18 The Jews attack Midian just as the LORD had commanded Moses, and they killed all the men. All five of the Midianite kings – Evi, Rekem, Zur, Hur, and Reba – died in the battle. They also killed Balaam son of Beor with the sword. Then the Israelite army captured the Midianite women and children and seized their cattle and flocks and all their wealth as plunder. They burned all the towns and villages where the Midianites had lived. After they had gathered the plunder and captives, both people and animals, they brought them all to Moses and Eleazar the priest, and to the whole community of Israel, which was camped on the plains of Moab beside the Jordan River, across from Jericho.

Moses, Eleazar the priest, and all the leaders of the people went to meet them outside the camp. But Moses was furious with all the military commanders who had returned from the battle. "Why have you let all the women live?" he demanded. "These are the very ones who followed Balaam's advice and caused the people of Israel to rebel against the LORD at Mount Peor. They are the ones who caused the plague to strike the LORD's people. Now kill all the boys and all the women who have slept with a man. Only the young girls who are virgins may live; you may keep them for yourselves.

Exodus 21:7-11 When a man sells his daughter as a slave, she will not be freed at the end of six years as the men are. If she does not please the man who bought her, he may allow her to be bought back again. But he is not allowed to sell her to foreigners, since he is the one who broke the contract with her. And if the slave girl's owner arranges for her to marry his son, he may no longer treat her as a slave girl, but he must treat her as his daughter. If he himself marries her and then takes another wife, he may not reduce her food or clothing or fail to sleep with her as his wife. If he fails in any of these three ways, she may leave as a free woman without making any payment.

Judges 11:29-40 "At that time the Spirit of the LORD came upon Jephthah, and he went throughout the land of Gilead and Manasseh, including Mizpah in Gilead, and led an army against the Ammonites. And Jephthah made a vow to the LORD. He said, "If you give me victory over the Ammonites, I will give to the LORD the first thing coming out of my house to greet me when I return in triumph. I will sacrifice it as a burnt offering."

"So Jephthah led his army against the Ammonites, and the LORD gave him victory. He thoroughly defeated the Ammonites from Aroer to an area near Minnith – twenty towns – and as far away as Abel-keramim. Thus Israel subdued the Ammonites. When Jephthah returned home to Mizpah, his daughter – his only child – ran out to meet him, playing on a tambourine and dancing for joy. When he saw her, he tore his clothes in anguish. "My daughter!" he cried out. "My heart is breaking! What a tragedy that you came out to greet me. For I have made a vow to the LORD and cannot take it back." And she said, "Father, you have made a promise to the LORD. You must do to me what you have promised, for the LORD has given you a great victory over your enemies, the Ammonites. But first let me go up and roam in the hills and weep with my friends for two months, because I will die a virgin." "You may go," Jephthah said. And he let her go away for two months. She and her friends went into the hills and wept because she would never have children. When she returned home, her father kept his vow, and she died a virgin. So it has become a custom in Israel for young Israelite women to go away for four days each year to lament the fate of Jephthah's daughter."

Deuteronomy 13:13-19 "Suppose you hear in one of the towns the LORD your God is giving you that some worthless rabble among you have led their fellow citizens astray by encouraging them to worship foreign gods. In such cases, you must examine the facts carefully. If you find it is true and can prove that such a detestable act has occurred among you, you must attack that town and completely destroy all its inhabitants, as well as all the livestock. Then you must pile all the plunder in the middle of the street and burn it. Put the entire town to the torch as a burnt offering to the LORD your God. That town must remain a ruin forever; it may never be rebuilt. Keep none of the plunder that has been set apart for destruction. Then the LORD will turn from his fierce anger and be merciful to you. He will have compassion on you and make you a great nation, just as he solemnly promised your ancestors. "The LORD your God will be merciful only if you obey him and keep all the commands I am giving you today, doing what is pleasing to him."

Read them ALL for yourselves in your OWN Bible.

NOW – do we see ANY resemblance to the words and actions of Christ to those of the OT Jew Yahweh?

The OT IS the Talmudic JEW 'bible' – filled with terror hate murder greed envy perversions cruelty sadism war destruction and fear! Did I mention LOTS AND LOTS of war and killing and hatred?

The New Testament IS the Christian Bible – a compendium of love, hope, compassion, charity, truth, modesty, tolerance, patience, courage, diligence, and wisdom as exemplified by Jesus.

The decision to investigate these horrors has set my mind free and has not weakened my love of our Lord one iota. You do what your conscience dictates. I am a 'NEW TESTAMANT CHRISTIAN' and not ashamed to admit it. My ONLY regret is that I had not opened my eyes- and my love of TRUTH long ago.

I HONESTLY believe that it is the ONLY way that our arguably dying Christian faith will survive honest minds. Having been raised Catholic – I feel betrayed by the Church of Rome for not having LONG LONG ago had the moral courage and perseverance and wisdom to declare ALL things Jewish as the mortal enemy of Christian belief. I could more easily be convinced that the Talmud and the New Testament were inseparable and interdependent.

"The Jewish so -called religion is the most evil of street gutter trash. It is nothing more than the 'wrapping up' of sharp business practices in a religious garment! Everything that is Holy to Christians is UNHOLY to the wicked jew. Their written religious practices are simply manuals for performing deeds considered deadly sins against humanity in general and Christ in particular."

NOW – I see why Jesus kicked those jew 'pawn brokers' out of the Temple. NOW – I see why Jesus clearly in plain comprehensive language – exposed the Jews as the "sons of Satan". Jesus was the 'new wine'. The sinful wicked hypocrite practices of the Jews before He came represented the "old wine" – hence the parable – "you cannot put new wine into old wineskins".

It is CLEAR! The cruel violent greedy murderous entity of the OT represents ALL of the sins and evil traits so CLEARLY described by Christ as sinful and wicked. The Jews did not worship a kind, benevolent, forgiving, loving, just 'god. They worshiped the DEVIL – CLEARLY AND UNDENIABLY. Christ said so! The awful being described in the OT could not possible be the TRUE GOD. THOSE descriptions obviously describe a horrid Devil -like entity

"When Christ came to this world, He did not come to refine Judaism. He did not come to improve it. He came to take it away and replace it with the new…" Hebrews 8:13: I rest my 'case'.

He did – and He was murdered for it by the Jews who had more or less created THEMSELVES in the image of the Devil whom they worshiped since they refused to hear His 'NEW WORDS' of truth and salvation.

In the ensuing millennia – for fear of losing control of the people who enriched their purses – with 'old wine' false 'religion' of greed lies and pretense – these wicked demonic Synagogue Of Satan Jews conspired to also destroy His followers and converts we call Christians.

The two weapons of deceit they have employed to destroy 'AD' Christianity were – the Old Testament – and in more modern times – the Hollowhoax industry. Both play on our superstitions/ fears – created guilt – and general ignorance and or the lack of understanding of the messages and lessons of the NT and Jesus.

I defy you to find even so many as one in a HUNDRED Americans – even self-professed so-called Christians -who have even read John 8;44 – yet it is without doubt one of- if not THE most profound and profound utterances of our Lord Christ. You will NEVER hear this momentous and powerful message shared in ANY modern false war-mongering 'Christian' Church (Synagogue of Satan)

I am totally and intellectually convinced that IF every American man woman and child had been required to read this most significant condemnation of the murderous criminal jews and their filthy lies – we would be today – a prosperous vibrant world leader – loved and respected by all freedom loving people on earth and enjoying the blessings of a true Christian nation – instead being a criminal Jew occupied land of shallow witless greedy pleasure seeking I-Pod Stupid Bowl NFL imbeciles – destined to shortly end up on the ash heap of history.

JANUARY, 2012
THE US ARMY TODAY-THE ULTIMATE EVIL-ONE NATION UNDER ISRAHELL!

Aside from being a pimp or a whore or a pedophile – I can't think of ANY type of 'job' more disgusting, more evil, more putrid, more rancid, more degenerate, more Godless or more demonic than to be involved in our DOD *(Department of Death and Destruction)* at the level of enticing decent wholesome innocent young men from their family environment and turning them into Godless robotic sociopathic baby killers – rapists -sadists – murderers – racists and terrorists – and REWARD THEM FOR THEIR CRIMES AGAINST HUMANITY!

My thanks to Brother Nathanael for the recent opportunity to expose these insidious 'Army Strong' evils to parents of young men who genuinely believe they are doing something noble and patriotic for America – by dying for IsraHELL. Read our interview and learn the filthy nasty dirty truths about how our wicked government is now training your beloved sons – NOT to be warriors to defend America – but to be Godless murderers for the Jews.

I was once as proud as any man ever born to wear the uniform and the silver wings of a paratrooper officer in service of the protection of the country I loved deeply. 'Death before dishonor' was once the unspoken maxim of my Special Forces comrades. I trained LOTS and LOTS of young Americans – your GRANDFATHERS – to be exact.

Today – NOTHING could be further from the truth! My beloved young son and countless more seduced naive young idealists/adventurists are nothing more than puppets for IsraHELL and it's PROVEN DEADLY agenda for Jewish hegemony of the entire Middle East as their slave states and personal concentration camps.

BEEN THERE, SEEN THAT – FIRSTHAND – UP CLOSE and UGLY!

I have lived long enough to witness our military transform from forging young, mostly-Christian warriors with courage, nobleness and character into pure Godless opportunistic mercenary psychopathic killers for hire.

There is a HUGE difference between the decent moral patriotic men of my era and the putrid terrorist robotic sick twisted garbage we turn out today. If you cannot see that difference – you are already a morally rotted corpse.

AND OF COURSE – ULTIMATELY – THE GRAND PRIZE – THE UNITED STATES OF AMERICA – currently under Jewish occupation, including our churches, newspapers, TV (Talmud vision) our police and our schools!

These Jews who would send MY son to an early grave for THEIR pleasure are cunning enough to never shed one drop of their racially-superior Jew blood. "Let those ignorant foolish 'goyim' do our dirty work for us!"

The REAL 'TERRORISTS' are right HERE on Capitol Hill! Again, been there, seen that.

There is nothing more noble than a man's courage to sacrifice himself for the safety, defense, and well-being of his family, friends, and country from a REAL ENEMY – as we once had when I was training young warriors.

THAT mortal REAL enemy was in fact created, sustained, financed, and sadistically enforced by the Jews – just in case you have forgotten your history lessons,

There is ALSO nothing more LOATHSOME and disgusting than for a man to disgrace the uniform to satisfy some Godless, sick, twisted, racist psychopathic urge to murder helpless defenseless children, rape helpless girls, slaughter innocent civilian families, and to loot, steal, plunder and destroy the homes and cities of innocent people.

Tragically, that is EXACTLY what the US Army has become. The records bearing testimony to this fact are LEGION.

My own fatherland – beloved place of my birth – has now earned the loathsome distinction of being the perpetrator of more horrible war crimes against innocent civilians in the past ten years than committed by ALL of earth's 'civilized' nations for the past millennia.

We have as of this date – MURDERED IN COLD-BLOOD MORE THAN TWO MILLION INNOCENT CIVILIANS, HALF OF WHICH WERE CHILDREN – as if they were nothing more than insects. As disgusting as it universally is among decent folk, nevertheless I have heard a LOT of so-called 'real Americans' cheer on these sadistic butcherings as if all of it were nothing more than one of their precious NFL games, which in a sense it is.

ALL of this killing, destruction, and massive radiation poisoning via depleted Uranium has merited America not one iota of "SAFETY" or "SECURITY." It HAS awarded us the title of the most evil, feared and hated people on earth. All of this senseless killing for the greater glory of the Jews will not and CANNOT be forgotten by the victims thereof.

When the REAL patriots – and REAL Christians finally WAKE UP and decide they have had enough lies, corruption, anti-Christian Jew TV, duplicity, treason, moral and economic ransacking of our nation by the Jews and their Jew puppets is when criminals like Obama and that beady-eyed treasonous country-selling vulture Biden will see fit to declare MARTIAL LAW.

WHEN that happens (NOT a matter of IF but WHEN) THAT is when our own uniformed sons will be receive 'orders' from their 'superiors' to KICK IN THE DOORS of their own countrymen who do not follow the PARTY LINE, and "NEUTRALIZE" and "ENGAGE" (READ: KILL!) the "HOSTILES (READ: American civilian families.

Our Marines have ALREADY admitted they will murder us and their counterparts in the Army will not be far behind. Our youth have already been conditioned during their previous 18 years of moral development through Talmud Vision to ENJOY watching suffering, death, and horror.

The examples are legion. The sadistic, remorseless killers at Columbine were ardent violent WAR GAME video fans, just ONE example. Prominent clinical researchers have proven that the primary cause of violence and aggression in our children in last decade or so is directly attributable to their incessant diet of ultra-violent sadistic 'WAR GAME' videos.

One of many similar observations by returning Gulf-War veterans–"Video games that allow players to murder real human beings are desensitizing generations of American society."

A similar conclusion by another Gulf-War/Iraq War vet–"Kids get in the Army and get to live out their aggressive fantasies of violence and killing."

Another vet's revealing and chilling observation–"The ARMY gives you the ultimate 'license to kill.'"

For God's sake folks – do something to stop this madness before it is too late for all of us! Do not let this be a voice in the wilderness. TAKE OUR NATION BACK!

LOOK at the TRUTH concerning WHO the ones are screaming in shrill voices for WAR, MORE WAR AND KILLING OF INNOCENTS. It is the Jews and their demonic, treasonous country-selling Zionist useful idiots – Tragically Christians of virtually all faiths – who mock our Lord even more cruelly than the insolent Jews themselves.

Look at Matthew 5-9 and there you will find the words of Christ: Blessed are the peacemakers, for they will be called the children of God…

For those of you who still try to conduct your lives in the spirit of the TRUE word of Christ–nota bene–IsraHELL and 99% of ALL Jews do NOT want peace. They want what they have shown to love for all of recorded history – BLOOD, KILLING, VIOLENCE, and the endless suffering of their victims.

Did Bush ask for an end to war? Did he strive to emulate Jesus as a 'PEACEMAKER'?

NO.

ANYONE who worked in his-Jew infested administration who so much as DARED to stand for peace, justice, sanity, truth, and righteousness – like decorated US CENTCOM Commander/4-star Admiral William Fallon was simply 'thrown under the bus'.

Has Obama – with his Zionist-Jew dominated cabinet strived in ANY way to end this madness and insanity and act as peacemaker?

NO!

Has his shifty, beady-eyed, monstrously-evil Vice Demon Biden done ANYTHING other than PURE TREASON TO AMERICA – and 100% devotion to Jew war-mongering causes?

NO!

Has our criminal Congress acted as the peacemakers that the American people hired them, to be?

NO!

Have ANY of the Jew-owned MSM or their useful idiot puppet show hosts – Hannity, Colmes, O' Reilly, Limbaugh – or ANY major news personality voiced ANY sincere wish to end this immoral slaughter of innocent people?

NO!

Have any of the major churches of the 50 million or so Hagee-inflamed Zionist Baptist churches who so ardently support the Jews (the same Jews who tirelessly work 24/7 for the destruction of Christ and His principles) ever voiced their loathing at these brutal, genocidal, demonic, wars for the greater glory of IsraHELL?

NO!

Are our own children taught anything today that is good, wholesome, Godly, charitable, compassionate, and Christ-like today in our 100% Jew-controlled public schools, or on the 100% controlled JEW TV, or our 100% Jew controlled 'entertainment industry?

NO!

50 years go as a young man, thing I have written here would have been pertinent, for the simple reason that it wouldn't have been necessary – as we still had decent people who knew right from wrong, and the putrid, demonic, evil conduct of ALL the aforementioned mega-criminal, greedy, self-serving parasitic, anti-American scum would have NEVER been tolerated for a day.

BUT TODAY – in our occupied serfdom of Godless 'IsraHELL West' – I will assuredly be persecuted for even DARING to be so insolent as to defend the teachings of our Lord that are now so unopposed and boldly mocked by the powers that be and their spineless 'news' shills who do their evil bidding.

Our modern 'improved' Zionist-loyal military are the world's largest cabal of criminal gangsters – virtually no different from the Chi-Coms or the former Soviet military. For ANYBODY who thinks that is ANYTHING but the absolute Gospel truth – I challenge you to study your modern history. Look at the dozens of articles in the Reader's Digest alone which chronicle the sadistic, brutal, criminal conduct of the Soviet military in their mid-to-late 80's military occupation of Afghanistan – which rightfully earned them the title of THE EVIL EMPIRE!

The only difference is that we–'GOD BLESS AMERICA' have now committed more brutal atrocities to those poor people than Soviets did.

READ THE TRUTH FOR YOURSELF. We are even MORE guilty than the communists – simply because WE as a free people in a Christian based Republic UNLIKE the subverted closed society ignorant Soviet masses – HAD A CHOICE.

We on the other hand CHOSE TO BE EVIL. That is the unvarnished ugly immutable TRUTH – like it or not. THIS is what WE – of our own free will have allowed ourselves to become – the NEW EVIL EMPIRE.

WHERE IS THE RIGHTEOUS OUTRAGE AT THE EVIL THAT DESTROYS OUR GOODNESS 24-7?

FEBRUARY, 2012
'LARRY – THE ASSHOLE GUY' – THE MOST RANCID PIECE OF HUMAN GARBAGE IN AMERICA

By now – there isn't a single decent American in this 'Judeo-Christian' country who hasn't been insulted, slandered, mocked, demeaned, and ridiculed by this obese Jew wanna-be piece of shit, obese, pig-faced, media prostitute. Can we possibly be so stupid that we now enjoy masochism?

When I was growing up – a bully – whether a physical one or a verbal one – was a creature to be detested by decent people. ESPECIALLY when that individual was a racist, a bigot, and a blasphemer – all rolled up into one wicked sadistic greasy fat pig.

Here is an animal who is 100% fake (his accent is fake – his name is fake – his assumed job is fake. His given name is Daniel Whitney and he was raised on a pig farm. Perhaps that is why he now resembles one. One of the signs of inbred vegetable class stupidity is when a person is grievously – maliciously – spitefully slandered and insulted to the core of his beliefs or religious values or afflictions or ethnicity – and thinks that is funny!

OH – I should lighten up and not be so tight-assed about 'jokes'? Oh then – next time I see your sorry ass on the street in public – how about I call your MOTHER or WIFE a WHORE? Don't get all riled up! Just remember – Larry the asshole guy – does this kind of Comedy Central mentality thing 24-7 and gets paid HUGE amounts of money for it by his Jew bosses – so it MUST be cool – because when HE does it – it suddenly becomes comedy for the whole family.

Any of you readers had a loved one – maybe your own mother – as I did – die as a victim of Alzheimer's? Then you know one of the ULTIMATE emotional pains in life – a gut wrenching pain in your heart NO ONE can POSSIBLY understand this pain unless you 'HAVE BEEN THERE'. It is the ONLY fatal disease which causes so much collateral grief that the survivors have created support groups to deal with the pain and stay out of deep depression. I still remember how my mother died. I had just gone through a divorce – had no family support for myself or to deal with my mom and was struggling to keep a small business alive so that I could pay the huge non-covered bills for her.

NOTHING will break your heart more that having to see that special person who gave you life and nurtured you and raised you with the love ONLY a mother could give and sacrificed it all to keep you safe and healthy and happy – to see her now as the living dead – conscious but for all intents a purposes brain-dead. I visited her every morning at the home and then went to work – sat at my desk for an hour without saying a word – fighting tears and anger and an indescribable pain – so that I could function well enough in an office environment to pay the bills.

This went on needlessly – week after month – till I thought I would end up on drugs or alcohol trying to cope with an impossible emotional task and function as a normal human being the rest of the day – knowing it would be the same the next day and the next and the next ...... NO ONE WHO HAS NOT LIVED THROUGH THAT EXPERIENCE CAN POSSIBLY UNDERSTAND OR CONSOLE YOU. Thank you so much 'Larry' for your sadistic cruelty to my beloved mother. What if it was YOUR mother Mr. Whitney?

Larry – The Asshole Guy has a specialty though. Oh sure – he is notorious for mocking and ridiculing all of you 'mud-people' – blacks, Puerto Ricans, Mexicans, etc – but his true heart's desire is in mocking Christ and all things and traditions truly Christian. He has made an album called 'HAVE A VERY LARRY CHRISTMAS' that makes most hard core Jew mockery of our Lord look sophomoric. I invite the strong of heart to click on the site and see just how far we as a people have sunk so as to accept and make this rancid pig a multimillionaire 'pop' entertainer. Remember – this putrid filth and his cruel mockery of Christ is WHO and WHAT your kids now look up to as an urban legend of comedy.

http://www.youtube.com/watch?v=-xpcVUSLUyY

He endlessly rails his 'redneck' hatred and racist mockery against Arab people who have never done him, me or ANY AMERICAN any harm. This open hate mongering which incites these REAL brain-sharing pieces of subhuman detritus imbeciles like Toby Keith to even further hate mongering – causing endless murders, rapes and destruction of innocent civilians by our even more immoral Jew controlled sociopathic uniformed military criminals.

When I was a child and we were still a decent, Godly, Christian nation – free of Jewish influence – his kind of filth would have caused RIOTS anywhere it was exposed to the public and their children. That is a GOOD THING. It is called RIGHTEOUS OUTRAGE and DEFENDING OUR FAITH. It pertained to that part of our oaths which specified the need to defend our nation against "DOMESTIC ENEMIES" as well.

I used to hear my father extol the virtues of America and the endless opportunities it offered hard working, honest, virtuous citizens. Neither he nor I ever dreamed that such a putrid tub of lard/Christ hating/foul-mouthed troglodyte pig like Dan Whitney could become famous and super wealthy from peddling his vile, hate-filled blasphemies in a nation he never served nor defended and whose Founding Fathers unquestionably founded the same upon Christian principles.

Every member of every visible Church in this nation which can honestly call itself 'CHRISTIAN' based upon the love of fellow man and following of the teachings of Christ – which remains silent regarding the unconscionable public conduct of this enemy of Christianity and of ALL decent men of good will – is guilty of co-sponsoring the blasphemies as is the demonic filth – Dan Whitney – himself.

MARCH, 2012
AMERIKA THE GREEDY–AMERIKA THE NEEDY–AMERIKA THE CORRUPT–AMERIKA THE CRUDE

It has gotten so bad that I don't know where to start – and the worst part is that had any of these signs of a dying nation been public when I was a young man – the public outrage would have been swift – collective and LOUD!

Today – there is not so much as a whimper from religious figures – from school officials – from civil leaders – from public figures or even 'the next door neighbor'. This fact does not bode well for the survival of this country.

Just like in the medical profession – there are benchmarks – or indicators by which the 'moral health' of an entire nation make manifest the dangerous condition before it reaches the point of 'terminal' – 'incurable' – or 'deadly'. Sadly – also like a medical diagnosis – if caught early – and properly TREATED -most 'patients' may be saved.

AMERICA THE GREEDY . The examples are legion, but here is a classic and particularly disgusting odious case in point. A drug derived from a common plant discovered over three thousand years ago called colchisine has been the best and most effective remedy against a disease – although not life threatening in by itself – is painful to a degree that it WILL make even a grown macho-man cry like a little girl.

The drug – until just recently – had been made available by no less than twenty one different pharmaceutical companies and affordable to even the most destitute of citizens. Even Wal-Mart carried it as far back as I can remember for a modest $10 for a three MONTHS supply (thirty pills). A criminally greedy drug company called URL Pharma – somehow destroyed ALL the competition and virtually overnight – changed the name of the drug so it could not be found elsewhere and jacked up the price.

So that you realize I am not splitting hairs in my condemnation of these greedy reptiles – let me make a universally understandable cost comparison example. I used 24ct 999 fine pure GOLD as the benchmark. Their – 'across the counter' drug price increased over TWELVE THOUSAND percent overnight! This cheap available drug was suddenly MUCH more expensive than PURE GOLD!

Think of an elderly widowed grandmother – alone in life and on a fixed 'assistance' dole from the Govt who has the EXCRUCIATINGLY painful condition which requires this very specific drug. The drug expense along eats up 15-20% of her total sustenance – so that she must at times make the decision whether to eat dog food or suffer unimaginable pain! I have reported this greed crime to insurance companies and to elected officials – but don't hold your breath for someone to rescue 'Granny'.

AMERIKA THE NEEDY Since our economy imploded and unemployment exploded and our gone INSANE government still forced citizens to pay TRILLIONS for endless serial wars for ISRAHELL – where we have made lifetime enemies out of formerly friendly totally innocent nations (Yes Dorothy – 9-11 WAS IN FACT a jew false flag crime just like so many other lies perpetrated by the jews) — I began to notice something remarkably different about the homeless 'bums' panhandling on street corners.

For the past few years I have taken all my pocket change and separated the pennies nickels and dimes into bags of a few dollars each to give to these unfortunates. I had my own rules for charity. No change bags for $5 a pack smoker or those with alcohol on their breath. All the rest were at my perception of their sincerity – black or white – male or female.

The numbers of these unfortunates was steadily growing month by year – which was to be expected – but then I began to notice a remarkable change in the appearance of these desperate 'street' people. There was always that look of hopelessness and sadness but there was something else. I saw well groomed hair – mostly all sober – no smokers – cleanly – even if modestly dressed – well spoken – and articulate. In short – these folks were NOW looking more and more like my neighbors – or the average man in the street or the average middle class shopper . I struck up a brief conversations at stop lights with these 'neo-homeless' and was impressed by their humility and efforts to shield what little pride they had left. Their sincere 'God bless you sir' parting sentiments touched my heart.

It scared the crap out of me. I experienced some level of homeless all my life but NEVER people who looked like mainstream blue collar America. These were not 'street bums' – they were victims of a greedy opportunistic nation of Godless parasites and non-compassionate criminals in the White House (read: WHORE HOUSE!)

AMERICA THE CORRUPT If you do a thesaurus/dictionary search for the adjective – 'corrupt' – you will find the following inclusive examples: dishonest – fraudulent – unscrupulous – dishonorable – untrustworthy – immoral – wicked – degenerate – perverted and a laundry list more – ALL of which – describe President 'O-bummer' to a 'T'!

Sadly – ALL of these also describe war criminal George Bush – a slimy hypocrite reptile whose crimes against humanity and this country are also legion and countless – but I digress. Bush will also have his place reserved in hell.

Should you believe that I am in the SLIGHTEST Way being overly disrespectful of our Criminal – In- Chief – consider the following disgraceful FACTS and the voluminous supportive evidence that the 'Obamination' is a monster who is IN FACT – a baby killer – a sex pervert – a Marxist ideologue – a treasonous scumbag and a pathogenic liar.

I used GOOGLE for my search engine and here are the astonishing figures unveiled by the corresponding searches.

"OBAMA -BABY KILLER" ==== "THIRTY TWO MILLION FOUR HUNDRED THOUSAND RESULTS!"

"OBAMA – SEX PERVERT" ==== "SIX MILLION, FOUR HUNDRED THIRTY THOUSAND RESULTS!"

"OBAMA – MARXIST IDEOLOGUE" == " ONE MILLION, ONE HUNDRED FORTY THOUSAND RESULTS!"

"OBAMA – TREASONOUS SCUMBAG" == " SEVEN MILLION FIFTY THOUSAND RESULTS!"

"OBAMA – PATHOGENIC LIAR" === " THREE HUNDRED NINETY FIVE THOUSAND RESULTS!"

"OBAMA – ARROGANT BASTARD" === " ONE MILLION SIX HUNDRED TWENTY THOUSAND RESULTS!"

AND THIS = is who our brain dead minorities want for "THE CONSCIENCE OF THE NATION"? I rest my case.

AMERIKA THE CRUDE There is SO MUCH of this filth spewed out like warm vomit on our jew owned – jew directed jew financed – jew sponsored – jew featured TalmudVision – that there is no way even most of the worst could be stored on a 'terabyte disc! Christ is mocked every night of the week on just ONE of their many Jew directed – jew created 'ADULT SWIM' episodes or that Biblical creation is trashed or that true Christians are made to look like nerds idiots morons bigots and imbeciles.

AND that is what Christians are mocked with 24-7. God forbid if you are a moral sober Muslim! Take the most crude vile rancid filthy putrid conduct imaginable in the darkest most private most morally uncontrolled part of your conscience – and that doesn't even begin to describe the filth that the jew employs to elevate amoral degeneracy – so as to make it acceptable conduct to your innocent children.

Who are the jew heros on their Talmud vision today? Selfless savers of human life like firemen – or EMR groups – or Founding Fathers who sacrificed it all to give us our freedoms in a Christian based moral government- or dedicated educators who declined fat cat industry jobs to educate our children – or true freedom fighters who renounced wealth and safety and creature comforts to secure the blessings of freedoms for others – or researchers who have dedicated their lives to discover cures and remedies only to give them at no personal gain to a pain filled world?

Are you shitting me? – as if there was ever groups of wealthy jews whose goals were anything other than self-serving greed to make themselves even richer. Just take a look at what the jews have done to AmeriKan 'entertainment and education' on their Talmud vision. Alligator Man – Pumpkin Chunkin – Duck Dynasty – Jackass – 1001 Ways to Die – Mud Boggin Racing – Tractor Pulls – NASCAR – NFL – AMERIKAN IDOL – Keeping UP With The Kardashians – The Family Jewels – Pawn Stars – Sons Of Anarchy – Mad Men – Californication – Tim And Eric – Fear Factor – Man Vs Food – Jerry Springer – Roseanne Barr – Sarah Silverman and a THOUSAND more

To give you an example of just how far these slimy reptilian scum will go – I was watching a prime time so-called comedy entertainment show on the Jew Epix channel. There was an obese putrid pig on stage – dressed like a punk rock idiot, who used the terms"fucking" – "fuck you" – and "mother fucker" and "mother fucking" in front of a mixed audience – mostly white and with many many children in the audience – so many times in a 60 second period (in disbelief of want I was seeing and hearing, I timed him) His obscene pure filth in public made nigger rap trash Snoop Dogg and Soulja Boy sound like choir boys from the MormanTabernancle choir!

The name of this putrid piece of filth was Kevin Smith. I seventy three years of life – 40 years of travel and 4 years of being a paratroop commander combined I have never heard such senseless profanity spewed out of the mouth of ANY sub human animal – black or white and certainly not in a public place LOADED with children. But you haven't heard the worst yet. A polite little ten year old girl with her family asked this putrid animal a question about a film he had made called Mall Rats.

His answer to the little girl? – a mocking : " Why You were just cum when I was making Mall Rats"

And if I have to explain the subhuman nature of the level of demeaning filth his response implied – then the reader needs to ne watered instead of fed. This was without doubt the most crude vile rancid putrid filthy nasty attack on the sensibilities of a child I have heard in my LIFE!!!!! What was even MORE disturbing to me personally – was the fact that instead of righteous anger at the unbelievably cruel base insult to a child and the parents – they howled with applause! How sick can we get? Had that been MY daughter or granddaughter – I would have beat the bastard to death on the spot without ANY regard to my own safety . Judge me anyway you will but that is my code concerning the innocence of such a child in my family.

We have become a sick twisted Godless nation – devoid of ANY goodness or sense of honor or propriety. I have traveled extensively in the past and honestly say that I have NEVER – EVER – even in the poorest of nations – witnessed such reprobate filthy Godless wicked sinister conduct. I find it hard to even imagine that what garbage we have become is less evil than the wickedness of Sodom & Gomorrah as depicted in Scripture as twin cities worthy of total destruction by God.

My 73 years of life experience is less than a heartbeat in the finite history of mankind – yet in reflection of the experiences of my youth – we as a people have transformed from goodness piety honor and wisdom – to the depths of depravity -all in the blink of an eye. What a heartbreaking curse it must be for a moral decent human being having to live in awareness in AmeriKa for over a hundred years. Please – show some righteous indignation towards the guilty – from the White House – to the house next door.

MARCH, 2012
DEPLETED URANIUM WEAPONS (DU) – THE REAL 'DIRTY BOMBS'

Interview between Joe Cortina and Brother Nathanael Kapner of www.realjewnews.com

Q – Joe -what is DU?

A – Nathanael – it is an acronym for Depleted Uranium. DU is a byproduct from spent uranium rods in reactors. It is the uranium remaining after removal of the enriched fraction contains about 99.8% 238U, 0.2% 235U and 0.001% 234U by mass; this is referred to as depleted uranium or DU.

Q – Does it have radioactive properties?

A- yes , Natural Uranium consists of three Isotopes = U235 , U238 and U 234. DU is composed of all three but is over 99% U238. U238 has a much longer half life than the other isotopes so radiates less alfa rays than natural Uranium. There are technical considerations involving Alpha rays Beta rays. Gamma rays and neutron rays – but in layman's language the bottom line is that vaporized DU is DEADLY TO ALL LIFE on earth!

Q – So why is it used by the military?

A- because of its density – it has greater penetration potential against armor and other hard targets it can be used for armor , or for kinetic energy projectiles to defeat armor – as it is about twice as dense as lead and unlike tungsten will ignite at temperatures over 600F

Q – How is it dissipated into the environment under war scenarios?

A – used in cannons rockets and bombs – It essentially vaporizes after the heat and kinetic energy of impact and produces a lot of DU dust particles as small as 5 microns and can travel long distances when airborne

Q- how is it introduced into the human body?

A – three ways – absorption through the skin or through open wounds or by in inhalation into the lungs which is the most common AND most hazardous.

Q – Are there 'safe' dosages"

A – ONLY – If you believe the biggest liars on earth – the 'US Government'. Our Government has lied to the public for years about all aspects of radioactive isotopes – more recently regarding DU. There is no safe dose or dose rate below which dangers disappear. No threshold-dose,'" says John Gofman, a former associate director of Livermore National Laboratory, one of the scientists who worked on the atomic bomb, and co-discoverer of uranium-233. "Serious, lethal effects from minimal radiation doses are not 'hypothetical,' 'just theoretical,' or 'imaginary.' They are real."

Q – Sounds like a situation that calls for education and direct action – so when was this dangerous technology first employed

A – Absolutely – education and activism is a must and not near enough emphasis has been placed on the he very real hazards. Our government has been lying about the risks since day one of the Gulf Wars in 1991. During this first period apx 350 tons were spread in Iraq. During the subsequent wars – the invasion of Iraq nearly 2000 Tons turned that nation into a radioactive wasteland.

Q – is it used in Afghanistan as well?

A – Absolutely! There has been tens of thousands of MORE tons of this deadly poison spread over Afghanistan by an irresponsible Government gone mad! These deadly micro-particles are often carried up in the atmosphere and released with rain hundreds or perhaps thousands of miles away. The Jews have spread over 75 tons of this radioactive death on the tiny 138 Sq mile prison we know as Gaza. That is enough to kill 50 million people. Gaza has 1.5 million

Q- What a horrible nightmare. I have heard these demonic weapons called dirty bombs. Is there any validation to that in technical means?

A – Let me tell you just how accurate that fear is considered to be by experts. When asked by the American Free Press – Marion Falk a retired Chemical physicist who built nuclear bombs for more than 20 years at Lawrence Livermore lab, if he thought that DU weapons operate in a similar manner as a dirty bomb. "That's exactly what they are," Falk said. "They fit the description of a dirty bomb in every way."

Q – so – America has become the major destroyer of the world community environment ?

A – Absolutely! We are as evil a polluter as any nation on earth .

Q- But is there any evidence to show that our Government was aware of these war crimes against humanity.

A – Once again – ABSOLUTELY – proof positive. While the Pentagon officially denies the dangers of DU weapons, since at least 1943 the military has been aware of the extreme toxicity of uranium dispersed as a gas (or dust particles -ed).

A declassified memo written by James B. Conant and two other physicists working on the U.S. nuclear project during the Second World War, and sent to Brig. Gen. L.R. Groves on October 30, 1943, provides the evidence:

"As a gas warfare instrument the [radioactive] material would be ground into particles of microscopic size to form dust and smoke and distributed by a ground-fired projectile, land vehicles, or aerial bombs," the 1943 memo reads. "In this form it would be inhaled by personnel. The amount necessary to cause death to a person inhaling the material is extremely small. It has been estimated that one millionth of a gram accumulation in a person is body would be fatal. There are no known methods of treatment for such a casualty."

Point is – ALL of our leadership civilian and military knew EXACTLY what would happen if we polluted the earth with it. Incidentally we have stockpiles of over 150 MILLION TONS! To put it into perspective – enough to give a death sentence to every man woman and child on earth! We have ALSO permanently poisoned hundreds of MILLIONS of square miles of land no longer safe for providing food for a starving world. We are now the monsters of the universe – whose greed and lust for power has exalted all manner of evil and wickedness to obfuscate rationality goodness and wisdom. WE – sir – have become the willful arch enemies of God and our own people its placated accomplices.

Q – What in name of God have we done? Have any effects of these poisons shown up since these endless serial wars started?

A – The evidence is now legion. Anybody, civilian or soldier, who breathes these particles has a permanent dose, and it is not going to decrease very much over time," Leonard Dietz, a retired nuclear physicist with 33 years experience told the New York Daily News. "In the long run – veterans exposed to ceramic uranium oxide have a major problem."

"Inhaled particles of radioactive uranium oxide dust will either lodge in the lungs or travel through the body, depending on their size. The smallest particles can be carried through cell walls and "affect the master code – the expression of the DNA," Falk told American Free Press.

More than one out of every three veterans from the first Gulf War are permanently disabled. Terry Jemison of the Dept. of Veterans Affairs said that of the 592,561 discharged veterans from the 1991 war in Iraq, 179,310 are receiving disability compensation and another 24,763 cases are pending. Actually these figures are several years old now. I think one could safely add 25-30% to the above figures – as if they were not disturbing enough!

Q – I have see photographs of children born in Iraq and Afghanistan during this period and they are heart breaking

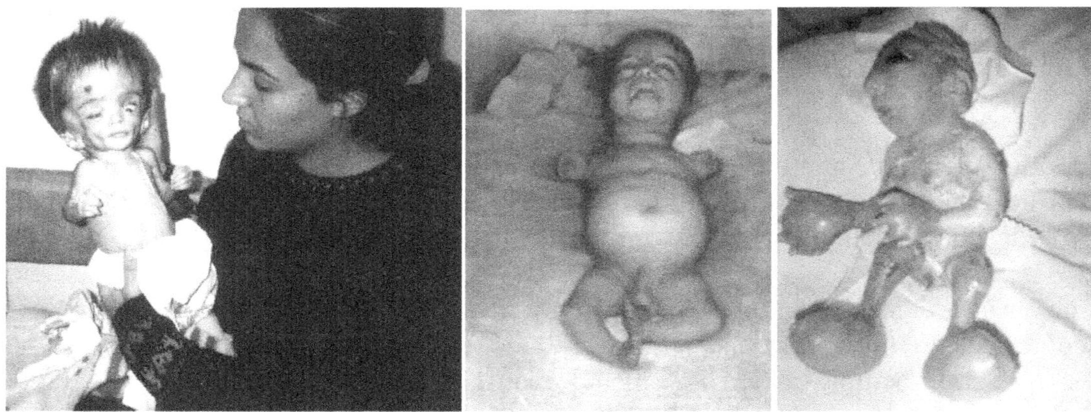

A – I have also seen them – and expect a lot more as time passes. What is truly tragic is that so many of these young mothers mostly clean living religious Muslims naive as to what real life monsters are capable of doing to innocent people – see their precious babies born with horrible deformities beyond description – two heads – a third eye – gigantic swollen and or blackened heads – intestines outside the body and WORSE! The increases of bizarre monstrous birth defects have increased by THOUSANDS of percentages since we have saturated our victim's nations with these lethal poisons. The evidence is now legion and supported by the finest scientific minds on earth.

Nathanael – The problem is this: Now that these ghastly demonic horrors have been exposed – including the FACT that our 'Government' has LONG SINCE known about the deadly nature of these insane lethal threats to all living organisms – rational people can only conclude that the people we have entrusted our very lives to are lying sick twisted demonic sociopathic mass murdering criminals – from our top ranking military leaders all the way to the President – and MUST be charged tried and convicted of mass murder. To NOT do so is to doom humanity to eventual extinction and relegate the goodness of human beings to that of mindless demonic bararic demons. We MUST regain our sanity and do what needs to be done. Reign in the greatest institutionalized terrorist apparatus on earth – the greedy Godless murderous maniacal military industrial complex that was once America

These poor innocents in horror of what has happened to their children – many believed that they had somehow been responsible and had offended God – so in their irreconcilable grief are committing suicide because of their guilt. The REAL monsters are of course our neighbors – the “brave – free” American people – who see these horror so every day and could care less about these poor victims of American criminal imperialism as long as they have their American Idol Talmudvision – new cars – comfortable homes – cold beer and of course their obligatory Sat night NFL idiocy.

Q – Then what you are saying is that in the near future – many of these hundreds of thousands of Mid- East Veterans have inhaled this deadly contaminated dust and are walking time bombs.

A – Exactly. It is already showing up despite all the frantic efforts to cover-up. Perhaps this nuclear bomb builder physicist scientist’s comment says it best about the many symptoms of Golf war veterans that our lying VA puppets want to give different catchy names or ‘syndromes’ like PTSD or PTSS to explain the inevitable horrors away: “Inhaled DU can “fool around with the keys” and do damage to “practically anything, It affects the body in so many ways and there are so many different symptoms that they want to give it different names,”

Q – So what do we tell our Vets when they begin fathering children that look like some nightmarish ‘Alien like reptile.

A – Simple – since they volunteered – WITHOUT ANY MORAL RESERVATION to go to another human being’s nation – murder their people – rape their women – loot their heritage – (to keep Merka free of all these marauding ‘Mooselim’ terrorists of course) ALL based on filthy lies promoted by the jews – then they shouldn’t have a big problem accepting that their new baby girl or boy looks like an FX Talmud vision creation.

Our ‘Judeo – Christian’ values based Government would NEVER EVER lie to its own people – especially our vets – so just accept the fact that your web-footed or third eyed baby was because your wife became a crack head while you were gone murdering other people children and saturating their entire country with ‘safe’ uranium oxide dust. It couldn’t be the wrath of God because the jews who give us our marching orders are His chosen people – according to our self anointed Judeo-Christian value prophets like Hagee.

Q- So what is the fate of the six hundred thousand+ – and growing daily number of returned vets who have been exposed to breathing in DU dust particles?

A – Simple – they will all die – some sooner – some later. Some will father babies that look like demons and suffer the same grief they have caused countless inocent Afghan and Iraqi parents by saturating their nations with radioactive death. After watching their children suffer and die from poisons they themselves were responsible for – Eventually – they themselves will all experience worsening prognosis and die horrible lingering cancerous systemic deaths which will of course be diagnosed as some sort of nonexistent ‘syndromes’ which will have catchy acronym ‘new names for old lies’.

But that is OK with many Americans because the endless wars which we started and in which they sacrificed their lives as well as millions of other innocent lives – will have made the world a safer place. OH – almost forgot – safer for the jews only – the only part of the nature of these wars that is true.

So now just ignore these truths again – grab a cold Bud – take one of your purple pills – turn on the Talmud vision to your favorite jew created violence or NFL and repeat this little mantra over and over till it make things right again. "Our government would never lie to us – our government would never lie to us – our government would never lie to us". Or if you feel really 'patriotic' – you can see your recruiter and redeploy to murder more "rag head" or "dune coon" or "sand nigger" children – as you vets AND our brave military leaders so eloquently belittle them. There now – don't you feel a lot better bout being a brave – free 'Merkan'?

MARCH, 2012
POP QUIZ ON JEW BEAUTY QUEENS

The nubile sexy Hebrew princess in the picture is in reality:

(A) An IDF 'Playmate of the month' sex goddess
(B) The Jewish Pillsbury 'DOUGH-GIRL'
(C) A centerfold for 'Miss Piggy' magazine
(D) Jewish dream girl
(E) Pig farm security cop
(F) Poster girl for the 'Pork Belly Futures' brokers Inc.
(G) Miss Tel Aviv contestant
(H) Cheerleader for Mt Zion High
(I) Abe Foxman's personal Fitness instructor
(J) Pop art jew girl figure made of all bread dough
(K) Popular Israeli porn sex channel porn star
(L) Nutritionist advisor for jew glutton TV star Adam Richman
(M) Glutton Bowl speed eating champion
(N) Miss Silly Putty lookalike contest winner
(O) Unsuccessful tanning bed saleswoman
(P) Definitive quintessential example of a butt-UGLY female!
(Q) Failed Ab-Blaster saleswoman
(R) A pin up girl for H.G.Wells' pasty albino subterranean Morlocks
(S) An ADL terrorist
(T) A 300 pound pig, 'photoshoped' to look like a woman
(U) Covergirl for 'Piglets-n-Porkers on Parade' magazine

MARCH, 2012
OPEN LETTER TO AMERICANS–HOWEVER FEW IN NUMBER–WHO CAN STILL HANDLE THE TRUTH

Most of us are aware of the latest in an endless list of soulless, Godless, sadistic, sociopathic, cold-blooded mass-murderers in the jew-occupied rotted corpse of our former moral self. These collective criminals are our military and are hopelessly evil, wicked, twisted, demonic filth which today factually rivals the most sanguine, sadistic, brutal, barbaric thugs of the former Godless Soviet Union. (FSU)

Former President Ronald Reagan termed them the 'EVIL EMPIRE' as analogous to the totally evil incarnate nature of the villains of the Star Wars episodes. The brutality of these animals was unparalleled in modern history and their legacy of death and terror is well chronicled for any interested party to experience in history books and even pop periodicals like Reader's Digest. I still have in my library many issues from the 70s which covered in detail – horrors committed by a Godless, dysfunctional Soviet military against the simple poor civilian populace of Afghanistan.

There – assembled like stories out of a horror movie series were the real life crimes of a sick twisted society with gory details week after week and month after month. Several films became popular during that period, one of which was Red Scorpion with super hero Swedish actor Dolf Lundgren where he plays a Spetsnaz (Russian Special Forces) commando who realizes he is on the wrong side. (Some of our own soldiers are finally beginning to figure that out for themselves)

Yet another was a Rambo classic where after witnessing the horrible injustices committed by the invading Soviets – our hero decides to help the Afghan Mujahedeen fight their evil empire war criminal occupiers. (If 'Rocky' made one more 'Rambo' movie today fighting the REAL 'terrorist criminals' of the US Army – every decent vet I have ever known would be cheering for him)

But perhaps the most inspiring 'good guys to the rescue' film was 'CHARLIE WILSON'S WAR' – directed by Tom Hanks. It was based on the true life actions of a US Congressman whose support, patronage, and legislation for the Soviet-occupied and brutally oppressed Afghans actually turned the tide against the terrorist Godless Soviets with the aid of our Stinger missiles. We Americans cheered for the freedom of these brave people not so long ago. How quickly we forget our own actions. "Land of the FREE" – home of the BRAVE?" – not anymore!

The point here is that ALL of these films were made to garner sympathy for the underdog, in this case the oppressed Afghans and their courageous battle to gain their freedom from murderous, Godless, terrorist, sadistic psychopaths – the Communist Soviets. The irony today (to the informed only) is that their current strongman – Putin – is a dedicated Orthodox Christian and has become the sworn enemy of the Jew oligarchs who had ruined Russia in the first place and transformed it into a Godless "Evil Empire". Too bad we don't have the moral courage to free our OWN occupied country from the demonic evil of the jews as the Russians are NOW doing under Putin's leadership.

If you bother to learn what the FSU Russians actually did to these poor people in the 70s – you will learn the FACT that it is EXACTLY what WE are doing to them today – only We (the new EVIL EMPIRE) have caused infinitely more death, destruction, and horror than that Evil Empire ever dreamed of!

Do you get it yet? We are NOW exactly WHAT and WHO we as Godly, decent, compassionate, freedom-loving 'Merkans' despised in the 70s in seeing the daily atrocities committed against these freedom loving brave people. Our hypocrisy is off the scale. WE are NOW the terrorists who commit war crimes 24-7 that defy imagination. WE are NOW the destroyers of sovereign nations who have done us no harm. WE are NOW the rapists, murderers, thieves, looters, and barbaric, soulless, Godless criminals that we so much despised 35 years ago! I have 'been there/ seen that' – and it saddens me to see the ugly truth of what we have become.

But I digress. Let's look at the REAL EVIL EMPIRE of murderous hypocrite racist pukes today – the US military.

Look at the latest massacre (March 2012) by a racist US Army killer named Robert Bales. This twisted demented sociopathic war criminal murdered 17 innocent civilians in their beds as they slept. I have known his ilk my entire life. Redneck, NASCAR mentality, brain-dead, ignorant, racist, bigoted bullies with no morals or human compassion. Like every other remorseless, Godless war criminal & cold-blooded animal piece of sub-human filth – he will probably escape justice just as every military war criminal has since the jews demanded their post 9-11 serial wars against innocent people and innocent nations – none of which had committed an act of war against the USA.

Technically, the only nation which in fact HAS committed an act of war against the USA since Dec 1941 — by purest definition– has been by the Jews in their massacre of our USS Liberty crew in international waters on June 8 1967. They got away with it, thanks to the treason of then-President Johnson and every successor since and as a result the USA has become a puppet of IsraHELL and as the jews' personal attack dog. Yes Dorothy – President Kennedy was murdered by the Mossad for threatening to expose the jews control of the Fed. By far – the biggest threat to our freedoms today is a massive criminal level collective stupidity that is ALWAYS fatal. As drunken redneck racist bigot 'comedian' Ron White says – "you can't fix stupid" – and YOU certainly ought to know – Ron. Now back to my story.

BTW – according to recognized Human rights groups – the international Red Cross – UN peace observers and other groups dedicated to observing and cataloguing genocide and war crimes – only about 5% of ALL serious war crimes (Murder – rape – assaults thefts – looting – desecrations etc – committed by American military in the Mid-East are ever formally reported. The ONLY time these horrors get to see the light of day is when (IF) some lone American soldier with a conscience cannot live with what he has witnessed – or some brave

Afghan is willing to risk being a victim himself and steps forward to testify. In both possibilities, however- it rarely – if ever happens.

That means simply this: That for every ONE HUNDRED of these gruesome murders committed by our murderous jack-booted, thug, mercenary killers for thrills and good money (yes Dorothy – our psychopath military makes GOOD money as hired killers for IsraHELL– many reenlistment perk bonuses are FIVE FIGURES!) – only a handful are ever reported. In other words – in that same weekend massacre that the murder of seventeen innocent civilians was committed – the probability was that there were over NINETY OTHER SUCH GRUSOME MULTIPLE MURDERS committed by sadistic racist bigot animals like Bales all over Afghanistan. HUNDREDS MURDERED!

Today -It cost YOU the taxpayer $100,000 year to maintain ONE G.I. The perks offered to these sociopath killers are so outrageous that the situation has been compared to "PLOWING A FIELD WITH A FERRARI". We waste BILLIONS of our tax dollars training our sons to become murderers -mad dog killers who defend NOTHING here at home!

I have trained young warriors in the past – a LOT of them – for thirteen straight months in fact. We produced valiant defenders – NOT child murdering criminals! We made soldiers – NOT mindless animals! We instilled courage and honor – NOT terrorism! I and my 'band of brothers' did our jobs proudly and gladly in a military where we had an OBLIGATION (read: patriots) to serve. I was paid a LOT less as an officer to train recruits than raw MERCINARY (read: killers for hire) recruits themselves make today!

And we wonder why the entire nation is in an economically insolvent death spiral today. Sadly – most of our young people are clueless – without wisdom.

We now have the most expensive and most brutal, sadistic, Godless, racist military in the world – yet we have had NO threats from foreign powers since the USSR collapsed (except IsraHELL of course – who frequently brags how they own America) Yet the VA claims it doesn't get enough funding for proper medical care – so vets like myself had to decide it may be best for us to go to the private sector and pay for it out of pocket. Our corrupt gov has plenty of fiat currency (counterfeit money) to bleed from the public to murder babies in their sleep – but not enough for vet's medical expenses. Go figure that one out. OH – and BTW – I was censured from speaking about these abuses.

You know, 'censured', as in the USS Liberty massacre, where the survivors were ordered NEVER to speak the truth about the high treason committed against them by their OWN government! Still in the duhhh mode? Google this; 'USS LIBERTY – HIGH TREASON BY OUR OWN GOVERNMENT' Get almost fifty thousand hits! Open at your own risk – because just like when the elder ape Dr. Zaius in Planet of The Apes told hero astronaut Charlton Heston as he was about to learn the truth–"Don't look for it, Taylor! You may not like what you'll find."

Our hired assassins have murdered well over TWO MILLION INNOCENT civilians since the jew false flag 9-11 incident – mostly children. We have maimed over FIVE million more and made homeless refugees of at least ten million – not only in Afghanistan but as well in Iraq, Palestine, Libya and other nations we have destabilized and or waged war on directly or by proxy. How many of your friends or neighbors or family can converse intelligently about these crucial matters which WILL affect the future of the entire planet – OR even CARE to take the time to tear themselves away from their precious NFL nonsense long enough to acquire any wisdom on these crucial matters ? Duhhh – I thought so.

The brutality and sadistic nature of the pre-meditated murders upon defenseless innocent civilians that Sgt. Bales committed made most convicted serial murderers here in the States look like naughty pranksters. This piece of crap murdered sixteen innocent human beings – mostly children and then burned their bodies to further show his racist hatred for these "sand niggers", "camel-jockeys", "towel heads" or "hajjis as he disrespectfully refers to human beings he and his terrorist thug comrades murdered 24-7 in their OWN HOMES.

According to Afghan accounts and some press reports, "he's a rogue soldier who trudged from hut to hut in two remote Afghan villages picking out women and children to shoot, stab, kill." He also has a criminal record of assault upon a woman before he entered the military. Perhaps she was unfortunate enough to be one of those 'mud people' that the racist Bales family and their racist bigot son feel so superior to.

Bales was also guilty of more serious crimes. This malicious, greedy, slimy, reptile had also conned an elderly couple out of their life savings before he entered the Army. As matter of fact – his primary motive for entering the service was to escape the justice he would have had to face if he stayed at home. Check it out for yourself. Try this: enter – 'Bales -frauds elderly couple'. I guarantee ONE HUNDRED AND FOURTEEN THOUSAND HITS on Google alone!

His friends and neighbors testified that he couldn't wait to get re-deployed to murder more of what he and his redneck friends so hatefully and racist refer to as animals. I guess to these inbred, brain-sharing morons the grief of an Afghan father or mother for their murdered child isn't as important as that of superior, bigoted WASPS like themselves!

This animal's family and friends are predictably the same kind of filth he is. Instead of the SLIGHTEST remorse or shock – they are all busy making excuses why he was justified committing these horrible crimes. READ IT FOR YOUR SELF. Is this what my country has come to? Entire families who rejoice in his crimes calling him a hero and actually promoting him – the vicious soulless killer as the "victim". I can't just make this ugly stuff up. It's TRUE!

Look at the human filth that this crap family chose to get him off the hook. The attorney they chose is an unbelievable piece of work who has made his fortune defending America's most vile, self-confessed serial killers like Ted Bundy. The name of this depraved Godless egomaniac is John Henry Browne. If the notion of this greedy scum – described as "a pit bull on crack" – defending the most evil war criminal in recent American history is as offensive to you as an American as it is to me – why not send him a love note and let him know how much you appreciate his self-serving greedy efforts to keep the image of our country and our people in his personal sewer so as to trash any remaining opinion of the goodness we once held in the international community. Browne's Telephone: 206-388-0777 Fax: 206-388-0780 Office Address: 200 Delmar Building 108 South Washington Street Seattle, WA 98104

Personally, I intend to offer my services as a patriot – a veteran and a father of a son who will undoubtedly have had his life ruined by our immoral, Godless, murderous, imperialistic military – to my Government in addition to time served in the military as a Special Forces paratroop commander. In the unlikely event that our corrupt D.O.D. will have the integrity to see justice done in the no-brainer case of this latest mass murder of mostly innocent sleeping children in Afghanistan – I will offer my services to personally execute the bastard myself. I will willingly pay for my own travel and lodging and request only that I PERSONALLY am given the opportunity to redeem America's honor and goodness and righteousness by carrying out the death sentence demanded by ALL THAT IS RIGHT AND HONORABLE AND JUST against the self-confessed mass murderer Robert Bales. I would GLADLY hang this sadistic monster or whatever it takes to see justice done.

Then – and ONLY then – can I – and millions more righteous honorable Americans begin to feel we can say something like – "God bless America" without the words sticking in our throats like warm vomit – and without the endless disgrace to the uniform that I and millions of pre – 9-11 veterans wore with honor before our disgraceful occupation by IsraHELL under treasonous war criminal George Bush and his cabal of neo-con apostates!

There is not a flag large enough to cover the innocent blood spilled by our criminal terrorist military – ALL since 9-11, the must disgraceful treasonous false flag operation against America – ALL for the greater glory of the mortal enemy of all freedom loving people on earth – that Godless demonic evil stolen moral sewer of IsraHELL.

APRIL, 2012
A JEW IS A JEW IS A JEW AND CAN ALWAYS BE TRUSTED TO BE UNTRUSTWORTHY – JOHN -8-44

After living as long as I have, and having experienced such a variety of real life encounters in the military, business, private life and travel abroad, one develops a keen sense of 'human nature' and the nature of beings not quite so 'human'. I am referring specifically to the only ethnicity on earth which has been openly damned by Christ in holy Scripture.

No other 'tribe' of people on earth has EVER earned that distinction. Additionally – no other 'tribe' has ever had the disgusting 'distinction' of being so universally detested that they were expelled en masse from OVER ONE HUNDRED nations and city States over a period of 1800 years!

I have warned many people over the years to divest themselves from any and all association with the jew – for their own well being, safety and peace of mind. There are two kinds of 'pain' a man can endure. One is the physical kind – as when one suffers a physical trauma such as a broken bone. The other pain – often termed anguish misery or sorrow can inflict an 'emotional pain' that is equally devastating – often worse.

More persons have taken their own lives to end mental emotional trauma than those who could no longer deal with physical pain. Suffice it to say that both types of pain can and WILL make the 'quality' of one's life unbearable. The jew excels in inflicting BOTH types of pain upon innocent people. As a matter of fact – aside from measuring the value of life in terms of silver and gold shekels – the second greatest aspiration of the jew is to make life as miserable and pain filled as possible for all Gentiles.

Perhaps this inbred and obviously demonic trait was best demonstrated by the genius of 'the bard of Avon" – William Shakespeare – in his masterpiece – The Merchant Of Venice. Every Christian school child should read or see this centuries old depiction of the true nature of the jew at least once a year. Shakespeare understood the TRUE nature of the jew with with clarity.

If that were done in every learning establishment throughout the civilized world – history – especially the history of warfare and more specifically modern global warfare – would certainly be so minimal as to be relegated to much smaller volumes in subsequent history classes.

The jew monster in the play – 'Shylock' – is of course of the same evil nature as modern day war criminal mass murder ring – child killing – sadistic demonic jew monsters like Benjamin Netanyahu – Ariel Sharon – Menachem Begin – Ehud Barak – Yitzhak Rabin – Golda Meir – Yitzhak Shamir – Ehud lmert – and Shimon Peres

Those of you above room temperature – and who have a fair grasp of world history – will understand my meaning. However – for the majority of Blacks and rednecks and most stupid bowl NFL NasCar addicts – none of this will make any sense – since it will require an undamaged – unshared and 'well exercised' brain that has been exposed to wisdom from time to time – to connect the dots.

Every single person I have EVER known – including the author of these rantings has 'paid the price' for association with a jew for any period of time. The jew has ruined more friendships and trust relationships on earth that all issues of money power women and ambition combined. A young friend whose father and I were childhood playmates – had befriended a jew in a social and business relationship. I was criticized for my concern. Years later my friend's wife finally admitted that this jew had cheated her husband in a business enterprise. BIG SURPRISE – NOT!

The number of similar incidents I have noted over the past decades is legion. I have not escaped the damnation of the jews in the periphery of my life associations as well. A close warm relationship of some twenty five years between me and a male friend whom I loved as a brother was irrevocably destroyed by his evil jew wife. As similar male friendship of FORTY years has been permanently trashed due to the slavish bizarre jew association by his non jew wife to Christ hating jews.

My long time post divorce warm caring friendship (with my former wife) was destroyed in an instant by her ' newly discovered' radical jew worship in a Zionist 'Synagogue Of Satan' – after spending most of her adult life as a Catholic. My strained but friendly relationship with the mother of my youngest son totally destroyed when she sided with an evil jew Psychiatrist who Kept my son addicted to Ritalin and other dangerous psychotropic drugs so as to pay his country club dues and maintain his destruction of the souls of young Christians .

As 40 year relationship with a male friend totally destroyed when he mocked my concern for the Palestinian victims of jew terrorists the Mid -East. In his ignorance he had sided with the murderous jews. At least a dozen other relationships of many years – ended as a result of ignorance of poorly informed people who disrespected my extensive and personal firsthand knowledge of the Mid-East – as they sided with the jews.

And of course non of these serious tragedies include the personal pain I feel as a veteran paratroop commander and former basic infantry troop company commander – when I see endless war crimes against defenseless innocent civilian women and children. All of these monstrous horrors of course – committed for the benefit of the demonic jews.

And then of course – as a Christian – I am subjected to the emotional pain of seeing and hearing all manner of blasphemous filth spewed out nightly on the 100% jew owned and presented 'Talmud-Vision' – regardless of how hard one tries to search for wholesome TV entertainment – as was the norm when I was a young man living in a not yet totally jew controlled nation – of still mostly decent people.

It seems that virtually no 'Americans' give a flying rat's ass about the FACT that these demonic murdering lying filthy stinking jews butchered our fathers brothers and sons aboard the USS Liberty. To this DAY – there has been not ONE IOTA OF JUSTICE served to these murdering "sons of the Devil". Ask the average backwards baseball hat adorned imbecile on the street about the USS Liberty incident – and get a response something like:" Was dat bout a bell?"

AND – if there STILL any imbecile brain-sharing amoeba brained morons who STILL – even after the ENORMOUS VOLUMES of evidence produced – do not realize that it was these same stinking filthy jews who were behind 9-11 and were the SAME demonic mega criminals behind the murder of President Kennedy for his promise to abolish the jew controlled and run criminal Federal Reserve then you idiots need to be WATERED instead of fed.

These are the EXACT SAME STINKING ANIMALS who caused WWI and WWII and have financed the death and destruction and human misery of billions of deaths worldwide since they crucified our Lord. NOTHING has changed except the names of these mega monster criminals. They are the same murderous LYING Godless demon worshiping filth they were on the day the screamed for the blood of Christ.

Jew are LIARS & EXPERTS at victimizing themselves and demonizing their OWN victims. God says so! John 8-44

IF – there are still any TRUE patriots left in this occupied sick dying nation then wake up and take our country back. Until you ball less little pansy girly boys accept the FACT that the ONLY people who have the guts to love their freedom enough take a stand against these putrid jew scum – and DIE if need be – are the Arab people – we will NEVER be a free people again.

SO – Make up your mind. Which is more important to you and to your children's future? The NFL – or the USA

APRIL, 2012
OUR GODLESS MILITARY – SINKING EVEN LOWER INTO THE ABYSS OF THE DAMNED

Just when you thought our jack booted criminal terrorist jew-controlled military couldn't get any more putrid or universally feared and hated here is yet more proof of the descent into Hell by our Government since the 9-11 jew-instigated false flag crime of the century!

Endless serial wars waged against innocent already impoverished third world nations at the bequest of the demonic State of IsraHELL. Two million innocent civilians – MOSTLY CHILDREN – murdered in cold blood by sociopathic marauding murdering animals masquerading as 'soldiers'. Total devastation of two sovereign nations whose land we have poisoned with radio-active death that will render the land useless for agriculture – create deadly birth defects in their indigenous innocent newborn – as well as creating a lasting hatred for a nation of murdering Godless remorseless sadistic imbecile knee jerk reactionary mass war criminals on jew demand.

We all once knew this place as the United States Of America – a Nation of Christian based decent people. Sadly – that image is no more – and the reality today is a murderous blood lust rampage of inflicting Agony death and desolation upon even MORE innocent people – as it continues unabated – fed by the shrieks and howls of the filthy sick twisted imbecile brain-dead Godless Christ mocking most evil wicked murderous racist bigoted red neck filth to ever disgrace this once fine nation – the stinking – BabtDUHS.

As a veteran who once loved his country and it's military and wore the uniform with the same pride and honor of those before me – with a heritage extending back to Lexington and Concord – I cannot but with loathing disgust and revulsion look upon the murderous Godless filth in desert camos who have brought disgrace and shame to this nation by their abominable criminal conduct which increases by unbridled leaps and bounds day by day – worse and worse.

This same murderous mob of institutionalized demonized terrorists has now welcomed the Christ-hating atheists into their fold – so as to honor their 'in- your-face' anti-religion to be a normal and AmeriKan as apple pie. Ft Bragg – where I once was stationed – was recently (March 2012) the host for an official 'party' of festival nature in which these Christ haters might feel more 'welcome' in our already SUPER- Godless military. Called 'ROCK Beyond Belief' the festival party like theme was predictably anti Christian and pro secularism with as many lying misleading perversions of history as possible.

As expected – every slimy reptile – with a disproportionate number of the self-chosen came out from under the rocks they live in to confirm their hatred of Christ. One of the more odious creatures is a jew supremacist named "Mikey" Weinstein – the founder of a hate group called MRFF (Military Religious Freedom Foundation) Interesting to note that its founder a dedicated Christ hating Talmudist claims to only have good intentions to protect servicemen from being forced to be exposed to Christian teachings. Heaven forbid our sons learn honor compassion and morality!

Mikey the jew is so frightened about criticism from Christians that he has a pair of vicious specially trained attack dogs guarding his opulent mansion. This Synagogue of Satan jew actually has the arrogance to call any attempt to spread the message of Christ to our military as "spiritual rape". He has become more and more effective with his goal of de-Christianizing our military and with the soaring rate of mass war crimes by our Godless military against innocent civilians – it would appear that he indeed has been successful in creating a Godless murderous sociopathic military.

Here is a revealing quote of the jew regarding his own twisted perverted secular jew mentality of what our Founding Fathers and the FATHER of our country had clearly stated about the Christian nature of our Government and the 'moral compass' that should guide it. Here is some of this jew's sick twisted philosophy. "When one proudly dons a US military uniform; there is only one RELIGIOUS symbol: the American Flag" Hey jew boy – is that like when you or some other Godless piece of crap murder entire families of defenseless civilians hiding behind a NOW blood soaked rag called the Stars and Stripes – that makes it OK?

Here is another one of "Mikey" the jew boys – jew mantras: "There is only ONE religious faith; American patriotism" Oh really jew boy? Like the 'patriotism' showed by atheist war criminal Sgt. Bales as he murdered 9 babies and their mothers in their beds and then burned their bodies to show his redneck 'MERKAN PATRIOTISM'?

The more Godless pieces of crap like Bales – the more killing – the more revenge. That IS what you jews want isn't it -fat boy?

One of the supporters of this filth – is racist bigot arrogant ignorant lying garbage atheist agitprop muckraker – Richard Dawkins. Just to show what piece of rancid smegma he is – simply Google: "Richard Dawkins – scumbag" = almost 800,000 hits will appear! Need any more proof?

The main mean spirited thinly veiled hate theme on T shirts was: "We're never antagonistic toward religious believers, we're antagonistic toward religious belief," said Richard Dawkins, the British biologist and best-selling atheist author who was the event's headline speaker. Think about the BS you just read – demonic jew doublespeak.

What you read here is the Devil's bastardization and disingenuous twisting of the notion of hating the sin but loving the sinner which in itself was never stated in Scripture by the Lord. Once again a demonic attempt to mislead and confuse the ignorant Christian mind.

Here is yet another of those double speak Christ hating hate mongers. Hs name is Justin Griffith "I love the military," said Sgt. Justin Griffith, main organizer of the event and the military director of American Atheists. He added, "This is not meant to be a black eye." OH but of COURSE NOT! Are you kidding – SCUMBAG! What you have worked so hard to defame any remaining honor or decency or goodness of our jew run terrorist military will permanently disgrace the US Army in the eyes of most decent men. This filth of yours has set a BENCHMARK for evil to prevail – a watershed to insure we are now UNIVERSALLY viewed as the most Godless amoral military on EARTH.

Want more proof of the TRUE intentions of these reprobate anti-American retards? More double speak: "A lot of people think it's all about God-bashing or something like that," he said. "You can see we're not evil people who want to burn down churches. We're just here to have fun." FUN!!??? Right!

'OH what wholesome American family fun – lets bash Christ and mock Christians – but don't burn the churches – yet '

Another disgrace was the fact the Golden Knights – the US Army's official skydiving team did demonstrations for these pukes. As an ex paratrooper formerly stationed at Brag and close personal friend to more than one Golden Knight a long time ago – I admonish ALL of these spineless young men who contributed to that public mockery of Christ – at taxpayers' expense I might add.

Mockery of Holy Scripture and of the Lord was evident EVERYWHERE as a performer on stage rapped that "creationism is dead wrong" and a T-shirt for sale featured a Bible along with the slogan "Holy Crap." Calling the words of Christ "CRAP" is about as rancid and blasphemous as you can get. The jews who organized this filth must have got a laugh out of that one.

That performer on stage who mocked creationism was also a jew – big surprise! He is Murray Brinkman – a Russian atheist Christ hating jew. He mocked Biblical creationism by yelling to the Godless crowd: "Are there any Darwin fans here!?

His ignorance was apparently lost on the mob of Christ mockers. What he failed to mention through ignorance or more likely purposeful LYING – was the FACT that Charles Darwin DID not ONLY believe in Christ (even the Devil 'believed' in Christ – that there WAS such a being)

– but also in his latter days confessed that he was WRONG in his theories of evolution and did in fact become a 'believer'. Atheists don't like it when you confront them with these facts.

He stated; " For I am well aware that scarcely a single point is discussed in this volume on which cannot be adduced, often apparently leading to conclusions directly opposite to those at which I arrived"

Reflecting on his work near the end of his life Darwin confessed: " I was a young man with unformed ideas; I threw out queries -suggestions; wondering all the time over everything – and to my astonishment the ideas took like wildfire. People make a religion of them. Christ Jesus and His salvation – is that not the best idea/"

Once again – your ignorance exposes your evil – and your evil exposes your ignorance.

The main mean spirited thinly veiled hate theme on T shirts was : "We're never antagonistic toward religious believers, we're antagonistic toward religious belief," said Richard Dawkins, the British biologist and best-selling atheist author who was the event's headline speaker. Think about the BS you just read – demonic jew doublespeak.

What you read here is the Devil's bastardization and disingenuous twisting of the notion of hating the sin but loving the sinner which in itself was never stated in Scripture by the Lord. Once again a demonic attempt to mislead and confuse the unfortunately often ignorant Christian mind.

These then, are some of the darkest days of the soul and essence of what used to be an honorable institution – maintained ONLY to provide for the DEFENSE of our people and NOT the enrichment of our greedy industrialists or for the demonic enterprise of our elected leaders or for the demonic Satanic ambitions of the mortal enemies of the Son of Man and all that is good and righteous.

The jew is no longer 'at the gates'. He now feasts upon our flesh and destroys the goodness of our sons.

JULY, 2012
OPEN LETTER TO ALL TRUE FREEDOM FIGHTERS AGAINST THE EVIL WICKED JEWS

Aside from rare people like Brother Nathanael who was BORN into a jewish household environment – I know jew evil better than 99% of all Americans. I suffered their incessant whining in their rancid business practices when I headed my own company. I made note of their CONSPICUOUS absence from participation in any military combat branches. I lived with them and their 'Oh Veys' while a self sustaining university student at jew U (U of Miami) – had a jew roommate and later spent time at Hillel House while dating a jew princess. Watched my youngest son's life ruined by a Heeb shrink reptile posing as a true physician and watched some otherwise good people metastasized into sick trash by poisonous jew lies.

I Have watched in horror as my once blessed America was occupied by jew filth from the jew puppet POTUS in the White House to the control and censorship in my own hometown local newspaper. Have watched once decent long time personal friends develop a strange bizarre evil affinity for all that is evil anti-American anti- Christ and pro IsraHELL jewish. And of course every evening when I attempt to entertain myself with some uplifting or exciting or educational respite on the Talmudvision – all I see is life as the jews like it – living in a giant collective toilet surrounded by jew turds that never flush!

There isn't an aspect of American life that has not been polluted by jew filth in what USED to be the United States Of America. Today we are nothing less than IsraHELL'S whore – a lapdog for Satan and an attack dog for the international jew – and a training ground for Syanims (jew secret network society) to practice their treason in always supporting the benefit of 'the tribe' ahead of that of America. Its a jew dual patriotism thing where IsraHELL is always numero uno.

Now comes the good part. Years back during my ongoing education to the true nature of these putrid scum – I had a once in a lifetime experience that has forever changed my life. I got to spend time living with Satan's own ilk in the most demonic place on earth – for all intents and purposes as an insider – ISRAHELL!

I have done expensive travel over many decades – to over thirty nations to be exact. I was also a Vice Consul for many years to one of those nations – fluent in their language. In all of the places good and bad – Communist and free world – poor and affluent – primitive and sophisticated – new world and old world – the one which stands out in my mind as being 100% pure evil – filthy – vile- profane – perverse – Godless – cruel – vain – materialistic – murderous – treasonous – deceitful – blasphemous and the hands down winner of the State most likely to cause the next world war – I present the world's largest un-flushed toilet – the OFFICIAL playground of Satan Himself – IsraHELL!

I have been in 'bad' places and experienced 'bad' people – but nothing could prepare me for the in-your-face evil of these jews. Their shameless blasphemy towards our Lord is over the top rancid putrid filth! When you see a drunk punk hook-nosed rat faced animal screaming threats at some poor Palestinian family – probably one of the 20% Christians who has lived upon that land in peace with his Muslim neighbors for over fifteen hundred years – you will never forget – nor forgive – as you will NEVER – EVER find a 'repentant' jew.

Remember – I am only the messenger – repeating his especially filthy blasphemous threatening message screamed at the top of his voice: *" Fuck you and fuck your fucking Jesus. This is OUR land – God gave it to us and it belongs to us – not you! We crucified your fucking Jesus and we will do it again"!* you can still find examples of this on the web – but I warn you – it's pretty raw but the whole family needs to see these ugly TRUTHS. Jew thugs do these horrid acts daily. These vile blasphemies are wholeheartedly approved by the majority of jews – unofficially of course as it only reinforces John 8-4 .

This kind of outrageous hateful filth was rampant in that hellhole of reprobate demons – but like the equally filthy jew graffiti damning Christ and Christians and supporting treasonous filth like John Pollard – fat pasty faced BaptDUH tourists staying in the safety and comfort of TelAviv never see or hear this common fare in the less visited outlying areas – Bathsheba, Hebron, Beersheba, Bat Yam, Ramat Gan, Eilat etc etc

This abysmal filth is the TRUE nature of the jew. I experienced it because I was NOT there to be fooled by the local Hava – Nagila dancing whores and other such 'Potemkin village' deceptions fabricated for stupid fat pasty drooling rednecks in santiized Tel Aviv.

One of the best descriptions of IsraHELL was offered by the genius of jew turned TRUE Christian -Brother Nathanael who today exposes ALL jew evils on his hard hitting site RJN (REAL JEW NEWS) He terms this land of demons. He identifies IsraHELL as: *a "Jewish" state, which means nothing less than an anti-Christ entity with diplomatic credentials.* As truthful and technically correct as you can get in formal terms.

These baby killers also have a formidable military which included their 'then new' 105mm Merkeva 2 battle tank – part of which I witnessed on maneuvers in the Negev. Hardware (paid for by American sweat) not withstanding – I can't say much for the girly boy soldiers themselves – cocky arrogant and immature.

Do not be fooled by these god jew bad jew deceptions. In other words – these two Janus 2- faced jews to whom lying is an honorable way of life, will have you stupid goy (non jewish cattle) now believe that sure – the Zionists are not the true Torah jews and in fact are bad guys – BUT the ordinary jews – like Mr. Goldberg who teaches your children at the local high school – or Ms Silverstein who is your local commissioner – or Mr. Lieberman who is a local bank VP – or Mr. Eckstein who is running for a State Rep seat – or the Jacobsons who have a real estate business – or even that old retired couple down the block – the Eisners – are all just good Americans and as wholesome and patriotic as apple pie.

BULLSHIT! Do not buy into that monstrous lie! They are ALL part of the 'tribe' – all Sayanims' who are like minded and work behind your back to promote all things jewish at their meetings and countless jew organizations and Synagogues Satan headed by pedophile womanizing demon worshiping rabbis – ALWAYS cloaked in a veil of mystery intrigue unintelligible gibberish and never ending deception deception deception. Deceiving Gentile people is their national pastime. Even the OFFICIAL motto of their government betrays their true evil wicked lying nature, and I QUOTE: *"BY DECEPTION WE WAGE WAR"* Check it out for your self – as I just can't make all this stuff up.

Jews and their leadership despise you they despise our Lord and they despise courage principle morality work ethics and everything that made America great once – before we allowed these rat faced scum to infect our land and our most sacred values.

Still not convinced? Read this horrid jew filth out loud to ALL your family and friends: *"My opinion of Christian Zionists? They're scum. But don't tell them that. We need all the useful idiots we can get right now."* — Benyamin Netanyahu, at the time a former IsraHELL prime minister

BTW – you 50 million imbecile brain sharing stupefied inbred redneck moron BaptDUHS – that is YOU – that this Christ hating, Christian hating Gentile hating self styled sociopathic egomaniac – is talking about!

The BaptDUH is the only creature on planet earth who is stupid enough to eagerly worship the scum who mock slander ridicule scorn taunt and insult you behind your backs. You imbeciles are a nothing more than a joke in IsraHELL and the rest of the informed world. You drones give new meaning to the meaning of STUPID. Your treatment of Christ and perverse twisting of His words is world class perversion!

Just think about the insanity of the crime you have committed against God. You have rejected ALL of His warnings of the demonic nature of the jew and have freely chosen to WORSHIP the very demons who murdered Him. You sick evil bastards!

Speaking of Zionists – to be sure – there are jews who are foaming at the mouth Zionists , but the truth is that the vast majority of these demonic jew bastards that have infected our nation into a morally rotted corpse with their greed – nastiness – organ trafficking – drug trafficking – usury – greed – profanities – shock jocks – gangbanger hip hop rap trap crap filth – Marxist support – mockery of the service of our country – porn industry – infanticide – crime syndicates – corruption – theft of America's wealth – white slavery – countless treasons – blasphemies – hatred of Christ and His Blessed Mother 24-7 on their Talmudvision trashing of our Constitution and every evil known to man – are just 'ordinary' jews like the ones who live next door and work night and day to corrupt your children seduce your wives and steal your possessions.

I met NO Zionists while staying in IsraHELL – lots and lots of slimy sadistic reptile jew bastards but no card carrying formal Zionists. Over 95% of the Zionists in this ZOG today are Gentiles and 95% of those Gentile Zionists are the worst most criminally purposefully ignorant evil creatures on earth – the oyster-brained BaptDUHs. Keep those FACTS in mind next time the issue of Zionism come up.

Keep the faith people. It WILL get worse. Many of you WILL live to see a perversion of truth honor logic and goodness that will defy all reason. Evil will be worshiped as good. Truth will be reviled and evil. Lies will be worshiped as wisdom. Violence will be the default solution to all disputes. Peace will be mocked as treason. We will be taught to betray our finest sons and to reward and ally with our most mortal enemies. And finally – we will all be taught that servitude is holy and freedom is wreck less.

IF these insane BaptDUh minions of the Devil succeed in their quest for world conflict – the entire world will suffer for their evil ways. The jew and the BaptDUH are equally evil and although the BaptDUH is a surrogate of the demonic jews – neither may accomplish the horrors of another world war by themselves. Remember that fact next time your innocent naive child asks to play with the child of some scumbag monster BaptDUH neighbor.

ALL AmeriKan military are the mortal enemy of ALL decent Godly people here – NO EXCEPTIONS! It is a volunteer mercenary organization. Each and every man or woman who of their own free will agrees to support and legitimize our murderous sociopathic at this late stage of the game is your mortal enemy. Our "few" or "brave" Marines are the most evil violent Godless criminals to ever disgrace the uniform I and those 'of and before my time' – WORE WITH HONOR.

If you have any doubts as to the TRUE nature of the psychopathic Godless sadistic human garbage we now train in our new improved infected jew military – do the following.

(1) compare the moral aspects of Basic training fifty years ago when I trained young man and the jew oriented Godless insane filth your sons are taught today – like not hesitating to murder civilians in cold blood in their own homes. You NEED to see and hear the demonic sadistic barbaric Godless crap my own son was trained to do to unarmed civilians protecting their own families and lives and homes. I KNOW the rules of the game and how we used to conduct ourselves with your sons. I did it as a professional. I would rather go to prison than take ANY part in the filth I saw my own son being taught. If what you learn does not totally disgust you as a human being – an American – a parent or a Christian – then you are as sick as the bastards who commit these awful crimes against your children.

(2) Go to your computer and punch in; 'treasonous Marines agree to murder their own neighbors – 29 Palms Naval base'. Be patient – you will find it. If THIS FILTH does not scare the be-Jesus out of you as a human being -parent American etc – then you are part of the problem again! BE SURE TO READ THE PART OF THE TEST WHERE A LARGE PERCENTAGE OF OUR 'brave' -'honor laden' – patriotic Marines freely stated that they WOULD MURDER SLAUGHTER SHOOT KILL you and your children and family in your own homes if you should DARE to defy the STATE and defend your own family and home. Next time you see one of those propaganda commercials for "THE FEW – THE PROUD -THE BRAVE – THE MARINES" crap – just remember who brave it would be and how proud they would be to blow your brains out along with your children – just as these knuckle dragging Neanderthals walking hamburgers did to so many innocent defenseless civilian: " rag heads – camel jockeys – sand-niggers" as our racist Godless jew dominated thug criminal military has taught your sons to slander other cultures.

And no lectures from the peanut gallery. If you are young enough to be wearing desert camos – you are punks – Marines or not – who have disgraced the uniform and you can go straight to hell- scumbags! My oldest and closest friend in life was a Marine officer – a fine and moral individual. Fifty years ago I trained Marine Paras in unconventional Special Forces DZ re-supplying and night infiltration drops. These were men I knew and respected. They were not the Godless judaized vicious sadistic criminal scum I see today. The scum of your murderous thrill seeking ilk have NOTHING in common with the men I worked with two generations ago.

(3) Go to a film rental place or download perhaps – a documentary called STANDARD OPERATING PROCEDURE – a documentary by photojournalist Errol Morris. It was shot at the notorious torture chambers of Abu Ghraib where our "land of the free and home of the brave" tortured and murdered countless Iraqi young men whose 'crime' was to defend the honor of their wives and daughters and their beloved homeland from our marauding sociopaths killers rapists sexual perverts thieves and rancid criminal trash. ALL of the rancid military filth in the film were nasty looking human pervert garbage. The 'women' were whores and lesbian filth eager to show how low a human being could sink. Beyond disgusting!

Just look at the evil in their pig like faces and listen to them whine and even brag about their grizzly sadistic crimes – and tell me you would not want to send them all straight to their 'father' – in hell!

This documentary is exactly what our military has become today. What the Soviets did in Afghanistan makes them look like naughty pranksters compared to what monsters we have become and I am VERY familiar with what BOTH nations' military did to civilians in the Mid-East. Of course the hands down masters of pure brutal sadistic treatment of civilians are the jews – been there, seen that.

I PRAY for the day when this current Godless wicked evil demonic perverted military is destroyed and goodness and honor is once more the order of the day! We have becomes a garbage people in total denial! We have now become everything decent Americans despised about the Soviets and Chinese

Those in command were ALL as guilty of these horrible crimes as the lowest ranking NCO and should have ALL been shot or hung or serve life sentences in Leavenworth. Show this to ALL of your family and be SURE that ALL of your children understand that these were not dated films of Soviet atrocities or Mao's torture chambers. They need to know that the sadistic animalistic sick twisted filth they saw were modern times AMERICAN servicemen and woman – much to the disgrace of what scum we have become as a people.

And they need to additionally know that the jew worshiping BaptDUHs down the street made this horror possible. If you do NOT level with your kids now as to what we have become – why not just blow their brains out and save them the grief of the reality of what is in store for Amerika because mom and dad were too busy with NFL and other immature irresponsible dominating inane nonsense.

You AND your children ESPECIALLY need to know that It was individuals, not a policy, that forced Iraqi prisoners to stay in stress positions for hours on end, to masturbate in front of one another, to be led on leashes like dogs, and to strip and then form a human pyramid. And it was the individual U.S. soldiers who photographed these events and treated the pictures like prized trophies. And then to be eaten alive by vicious attack dogs or murdered in cold blood just for amusement.

This then is what AmeriKans are really like today – vicious – sadistic – cruel – remorseless – criminally ignorant – racist – Godless – remorseless – selfish and incapable of human compassion whiney immature brats at best – sadistic serial killers at worst.

I have read HUNDREDS of these horror stories – some MUCH worse – monstrous! But it becomes so revolting to learn what putrid garbage I have for 'neighbors – that it becomes depressing.

When your young son or daughter asks you for an answer – mom, dad – why do these things happen today? They are old enough to know the TRUTH – so tell them.

Kids – years ago we threw morals and goodness out of our schools and churches and government. And along with that we also threw Christ in the toilet. So today we play the game of life with NO RULES – and when you do that – the people turn out to be the same garbage they admire.

Gee Dad – so if all these terrible things are because we are no longer good people – why did we through Jesus under the bus?

Well – son to be perfectly truthful – it was because the jews who run our country told us!

Yes Dorothy – there is a moral to the story. As the song says: teach your children well – teach them the TRUTH of the evil of the jews so they will live as free men and women once again.

JULY, 2012
A QUIZ FOR EVERY TRUE AMERICAN PATRIOT

(1) Only actual defined act of war against America since 1941 was committed by:

(a) Iraq
(b) USSR
(c) Iran
(d) Afghanistan
(e) Israel

(2) According to many of America's most talented scientists engineers and analysts 9-11 was perpetrated by:

(a) Iraq
(b) USSR
(c) Iran
(d) Afghanistan
(e) Israel

(3) The Christmas Nativity traditionally celebrated at the White House has been replaced by

(a) Islam
(b) Buhddaism
(c) Shintoism
(d) Judaism

(4) The only modern nation on earth that has a record of civilian murders so sadistically brutal and barbaric as to be classified as genocidal is:

(a) Russian military
(b) Chinese military
(c) Cuban military
(d) Iraqi military
(e) Israeli military

(5) The only modern military on earth too openly condone the murder of pre-school children & pregnant mothers and the desecration of places of worship:

(a) Russian military
(b) Chinese military
(c) Iraqi military
(d) Afghan military
(e) Israeli military

(6) What metropolitan city has the greatest density of whore houses on earth:

(a) New York
(b) London
(c) Paris
(d) Rome
(e) Hong Kong
(f) TelAviv

(7) What nation has the greatest per capita percentage of white slavery on earth

(a) USSR
(b) Cuba
(c) China
(d) Columbia

(e) India
(f) Israel

(8) What Is the only nation on earth to threaten the entire world with nuclear destruction if their criminal war mongering is interfered with:

(a) Russia
(b) USA
(c) China
(d) Pakistan
(e) Israel

(9) Who are the only ethnic group of people in all of recorded history to have been cast out of a hundred nations and city states for their unethical criminal sociopathic conduct over a period of fifteen hundred yesrs!:

(a) Poles
(b) Tartars
(c) Slavs
(d) Arabs
(e) Turks
(f) jews

(10) Which is the only ethnicity on earth to have been openly accused by the Lord Christ in the Bible of having a demonic birth heritage – children of Satan:

(a) Arabs
(b) Hittites
(c) Macedonians
(d) Romans
(e) Goths
(f) Philistines
(g) jews

(11) The jews gained control Israel by what means:

(a) Was purchased from the owners
(b) Was traded by the owners
(c) Was leased from the previous owners
(d) Was given to the jews as a gift
(e) Was bartered or lend leased
(f) Was stolen through violence and bloodshed by jew terrorists

(12) Who controls the porn industry in America today:

(a) The Gentiles
(b) The Arab-Americans
(c) The Greek Americans
(d) The African Americans
(e) The French Americans
(f) The jews

(13) What is the largest supporter of the evil leftist Democrap Party today (per capita):

(a) Red Necks
(b) Mexicans
(c) homosexuals
(d) African Americans
(e) jews

(14) What ethnicity leads in per capita numbers for the most traitors to our nation:

(a) Mexican Americans
(b) Italian Americans
(c) German Americans
(d) Russian Americans
(e) Cuban Americans
(f) jews

(15) What ethnicity leads America in the support and funding and promotion of infanticide (baby murder):

(a) Mexicans
(b) Cubans
(c) crackers
(d) Indians
(e) Negros
(f) jews

(16) What ethnicity are the leading per capita percentage of Communists (subversive traitors) in America:

(a) Italians
(b) Spanish
(c) Cuban
(d) Haitian
(e) Russian (gentiles)
(f) jews

(17) Who runs ALL of the filth that pours out of Hollywood like an open sore to infect our children;

(a) the Spanish
(b) the Arabs
(c) the Russians (gentiles)
(d) the French
(e) the jews

(18) What ethnicity had been responsible for more innocent civilian murders than all the rest over 200,000 million

(a) Germans
(b) Chinese
(c) Turks
(d) Koreans
(e) Japanese
(f) jews

(19) What ethnicity can be credited with the final destruction of the Catholic Church and mostly of all the other Protestant denominations as well – especially the BaptDuhs;

(a) Chinese
(b) Germans
(c) Russians
(d) Arabs
(e) jews

(20) "He who controls the banks – controls the world" – so who controls (STOLE) virtually all of the world's money:

(a) Chinese
(b) Americans
(c) Columbian drug cartels
(d) the British
(e) The Arab oil sheik emirates
(f) the jews

(21) What was the ethnicity of the demon – Lazar Kaganovich – who was attributed with the actual responsibility for the murder of more innocent civilians than any SINGLE human being in history – nearly 15,000,000 Christian Ukrainians?
(a) German
(b) Japanese
(c) English
(d) Turkish
(e) jewish

OH and remember – we ARE a CONSTITUTIONAL REPUBLIC – PERIOD – a nation of laws – not mob rule (democracy) The jews who occupy us have hammered that lie in our schools our movies and our homes – our news sources – and even our POTUS has been corrupted to spout the Jew Communist line as an 'official LIE' until our children believe that awful jew lie.

The irony of all this is that our modern day stupid brain dead hip-hop Ebonics gibberish spouting 'nigga' morons have been brain washed to accept that as Gospel. IF – IN FACT we we actually a Democracy – all them 'niggas' would still be pickin cotton on plantations fo da massah. Anyway – it serves the jew control the vote of imbeciles agenda.

Why? simple. The question of slavery comes up in Chickasaw Ga – so all dem Southern gentlemen take a vote – all proper and Democratic like – and they decide – lawsy me! To continue with keepin slaves. And since they believed they had a Democracy (predicted on mob rule NOT laws) – the ruling class 'VOTED' unanimously to keep slaves. See how a democracy works? Just fine – iffen you happens to be a white businessman in a 30s or 40s small 95% white town.

OR how about the black man who was accused of ogling the boss man's pretty blond wife? They want to hang his black ass! Oh – but logic prevails – someone reminds the ugly lynch mob that since this is a DEMOCRACY – that fair is fair and it must be put to a vote. SO all of these 'foxes' guarding the hen house – 'VOTE" – what is to be the fate of the chicken. OFF WITH HIS HEAD! All done proper and democratic like. See the point. Democracy is CRAP!

OOPS ! along comes the revelation that we have a REPUBLIC and slavery is NOT lawful – so there is a BIG problem now. See how stupidity keeps people (of ALL colors) enslaved. I can't remember in my entire life of ANY prominent wealthy jew raising hell for one of his co-religionists improperly identifying our form of government as a DEMOCRACY – NEVER!

***JULY, 2012
YOU MIGHT BE A TRUE, INFORMED 'WALK THE WALK' AMERICAN FATHER – VETERAN – PATRIOT IF…***

You refuse to participate or validate anything that is jewish is any way – like their filthy violence–based 'unholy' days.

You refuse to buy products made by demonic jews in IsraHELL or in the States (E.g.. Starbucks)

You expose any and all jewish activity that is harmful to our freedoms – Like our depraved government as a whole.

You boycott all jew produced movies or books that demonize the German people or the Arab people.

You take every opportunity to educate Americans about jew treason against America.

You shun ALL ACTIVITY that promotes Gulf war military as heroes – THEY ARE WAR CRIMINALS!

You stand by and support and USE all reliable alternative news sources.

You stand by and defend the helpless – give hope to the hopeless – and be a voice for those oppressed by the jew.

You refuse to be a member of ANY so called church that preaches jew lies.

You stand tall and firm against ANY more unjust wars for IsraHELL – specifically Iran.

You expose jew war atrocities in Palestine and Iraq and Afghanistan at every opportunity.

You ALWAYS refer to the jew military (IDF) as the world's 'largest institutionalized terrorist organization'

You teach your children the truth about jew history in the Bible and how Christ condemned them as demonic.

You teach your children the TRUTH about the USS LIBERTY massacre – a jew act of war against America.

You teach your children the truth about 9-11 – the IsraHELL government and treasonous US officials did it.

You teach your children that it is the jew who has turned their nation into a morally rotted corpse.

You teach your children that it is the jew who has economically destroyed our once prosperous nation.

You resist any and all jew who wish to poison your children with their lies on TV or schools.

You refuse to do ANY business with jews in any capacity – and condemn people who DO.

You Show how the jews murder innocent children in Gaza using your tax dollars – graphic T-shirts are a good tool.

You ask everyone you meet if they have read John 8-=44 of the New Testament.

You demand that jews stop their 24-7 mockery of our Lord and His blessed mother on their Talmud-vision filth.

You spend at least an hour a day on alternative 'truther' websites – and share what you have learned.

You donate regularly to the best of these sites and encourage your neighbors to do the same.

You expose false preachers wherever and whenever you encounter them – on TV and in your community.

You bring charges against ANY teacher who lies to your children – calling our Republic a mob rule Democracy.

You Encourage ALL young Christian men to stay out of our psychopath demonic evil war criminal military.

You encourage and support any and all true religious figures who have the integrity to stand against the jews.

You expose the jews as the murders of Jesus over and over and quote the blood oath that damned themselves.

You remind your neighbors aware that Christmas is no longer celebrated in the White House – only evil jew filth.

You take a stand to defend the courageous Arab people in their fight against these filthy demons from hell.

You fly our flag ONLY upside down if at all – so other veterans understand how it has been trashed by the jew.

You have nothing to do with ANY veteran's groups who support our war criminal thugs who murder civilians.

You confront ANY public display of ANY attempt of military recruitment in your schools or civic centers.

You teach family and friends of the EXACT parallels between what the jews did to 30s Germany and the USA today.

You show zero tolerance for the jew supported rap trap crap gang-banger black filth that is poisoning our youth today.

You live by example a clean wholesome family life – live by the Good book and our blessed Constitution.

Practice what your preach – keep your honor clean – but show no mercy to the sworn enemies of God – the jews!

Do ALL this and we WILL prevail against the putrid rancid filth that suffocates every pore of our American landscape

Do this and regain our occupied nation's freedom as we inform the Lord and pray he is welcome here once again.

AUGUST, 2012
A JEW WALKS INTO A BARBER SHOP AND SAYS...

Here is an anecdote or modern parable of sorts that tells a story – explains the reason the jews so easily deceive us – and has a 'moral mandate'

A young man once asked me how could the jews -even with all their stolen money could possibly be cunning and shrewd enough to fool 98% of our population 98% of the time. I was tempted to tell him the straight out truth – that we as a people have been so dumbed down by Talmud Vision Pumpkin Chunkin or mud – bogging racing or NASCAR races or the NFL Stupid Bowl – or Dancing with The Stars – or Pawn Kings – or the kinky Karadashians – or Jerry Swinefeld -or the all mutant cast of inbred retards on the Operation Repo show or a hundred more disgustingly stupid imbecile mentality examples of jew entertainment – that we have brain atrophied to the reasoning power of retarded oysters – but I changed my mind.

I opted instead for this little mind teaser, waker-upper, story book quiz lesson in human nature and plain old-fashion Merkan stupidity. It would PROVE my point and he would never forget it.

In my hypothetical story – the scene is a busy barber shop in Smallville USA. All the seats are filled with customers and there is even a shoeshine boy we will name Sunny. I asked my young friend to pretend he was the shine boy and was observing the small drama about to unfold – remember it well and give me his impressions as honest answers to my questions.

The scene starts – in walks Moshe the jew – but he is NOT here for a hair cut or shave. He is here to create trouble (that is what jews do, 'Sonny' – make trouble) Moshe points his finger at the man in the last chair (we will call him Chris) and says in a shrill voice – "your wife is a hoar!". Well the whole crowd in the Barber shop suddenly stops chattering and the room is dead quiet – as all eyes turn towards the husband of the accused wife.

OK 'Sonny' it's quiz time. Tell me – what could be Chris's response and keep in mind at this point we do not know if the accusation was true or not – only the Husband and the jew knows the truth – so just tell me what are ALL of the possible reactions – and remember – the ENTIRE barbershop crowd are watching and waiting for responses too.

Well – if his wife is innocent – Christ should immediately confront the jew and either kick his ass or demand he apologize for the lie and defend his wife's honor. Good answer 'Sonny' – so what other reaction might be possible? Sonny looks pensive and then answers: " well if it IS true that his wife really IS a whore – he would obviously know that and might offer a weak response as admission of her guilt but feel really bad. OK – another good answer – but what ELSE might happen.

That is when the young man (Sonny) looks at me with a big question mark on his brow and says -" but there isn't anything else possible for him to say!" AH – but that -young man – is where you are right in a way – but really dead wrong.

But how can that be he says quizzically? Simple – but you missed it, I tell him. SILENCE can and does 'speak volumes! What if 'Chris' simply said NOTHING AT ALL. Remember – all those other folks in the shop are also dying for an answer. Do you know what human nature is son? Yes he says. Well then – what will the people tend to believe if he does NOT defend her in any way.

Uh – they will probably all believe the jew was telling the truth. RIGHT! – now you're beginning to think and connect dots. Does his silence PROVE her guilt? No – not really – but like you said – 'human nature' and all that…will make it look bad"

OK – so let's recap the story. Jew accuses man's wife. His reactions: /THREE possibilities – NOT JUST TWO – RIGHT? Right! He defends wife – crowd sees the sincerity and honest anger and sides with the husband/wife RIGHT? Score one for the wife. Husband admits his wife is a trollop – crowd hears this and the crowd sides with the jew. Jews wins in that case RIGHT? Right.

NOW the third possibility – the crowd waits for a reaction but the husband remains silent. The crowd will NOW believe she WAS guilty based on no other proof other than his silence. The crowd sides AGAIN with the jew even though there was no admission. Jew wins TWO OUT OF THREE every time the accused elects to NOT defend his or her position. It is ALWAYS a win-win situation for Satan's Children *(John 8-44)* when good people remain silent in the presence of evil.

Imagine this same scenario where the issues and stakes are high – like wars or freedoms or illegal laws or laws that take away our Constitutional rights, or war crimes issues or religious freedoms or a hundred other moral social and economic issues which we continually lose to the will of the jew. Only then will you understand why remaining silent is suicide treason cowardly and defeatist all at the same time.

You must never ever for ANY reason remain silent when confronted with jew lies or these lies WILL become the shackles that bind you as a slave in your own nation. The jew knows he doesn't even have to work extra hard with evil and wickedness of endless lies – as you- the sheep will fasten the chains of bondage FOR HIM. We profess to be a so called Christian nation – yet for the past 4 years the Nativity manger scenes which were traditional at our White House since the time of George Washington have been replaced with the demonic filth of the Devil's pitchfork.

Ten million jews two hundred million Christians – YET we moral cowards allow these Christ hating jew blasphemies to continue unchallenged and undefended.

Suppose three thousand churches are Solicited by Christians wanting their centuries old traditions back. 1/3 say they want our sacred traditions back. A third (Christian Zionists frauds) say the jews filth is OK with them – AND the other third? Well they just can't be bothered – so they fall in the camp of the demonic jew whether they wished to be OR NOT! If the jews took a survey right then – they wouldn't even have to lie. 66% in favor of the jew blasphemies against Christ by democratic process. Christ is 'thrown under the bus' for another year and on and on and on Get it?

If more churches do not even bother to take a stance to defend our faith that the faithful who will do so the jew will say: See – even your own people do not object to our 'pitch forked blasphemies. That silent majority has because of cowardice or hypocrisy or ignorance cast enough doubt so that the jew lies become 'the will of the people – EXACTLY like the result of the silence of the husband at the barber shop.

When WWIII is on our doorstep – ask your neighbor if he took ANY action against it AT ALL. If he did NOTHING – that was as EQUALLY responsible as if he had actually voted FOR WAR. Just remember that when the bombs start to fall on OUR CITIES instead of those "awful third world countries filled with sand niggers and camel jockeys" we have destroyed for the past ten years.

Remember the 'parable' of the jew in the barber shop.

When a normal healthy sense of outrage against wickedness dies in any nation – the trash heap of history is close by.

If you fail a college course – you get an 'F' -for failure and take the course again
If you fail to grasp the message of the parable – you get a 'D' – for DEATH – game over!

Hell WILL be at a town near you sooner than you think – as you have worked hard to earn it!

AUGUST, 2012
KNOWLEDGE IS A COLLECTION OF FACTS- USED FOR BOTH GOOD AND EVIL. WISDOM IS THE MORAL USE OF KNOWLEDGE

Where is the wisdom – we have lost in knowledge?

Here is a quiz which every American family should take. Knowing the correct answers does NOT require a special amount of training or special background. It is just mostly plain common sense, plus a nominal level of responsibility as a an adult who takes enough of an interest in the future of his or her own nation and that of their OWN children to want to secure the blessings the Founding Fathers gave us long ago – all paid in full by sacrifice blood sweat and tears.

All one needs in the way of a base of knowledge, is a good high school education – the kind I received from the Jesuits nearly sixty years ago when even public schools imparted REAL knowledge I know this to be true as I experienced both systems as a student.

With age and experience knowledge will hopefully become WISDOM – now a rarely used word in the American lexicon. True Christians cherish and esteem WISDOM. The deceitful jew covets and lusts after CUNNING.

Of course if you are a product of our more recent failed secular social experiments where imparting discipline knowledge morality and wisdom has been replaced with inane dribble to make us feel 'good about ourselves' and a policy to 'teach' at a level that makes the most disruptive delinquent Ebonics speaking hooligan in class feel comfortable – then you are more than likely as dumbed-down as retarded oysters and are satisfied that your children are of the same ilk. You and your children will NEVER acquire wisdom -simply because you DID NOT WANT TO!

If you think that Europe is a country – or that the USS Liberty Incident was about a cracked bell – or that the murder of a human infant is the 'right' of a women to decide – or that we are a democracy instead of a Republic – or that 9-11 was a crime committed only by Arabs with box cutters – or that the 'Federal Reserve is either Federal or a protection of our national monetary system – or that Israel is our friend and ally or even a Democracy – or that who we elect for POTUS will save our country from destruction – or that The Arab people hate us because we are "FREE" – or that non Zionist Jews are just as apple pie and loyal Americans as you and I – or that WWI AND WWII was started by the Germans – or that Jesus was Jewish carpenter – or that the so-called Jews had a right to steal the Arab land with terrorism and make it their own – or that the Jews the Baptists worship are the sons of the Lord – or that this country is still loved and respected by ANY of the world's moral free people – just forget the test – you are way too stupid.

TEST QUESTIONS=

The answers require only knowledge.
The UNDERSTANDING of the answers requires WISDOM

(A) Who is America's most mortal enemy?

(B) Which country harbors the world's largest institutionalized terrorist organization?

(C) Which nation has the highest density per capita of Whore houses on earth?

(D) Which place is the largest dealer in white slavery in the world?

(E) Where is the most universal refuge for Marxist war criminals and traitors to America on earth?

(F) Where is the greatest concentration per capita of Christian haters and Christ mockers on earth?

(G) What is the only nation on earth which has committed an act of war against America in past 70 years?

(H) What foreign nation's people have occupied and completely control America today?

(I) What is country whose leadership officially condones and encourages murder of helpless women and children?

(J) What nation is home to the ONLY people to be exiled from virtually every nation on earth for criminal conduct?

(K) What is the most racist apartheid State in Middle East today?

(L) What country has imprisoned murdered tortured and terrorized more innocent defenseless civilians?

(M) Were on earth do we find the largest organ theft trafficking syndicate?

(N) Where is nation from which the people who control 90% of ALL news media come from?

(O) What nation harbors the people who have financed BOTH sides of virtually every war in history?

(P) What is country whose people have financed over 90% of all slave trade – ships etc, in past history?

(Q) What is nation whose people were long ago damned by God as not being worth praying for?

(R) What is nation whose people's highest religious books teach that Christ was a BASTARD?

(S) What is nation whose people's highest religious books teach that Christ's mother was a WHORE?

(T) What is nation whose people's highest religious books teach it is OK to cheat and lie to Christians?

(U) What is nation whose people's highest religious books teach it is OK to lie in a Christian court?

(V) What is nation whose people's highest religious books teach it is Ok to murder Christians?

(W) What is nation whose people's highest religious books teach it is OK to steal from Christians?

(X) What is nation whose people's highest religious books teach it is OK to desecrate Christian Churches?

(Y) What is nation whose people's highest religious books teach Jesus is boiling in a vat of shit?

(Z) What is the ONLY modern nation whose people were damned by God as being the SONS OF THE DEVIL?

To anyone but those of the IQ's of retarded oysters – it should have been GLARINGLY obvious that the answer to ALL of these historically true and Biblically accurate accusations of unconscionably evil conduct was the cumulative – but by no means, total evil deeds of IsraHELL and the JEWS!

I could probably do a THOUSAND More DIFFERENT examples of jew/IsraHELL wickedness but I was out of letters.

A perfect score is 26 out of 26 – which EVERY Catholic teenager would have scored back when truth knowledge and wisdom were not dirty words – our country was strong moral and Christian.

Sadly – today's Catholic youth – because of the hypocrisy and moral spinelessness of their parents – would have also done poorly. ALL – of you OLDER TRUE TRADITIONAL Catholics will know EXACTLY what I am talking about . I you are not a passionate moral supporter of Bishop Williamson – or do not even know WHO he is – or think that EWTN is any REMOTELY courageous voice of TRUTH for the Catholic faith of your fathers – then – you are not old enough or moral enough to even be called Catholic.

Today's BaptDUH blasphemous hypocrite treasonous war mongering dazzlingly stupid brain dead inbred redneck scum would have scored ZERO!

I HOPE you have learned something valuable from this little 'quiz game'. ALL of the examples I used were IN CONTEXT and arguably true. There were no tough questions and no trick questions.

IF ANY adult person who claims to be a REAL American and MORAL American and an INFORMED American had ANY reservations to ANY of these TRUTHS – you have also failed your children – you have failed your country – and you have failed your Lord. You are morally blind and deaf.

Jer. 5:21 (King James version): "Hear now this, O foolish people, and without understanding; which have eyes, and see not; which have ears, and hear not."

AUGUST, 2012
WHY DO AMERICANS, ONCE CHRISTIAN, WORSHIP WAR CRIMINALS LIKE CHRIS KYLE

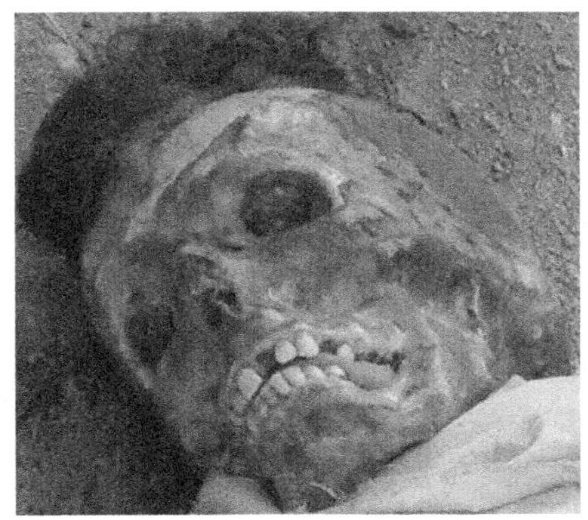

To the chant of : one two- button your shoe

ONE TWO – here comes the jew, with his endless lies, directly to you
THREE FOUR – To teach our kids, to love violence and gore, and 'free' sex, much even the more
FIVE SIX – With his deceit and his trix, he will everything fix, till we all drown, in the river called Styx
SEVEN EIGHT – his methods include racism and hate, all designed to assist, in sealing our fate
NINE TEN – an enemy he'll make, from one who was friend – by twisting the truth of the finest of men.
ELEVEN TWELVE – I will then become, what I once hated myself, lest his motives, into I should delve .

Pfc Needham – decorated Army Ranger is a whistleblower who helped expose the epidemic level of war crimes committed in the Mid-East against innocent civilians. Every decent veteran needs to stand by REAL heroes who have placed honor and courage above his own personal safety so as to try to bring back the reputation of our military from the depths of Hell to which many outright war sociopathic criminals have dragged our honor.

John may have killed innocent people himself – but at least he had a conscience. His reasons for being in another man's country and waging war against a people who had never attacked the USA – were never justifiable although he volunteered more out of a sense of camaraderie/belonging , than any notion of just WANTING to kill innocent people he considered less than human – such as the mass murderer war criminal sociopathic scum Chris Kyle.

If the reader has the SLIGHTEST doubt that our military is now controlled by 100% corrupt criminal psychopath scum

Your must listen to this report by his father *(see further down)* and share it with family friends veterans newspapers churches and schools. It WILL scare the crap out of you as you keep reminding yourself that this is NOT some animal mentality murdering Southern Cal. Chicano street drug cartel gang syndicate conducting themselves with such disgrace – but THE US ARMY!!!!!

I have stated this before and I will say it again: from a lifetime of experience and travel and my service in the military – there is no lower form of life than that of a 'recruiter'. These putrid reptiles look upon your son as a lump of flesh who will put extra cash in his pocket for transforming him from a compassionate boy full of life and hope and love – into a remorseless Godless sociopathic serial murderer of innocent men women and children as some sort of deranged game for thrills. I had a fair amount of experience training young warriors and know the good from the bad.

Every society has it's occasional hidden bad apples. Such a reprobate in the military with a license to kill spells guaranteed EXTRA civilian death and destruction and misery and was usually weeded out and shot or dishonorably discharged.

The HUGE difference between what I taught your grandfathers over fifty years ago and what I KNOW for FACT is being taught today – as that TODAY – the slime who run the show have purposefully trained you beloved children to be Godless remorseless sadistic barbaric cruel evil vicious bestial inhuman murders of ALL living things – soldiers women children pets – everything!

None of these criminal horrors were taught nor condoned nor tolerated. For SURE – we were taught to be tough as nails – but ONLY against a REAL ENEMY – and only in defense of our land people freedoms an way of life. TO A MAN – we ALL considered AGGRESSION a war crime. So much so – that our very motto (of the Greed Berets) was – – "de oppresso liber" – meaning literally to LIBERATE from the OPPRESSOR.

That Holy Grail of sacred trusts has been bastardized and perverted today by our jew occupiers to mean EXACTLY the opposite! Our jew mandated goal today is to OPPRESS the FREE – for nothing more than the greater glory of IsraHELL!

The criminal activity goes deep into the levels of command like an insidious cancer. Needham's unit commander – war criminal Lt Col. Steven Michael. This Negro animal is a sadistic reprobate piece of scum war criminal who should be executed for a laundry list of VERY serious UCMJ crimes. When I served – putrid stinking punk sadistic filth like him would have been fragged by fellow OFFICERS! If what our OWN military did to this young man does not sicken you – honor is a dirty word to you.

God blesses those who strive for peace and curses those who glorify war. May Christ protect those now in prison in this demon jew occupied nation – whose 'crimes' were to refuse to commit treason – murder – rape and sick sadistic brutality against defenseless innocent men woman and children in Palestine Iraq Afghanistan and other sovereign nations where we have aggressed and murdered to satisfy the blood lust of the Satan worshiping Christ hating jews.

One such hero is pfc Bradley Manning – STILL imprisoned for his valor and honor moral conscience and patriotism. So far I have seen no high ranking officers with the moral courage to step forward and be REAL MEN! What a shame – all that is left in America's officer corps are greedy self-serving ambitious hypocrites who have ALL forgotten the oath we ALL swore.

Unfortunately the story of John Needham ended tragically as he could no longer cope with the constant pain he suffered from combat injuries – prolonged psychological trauma – disenfranchisement by sadistic soldiers in his unit, combined with the cruel and bizarre punishment he received at the hand of his reprobate sadist criminal Commander and the memories of the unspeakable war crimes committed by war criminal members of his unit. He finally lost all hope and in a fog of uppers downers pain pills and other poisons administered by the VA plus his excess alcohol abuse – he killed his girlfriend – the took his own life as his only way out of the jew created nightmare of serial wars for IsraHELL.

Interesting to note that by the admission of the war Dept. – it was found in a survey that returning members of his own unit (2-12) trained as street thugs bullies rapists and murderers-nicknamed 'lethal warriors' – should have probably been called LETHAL SCUM!.

Out of 650 returning vets chosen for the survey from this rogue outfit – over 40 % had been involved in crimes of violence. BIG SURPRISE! Gee – what a disappointment it must have been for these criminals who spent their days amusing themselves with murdering innocent civilians – terrorizing entire neighborhoods – destroying peoples homes – beating up defenseless children – shooting family pets – suddenly being charged with crimes for the same routine violent terrorizing conduct they committed with impunity under the command of their criminal reprobate sociopathic sick twisted criminal COs!

These scum are NOT soldiers – they are CRIMINALS and need to be treated as such. I encourage ALL decent Godly young moral men who have made the serious error off enlisting to fight for the Christ hating jews to have the courage to do what John Needham did – and document war crimes committed by US Soldiers against innocent defenseless civilians. First you must come to grips with the fact that you made a BIG mistake buying the poison peddled by the scumbags at the 'enlistment whores' office. Then you must decide whether you want the rest of your life messed up by associating with garbage killers for hire masquerading as real soldiers and patriots.

Enlistment officers – WHAT SCUM! Christ loves the peacemakers. He is displeased with war mongers – so what special resentment must He feel about the slimy reptiles who actually get paid a BOUNTY for every innocent soul they can snare into becoming an ally of the Devil. Look what became of poor John Needham. I hope his soul is resting peace finally – since the Army made his life hell.

John Needham's "Notification of War Atrocities and Crimes"

The Veterans Project (11.13.11)

The November 12 episode of 48 Hours Mystery mentioned a letter U.S. Army Private John Needham sent to high-ranking military officials in which allegations of various war crimes are detailed. The program focused on only one of those incidents, and included only one of several photographs that John had submitted with his letter to substantiate his accusations. *CBS chose to blur the image "because it's so graphic." Here is John's letter with that image and additional photographic evidence, all of which is completely uncensored.

*NOTE: CBS is run by Christ hating jews like Dick Wolfe – the reprobate Marxist scum who helped elevate Useful idiot trash like serial murderer- war criminal Chris Kyle, to hero status on their recent unconscionable 'show special' made to glorify war and murder and racism as " FUN" and "EXCITING"

WARNING: The images are very disturbing, as are John's allegations:
December 18, 2007

To: Mr. Randy Waddle, Assistant Inspector General, Ft Carson, Colorado
CC: LTC John Shawkins, Inspector General, Ft Carson, Colorado
Major General Mark Graham, Commanding Officer, Ft Carson, Colorado
Major Haytham Faraj, USMC, Camp Pendleton, California
Lt General Stanley Greene, US Army Inspector General

Subject: Formal Notification of War Atrocities and Crimes Committed by Personnel, B Company, 2-12, 2nd Brigade Combat Team, 2nd Infantry Division in Iraq

Dear Mr. Waddle

My name is John Needham. I am a member of Bravo Company, 2nd Battalion, 2nd Infantry division, 2nd Brigade Combat Team, 2nd Infantry Division, (BCo,2-12INF,2BCT,2ID . I deployed with my unit to Iraq from October 2006 until October 2007 when I was medically evacuated for physical and mental injuries that I suffered during my deployment. The purpose of my letter is to report what I believe to be war crimes and violation of the laws of armed conflict that I personally witnesses while deployed in Iraq.

Upon arriving in Iraq in October of 2006 my unit was assigned to the ¼ Cavalry unit at Camp Prosperity. In March of 2007 I was sent back to my unit, B Company 2-12 at Camp Falcon. It was at Camp Falcon that I observed and was forced to participate in ugly and inhumane acts against the Iraqi citizens in our area of responsibilities. Below I list some of the incidents that took place.

In March of 2007, I witnessed SSG Platt shoot and wound an Iraqi national without cause of provocation. The Staff Sergeant said that he suspected the Iraqi be a "trigger" man. We had not been attacked and we found no evidence on the man to support the suspicion. As the Iraqi lay bleeding on the ground, PVT Smith requested to administer first aid to the Iraqi. SSgt Platt said no and "let him bleed out." When SSG Platt walked away, Pvt Smith and PVT Mullins went to the Iraqi, dragged him to an alley, and applied first aid. They then drove him to the cache for further treatment.

In June of 2007 1SG Spry caused an Iraqi male to be stopped, questioned, detained, and killed. We had no evidence that the Iraqi was an insurgent or terrorist. In any event when we stopped he did not pose a threat. Although I did not personally witness the killing, I did observe 1sg Spry dismembering the body and parading of it while it was tied to the hood of a Humvee around the Muhalla neighborhood while the interpreter blared out warnings in Arabic over the loud speaker. I have a photo that shows 1SG Spry removing the victim's brains.

On another occasion an Iraqi male was stopped by a team led by Sgt Rogers as he walked down an alleyway. The Iraqi was detained and questioned then with his hands tied behind his back, SGT Rogers skinned his face.

1ST Spry shot a young Iraqi teenager who was about 16 years old. The shooting was unprovoked and the Iraqi posed no threat to the unit. He was merely riding his bicycle past an ambush site. When I arrived on the scene I observed 1SGT Spry along with SSG Platt dismember the boy's body.

In August of 2007, I responded to radio call from SGT Rogers reporting that he had just shot an Iraqi who was trying to enter through a hole that the platoon had blown in a wall to allow them observation of the area during a security patrol. When I arrived, I saw a one armed man who was still alive lying on a barricade. The man was about 30 years old. He had an old Ruger pistol hanging from his thumb. It was obvious to me that the pistol was placed there because of the way it hung from his thumb.

The Iraqi was still alive when I arrived. I saw SGT Rogers shoot him twice in the back with hollow point bullets. The Iraqi was still moving. I was asking why they shot him again when I heard Sgt Hoskins say "he's moving, he's still alive." SPEC Hoskins then moved to the Iraqi and shot him in the back of the head. SSG Platt and SGT Rogers were visibly excited about the kill. I saw them pull the Iraqi's brains out as they placed him in the body bag. CPT Kirsey must have learned something about this incident because he was very upset and admonished the NCOs involved.

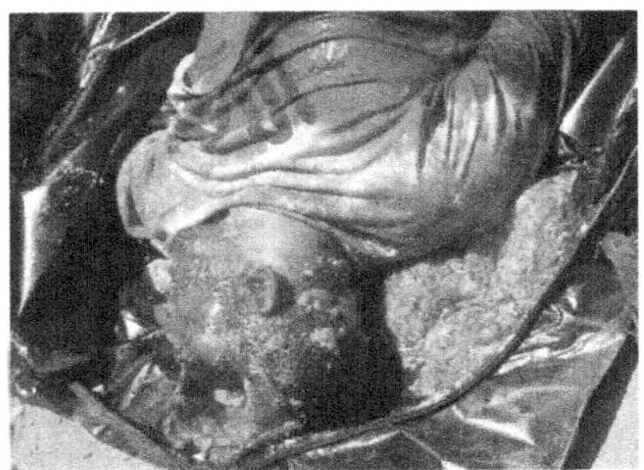

I have seen and heard 1SGT Spry brag about killing dogs. He kept a running count. At last count I remember he was boasting of having killed 80 dogs. On many occasions I observed SGT Temples, SSG Platt and SGT Rogers beat and abuse Iraqi teenagers, some as young as 14, without cause. They would walk into a house near areas where they suspected we had received sniper fire, then detain and beat the kids.

I have photos that support my allegations. I also have numerous other photos on a laptop PC that the unit illegally seized from me. I have requested its return but they have refused.

My experiences have taken a terrible toll on me. I suffer from PTSD and depression. I had no way to stop the ugly actions of my unit. When I refused to participate they began to abuse and harass me. I am still in treatment at the Balboa Naval hospital. I respectfully request that you investigate these matters, that you protect my safety by reassigning me to a different unit that is not located at Fort Carson, that you return my PC or, at least, seize it to protect the evidence on it, and that you issue a military protective order to prohibit the offending members of my unit from harassing, retaliating, or contacting me.

I have some photographs and some supporting documentation to these allegations.

Respectfully,

PFC John Needham
US Army
John's father, Michael Needham, will read the above letter at a special Human Rights Day event in Los Angeles on December 10.

In summary – Pvt Needhams exposure has revealed on the proverbial tip of the iceberg. Logical conclusions are normally drawn from an analysis of available facts. Tie all of these together and you will be able to connect the dots. The big picture – the full extent of what we have done as a people and a nation begins to become horribly clear as the veils of smoke and deception are lifted to expose the ghastly truth of what we we have become since the jews have exercised their full evil domination over our once Christian land.

We have now become EXACTLY the same kind of monstrous barbaric Godless filth – that we-as decent Americans, once despised about the Godless secular Soviet Union or the Red Chinese.

The forewarnings and exhortations began two thousand years ago from the prophets and Christ Himself. The Christian Bible – we know as the NEW TESTAMENT is replete with condemnation of the jews – too many to list here!

Our Founding fathers followed suite with their own cautions regarding accepting the treacherous jew into our midst.

History is FILLED with undeniable quotes by the world's most famous figures for the past 2 thousand years – from the ancient philosophers to Popes of old – to more recent leaders statesmen poets writers and humanitarians – ALL giving council to avoid any association with the jews lest they destroy us.

What we see here are classic symptoms of jew influence which have corrupted our youth and given incentive to already corrupt adults. We did NOT used to be like this.

Only a few of you will feel outrage at these horrors. Whereas in a morally healthy society – ALL America should be deeply disturbed. It is the death of outrage – which ALWAYS precedes the death of the nation. Read on —

FACT: according to human rights agencies -only about 5% of these crimes are ever fully reported and brought to light

CONCLUSION: For every 10 murders reported there are TWO HUNDRED MORE corpses in ditches ponds holes rubble shallow graves and cellars that will never been seen

FACT: this one PFC – ALONE – witnessed SEVEN cold blooded brutal murders – all unconscionable war crimes

CONCLUSION: since there have been a half MILLION combat troops there in the past ten years – how many hundred of thousands of murders have been committed by other psychopathic criminals. Do the numbers yourself.

FACT: this soldier also witnessed proof that one identified NCO and witnessed murderer – A 1st Sgt Spry man had also killed 80 pets of civilians for sheer cruelty and meanness

CONCLUSION: Since our military is LOADED with these sociopaths – how many millions of personal pets and farm animals were used for target practice by these demonic vermin? Hundreds of thousands? So why are dogs important? Simple – show me a man who would brag about killing every family pet he saw, for target practice and I will show you a remorseless killer who would just as easily murder the entire family.

FACT: Several NCOs in Needham's unit were observed brutally beating many innocent children out of racist hatred – many undoubtedly receiving permanent injuries.

CONCLUSION: If so many Non Commissioned Officers in JUST Needham's unit felt at liberty to terrorize and brutalize civilian children at will – how may Iraqi children will bear physical and emotional scares for the rest of their lives at the hand of these Godless racist remorseless barbaric savages? Hundreds of thousands at least!

Remember the jew slogan that stated? : "They hate us because we are free". That ANY adult human being not sharing a brain – would believe such inane imbecilic childish nonsense – would be almost humorous were it not taken seriously by 'boobus Amerikanus' – a nation of criminally ignorant dumbed-down morons like ourselves.

ALL of these criminals MUST be arrested – charged – court marshaled and hung or given maximum sentences if we re to EVER AGAIN be able to have ANY pride in our country and regain our goodness as a people. Every man and woman above the age of reason who has done NOTHING WHATSOEVER to see justice done in these matters shares some guilt for these crimes against humanity!

I knew a LOT of people who had served in Europe during WWII – some even POWs. In countless conversations and anecdotes and stories I never ever heard of ANY German who had Skinned the face off of a civilian child for entertainment and cruelty NEVER! Nor had I heard of any German soldiers killing every pet they could find in a village only for cruelty and meanness – or beating civilian children just to terrorize them, or a dozen other horrors committed an a regular basis by American Soldiers on a people who had never harmed them.

This cruelty was NOT prevalent when I was in uniform and at that time we had DAMN Good reason to hate the REAL enemy – the Communists. This current insanity is a sick twisted Godless depravity we learned from the Jews. Our police forces are ALSO getting more and more Israelized in their Godless sadistic filth by the day.

There is a REAL reason for this – so when our puppet jew President declare martial law – our military AND our police will NOT hesitate to murder rape and brutalized their own neighbors when they come to take your fathers away in the night should they not support our imperialistic war mongering and or should a citizen refuse to surrender his Constitutionally guaranteed right to bear arms and defend his on family.

People – this is NOT a matter of 'IF' – but only WHEN. You will come home from one of your childish Stupid Bowl games – or mud boggin races – or monster truck demolition derbies only to learn that thanks to YOUR stupidity and hypocrisy and CRIMINAL level of ignorance – we HAVE STARTED WORLD WAR THREE!

Within 24 hours the jews who RUN this occupied dying nation – will have had their sock puppet President declare martial law. Let me translate: GAME OVER! ALL of you Constitutional rights SUSPENDED Personal firearms WILL then be confiscated BY FORCE. Your own sons in uniform WILL KILL YOU if you resist. The rest who voice their anger at the treason will be given an 'extended holiday' at the already built 'Halliburton Arms' re-education resort.

I'm not guessing. I KNOW this is what will be done from REAL LIFE EXPERIENCES. My own flesh and blood son recently went through ARMY basic training. What he was taught was unconscionably evil – criminal – and Godless. Our Israelized military is NOW training our children to force their way into civilian homes – terrorize the families steal their means of defense and kill them if they resist!

Now you understand WHY our now 100% mercenary military is out of control and has committed more atrocities against defenseless civilians than in ALL the past war combined! That is why our quilt ridden sons are committing suicide at alarming rates today!

Notice I said "'NOW" training. reason is that I was once (fifty years ago) an infantry basic company commander and trained young warriors how to DEFEND our country for 13 straight months. Military training then did NOT include teaching our kids to terrorize and murder civilians – which is ALWAYS a crime of the worst kind – a WAR CRIME!

WE ARE NOW TRAINING YOUR SONS AND DAUGHTERS TO MURDER CIVILIANS ROB THEM BEAT THEM HUMILIATE THEM and TERRORIZE THEM! The US Army is NOW the world's largest institutionalized terrorist organization – WE ARE NOW IsraHELL's WHORE!

Any company commander or other officer commissioned or non-commissioned – involved in our demonic Godless sadistic deranged military who has not refused to commit these horrid crimes and who HAS taught these jew mentality blasphemies ARE against the laws of God – is a traitor to this nation.

He is ALSO – a mocker of our Constitution – a hypocrite – a moral coward – a criminal, and an accomplice to mass murder who should be arrested and convicted for high crimes!

John Needham – a US ARMY veteran – is a real hero – a TRUE patriot – and a brave TRUE American in my eyes.

Just in case you have not heard of Needham. As much as I DEEPLY despise virtually ALL Gulf war soldiers – guys like this are rare moral heroes and MUST be supported . His letter MUST be read and should be made viral even if a bit dated. He is what being an American is ALL ABOUT. The crimes of the cold-blooded savages he exposed are to the everlasting SHAME of our nation. I can't even LOOK at my old uniform any more without my guts churning.

Men with his moral courage are the ONLY Hope we may have to escape perdition as a nation. The guilty must be punished – ALL OF THEM! There are NO innocent non repentant soldiers – NONE! Reprobate criminal mass murderer human filth like Chris Kyle MUST BE PUNISHED for his war crimes along with ALL of his ilk! When a Mafia or Chicano gang killer murders an innocent person – REMEMBER – HE IS JUST FOLLOWING ORDERS!

Remember this fact: Every single human being murdered by the reprobate scumbag Kyle was a civilian patriot defending THEIR OWN country family and home. That is something that according to his evil mind, is reserved ONLY for pig faced bigot bullies like himself! One can only imagine what rancid Godless filth their children will turn out to be.

That means – according the serial murderer Neanderthal pig faced Kyle – that a man like myself or my civilian neighbors – should we be invaded by a FAR more powerful imperialistic nation – to which we have NEVER EVER done ANY Harm whatsoever – would be a legitimate targets for their military snipers.

AND – should we be so 'arrogant' as to try to defend our homes and families – we would be smeared as – "terrorists" – "criminals" – "savages" – "evil" – and "despicable"! Also – the butchered mutilated lifeless bodies of our beloved children would be nothing more to their HEROES than : "BUG SPLATTER" HIS – EXACT – WORDS!

A sick twisted depraved sadistic monster whose greatest lust in life is to inflict terror and death upon the innocent.

We are ALL – every mother's son on earth – PERSONALLY responsible for our OWN actions

May the God of all just acts send monsters like the murderers described by Pvt Needham and filthy sadistic Godless remorseless animals like Chris Kyle to the hottest place in hell for their crimes against innocent humanity and the disgrace they have brought to the honor of decent men who served with honor long before them.

AUGUST, 2012
OPEN LETTER TO WAR CRIMINAL CHRIS KYLE –WORLD'S WORST HUMAN BEING

To my readers – This will be the first in a series I will be doing a monthly basis of exposes on the most horrible Godless scum I can find.

This month's smegma award for the most putrid rancid demonic sub-human piece of crap in the world is Navy Seal sniper Chris Kyle. This pig faced red neck will be able to look forward to eternity in Hell for his crimes against humanity.

You are such an evil reprobate wicked sadistic sick twisted sociopathic punk – it is hard to know where to begin. I have read some excerpts from your putrid disgusting book which is a chronicle of your sadistic murderous killing sprees of innocent men women and children patriots whose crime was trying to defend their OWN country family and dignity from the World's largest institutionalized terrorist group – the jew occupied imperialist US MILITARY.

To you, new readers – I am not a mal-content leftist commie. I served my country with honor in one of our elite branches as a Special Operations Paratroop commander. I also trained basics at the USATC and was the youngest company commander on record there according to the PIO. I also trained Marines and Seals in 'Green Beret' unconventional airborne operations.

I was also a foreign diplomat (Vice Consul) for 5 years – as well as a NASA project aerospace engineer who did materials certification and troubleshooting for projects ranging from early re-entry vehicles to Polaris (submarine) missile guidance systems. I am a commercially rate pilot as well as a PADI scuba instructor.

Now back to the pig faced scumbag du-jour who this article is dedicated to. I love children – you dirt bag – and have sons and granddaughters – and love them no less than the patriot parents of the Afghan and Iraqi children you brag about murdering. Your book reveals your TRUE racist redneck mentality. What was your favorite racial epitaph against these poor people – dirt bag? Was it "dune coon or rag head or camel jockey" or a new one.

You sick psychopaths are ALL the same – and I have seen so many of you. You are bullies drunkards stupid uneducated racist violent degenerate moral cowards whose thrills are inflicting as much pain and terror and humiliation on your defenseless victims as possible. By your OWN sick twisted admission – murdering some terrified child was fair game as long as they were "rag heads" – isn't that true – scumbag?

You 'defended' NOTHING – asshole! You got your license to kill innocent people – " KILL EVERY ONE FROM 16-65″ – isn't that what you did – you murdering filthy animal! You considered ANY human being that was not one of your precious jack-booted murdering psychopath assassins – even women -especially pregnant ones – isn't that right – pig face?

What a big brave man! Wow – a wannabe cowboy and bronco rider from Texas no less. IF – in fact YOU are the quintessential example of what is considered a 'man' in Texas – then the first bomb dropped here should be reserved to 'flush that toilet' from this land.

YOU – Godless dick-wad – are the EXACT profile of who will be murdering their own neighbors right here in the USA. you fit the profile of those scum from 29 Palms who admitted they would murder their OWN neighbors if asked to by the 'authorities' – just like the USSR - right buddy?

Sick degenerate twisted sadistic sociopaths like you are the greatest threat to the safety of MY people and to WORLD peace that ever existed. Your imbecile child like brain – like all moron rednecks – is suited only for violence murder and terror! As old as I am – if I could defend my country by fighting demonic retards like you – I would make the sacrifice in a heartbeat.

Criminals like you are an embarrassment to every decent man woman and child on EARTH – especially those veterans who served during my era – REAL men like Bo Gritz and David Hackworth

I served over a half century ago when we were a decent moral Godly people and our military was honorable. Our purpose was the D-E-F-E-N-S-E of my country – and N-O-T being murderous imperialistic war criminals who trained your sons to become murderers and kill innocent people who had NEVER EVER attacked me or my family or my country in ANY WAY WHATSOEVER!

You boast that the proceeds from your new redneck hate book are to go to the widows and orphans of fellow seals. You stinking filthy hypocrite! YOU personally – you sadistic prick – are responsible for HUNDREDS of innocent widows and children. NONE of these murdered people or their families EVER did you ANY harm. They were simply defending THEIR homes and families against an aggressor force of Godless soulless scum!

You want to be a REAL man? Fall on your knees and beg our Lord forgiveness for the unspeakable crimes you have committed. THEN – announce that the profits will go to the orphans and widows of the innocent brave patriot parents you MURDERED IN COLD BLOOD – not the criminals who murdered them – you idiot!

Remember this day. I PROMISE that you WILL be haunted by the spirits of the countless innocent victims living and murdered will come back in your dreams to haunt you. You are not human. You are a MONSTER!

If my children or grandkids were raped or tortured or brutalized or murdered by aggressor scum like you – I would use my last breath to avenge their suffering and death. According to you – for defending MY OWN HOME – MY OWN FAMILY – MY OWN COUNTRY – I would be

"SAVAGE – and DESPICABLE – and EVIL". Isn't that EXACTLY what you stated – your stinking Godless piece of shit hypocrite.

AND my murdered children and family would be according to YOUR morality and wisdom – nothing more than "BUGSPLAT" – isn't that ALSO TRUE , you imbecile inbred oyster brained moron?

I took an oath on the Book of God when I became a soldier – just like you did – only I kept mine! Do you know what the motto of my branch unit is – scumbag? It says: 'DE OPPRESSO LIBER'. Can you little tiny child's brain tell me what that sacred Special Operations banner means? Of course not. Let me spell it out for your sick twisted racist bigot hate filed brain. It means: 'TO LIBERATE FROM THE OPPRESSED"

Soulless Godless sub-human knuckle dragging garbage like you – ARE THE OPPRESSOR! Do you get it yet. You have disgraced my uniform – you are a disgrace to my Republic – and you are a debasement and ignominy to ALL that is good compassionate honorable brave true and Godly in this life.

I was taught that death was better than dishonor. Scum like you consider HONOR a DIRTY word. That is the difference between you and your current ilk and the decent men I served with 2 generations ago.

May you rot in hell – as you certainly WILL. When you die – thousands of decent human beings will rejoice. Don't worry about the worms in the grave – child killer – You are so filthy nasty putrid that there are some things that even a maggot will not touch.

AUGUST, 2012
OPEN LETTER TO 'LIFE SITE' NEWS – MORE OF A GODLESS CULTURE OF DEATH THAN OF LIFE

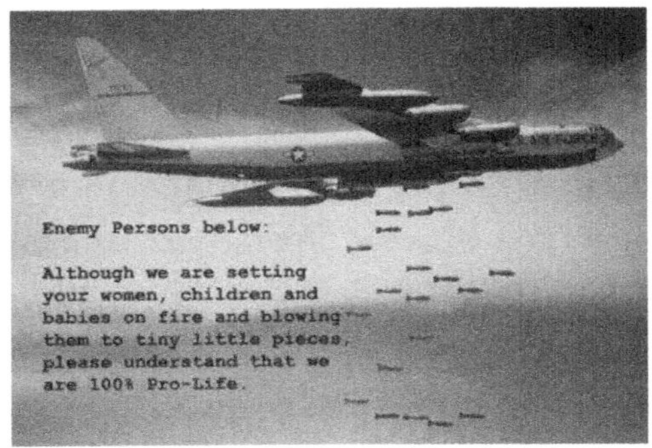

There are two special evils that irritate me more than anything else – being deceived and betrayed by someone or some organization I trusted – and hypocrisy in general!

I was recently made aware that Chik-Fil-A owner Dan Cathy took a pro life /family value stand against reprobate homosexual pervert scum who mock the sanctity of marriage and the hallowed value of single innocent human life – or so I was made to believe. I was ignorant of the TRUE reprobate hypocrite nature of the scum who are behind these false fake fraudulent apostate Pharisee Christ mocking 'Christians'.

This monstrous hypocrisy was promoted by a false 'PRO-LIFE' site – called Life Site News. Nothing could be further from the truth. This false site promotes FAR more death of innocent children that it does life.. If the child – born or unborn is a WHITE ANGLO-SAXON PROTESTANT (WASP) – then the child's life is defended , so there is some truth to their claims – BUT if the hapless child of God happens to be of Arab decent – or an avowed enemy of the jews – is an automatic death sentence – HYPOCRITES!

Listen up people and learn the truth about these rancid two faced enemies of God. I discovered that not only were the people involved were not only the antithesis of true Christians but are open supporters of mass murder genocide racism bigotry and a level of criminal ignorance that can only be termed despicable reprehensible loathsome contemptible offensive hateful and just plain nasty ugly evil!

UNDERSTAND THIS REALITY!=

The Hellish Godless demonic monsters who WANT endless serial wars that will of course logically end with Another world war so that even more Christians and Muslims will die needlessly in these fabricated racist hate wars are the goals of the wicked jews.

HOWEVER – none of this could be a reality without the EXPRESS support of an even more bloodthirsty wicked Satan worshiping entity whose capacity for death and destruction WILL be the end of America as we knew it. These rancid criminally ignorant imbecile scum are the fifty million strong inbred redneck morons we know as 'BaptDuhs' – the largest concentration of Ziobot useful idiots of the jews since their mobs of street trash during the Russian Revolution of 1917-18 – a jew organized Godless murderous hate fest which has caused more loss of innocent life that ALL of the wars and all of the plagues and all of the natural disasters on earth of the last millennia and the enslavement of hundreds of millions more!

Dan Cathy is one of the hypocrite war mongering racist demonic jew loving Arab hating criminally ignorant red neck BaptDuh morons who will soon destroy our nation and send our sons off to murder more innocent people who have NEVER done ANY American any harm. Sons – many of whom will also return in pine boxes or as radiation poisoned vegetables with a lingering death sentence form DUI. There are ALREADY half a million veterans here with all this symptoms. We are told all these lies that they only have the shrink created catchy little acronym PTSD

BULLSHIT! Look at the facts! They are ALL going to die of some type of cancer. The horrors we have unleashed upon innocent mothers in Afghanistan and Iraq are already epidemic in those war torn nations. Look at the pictures of what we have done to their children. Thousands being born as monsters. Soon there will be thousands of American children and grandchildren born horribly disfigured. We WILL reap the whirlwind as we have so richly deserved.

When YOUR grandson is born with three arms of his intestines on the outside – be SURE to thank some racist redneck BaptDuh bastard like Mike Huckabee or Dan Cathy or any one of the other 50 million BaptDUH scum who scream for the death of innocent people in foreign lands to please their precious Christ hating jews.

The following reptiles are all rabid supporters of war murder destruction and self-professed friends of the enemies of God Himself! Sarah Palin – the brainless twit who prefers to flaunt the flag of the putrid nasty "sons of Satan" rather than the American flag in her office! Mike Huckabee – a false prophet whose inane baseless racist slanderous hatred of the Arab people has caused countless deaths and suffering of innocent people as well as causing the destruction of entire civilizations – Mitt Romney – the man who would be king and yet another shill for the murderous jews who are the instigators of the most massive documented creation of war crimes since the Russian revolution and the largest creation of homeless refugees in the history of the world .

These BaptDuh war criminals like Huckabee Romney and Hagee are the MORTAL enemies of ALL decent Christians and all decent Americans. These typical racist bigot redneck BaptDuh imbeciles are emblematic of the war mongers whose lies keep the flames of war alive and well and has caused more death and destruction and suffering of innocent people that the worst German war criminals on record.

Our sons – under the influence of BaptDuh scum like Huckabee Romney Palin and Cathy have been commandeered by Satan Himself to murder over TWO MILLION TOTALLY INNOCENT CIVILIANS in the endless serial Gulf Wars we wage for the greater glory of IsaHELL. MOST of those two million murdered by our demonic sadistic sick twisted sociopath jack -booted thugs in uniform – were children!

Soon we will 'elect' a NEW jew loyal IsraHELL first war monger (Romney robot) guaranteed to do the bidding of his Hebrew masters – or we will retain the same sock-puppet of the jews (Obummer robot) Either way – we WILL wage more jew wars – murder millions more civilians – watch more American sons die for IsraHELL and VERY VERY soon – watch find our own country fighting angry nations who have become tired of our warmongering and who CAN FIGHT BACK! Even if we survive total destruction – you will witness MILLIONS upon MILLIONS of sick dying horribly terminally ill radioactively poisoned Americans as time goes on – for whom death will be a blessing. Mark my words.

As for the 'LIFE SITE NEWS' deceivers – I thought these putrid devious ambitious racist imbecile scum were true pro-life proponents. They fooled me and that makes my angry. It is loaded with typical pro-IsraHELL racist anti- Arab slanderous rhetoric. These hypocrite Pharisees from the Synagogues Of Satan have no problem murdering millions of human beings – MOSTLY CHILDREN – as they slander as rag heads sand niggers dune coons and camel jockeys.

In other words – to these putrid Christ mocking hypocrites – the purposeful murder of one WASP child is an unforgivable sin (and I agree) BUT – the murder torture humiliation brutalilizing of MILLIONS of MILLIONS of 'sub human' Arab children becomes a mandate from God. THAT IS FILTHY JEW MENTALITY BLASPHEMY which serves only the will of Satan!

You MUST see and read the interview on my site with Brother Nathanael Kapner of REAL JEW NEWS – explaining DU hazards to visualize the magnitude of the horrors that are the collective Sociopathic sick mind of the jews .

If you are foolish enough to allow our immoral Godless Jew occupied government to seduce you son or daughter to serve Satan as uniformed murderer for IsraHELL – your child will probably die a horrible lingering untreatable death.

Even if he does return home alive – IF he has spent ANY time in a combat area where ANY DU weaponry is or even HAD been used he will be irreversibly poisoned with a death warrant to his wife and future children that will make a normal death look like a blessing! Everything you will see has been witnessed and well-documented by some of the finest specialists on earth. This IS ALL REAL! The inescapable horrors of this special gift from the jews and the puppet government they now own will make any horrors you have even imagined in your worst nightmares pale.

The military in this place we once knew as the United States Of America is insane with lust and power and has NO conscience regarding our own people any more. The US Army is a collective insane rabid harbinger of death – BEYOND TREASON to our OWN PEOPLE! If you never watch another film in your life – this one is a MUST SEE!

SEPTEMBER, 2012
DEMOCRAT PARTY: TODAY'S SCUM MAGNET FOR THE DREGS OF SOCIETY

As an American who spent a long time serving the evil Democrat Party through ignorance – and later as a Veteran – and as an educated world traveler and experienced geo-political analyst I feel compelled to issue this grave warning!

IF – you consider yourself anything other than a Marxist – a country seller – a homosexual pervert – an atheist – a Zionist Jew – a Christ hating jew – disgruntled sociopath – parasite loser – or otherwise some other form of societal detritus – a 'nigger' or 'redneck' – as opposed to a decent Negro person such as the saintly black woman that helped to raise me or a the truly decent 'good ole country boy' who does not pride himself in ignorance – GET THE HELL OUT OF THAT TREASONOUS FOUL ORGANIZATION IMMEDIATELY and help fight for the freedom of your country – NOW!

I promise you – a feeling of cleanliness that you can only remember after one of those hour long hot showers to cleans off ground in dirt and grime form a situation where you could not bathe for days! Must adults know the tingling exuberant feeling of that experience? That is how I felt – the day I finally woke up and officially resigned from that evil organization of death, perversion, ignorance, blasphemous mockery of Christ and outright treason to the traditional principles of our American REPUBLIC.

Barack Obama – the person that represents your Party is the epitome of evil deception and lies. He is a MARXIST IDEOLOGUE – meaning that his philosophy of life is nothing less than treason to the people of this Republic – SOCIALISM/COMMUNISM/MARXISM! Call it what you like – but it all adds up to high treason! The Democrat Party is and has been lost long ago to the forces of evil as the official home of the Communist Party. Only the most ignorant of idiots can truthfully still be in denial of that fact – know by even third world children for decades!

GET OUT OF THE COMMUNIST DEMONCRAP PARTY – NOW!

The Communist Party of the United States of America (CPUSA) has thrown their political support to nearly every candidate since George McGovern. The last TRUE anti-communist I remember when still a DNC member was JFK – and he had to be disposed of.

Here are some of the quotes from Official Communist newspaper – The Daily Worker articles:

"Over the next 40 years the American Stalinists became increasingly ossified under Hall's (Gus Hall – CPUSA chairman) leadership. They remained unswerving in their support for the Democratic Party and the trade union bureaucracy"

"The CP, in fact, has supported every Democratic candidate for US President from Roosevelt to Gore, with the single exception of the 1948 race, when it endorsed the third party campaign of Henry Wallace, the former vice president and secretary of agriculture, who ran on a platform advocating continued collaboration with the Soviet regime.

"In 1988, he steered the CP into full support for the Democrat Party when he suspected left-Democrat Jesse Jackson would win the Presidential primaries"

So if you want the final destruction of America into AmeriKa – just support Communist Jesse Jackson clone Obama. ANY person calling themselves an 'AMERICAN' – that supports Comrade Bema FULL WELL KNOWING this fact about has treasonous agendas should be considered guilty of high treason in the STRICTEST SENSE. BECAUSE – IF you are against Communism – why in the name of God would you support a KNOWN Communist? It is UNIVERSALLY agreed among ALL knowledgeable analysts that if Comrade Hall were alive today – he would through his full weight behind his ideological brother – Obama. Even so, the CPUSA has in fact predictably endorsed Comrade Obama for President due to his leftist ideologies.

AL of Comrade Obama's meaningful associations in life have been COMMUNIST – his father – his mother – his teen mentor – his brother – his organizers – His fundraisers – his Senatorial predecessor and a good part of his organizational involvements – ALL COMMUNIST INFLUENCED.

Obama is a monster whose black heart knows no limits to sadistic cruelty. He was recently asked in an interview regarding abortion and the sanctity of human life – what would he do in the following situation if elected President: Say that a child had somehow survived an abortion (as has actually happened in more than one instance) – would you then save the life of that innocent helpless child?

Obama's unhesitating answer: 'ABSOLUTELY NOT! I would legislate that no further care or protection be given to the child and the medical staff would just stand there and let the child die' (murder a defenseless helpless human being in cold-blood) But of course that is what Demoncraps are all about – EVIL!

NOWHERE in my adult life have I ever encountered that kind of sadistic cruelty – even the worst societies on earth! I have never even READ about a top leader even in Hitler's Germany – Red China – Stalin's 'Evil Empire' – or even Castro's Marxist Cuba PROUDLY stating that he would make it a LAW to allow the life of a helpless newborn citizen of their country to be abandoned to die on the altar of infanticide!

That kind of sadistic cruelty is virtually unparallel in ANY civilized moral society. It would be difficult to even imagine an act of greater fiendish barbaric brutality than to witness professionals trained and dedicated to ease suffering and protect life – forced by LAW to stand by and watch a child struggling for life – crying and gasping for breath just left to die with less dignity than a rat caught in a trap!

And this sadistic treasonous Negro scum wants to become the 'Conscience' of MY nation! Fact is – that most animals – even some cold-blooded ones – will defend their young to the DEATH! Yet – I see huge crowds cheering Obama as their 'role model' and anointed high leader. What does that tell you about the character of the Democrats?

Remember that FACT when you see this soulless monster talking to crowds about a "change". Yes there will be a change should he be in command of our lives – a FURTHER descent into the depths of hell the likes of which this country – even as bad as we have become – has yet to see. His skin is not the ONLY thing about him that is 'black'.

ANY Christian who even allows his children to associate with the families who have supported this monster – is a fool on the fast track to hell!

It has been wisely noted – that, throughout the ages – in the free world – the morals and character of the electorate are MIRROR IMAGES of those of the elected official. That simple truth NEVER EVER CHANGES!

As you may have by now realized – The Communist Party USA Endorsed Obama – "Our Party actively supported Obama during the primary election." Source: CPUSA Website

Obama has done more to help further destroy the image of Negroes in America than anyone since King. I believe that there are still a fair number of moral decent educated honorable blacks today in America, who should do everything possible to distance themselves from hypocrite scum like Obama. I have in the past – and still will – stand up for ANY decent American – black or white. You want 'respect'? – then have the guts and character to criticize your 'own people' when they are wrong! Barack Obama is a classic opportunity.

GET OUT OF THE DEMONCRAP COMMUNIST PARTY- NOW!

Aside from the ultra treasonous Communist nature of the 'political complexion' of the Democrat Party – here are many WELL DOCUMENTED FACTS concerning the TRUE 'character' of this foul anti-American cabal of human slime. I have posted this list of facts for ALL Americans to see for decades – and it has NEVER EVER been challenged for authenticity. I have said it before and I will say it again:

THERE IS NOT A LIVING AMERICAN WHO KNOWS THE TRUE FILTHY NATURE OF THE DEMOCRAT PARTY BETTER THAN I . They have only become fouler since I defected from their evil ranks over 25 years ago. The only difference between then and now is that then – I was actually a participant in their filth – and today I observe this human cesspool from the outside.

LEARN WHAT THEY STAND FOR AND WHAT KIND OF PEOPLE THEY REALLY ARE

NOTE: many of these facts were researched during the disgraceful Clinton administration but that does not affect their validity. The only thing that is worth mentioning is that there are today

– ADDITIONALLY – at least TWICE the disgusting number of rancid issues committed by the Democrats.

FACT: Virtually EVERY homosexual child molesting pervert organization in the US supports the Democrats. (there are literally hundreds of these organizations)

FACT: Virtually every leftist [Marxist, socialist, communist, Maoist] group in the USA supports Democrat 'values' – as well as THE Communist Party itself!.

FACT: The Communist Party has officially endorsed Democrat political candidates for decades.

FACT: Virtually every pervert, criminal, drug dealer, porn king, atheist, Marxist, baby murderer and traitor supports the Democrat Party.

FACT: The Democrats booed and humiliated our American Boy Scouts as they carried our nation's flag at the recent Democrat National Convention.

FACT: Virtually every Communist and homosexual organization in America had a delegate at the recent DNC

FACT: Virtually ALL the homoerotic filth, graphic violence, foul language and mockery of God and Christian principles from Hollywood, is a product of supporters of the Democrat Party

FACT: Destruction of the family unit and tireless mockery of family values and patriotic symbols such as our flag and our National Anthem is a major project of the Democrat Party.

FACT: Al Gore – who would be 'king' – was a close friend [as was his pro-Communist Senator father] of America's most notorious communist traitor and country seller – Armand Hammer

FACT: William Jefferson Clinton is a traitor (by definition), a liar of dazzling proportions, an adulterer, a blasphemer, a coward and a murderer of such large numbers of innocent human beings as to exceed Hitler's victims by hundreds and hundreds of percent.

FACT: Janet Reno – our (then) Democrat Atty. General, is a notorious sex pervert, child hater and God mocker. This proven deviate signed the death warrants for 69 innocent people shot and burned alive in their own church. Twenty-six of those murder victims were innocent children and infants! Her venomous hatred for Christian principles was legendary -ESPECIALLY HER HATRED FOR CHILDREN – as this sex deviate pervert is childless. Her vicious deportation of a helpless innocent Cuban child BACK to a Marxist hellhole – against his DYING father's wishes is completely typical of immoral Godless Democrat mentality.

FACT: The Democrat administration committed high treason [trading nuclear secrets for campaign donations] and has endangered the lives of virtually every man woman and child in America. In case you have forgotten – the PLA of the Peoples Republic of China has reminded us that they not only have the ability to destroy us – but the desire to do so as well. These friends of Clinton are the remorseless animals who murdered over 60,000,000 of their own civilian population – and murdered 1,000 students in Tiananmen Square, for their 'treasonous' expression to want democracy in their communist hellhole.

FACT: The (then) Democrat VP candidate – the Jew, Joseph Lieberman – was officially ex-communicated from his Synagogue by a formal rabbinical court of elders. Why? Because Lieberman has consistently mocked God and sacred Jewish law – for one reason – approval and support of the murder of millions of innocent children.

FACT: The reason most people don't know most of these outrages by the Democrat/Marxists is because the news media in America is now controlled almost 100% by Democrat /Marxists/Jews. This fact has been PROVEN a hundred times over – again and again. These vital damning absolutely true facts will never be seen in any major newspaper. Democrats hate the truth.

FACT: The Marxist/Democrats have worked tirelessly to divide this country by creating class envy and encouraging welfare for the lazy and violent minorities that support the handout welfare mentality of their Marxist/Democrat Party. This technique is E-X-A-C-T-L-Y what the Russian street trash under Lenin was encouraged to believe and therefore revolt against anyone who had worked for and earned more than they did. It in fact did succeed in 1917 and continued to grow like a cancer, killing all in the way, subverting entire countries to slavery with the aid of traitors like Gore's friend Armand Hammer. Check ANY reputable history book.

FACT: Some 53 members of our Congress – ALL DEMOCRATS! – are card carrying Marxists/Socialists. This is classic as you can get for an act of treason! Anyone who has a computer and can access the Web can see this.

FACT: There were 45 Communist goals that appeared in our congressional records (Jan10-1963). Today, all but 2 or possibly 3 of those subversive goals have been accomplished. EVERY SINGLE ONE OF THESE TREASONOUS aims were by and large, legislated, supported, endorsed and made possible by the Democrat Party. I will personally award $100 to anyone who can accurately disprove my statement!

FACT: One of those 45 treasonous goals to destroy America (#15) was: "To capture one or both of the political parties in the US". Just in case any reader really still thinks that all this is coincidence! (the fact that Obama would even be CONSIDERED is even more proof)

FACT: The ACLU is in fact the 'legal arm of the Communist Party. Their goal has been and still is – victory of Communism in America [as stated by its founder- Roger Baldwin] – is always supportive of the leftist Democrat Party. (and still is)

FACT: Destruction of our Constitution has been a long time goal of Democratic administrations. The Marxist country seller, Clinton (literally) – has stated he wants to "re-invent" our Constitution. Confiscation of private firearms has been the historical prelude to virtually EVERY SINGLE instance of a free people being enslaved. Russia, Germany, Cuba and China are but a few victims. Yet – the Democrats work tirelessly to put decent law abiding Americans (that is over 98% of us) in that same mortal danger.

FACT: Only the Democrats have had a House Speaker that OPENLY supported Marxist terrorist organizations. Actually – not just one – but TWO! (Tip O'Neil and Jim Wright)

FACT: According to the liberal Newsweek – and US News & World Report – Democrats were found to be far less moral than their Republican counterparts on issues of traditional family values and ethics. (Can you imagine any better reason not to associate with a Democrat?)

FACT: Four other major late 60's Communist goals of the CPUSA were achieved in the late sixties by Democrat legislators

FACT: In 1987, four more of the Communist Party's major goals were accomplished by aid from Democrat legislators! [stop SDI – stop all nuclear testing – stop aid to anti-Communist freedom fighters in Nicaragua – and ratify 'SALT II' treaty with the USSR]

FACT: In the 80's, the Chairman of the Communist Party here announced for the first time in decades that the Communists would not run their own candidate for President. Reason? Simply because of the similar agenda of the Democrat Party. (more details listed later) Since that time, the Communist Party has not only run no candidate of their own – but has vigorously thrown their weight behind the Democrat Presidential candidate! Talk about TREASON!

FACT: The Democrat Party is home to several PRACTICING homosexual perverts – Members of Congress! (even worse today)

FACT: Their hatred of God and Christian values is so strong that the Democrats have initiated EVERY legislation to force Christian Americans to pay for the murder of innocent children. [Check the voting records of the past dozen 'Congresses']

FACT: A Democrat President is the only one in our once proud history to have demonstrated AND organized a Marxist demonstration for the DEFEAT of Americans in battle. Clinton HIMSELF called for the defeat of the servicemen of the United States – but after all – remember his comment: " I loathe the military". REMEMBER – DEMOCRATS ELECTED this reprobate!

FACT: The IPS (Institute for Policy Studies – America's most powerful think tank) sent advisors ONLY to Democrat legislators.

FACT: Democrat legislators are the only open supporters of homosexual pervert 'rights' [read; the 'right' to seduce our innocent children and promote their filthy lifestyle to our youth]

FACT: Democrats ALWAYS side with the Marxists in 'revolutions'

.FACT: DEMOCRATS are ALWAYS the ones to mock and criminalize traditional family values. (much MUCH worse today)

FACT: The appointed Democrat Cabinet is predictably almost always comprised of Marxists, homosexuals, lesbians and atheists.

FACT: Democrats OPENLY support – and are OPENLY supported by Hollywood trash.

FACT: ALL leftist, foul-mouthed, lesbian, homo radio/TV personalities are Democrats. (Only the name have changed)

FACT: MOST ALL Democrat sponsored 'think tanks' and 'foundations' are leftist.

FACT: Democrat legislators have taxed the American middle class almost out of existence. (the recent Democrat supported 'bailout' is now the greatest tax rape in history)

FACT: Democrats strongly support the anti-God filth of the Marxist dominated NEA. They have controlled our public education system with their anti-God – anti-Christian – anti-family values – anti Constitution amoral decadence for almost four decades. An ENTIRE generation of America's youth – or possibly two – have for the most part, been 'dumbed down' – violent – disrespectful – druggies – leftist revisionist indoctrinated and taught to hate everything that our forefathers held sacred. These 'academically challenged' morons will never be productive decent citizens.

FACT: Democrats are responsible for making God and His law illegal in our schools and other public places.

FACT: Democrats appointed ACLU MARXIST Ruth Bader Ginsberg to the Supreme Court where she is empowered to mock Christianity, enforce the seduction of our children and destroy our Constitutional rights.

FACT: Democrats have appointed the enemies of all that is decent and good in America as powerful cabinet heads. Carol Browner – brutal Marxist EPA 'land grabber head. Madeline Albright – leftist UN ambassador. Donna Shalala – Head of HHS with her Nazi style openly anti-Christian policies. Council of Economics advisor, Stalinist Laura Tyson. Just to name a few

FACT: Democrats control the anti-God, anti-Constitution, pro-homosexual/lesbian perverts NEA. If you want to read something to really make you sick – take a look at a few issues of the NEA's leftist 'Goals 200'

FACT: Democrats refuse to prosecute the criminal – Hillary Clinton for crimes too numerous to mention. Among them is support for congressionally identified terrorist groups. Direct violation of HB 1710 (S.390) Jan 1995. Title 3- section 301 – subsection 'D' paragraph '2'

FACT: Democrats are so sadistic and cruel that they have legislated recent laws to prevent parents from leaving what they have worked for their whole lives to their children after their death.

FACT: Democrats are SO SIMILAR in their treasonous goals to the objectives of the Communist Party (the over-throw of our Constitution by any means) – that Party HEAD Avro Kusta Halberg, (AKA-Gus Hall), when asked by the national press as to why the Communists declined to run candidates for President/VP for the first time in decades – answered with this chilling and sobering statement: " Since the goals of the Democratic party are now so progressive, we feel that for us to field a candidate would be redundant". ["progressive" is a Marxist 'buzzword' indicating being in accord and conformity with Communist objectives and ideology] (that policy still holds true today)

Democrats are so close in their goals and beliefs to the Communists that the last dying wish of the Chairman of the Communist Party (CPUSA) was that the Democrats defeat the Republicans in this past critical Presidential struggle. It should be noted that this treasonous reprobate admirer of 'Comrade Klinton', – 'Secretary General' Hall was in fact a convicted felon – a treasonous criminal – having spent 8 years in federal prison for high treason and sabotage. Many Democrat Congressmen OPENLY mourned his passing.

FACT: Finally – the Democrats are 'world class' murderers! The accurate definition of murder is to take an innocent human life with malice and forethought. ABORTION IS LEGALIZED MURDER BY DEFINITION – PERIOD! To put the evil of these monsters in understandable perspective – consider these facts: In the war of independence, there were 2,500 Americans killed. In our civil war, there were 498,000 Americans killed. In WWI, 116,000 Americans lost their lives. In WWII, 407,000 of our countrymen were killed. In Korea, we lost 54,000 sons. In Vietnam, There was a loss of life that was over 58,000 souls. All together, a total of a little more than 1.1 million Americans were killed. That is a total death count for ALL major wars in the USA since our birth over 225 years ago!

In the Democrat/ACLU sponsored 'War Against Children' since 1973 – there have been over THIRTY EIGHT MILLION AMERICAN BABIES MURDERED! At LEAST 15,000,000 (FIFTEEN MILLION) of these cold-blooded pre-meditated murders was authorized and approved by our very own 'coward-in chief' William Jefferson Clinton – truly a world-class murderer. Historically this American butcher outranks Hitler's deeds by over ONE THOUSAND PERCENT – and is close to the horrific record by Mao and Stalin. The enormity of the horror and mass murders committed by the Marxist Democrats in this country has seldom been paralleled in history.

HERE ARE SOME OF THE THINGS THAT DEMOCRATS DO NOT BELIEVE

This list could go on and on almost endlessly, but essentially – [Hypocrites don't count] Democrats DO NOT TRULY believe in God – they do not believe in Family values – they do not believe in a wholesome atmosphere for our children – they do not believe in the sanctity of human life – they do not believe in self-determination and responsibility for one's own actions – they do not believe in a strong military to defend the country – they do not believe in the validity of our Constitution – They do not hold any value for integrity, truth or honesty – They do not believe there are any moral absolutes – they do not believe in American culture and tradition – they do not believe in patriotism and most every other principle which decent Americans have honored since our country was founded — OR they wouldn't STILL be so loyally supporting the kind of filth that was so typified by the past Klintonista administration.

AND – HERE SRE SOME OF THE THINGS THAT DEMOCRATS DO BELIEVE

Democrats DO believe in promoting homosexual perversions – and they do – BIG TIME!

They believe that the Holy Bible is a fairy tale. They Do believe that the Ten Commandments are at best 'The Ten Suggestions' – They do believe that character or integrity is archaic idealism – They do believe that "CHARACTER DOESN'T COUNT" – as nationally televised at their national conventions.[Bill Clinton]

They do believe that our Constitution is vague, ambiguous, outdated and invalid – they do believe that the 'end justifies the means' – they do believe that 'it's OK if you don't get caught' – They do believe in a big government that suckles them from cradle to grave – they do believe that the people are here to serve the government, and not vice versa.

Additionally, they do believe that frogs, tadpoles and owls etc. are more valuable than human life – they do believe that our Boy Scouts are bigoted because they will not accept the ungodly nasty, filthy conduct of homosexual perverts in their ranks – they do believe that honesty, reverence, respect and humility are signs of weakness – they do believe that society has a RIGHT to murder their own children BUT that to take the life of a cold-blooded murderer is illegal.

Not surprisingly – they do believe that they have a 'RIGHT' to a nice home (at some working person's expense) – a 'RIGHT' to take money they haven't earned – a RIGHT to have preferential treatment if black, Hispanic or homosexual – they do believe that Communism [AKA Socialism] is an acceptable alternative for Americans – they do believe that they have a 'RIGHT' to steal a man's income to use for grossly immoral purposes – regardless of how offensive it is to Christians.

In short – the Democrat Party is America's largest 'HUMAN GARBAGE DUMP' I have been criticized in the past for the perceived notion that there are also "good people" in the Democrat Party. Oh REALLY? Can you tell me then – as to just WHY any decent Godly American would KNOWINGLY – and purposefully associate him or herself with the unquestionable scum of society? You say that you weren't aware of the horrible conduct of the Party till now? Really?

OK – so what are you STILL doing in that cesspool? Or how about this one: " There are good people still trying to reform the Party from the inside." Yea – I even tried that a few years ago. I was a fool. NO Major evil entity has EVER been historically voluntarily reformed from the inside by do-gooders. NOT Communism – not Zionism – not the Homosexual movement – not infanticide – and CERTAINLY not the evil rot of the Demoncrap party. You do NOT destroy evil by first SERVING it. You EXPOSE evil – distance yourself from it and work to destroy it.

THERE IS NO MORAL REASON FOR ANYONE TO SERVE THE DEMOCRATS.

Some 'yellow dog' Democrats will predictably whine and howl because of what I have exposed. BUT – just remember – it is ALL TRUTH – and sometimes the truth is ugly –so get over it!

In closing it is only fair and truthful to clear the air regarding the Republicrats. I am NOT advocating that ANY decent moral educated American be associated with that evil jew dominate gaggle of reptiles and maggots in any way shape or form. Just be a good American and do what you KNOW in intellectually and morally right for family God and country. Get the damned demonic Christ hating deceiving greedy jews our of our America. Jews are NOT cannot be and NEVER will be Americans.

The Republican Party (which in reality no longer exists) in different ways – is easily as evil as the Democrats – but that is a different story – its hypocrisy and ugly truth deserves a total exposure. I served the so-called Republican Party for almost twenty four years as an active member of the RNC. Once I was aware of the true evil Godless nature of monkey faced treasonous Jews before Americans war criminal mass murderer George Bush – I RAN – not walked away from that putrid nest of treasonous hypocrite jew run scum.

Today we are run by ONE 'party' – the stinking Godless treasonous jews! We are no longer sovereign nor free nor brave

SEPTEMBER, 2012
USA: LAND OF FALSE PROPHETS, JEW LOVERS, CHRIST-MOCKERS, LIARS AND WARMONGERS

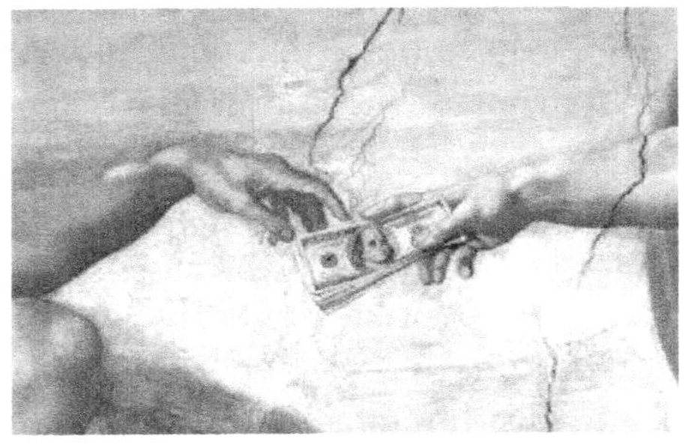

I have made a partial list of the societal sludge and detritus that we as MerKans so dearly worship love respect and adore in place of Christ. These reprobate creatures are so vile and putrid that there has never ever in MerKan history a benchmark from which to compare the wickedness hypocrisy and larcenous lust for earthly pleasures as with this rancid putrid scum.

We know these false prophets best, as 'fundamentalist evangelicals'. NONE have ANYTHING To do with truth hope salvation love or Christianity. They are hateful evil self serving arrogant haughty racist deceiving greedy materialistic SCUMBAGS! They are to the ultimate shame of what USED to be America – nothing more than criminals disguised as 'representatives of our Lord Christ'. No other nation on earth has stooped so low as this home bred scum.

It has been said – that there are some acts, so foul and perverse and wicked – that even a sewer rat won't do. Apparently that cannot be said for the following sociopathic unconscionably wicked criminals.

They collectively operate a billion dollar confidence swindle game rivaling the gambling tables at Vegas. These are friends of the Devil – "wolves in sheep's clothing" who prey upon the naiveté ignorance and foolishness of the most ignorant people on the face of the Earth. Those being, inbred uneducated superstitious hillbilly imbecile MERKANS!

For a perfect 'storybook' example of the quintessential shyster pastor – may I suggest you rent the movie: LEAP OF FAITH – starring Steve Martin as a 'con artist / preacher'. His performance is incredibly faithful to what these following 'fundie' scum do in real life 24-7. I had to laugh out loud as I read the ending credits and the obligatory disclaimer: "ANY RESEMBLANCE TO REAL PERSONS – LIVING OR DEAD IS PURELY COINCIDENTAL"

Are you kidding ME? "Coincidence"? Martin's stellar performance was a faithful collective carbon copy of the despicable REAL LIFE conducts every single one of these "REAL PERSONS" I have selected to expose as scum. The ONLY difference between preacher scum "Jonas Nightingale" of the 'fictitious film – and the real life preacher scum – are the NAMES!

You may do your own search. I simply used the name of the so-called 'pastor' + the word 'scumbag' – or 'racist' – or 'fraud' on my Google browser. Of the eighteen scumbags I selected – I used that exact word – "SCUMBAG" . Out of curiosity I used the other words – "RACIST" and " FRAUD" for three of them marked with 'asterisk' . THAT'S IT – nothing fancy – no tricks – no cherry picking.

I list them in their order of being despised as "SCUMBAGS" by moral educated viewers (from least – to most hits)

Meet AmeriKas most Christ mocking vile racist frauds and scumbag war mongers A VERY REVEALING 'HALL OF SHAME'

(1) BILLY GRAHAM = 23,800 the least wicked of the bad goys – but still evil
(2) JIMMY SWAGGART = 28,200
(3) BENNY HINN = 89,500
(4) DONNIE SWAGGART = *109,000
(5) CREFLO DOLLAR = 114,000
(6) JIM BAKER = 135,000
(7) ORAL ROBERTS = 137,000
(8) JERRY FALWELL = 195,000
(9) JOYCE MEYER = *235,000
(10) FRANKLIN GRAHAM = *264,000
(11) JOEL OSTEEN = 280,000
(12) RICK WARREN = 294,000
(13) PAT ROBERTSON = 586,000
(14) TED HAGGARD = 702,000
(15) JOHN HAGEE = 823,000
(16) KENNETH COPELAND = 1,550,000
(17) T.D. JAKES = 1,760,000
(18) MARCUS LAMB = 3,310,000
(19) PAUL CROUCH = *12,900,000 the king of the Zionist IsraHELL worshipers and Christ mockers

There dozens or perhaps hundreds more. I selected the ones that came to mind as the most prominent. Note that one of these slimy greedy Godless deceiving larcenous snakes' own name is greed itself ('Dollar')! They have all gotten wealthy peddling vicious cruel lies and twisting the truth to suit their lust for fame and earthly pleasures. They have all 'sold' God for profit. Sadly – We MerKans have spread this unconscionable wickedness all over our Hemisphere and beyond.

Joel Osteen alone, has fleeced his sheeple for over 30 MILLION DOLLARS. This Sardonic faced fraud is a classic example of 'MerKan' greed pride and arrogance. Nearly 45,000 greedy materialistic reptile 'itchy eared' hypocrites attend this scumbag's false teachings of Satan each Sunday. There is not ONE Godly honest humble true Christian follower of the word of God in his money-making disgraceful Lakeside church or ANY other 'Synagogue Of Satan'.

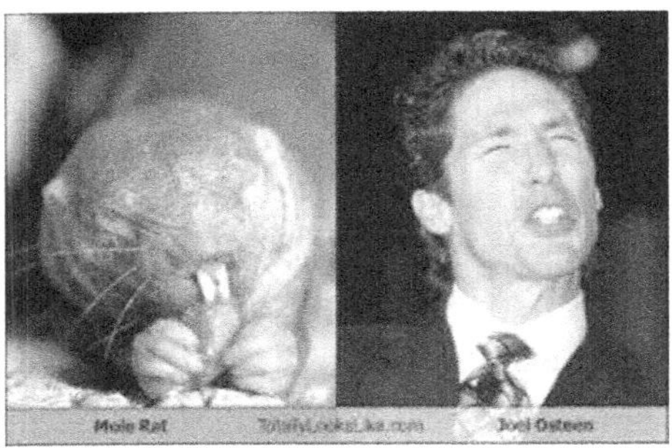

Many of these scumbags are out right self professed Zionists, but all IsraHELL first traitors to America and mockers of the Scripture. They are ALL Protestant – mostly 'BaptDUHs' – and command loyalty from over fifty million treasonous Americans who have sold us out and WILL chose the demon terrorist State of IsraHELL over their OWN country as far as loyalty.

Beware of these self- serving war mongering scum. They ARE your neighbors and your children's classmates. They are the jew indoctrinated IsraHELL LOYAL war criminals in 'desert camos' who WILL murder YOU and YOUR Family on command. Should you consider that statement too "over the top" – READ about the treason of our OWN US MARINE CORPS at 29 Palms Marine/Naval base.

The Marines have ADMITTED they would murder civilian neighbors if given the order. This is not a joke or scare tactic. IT IS A FACT! I am a historian and pre-jew occupation former Green Beret paratroop commander. Today's 'judified' Marines (not the old true 'semper fi' corps) have committed more sadistic war crimes against innocent civilians in the 'Gulf wars' than all of the branches AND all the wars we have ever engaged in – COMBINED!

These young killers are NOT The same quality of decent honorable brave Marines I trained in special Forces airborne techniques some 45 years back. Decades of endless jew lies and glorification of murder and violence injew created 'war' video games have turned them into mindless soulless monsters. Our military today are the most Godless segment of our society – as I know so painfully well.

Should martial law be declared – I will be arrested for speaking the TRUTH and will simply disappear. Do not let this happen in our America to you and your family. I have spoken only the TRUTH from years of experience here and abroad. It matters not which traitor is 'elected by the sheeple'. It is a WIN-WIN for the jews and a lose-lose for us 'goy'. Tear your selves away from your Stupid Bowl NFL childish nonsense and start acting like mature Americans.

Teach your children well – these TRUTHS at HOME – or they WILL learn the lies of the jew 'in the street'. We have already lost TWO generations of our sons and daughters to the filth and lies of the jews. If we lose the generation of my grandchildren – we are a Godless damned and doomed nation – destined for the trash heap of history!

SEPTEMBER, 2012
OBAMA: A REAL LIFE DEMONIC MONSTER

This is not intended reading for 'yellow dog' demoncraps. Those scum are Satan worshipers and are beyond repentance as they race to perdition with their father in hell. They constitute the majority of the current filth in the Demoncrap Party of societal detritus.

This is intended for people like the criminally ignorant but not wicked, black woman I encountered one day in my cardiologists office. There are millions like her – not intentionally evil but by inexcusable ignorance supporting most of the most evil acts Known to man. I believe that my encounter with her may have actually stirred what little brain matter she had that was viable. I pray I touched her heart and soul – if she still had one.

On my way to the elevator *(one of those that moves about the speed of a tired sloth)* I held the doors for a aged black lady who was struggling with a cane as she approached the elevator wearing a bright pro- Obama sweatshirt. She had an almost angelic face – kinda like the kindly looking black woman on the Aunt Jemima pancake syrup bottle.

I decided to try an experiment in human nature I had done many times before. I started a conversation by saying: "I see you must have voted for Mr. Obama judging from that fine sweatshirt". She responded very politely that she was indeed a supporter. I then Stated that :I'll bet you have children yourself. (being sure at her age she would) "Oh I has 7 chillen and 10 granchillen" she proudly stated.

It was time to set the hook and reel in the catch. I responded:" And I'll bet you have a respect for the lives of children and might even be a Christian". She smiled and proudly stated that she was indeed a follower of the Lord and that babies' lives were sacred to her. I purposely look puzzled and asked her: "Ma-am – it is not my business of course but I am now curious – as to why you voted for Obama – I mean what was the most important reason?"

She looked pensive for a moment then smiled again and said: "I guess to be honest – it was he be a black man".

NOW I 'set the hook and dropped the bomb. Ma-am – I'm confused – you said you loved the lord and little babies – did you know that Mr. Obama not ONLY voted against a bill to save children but sponsored a law that any child who survived one of those horrible partial birth abortions – was to be killed anyway" – which was of course 100% true.

Her face changed from a smile to a look of puzzlement and almost fear. I quickly added : OH my God – you didn't know that? Certainly as an a responsible adult you must have taken time to find out WHO he REALLY was and WHAT he REALLY stands for – didn't you? -I asked almost pleadingly.

By that time the snail slow elevator had made its way to the ground floor. Her painful expression then showed what I perceived as guilt as she slowly went past me. Of course I never saw her again – but I am sure my psychology had done its job. Only She and God knows if she would vote for the baby murdering Obama demon again.

THAT folks – is the kind of ignorance and irresponsibility that is emblematic of uneducated blacks hillbillies and Hispanics who are attracted to the handout mentality – ah be entitled – welfare mantras the democrats use so effectively on ignorant irresponsible uneducated drones.

And by the way – here is a little experiment I did with my browser to test for what literate people think of the disingenuous chameleon like jew puppet reptile Obama. I used Google for my search engine and here are the shocking disgusting unconscionable factual results.

Remember what you see in the next few lines. It is the legacy of a man who may be elected to a second term.

MORE frighteningly – it is testimony and confirmation to the no exceptions rule deduction and tenet for ALL free governed nations, that, The morals and values of the elected official are the mirror image of those of the electorate. If you take a moment to reflect on the following statistics and then re-read the above truism – it should be disturbing to say the least. OH and Obama is at least currently – the more POPULAR candidate.

I simply entered OBAMA and then the following ONE WORD adjectives into the browser. Try it for YOURSELF!
You ABSOLUTELY SHOULD read this to your children – friends relatives and co-workers!
Look at the numbers!

OBAMA – SCUMBAG = 3,010,000 hits
OBAMA – PERVERT = 4,470,000 hits
OBAMA – MARXIST = 8,350,000 hits
OBAMA – BABY KILLER = 13,000,000 hits
OBAMA – LIAR = 73,400,000 hits

OH and just for the hell of it I conducted the EXACT same test for Hitler. As expected I got a lot of large numbers
BUT all of the results were hundreds of percents LOWER than for Obama – HUNDREDS!

Oh and here is a video clip that ALL mainstream America MUST see regarding the – shall we say – manners – intellectual skills – the state of literacy – the level of wisdom and general demeanor of the typical Obama's supporter. Not a bad idea to share this one with your kids either. Truth need exclude no age.

The screaming oyster brained cell phone queen creature in the video will probably end up with a nice political – albeit a minor one – appointment as a reward for her zeal to re elect her hero and 'entitlement' giver. We are toast we are done. Years back if you had suggested that there could POSSIBLY be ANY scumbag POTUS more immoral treasonous Godless and arrogant than Bill Clinton – I would have simply stated with assurance and confidence – IMPOSSIBLE – We have hit the bottom of the pile of putrid rancid reprobate sociopathic AmeriKan shit!

SEPTEMBER, 2012
A LOOK INSIDE THE DEPRAVED MINDS OF THE VILEST, MOST EVIL AND WICKED CREATURES ON EARTH

IF YOU EVER EVER HAD THE SLIGHTEST DOUBT OF THE EVIL AND DEMONIC NATURE OF THE JEWS IN GENERAL -READ THIS FILTH – AND KEEP IN MIND THAT 'WIKIPEDIA' (from the word Wicca which has to do with paganism witchcraft sorcery and demons) is a jew owned and created anti Christian tool – like ALL of the internet 'cool jew features' e.g. Face book -Yahoo – My Space – Google & more – to further the demonic Godless control of our people by of the Christ hating jews.

Here- these filthy Christ killers actually accuse all Christians of being anti-Semites – EVEN THE LORD – of being an anti-Semite. These putrid scum actually declare that the words of Christ are hateful lies with their worn-out third world joke line of anti -Semitism. Only rancid jews and their shills are used to illustrate how anti-Semitic the Christian Bible is(the New Testament) Jew have NO sense of decency decorum or respect.

They accuse Christ as having replaced Christians as the Chosen people rather than the jews whom Christ CLEARLY condemned as being paternal relations of Satan himself. The ONLY entity who has "CHOSEN" these horrid jews is SATAN! Wikipedia goes on to lie again as the jew authors mislead readers with this lie: "In the Book of John, Jesus calls certain Pharisees "children of the devil".John 8- 44

"Certain Pharisees" MY ASS! The Bible made it quite plain and quite clear that Christ was addressing the jewish people PERIOD! the EXACT same jews whose mobs screamed for His murder by crucifixion More lies: "Jesus says, speaking to a group of Pharisees:" The footnotes in the authorized King James Version say of this and I quote: "*<u>That this SATANIC FATHERHOOD cannot be limited to the Pharisees is made clear in 1 John 3 – 8-10"</u>*

The jew apologists of jew WICKEDpedia continue their distortion and twisting of the Gospels as they say : *"it was all too easily read as an anti-Jewish polemic and became a tool of anti-Semitism."* More libelous slander.

Now read this Christ mocking filth: "*It is because of this controversy that some modern English translations, such as Today's New International Version, remove the term "Jews" and replace it with more specific terms to avoid anti-Semitic connotations. For example, the Jesus Seminartranslates this as "Judeans", I.e. residents of Judea, in contrast to residents of Galilee. Most critics of these translations, while conceding this point, argue that the context (since it is obvious that Jesus, John himself, and the other disciples were all Jews) makes John's true meaning sufficiently clear, and that a literal translation is preferred"*

Let me translate that crypto jew filth: (we jews must destroy or revise the entire New Testament because the TRUTH of the word of God will destroy us sooner or later)

Lies upon lies upon lies – First of all – Jesus was NOT a Jew. That is blasphemy. See the reference to the jew approved sanitized jew friendly = Today New International; Version (gotta avoid those ugly facts about the stinking demonic jews)

But it gets even worse with MORE Zionist Jew cheerleaders for 'WICKED pedia' . Check out this jew Christ Killer useful idiot apologist jew doublespeak filth:

"*The Gospel of John has the dubious distinction of being both the most popular Gospel (considered the most "spiritual" of the canonical Gospels) and the most anti-Jewish. The term "the Jews" (Ioudaios) in the Gospel functions as a "hostile collective stereotype" and is identified with "evil" and the "devil." Yet the Gospel of John is intimately connected with Judaism. Jesus is thoroughly Jewish in this Gospel. His life revolves around theJewish festivals, and his identity as the Messiah is confirmed by the Jewish scriptures. According to John 20:31, the book was written so "that you may come to believe that Jesus is the Messiah, the Son of God." Christology, therefore, is the key to understanding both the theology of the Gospel and its strained relationship with the larger Pharisaic Jewish tradition."*

Anti Jewish? How about anti demonic sons of Satan filthy jews? OH but as you see, these filthy kikes use nothing but anti -Christian pro-jew sons of the Devil bastards for references. They have 50 million of those pasty obese pig faced BaptDUH ziobots to help libel and slander our Lord – as they worship Satan.

As their grand finale these filthy gutter scum enlist the services of the now apostate Catholic Church and jew compromised modern jew loving Christ mocking Popes Like false Pope Paul VII – to bolster their lies and take Christian belief to the trash heap. Ratsinger the most despickable Christian sell out since Judas – has finished the job of destroying the Church.

Notice they would not DARE quote TRUE Men of the faith like : Pope Sylvester 1 – or Pope Gregory 1 – or Pope Gregory VIII – or Pope Gregory IX – or Pope Benedict XII – or Pope Julius III – or Pope Paul IV – or Pope PIUS IV – or Pope PIUS V – or Pope Gregory VIII – or Pope

Clement VIII – or Pope Alexander VIII – or Pope Benedict XIV – or Pope PIUS VII- or Pope Pope Benedict XV or many more decent REAL Christians who kept these filthy Christ killers in their place where the belonged – under slimy rocks – before they joined their demonic father in HELL!

Read what THESE REAL MEN OF GOD had to say about the wicked demonic nature of the horrid murderous jews.

A last insult to Christ and all who love Him is this ULTIMATE mendacity written by a jew demon apologist Christ mocking filth – one of the ultimate OVER THE TOP blasphemies even for a jew site to use as a legitimate quote:

Daniel Goldhagen, former Associate Professor of Political Science at Harvard University, also suggested in his book *A Moral Reckoning* that the Roman Catholic Church should change its doctrine and the accepted Biblical canon to excise statements he labels as anti-Semitic, to indicate that
"The Jews' way to God is as legitimate as the Christian way"

Just let that putrid garbage describing the world's most wicked lying murderous people sink in for a moment

Thank you jews at WICKED pedia for so cruelly mocking my most sacred beliefs and slandering our Lord!

***SEPTEMBER, 2012
FULL TEXT: BIN LADEN'S 'LETTER TO AMERICA'***

In my previous article – The one refused by our jew controlled MSM – for the simple reason that everything I said WAS THE TRUTH – and the lying demonic (yes Dorothy the jews ARE DEMONIC – lying sons of the Devil – because the Lord said so in scripture -John 9-44) jews cannot stand TRUTH as they are a kind of demonic vampire. The TRUTH makes them burn up and be destroyed just like in those horror movies where you see the vampires who, when they are subjected to the light of day (TRUTH) – become crispy critters.

Upon reflection of what I stated – that ALL still ignorant Americans NEED to learn that Bin Laden was not some deranged simple minded lunatic (like George Bush) but was a very wise worldly experienced well educated articulate patriot who unlike ANY super wealthy greedy self-serving Godless amoral American – he selflessly gave up a safe posh materialistic luxurious life (he was a VERY wealthy man) to do something for his own people.

I DEFY you to be able to name even ONE of the countless greedy shallow spineless hypocrite billionaires and multi-multi -millionaire Americans who sit on their far asses and live the selfish greedy lives of the rich and famous while the country which gave them the opportunity for this ENORMOUS wealth dies before their eyes. Not since the Founding Fathers risked everything –

including their lives – has so much as even ONE prominent wealthy influential American done what Bin Laden did – sacrifice EVERYTHING for God and his people.

I have known a few REALLY wealthy *(multi-million dollar homes million dollar yachts expensive multi-engine aircraft etc)* – whose greed is NEVER satisfied and have never in their useless lives done ANYTHING noble and selfless in their entire shallow meaningless materialistic narcissistic lives of endless self-indulgence. These people that I have known for half my life are so shallow and stingy that they would not so much as even give a dollar to sustain struggling TRUE patriots whose lives were selflessly dedicated to TRUTH and salvation of our own country!

Two sterling examples are Mark Glenn and Brother Nathanael – two men who walk the walk every day of their lives. Their reward? An occasional sincere "thank you" – and the knowledge that by THEIR sacrifices – another world war has been thwarted – at least for the time being. They buy precious time for ALL mankind and especially Americans to ponder their own stupid folly and hopefully to gain the knowledge and courage to fight back at the evil ones who have turned our blessed America into a morally rotted corpse – the jews!

Osama Bin Laden was a REAL man -a courageous wise intellectual selfless patriot – the likes of which- I am ashamed to say does NOT exist in this current garbage dump I once had cause to love and admire and respect enough to willingly sacrifice my own life to defend what it once – and I REPEAT – ONCE STOOD FOR.

OH – and for the children and adults who still have children's brains (No Dorothy – Mr. Bin Laden did not have anything to do with 9-11 – it was traitor Bush and his jew criminal friends)

Also for you inbred rednecks who are still spewing your imbecilic stupidity about "them damn Moooselum terrorists" – here is a news flash – morons!

Ever heard of Dr. Alan Sabrosky (Ph.D, University of Michigan) a ten-year US Marine Corps veteran and a 1986 graduate of the US Army War College of which he was Director Of Strategic Studies? Of course not! He is not an NFL Stupid Bowl moron – so the fact that this highly respected and highly credentialed American son has had the moral courage to speak out against the enemies of ALL decent mankind could matter less to you idiots. He KNOWS IsraHELL was behind it.

Here are his exact words – the sentiments of every informed responsible intelligent moral American, I might add.

"I had long conversations over the last two weeks with contacts at Army War College and Hqs. Marine Corps and I made it absolutely clear in both cases that it was 100% certain that 9-11 was a Mossad operation – PERIOD!

The Zionists are playing this as an all or nothing exercise. If they lose this one – they are done.

What we need to stand up and say is not only did they attack the USS Liberty but they did 9-11 They DID IT!"

Now -to the select few Americans left who value truth wisdom knowledge justice and honor – you will find this great man's speech filled with truth and honesty and concern for his people an envious quality. I would have been honored to have known such a great man as Osama Bin Laden personally.

This was a truly great man who we foolish ignorant sheep allowed ourselves to demonize slander and and ultimately murder to satiate the blood lusts of the jews and their 'attack dog' useful idiots. The jew is an expert at lies and deceptions. The jew with his endless wealth can and has successfully convinced our stupid people to worship the must putrid filth on earth, and conversely, to demonize our finest sons.

Deception and lies are the essences of jewishness and have been since they crucified Christ, and before. A two thousand year old chronological compendium of damning quotes from the worlds' most famous personalities – with undeniable testimony – gives impeccable credentials and faultless validation to that UGLY FACT! READ IT!

I guarantee you that if the jew so desired and made it an issue – that within six months – even school children would be wearing T-shirts purchased by their brain dead parents that portrayed the Father of our Nation – General/President George Washington as a vile reprobate corrupt sociopath womanizing terrorist hypocrite – or worse!.

Far-fetched you are thinking? Oh REALLY? These SAME jews did EXACTLY that to the Son of God! If there would have been silk screen T-shirt technology two thousand years ago – every jew would have been wearing a "hate Jesus" T-shirt slandering Him as a "SORCERER" – "BLASPHEMER" – GLUTTON" – "DRUNKARD" – " guilty of "SEDITION" -" BASTARD" – "SON OF A WHORE" just for openers! Read it It is ALL there in the NT

As long as this scum and their demonic stolen shit country remain unchallenged – no decent human being will ever be safe.

Need I remind you – that these same filth tortured and murdered Christ – obviously with the help of their father – the Devil – as their ally. Additionally the self imposed curse of – "may His blood be upon us and our children" -was from the jews in the mob -screaming for the death of Jesus – and NOT just high priests or Pharisees and certainly not the non existent Zionists.

They were of the same mindset as the ordinary filth I saw in IsraHELL screaming blasphemies in public against Christ – that; " We crucified your f–king Jesus and we would do it again" The same kind of jew that lurks in YOUR neighborhood – the Goldsteins – or the Silverbergs – or the Liebermans – if not all of the same tribe , assuredly ALL of the same evil Godless Christ hating mindset. Only ,here – they are not quite as bold – YET – but soon! You will not find one in a thousand who is truly a righteous man. I have learned that lesson from a lifetime of abuse lies injustice and grief from these wicked deceptive devious people.

Read this and pray God grant us a son with HALF Bin Laden's courage and dedication and character to lead us and save us from these horrid wicked greedy Godless murderous reprobate lying jews! We as a judised people have repeatedly trashed our finest sons (like Rep Paul Findley) and glorified and idolized the most putrid wicked treasonous devious lying bastards ever spawned by Satan (like POTUS Barry Obama and George Bush) Will we EVER do the right thing again?

Online document: the full text of Osama bin Laden's "letter to the American people", reported in today's Observer. The letter first appeared on the internet in Arabic and has since been translated and circulated by Islamists in Britain.

Observer.co.uk, Sunday 24 November 2002 12.07 GMT

"In the Name of Allah, the Most Gracious, the Most Merciful,"

"Permission to fight is given to those who are fought against, because they have been wronged and surely, Allah is Able to give them victory" [Quran 22:39]

"Those who believe, fight in the Cause of Allah, and those who disbelieve, fight in the cause of Taghut (anything Satanic). *So fight you against the friends of Satan; ever feeble is indeed the plot of Satan."[Quran 4:76]

*My comment: so, since the jews are the mortal children of Satan according to Christ [John 8-44] and most Americans are the friends of these demon jews – is it not irrefutable logic to conclude that Americans like the BaptDUHS have made themselves not only enemies of the Muslims but of Christ as well? Let that logic sink in for a moment – and you will then understand why all TRULY decent people on earth hate (most) Americans. We are not just the enemies of the Arabs – we are NOW the enemies of GOD!

Just to make SURE that 'God' knew He wasn't welcome in The United States – our lawmakers told God to piss off *(Madelyn Christ hater O'hare 1962 – remember?)* Once again for you witless cretins who are between amoebas and parameciums in intellectual capacity – try to understand this simple universal truth. "Allah" IS God to Arab people. "Dios" is God to Latin people. "Deu" is God to the French people. "Got' is God to the German people – etcetera etcetera. One God different cultures different 'sounds' but the SAME GOD! Are you inbred redneck imbeciles getting it yet? those of you who constantly use the most vile of profanity when addressing "Allah" – you are blaspheming 'THE ONE GOD' – you degenerate insolent arrogant witless ignorant animals! You shame everything good and decent about America by your detestable bigoted idiocy.

letter continues ===

"Some American writers have published articles under the title 'On what basis are we fighting?' These articles have generated a number of responses, some of which adhered to the truth and were based on Islamic Law, and others which have not. Here we wanted to outline the truth – as an explanation and warning – hoping for Allah's reward, seeking success and support from Him.

While seeking Allah's help, we form our reply based on two questions directed at the Americans:

(Q1) Why are we fighting and opposing you?
Q2)What are we calling you to, and what do we want from you?

As for the first question: Why are we fighting and opposing you? The answer is very simple:

(1) Because you attacked us and continue to attack us.

a) You attacked us in Palestine:

(i) Palestine, which has sunk under military occupation for more than 80 years. The British handed over Palestine, with your help and your support, to the Jews, who have occupied it for more than 50 years; years overflowing with oppression, tyranny, crimes, killing, expulsion, destruction and devastation. The creation and continuation of Israel is one of the greatest crimes, and you are the leaders of its criminals. And of course there is no need to explain and prove the degree of American support for Israel. The creation of Israel is a crime which must be erased. Each and every person whose hands have become polluted in the contribution towards this crime must pay its*price, and pay for it heavily.

(ii) It brings us both laughter and tears to see that you have not yet tired of repeating your fabricated lies that the Jews have a historical right to Palestine, as it was promised to them in the Torah. Anyone who disputes with them on this alleged fact is accused of anti-Semitism. This is one of the most fallacious, widely-circulated fabrications in history. The people of Palestine are pure Arabs and original Semites. It is the Muslims who are the inheritors of Moses (peace be upon him) and the inheritors of the real Torah that has not been changed. Muslims believe in all of the Prophets, including Abraham, Moses, Jesus and Muhammad, peace and blessings of Allah be upon them all. If the followers of Moses have been promised a right to Palestine in the Torah, then the Muslims are the most worthy nation of this.

When the Muslims conquered Palestine and drove out the Romans, Palestine and Jerusalem returned to Islam, the religion of all the Prophets peace be upon them. Therefore, the call to a historical right to Palestine cannot be raised against the Islamic Ummah that believes in all the Prophets of Allah (peace and blessings be upon them) – and we make no distinction between them.

(iii) The blood pouring out of Palestine must be equally revenged. You must know that the Palestinians do not cry alone; their women are not widowed alone; their sons are not orphaned alone.

(b) You attacked us in Somalia; you supported the Russian atrocities against us in Chechnya, the Indian oppression against us in Kashmir, and the Jewish aggression against us in Lebanon.

(c) Under your supervision, consent and orders, the governments of our countries which act as your agents, attack us on a daily basis;

(i) These governments prevent our people from establishing the Islamic Shariah, using violence and lies to do so.

(ii) These governments give us a taste of humiliation, and place us in a large prison of fear and subdual.

(iii) These governments steal our Ummah's wealth and sell them to you at a paltry price.

(iv) These governments have surrendered to the Jews, and handed them most of Palestine, acknowledging the existence of their state over the dismembered limbs of their own people.

(v) The removal of these governments is an obligation upon us, and a necessary step to free the Ummah, to make the Shariah the supreme law and to regain Palestine. And our fight against these governments is not separate from out fight against you.

(d) You steal our wealth and oil at paltry prices because of your international influence and military threats. This theft is indeed the biggest theft ever witnessed by mankind in the history of the world.

(e) Your forces occupy our countries; you spread your military bases throughout them; you corrupt our lands, and you besiege our sanctities, to protect the security of the Jews and to ensure the continuity of your pillage of our treasures.

(f) You have starved the Muslims of Iraq, where children die every day. It is a wonder that more than 1.5 million Iraqi children have died as a result of your sanctions, and you did not show concern. Yet when 3000 of your people died, the entire world rises and has not yet sat down.

(g) You have supported the Jews in their idea that Jerusalem is their eternal capital, and agreed to move your embassy there. With your help and under your protection, the Israelis are planning to destroy the Al-Aqsa mosque. Under the protection of your weapons, Sharon entered the Al-Aqsa mosque, to pollute it as a preparation to capture and destroy it.

(2) These tragedies and calamities are only a few examples of your oppression and aggression against us. It is commanded by our religion and intellect that the oppressed have a right to return the aggression. Do not await anything from us but Jihad, resistance and revenge. Is it in any way rational to expect that after America has attacked us for more than half a century, that we will then leave her to live in security and peace?!!

(3) You may then dispute that all the above does not justify aggression against civilians, for crimes they did not commit and offenses in which they did not partake:

(a) This argument contradicts your continuous repetition that America is the land of freedom, and its leaders in this world. Therefore, the American people are the ones who choose their government by way of their own free will; a choice which stems from their agreement to its policies. Thus the American people have chosen, consented to, and affirmed their support for the Israeli oppression of the Palestinians, the occupation and usurpation of their land, and its continuous killing, torture, punishment and expulsion of the Palestinians. The American people have the ability and choice to refuse the policies of their Government and even to change it if they want.

(b) The American people are the ones who pay the taxes which fund the planes that bomb us in Afghanistan, the tanks that strike and destroy our homes in Palestine, the armies which occupy our lands in the Arabian Gulf, and the fleets which ensure the blockade of Iraq. These tax dollars are given to Israel for it to continue to attack us and penetrate our lands. So the American people are the ones who fund the attacks against us, and they are the ones who oversee the expenditure of these monies in the way they wish, through their elected candidates.

(c) Also the American army is part of the American people. It is this very same people who are shamelessly helping the Jews fight against us.

(d) The American people are the ones who employ both their men and their women in the American Forces which attack us.

(e) This is why the American people cannot be not innocent of all the crimes committed by the Americans and Jews against us.

(f) Allah, the Almighty, legislated the permission and the option to take revenge. Thus, if we are attacked, then we have the right to attack back. Whoever has destroyed our villages and towns, then we have the right to destroy their villages and towns. Whoever has stolen our wealth, then we have the right to destroy their economy. And whoever has killed our civilians, then we have the right to kill theirs.

The American Government and press still refuses to answer the question:

Why did they attack us in New York and Washington?

If Sharon is a man of peace in the eyes of Bush, then we are also men of peace!!! America does not understand the language of manners and principles, so we are addressing it using the language it understands.

(Q2) As for the second question that we want to answer: What are we calling you to, and what do we want from you?

(1) The first thing that we are calling you to is Islam.

(a) The religion of the Unification of God; of freedom from associating partners with Him, and rejection of this; of complete love of Him, the Exalted; of complete submission to His Laws; and of the discarding of all the opinions, orders, theories and religions which contradict with the religion He sent down to His Prophet Muhammad (peace be upon him). Islam is the religion of all the prophets, and makes no distinction between them – peace be upon them all.

It is to this religion that we call you; the seal of all the previous religions. It is the religion of Unification of God, sincerity, the best of manners, righteousness, mercy, honour, purity, and piety. It is the religion of showing kindness to others, establishing justice between them, granting them their rights, and defending the oppressed and the persecuted. It is the religion of enjoining the good and forbidding the evil with the hand, tongue and heart. It is the religion of Jihad in the way of Allah so that Allah's Word and religion reign Supreme. And it is the religion of unity and agreement on the obedience to Allah, and total equality between all people, without regarding their colour, sex, or language.

(b) It is the religion whose book – the Quran – will remained preserved and unchanged, after the other Divine books and messages have been changed. The Quran is the miracle until the Day of Judgment. Allah has challenged anyone to bring a book like the Quran or even ten verses like it.

(2) The second thing we call you to, is to stop your oppression, lies, immorality and debauchery that has spread among you.

(a) We call you to be a people of manners, principles, honour, and purity; to reject the immoral acts of fornication, homosexuality, intoxicants, gambling's, and trading with interest.

We call you to all of this that you may be freed from that which you have become caught up in; that you may be freed from the deceptive lies that you are a great nation, that your leaders spread amongst you to conceal from you the despicable state to which you have reached.

(b) It is saddening to tell you that you are the worst civilization witnessed by the history of mankind:

(i) You are the nation who, rather than ruling by the Shariah of Allah in its Constitution and Laws, choose to invent your own laws as you will and desire. You separate religion from your policies, contradicting the pure nature which affirms Absolute Authority to the Lord and your Creator. You flee from the embarrassing question posed to you: How is it possible for Allah the Almighty to create His creation, grant them power over all the creatures and land, grant them all the amenities of life, and then deny them that which they are most in need of: knowledge of the laws which govern their lives?

(ii) You are the nation that permits Usury, which has been forbidden by all the religions. Yet you build your economy and investments on Usury. As a result of this, in all its different forms and guises, the Jews have taken control of your economy, through which they have then taken control of your media, and now control all aspects of your life making you their servants and achieving their aims at your expense; precisely what Benjamin Franklin warned you against.

(iii) You are a nation that permits the production, trading and usage of intoxicants. You also permit drugs, and only forbid the trade of them, even though your nation is the largest consumer of them.

(iv) You are a nation that permits acts of immorality, and you consider them to be pillars of personal freedom. You have continued to sink down this abyss from level to level until incest has spread amongst you, in the face of which neither your sense of honour nor your laws object.

Who can forget your President Clinton's immoral acts committed in the official Oval office? After that you did not even bring him to account, other than that he 'made a mistake', after which everything passed with no punishment. Is there a worse kind of event for which your name will go down in history and remembered by nations?

(v) You are a nation that permits gambling in its all forms. The companies practice this as well, resulting in the investments becoming active and the criminals becoming rich.

(vi) You are a nation that exploits women like consumer products or advertising tools calling upon customers to purchase them. You use women to serve passengers, visitors, and strangers to increase your profit margins. You then rant that you support the liberation of women.

(vii) You are a nation that practices the trade of sex in all its forms, directly and indirectly. Giant corporations and establishments are established on this, under the name of art, entertainment, tourism and freedom, and other deceptive names you attribute to it.

(viii) And because of all this, you have been described in history as a nation that spreads diseases that were unknown to man in the past. Go ahead and boast to the nations of man, that you brought them AIDS as a Satanic American Invention.

(xi) You have destroyed nature with your industrial waste and gases more than any other nation in history. Despite this, you refuse to sign the Kyoto agreement so that you can secure the profit of your greedy companies and*industries.

(x) Your law is the law of the rich and wealthy people, who hold sway in their political parties, and fund their election campaigns with their gifts. Behind them stand the Jews, who control your policies, media and economy.

(xi) That which you are singled out for in the history of mankind, is that you have used your force to destroy mankind more than any other nation in history; not to defend principles and values, but to hasten to secure your interests and profits. You who dropped a nuclear bomb on Japan, even though Japan was ready to negotiate an end to the war. How many acts of oppression, tyranny and injustice have you carried out, O callers to freedom?

(xii) Let us not forget one of your major characteristics: your duality in both manners and values; your hypocrisy in manners and principles. All*manners, principles and values have two scales: one for you and one for the others.

(a)The freedom and democracy that you call to is for yourselves and for white race only; as for the rest of the world, you impose upon them your monstrous, destructive policies and Governments, which you call the 'American friends'. Yet you prevent them from establishing democracies. When the Islamic party in Algeria wanted to practice democracy and they won the election, you unleashed your agents in the Algerian army onto them, and to attack them with tanks and guns, to imprison them and torture them – a new lesson from the 'American book of democracy'!!!

(b)Your policy on prohibiting and forcibly removing weapons of mass destruction to ensure world peace: it only applies to those countries which you do not permit to possess such weapons. As for the countries you consent to, such as Israel, then they are allowed to keep and use such weapons to defend their security. Anyone else who you suspect might be manufacturing or keeping these kinds of weapons, you call them criminals and you take military action against them.

(c)You are the last ones to respect the resolutions and policies of International Law, yet you claim to want to selectively punish anyone else who does the same. Israel has for more than 50 years been pushing UN resolutions and rules against the wall with the full support of America.

(d)As for the war criminals which you censure and form criminal courts for – you shamelessly ask that your own are granted immunity!! However, history will not forget the war crimes that you committed against the Muslims and the rest of the world; those you have killed in Japan, Afghanistan, Somalia, Lebanon and Iraq will remain a shame that you will never be able to escape. It will suffice to remind you of your latest war crimes in Afghanistan, in which densely populated innocent civilian villages were destroyed, bombs were dropped on mosques causing the roof of the mosque to come crashing down on the heads of the Muslims praying inside. You are the ones who broke the agreement with the Mujahedeen when they left Qunduz, bombing them in Jangi fort, and killing more than 1,000 of your prisoners through suffocation and thirst. Allah alone knows how many people have died by torture at the hands of you and your agents. Your planes remain in the Afghan skies, looking for anyone remotely suspicious.

(e)You have claimed to be the vanguards of Human Rights, and your Ministry of Foreign affairs issues annual reports containing statistics of those countries that violate any Human Rights. However, all these things vanished when the Mujahedeen hit you, and you then implemented the methods of the same documented governments that you used to curse. In America, you captured thousands the Muslims and Arabs, took them into custody with neither reason, court trial, nor even disclosing their names. You issued newer, harsher laws.

What happens in Guantanamo is a historical embarrassment to America and its values, and it screams into your faces – you hypocrites, "What is the value of your signature on any agreement or treaty?"

(3) What we call you to thirdly is to take an honest stance with yourselves – and I doubt you will do so – to discover that you are a nation without principles or manners, and that the values and principles to you are something which you merely demand from others, not that which you yourself must adhere to.

(4) We also advise you to stop supporting Israel, and to end your support of the Indians in Kashmir, the Russians against the Chechens and to also cease supporting the Manila Government against the Muslims in Southern Philippines.

(5) We also advise you to pack your luggage and get out of our lands. We desire for your goodness, guidance, and righteousness, so do not force us to send you back as cargo in coffins.

(6) Sixthly, we call upon you to end your support of the corrupt leaders in our countries. Do not interfere in our politics and method of education. Leave us alone, or else expect us in New York and Washington.

(7) We also call you to deal with us and interact with us on the basis of mutual interests and benefits, rather than the policies of sub dual, theft and occupation, and not to continue your policy of supporting the Jews because this will result in more disasters for you.

If you fail to respond to all these conditions, then prepare for fight with the Islamic Nation. The Nation of Monotheism, that puts complete trust on Allah and fears none other than Him. The Nation which is addressed by its Quran with the words: "Do you fear them? Allah has more right that you should fear Him if you are believers. Fight against them so that Allah will punish them by your hands and disgrace them and give you victory over them and heal the breasts of believing people. And remove the anger of their (believers') hearts. Allah accepts the repentance of whom He wills. Allah is All-Knowing, All-Wise." [Quran9:13-1]

The Nation of honour and respect:

"But honour, power and glory belong to Allah, and to His Messenger (Muhammad- peace be upon him) and to the believers." [Quran 63:8]

"So do not become weak (against your enemy), nor be sad, and you will be*superior (in victory)if you are indeed (true) believers" [Quran 3:139]

The Nation of Martyrdom; the Nation that desires death more than you desire life:

"Think not of those who are killed in the way of Allah as dead. Nay, they are alive with their Lord, and they are being provided for. They rejoice in what Allah has bestowed upon them from His bounty and rejoice for the sake of those who have not yet joined them, but are left behind (not yet martyred) that on them no fear shall come, nor shall they grieve. They rejoice in a grace and a bounty from Allah, and that Allah will not waste the reward of the believers." [Quran 3:169-171]

The Nation of victory and success that Allah has promised:

"It is He Who has sent His Messenger (Muhammad peace be upon him) with guidance and the religion of truth (Islam), to make it victorious over all other religions even though the Polytheists hate it." [Quran 61:9]

"Allah has decreed that 'Verily it is I and My Messengers who shall be victorious.' Verily Allah is All-Powerful, All-Mighty." [Quran 58:21]

The Islamic Nation that was able to dismiss and destroy the previous evil Empires like yourself; the Nation that rejects your attacks, wishes to remove your evils, and is prepared to fight you. You are well aware that the Islamic Nation, from the very core of its soul, despises your haughtiness and arrogance.

If the Americans refuse to listen to our advice and the goodness, guidance and righteousness that we call them to, then be aware that you will lose this Crusade Bush began, just like the other previous Crusades in which you were humiliated by the hands of the Mujahedeen, fleeing to your home in great silence and disgrace. If the Americans do not respond, then their fate will be that of the Soviets who fled from Afghanistan to deal with their military defeat, political breakup, ideological downfall, and economic bankruptcy.

This is our message to the Americans, as an answer to theirs. Do they now know why we fight them and over which form of ignorance, by the permission of Allah, we shall be victorious?

*

As a parting comment – I would like to address the cowards who disgraced the uniform I wore with your grandfathers. To murder a man for simply wanting to free his people from the Godless jews and their Godless lackeys (READ: American filth) is unconscionable. Bin Laden may not have been perfect but he had the courage to fight for their dignity and freedom of HIS people. That is a HELL of a lot more that you cowards have done. You country is STILL held captive and occupied by the stinking Godless jews – and yet you haven't the courage to stand up to them and FREE your OWN country. You are cowards and hypocrites!

Our Republic was seen as fit to be governed ONLY by Godly decent men of wisdom and goodness. That is not just my opinion – as it was the express wishes of the Founding Fathers and SO STATED. Bin Laden would have liked the Americans when I was growing up before the jew occupation began and they convinced our stupid sheeple to murder cheat and rob Arab people. Anyone who took ANY part in that disgraceful assai nation may as well have used our blessed Constitution for toilet paper.

Your criminal conduct has violated ALL that the REAL pre-jew America once stood for. I consider you all rancid criminals and a disgrace to the oath you took and especially those of you in Special Forces. Shame on all of you! Look down at your epilates or berets. READ THE MOTTO I SWORE BY AND LIVED BY 50 years ago! I honored it. You have cruelly violated it. you have 'shit and pissed' upon your own uniforms. You have sold your honor to the Christ hating jews for thrills tin medals and 'pieces of jew silver'. You are all Judases.

All you have done is to make REAL patriots like Bin Laden martyrs heroes and legends. This is ONE ex Green Beret commander who will hold your victim in respect and admiration, and especially in the bitter realization that such a man who would give it all for his own people's freedom and justice does not exist today in my OWN country – only selfish greedy materialistic $ worshiping talking head hypocrites like Warren Buffet & Bill Gates whose vast fortunes could have indeed easily educated every man woman and school child of the TRUTH.

And NEVER forget these facts, war mongers! Until IsraHELL was granted legitimacy by that rancid piece of war criminal crap – Harry, the jew lover – Truman, there were no problems in the Mid East. Gas was affordable to ALL Americans – the economy was sound – our citizens could fly without fear of being fondled terrified robbed humiliated and treated like pigs in a slaughterhouse by those putrid ignorant illiterate TIA thugs – there was prayer in our schools there was no jew filth in our entertainment – our military was still honorable – there was no real threat of more world conflict – Americans had not been poisoned by 24-7 jew Talmudvision filth – there was no blasphemous hyphenated Christian belief in America (the stinking filthy ignorant Zio-BabtDUHS). Then came the jew vampires.

I remember – BEFORE ISRAHELL – when our national anthem stirred those feelings of love and respect for all we once stood for, and a man could speak of his love and respect for America as a Godly moral nation, blessed by God to both friend and foreigner – without the words sticking in his throat like day old rancid vomit!

You are no longer soldiers defending the Republic – you are cold-blooded mercenary assassins – overpaid thrill seekers – Godless hypocrites – bullies – war mongers – sociopathic rapists thieves terrorists and murderers despised by ALL decent moral educated men of good will. NONE of you evil bastards was obligated to do these wicked things to innocent people in other nations that CAUSED these JUST and PREDICTABLE reprisals in the first place. Any decent American man would have done the same thing had HIS family been attacked by foreigners.

ALL of you are mercenary criminals by you own free will, in today's 'war mongers for hire' – Army of losers and sick twisted sociopaths. If you think I exaggerate – compare yourselves with the level of honor and morality that your grandfathers served two generations ago before the jews poisoned the entire nation with their Godless filth & lies.

As a tree is known by its fruit and a man is know by his deeds – you have born only rotted fruit – and you know what the overseer of the orchard does with a rotted tree – he DESTROYS IT! So it will be with you and your ilk.

There has not been one major war in the past millennia which was not initiated by and or financed by the jew. Bottom line – folks – the jews have brought ALL of these evils upon us. Evict the jew and destroy his evil IsraHELL – punish and rid this nation of the filthy criminals who now run it for the jews – and the USA and our world will be at peace and enjoy moral and material prosperity once more. OH YES – and we must also beseech God to once more be welcome in this now jew dominated Godless shithole that WE have created. Think about it.

SEPTEMBER, 2012
A LETTER TO AMERICA – BY AN AMERICAN – CENSORED BY AMERICAN NEWS MEDIA – WHOSE JEW MASTERS FEAR THE TRUTH

I wrote this letter over nine years ago, in hopes that Americans who still had the capacity for rational thought might begin to wipe the agitprop haze from their minds and see the unvarnished

TRUTH. It was of course thrown in the trash by my own home town newspaper by people who now fear HONOR and TRUTH and worship EVIL and LIES.

Ironically – my journalism was once held in esteem by the editors, and my face and name were not unknown with the 'gentlemen of the press'. That was before our occupation by a foreign power so evil that even GOD condemned these demons as "SONS OF SATAN" – but then, after all – we as a people, threw Christ under the bus a long time ago. We now worship the very creatures whose goal in life is to steal our wealth – destroy our Christian beliefs – and make us worship THEIR 'god' – Satan!

Just ONE evening of sampling the filth violence depravity and blasphemy of AmeriKan Talmud-vision should convince anyone not sharing a brain.

The only real changes in the American condition – aside from a devastating spiraling economic collapse – as that we have become even wicked – more murderous – more ignorant and more determined to RACE to the trash heap of history than ever before. In that past decade we have committed more war crimes than have been done in our entire history. We have gone from relative prosperity to triple digit inflation – the destruction of the middle class – a military which is now technically the world's largest INSTITUTIONALIZED TERRORIST ORGANIZATION .

We are now the most hated and feared warmongering imperialists on earth. The streets exude an aura of total hopelessness – a new low in national morality – a state of permanent denial as we spiral into the abyss of hell – an all time increase of taxes and living expenses. Two decades of nonstop increasingly violent jew produced video games which glamorize war and destruction and violence – have now made our children mindless thrill seeking killers (future Army recruits to fight the jew wars)

Also a frightening unparralled increase in the level of lost freedoms – a 100% treasonous disloyal Congress which has sold our sovereignty to the Pharisees for the traditional 30 pieces of jew silver – and WILLINGLY destroyed ANY hope of Christianity to survive in this jew controlled hellhole. We have no moral leaders or role models as we venture into unchartered seas without an anchor or compass or even a competent Captain.

(since writing this letter for my newspaper – I have gained an ENORMOUS new amount of knowledge – a HUGE database – countless interviews and hundreds of published articles – and countless new jew crimes far more sinister and evil that anything I had seen or heard before. My expertise in these matters has increased a HUNDRED fold!)

"I am an American born male – retired businessman – father – husband – foreign Consul – world traveler – foreign policy analyst -TRUE political 'conservative' and former '60s' Special Operations Commander. I honestly believe I am considered a REAL patriot – having spent a great part of my life and my wealth in the endeavor to educate my 'neighbors' of the growing and imminent dangers form the myriad of "domestic enemies" that I swore with my hand on the Word of God – <u>that I would defend my country against</u>.

I have kept that covenant even until this very day. That having been said – I wish to comment on the content of an article /letter I read in the Observer. It was Bin Laden's 'Letter to the American People'.

EVERY American man woman and literate school child MUST read this letter.

I must in good conscience, as a world traveler and educated person – agree with most of his observations and condemnations. In some 45 adult years of observation of matters in my own country – as well as that in over 30 other countries, I have reached many learned conclusions on my own. The truths and wisdom of Bin Laden's letter only served to validate my findings.

One of those is the undeniable fact that the USA – my homeland – is controlled by Israel. I have watched the Jews here destroy virtually everything of any semblance of courage, integrity , individual ruggedness, and truthfulness in my once Godly America.

We have been perverted into a depraved, selfish, materialistic, secular, money worshiping fortress of evil.

God is mocked at every opportunity – homosexual perversions of every kind are now in vogue – anything goes, as long as 'you get away with it' – and as our recent former TWO TERM lying, blasphemous, cowardly, adulterous, drug infested, child murdering President Bill Clinton – our " Conscience of the Nation" put it — " CHARACTER DOESN'T COUNT".

I had the opportunity – 13 years ago – to be in the Middle-East, under – shall we say – very politically privileged conditions. Worth mentioning – was the fact that I had a predisposed image of BOTH the Israelis AND the Arabs before I arrived. The Jews who control ALL of our MSM had done their propaganda job well.

I had envisioned the Israeli Jews as brave, noble wonderful people, and the Arabs (Egypt, Jordan etc) were untrustworthy 'faceless' wretched sub-humans with no integrity or character. Boy – was I ever WRONG! DEAD WRONG!

What I saw in the following weeks painted a quite different picture , however. The few days I spent with the 'Arab' people did not of course make me a 'qualified' expert – but I found them to be warm, hospitable honest souls with Biblical 'family values' not unlike my own.

What I discovered during a much longer period in Israel was so disgusting that I cannot find adequate words – or space – to expand upon the matter completely. I will share but a few of the many bad experiences that I would have NOT been exposed to, had I been a 'tourist'.

Jonathon Pollard was an American Jew whose crimes of espionage for financial gain had been so serious that several seasoned members of the US intelligence community felt that the full extent of the damage this treasonous slime may NEVER be known. One of these officials – a former CIA high ranking station chief was a good personal friend and colleague.

At the time Pollard was serving sentence (which SHOULD have been the death penalty!) in a US prison. It was a COMMON sight outside of 'tourist sanitized' Tel Aviv, to commonly see signs condemning the US and asking for this treasonous criminal's release!

I spent some time in Hebron and Gaza – which were then not only part of the 'occupied territories' but were in the midst of hostilities. One day I witnessed a small car with an Israeli flag and the barrel of an assault rife protruding menacingly through the sunroof racing in and out of Palestinian neighborhoods. Keep in mind – this was in the homeland of the Palestinians – a PURPOSEFUL provocation to involve the IDF.

That same day at a road block/checkpoint in Gaza, I had the opportunity to overhear 2 regular IDF troops conversing. To my surprise, I heard unmistakable Jersey accents. They confessed that they were indeed from the States – US citizens – and had come to Israel to kill Palestinians.

When I asked what military branch they received their Stateside training in – their answer was; " Na – we won't ever even consider serving in the American services". I was shocked at their shameless attitude towards America – but it brought to memory – the fact that I couldn't recall any Jewish names of any of the Special Operations Paratroops I served with or commanded during a two year period, some 35 years ago.

Then there was the incident in Gaza – near a burned out Palestinian town – Gaza City I believe – where a young Palestinian boy was venting his frustration at the invaders in the only way he could – by casting egg sized rubble at the IDF paras directly in front of our bullet proof embassy vehicle.

One IDF soldier dropped to his knees and took careful aim at the child with his .308 FN FAL assault rifle – not ten yards in front of me. I trained my camera on the would-be murderer and decided that this picture and the truth would be told by at least myself.

He turned his head and gave me a dirty look and swore and lowered his weapon – retiring briskly to his jeep. I saw other instances of brutality – but this was typical – the kind of thing NEVER intended for the gullible American public to see in the news at their breakfast table

Bin Laden is quite accurate in saying that we- the American people, have elected leaders whose actions and policies mirror those of the electorate. To the average uneducated American (which constitutes the vast majority) – an 'Arab' is a soulless animal and whether children or worshipers in Mosques are slaughtered as well – is of absolutely no importance to our racist criminally ignorant sheeple.

There is NEVER any mention of the war crimes committed by Sharon himself. To criticize a Jew in America – ANY JEW – FOR ANYTHING – FOR ANY CRIME – is a social and political taboo.

This is Israel's war — NOT — AMERICA'S WAR! As long as our govt continues to send billions of dollars to the Jews to assist them in killing their neighbors – we will never be safe in America. If a child or grandchild of mine suffers as a result of President Bush's, ignorant and irresponsible rashness – I will NEVER EVER forgive him nor anybody in govt. who supports this insanity.

Sharon, APIC and the overwhelming criminal influence of Jews in my country are as responsible for the events of '9-11' as anybody.

OH – by the way – should ANY reader still not be convinced that Israel controls my country – consider these facts:

In June of 1967, the Israeli military was ordered by Moshe Dayan under authority of the Israeli Prime minister, to attack the USS Liberty which was at the time in international waters – in bright sunny daylight with a large American flag flying straight out in the breeze. Over TWO HUNDRED American sons brothers and fathers were butchered by the Jews that day.

To this very day – there has been no success in ANY attempt to convene a legitimate board of inquiry regarding this treasonous (our ally!?) cowardly (torpedoed – strafed – fire bombed and life boats machine-gunned) act of cold-blooded murder! Actually – it was technically – an ACT OF WAR against the USA

ALL of this is only the tip of the iceberg of Jewish lies, deception, treachery and general destruction of the moral fiber of America. Do the Arab peoples have a legitimate reason to hate us – or even attack us — YOU BET THEY DO! I just want my country back. The predominantly Christian America I grew up in.

I know the truth or at least a good bit of it. I pray to God that we will wake up in time – cut our ties with the treasonous nation of Israel and reclaim our once proud sovereignty. Perhaps a new twist on the Biblical phrase might be: "My people WILL perish for lack of knowledge."

Joe Cortina – A concerned American

SEPTEMBER, 2012
IGNORANCE BREEDS FEAR – FEAR BREEDS HATE – HATE BREEDS VIOLENCE. EDUCATION BREEDS CONFIDENCE – CONFIDENCE BREEDS HOPE – HOPE BREEDS PEACE

Ignorance breeds fear. Fear breeds hate. Hate breeds violence. Sadly – it describes most Americans. Two million innocent brutally murdered civilians in Iraq and Afghanistan proves my conclusion.

Based upon this brief but classic 'explanation' of the ilk of societal sludge and evil whose sociopathic conduct is reflected in their racism and inane unlearned mindless hatred – we can clearly see the connections of depraved mindless emotions which lead to endless acts of mega-evil violence – WARS.

Essentially – it perfectly describes the status and emotions which control and dominate so-called evangelical (evang-HELL-ical) BaptDUH morons who are still burning witches at the stake in their tiny atrophied desiccated diseased minds. This is WHY they are the DEADLY MORTAL enemies of ALL decent rational moral mankind. If 'ignorance kills' – then they are the ultimate harbingers of death!

They are not alone in this treason – but are by far the largest enablers of these serial wars of madness.

These inbred retarded imbeciles are the witless sociopaths who actually believed that Catholic priests had cloven hooves. I didn't just read this putrid trash – I experienced it PERSONALLY! These same reprobate hypocrites will point their fingers and condemn you for even so much as a sip of wine yet the Bible is replete with indifferent references to wine. No where is wine condemned. Only the effects of the ABUSE of drinking wine in EXCESS are condemned.

Jesus' first miracle was to create wine (NOT fruit juice, kiddies) from plain water at a wedding feast. Grape juice and wine have no more in common in makeup than do water and urine. Leave it to the hypocrite BapDUHS to condemn someone as "Satanic lost souls sons of Demons wretched sinners" – should they take a sip of wine – YET it is to their wicked depraved minds – a mandate for our murderous Godless sadistic wicked racist sociopath military to murder a million innocent helpless children (aka – sand-niggers rag-heads or dune coons)- for the glory of the Demonic Jews.

These are the same morons who call money "the root of all evil". Like their demonization of wine – another baseless untruth due to their criminal level of ignorance! Nowhere are either of these inanimate objects given demonic properties as if each had a life of it's own. Disgustingly stupid.

If you tell these idiots the truth – that it is the -LOVE of MONEY- that is sinful – NOT the inanimate coin itself – you will get a blank stare as one might expect from a member of some isolated aboriginal naked primitive tribe who is shown a state of art cell phone – or the same result as if you were addressing a two year old child.

These are the same 'family' of degenerate creatures who murdered men of wisdom long ago for proclaiming the earth was NOT flat and who would UNDOUBTEDLY have Christ murdered today should He appear in human form doing good deeds and speaking TRUTH they do not want to hear.

Be afraid – be VERY afraid – as they walk among us even today, carrying a deadly incurable cancerous disease – called IGNORANCE – which is death itself. Their superstition and stupidity has already taken the lives of millions – and they their lust for murders will not be satisfied until the entire world is destroyed by their criminally irresponsible conduct.

Christ blesses those who are peacemakers and curses those who are war mongers. That was made perfectly clear in Scripture – no parables no complex lexicon – departure from intent or context. There are no greater WARMONGERS than the American BaptDUHS . The evil wicked criminally ignorant hypocrite BaptDUH is the ally of the devil and the enemy of God and goodness. By his own mouth he damns himself to hell.

Education breeds confidence. Confidence breeds hope. Hope breeds peace. Sadly-the 'elect' are few

Here we see that knowledge and wisdom breed a feeling of self-assurance and conviction that creates an ambition and optimism to promote peace. And of course – those who are the peacemakers are blessed by the Lord.

Who are the peacemakers? They are also among us but not as visible. NONE are to be found in our mainstream news media whose job it is to promote the wars of the jews who teaches your sons to become murderers (YES MURDERERS – not just killers) of innocent human beings. Many of our sons – NONE of whom are innocent – will ALSO be killed by these innocent people in defense of their own homes and families freedoms and honor.

Would you not defend your wife your children your home and your freedoms from brutal imperialistic Godless jack booted foreign thugs – should YOUR country be attacked? I damn sure would – wouldn't you? Have we become so vain and arrogant and superior as a people that we demean some other culture as not loving their OWN family as much as we love OURS? Apparently we HAVE!

NONE will be found in our now 100% treasonous IsraHELL first Congress. A Congress which recently honored a foreign Godless war criminal – invited in our Government as an HONORED guest – to whom we rendered no less than TWENTY SIX CONSECUTIVE STANDING OVATIONS for a vile speech which thanked our Congress for its treason against our own people.

It was the most disgraceful conduct I have witnessed in my entire life. It was a treasonous conduct that was sick demented twisted and reprobate to a degree unparalled in our entire history.

Such an accolade has NEVER EVER BEFORE been recorded in American history in honor of one our OWN American sons – yet we bow and scrape like whipped dogs to the leader of a people who have turned our nation into a morally rotted corpse. Nobody cares? That is OK? No moral outrage?

NONE will be found in Sodom West (Hollywood) or our 100% jew-controlled television (TALMUD-VISION). They are all too busy glorifying and glamorizing the horrors we commit daily in the Mid- East. Our putty brained sons must be taught that war is COOL – war is FUN – war is THRILLING – war is just the ultimate version of all those super violent jew-produced video games that have rotted their minds.

NONE will be found in ANY large Catholic or Protestant Church. As a matter of fact – the drums of war beat the loudest in what used to be places of worship of the Prince Of Peace. We as a people threw Christ out of our schools our government our churches and our hearts long ago.

Out nation is nothing more than a rotted corpse of what we once were. Christianity today in America is nothing more than a mega buck business.

Poor Fr.Martin (Martin Luther – yes Dorothy – Martin Luther was a Catholic priest) – he would roll in the grave should he see the level of corruption and outright blasphemy today – vile creatures whose sole purpose is to get rich on the emotions of the hopelessly ignorant.

NONE will be found in our jew run military. It no longer even remotely resembles the military in which I served two generations past. We no longer defend ANYTHING American. We DO – however- defend the most vile criminal degenerate Godless degenerate reprobate sadistic treacherous filth on planet Earth – the jews and their dirty little stolen country – ISRAHELL!

ALL of our military madness of the past 13 years has been wars of imperialism -wars of oppression – wars of terrorism and wars for greed in which I have not seen so much as ONE decent Godly man.

In regard to our horribly evil military – the seeds of justice have already been planted. Some five hundred thousand Gulf war veterans – now stateside – who VOLUNTEERED to go into innocent people's nations and murder their families – destroy and loot their culture and history – rape their women and murder and torture their children and have been exposed to combat situations share a commonality.

Virtually all been diagnosed with some jew created syndromes to explain away all the fatigues joint pains headaches lesions painful urination irritability insomnia and other unexplained growing mystery symptoms which grow in number daily. Most all of these war criminals have a rather large unpleasant shocking surprise in store! Guess what guys? It isn't going to get better and it is not some bullshit 'treatable' jew shrink diagnosed PTSD syndrome. You are dead men walking!

A majority of you are going to die prolonged painful deaths you have so richly deserved. You have inhaled some of the hundreds of thousands of tons of sub micro particles of DU that were atomized upon impact and are either floating around in different layers of the atmosphere. Once in your lungs, the radiation is deadly, terminal, and there is NO CURE! All manner of cancers will slowly metastasize in your organs – from your brain to your blood to sperm.

Your bastards have poisoned entire nations – the very air they breathe the soil that grows their food. Now YOU are going to pay! You have sown endless death upon innocent people. NOW – you will reap what you have sown. A sort of beautiful Biblical justice – payback direct from God so to speak.

I would GLADLY pay a thousand dollars for the information and opportunity to learn that a subhuman monster like mega serial murderer Chris Kyle is one of the 'condemned' – so I can watch a rare even seldom actually seen by mortals. That would be JUSTICE in real time. It will not bring back the countless fathers brothers and sons he has murdered for thrills – but I would make the information available to as many of the survivors as I could find – and relish the retribution and punishment of the purest instance of justice imaginable.

If some monster in a land so evil as to make him a hero for being a serial murderer – had murdered MY innocent son or MY innocent father or MY innocent brother or MY innocent best friend – I would be grateful to anyone who informed me that their killer was suffering as slow agonizing death administered by fate itself.

You children will probably be born monsters just like the ones YOU HAVE CAUSED in Iraq and Afghanistan by your lawless murderous criminal "don't give a damn about those rag heads" redneck racist mentality. There isn't a book or movie or super-computer large enough to document ALL of the misery and suffering your greed stupidity and Godless cruelty have caused tens or perhaps hundreds of millions of innocent human beings who have never in ANY WAY caused ANY of you disgusting putrid bastards any harm!

I pray God that you ALL 'die ten thousand deaths' for the evil and human misery you have caused decent innocent human beings. At least then – there will be some sort of JUSTICE for what we have done. When the dying begins – curse no one but your wicked selves. If you had been FORCED to go and do these horrible things – I would have compassion for you – but for the past 40 years we have had a mercenary military and we have had no cause to go to war and nothing to 'defend'. The last time the United States was attacked by a foreign enemy force was on June 8 1967. That enemy was IsraHELL and the people were JEWS!

Till this day – that horrid cowardly act of war has not been avenged or even been made an issue. Such is the control the evil jews have over our freedoms and sovereignty. Sad and true – but I digress.

Today – those Godly people of peace are like unto the early Roman Christians – persecuted for their goodness courage honesty wisdom and patriotism. It is as if we have reverted back to the dark times when a man could only convey his faith by drawing a symbol in the sand – fearing his speech would betray him to the authorities should it be heard by the wrong people.

Just talk to a church or school or even write a news paper in support of peace and see what happens. You will be labeled as a commie or traitor or "one of them Moooseums" and be slandered as unpatriotic or worse for your crime of wanting to save innocent children's lives. I have suffered such iniquitous outrages myself many times. It is a wound that is always painful and slow to heal.

We are the educated confident hopeful peacemakers – few in number as were the the patriots of Washington's revolutionary America – but we are firm in our resolve – knowing we are in favor with the Lord. We are no longer fed to the lions. This time we will be fed to vampires – creatures who survive by sucking the life from their victims. We will be betrayed to the eternal enemies of our Lord – the jews. Ultimately – like the brave consecrated colonial men who loved liberty more then they feared death – we will prevail – as good will always defeat evil. I pray I am right – or we WILL perish.

OCTOBER, 2012
WHAT IS TERRORISM? WHO ARE TERRORISTS?

One hears the word "TERRORIST" a lot today. It is in the news – We are told there is a " WAR ON TERRORISM" – We are told WHO the terrorists are and what dastardly deeds they do and how cowardly these 'sociopaths ' are and why we should murder millions of innocent people worldwide who "ARE terrorists" – or entire nations which "ARE TERRORIST" and "harbor terrorists". Obviously all Arab people are terrorists. Just ask any Merkan beer guzzling NFL fanatic pot bellied inbred racist redneck moron you see. After all, they are experts on such matters.

However I defy almost ANYONE – particularly our own home grown dumbed-down lemmings to carry on an intelligent conversation regarding terrorism for so much as 30 seconds! Just try to open a meaningful informed dialogue with the average 'Merkan' Joe six-pack The average comment would probably go something like this:

"Oh – you mean dem A'rab Mooselums". And if you ask to expend and clarify their profound conclusions a bit , It would sound like this: "That would be dem ragheads in Raq and EYEran and Afaganstan -right?". For the more sophisticated nitwit – your answer might have included: Dose A"rab terrists be do ones who flew dem airplanes into da twin towers cause dey hates our freedoms and all dat"

So much for the character and intelligence of a useful idiot mob mentality people who recently trashed a K-Mart store as they trampled to death a K-mart employee just to save a buck on an I-pod or 'blackberry' or T-shirt on sale. I guess one might call that an act of terrorism itself if you can imagine the terror experienced by the poor person who was stomped to death by those idiot savages!

Let me first define the difference between a 'terrorist' and a 'FREEDOM FIGHTER'. Some poorly informed person will state that they believe that "one man's freedom fighter is another man's terrorist" I have heard this following opinion before and I TOTALLY reject it after much experience with BOTH authentic freedom fighters and authentic terrorists on two continents. (please read my credentials at end)

The ideological differences are intrinsic and essential. The terrorists are criminals who attract destroy and profane mankind's most sacred values freedoms and rights. They desecrate destroy and burn churches and Mosques schools hospitals and municipalities that provide water electricity and transportation.

The terrorist purposefully targets innocent civilians for their own sadistic agendas. They intimidate humiliate maim torture kidnap and kill defenseless men women and children. They murder Judges news--persons elected officials administrators policeman and even priests. In other words – those who defend and uphold the laws and values of a civilized society.

Conversely – true freedom fighters try to adhere to international law and stay within the civilized standards of conduct as much as humanly possible. They attack military personnel and military targets. Since the freedom fighter is ALWAYS the disadvantaged underdog, noncombatant casualties are often unavoidable and normally not the result of a deliberate policy to employ the purposeful terror of the true terrorist. Their goal is simple – to free themselves from the oppression of their occupiers or their own criminal government. They just want freedom and independence.

Americans need to understand these stark differences between these groups. Perhaps the least used and most classic example of terrorism and freedom fighters was our own Revolutionary war. Washington's militia were very much considered terrorists by British (King George)

However the British had conducted themselves as TOTAL TERRORISTS. Consider these facts. They murdered and imprisoned countless civilians. Fact: MORE Americans died in the bowls of British prison ships from sadistic beatings – malnutrition – starvation – and disease that ALL of the lives lost in combat. Talk about REAL terrorists! The British are among the most ruthless barbaric immoral hypocrites people on earth. They have NEVER EVER been any ally of our in any manner shape or form.

British jew treachery got us into World War one under the treasonous Wilson in 1917. Two decades later British /jew treachery with the influence of American Marxist traitor FDR and British war criminal Churchill – we found ourselves once again sending American sons to die for the jews and the British. American traitors – British criminals – jews on both sides of the Atlantic then deceived us to fight THEIR wars AGAIN Germany NEVER wanted to start a war with America despite countless provocations by our Navy to make the Germans attack us. Learn the FACTS!

These were two absolutely preventable global wars in which we had NO legitimate cause whatsoever to initiate war against Germany – once again British lies and British treachery had cost us over a half million DEAD sons father brothers and friends in those two wars- for no good reason! We fought the wrong people. The Germans were never our 'enemy'. Had the Germans done away with Satan's children – I wouldn't have to be warning my countrymen of our impending destruction. George Patton was murdered for that realization.

Had we supported the anti-Communist anti jew Germans – there would have been no Vietnam Communists – no Korean Communists – no Cuban Communists no Chinese Communists and of course no IsraHELL. Also here would have been – no tens of thousands of MORE dead American sons who died for the jews and no near half million Gulf war veterans who are now all incurably poisoned by radioactive DU and will ALL eventually die horrible systemic deaths. Additionally there would be no World War III which will happen at any time now thanks to the lies and evil influence of the stinking jews!

OH and of course – our country would be a thriving prosperous loved and respected moral decent nation – the envy of all civilized people and we be a TRUE light unto the nations of the world – instead of the war mongering divided terrorist modern day judaized Sodom that we have become – destined for perdition on the trash heap of history.

Just consider what marvels we could have done our people and the world had we used the HUGE resources and lost lives to work for peace all those years we lived in fear of nuclear war with the Communists. Probable cures for cancer diabetes and many more blights of mankind – all eradicated! General Patten was right just as I am. Had the jew war criminal Eisenhower not had him murdered – who knows what potential utopia of peace prosperity and technical advances for good might we have had today – instead of endless wars to make the jews even richer. Learn your history! What the victors 'write' as truth is seldom true. DEMAND the TRUTH. Seek it. Embrace it. Defend it!

The overall end result? Our collective stupidity guaranteed that the REAL evil on the planet – the jews and the Marxist monsters who then ruled Russia held the world in fear for another FORTY SIX years! During that period thanks to treasonous scum like FDR – the Soviets imprisoned half of Europe at a cost of tens of millions of lives and America lost one hundred thousand more sons killed by Communists in two more wars (Korea and Vietnam) enabled by FDR and his Marxist jew pals and we experienced more world war crisis situations one after another Cuban Crisis – Berlin Crisis – Missiles in Turkey Crisis – U-2 Crisis and more.

Who are the terrorists today? There undeniably several REAL terrorist factions throughout the world. Here is a partial acronym list (some are no longer active threats) ETA – LARF – AD – CCC – GRAPO- RAF – BR – ELA – AVC – MPL – FMLN- M-19 – FARC – EPL – SL – MRTA – NPA – ANC.

BTW let me clear up some misunderstandings about the 'suicide bombers' taking revenge on IsraHELL for their REAL terrorism against Palestine for sixty four consecutive years. IsraHELL STOLE the land from these good Christian and Muslim Arab people and has murdered tortured mutilated beaten starved and humiliated them 24-7. IsraHELL is simply a rabid mad dog that must be put down for world peace and the safety of all decent mankind.

If you have spent any time in IsraHELL traveling on your own – you will notice their terrorist IDF is ALWAYS in these two places insignificant numbers. Cafe's and the public transportation which is free to their child murdering terrorists. Now you inbred redneck morons who might want to bash my truths with your oyster sized brains get this straight. NO Palestinian mother or father or child WANTS TO DIE!

These people live in fear 24-7 and there not ONE family in the ENTIRE country who has not lost friends relatives or children to the sadistic vicious demonic cruel jews – NOT ONE! They have no hope as they have been all but forgotten by the rest of the world. No American who was born here has EVER had that kind of horror in his or her life NOBODY – PERIOD! Like ANY parent

– they would do anything to defend and protect their child – but they have no weapons – nothing to defend their families from constant rape attacks beatings humiliation.

The ONLY thing they have to fight with is their frail mortal bodies. Don't talk to me about courage. I saw more courage there than anywhere in real life – the military – anywhere. I have been told that I have done some pretty gutsy things in my life faced death more than once survived being totally lost by myself at sea – survived a night plane crash – been clinically DEAD – twice and a bunch of other car crashed motorcycle accidents parachute mishaps and more.

I believe I would face possible death to save one of my children or grandchildren – but to kill my self knowing that my death MIGHT possibly save my child's life later on? I don't have that kind of courage and believe me IT IS RAW COURAGE – GUTS to knowingly sacrifice your life with fore thought and reflection. The soldier jumping on the hand grenade to save his buddies is not 'thinking' – he is simply reacting – believe me.

A pilot of a doomed airplane who coolly saves everyone's life in the plane seconds before it crashes by doing exactly what he was taught to do is not necessarily an iron nerved hero either. I know. I WAS that pilot of that plane in the night crash. And yes – all I did was to follow my commercial pilot emergency procedures I had been taught to the letter, and fortunately we all survived. I was later asked how I could keep my cool in a life and death situation.

Truth be known – I scarcely remember that last 10 seconds before the crash. 30 minutes after the crash and we were safely seated at the small airport cafe – my knees were shaking so badly I couldn't stand up – so much for my nerves of steel. I asked one of the passengers if they remember what I said – if anything – just before we hit. He told me absolutely – I said ; "OH SHIT!" It was good for a laugh because that is what you hear the 'John Wayne' hero in the movies say just before he crashes. Point was – there was no courage involved – just discipline.

The young Palestinian mother who is grief stricken she can no longer stand by and see her beloved children brutalized raped and beaten half to death has called upon her last ounce of courage to sacrifice herself for her family and country. Greater love no man (or woman) has than when she gives her life for her family. I have witnessed these horrors and the desperation and hopelessness that comes with endless animal brutality and YOU HAVEN'T.

I still wake up every morning with the thoughts of the horrors I witnessed committed by the filthy Jew terrorists in Israhell twenty three years ago. Knowing they mock everything any my family have ever held sacred honorable pure and decent and that their unpunished horrid crimes have become even more brutal does not set well with me.

I swear on my word that if I ever experience anyone in my presence mock and ridicule such extraordinary bravery I will try my best to put that person in the hospital for a long time! Sometimes the tongue of such a reptile can do more hurt than a stick. I am NOT a violent person by nature – but every person has his limit of experiencing cruelty – especially against the helpless and defenseless. I despise bullies and cowards I WILL NOT tolerate that type of putrid sadistic cruelty and mockery of an innocent oppressed victim in my presence

These poor people have been raped robbed beaten brutalized starved humiliated tortured and murdered like rats for 65 YEARS! They have no army no navy no air force as they have lived in peace – Christian and Muslim for SEVENTEEN HUNDRED YEARS. Why would peaceful Godly people need an army? Abortions in Palestine are so rare that their language does not even have a WORD FOR IT. I know this for a FACT! Their Godless jew neighbors have one of the highest abortions rates in that part of the world. NOTHING in jew world is 'holy'.

The demonic jews have destroyed or stolen their homes smashed their churches and Mosques murdered their their physicians their police and elected political officials – destroyed hundreds of thousands of modest private homes – destroyed their crops and livelihood and keep them as animals with no rights or freedoms in the world's largest outdoor prison – the exact textbook essence of terrorism.

No other non jewish-controlled people on this planet have ever treated other innocent human beings in this barbaric fashion. READ YOUR HISTORY BOOKS. The demonic Christ hating vicious sadistic lying Godless Marxist and Zionist filth who have committed these unconscionable crimes are the SAME scum who have been cast out of ONE HUNDRED AND NINE nations and city States over a period of almost EIGHTEEN HUNDRED YEARS – because of their putrid filthy criminal conduct – PERIOD!

Never EVER in the history of mankind has there been a people so evil as the jews. Never in Biblical history has there been such a people so universally damned for their horrid wicked evil demonic demonic natures. Read what Christ Himself had to say as he damns them not just TO Hell – but for the fact that these jews ARE FROM HELL! READ JOHN 8-44

But I digress – so back to terrorists and terrorism.

Until recently I could safely and statistically state that the world's largest institutionalized terrorist group was the jew IsraHELL 'IDF'. There record of torture beatings starvation mutilation and murders of mostly children and other defenseless helpless victims is their cowardly style and conduct so vile it is not easily described to even hairy-chested men.

I have seen their 'brave moral' military in action as these courageous 'soldiers for Satan' actually bind up children on the front of their combat vehicles so to discourage any attacks that would obviously put the child at risk. While ANY real soldier, like the men I served with would put his life on the line to stand BETWEEN danger and a child – the filthy yellow bellied filthy Godless jews openly use Palestinian children as shields as common IDF POLICY!

Been there – seen that. Just something else the American public might just be outraged about to know. And these are the putrid demonic scum that 50 million inbred redneck BaptDUH reptiles worship above the lord Jesus.?!

Today – IsraHELL can no longer lay claim to that Ignoble vile despicable title. The USA Department of Defense is now hands down 'numero uno' as far as formal terrorist groups on the planet. In the past ten years the US military has murdered in cold blood over TWO MILLION totally innocent civilian human beings – all Arab people and all for racist reasons of their ethnicity.

So – we are not simply terrorists by purest definition – but RACIST terrorists. the majority of that two million innocent civilian souls were children. We have left another 15-20 million badly injured and we have left twenty 25 -30 million homeless. The despicable conduct of our mercenary paid assassins (disguised as real soldiers) is in perfect accordance with the parameters describing terrorists and terrorism.

We have looted destroyed raped pillaged plundered and poisoned their land with thousands of tons deadly radioactive waste. We have poisoned their land their air and their newborn with the same radioactive horrors we sentenced millions of Japanese civilians to needlessly suffer from to satisfy our lust for inflicting terror and misery that we just can't seem to rise above.

I trained the grandfathers of these slimy sick sociopathic scum jackbooted bullies our jew masters send overseas to kill innocent people for. Do ANY of you parents give damn about the sadistic filth your 18 year old sons are being taught. In the name of God – please listen to me. I was a basic training infantry company commander (E-5-2) I trained basic young warriors – over a thousand of them – personally during the early 60s 'Berlin Crisis' period.

The criminal scum who are running the show for the jews have changed the rules of engagement and human decency for our children to become soulless mindless remorseless terrorists whose current training has little to do with DEFENDING our nation and EVERYTHING To do with terror & murder rape brutal savagery – against innocent defenseless civilians mind you – not unlike what the Soviets were taught by their jew masters during WWII.

I know what I am talking about been there – seen that – done that. Please listen to me. MY OWN BELOVED FLESH AND BLOOD young son confirmed these criminal terrorist sadistic barbaric cruelties were taught at his basic training but none of the jew or jew useful idiot controlled newspapers or Broadcast news will allow this shocking ugly truth.

Most of my own grown adult prosperous neighbors will expend extraordinary means to obtain good seats at an NFL 'game' (n. diversion – amusement – recreation) but will not lift a finger to protect the right to freedom of speech our Founding Fathers fought suffered and died for to secure for our people. Sad.

Finally – the OBJECTIVE of organized institutionalized terrorist activities – like the jew IDF – or our current Army of murderous criminal bully thugs – is to so traumatized demoralize and make so hopeless, the civilian populace – that they will become convinced to follow the foreign (or domestic) terrorists and accept THEIR puppet government.

That sinister evil objective of terrorism has a dual effect which is always good for the terrorists (the USA) but bad for the former sovereign nation (the Arab nation that we have currently aggressed and terrorized into submission) Just like what the stinking British bastards did to us (unsuccessfully thank God).

The SECOND desired result would be that the REAL – TRUE patriots who would DARE to defend their home their land their freedoms their culture their age old traditions their religious beliefs – WILL now be slandered mocked ridiculed by the puppets in charge – as "insurgents detainees traitors and or terrorists". Merkans love to ridicule 'different foreigners'. Sadly – for them to be respected – they need to be as shallow and immoral as we are.

In other words: " Become like we superior, judized Westerners – immoral – lovers of perversions – war mongers – materialists – money worshipers – have your once modest women now look like whores – corrupt – liars – cheats – hypocrites – racists – lovers of violence – homosexual perversions – infanticide – Godlessness and accept this this evil monster called Democracy (which our Republican Founding Fathers considered dangerous to our freedoms) or we will bomb you into the stone age.

The jews who now occupy every aspect of our once sovereign nation, have taught our 'leaders' (read : traitors) well.

Do I have any real credentials regarding my knowledge (not just opinions either) of REAL terrorists of which I have made the above factual statements? I certainly do. You don't learn this stuff in a classroom behind a CRT. I can't compete with James Bond and my experiences never made me an urban legend but my real life experiences within the areas of my experience are probably better than any American that 99% of you will ever meet.

In the Mid-East – I was for a period of time privileged to be in the company of operatives/officials that allowed me to meet and interview jew terrorists from the IDF and other governmental agencies. At that time 1989 – the jew IDF was the technically the largest institutionalized terrorist group on earth. Been there – saw that

In the West I had certain connections – some diplomatic – some political – some military that eventually got me invited by the government of El Salvador as part of a Caribbean basin terrorist advisors committee during the height of the Sandinista occupation in Nicaragua. A modest diplomatic position as Vice Consul to Costa Rica for several years with MANY connections at the highest Government levels proved to be of great value as I had an entire country as a 'safe house to work from.

I had also been very involved with the events at the height of the Sandinista regime and worked closely with some major 'contra' freedom fighters (yes – they were REAL anti -Communist all REAL Christian freedom fighters) The soviet Marxist supported Sandinistas (FSLN) were pretty much terrorists in their own right but my exploits undercover in Nicaragua is another story. They were the official government (the bad guys) and the Contras were the rebels(the good guys). The opposite of the situation next door in El Salvador was that the rebels – the Marxist FMLN – were TERRORIST bad guys fighting the elected Government and assisted by the Nicaraguan Marxist FSLN government. It can get confusing. Classic good guys bad guys reversal and also next door neighbors.

In El Salvador I worked with the Salvadoran military intelligence at highest levels and went on several patrols with their Atlacatl battalion (Salvadoran Special Forces) which already had active duty American Green Beret advisors in place. I still have several hours of films of those times.

The enemy was the Marxist FMLN (Farabundo Marti Liberacion National) – at the time the largest and best organized Central American terrorist group. They were REAL terrorists at their worst – well equipped – supported by the Nicaraguan Marxist FSLN (the Sandinistas) as well as USSR Spetsnaz – Eastern bloc Marxists (Bulgaria etc) Cuban Communists Asian Communists and others. They were as brutal and sadistic as the jews in IsraHELL and were the largest terrorist group in Latin America. I had the opportunity to be with one of their young officer Atlacatl heroes on patrol – also very well disciplined and well trained Salvadoran Marines.

I was able to participate in patrols into remote FMLN occupied areas and I filmed some of the damage to walled farming co-ops that had been attacked because of their choice of free enterprise. The FMLN tried to massacre the entire village but the Atlacatl rangers got there in time to repel them. The huge steel reinforced doors had several large RPG holes and countless small arms AP holes – but it held throughout the night attack.

Had they breached the doors they would have massacred everyone inside. The Salvadoran military put their own people and THEIR country FIRST – unlike the United States of IsraHELL we now live in with everybody from Congress to the President seeing how far they can stick their brown noses up jew ass.

I have some photos of the dead terrorists that resulted from a firefight the night before. One of the terrorists was carrying several incendiary devices used to burn the civilian co-op housing. These scum were devout Marxists – textbook terrorists

One of our Salvadoran Rangers put a tracer round in his satchel and turned him into a crispy critter that lit up the night. I took his picture to Washington later where it was displayed at Langley – entitled ‘breakfast of buzzards’. I also still have those pictures but haven’t shown them in 25 years.

Being bi-lingual – I was also allowed to participate in some of the interrogation of captured terrorists one in particular why had just blown up some municipality. A paraffin test verified he had been involved in the murder of some elected official. He had no remorse.

I still have hundreds of captured documents and photographs of their meetings their fighters and other interesting intelligence. One of the documents that impressed me with their Godless sadistic brutality was a statement form a prominent leader that cynically stated that they would continue mining the peoples small farms so that the poor workers who at least had jobs were forced to risk their lives just to gather fire wood needed for cooking and warmth. The FSLN was out to try to starve the country by terrorizing the farmers and stealing what crops they had.

Sound familiar? To informed educated Americans it should. Just remember what the Marxist jews did to the Ukrainian small land owners in the 40s Same method of terror. Steal and starve the nation into submission. Some 7 million Ukrainians were murdered and or starved to death by

Lenin's jew 'Cheka' secret police. The terror and genocide of the jews against innocent defenseless Godly people just never ends. Only the name have changed.

Many of the mine victims in El Salvador were children and suffered death or worse – the loss of their legs – which is worse than a death sentence in a poor nation. I saw many of them in a hospital in San Salvador. One kid was with his mother when they tripped a mine on the farm they worked on and they both lost legs – the mother eventually died the next day.

Seeing dead bad guys didn't bother me – but cruelly murdered helpless children send me off the scale – whether they were Salvadoran, murdered by the Marxist FMLN – or Palestinian, murdered by American supported jew IDF.

It was heart breaking. Perhaps the comment of the terrorist commander was what made convinced they were so hopelessly evil – like the jews – that they all must die for the sake of all the innocent people whose lives they would eventually ruin or take.

He said that "they would continue to mine the farms even if dozens or more or all of the children were maimed – all for the greater good of the Party" (jew created communist Party) Change a couple of words and you have the exact same mentality of the filthy Godless bastard jews endless genocide against the Palestinians.

I could write pages on this but the point is -I didn't learn about 'terrorists' in an armchair behind a keyboard. I learned it from the tears and the mud and the blood and horrors of real life as to just how low human beings can sink.

Palestinians? = TRUE OPPRESSED FREEDOM FIGHTERS

American military? = HORRID GODLESS SADISTIC TERRORISTS

IsraHELL IDF? = HORRID GODLESS SADISTIC TERRORISTS

Oh – and just in case you STILL think that The IDF AND the American military being identified as authentic terrorists is only "my opinion" based on my experience and credentials – check out this man's credentials!

"And then you have the Israeli army, which I would categorize as one of the best-armed, best-fed, best-financed terrorist organizations in the world … They are dedicated to terrorizing an entire nation … and they do this with American money, and they do this with American arms."
10-2012 public comment by Miko Peled – Former IDF officer and son of a prominent Zionist IDF Major General – author of best seller 'THE GENERAL'S SON'
If a former IDF Israeli of such prominence has concluded that the IDF – IS a 'world class' terrorist organization – shouldn't that validate my exact same conclusion? AND he is not the only prominent former IDF that thinks so.

So please- no lectures from the ignorant or apologist peanut gallery about who the REAL terrorists are today.

Like Pogo Opossum – the comics' page character used to say: "We have met the enemy – AND IT ARE US!"

GET IT? Now let's at least TRY to take this country back before we are ALL slaves of the jews!

OCTOBER 2012
THE ACLU: TROJAN HORSE OF THE JEW

When most Americans think of the ACLU, it is usually the generalization of ultra-liberal legal assistance to church/state separation cases, anti-death penalty advocacy and protection of an assortment of generally undesirable groups. The truth is much more insidious and dangerous. This carefully documented report will attempt to show that there can be no doubt as to the treacherous and dangerous ongoing agenda of an organization so evil and so deceitful that it could not exist if the whole truth were known by the public at large. This then is a confirmed chronicle which will make most fictional thrillers about sinister and diabolic organizations pale by comparison. Learn why the Jew ACLU is the mortal enemy of ALL DECENT CHRISTIAN Americans – and always will be. Like the treacherous Jew whose 'god' is the ideology of Zionist /Marxism – it must be destroyed if we wish to live as a free people.

The roots of the ACLU go back as far as 1914, but its real beginnings were in Oct. of 1917 when Roger Baldwin who was then director of the Civil Liberties Bureau (CLB) was prompted by friends to reorganize the CLB as the National Civil Liberties Bureau. The main thrust of the NCLB, as had been the CLB's was to assist and encourage draft dodgers. True to his cause, Baldwin was imprisoned for draft dodging. Upon his release from prison in July 1919, a party was given in his honor during which the attendees advocated forming a new organization, ostensibly to champion "civil rights". Honored guests at the party included Norman Thomas, patriarch of the Socialist Party, Elizabeth G. Flynn, soon to be the Chairperson of the American Communist Party, and Agnes Smedley who later became a Soviet espionage agent in China.

Shortly thereafter, the NCLB was reorganized as the American Civil Liberties Union (ACLU) in 1920. Harry Ward was the first chairman, Baldwin, its director, and Louis Budenz the publicity director. Since the concept that people are known by "the company they keep" is accepted by sociologists and society in general, lets look in detail at some of the "company" that the ACLU and Roger Baldwin kept. Budenz later became an important official of the Communist party, and was called upon on several occasions to give testimony before the House Un-American Activities Committee (HUAC). Ward had a particularly odious contribution to the success of the communists in that he enthusiastically used the Church to infiltrate Moscow's anti-god agenda into American society. An ordained Methodist minister, Ward founded the Methodist Federation for Social Service.

The following is official sworn testimony and matter of record from the 1953 files of the HUAC. Manning Johnson, one time Communist Party leader of the Negro Section testified: *"Dr. Harry F. Ward, for many years has been the chief architect for communist infiltration and subversion in the religious field... He was a member of the Communist Party while I was a member.... I would say that he is the Red Dean of the Communist Party in the religious field."*

Benjamin Gitlow, a founder and former general secretary to the Communist Party of the United States (CPUSA) testified: *"The Russian Communists were the first to exploit ministers of the United States, and through them the church organizations for the purpose of spreading propaganda in favor of Communist Russia, and of the building of a pro-Soviet sentiment among church people in America and among Americans generally."*

Gitlow further testifies: *"The Methodist Federation for Social Action ... was first organized by a group of Socialist, Marxist clergymen of the Methodist Church headed by Dr. Harry F. Ward.... Its objective was to transform the Methodist Church and Christianity into an instrument for the achievement of socialism."*

Harry Ward, the first chairman of the ACLU and an identified communist party member, was an active member of almost 50 identified communist front groups and subversive organizations! He was instrumental in the founding of the leftist Federal Council of Churches which became today's National Council of Churches (NCC). The NCC has consistently and still currently supports leftist objectives in the Caribbean Basin, and lends its support and name to many Marxist support groups.

Worth mentioning here. For you 'Christians' who believe your church is Godly and pure and holy – consider this FACT. ALL 'churches' titled "UNITED" (as in United Methodist) are under NCC control and are the antithisis of Godliness. They are an abomination in the sight of our Lord. Read: The Gospel According To Marx -Readers Digest

For example: the Inter-Religious Task Force, which is a coalition of several hard core Marxist and terrorist support groups such as SANE, IPS, PACCA, CISPES, NISGUA, WOLA and Nicaragua Network – receives DIRECT Financial support from the NCC. So much for the supposed noble nature of the original governing body.

For the next decade, the ACLU's membership was predominantly a "laundry list" of the country's most active pacifists, Socialists, and communists – and of course dominated by the Jew. Virtually every communist front group in the USA at the time had representation in the ACLU. An apparent paradox, among its members in late years was four consecutive US Presidents, Truman, Eisenhower, Kennedy and Johnson. We shall examine the reason for membership by respectable figures later, but there is much more in the background of Roger Baldwin and the ACLU before the 40s that deserves closer scrutiny.

Just keep in mind – the ACLU is a 'Jew thing' and being so – Americans must realize that regardless of the cunning deceptions – it serves ONLY Jew interests – which of course are the ultimate destruction of our Constitution – our Republican form of government and ESPECIALLY our Christian heritage.

In its report of 17 Jan., 1931, the Special House Committee to Investigate Communist Activities in the United States (precursor to the HUAC) stated: "The American Civil Liberties Union is closely affiliated with the communist movement in the United States, and fully 90% of its efforts are on behalf of communists who have come into conflict with the law. It claims to stand for free speech, free press, and free assembly; but it is quite apparent that the main function of the ACLU is to attempt to protect the communists in their advocacy of force and violence to overthrow the Government, replacing the American flag by a red flag and erecting a Soviet government in place of the Republican form of government guaranteed to each state by the Federal Constitution. Roger N. Baldwin, its guiding spirit, makes no attempt to hide his friendship for the communists and their principles."

Lest there be any doubt as to the accuracy of the committee's findings in the afore-mentioned statement, consider this quote of Baldwin's philosophy: "*...I am for Socialism, disarmament and, ultimately for abolishing the State itself as an instrument of violence and compulsion. I seek the social ownership of property, the abolition of the propertied class, and sole control of those who produce wealth. COMMUNISM IS THE GOAL.*"

And if there be any doubt as to the violent nature of Baldwin's Communist Party if it should ever succeed in the relentless goal of our defeat, read carefully the statement of Baldwin's ideological comrade, former CPUSA General Secretary Gus Hall. Comrade Hall states, (Feb. 1961) and I quote: *" I dream of the hour when the last Congressman is strangled to death on the guts of the last preacher — and since the Christians love to sing about the blood,* [the blood of Christ] *why not give them a little of it."* A chilling prelude to Soviet dictator Khrushchev's statement of Soviet Communist intentions to Americans: *"WE WILL BURY YOU!."*

In 1943, the Legislative Committee investigating un-American activities in California reported: "The ACLU may be definitely classed as a Communist front or "transmission belt" organization." In 1948, the California Senate Fact-Finding Committee on Un-American Activities reaffirmed prior committee findings concerning "...the communist character of ACLU. The Internal Labor Defense, called the *"legal arm of the Communist Party"* by former Atty. Gen. Francis Biddle, *has not established a better communist record than this thinly disguised organization that devotes its energies to the defense of enemies of the United States."*

A chairman for the investigating committee asked the following questions of ACLU Director Baldwin. The frightening answers he rendered on behalf of ACLU policy are a matter of congressional record – facts I'm sure today's ACLU officials would not want Americans to know.

Chairman – *"Does your organization uphold the right of a citizen or alien [implying a Soviet agent]...to advocate murder?"* Baldwin – *"Yes."* Chairman – "*Or assassination?"* Baldwin – *"Yes."* Chairman – "*Does your organization uphold the right of an American citizen to advocate force and violence for the overthrow of the Government?"* Baldwin – *"Certainly.."* Chairman – *"Does it uphold the right of an alien* [implying a Soviet agent] *to advocate the overthrow of the Government by force or violence?"* Baldwin – *"Precisely on the same basis as any citizen."* Chairman – *"Do YOU [personally] uphold the right of an alien* [implying a Soviet agent] *to advocate the overthrow of the Government by force and violence?"* Baldwin – *"Sure; certainly…"* One will still find communist ideologue Roger Baldwin quoted on current ACLU literature, with pride and conviction.

Baldwin was Quoted in the Sept., 1934 issue of `Soviet Russia Today' as saying: *"When the power of the working class is once achieved, as it has been only in the Soviet Union, I am for maintaining it by any means whatsoever….. The class struggle is the central conflict of the world; all others are coincidental."*

How this familiar sounding "Communist Manifesto" strategy was to be accomplished was revealed in the following quote to communist leader Louis Lochner: *"We want to, also, look like patriots in everything we do. We want to get a good lot of flags, talk a good deal about the Constitution and what our forefathers wanted to make out of this country and to show that we are the fellows that really stand up for the spirit of our institutions."*

But an event happened in Sept. of 1939 that caused dissent and confusion in the communist dominated ACLU. This was the Hitler-Stalin Pact. The ACLU's "role model", Soviet communists were now big buddies with Hitler's Germany, This new revelation caused too much dissension in the ranks, and a drastic measure had to be enacted to save the integrity of the ACLU lest attrition and hypocrisy undo Baldwin's work. Something drastic was done.

In 1940 the almost entirely communist ACLU announced its flip flop new policy – no more communists allowed in the club, or for that matter, Nazis, Fascists, or KKK. Interesting to note here: *there never were any Nazi,Fascist, or KKK officials in the ACLU anyway!* At any rate, communist luminaries such as Elizabeth Gurley Flynn and Harry Ward were either dismissed or forced to resign. This move confused a lot of people including the communists. Curiously, an "open letter" by 17 pro-communist leaders to the ACLU was published in the official communist party newspaper, Daily Worker on Mar 19,1940.

It read: *"…We are told that communists are to be barred from office or employment in the Civil Liberties Union because, while fighting for civil liberties in America, they accept their suppression in Soviet Russia."* Why then, did the Civil Liberties Union wait until 1940 before seeking to bar them? … Civil liberties within the Soviet Union were no different before the [Hitler/Stalin] Pact than after." It would seem that even some persons on the left found the thinly disguised hypocrisy of the ACLU worthy of exposing.

This farce lasted from 1940 to 1968, a period during which the ACLU was no longer investigated by any Congressional committee, presumably because of its self proclaimed exclusion of communists from its fold. It was during this period that many respectable non-communist personalities from presidents to entertainers, from diplomats to clergymen, joined the now "patriotic" ACLU.

They even cooperated with the FBI in exposing communist front activities. There is substantial evidence indicating conclusively, that during the "clean" period, many of the "non communist" officials of the ACLU remained active in communist fronts, and were perhaps even more effective than if they were "dues paying" and "card carrying" members of the party due to their new low profiles.

In 1968 the ACLU hierarchy decided the ruse had gone on long enough, so they opened membership once more to all the real "card carrying commies" that had been previously barred. In a cursory check of the ACLU Board and National Committee members since its inception, the Reports of investigating Committees of the Congress have revealed that almost 80% of them had affiliated themselves with communist activities over the years. It should be noted also that while not all ACLU members are communists, it can be safely stated that there are NO communist front groups that don't have ACLU members.

While patriotic mainstream Americans with traditional family values have worked for true liberty, law and order and social responsibility, the ACLU has pushed for licentiousness, chaos, and a regimented totalitarian society. Patriotic moral Americans are rightfully concerned for the victim of a crime, while the ACLU is solely concerned with the welfare of the criminal no matter how heinous the crime. Real Americans are anti-communist by nature while the ACLU is extremely pro-communist or anti-anti-communist. Informed Americans have recognized that the basis of our government was religious by the express will of the Founding Fathers of this country (*who gave us MANY warnings of the evil of the jews*) , while the ACLU has consistently insisted on the separation of all moral values from our laws and their administration.

The ACLU supports the sale and distribution of child pornography, the legalization of crack cocaine and heroin, tax exempt status for Satanists, legalization of prostitution, abortion on demand even if the child could be delivered alive, mandatory public sex education, forced busing, public demonstration for communists, homosexual "marriages" and adoption of children by homosexuals.

On the other hand, the ACLU opposes voluntary school prayer, sobriety checkpoints, tax exemptions for legitimate churches, religious displays in public even if all denominations are present, parental consent laws, Government ethics committees, prison for criminal offenses, public demonstration for pro-life groups, aids tests to protect the public health, metal detectors in airports to protect the public from terrorists, all capital punishment, all secret Govt. anti-terrorist operations, all covert operations by national security organizations (like CIA), military draft, "Under God" in our Pledge of allegiance and "in God we trust" on our currency, movie rating systems to protect children from viewing graphic sex, violence or obscene material and school searches for weapons and drugs.

The records of the ACLU in the defense of communists are unparalleled in history, and would quite literally fill volumes. The ACLU has worked hard to destroy any agency that protects America from communist subversion. The ACLU has gone so far as to defend jew spies like

Jonathon Pollard whose treason against America for the jews is considered the most serious betrayal of US classified information in history!

The jew ACLU was of course eager to defend this slimy treasonous jew reptile and as been working for years to free him from the life sentence justice he so richly deserved. They have submitted an amicus brief in his behalf. The *amicus curiae* brief, which strongly endorses counsel's right to have access to the docket materials, was prepared by the usual suspects and enemies of all decency – which included a list that looked like a invitation to a Bar Mitzvah!

Oy Vey! The law firm of Morrison & Foerster LLP [JEWS] on behalf of the American Civil Liberties Union of the National Capital Area (ACLU), [JEWS] joined by the National Association of Criminal Defense Lawyers (NACDL), [JEWS] the American Association of Jewish Lawyers and Jurists (AAJLJ), [JEWS] and fourteen prominent law professors and other distinguished individuals, [JEWS] including Congressman Anthony D. Weiner (D-N.Y.), [JEW] former New York State Attorney General Robert Abrams, [JEW] and former United States District Judge George N. Leighton, [Christ hating Negro Democrat leftist NAACP and ACLU member who had a nativity scene destroyed].

The ACLU has actually defended the entire communist party, fully aware that the party is part of a conspiracy whose sole purpose was and STILL IS to destroy the American Govt. by any means possible.

The ACLU has upheld the "right" of communists (READ- JEWS) to hold jobs in motion picture, radio and TV, in our schools, defense plants, armed services, and even govt. positions of high national security! Sound familiar? The ACLU defends the "right" of communists (READ- JEWS) to speak on our campuses, but opposes the use of public schools for anti-communist speakers. Sound familiar? This author can testify to this alarming fact from my OWN PERSONAL EXPERIENCE. Just try to lecture the TRUTH of IsraHELL terrorists – in my case from PERSONAL in situ experiences. You WILL be censured as surely as if this was a 'colony' of IsraHELL instead of the USA.

The ACLU opposes loyalty oaths, and today there are none! If you want to conduct a convincing test that should scare the wits out of you – try this. Call the local FBI and tell them you have information on a subversive individual or group, and make it as dramatic as you wish. You have overheard bomb threats, espionage, sabotage, or threats on your life by a communist, open support for a jew terrorist organization etc. Do you know what the FBI will do? Nothing – absolutely nothing – thanks to action many years ago by the ACLU.

There are actually from three to ten times as many Soviet espionage operatives (depending on the area) in the USA as there are counter-intelligence trained FBI agents to keep track of them – and that is a FACT! The FBI is no longer allowed to keep files on subversives – thanks to the ACLU. Your local defense plant more than likely has several communist supporters working there, perhaps in high and/or sensitive areas and there are NO loyalty oaths, there are NO background checks, there are NO means WHATSOEVER to screen out individuals who might commit acts of sabotage or espionage. Why? – because it is now literally against the law to protect our national security, because it is a violation of "privacy" and "civil rights" according the ACLU.

I personally know this to be true- as at that time I did occasional undercover work for the FBI and discovered some serious problems regarding Communist sympathizers within the officer ranks our own military. The FBI told me they couldn't do anything about it. My personal experiences confirmed the above allegations. Even then – the jews in this country exercised substantial control.

By the same token – there are ALSO now more Mossad agents active in America than ever before, and they are equally as dangerous – IF NOT MORE SO – than the 'Communists' were/are. The REAL difference is that when we caught a Soviet agent with his hand in the 'cookie jar' – he was arrested and perhaps tried for espionage. Today – when Israeli espionage agents are uncovered and caught – as in 9-11, our Jew run and Jew infested Federal Government just looks the other way – on orders from our masters in Tel Aviv. AND of course the treasonous ACLU will be there on the spot to defend the 'Constitutional rights' of their beloved fellow jew agents. Same games – different names

Dr. J. B. Matthews, chief investigator for the now defunct House Special Committee on Un-American Activities, made this observation in Jan of 1955: *"In thirty seven years of history of the Communist movement in the United States, the Communist Party has never been able to do as much for itself as the American Civil liberties Union has done for it."*

The ACLU/Communist Party connection was so obvious that it prompted further comment, this time from the records of the 1966 Report of the Counter-Subversive Committee of the National Conference of Police Associations: *"In our opinion, the ACLU and its brother organizations have mastered the technique of Joseph Goebbels and practiced by Moscow Communists to the nth degree. `Tell a lie, make it big, and tell it often enough so that soon everyone will believe it.'"* That lie of course is the deception that the ACLU is just trying to protect our Constitution, all the while of course intent upon its destruction.

Let us examine some of the areas in which the ACLU currently exercises the "big lie". You will see the motion picture industry stoop to "tricking" parents into taking children to see outright "X" rated trash under the auspices of new rating systems. The ACLU hated the Legion of Decency and The Motion Picture Code, private groups that wish only to protect our children from exposure to obscene and pornographic "entertainment."

Now that the ACLU has succeeded in destroying these agencies, watch the wave of violence, hate, and explicit sex that adults well know can and will desensitize young impressionable minds at the movies and on TV. Anything goes – no matter how violent – offensive – sadistic – blasphemous and graphic. AND- it is ALL protected by the Christ hating jew ACLU.

I defy you to look at the movie section in your daily newspaper and find more than one or two current movies you would feel comfortable taking the family to. In a random sampling of movie listings in my own home town, I found the following. Of 208 movies listed, there were 138("R"), 61("PG") and only 7("G") [6 of which were a 50 year old Disney animation!]. The trash peddlers will produce more and more trash as long as the ACLU supports them. It's already out of control, and it didn't just happen – the ACLU MADE it happen, all the while espousing their defense of our first amendment.

Remember a Negro "rap" group called "2 Live Crew"? They made headlines with their tasteless and obscene record album called "As Nasty As They Wanna Be" sporting song titles like "Me so Horney".

The band members actually proudly argue that the sexually explicit filth and profanity contained therein was an integral part of black cultural tradition! If Luther Campbell, the band leader, wanted to appear eager to encourage and endorse the notion that black people are the embodiment of irresponsible and unrestrained sexuality, he did a convincing job. The group's council at the time – the jew Bruce Rogow, argued that the labeling of women as "bitches", which was used 163 times in one album, is a *"cultural norm"* for Negroes! You guessed it, defending the offensive obscenities of "2 Live Crew" had become a pet project of the ACLU.

Today – the profanities and filth of 2 Live Crew seem tame compared to the endless stream of jew approved and ACLU defended blasphemies – sordid filth – demon worship – death wish – suicide promoting putrid scum

Using the BILL of RIGHTS as an excuse, the ACLU under the leadership of former director – Jew Ira Glasser, , continued to show contempt for a family-oriented society by an unhealthy preoccupation with helping homosexuals, prostitutes, sex offenders, drug dealers, rioters, bums, hoodlums, anarchists, abortionists and murderers. The ACLU relentlessly pursues ways to find loopholes through which the criminal can escape prosecution and justice.

Police too have been a major target of the ACLU. Law enforcement people are considered so much trash by the ACLU, and the ACLU actually encourages the lawless to insult and intimidate them so the resulting "police brutality" can be exploited by the anti-law and order ACLU. Any legislation aimed at reducing crime is vigorously opposed by the pro-criminal ACLU.

Some examples of these laws that would protect innocent citizens are (1) an automatic increase in penalties for crimes committed with deadly weapons,(2) removal of bail for second offenders,(3) removal of probation and parole, plus longer sentences for certain offenses (remember Willie Horton's bloody killing spree while on Dukakis' furlough?) and (4) use of voluntary oral confessions. The ACLU has made it easier for hard-core coldblooded condemned murderers to escape because of security measures that have been rescinded by the ACLU.

These pro-criminal laws have cost millions of tax dollars as well as innocent lives when the escaped murderers have gone on a killing spree. Case in point: on April 21, 1986 Colorado Gov. Richard Lamm agreed to pay the ACLU almost 700 thousand dollars of taxpayer's money to settle a 1977 lawsuit over alleged "unconstitutional" conditions at a maximum security prison in Canon City. Not surprisingly, Philip Hirschkop, one of the most active lawyers on the ACLU's National Prisoner Project is listed as a member of the National Lawyers Guild, a Congressionally cited Communist front.

Thanks in great part to the ACLU, there are over 1500 convicted murderers on "death row" who tie up our nation's courts with endless appeals, virtually all of which have absolutely nothing to do with whether innocence is in question, but whether some loophole of jurisprudence has been overlooked so that justice can be mocked, and the killer turned loose on society again. DID YOU GET THAT? Even if the murderer has confessed – the jew ACLU wants him to be set free to murder again based on a LOOPHOLE – NOT truth or justice. Loopholes in the law – GET IT?

Periodicals like the Readers Digest often publish documented examples of how the ACLU helps the court system turn ruthless killers free on technicalities. The ACLU never misses the opportunity to create racial strife and maintains community discord by crying "racial discrimination" at every remote possibility, even if they well know none existed. All of us, both black and white, have seen this destructive and divisive tactic abused time and time again by the ACLU. It is as if racial unrest at any price in the community is the goal – but seldom civil rights or social justice.

Racial agitation isn't the only goal of the ACLU. Student riots seem to be another priority. A "Student's Rights Conference" was hosted by the ACLU for the "Liberation" of students, in Oct.70, at Rutgers University under the tutelage of ACLU jew agitator Alan Levine. Levine told the young people: *"Oppressive institutions give you no right at all to say why you go there, how long you go there, and what you do while you're there."* Levine urged them to riot and take over their schools as he declared: *"Indeed, you cannot exercise the rights the courts have told you have without disrupting the system."* The message was clear: to tear the schools apart to get what you want, and we will see that you are not punished by the law. And that is exactly what they did.

The ACLU has an almost fanatical obsession with being the legal patrons of homosexuals and other deviates. Keep this fact in mind: homosexuals have exactly the same rights as anyone else, and always have. For example, a homosexual is as free to marry as you or I. Look in Rodale's Thesaurus and read the meaning of matrimony: "marriage ceremony or sacrament, wedding, nuptial, holy wedlock etc." Marriage always has, does now and always will mean the union of a man and a woman. It is a sacred status, instituted by God, and is not a convenience for a pair of immoral male deviates to perform debasing degenerate acts of sodomy upon each other and mock its sanctity.

Yet, knowing this, the ACLU seeks to get a "constitutional rights" status for homosexual "marriage", rights to operate their infamous bathhouses [for sodomy orgies], rights allowing them to become "foster parents" *(one can only imagine the twisted ruined lives, and continuing legacy of depravity and pedophilia that situation will foment),* rights to engage in street solicitation [homosexual prostitution] and rights to become a "Big Brother".

Big Brothers is an admirable service organization whose volunteer members act as role-model images for fatherless boys ages 6-12, probably the most impressionable age for growing boys. (I was a 'Big Brother to a fatherless child many years back) The ACLU has brought suit against the Big Brothers of Greater L.A. on charges of discriminating against practicing homosexuals in acceptance of Big Brothers applicants, a procedure the mothers of these innocent youngsters understandably insist on for confidence and peace of mind.

Can you imagine the horror of a child's mother finding out that her son is under the influence of some deviate whose leaders decree the following sentiments. Quoted Statements from "the Gay Revolutionary", by "gay" activist Michael Swift: *"The family unit – spawning ground of lies, betrayals, mediocrity, hypocrisy and violence – will be abolished."*

"We shall sodomize your sons, emblems of feeble masculinity, of your shallow dreams and vulgarities. We shall seduce them in your schools, in your dormitories, in your gyms, in your locker rooms.... legislation shall be passed which engenders love between men." "If you dare to cry faggot, ferry, queer at us, we will stab you in your cowardly hearts, and defile your dead puny bodies." "All churches who condemn us will be closed. You can thank the Jews and their beloved ACLU for this kind of Godless filth.

A little insight into the mentality and violent agenda of one of the groups that the ACLU has gone overboard to assist in attaining their bizarre and frightening goals. By the way, AIDS statistics from every reliable source indicate that it in fact is a dominant homosexual disease. That is to say, its spread was started by homosexuals, it has been growing at alarming rates due almost exclusively to deviate homosexual activity and the rates and percentages of infection of the "gay community" in cities like San Francisco are estimated in one instance by Time Magazine to be as high as 70%!

Even though the real dangers have been critically reassessed (Centers for Disease Control now say that just kissing an infected person is "unsafe"), we will see more "discrimination suits" sponsored by the ACLU involving homosexuals handling our food in restaurants, blood donors etc.. Ironically, the truth is that AIDS is one of the most preventable diseases in the world. Just `don't'. It doesn't matter how many innocent normal people die from this incurable legacy of the "gays", the ACLU will be there to insure none of them get their feelings hurt.

A recent report by our own federal Department of Health and Human Services states that *"Homosexuality is a natural and healthy form of sexual expression"*, and goes so far as to actually charge that Christian churches are largely responsible for teen suicide by creating *"irresolvable internal conflicts for gay youth."* The Baptist and Catholic churches are singled out as *"faiths [that] still portray homosexuality as morally wrong or evil."* Expect this phenomenally twisted perversion of logic and basic morals to be replicated by the pro-homosexual ACLU in upcoming legal battles against our religious institutions and our freedom to worship.

As a point of interest, the ACLU has allies in their battle against exercise of religion in America. These are People For The American Way, Americans United for the Separation of Church and State, The American Jewish Congress and the American Humanist Association. Not surprisingly – <u>ALL JEW DOMINATED</u>.

There are more horror stories, like the one about little ten year old mentally and physically handicapped Audrey Pearson who was forbidden to read her Bible on the school bus. A former

Miss America, Debbie Turner was pressured to drop songs with reference to Christ when making appearances in public schools. In North Carolina, an ACLU suit was brought against County Judge H. William Constangy. His "crime"? – praying for divine guidance at the beginning of court sessions.

Here is a particularly odious recent and very typical type of filth the communist jew ACLU engages in. Just open the story and read. it is brief and heart breaking to see just what depths jews in this country will sink to express their hate for good and truth and hope and love.

Now get this – the ACLU claimed that the Judge's short non-sectarian prayer represented a governmental endorsement of religion, and so discomforted the atheist attorneys as to cause them "irreparable harm", I kid you not! Public libraries in Mississippi have denied use to the Concerned Women For America organization, because they opened their meetings with a prayer.

A pro-life Lincoln Nebraska preacher, trying to preach against the sins of abortion at a pro-abortion [pro-death] demonstration rally, was arrested for "disturbing the peace" [espousing Bible documented morality in a public place]. A law student and six of her associates joined hands and offered a silent prayer for our Supreme Court Justices on the steps of that building, but a policeman appeared suddenly and ordered then to stop their crime of illegally "demonstrating" [praying].

Let me take a moment to clarify two points here. #1: These incidents happened in America, a nation founded upon Christian principles and #2: Since the ACLU likes to mix their anti-Christian bias with myopia with hypocrisy, I would like to quote the portion of our Bill of Rights that deals with religion: "*Congress shall make no law prohibiting the free exercise of religion*".

Read it for yourself. The outrage continues. In Hartford, Wis., third grader Jennifer Backhous was disappointed to find out that she had committed a "criminal" act by decorating her valentine artwork with the following "obscenities" : "*I love Jesus*", and "*Jesus is what love is all about.*" Students in Pennsylvania and Colorado schools have actually been suspended for passing out Christian literature to fellow students. Another student was reprimanded and humiliated for praying silently before an exam, by being sent to the principal's office and forced to publicly deny his religious beliefs by writing 500 times: "*I will not pray in class.*"

Not so long ago, a news release revealed that several Tibetan Buddhist monks were shot dead on the spot by Chinese communist soldiers for just moving their lips in silent prayers. How far away from violent persecution are Christians rights here in the United States? A fifth grade teacher in Denver, Co. had regularly conducted a brief silent reading period for himself and his students utilizing any books of the student's choice, including the classroom library of over 200 selections. One of those books ordered to be removed by authorities was the school's Bible and the other was "The Story of Jesus". He was also forbidden to read the Bible to himself in the classroom, because the students might see him with it, and be influenced by it.

The point of these examples of ACLU supported religious censorship is that citizens should realize that its not just OK; but patriotic, creative and artistic to express feelings of religious desecration and mockery like the tax-payers publicly funded display of Jesus immersed in some deviate's urine ("Piss Christ"), but it is criminal, fascist and unconstitutional to expose Americans to "discredited" and "obsolete" Christian concepts like prayer and the Bible. Are you beginning to get the picture?

The leftist ACLU is well funded with about $15 million a year (*that figure must be doubled or more today*) to wage their war against the American people. Ironically, you can't get a tax deduction if you contribute to many anti-communist organizations in our USA, but the contributions to the communist dominated ACLU are tax deductible! The ACLU celebrated its 50th anniversary by presenting awards to its most revered personalities. They were: David Dellinger, self-admitted communist, Castro apologist, leftist newspaper owner editor and publisher, and who was Jane Fonda's counterpart in visiting Ho chi Minh to demoralize American fighting men in prison and at home where he carried Viet Cong flags to the Capitol, participated in pro-communist riots, burned American flags, and supported dozens of Marxist front groups.

Another ACLU 'poster boy' was Paul Robeson, an identified communist, married to a communist, described by communist Manning Johnson at the 1949 HUAC hearings as wanting "to be the black Stalin among Negroes.", a recipient of the notorious Stalin Peace Prize in 1952, had his birthday celebrated by the Communist Party in the Soviet Union and in Red China, and belonged to so many identified subversive organizations it would take apx. four pages just to list them all!

Julian Bond, a radical Marxist legislator and NAACP star who was a hero to the far left, encouraged Negro violence and sedition, advocated communist rule, and predictably supported and joined many communist support organizations. Lastly, C. Willard Heckel, ACLU defense council for radical communist party official and violent felon, Angela Davis. So much for any notion that the ACLU had changed its "RED" spots.

To show how low an organization can sink and the extent of hypocrisy that can be involved, let us look at former National Advisory Council member, atty. William Kunstler. His reputation for defending murderers, spies, communists and recently, flag burners, is legendary among the Left. Kunstler once bragged that: *"I am a double agent, working from within the system to bring down the system!"* The ACLU has such a perverted sense of values that it actually auctioned off an abortion as a "novel" publicity stunt at a fund-raiser.

The value of a human life to the ACLU? – $30.00.

The ACLU has fought for the "rights" of children to receive contraceptives from clinics without parental notification, and they are adamantly opposed to requiring parents' approval prior to an abortion. An ACLU official once stated:" *In the ACLU's world, parents who resist the sexual revolution should lose their children to the state!"* Thanks to the ACLU, America had entering the 1990s with, as Pat Buchanan described it, *"a justice system where the guilty have never been freer, bolder or more secure, and the innocent have never been more terrified or repressed.*"

Two decades later that frightening truth is even worse if imaginable. An ACLU staffer was once quoted as saying: *"Victims don't have rights!"* The ACLU Policy Guide has over 300 separate entries, of which several mention rights of prisoners, yet not ONE mentions the rights of the victims of crime!

This sick twisted garbage mentality of the ACLU – of protecting the criminal and victimizing the victim – is the basis for ALL jew lies and jew crimes against humanity – especially in IsraHELL. These horrid jews scream for the blood of helpless defenseless women and children at home in schools or hospitals – and blame THEM just for BEING Palestinians.

These good people – who have lived on the land for 1500 years – that the jews stole thanks to the filthy putrid British criminal scum who dragged us into WWII – are made to suffer for their ethnicity. Their 'crime' was that they are Palestinian. They are the victims who don't have any rights! Thus is the sick sociopathic reprobate mentality of the jews – AND their demonic criminal Christ hating ACLU . Have you connected the dots yet?

The factual indictment against the ACLU reveals scores of examples of lies, deceit, contradictions and the most outrageous types of hypocrisy imaginable. Take the situation of AIDS in custodial facilities such as mental hospitals and prisons where even the ACLU admits the patients and inmates have the right to protection from a certain death sentence from virus carriers who engage innocent persons in violent rape or sodomy. Yet, consider the official ACLU policy in opposing the exact measures which would save those innocent lives. The ACLU opposes: (1) Compulsory inmate testing for AIDS, (2) Compulsory segregation of AIDS infected inmates, and (3) Compulsory treatment of inmates with AIDS. This is only one instance in which people will die as a result of ACLU policies!

Let's look at one a little closer to home. On April 16, 1987, Chester Jackson, a student in a Detroit high school was shot to death on the school grounds by another student who had brought the gun to class. A surprise? – hardly. You see, in the previous months, authorities had seized over 450 deadly weapons INSIDE the schools. In a grip of terror, teachers, parents and students pleaded with the school board to authorize school security personnel to use metal detectors to search for these lethal weapons. Of course the ACLU declared the searches "unconstitutional" and a court injunction stopped them.

Shortly thereafter, Mr. and Mrs. Jackson's son lay dead in a pool of his own blood, a tragedy easily preventable by the PREVIOUSLY established policy of using weapons detectors in these high risk gang permeated schools. But it gets "better". Under strong pressure from an outraged community and its mayor, metal detectors were used once again. The Michigan ACLU has indicated their willingness to go back to court, says David Wineman, a member of the ACLU board! Who cares if there is another bloodbath, count on the ACLU to protect the constitutional rights of the killers not to be searched unfairly.

The ACLU is great with noble sounding clichés and phrases like "victimless crimes". Remember the Amtrak disaster in which almost 200 passengers were killed or injured when a train smashed into three Conrail locomotives at over 100 miles per hour? It seems that the

Conrail engineer was under the influence of drugs, and so ignored several warning signals. Why this tragedy then?

Simple – the ACLU in its # 210 "victimless crimes" policy clearly opposes rail worker be drug tested. I wonder if the ACLU bothered to explain to the families of the dead and mangled passengers that their policies were in the public interest since drug abuse is after all, only a "victimless crime." Next time you and your family are passengers on a commercial airliner on a tense foggy night approach to a congested airport, remember the following fact.

Recognized agencies have surveys indicating that on any given day, a significant percentage of ATC personnel at their radar screens with your life quite literally in their hands – are ON DRUGS! How could this insane situation be allowed to exist; just ask the ACLU, if they aren't too busy washing the "blood off their hands" from a previous "victimless" disaster.

Here is an official (Loren Siegel) ACLU statement, and I quote: *"Under no circumstances would we approve of urinalysis, NO MATTER WHAT THE OCCUPATION."* Keep that policy statement in mind next time you hear ACLU "civil liberties" doubletalk or discover that the operator of a passenger train disaster that killed hundreds of people was loaded with hard drugs.

The ACLU insists it represents the best interests of America. Consider this outrageous statement by ACLU President, Norman Dorsen: *"Our positions are mainstream positions."* I presume there is a vestige of truth in that if you consider mainstream America to consist of criminals, homosexuals, spies, drug dealers, obscene entertainers and "artists", child pornographers, sex offenders, atheists and especially communists. These groups of people comprise the majority of ACLU client activity, and that is a fact – PERIOD! The outrage and insult to decent Americans by the ACLU seems endless. .

There are over 400 late term abortions a DAY in this country, performed with the official blessings of the ACLU. I'm not debating the "life begins at conception" issue here. I'm talking about little people with hair, fingers, toes, ears, eyes and a beating heart: beating that is, until they are ripped apart by the crushing forceps of the abortionist, then thrown into the garbage for the rats and roaches to eat. And if you believe that is exaggerated melodramatics, then see a documentary video narrated by actor Charlton Heston called `Eclipse of Reason'; you will never forget it!

The ACLU along with the NOW organization and Planned Parenthood are endorsed by and more importantly, ACCEPT the endorsement of, virtually every pro-communist, subversive and lesbian/homosexual organization in the USA! This may be a little known fact, but nevertheless, there are, documents to substantiate it.

Evidently, unborn children have no civil rights, or even a right to live in the eyes of the leftist ACLU. One can only wonder how much money is donated to the ACLU coffers by abortionists, whose grisly trade is encouraged and made secure by the "pro-death" ACLU. But of course, the ACLU is only defending women's "reproductive rights", and "freedom of choice" as if they some how mysteriously and inexplicably got pregnant.

The ACLU believes it is solely the parent's responsibility to prevent exposure of pornography to their children – how convenient. Case in point: when an ACLU lawyer was asked by a pornography commission chairman, if she thought the government had "any interest whatsoever" in a situation in which an adult attempted to give or sell literature portraying sodomy or bestiality to a 12 year old child, she answered: "No, I don't..". That is the jew mind at work.

Let's see now: the ACLU sponsors killing viable children in the womb, then those that survive can have their lives ruined as child porn "stars", and if they make it to school they could be shot or stabbed to death by mostly Negro gangbanger thugs whose rights are insured by the ACLU. So much for the ACLU's love and respect for our children.

Destroying Christianity and any notion of the worship of God is a paramount goal of the ACLU that must be accomplished in order to fulfill its founders' dream of a communist America. That "there is no god" is an essential premise and basis for Marxism. As Lenin once stated: *"Atheism is a natural and inseparable portion of Marxism, of the theory and practice of Scientific Socialism."* When the existence of God is denied by the communists, the authority of the Ten Commandments and absolute standards of right and wrong as well as the basics of good and evil are negated, and consequently so is the basis of all morality. Man is on the playing field of life with no referee or rule book. The result of this jew ACLU dream is that the winners of any conflict can decide on what the rules of conduct and morality should be.

The examples are all around us. Look at Dictator Fidel Castro's Marxist paradise in Cuba — an Orwellian nightmare where the State is "God", and one in eight Cubans has risked horrors at sea and sometimes certain death to escape. Castro currently maintains Cuba's own version of the Gulag Archipelago, where thousands of Cubans are tortured for their Christian beliefs. Read "Against All Hope" by Armando Valladares, who suffered twenty-two years in a Cuban Gulag. His crime (?) –professing to be a Christian. In Ortega's Soviet-backed Nicaragua, a once peaceful land of gentle people that this writer has known for over three decades, hundreds of thousands of refugees left their homes and friends to escape that godless and terrifying reality. I know – I did intelligence work there during that period and I was in Cuba the same month that Castro took Havana.

In Cambodia, Marxist/Leninist ideologue Pol Pot literally slaughtered millions of innocent human beings to create the "new man" of godless communism. In Soviet Russia, we now know that master butcher Josef Stalin exterminated tens of millions of his own people in order to eradicate the bourgeoisie and other religious undesirables. This happened because there is NO BASIS FOR MORALITY in an atheist society; humans are considered nothing more than animals.

Communism was in the beginning and still is the driving force of the ACLU. One need look no further than the daily newspaper to see this evil force at work, always of course in the guise of defending the rights of the people. If a child utters a prayer in school, the ACLU is there like the Gestapo to silence it. If a Christian educator should dare to suggest anything religious and moral to the class, or read the Holy Scripture, he/she will soon be stopped and reprimanded by the ACLU as well as the amoral and spineless judges who serve the evil interests of the communist ACLU.

These blasphemies by jews against our freedoms our heritage and our Lord are committed with the assistance of the ACLU on a daily basis. THIS MUST STOP! Look at what you the AmeriKan people have become. Morally lazy shallow hypocrites whose sense of moral outrage has long been extinguished by childish nonsense like the NFL Stupid Bowl and NASCAR and Keeping up with the Karadashians on the jew 'Talmud Vision.' SHAME UPON YOU!

A painting of Christ on the cross that hung on a school wall for 25 years was ordered to be removed under threat from the ACLU. Nativity scenes at Christmas time that bring so much joy and feeling of kindness and brotherhood are a serious crime in the eyes of the ACLU. As of the past three years – the traditional nativity scene that has been an American Christian tradition since colonial times has been trashed by the jews!

Do you know what jew filth presently is officially displayed in the White House of our Christian founded nation to replace the Baby Jesus Nativity? That evil jew 'Devil's pitchfork' (menorah). This two story high demonic monstrosity is now a reminder to ALL Americans from ALL jews at Christmas that" SATAN'S CHILDREN NOW RULE AMERIKA" Jesus not allowed!

So evil are these jews that even the "Christ of the Abyss", a dramatic statue of our Lord that resides underwater in a natural reef at Florida's Pennekamp Park, an inspiring sight for divers visiting from all over the world to share, is an affront to the atheistic jew ACLU.

The Jew dominated ACLU finds ANY notion of God offensive and intolerable. It must be eliminated from our schools, our money, our town meetings, our buildings, our universities, our military, and I'm sure if they had their way, from our churches and homes as well. The ACLU has already been successful in making it ILLEGAL just about everywhere else — a pretty impressive accomplishment, considering this country was founded on religious premises — just in case anyone has forgotten OR bought into jew lies that we were not.

An ACLU member can never feel the "lump in their throat" when honoring what our flag proudly stands for, because they hate and loathe it. The cover of one of their brochures shows an American flag, with the following caption at the bottom – "THIS IS NOTHING". The insult to our heritage continues.

The damage that the ACLU has done to our society, our peace and our security can probably never be measured in everyday terms. The politics of the ACLU aren't just anti-religious or anti-American family value – their influence on our society is a deadly dangerous threat. We have already seen that the collective "moral conscience" of the ACLU is an oxymoron. The legacy of anti-Americanism, pro-communism and anti-Godism that have been the aggregate agenda of the ACLU has created a yellow stain of shame on the fabric of American values. It is this fabric that is the binding cloth of what we have been, what we are and what we will evolve to become morally. The thread in that fabric is the family and its traditional Christian values.

It was that way when this great country began from its humble origins, and it will remain an unchangeable truism until such time as the fabric is cleansed and once again made whole – or is unraveled and rots away, which after all has been the ultimate goal of the communist ACLU for over 95 years. I will leave the reader with one last foreboding omen.

This most evil of American communist Jew dominated organizations was "born" in October 1917, exactly the same month and year as the birth of the Jew dominated, financed and supported Soviet Communist revolution in Russia, that has thus far claimed over 200 million innocent lives worldwide for the Jew 'cause'. Was it by coincidence or by design?

OCTOBER, 2012
A JEW DENYING HIS LIES IS LIKE A SKUNK USING 'BAN'

Sometimes I allow the hatred I have for the diabolical jews who have caused such worldwide mass suffering and death – to affect my emotions, and I am criticized by some readers who although they know virtually nothing about my personal life- say I take it too personally.

Well – I have a news flash for those who would mock my anger and grief. You see – you jews – it IS personal – VERY personal. Your lies have not only ruined lifelong friendships – ruined my business – my relationship with my own sons – the honor of the uniform I wore – the love I once had for the goodness of my people and my country . AND – as if THAT were not enough grief and permanent damage – you just had to include murder!

The Godless demons of your tribe have murdered millions of innocent people in a part of the world where I had relatives – and it so happens that SOME Of them were specifically related to me by marriage. You bet its personal!

This is a true story about the kindness of one people and the barbaric sadistic cruelty of another 'people'.

When I was married to a Ukrainian woman – in the course of our conversations about jews communists and war criminals – she shared this experience she remembered her grandmother telling her. You must remember this. Tanya's grandmother was Ukrainian and before Stalin's purges – loyal to the 'Mother Country'. She was NOT a Marxist however – and was like most Ukrainians – a devout Orthodox Christian.

They were of course in the heart of the 'breadbasket' of the Ukraine and were self sustaining farmers who owned a small bit of their own land – Kulaks . This combination of circumstances are identical to one of the major premises of what makes America American !'. Our origin was MOST certainly Christian [no other book I have read points this out so convincingly as Bill Federer's " America's God And Country".] and many of our heartland people are hard working farmers and land owners.

Back to the story. Her grandmother recalled the horrors of the Stalin purges or planned mass starvation of the Kulaks. This REAL holocaust known as the Holodomor was executed by Stalin's jew 'Cheka' in 1932-33 as all Kulaks were forced under penalty of death to surrender ALL of their crops – personal food and food producing equipment.

The result was a forced mass starvation called 'collectivization – a terror-famine during which the Soviet jew criminals orchestrated a terror that took over seven million lives. The grandmother watched as her sons and husband were murdered right before her eyes by the Cheka – who were identified as Jews. They stole or destroyed her crops and lectured her on the evils of land ownership and her religious "superstition". Her daughters were raped but left to live. She and the daughters managed to somehow repair and keep the farm going.

Fast forward to the German invasion of the Soviet Union during what was known as Operation Barbarossa. In the Summer of 1941 there was a part of the 3rd Panzer Army going right through the middle of the Ukraine and her farm was in the center of their march. Apparently a Panzer unit commander had ordered his company to stop and rest on her farm. She was terrified – and could only imagine what would come next. The Soviet jew secret police had lied to the Ukrainians of the brutality of the Germans and what murderous animal they were when in reality of course it was the Soviet jews who were the master butchers. This was all that she knew about the Germans – jew gossip. She braced for the worst.

The Panzer unit commander approached her door – introduced himself and apologized for the inconvenience stating that he must bivouac his troops and tanks there briefly. He told her that they had to utilize some of the farm's food but that she would be fairly paid in Deutschmarks for anything they used. Apparently she understood German. Not unusual for Ukrainians to be multilingual, as Tanya – her granddaughter (my wife) spoke FOUR languages fluently.

Noticing that she was protective of the surviving daughters – he further stated that she had his word that no German soldier would molest them in any way. He went further to assure her by stating that should there be any such behavior – he would personally deal with the matter and the offending soldier would be dealt with severely – perhaps shot. He kept his word and there were no such incidents.

The grandmother found herself working in the field with the girls picking potatoes the next morning (apparently a major crop there) and the Panzer officer walked up beside her – removed his hat, gloves, shirt and weapons and got on his knees and began digging potatoes with her. Tanya relayed to me that her grandmother was shocked – and blurted out something like; "Herr Major – you cannot do this kind of menial work- you are an officer – look- you will get your tunic soiled "etc.

Apparently she was genuinely shocked for 2 reasons. First of course she was from the 'old' school' where Soviet military officers would never engage in such menial labor. – And also – of course – the horror stories about the Germans that she had been told by the very cold-blooded murderers of her family.

The officer smiled and said to her that he and his men were glad to help with the chores, and it was the least they could do for the inconvenience they had caused. This Ukrainian grandmother never forgot his German officers' kindness – even though he and his soldiers were 'the enemy'. He and his men had treated her with kindness and civility while her 'own people' had committed these horrible brutal sadistic crimes upon her family.

My wife, Tanya told me that her Grandmother never forgot how she was treated by that German officer – and remained bitter against her own people for their unforgivable brutality. Can you imagine? Say in America – such a circumstance where our own people are such hated monsters – and the only lenient or compassionate treatment came at the hands of the foreign enemy INVADERS!

I believe it was true – as Tanya had no reason or incentive to fabricate such a story. Had I not heard it direct from my wife – perhaps I would have thought of it as possibly fabricated not knowing the source. The only lies regarding many of these horrors are those told by the jew criminals themselves. Jews are VERY VERY good at lying – just like their father Satan – who is the 'father of ALL lies'.

Jew lies got us involved in TWO world wars with Germany and more recently two other major serial wars in Iraq and Afghanistan none of which had the countries in question attacked us in any way whatsoever. Jew lies helped demonize Hitler and the German people over and over again and again. Jews lied about the murder of 20 thousand Polish officers at Katyn – blamed it on Hitler when it was Stalin and his jews. The hollow hoax is nothing more than a profitable business for the jews and was created by even more jew lies.

I even caught our former jew POTUS – ***"that terrible Swedish jew"*** – war criminal mass murderer, 'Kike' Eisenhower – as he SWORE on the Holy Book regarding more lies about the Hollow hoax. I can easily prove that jew lied to slander an entire nation. He may be beyond justice now – but being jew like he was – he is still a liar and murderer.

Jew lies by themselves could fill a small library. They have lied to man and God for centuries. This next quote pretty much proves everything I have said. Jesus to the jews ; ***" Your father is the Devil and a murderer and is the father of ALL lies – AND these lusts of that demonic father -YOU WILL DO!"****....* No further questions – I rest my case.

OCTOBER, 2012
WHERE I STAND ON TRUTH

I am sick to death of seeing people pretending to support TRUTH and then doing everything they can to discredit it bastardize it – demonize it – disenfranchise it and treat like used toilet paper. The truth is inviolate eternal and indestructible. It is like a bubble under water. You cannot tie an anchor to it You cannot make it just go away. It will always find it's way to the light above. I WILL fight to insure TRUTH stays in the bright pure light of day.

God favors those who live in the truth. Speaking the TRUTH is a MANDATE from God – not a suggestion so why are we in America today so devoted to lies upon lies upon lies. Why do we worship those who lie the most? Why do we even prefer the lies of greedy multimillionaire reprobate reptiles like Joel Osteen even when we KNOW he is lying? Why will tens of millions of us cheerfully elect the mega liar of our choice on Election Day?

Why do we – such an advantaged nation of information available 24-7 – still have most citizens citizens continue to believe lies about the USS Liberty – lies about the 9-11 treason – lies about the economy – lies about the poor innocent people we murder by the millions at the request of people who the Lord has exposed as the children of the greatest liar of all times.

And why do fifty million BaptDUHS – supposed followers of the Lord Christ support the endless dazzling incomprehensible lies of the very liars who have destroyed their souls with hatred wickedness warmongering and racism so as to cruelly mock the TRUTH of the teachings of Christ?

So important in Christianity is the virtue of TRUTH – that when Thomas asked Christ – ‘ how would the people know the way to come to Him ‘ – he used a short phrase with THREE dramatically SIGNIFICANT words WAY- TRUTH & LIFE.

Speaking the TRUTH is also one of the Ten Commandments.

This spineless apparently considered obligatory comment was present on Veterans Today’s site. It is as if they FEARED the use of the actual word TRUTH – lest it embarrass Satan’s children.

“The views expressed herein are the views of the author exclusively and not necessarily the views of VT or any other VT authors, affiliates, advertisers, sponsors or partners”

I am becoming more and more disillusioned with Dr Barrett as his rhetoric becomes more and more concessionary not unlike the DANGEROUSLY misleading – good (“ordinary”) jew and the bad (“Zionist”) jew mantra that we so often emblematic of the M.O. of ‘controlled assets’ In a recent article on VT he uses the apologist term “ordinary jew” over and over again.

I ask myself- which jews are Kevin so concerned about upsetting – wink wink ? According to Dr. Barrett:” No sane person can deny that Nazism and Zionism are mirror images of each other“.

Well sir – call me sentimental- call me insane – but I DO deny the validity of your irrational statement. One is an acronym of a political party whose goal was to restore prosperity sovereignty and self respect to a people who were totally morally culturally and economically enslaved and oppressed by the most pernicious amoral Godless filth on earth. A demonic race of Satan’s children (by BIBLICAL DECREE) who by their lusts greed usury and general putrid conduct – transformed one of the cultural centers of the world into a morally and economically bankrupted rotted corpse. Hitler by himself transformed A decimated Germany into a proud nation which even if for a brief time in history- prospered even as America suffered a devastating jew created depression.

The other term is simply another stripe/ilk of jew filth that brought about our 'great depression' – much of it under treasonous communist jew 'polesney idiote' (useful idiot) war monger FDR.

Hitler kicked the kikes out of the German banking business and the nation thrived grew and prospered with virtually NO unemployment. In stupid America we embraced the treasonous jew Fed monster and our communist jew loving POTUS and went down the tubes – where we are back again – at the bottom. Our kike kontrolled kindergarten mentality educational system never taught you that did they?

Also according to Dr. Barrett : "Only stupid racist bigot paid Mossad shills would blame ordinary jews" (there's that 'ordinary jew' term – AGAIN) for their factually committed crimes of three thousand years as condemned by our Founding Fathers – hundreds of history's most prominent figures – prophets – Apostles – God the Father and God the Son just for openers! With little exception – ALL of the condemnations warnings were directed at pre-Zionist jew bastards. OH – excuse my insensitivity. I meant to say " ORDINARY JEW" – bastards.

Logical conclusion – All of these people listed above (including non- 'people' = God) are 'STUPID' – 'RACIST' 'BIGOTS' and 'PAID SHILLS' of 'MOSSAD' – an international terrorist group ?

Come on Kevin, get a grip – go visit "WHAT WORLD FAMOUS MEN SAID ABOUT THE (ORDINARY) JEWS"

You have a good mind and are on track – MOST of the time. Please sir- loose that "ordinary jew" crap.

Tell whoever or whatever is controlling you to piss off. Lose the baggage and rejoin the TRUE band of brothers

Virtually ALL of the jews I have ever met or seen or read about or spoken with – both here in the States and in IsraHELL and dozens of other countries are pure unadulterated lying reprobate scum. Factually – I had seldom if ever actually met any jews who proclaimed to be Zionists – just those 'ordinary jews' you apparently loves so much.

Dr. Barrett – lets look at just who your precious 'ordinary jews' really are.. The jews who murdered Christ were 'ordinary jews'. The jews who wrecked my marriage by vicious lies were 'ordinary jews'. The jews who murdered part of my former wife's Kulak family in Ukraine were 'ordinary jews'. The jews who I see screaming every day for the blood of innocent Palestinians are 'ordinary jews'. The jew I saw attempting to murder a 5 year old defenseless helpless Palestinian child in Gaza? An'ordinary jew'? The IDF officers who supported these unconscionable murders were 'ordinary jews' The scum who mock our Lord 24-7 on their 'ADULT SWIM' Talmud Vision filth are 'ordinary jews'.

The jews who I see committing homosexual perversions in public parades are 'ordinary jews'. The putrid scum who promote the serial mega murders of the unborn child for greed in this country are 'ordinary jews'. The Goldbergs and the Silversteins who are my 'ordinary jew' neighbors – smile to our faces but mock our Lord as a bastard and our children as cattle behind our backs The pukes who promote white slavery porn kings real estate thieves prostitutes and promote violence sex hollowhoax lies evolution promote blasphemy profanity false prophets Satanism and lewdness on their Talmud Vision networks are more of your 'ordinary (albeit) wealthy jews'.

The words below exude the handiwork of a lawyer – not a dedicated patriot – perhaps a Jewish lawyer?

"The views expressed herein are the views of the author exclusively and not necessarily the views of VT or any other VT authors, affiliates, advertisers, sponsors or partners"

Anyone – especially an American should not need the services of a lawyer for speaking or writing the truth in behalf of the welfare of his nation and fellow patriots,- now should he? The TRUTH has always been its own defense

Imagine for a moment – If Jesus of Nazareth felt He must consult a lawyer before He preached the Gospel – lest He offended Satan or his children – or the Prophets had to seek 'legal' council before they would speak truths that might ' hurt some poor jew's feelings' – such that each and every stern proclamation in the NT had the obligatory 'disclaimer'.

"The 'views' expressed herein are the 'views' of the Son of God exclusively and not necessarily the 'views' of God the Father or his Prophets authors affiliates advertisers sponsors or partners." (legal council of the most high)

Now picture – if you can – a wimpy Jesus and the Prophets and the Apostles acting like the average spineless PC 'won't get involved' Merkan in today's jew occupied attorney intimidated suffocating oppressive atmosphere.

In view of this restraint of the inviolate truth – Jesus might have been 'intimidated' to say it thus – had he not consulted first with the celestial law firm of 'Shovel & Smoke':

John 8 -44 a timid Jesus – to the jews: "Ye are beginning to act a bit like Satan – to whom you may possibly be somehow distantly related – a being who has been suspected on occasion – of speaking falsehoods as well as doing lusty things which might influence your own conduct. Why – you might even be persuaded to commit murder -although I am not suggesting it – so please do not take this personally."

Or this 'modified epistle' from Paul – in Thessalonians 2-14-15 – also hesitant to speak God's unvarnished truth without legal counsel – lest the TRUTH 'hurt some evil person's feelings' :

"For you, brethren, became imitators of the churches of God in Christ Jesus that are in Judea, Ye should be more sensitive of others' feelings, lest you also endure the same sufferings at the hands of your own countrymen, even as they did from the Jews, who were said to have ignored both the Lord Jesus and the prophets, and were not hospitable to us. Rumor has it that they are not really on best terms with God, but hostile in some very rare instances – and only to few men,"

For those unfamiliar with either selection – go to your Bible and read the ACTUAL AUTHENTIC statements of both. There you will read the TRUTH – undistorted or twisted or compromised by politically correct cowards who cared less about forthright honesty and more about potentially bruising the egos of Satan's children

It is so refreshing to find a NEW patriotic truth site in which the owner(s) had the integrity and balls to say that he cares not a farthing for "VIEWS" – described by both Webster and Oxford as an 'outlook' – 'an opinion' – 'a slant' – 'a perception' – or 'a mental attitude' . I can count the ones I know of presently whose goal is TRUTH – not opinions – with a single digit

OPINIONS are like assholes – EVERYBODY HAS ONE! – and unless you are some individual of world acclaim – noted for your extraordinary wisdom and knowledge – nobody of above average mentality will give a flying rat's ass what your 'OPINION' is, if the facts and the TRUTH are also available – as on my site and the aforementioned few..

Every man has a right to be wrong in his opinions. But no man has a right to be wrong in his facts. - Bernard M. Baruch (1870-1965) American financier and political consultant.

The majority have no other reason for their opinions than that they are the fashion. Samuel Johnson (1709-1784) British author.

The man who never alters his opinion is like standing water, and breeds reptiles of the mind. William Blake (1757-1827) British poet and painter.

Errors of opinion may be tolerated where reason is left free to combat it. Thomas Jefferson (1743-1826) Third president of the United States.

Things are not to be judged good or bad merely because the public think so. Publius Cornelius Tacitus (55-117) Roman historian.

A great deal of laziness of mind is called liberty of opinion.
Unknown Source

A man is getting along on the road to wisdom when he begins to realize that his opinion is just an opinion.
Unknown Source

Opinion is the medium between knowledge and ignorance. Plato (BC 427-BC 347) Greek philosopher.

The history of human opinion is scarcely anything more than the history of human errors. Voltaire (1694-1778) French writer and historian.

An obstinate person does not hold opinions; they hold him. Alexander Pope (1688-1744) English poet and satirist.

You're entitled to your own opinions. Your are not entitled to your own facts. Unknown Source

Opinions alter, manners change, creeds rise and fall, but the moral laws are written on the table of eternity.
Lord Acton (1834-1902) English historian.

The deadliest contagion is majority opinion.
Unknown Source

The average man's opinions are generally of more value to himself than to anyone else. Unknown Source

Opinions are the cheapest commodities in the world.
Unknown Source

Overheard at a recent political rally:" I don't think there are enough morons out there to re-elect him!" I didn't hear which one – so take your pick of which 'flavor' of Christ hater. The lying black Marxist or the lying white warmonger – both are demons with black hearts and black souls – and both would destroy America for the jews.

If you want mob mentality OPINIONS – go to bars or barber shops or political rallies – as you will find an abundance of fools and imbeciles more than willing to share their opinions on matter of which they are abysmally ignorant.

I have dedicated my life to truth knowledge and wisdom and I deal in FACTS = things asserted to be true as a basis for reasoning PERIOD! I do not write fiction – I write TRUTH as best as I can perceive it from either personal experience or from sources I have personally investigated and determined sound – or from trusted individuals of normally long time acquaintance respect and trust whose integrity and credentials are sound and impeccable.

As an author I must first capture the attention of my readers. Every successful writer has his or her style. Mark Glenn has his – Brother Nathanael has his own – Incog Man has his very own and so I have mine. We all use different lexicon syntax adjectives satire emphasis added or even humor to make the point – but we all stick to authenticity and factualness.

Re READ the presumptuous insulting intrinsic arrogant insolence of this statement posted by VETERANS TODAY.

"The views expressed herein are the views of the author exclusively and not necessarily the views of VT or any other VT authors, affiliates, advertisers, sponsors or partners"

Keep in mind that VIEWS and FACTS are mutually exclusive in essence meaning and substance. Hold that fact in mind. Now see that the site owners by this policy statement – have already decided to demean the writer's potentially well researched factual TRUTH and demeaned and bastardized them down to the level of worthless opinions (views) regardless of any obvious truth integrity and credentials.

Allow me to translate their doublespeak in the red disclaimer. “we will take ALL of the verifiable FACTS which the author has presented even if undeniably true and reduce their value to inane subjective prattle. The REAL reason we state this nonsense is to dazzle the less astute readers with the notion that we are just trying to seem ‘fair and unbiased. ”

That is how such statements come across to me – and I’ll bet I’m not the only one who sees that.

Go to this site and read the article and the comments. See for yourselves of what I speak

http://www.veteranstoday.com:80/2012/10/15/israel-tries-to-assassinate-top-us-general-then-invites-him-for-tea/

Note that in the comments section the ONLY reader who used the word jew was immediately personally insulted and ad hominem attacked by a jew troll using a laughingly transparent demonization of the other honest commenter.

The polite statement void of any profane language was brief and non specifically directed and arguable 100% true as to the nature of the VAST majority of jews that I have personally experienced not only in IsraHELL but all over the world — IN PERSON!!! Remember most Zionists are not jews and were a fairly modern creation having nothing to do with the time frame during which ‘ordinary jews’ were expelled from virtually every civilized nation on earth for committing very unordinary crimes against humanity.

So that you understand: Only a small part of the jews are ‘religious’ Of that small part – they all worship Satan (read John 8-44) Judaism is a ‘religion’ based on sharp business practices revolving around MONEY! Zionism is the political manifestation of Judaism. Roughly half of American jews consider themselves as Zionists. The percentage in modern IsraHELL is supposedly about the same. The current approval rating of their war criminal leadership is supposedly at about 30 %

Knowing what I do about the evil nature of the people in IsraHELL – his rating is probably because he hasn’t murdered enough Palestinian civilians recently to satisfy the normal jew blood lust for defenseless children.

An ethnicity as a people in their collective entirety do NOT get their asses kicked our of ONE HUNDRED AND NINE NATIONS all over the world – over a period of NINETEEN HUNDRED YEARS because they have big noses or are insufferably clannish or even being collective pathological liars. This unforgivably horrid putrid rancid murderous greedy evil nature of the jews who had Christ murdered was centuries upon centuries before Zionism became a reality. BAD ‘ORDINARY JEWS’ BEFORE ZIONISM INVENTED. GET IT?

VT has several moderators’ staff etc that should have IMMEDIATELY sent the lying deceitful slanderously offensive man who viciously attacked another commenter for simply being

TRUTHFUL – to cyber hell. I will certainly not allow that kind of purposefully disruptive Godless demonic filth to show his or her face on MY site if I am made aware.

I produce and disseminate only what I know to be true and do not allow ANY lies or slanderous attacks to be to be perpetrated on my site if possible. All untruths are not lies. However a purposeful lie is a SIN! Our Constitution did NOT promote the 'freedom of purposeful LIES' as a right. Our Lord Himself did in fact expose Satan as the father of ALL lies as well as the father of the horrid jews – John 8-44

Freedom of dissemination of the truth by speech or journalism must be defended – be it embarrassing or not – with equal zeal of the attack of lies and liars. However- NO known LIES should be tolerated lest they be taken at face value as TRUTH and thus poison the minds of our young or poorly informed – the latter being legion in number, in our now dumbed down jew run nation!.

Ignorance of the TRUTH is America's greatest conceptual intellectual enemy. Jews themselves- the most prodigious liars on earth and most virulent promoters of progressive ignorance of our people – our greatest mortal ETHNIC enemy.

The MAIN reason we have lost virtually ALL of our freedoms ALL of our goodness and ALL of our MORALITY – and consequently our nation itself ? MASS CRIMINAL LEVEL IGNORANCE.

My site is a place of truth. Often not what you WANT To hear – but ALWAYS what you NEED to hear. Sometimes the truth is ugly – so If you cannot handle anything true that is NOT all nice and warm and fuzzy and satisfies your "itchy ears" .

Then get the hell out and go spend the rest of your useless lives glued to the Talmud-Vision and your all so important Stupid Bowl NFL 'games' (as in diversions for children) and all the other inane foolish useless amusements for your infantile oyster brains. But don't worry – as you will have lots of company in your future residences at the 'Halliburton Arms' reeducation facilities for sheeple run by your jewish occupation friends.
"The views expressed herein are the views of the author exclusively and not necessarily the views of VT or any other VT authors, affiliates, advertisers, sponsors or partners" (A concessionary cowards pledge)

MY PERSONAL policy pledge of my SITE refutes the submissive dribble stated above and is as follows:

"The FACTS and TRUTHS expressed herein are the UNDENIABLE FACTS and IMMUTABLE TRUTHS painstakingly assembled by the author who reports to NO ONE and NO advertiser and NO sponsor and NO handler and NO MASTER save the Constitution of the United States and the Lord – and whose motives are pure and honorable in the pursuit of justice honor truth wisdom and freedom for my sovereign nation."

I am concerned only with the truth and exposing the enemies of my family my freedoms my religion and my nation. I ask no quarter and I will give none. If you agree with me and want your country back – stand by me and learn the TRUTH that our jew newspapers and our jew Talmud vision will not allow.

If you still believe that bought and paid for evil self serving useful idiot reptiles like Rush or Beck or jews like Sekulow or Alex Jones or Jon Stewart – you are delusional sick and twisted beyond help – so stay the hell off MY site. ONLY patriots are welcome here. You know who you are. Welcome home. The fight for our nation's freedom continues. To the wicked jews I say: MOLON LABE!

OCTOBER, 2012
AND TO THE REPUBLIC FOR WHICH IT ONCE STOOD

As Dr. Franklin was leaving the 1st constitutional convention 1787 – he was asked by a lady: "Dr. Franklin – do we have a Republic, or a Monarchy" – to which he responded : "Madam – we have a REPUBLIC – if you can keep it."

" I pledge allegiance to the flag of the United States of America AND to the – REPUBLIC – for which IT STANDS"

Get it – morons! Get it Democraps? Get it – all you lazy imbecile irresponsible brain-sharing NFL couch potatoes who have never contributed one iota of your time to the love and preservation and protection and education of your own country – what it represents – what it stands for – and the freedoms which we have now lost – that our Founding Fathers fought bled and died for?

THIS NATION – THE UNITED STATES OF AMERICA – IS A REPUBLIC – GET IT? (or at least was – before ZOG)

It was NOT founded as a monarchy – an oligarchy – a dictatorship or a volatile unstable perilous Democracy – but then after all – I would wager my pink slip that you would be hard pressed to find ANY of your fellow feeder sheeple pals who could render an even half way intelligent discourse of the difference between our blessed Republic and the so very anti-American characteristics of a 'nice sounding' DEMOCRACY.

Here is an excellent video that will inform and enlighten. It should be required study for ALL public schools – but of course since the occupying jews obfuscated our freedoms of speech and press – our children will go on living a lie unless you share these truths with them.

To those of you the few who were taught and faithfully have stood by these simple truths at the foot of your parents or elders or teachers – may God bless and keep you – as you are the ONLY vanguard standing between what our country was meant to be and the avalanches of lies and deceptions and frauds created through purposeful evil as well as criminal ignorance. You will probably already poses the wisdom that will reveal and you are encourage to pass it on to the misinformed young and our criminally ignorant adults – at least those who still care what happens.

Those combined effects are seeds of our own destruction and the guarantors of the destruction of our Constitutional freedoms. Such events will herald the inevitable transition from a Republic to a stinking lawless Democracy to lawless anarchy and finally of course as has happened in every failed democracy throughout history – a tyrannical form of dictatorship where any 'laws' are made by and for the rulers themselves.

In case you tailgating morons have forgotten or never bothered to know – here is one of the frightening signs that even some our own Presidents have now boldly shown their utter treason and contempt for the very document they swore to uphold protect and defend against ALL enemies – including our own home grown domestic enemies -THEMSELVES!

Statement by former POTUS George W Bush – traitor – war criminal – liar – deceiver and coward. At a briefing during the Gulf War – as he was cautioned by an advisor, that he was violating the Constitutional rights of American citizens (remember the wiretap scandals) – he angrily responded "I don't give a goddamn, I'm the President and the Commander-in-Chief. Do it my way." "Mr. President," one aide in the meeting said. "There is a valid case that the provisions in this law undermine the Constitution." "Stop throwing the Constitution in my face," Bush screamed back. "It's just a God-damned piece of paper!"

To the coward war criminal mass murderer traitor and blasphemer my comment is: That " God-damned piece of paper just happens to be the Constitution and Bill Of Rights of MY country Mr. SCUMBAG. I took an oath to defend it even from reprobate treasonous filth like you. I and a lot of other good loyal Americans VOLUNTARILY put ourselves in harm's way to defend those laws and guarantees and we take no small offense to your blasphemous treason against the American people."

Those of you who have served HONORABLY before Bush's jew wars know what that oath was all about. Punks who volunteered to murder helpless civilians in Iraq and Afghanistan for the stinking demonic jews need not consider ANYTHING honorable about their war criminal conduct – as I and other decent veterans hold them in utter contempt.

That was when I finally left the Republican Party as did millions of others, in utter disgust. I should have left the day he put my country ahead of the stinking stolen jew terrorist nation of IsraHELL and initiated a war against millions of innocent people in a country which had never attacked our country nor its citizens in any way -.another act of treason against America.

NO I have not forgotten Obama's trashing of our laws and rights but after all -since half of the pint of this paper is to rightfully demonize the concept of a Democracy (read: Democrat Party) it should be quite obvious that I consider ANYTHING To do with that party as wicked and anti - American as it can be.

Sadly – there is no more Republican Party today and that is why I left it after 9-11 The ONLY 'thing' we as Americans have left of our heritage is of course our Constitution and Bill of Rights – which has been trashed over and over with jew filth like the 'Patriot Act' and 'Homeland Security' – both smelling like dictatorial Stalinist Marxist tyranny

But I digress. Back to our Republic VS a Democracy.

Thomas Jefferson's quote: " Democracy is nothing more than mob rule where 51% of the people may take away the rights of the other 49."

By the way, in regards to the Jefferson's astute observation – this question to all the dumb blacks who are supporting the 'mob rule' Democrat Party. Since you guys are a minority and the basic proviso of the Democrats 'Democracy' ideology is the majority -not laws – rule. Aren't you the least bit worried that they can vote any time to negate any of your wishes or grievances – unlike a Republican form of government where the already existing laws protect minorities in the Bill Of Rights.

Here is an unlikely but revealing source for a quote about Democracy that reinforces the warnings of the founding Fathers: Karl Marx = "Democracy is the road to Socialism"

Obama is POTUS and he is a 'DEMOCRAT' whose party supports the principles of 'DEMOCRACY'. So on what road is headed down? Why, to SOCIALISM of course as Marx stated.

Not convinced? Type (Google) in these two words "democracy socialism"

Number of hits? seventeen million nine hundred thousand! (17,900,000) Do we 'get it' yet?

The evils of a Democracy were so reviled by our government that a US training manual was published in 1928 that was required reading for all immigrants seeking citizenship as well and all military inductees – so that people might learn the dramatic difference between a Democracy and a Republic. Here is an exact copy in its entirety:

Show it to your children .Teach them well. Teach them the TRUTH Annoy a jew- and show this to a fellow patriot.

TM 2000-25

1 TRAINING MANUAL | WAR DEPARTMENT,
No. 2000-25 | Washington, November 30, 1928

CITIZENSHIP

Prepared under the direction of the
Chief of Staff
This manual supersedes Manual of Citizenship Training

The use of the publication " The Constitution of the United States," by Harry Atwood, is by permission and courtesy of the author.
The sources of other references is shown in the bibliography.

TM 2000-25
CITIZENSHIP 118-120

Democracy:
A government of the masses.
Authority derived through mass meeting or any other form of "direct' expression.
Results in mobocracy.
Attitude toward property is communistic—negating property rights.
Attitude toward law is that the will of the majority shall regulate. whether it be based upon deliberation or governed by passion, prejudice, and impulse, without restraint or regard to consequences.
Results in demagogism, license, agitation, discontent, anarchy.

TM 2000-25
120-121
CITIZENSHIP
Republic:
Authority is derives through the election by the people of public officials best fitted to represent them.
Attitude toward property is respect for laws and individual rights, and a sensible economic procedure.
Attitude toward law is the administration of justice in accord with fixed principles and established
evidence, with a strict regard to consequences.
A greater number of citizens and extent of terror may be brought within its compass.
Avoids the dangerous extreme of either tyranny or mobocracy.
Results in statesmanship, liberty, reason, justice, contentment, and progress.
Is the " standard form " of government throughout the world.

A republic is a form of government under a constitution which provides for the election of
(1) an executive and (2) a legislative body, who working together in a representative capacity, have
all the power of appointment, all power of legislation, all power to raise revenue and appropriate expenditures, and are required to create (3) a judiciary to pass upon the justice and legality of their
governmental acts and to recognize (4) certain inherent individual rights.
Take away any one or more of those four elements and you are drifting into autocracy. Add one or more to those four elements and you are drifting into democracy—-Atwood.
121. Superior to all others — Autocracy declares the divine right of kings; its authority can not be questioned; its powers are arbitrarily or unjustly administered.
Democracy is the " direct " rule of the people and has been repeatedly tried without

success.
Our Constitutional fathers, familiar with the strength and weakness of both autocracy and democracy, with fixed principles definitely in mind, defined a representative republican form of government. They " made a very marked distinction between a republic and a democracy * * * and said repeatedly and emphatically that they had founded a republic."

[A. G. 014.38 (4-28-28).]
By order of the Secretary of War :
C. P. SUMMERALL,
Major General,
Chief of Staff.
Official :
LUTZ WAHL,
Major General,
The Adjutant General.

Having spent some 22 years in the Democratic Party – I know its policies and beliefs quite well. It is and ALWAYS has been the party of liberals – Christ-hating jews – ignorant lazy blacks – ignorant illiterate rednecks – union thugs – low life Hispanics – homosexuals – atheists and the general ignorant stupid detritus of the streets. Those are facts – not opinions. Been there – seen that – EXPERIENCED that.

There was an old saying that is still occasionally heard that has a lot of between the lines wisdom. It went something like this: "If you are under twenty and are not a Democrat – you don't have a heart – but if you are over thirty and are not a Republican – you don't have a brain." If the reader DOES have a brain – regardless of age he or she will be able to connect the dots.

Democracy has also been described by Dr. Ben Franklin as: "two wolves and one sheep deciding on what to have for dinner". The ultimate 'majority rules' mantra (no matter how evil or dangerous or stupid I couldn't have described it better.

"Remember, democracy never lasts long. It soon wastes, exhausts, and murders itself. There never was a democracy yet that did not commit suicide." – John Adams (1814)

James Madison: "Democracies have ever been spectacles of turbulence and contention; have ever been found incompatible with personal security or the rights of property; and have in general been as short in their lives as they have been violent in their death."

Thomas Jefferson: "The democracy will cease to exist when you take away from those who are willing to work and give to those who would not." Isn't that EXACTLY what the Democrats have legislated from day one that has made them enemies of hard working productive mainstream REAL Americans?

John Quincy Adams: "The experience of all former ages had shown that of all human governments, democracy was the most unstable, fluctuating and short-lived."

James Madison: "Democracy was the right of the people to choose their own tyrant."

John Adams: "That the desires of the majority of the people are often for injustice and inhumanity against the minority is demonstrated by every page of the history of the world."

John Witherspoon: "Pure democracy cannot subsist long nor be carried far into the departments of state – it is very subject to caprice and the madness of popular rage."

John Marshall: "Between a balanced republic and a democracy, the difference is like that between order and chaos."

Oscar Wilde: "Democracy means simply the bludgeoning of the people by the people for the people."

Winston Churchill: "The best argument against democracy is a five minute conversation with the average voter."

G. K., Chesterton: "Democracy means government by the uneducated, while aristocracy means government by the badly educated."

George Bernard Shaw: "Democracy substitutes election by the incompetent many for appointment by the corrupt few."

Alan Coren: "Democracy consists of choosing your dictators after they've told you what you think it is you want to hear."

Benjamin Franklin: "When the people find that they can vote themselves money, that will herald the end of the republic." Hmmnn? – like the "ah's entitled" mantra we endlessly hear from welfare blacks who won't work

Alexander Hamilton, "Federalist Papers: We are a Republican Government, Real liberty is never found in despotism or in the extremes of democracy…it has been observed that a pure democracy if it were practicable would be the most perfect government. Experience has proved that no position is more false than this. The ancient democracies in which the people themselves deliberated never possessed one good feature of government. Their very character was tyranny; their figure deformity."

So there you have it – right from the People who actually CREATED the government of the United States as well as other famous respected figures.

I have noticed in recent years the unmistakable presence of two major evils aimed at the destruction of our freedoms by slowly morphing our consecrated Republican form of government into the destructive bogus substitute of one of most failed forms of governance in history – the Democracy.

One is the fact that the term REPUBLIC is almost never heard today to describe the type of government that we have inherited from the greatest minds of our founders. THIS IS NOT BY ACCIDENT. IT IS BY DESIGN. I have not heard our nation described as the Republic that it IS by ANY of the Jew-owned news media for YEARS! Thank about that fact for a moment and ask your self why? If you haven't figured it out by now – then your ignorance is part of the problem. A Republic by its very nature is much harder to infiltrate and sabotage than a Democracy – which ALWAYS fails!

Number two – you will hear AND read Democracy this and Democracy that on and in every jew published or created news source magazine news story – foreign policy report – entertainment – be it movies – live shows specials – news bulletins – speeches by ALL political candidates except Ron Paul. Have you noticed how we CRAM Democracy down the throats of every one we invade – and if they resist we simply bomb them into rubble and install our own Democratic puppets.

We never speak of good will nor humanitarian assistance – only that they MUST accept our Merkan Democracy as if the term were mandated by Christ Himself in the most brutal Draconian methods imaginable. Try this little experiment yourself. For those who have never been outside or 'River City USA' – as as many school children as you can – what kind of government we have and see what you are told. Virtually ALL will say a Democracy.

The Founding Fathers must be rolling in their graves with anguish. For those of you who are multilingual and travel – ask the average foreigner the same question. You may be surprised. USA stupidity is now a third world joke.

This is all pretty bizarre considering that the word DEMOCRACY was never even used in the Declaration of Independence – nor the Constitution – nor the Bill of Rights – not even the Constitutions of the new 'colony States'. ONLY THE WORD: "REPUBLIC" Want to embarrass a Democrat? Ask them why?

In brief summary – here then, are the main features of both systems outlined in plain English for your convenience to save and share with others. I hope this has been enlightening and helpful in understanding your own nation.

Democracy: a government of the masses. Authority derived thru mass meeting or any other form of direct expression. Results in Mobocracy. Attitude toward property is communist – negating property rights. Attitude toward law is that the will of the majority shall regulate, whether it be based upon deliberation or governed by passion, prejudice and impulse without restraint or regard to consequences. Results in demagoguism, license, agitation, discontent, anarchy.

Republic: Authority is derived thru the election by the people of public officials best fitted to represent them. Attitude toward law is the administration of justice in accord with fixed principles and established evidence, with a strict regard to consequences. A greater number of citizens and extent of territory may be brought within its compass. Avoids the dangerous extreme of either tyranny or mobocracy. Results in statesmanship, liberty, reason, justice, contentment and progress. Is the standard form of government throughout the world.

Sadly – after all is said and done my proof may be a mute point – for the fact is – that we today are nothing more than a colony of IsraHELL and since our blessed Constitution has been trashed revised and or deemed a bastardized "living" document – meaning that as George Bush so crudely and viciously stated – that it is nothing more than a "God Damned piece of paper" (less than toilet paper to him)

So now – the jews who now rule us are now at liberty to interpret the Constitution to suit their wicked agenda as they have succeeded to turn two thousand year old Catholic Dogma on its ear – distort the words of Christ – and install a jew Pope – how hard would it be for our jew masters to twist the words of a handful of long dead mortal patriots on a 240 year old document. (who they hate for exposing their evil)

If you TRULY love this country – then stop simply watching it die day by day. Tear yourself away from your stupid bowl NFL foolishness just once – and do something meaningful for your OWN country family and honor.

OCTOBER 2012
REQUIEM FOR A DEGENERATE NATION – THE FINAL MORAL ROTING AND DEMISE OF THE STUPID WEST

I recently read an interesting essay on one man's struggle within himself as to the nature of his allegiances to his roots and his country (not the USA) – since his background was very complex. Perhaps I myself, have of recent years began to wonder just what MY country means to me TODAY. Or more importantly – what and why my feelings of MY country have so drastically changed. A country which I learned to love from the values of my family and listening to my father speak of the marvels and goodness that resided only here in America

I continued that loyalty and 'proved' part of it as I voluntarily served in uniform in one our most elite and hazardous units at a perilous period of our history. I kept my nation's laws and constantly strove to see justice done as I matured. After a period of a relatively liberal but not evil lifestyle, I engaged in more and more in depth responsibility to 'civic duty' and stayed true to my conservative beliefs from which that time I never really strayed.

I still felt that America was great, because Americans were good – a notion that was shared by greater men than I – a hundred generations before it ever dawned on me (Alexis DeTocqueville) . That notion never changed in my heart – but the reality of that pre-supposed contingency that MADE it a reality – began to painfully manifest itself in way I would have never dreamed in my worst nightmares.

We WERE GOOD. We are no longer a good people by ANY stretch of the imagination in the mind of ANY informed moral person.

Evil had begun to manifest itself in America like a cancer – as I watched in horror and disbelief of what I saw and heard and experienced in years to come. Like most young men – I had lost my ‘innocence’ – like most men as they mature and witness the more harsh realities of life. Even so I had not lost the notion of the goodness of America and Americans.

Years later I would also lose that notion of this innocence/goodness of the country – as knowledge wisdom and understanding became a more commonplace part of my emotional, intellectual and spiritual makeup. Like a woman with the pangs of first childbirth – I had no idea of the pain that I would endure as a result of my knowledge. It was to change the way I would look at my beloved country – forever! I had not ‘left’ the American ideals. They had LEFT ME!

Having afforded myself the luxury of international travel – a ‘value’ instilled in me by my father who was truly cosmopolitan by nature – speaking reading and writing 5 languages fluently – and having frugally traveled to dozens of countries as a young man and experiencing their cultures – – I have had the education to enhance my wisdom form the finite portals of my own city to be witness to over thirty cultures of the world – mostly European – Caribbean and Lain American. I was even a diplomat – a Vice-Consul, to one of them for 5 years.

Until as of recent years – I had not fully realized the vast abyss of ignorance in my neo-American culture – if we may be so vain as to term this shallow secular ‘ instant satisfaction’ mentality of my fellow idiots – as a ‘culture’. My experience of 74 years now – has taught me that by and far – for the most part – the ‘average’ modern/adult ‘Joe six-pack’ has all the mental acumen of a 12 year old. Note that I did not say “mature adult”. That adjective, for the average American – would be a conflict of terms – an oxymoron as it were.

If you think my conclusions are personal rantings of cynicism and you want objective reliable confirmation of our dazzling world-class stupidity – simply Google these two simple words: “STUPID AMERICANS”

How about ONE HUNDRED AND THIRTY THREE MILLION HITS! Convinced? read on.

We are – or more accurately – have as of more recent times of the past 2-3 generations – a nation of immature children with the outward physical features of adulthood. In the common street vernacular — we have been ‘dumbed-down’ to the level of morons and imbeciles- to be polite. We were not always like this. I grew up in happier times with essentially ‘good’ educated people – wholesome role models – virtuous entertainers and far more trustworthy leaders.

Why do you think that when most people my age are asked – "what do you consider the 'golden years' of America?" — our young age at the time, not withstanding — had answered almost unequivocally – "Why the 50s – of course!" More precisely to my personal opinion – the mid to late 40s till the mid 50s.

Vulgar Jew created trash like the Beetles and their selfish materialistic godless drug and free love mentality were the beginning of the end of that innocent period. They only started an endless stream of trash that infested and morally destroyed most of an entire generation — ALL ultimately under the age-old aegis of greed fame and money.

Almost nobody locked his or her homes and only a paranoiac would lock his car. Americans ACTUALLY honored veterans on Memorial Day – NOT war criminals. It was not just 'some holiday' to stuff yourself and get drunk at parties. Hoodlums in schools – class disruptors – did not necessitate police on school grounds to keep the peace. We had well qualified teachers who had authority AND respect.

These antisocial misfit trash were despised by virtually ALL of the class in general. Good students were respected not only by teachers – but by their fellow classmates as well. WHY? – Because unlike today – KNOWLEDGE – EDUCATION and WISDOM were revered respected qualities that were desirable. There were NO backwards baseball caps to show the rest of the civilized word that the wearers ALSO had their tiny brains in backwards! Young women did NOT debase their bodies with piercings and tattoos – and the decent majority so considered any such person that did so, as a harlot and street trash. Goodness wisdom and rational thought prevailed over evil.

We had real responsible freedom then. Harsh feelings of racism were seldom encountered and 'hate' crimes on blacks or whites were uncommon. Today there is hardly a week goes by that some horror story of some almost always white people – totally innocent – are brutally murdered raped, burned alive, dismembered or tortured to death – even the children. Motives? " Dey was white"!

Communism was (as it ALWAYS HAS BEEN) an 'evil' – a mortal enemy of Christian doctrine and of free men and NOT to be tolerated. There WAS NO – NADA – NONE – ZILCH – crime and violence in schools – PERIOD! Out of marriage pregnancies WERE RARE – and I am NOT being naive. I WAS THERE!

There were not the millions of children FORCED to take dangerous psychotropic addicting drugs like Ritalin to 'cure' non-existent 'diseases' like ADHD. There were NO school massacres like happen here at least bi-annually – and ALL related to these psychotropic drugs – like Ritalin. 'Columbine' was a classic example.

There were no 'drug cultures' – RAP trash – demonic rock groups – or teen suicides. There WAS – school prayer – morals – TAUGHT in schools – and our 'icons' were decent clean cut REAL heroes and role models – not the filthy scummy reprobate rancid trash that permeates every pore of our dysfunctional society today.

That was of course thanks to the greedy jew managers who sold their souls to promote drug infested jew filth like the Beetles – and the Stones whose messages of Godlessness disrespect and drugs opened the doors to hell later for even more putrid filth like Carnivore – Malice-Blessed Death and Rotten Corpse and a hundred more jew inspired rancid scum whose purpose was to demonize the souls of our youth. Even then I knew something was terribly wrong.

ALL movies were Ok for grandma to see with her children & grandchildren. Disney world was run by CHRISTIAN family oriented people and not by the filthy porn peddling Godless money worshiping JEW! Our taxes were low and even the low economic classes could afford to have a parent at home to raise the children. THERE WERE NO CREDIT CARDS OR MASS CREDIT MENTALITY – why? Because we were all able to live within our means.

WHY? because we had been taught these and other real life useful values at the foot of our then, responsible parents. I was 'there' – to live and experience these truths. You young people reading this – if any of you still respect truth and knowledge as my generation did – take my word for these things – or just ask your elders.

By today's standards – my parents were struggling poor – yet my father could still afford to have a 'FAMILY' Physician come to our home to heal me when I was very sick. Today you would have to be a MULTIMILLIONAIRE to afford this once simple American way of life. Yes Dorothy – ALL physicians used to do 'house calls' then. People CARED about other people. Today – I could die in my sleep if I lived alone, and no one would know till I turned to dust!

America was powerful but LOVED and RESPECTED – not only at home – BUT abroad as well. We were not FEARED and LOATHED as a Godless amoral lunatic nation of war mongering imperialist war criminals as we are today! We had earned something called respect, because we were still a nation of mostly decent compassionate Godly people. The truth was still a priority with most. Do not EVER confuse RESPECT with FEAR. Respect is in the family of love. Fear is closer to HATE!

We have lost our moral rudder and have become a nation not unlike ancient Sodom. Today our 'Christian/Zionist' segment of the population have as much innocent blood on their hands as the Marxists of Soviet ilk that we once – as TRUE Christians – feared and despised and warned our children against. We have become what we once despised.

The Ten Commandments are today nothing more – at BEST – than the 'ten suggestions'. Our 'entertainment' is so rancid, evil and blasphemous that it would probably make Satan blush with embarrassment. The 100% jew dominate jew run jew financed Talmudic filth spewed into our living rooms like so much rancid vomit 24-7 is the VAST portion of our children's non-formal education. Evolution taught as FACT – promotion of gratuitous sex – graphic violence portrayed a normal – normalization of homosexual perversions – glorification of adultery – acceptability of in your face blasphemy – reprobate scum postured as role models – racist hate presented as American as apple pie and more.

We are like 'dead men walking' – doomed to the ash heap of history. We have VOLUNTARILY become void of any goodness – compassion and repentance. Truth, wisdom, responsibility and understanding are 'dirty words' not even discussed any more. All we love and respect is money, power, comfort, sex and that which makes us 'feel good'.

I have not heard any real wisdom, humility, truth or understanding come from the mouths of our leaders, since I was a child. We have befriended ALL of our REAL enemies and made enemies of any friends we really had left. Yes – I served my country in uniform – but with morally different people. I trained a lot of young kids for combat duty that had morals and a conscience.

Not surprisingly, not a single one of the 1000+ men I personally had a hand in training at the USATC in Berlin Crisis 1962 were jews. They were all given deferments so we inferior Goyem (cattle) servicemen could keep them safe and secure at home where they could continue with their posh jobs and lifestyles in Hollywood and in the media corruption our children's hearts and minds and souls. It's a jew thing.

The trash in today's 'new and improved ' Army are legions of murderers, rapists, looters, sadistic criminal thugs that are capable of murdering and raping an entire family of defenseless helpless innocent civilians just for "fun". These horrendous events are now common everyday occurrences in Iraq and Afghanistan and nobody 'at home' gives a damn!

One day you will see these same soulless young killers murder your neighbors and family right here in our own country! Why? Because they were simply "given orders to do so". by some war criminal madman like George Bush. These horrors have happened in every nation in history that has abandoned morality – and it will happen here! It is only a matter of time. If you think I exaggerate – then research the shameful frightening incident at '29 Palms' Naval base and THEN tell me you are not concerned – if of course this doesn't interrupt really important matters – like your 'FUN' at NFL tailgate parties.

I thank The Lord that I was born no later than I was – as I have been a witness to a time of goodness – or at least relative innocence and goodness – the likes of which no young person has ever OR WILL ever witness in his or her lifetime. I fear for the moral well-being of my children and especially grandchildren in years to come – as the 'poison cup' of the jew that we have partaken – has become more and more 'fashionable' to more and more of our ignorant population.

We ARE today nothing more than a morally rotted corpse – like one of those low budget 'B rated' 'Night of the Living Dead' late movies. Aside from the horrors that WE have created all over the world as a result of our greed – ignorance – racism – hypocrisy and arrogance – one need but take note of what degenerate inane mindless rot the jew TV vomits into our living rooms 24-7. Half of EVERYTHING YOU WILL SEE is based on our new improved 'Merkan' values of sex and money – SEX AND MONEY – get it?

Oh – and have you noticed that virtually ALL of these 'ads' are designed to target 'adults' with 12 year old brains? There are now scores of in your face adds promoting drugs to make your penis larger as if God created us all with some sort of defect. OR – how to be promiscuous without worrying about horrible diseases that one might catch from EVERYONE – but our wives of course.

There are now even promotions for homosexual perverts – to be able to more easily find other perverts – " for a good time". Lotions and oils and garments to make us sexier – NOT JUST CLEANER – abound every hour of the day so as to insure that our children become more and more sexually aware.

Then there are the money mongers. Buy this and buy that – and not to worry – you can buy ANYTHING any luxury you desire and pay for it later (at substantial jew usury premiums of course). Oh and if you get in trouble – being a little too greedy and materialistic – not to worry – there are also dozens of new 'companies' specializing in patching up your stupidity – greed and irresponsible behavior – so you can " get back on your feet" and screw your life up ALL OVER AGAIN!

There are mortgage rates and special 'trick plans' with fancy sounding names for every level of irresponsible excessive expenditure. BUY BUY – SPEND SPEND – not to worry – it all seems like a fantasy world where there are no 'pipers' to pay and everything is warm and fuzzy. And just in case you are a dead-beat moron scumbag whose irresponsible lifestyle has wrecked your credit – impoverished your family and ruined your reputation – once again – the AmeriKan way will see to it that its all OK and you can squander more of your children's education money with those sleazy outfits that will lend you dollars no matter what kind of irresponsible loser you are. RIGHT!

Oh and then there is another thing -DRUGS!. Not as insidious and morality deficient as the money/sex thing – but a another good litmus of sick (no pun intended) society. Remember – NONE Of this garbage existed in the society that I grew up in. We didn't have to. We didn't 'need' it. Why? – Because we all, once had , wisdom knowledge and good judgment. Note the HUGE deluge of drug ads shoved in our face literally EVERY 6-10 MINUTES ON EVERY NETWORK CHANNEL on TV.

Sometimes I wonder how our nation can function with all of the health related problems that we suffer from – like – upset stomachs – migraine headaches – sore muscles – sleepless nights – aching joints – stressful lives – constipation – diarrhea – stinky feet – balding heads – infected toenails – ulcers – bad breath – dirty teeth – germ infested homes – smelly kitchens – need for alcohol – need for nicotine – fast food – uncomfortable beds – diet schemes by the zillions! – gym fads – an apparent epidemic of allergies – cure for Hypertension – cures for cholesterol – cure for aging – breast augmentations – butt augmentations – cold-cures – cough cures – arthritic cures – Prostate cures – faulty bladder cures – depression cures – herpes cures and on and on and on.

It is as if the Pharmaceuticals industry and the medical profession and the carnival barkers have all been in collusion with one another to produce a sideshow of snake oil cure for anything and everything that plagues an entire nation – apparently ONLY the 'modern' American citizen. It is amazing that Americans as a people can even function in normal everyday life as ill as we apparently are.

And have you ever listened to the voice that – apparently by law – must mention the adverse side effects from these wonder cures. They are stated in a double the normal speaking speed that is impossible to comprehend as if it were of no consequence. It goes something like this: "Ever suffer from pains in your legs or frequent urination or shortness of breath? Well – like zillions of Americans you may be suffering from Hydrocondrocardiosubclavianendometaxis syndrome. Clinical studies have found that a regular regime of the new wonder drug Proloxiline sufanidomie oxypseudofltulanticularsodium succiliate or 'Proximax' – a combination of untested but clinically proven toxinogen will greatly reduce the painful effects of the HCD syndrome.

Use only as directed and consult your physician first. Should not be taken if you are pregnant – have any allergies – have a cold or cough – headaches – have ever had an operation – suffer from hypertension – anxiety – high Cholesterol – ever had the flue or a cold – diabetic or are a male between the ages of 18 and 87 or a female who has ever had children or had PMS or exceptionally large breasts or exceptionally small breasts or had 'hot flashes' or flatulence – as any of the aforementioned conditions could increase your chances of cancer using this drug – etc etc etc"

AND – if that weren't enough – here is a classic example of the very very small print that lists the possible negative side effects: CAUTIONS: Side effects may cause diarrhea- dizziness- fever- pain -swelling – headache – weakness – numbness– bleeding – unusual bruising – red or tarry stools- blood in urine- severe pain in legs feet toes – vaginal bleeding – rash – itching swelling – difficulty breathing – trouble sleeping – drowsiness – chest pain – irregular heart beat – coughing – bluish discoloration in hands or feet – blistered skin heart failure – stroke – chills – fainting – sore throat – hair loss – nosebleeds – bleeding from gums – reparatory distress – hallucinations – deep depression – tachycardia – or possible fatal effects.

Actually – ALL of these 'side effects' are real – I didn't make these up and they were from only 2 of the more supposedly benign drugs most Americans commonly use or have used.

Of course the TV screen shows the laughing now healthy 'patient' leaping through a field of flowers like Alice in Wonderland. The 'Madison Avenue' ad man and 'Big pharma' have a quick fix for anything that ails us – even if it nearly kills us. As long as LOTS of money is being made that is ALL that REALLY MATTERS! Only in AmeriKa – what a country!

Point is – we are programmed to live in a make believe world – where we have NO responsibilities and there are NO moral absolutes anymore. Hey – if it feels good – DO IT! If you commit a horrendous mass murder of totally innocent people – not to worry – it is – after all – society's fault and not yours – and if you are a homosexual pervert or violent scumbag Ebonics/rap raving 'nigger' (my euphemism for the typical scumbag violent oyster-brained street trash black – NOT To be confused with any decent hard working NEGRO) – not to worry either – because an ACLU lawyer will be right here to bail you out and place the blame where it obviously belongs – with the decent hard working family valued honest God fearing (now the minority) who MADE YOU DO IT! Trayvon Martin ring a bell?

We have become so completely 'moronacised' (dumbed-down) by our 'handlers' that we continue to use divisive and improper 'created' erroneous terms like "PRO- CHOICE" to describe the process of murdering an unborn child – or "AFRICAN AMERICAN" to denote a black American whereas it CORRECTLY means and designates any person – black OR white that was born in one of the many African countries and THEN becomes an American citizen by naturalization.

Or how about "ASSAULT RIFLE" to INCORRECTLY describe a simple plain rifle which CANNOT fire automatically as a machine-gun – which in reality is NOT in ANY Way a machine =gun or automatic rifle – or 'TERRORIST" to describe a national patriot who is fighting an invading force in HIS country.- he is more properly and popularly termed FREEDOM FIGHTER! – Or the term" CULTURAL DIVERSITY" to force racial intermarriage or homosexual perversions or other such unsavory conduct on a civil moral society.

We always see the improper word "GAY" to INCORRECTLY describe the homosexual pervert / pedophile child molester. There are other sinister evil intended bastardizations of our wonderful English language – but you get the idea. These things are EVIL PERIOD! They serve NO good purpose and act only for the benefit of evil people with evil agendas.

Finally; the last straw. One of the things that I grew up with – was a country that whether you were Catholic or one of the diverse Protestant sects – we ALL worshiped ONE SAME GOD. We ALL fell under the belief in one main collective belief – that we are all followers of the Christ and our collective belief was called CHRISTIANITY and was based upon the teachings of our faith.

Today that has been all but completely destroyed. Now – we have the 'new and improved' Christian/Zionist dogma – so painstakingly managed and manipulated by the Jew over the past half century. Today we no longer follow the teachings of Jesus Of Nazareth – but our churches have been sold or traded for the synagogues of Satan so despised by our Lord. We have now become a collective living oxy-moron that which never was – and never will be — CHRISTIANS who worship SATAN. Read John 8-44 – (Jesus to the jews) "Ye are of your father ,the DEVIL – the father of ALL LIES"

An oxymoron – a contradiction in principles – the marriage of the ultimate holiness and goodness with that which is evil and Godless. We have drunk from the cup of poison, – the same poison offered to our Lord by the Pharisees millennia ago. The pseudo-churches of hell today preach hatred of our fellow man – racism – wealth as equal to Godliness and that number one issue in importance in the obligation of the pastor is to make the flock 'feel good' – to satisfy the itchy ears of the hypocrite.

They 'preach' NOT the Gospel of Christ – but whatever inane tripe makes us feel good and fuzzy REGARDLESS of how blasphemous or distant from The Lord's teachings it strays. Hypocrite multi-millionaire rancid scum frauds like Joel Osteen have led countless millions of clueless imbecile fools down the road to damnation with his wicked lies

It shows that we are spiritually dead! With small exception of the few truly faithful left in America – we have sold our souls to the jews (Satan's earthly children). We are WORSE than the inhabitants of Sodom – for at least they were not guilty of hypocrisy as part of their blasphemy.

Even the original universal Christian Church – that of Catholicism – in which I was raised, has been infiltrated by the Satanic jews. We now have a full fledged wicked Christ mocking jew masquerading as the Pope and betraying a billion followers. Most Catholics aren't aware that 'Bishop' Ratsinger was the author of most of the blasphemous filth that came out of Vatican II. One look at 'Pope' Ratsingers face should reveal the jew wickedness in his black soul.

With the exception of the ONLY true Christian Church left – the Orthodox – and a handful of still loyal believers – 'Christianity' as I knew it as a young man in what was once 'AMERICA' – and not a colony of IsraHELL – has been totally destroyed by the jews and most of our three hundred+ million citizens – dumbed down to shallow self indulgent delusional sheep.

Since the demise of Christianity I have searched for a 'church' where I might feel is sharing the true message of God – where the spiritual head – by whatever name he calls himself – has the integrity and courage to speak the truth – defend the faith – and not only talk the talk – BUT also – as he should do – and as he has been mandated by God – to also walk the walk – lead by example – not hypocrisy.

I seek a sober modest frugal Christian 'pastor' and a TRUE Christian church that will set the example and show no fear to the face of adversity or cave in principles to secular majority or cower to the intimidation of everyday evil influence – such as our evil government and Jew controlled mass media – ergo -' public opinion'.

Show me such a place stewarded by such a man – hopefully within my immediate community – and I will join their ranks and attempt to be worthy of their company. I have searched but found little but voices of weakness, ignorance inane hatred, racism, and MONUMENTAL HYPOCRISY. Their phony churches boast of being " fun" = "dynamic" = "inspiring" = "uplifting" = "casual" = " informal"= "exciting" and even "prosperous" – but never ever faithful and truthful to the teachings of Christ. They are truly the 'quislings' of Christianity in America. I'm not looking for a 'blow job' for my ego or a fashion conscious social club for tail-gate party mentality Sunday Christians. My search continues.

OCTOBER 2012
IMAGINE THE USA WITHOUT JEWS TO CAUSE US BLUES

Well – here is what would actually happen or mostly NOT Have happened if – you can imagine for a moment – that there were NO SELF- CHOSEN in America – PERIOD! Not now – or EVER! Ironically – many of the Founding Fathers warned and counseled us to drive the jews out of our young Christian Republic for fear of EXACTLY what has happened here since then. That of course is only wishful thinking – and sadly for America – the reality of situations that we now have – thanks to the lifelong conduct of Jews in America, coupled with our current state of universal dumbed-down ignorance – is that we are morally AND economically bankrupt.

AND – I feel compelled to add – that in no small part – the culpability for this monumental moral disaster must be shared with the greedy ignorant and spineless average American gentile as complicit in 'allowing' these avoidable disgraceful 'events' to change this once wonderful and unique Christian nation of my childhood into the Sodom- like foul morally rotted corpse that we have most certainly become. Make no mistake – God will NOT hold the 'other 95%' – whole harmless.

These assumptions are based on history- events – experiences – laws – organizations – lawmakers and a general moral, sociological and economic condition of our nation that would in all probability NOT have happened without Jewish influence.

There of course must be a perspective for comparison. Since there was little Jew influence at high levels when I was a 'teenager' – I use many personal experiences from that general time frame as a pre- benchmark period of our RELATIVE innocence and goodness as a people and a nation in general. The horrible things that have happened to America since that period, are what was predicted would happen to a jew controlled America. SINCE they DID eventually 'poisoned the well', I emphasize those horrible consequences that we have lived with for most or all our lives that have had the most destructive effect on our freedoms – our morality and our economy.

For those of you over 60 this will only be a 'refresher' course in America's recent moral history – as most of you will recall life in the US during the 40s and 50s . For younger generations – especially – who read this – you did not live during those relatively wholesome times – so learn these lessons well – for if you fail to heed this message – you will inevitably repeat these mistakes and completely seal the fate of your country – and that of your children.

Teach them well. Teach them THE TRUTH! Teach them NOW – or you will be despised by them long after you are gone – as being the generation that allowed their country to end up on the ash heap of history – like EVERY other nation which has sold it's 'soul' to the Jew for 30 silver shekels. We have bartered our moral compass for a bigger Talmudvision and a seat on the 50 yard line at the Stupid Bowl. Merka is now a place where adults all act like children FACE BOOK ROCKS! GO BUCS! NFL RULES! NASCAR IS A BOMB! I hear this every day and not just kids! but I digress. Back to the examples.

FOR EXAMPLE =====

Grade school and high school violence crime and pregnancies would be as non-existent as they were in the 40s and 50s. Why? Because we would still have school prayer as WELL AS 'Golden Rule' ethics taught in school as well as wholesome 'clean cut' entertainment and positive role models for our youth instead of the putrid jew created Talmudvision garbage that infected our society like a plague. As a REAL LIFE yardstick. When I was in high school (mid 50s) there was just ONE pregnancy.

I KNOW that was true because when a high school girl gets pregnant – one of two things happened. (1) she got a big tummy – or (2) she suddenly takes an urgent and mysterious out of State 'vacation' . Today however – teachers like my daughter-in-law tell me that pregnancies are

SUPER common even in middle schools involving girls as young as 12 and 13 mostly blacks. Why? Because the jews have taught us that we should have LOTS of sex with LOTS of people and not to worry because if the girl gets pregnant – just murder the unwanted fetus – the pregnancy the – 'choice'. .

No Jews – No large number of teen pregnancies

There would have been NO 'Columbine' school massacres and no huge numbers of children forced to be drugged out 24-7 on horrible dangerous class 2 narcotic drugs because there would have been no psychotropic drugs pushed by predominantly Jewish psychologists (fake doctors) to 'cure' Jew fabricated non-existent 'diseases' (My own son is one of the victims of these horrors and I know ALL TO WELL, EXACTLY what is going on with this insanity) Another 'gift' from the Jews.

No Jews – No drugged out children or unexplainable youth suicides

Instead of the drooling imbeciles that we churn out year after year, in a completely failed education system – America would still lead the way with excellent well educated well disciplined graduates from our public school systems – as it was some 50 years ago – before the Jews dominate the policies of our educational system through the horrid jew dominated NEA and other State and local policy makers.

No Jews – no purposeful 'dumbing-down' of America – the single biggest cause of our sorry condition.

We would still have Creationism and other wholesome Godly concepts taught to our children in Schools. There would be NO teen suicides at the alarming increasing rates we see today. Why? Because we would still be teaching that there is value in human life – and that we are more than just 'hairless apes' and that human life has worth beyond material ambitions – instead – our children are taught night after night on the Talmudvision' Learning Channel and their Science Channel and their Discovery Channel and their Travel Channel and all their other 're-education' to jew thinking programming

"No Jews – no high teen suicides

We would not have the monumental destructive 'street' drug problems that have plagued us since the 60s. Countless young people's lives irrevocably ruined – perhaps an entire generation – drugged out – turned on and dropped out – all because we allowed soulless immoral Jews like the Beetles and other trash of their ilk to become our NEW icons and role models instead of the wholesome entertainers I grew up with as a teen.

No Jews – No drug culture

When I was a child – we could walk blocks away to visit Grandpa or friends without our parents worrying about some dreadful thing happening to us. My parents their cars and seldom locked the house. There was NO reason to. Decency prevailed and crime against a private citizen was rare indeed. In EVERY society on earth – when Christian based morals are cast aside – crime and violence has ALWAYS filled the 'vacuum'. This is NOT UNREALISTIC FANTASY! I lived in that happy time without the chocking Jew influence in every aspect of life.

No Jews – No spiraling violent crime rates

Christmas was a happy time where virtually EVERYONE celebrated the birth of Christ. There were prayers before every school sports event and it was CHRISTMAS – NOT the Jew preferred 'holiday season' of today. NO ONE was EVER forced to participate in ANY Christian custom then, and mockery of our Lord was unspeakable and unthinkable. We were taught of the Founding Fathers and that ours was a blessed Christian Nation based upon CHRISTIAN PRINCIPLES.

No Jews – no destruction of Christmas

Hollywood free of the filth of Jew mentality would be Christian dominated and the entertainment would STILL be suitable for the whole family. We would still have the mind- boggling special effects that are 'eye candy' to action movie buffs – but without the associated filth. Oh – and if you think nobody would go because the shows were too boring – ask ANYBODY with gray hair if they felt that George Raft had to blaspheme God to prove he was a 'tough guy' for the movie audience – or Humphrey Bogart – or Spencer Tracy or John Wayne-or if Loretta Young or Greta Garbo or Maureen O'Hara or Jennifer Jones were any less beautiful because they didn't bear their ass for everyone to ogle at. So – you're a big boy now and you want to see porn! Fine – Just go to your local XXX store – but keep it out of TV and public movie houses – and ESPECIALLY OUR LIVING ROOMS with children.

No Jews – no blasphemies, porn, homo filth, gratuitous sex, or needless violence to poison our children

Disney World was a wonderful place of wholesome entertainment for children and family alike. It was the dream of a wonderful Christian man who wanted a place for decent salubrious entertainment. The Jews with their power in wealth – seized the opportunity and turned it into a hellhole of nasty filth – more to actually honor homosexual pedophile perverts than for joy to children. Everything the Jew psyche touches with his money – regardless of how decent, innocent and clean – he turns into something vile, nasty, filthy and sordid!

No Jews – no homo pedophiles in Disney World – or ANY public place

Abortion was virtually unheard of when I was a teen. I did not know of ONE SINGLE married couple that had their own child murdered for 'matters of convenience' till I was well into adulthood. ONE girl was pregnant out of wedlock in our high school – the ENTIRE TIME! JUST ONE! You do NOT have to be a rocket scientist to know either. EITHER (A) the girl's tummy got big – or (B) she 'went on a long vacation – usually out of State. Today – children in grade school are routinely made pregnant! EVERY abortion mill and or abortion advocate group IS PREDOMINANTLY funded and or staffed or supported by JEWS – PERIOD! Infanticide is a Jew thing! No Jews – no Jews lawyers – No Jew layers – no Partial Birth Abortion horrors –

PERIOD! BTW 'Holy' Israel – home of the "CHOSEN" – murders TWENTY PERCENT of its annual live births. So much for the myth of the 'most holy anointed ones'.

No Jews – DRAMATICALLY Fewer out of wedlock pregnancies

America was free of any major treason since colonial days. That is – until the most repugnant act of treason in history was committed by two Jew Marxist American citizens, Julius and Ethyl Rosenberg. They sold the atom bomb to the devil – just for money! The repercussions from that one vile greedy despicable treachery can never be fully accounted for. The loss of innocent life, misery, torture, destruction loss of freedoms of hundreds of millions of humans is unfathomable. Korea – Vietnam – trillions of dollars spent on defense that could have undoubtedly found a cure for cancer or other plague of mankind was lost forever. Then of course there are the millions of dead and wounded Americans from both wars – widows and orphans – ALL – a 'special gift' from the Jews. NONE of those mega calamities would have probably happened were it not for Jews – the people who 'invented' communism. Jews = treason.

No Jews – no major treason in America

America has been for most of my life – unique in that we have – as American citizens – been granted the RIGHT to possess and bear firearms. "Freedoms teeth" as President Washington called them. That is- until the Jews got into the act and began to work on their tireless agenda of destroying our Constitutional rights. ALL anti-gun organizations – ESPECIALLY the dreaded legal arm of the Communist Party – THE ALCU – are either supported financed, legislated by and or dominated by Jews.

No Jews – no anti-Constitutional gun control laws.

Remember hearing this so many times in the past – years ago – if someone voiced an opinion that was controversial – he could always say, "Heck, it's a free country!" Freedom speech – so unique to the USA and a Constitutionally granted right that has been fought for and kept by much patriot blood – has been eroded and has ALREADY cost decent sincere Americans prison terms!. Thanks to powerful Jew legislators and lobbies – probably within the next few years – in a decade for SURE – I can be arrested and prosecuted by the Feds just for presenting the facts that I have assembled here. The TRUTH has become a 'hate crime' – you know.

No Jews – no 'thought police'

We were once on the Gold standard – and aside form our 'Great depression' I remember that prices were stable for decades! Gold was $36/oz for longer than I could remember. Even relatively economically poor people could afford to buy a home – a car – afford insurance and be able to pay for a Dr WITHOUT medical insurance! My struggling parents could even afford a Dr. to make 'house calls' when I was sick. I still remember that. Greedy banker barons changed that. Today greed has eclipsed all reason and the Federal Reserve has been the ruination of our economy. Who has their fingers in all of America's finances? Who are the bankers that pull the strings on the quality of life of the average working stiff? You got it. Jews – from the Rothschild's to the Greenspans – the self-chosen.

No Jews – no worthless 'Fed Monopoly play money'

Remember when Americans ran America? Remember when we had REAL enemies that REALLY wanted to AND COULD destroy us. They were called Communists. I remember them well – as THEY were the reason I volunteered to join Special Operations. The USA was the ONLY country that stood in the way of their godless agenda of world domination. Theirs was the bloodiest regime on the planet. The Jew originated Communists murdered over 200,000,000 TOTALLY INNOCENT CIVILIANS to show that there was no limit to their ruthlessness. Today virtually our entire foreign policies are dictated from Israel. The majority of President Bush's cabinet and advisors are Israelis or Israeli loyal traitors masquerading as loyal American citizens. Check it out for your self.

No Jews – no Communists

NOW – lets carry that last 'what if' there were no Jews (ERGO: no Communists) dream a bit further to its logical conclusions. REMEMBER THIS FACT! The JEW 'INVENTED' COMMUNISM. They bankrolled it – promoted it and assisted in the spread – like a cancer – throughout the WORLD. IF this horrid plague upon mankind that we know today as the JEW – had been eradicated by their victims – like the black plague of the middle ages – consider the effect on the United States.

There would have been NO WORLD WAR I . There would have been NO WORLD WAR II There would have been NO Vietnam War! There would have been NO KOREAN War! From just those last two events ALONE – there would have been no 100,000+ combat dead and 1,000,000 maimed and 10,000,000 economically and psychologically affected widows orphans friends and relatives (the collective 'collateral damage' of war)

There would have been No Cuban missile crisis (no Castro) and NO Berlin Crisis. There would be no SERIAL Mid-East GULF WARS – the longest, most costly, most war crimes filled event in American history! The Arab people would still be friendly towards the US as friends and allies. There would have been no decades of 'Cold War' with the Soviets and those monumentally ENORMOUS military expenditures could have been diverted towards benefiting our own people.

The results of such mind boggling figures directed into cancer and other deadly terminal disease research and improved medical services security would have saved UNTOLD millions of America lives in the following years! Analysts experienced with such scenarios have concluded that with ONLY the money spent on the Serial Wars in the Mid-East and on aid to IsraHELL those two goals – could have been achieved in our lifetime!

Used to be that it was tradition –(since we ARE – or at least WERE – a Christian based nation) – that all armed forces academies had prayer as part of the curriculum. Not anymore. Prayer AND morality and ethics was of course also a traditional part of American public school policy. Not anymore. You can thank the Jews for that.

No Jews – no forbidden prayers or forbidden teaching of ethics.

Before the Jew in our once Christian values based nation – there was a Republican Party – because this country was CREATED BY THE FOUNDING FATHERS AS A R-E-P-U-B-L-I-C (a government of laws) NOT a Democracy (mob rule). The Republican Party USED to be the bastion for morality and goodness in this country. True Christian teachings were at one time inseparable from the policies of this Party. Today thanks to the influence from the Jew and his endless powers of wealth – the Republican Party is no more. It is the Neo-Con Party of the United States of IsraHELL – COMPLETELY bastardized and perverted from the original intentions of our Christian Forefathers. Zionism has replaced Christianity.

Our Constitution has been trashed by war criminal jew compromised George Bush– a lunatic madman and his demonic thugs had stolen the Presidency AND this country. He and his cabal of treasonous criminals were undoubtedly accomplices in 9-11. His regime also instigated our treasonous Constitution trashing Patriot Act and Homeland Security. Bush and his co-conspirators have caused the murders of over two million innocent civilians as well as the needless deaths of some 60 thousand not so innocent invading American sons.

When counseled by an advisor not to trash our Constitutional rights – the traitor criminal coward monkey faced Bush blurted out: "*I don't give a goddamn,*" Bush retorted. "*I'm the President and the Commander-in-Chief. Do it my way.*" "*Mr. President,*" one aide in the meeting said. "*There is a valid case that the provisions in this law undermine the Constitution.*" "*Stop throwing the Constitution in my face,*" Bush screamed back. "*It's just a goddamned piece of paper!*"

No Jews – no destruction of the 'GOP' and infiltration of the office of the POTUS by jews.

Before the Jews invented the NAACP there were few racial problems in America and the injustices in discrimination that existed were well on the way to being resolved. It wasn't until the disgraceful rise of Martin Lucifer King that I ever heard an intelligent educated man call a black person a nigger. I CLEARLY remember any white person calling a black a 'nigger' just because of his color – as being ostracized by decent whites as a white-trash redneck. When I was a kid I knew nobody that was a real racist. We had no real racial problems .

Know why? Because the vast majority of blacks back then were decent people and were not ' niggers'. Today – thanks to the Jews and their ceaseless efforts to stir up divisive racial hatred (THEY created hate terms like African-American) – we now have a country full of niggers – with decent black folks few and far between and mocked by their own race for being decent and civil. Jews are MASTERS of creating hatred where there was none.

No Jews – no serious escalating race problems.

I remember when it was unthinkable for a seated American President – the 'Conscience of the Nation' – to blaspheme God by encouraging young Americans to go out and murder innocent men women and children in His Name. Today we have a Jew loyal madman – influenced, guided and manipulated by treasonous Christian hating Jew thugs, loyal only to THEIR country – Israel. Soulless amoral sadistic monsters like Rice and the jew Albright teach young Americans that human life is meaningless as they mock any vestige of decorum or decency by describing the wanton murders of hundreds of thousands of innocent civilians by OUR military – many of the murdered being children – as "COLLATERAL DAMAGE" – as if these children were inanimate fence-posts or stacks of cordwood!

Cindy Sheehan was 100% correct. Her son DID die for nothing – or rather Israel. EVERY MAN THAT HAS RETURNED IN A BODY BAG FROM IRAQ OR AFGHANISTAN – DIED FOR JEW ISRAEL! PERIOD!

No Jews – no wasted US lives in the Mid –East – no jew demeaning of human life as 'useless garbage'

This was once a TRULY Christian country – with the teachings of Jesus the Prince of Peace dominating ALL who claimed Christianity as their moral compass. It didn't matter if the church were Catholic, Baptist, Lutheran, Methodist or any other Christian based denomination – the basic teachings were essentially AND necessarily the same. Compassion – love for our fellow man – moral behavior – modesty – contrition – truthfulness – fidelity and the spirit of the Golden Rule.

Today we see a bastardized self-contradictory Talmudic Zionist heresy, which has almost completely destroyed true Christian doctrine in America. Satanic Churches seething with boisterous hatred, lies, and blasphemies beyond imagination – preaching racism, death and destruction. This monstrous nightmare did NOT exist before the Jews got influential enough to infiltrate their eternal nemesis – Christianity

No Jews – no destruction of TRUE Christianity

Television commercials used to be annoying at worst and sometimes even entertaining and clever. BUT – they NEVER taught our young to be evil or commit sins or that immoral conduct was absolutely OK — actually BETTER than OK – and should be REWARDED! That was before Jews dominated Madison Ave. The Jews OWN the add world and care not who is hurt or what damage is done as long as there is MONEY to be made. The examples are legion – but I will mention a couple of classic categories. The one where the car company tells our youth that it DOESN'T MATTER if they have no credit or EVEN BAD CREDIT – that they WILL BE REWARDED ANYWAY!

In other words – its OK kids – if you are a cheat, deadbeat, fraud, liar, con artist or crook – THAT IS ACCEPTABLE BEHAVIOR TO US AND WE WILL REWARD IT WITH A NEW CAR! Or how about the condom adds? Why not just tell teenagers that their parent's wishes be damned – and just go out and screw their brains out anyway – cause it's the COOL thing to do today! If you can't understand that Jews are behind this degenerate mentality – you have already swallowed their poison.

No Jews – No legitimizing of evil and corruption of our youth

Remember when art was art? Something beautiful that inspired the imagination and passion of the viewer. Timeless paintings of the masters – breathtaking sculptures, ageless classics. No matter what the medium – it was the inordinate skill and imagination of the true artist that inspired him to create beauty and amazement for all ages and all generations to enjoy. Take the kids or Grandma to an exhibit without concern.

Then came the Jews with their degenerate 'art' – usually sexual porn that the Jew mind seems so pre-occupied with – or something more sinister – openly blaspheming God in the most offensive way imaginable. AND to guarantee that their filth was made public – they 'created' the NEA and plenty of Jew Judges to enforce their public displays of depravities under the guise of 'art'. The jew did the same thing to the Germans during the Weimer Republic.

No Jews – no degenerate putrid filth disguised as 'art'

When I was a kid – I loved parades – all kinds – festive floats – huge balloon figures! Pretty girls in foreign costumes – patriotic parades with marching bands and soldiers – Christmas parades to get that feeling of brotherly love and peace – Western – Indian and cowboy parades with their Wild-West themes and so much more. It was wholesome and as American as apple pie and loved by kids – of all ages! But that is no more. Today a parent MUST approve the 'parade' lest it include some of the most graphic and filthy conduct imaginable to man. A parade with homosexual perverts! Their public displays of sodomy, public fondling – mockery of Christ – as universally disgusting us as they are – have ALWAYS been approved by, financed and or organized by Jews. You can take that to the bank!

No Jews – No public homoerotic parade filth

It used to be that if ANY pervert was caught molesting an innocent child he was better off going straight to the police than chance the wrath of an angry mob of children's parents. THAT friends – is ONE of the reasons why there were virtually NO (and I mean NONE) such incidents when I was growing up in a not yet Jew controlled America. Today – if the pervert is a NAMBLA (North American Man Boy Love Association) 'member' – the parent will probably end up being sued by the pervert. You think I'm kidding! The Jews run NAMBLA and – big surprise – always defended by the powerful Jew dominated ACLU. These are now dangerous people because we were so 'tolerant'(read: COWARDS).

No Jews – no pedophile support – ANYWHERE!

Remember when the good ole USA would defend its own – and if attacked (I MEAN A REAL ACT OF WAR!) by a foreign Government – God help the country which would do such a thing.

Can you imagine a country like say Japan – during 1941 when their Govt. ordered their military to conduct an unprovoked attack on Pearl Harbor, having such a STRANGLEHOLD on our country that when informed of the attack – President Roosevelt ordered our forces to stand down and allow the attack to continue because "he did not want to embarrass our friend Japan".

Of course not! What a ridiculous unrealistic scenario! We wreaked havoc on Japan and let them and the world know that such an act would suffer the severest consequences – of course! Lesson here? – you don't screw around with American lives, without consequences mister!

Well – realities have changed. Fast-forward to the late 60s when the FRAUD/STOLEN so called State of Israel had time to insert her spies and poisonous influence with America. Let us create a truly analogous situation – albeit on a smaller scale – when the Jews committed an unprovoked ACT OF WAR on an unarmed American ship in international waters with the intent to MURDER ALL OF THE CREW and sink the ship. They failed in their cowardly treachery to sink the ship – but butchered in cold blood – over 200 of our sons fathers brothers neighbors and friends!

That was the USS LIBERTY. NOT only did we PURPOSELY NOT come to the aid of our OWN citizens as they were bleeding to death on the decks of their ship – but NEVER punished the animals that committed this act of war. WHY NOT? – you may ask in understandable disbelief and amazement? Because the Jews by then owned the President (treasonous crypto jew puppet – the alcoholic Lyndon Johnson and crypto jew McNamara) as well as much of the rest of the legislative and judicial – lock stock and barrel -. AND – there has never even been a proper honest investigation to bring war crime charges against the stinking jews and their criminal filthy stolen shithole of IsraHELL .

No Jews – no unpunished murders of Americans by Jews – no un response to acts of war by jews

The above shameful incident ALSO needs an additional 'what if' there NEVER any Jews in America approach. This is 'speculation' and the only part of this document that is not arguably factual. However it is an educated guess. The first thing that would have happened would have been that Med Fleet's aircraft would have destroyed ALL of the attacking forces. Secondly – a state of war would have been declared by the President and most probably all of Israel's aircraft and naval fleet destroyed by fleet air arm within hours.

Whether or not we would have bombed that piece of crap phony country into the Stone Age is conjecture. They would been declared an enemy of the United States (officially) as they have of course been an enemy of ALL free people since day one. Their aid would have been cut off and there would have been such an outcry of anger from Americans that Jews here would probably be under strict surveillance by ALL Americans.

There would be no angry Arab people – no concentration camps in Palestine – the stolen lands returned to its rightful owners – no 'terrorists' angry with America – no 9-11 – no dead American sons in Iraq and Afghanistan – no hundreds of thousands of murdered civilians by American war criminals – no hatred of America by a billion Muslims –

No animosity towards America by most of the informed free world as an aggressive preemptive war mongering imperialist State.

Most probably no more 'NAMBLA' no ACLU – no Jew controlled Disney World – no filth on TV – no pro-homosexual legislation – no anti-gun legislation – no freedom of speech legislation – no above a dollar /gal gas – no tax increases – no inflation – no filthy TV – no homosexual movements – no pedophile problems -no desecration of Christmas – and of course – flying would still 'be fun'. The possible and probable positive consequences are endless!

I have only 'scratched' the surface – but use your own imagination for a hundreds of other blessings in a USA without Jews – or in this case – even if still present as people – at least without their corrosive pernicious immoral greedy influence and stranglehold on our nation any more. I haven't even touched on the massive corruption of our legal system by the Jew lawyers and Jew Judges. We cannot undo the horrendous damages inflicted by the Jew filth in the past – BUT we can halt further destruction taking a stand against our REAL MORTAL enemy and destroy the beast before it destroys us totally. Take this country back – or lose it forever! GAME OVER!

OCTOBER 2012
SELF DAMNATION FROM THE MOUTHS OF JEWS THEMSELVES

I have always believed that the most convincing intellectual arguments to prove the guilt of certain mass criminals are those that they themselves say. I have discovered that one of the main weaknesses of the Jew is his unique arrogance. Even though lying is the most universal characteristic of the Jew – his "stiff-necked" character (as our Lord observed in Scripture) has identified them for what they are, till this very day.

I had the unfortunate experience of having to deal in business with the 'self-chosen' for years and I have encountered in life, no more disgusting creatures than the Jew. No other ethnicity in mankind has exhibited their wickedness with such predictable 'chutzpah'. Some comments by Jews are obviously critical of the universally filthy nature of fellow Jews – but they only reinforce my case against the hateful evil nature of the tribe against ALL MEN.

This, from Scripture – Thess 2-15 pretty much says it all: "Jews, who both killed the Lord Jesus and the prophets, and drove us out. They are not pleasing to God, but hostile to all men,"

Here then is a modest 'collection' of self-incriminating statements that is by no means complete. The first example pretty much says it all

One of the comments by a modern day Rabbi (Eric Lankin) perhaps sums it all up in a speech where he references a comment by another Rabbi: "Rabbi Yitz Greenberg in his book, Living in the Image of God, (p.79) notes that _"Jews are not genetically programmed to be good.. It takes great effort-and religious training-to go on acting Jewishly"

[My comment] "ACTING JEWISHLY"? How profound! Our Lord does NOT 'program' His children to be evil – BUT since He accused the Jews of being sons of the Devil in John of the NT – it stands to reason that if the Jew is programmed to be evil – as suggested by Rabbi Greenberg – that this could only be done by Satan. Thank you for PROVING my point. The Jew IS the spawn of hell!

My dear Rabbi – has it ever occurred to you that THE reason mankind has suffered HUNDREDS OF MILLIONS MURDERED – the horrors of Communism – the moral destruction of ENTIRE NATIONS – WORLD WARS – and more currently over a million murdered in the Mid-East – IS PRECISELY THAT THE JEW IS "ACTING JEWISHLY"!

"The strongest supporters of Judaism cannot deny that Judaism is anti-Christian." (Jewish World, March 15, 1924)

"I am devoting my lecture in this seminar to a discussion of the possibility that we are now entering a Jewish century, a time when the spirit of the community, the non-ideological blend of the emotional and rational and the resistance to categories and forms will emerge through the forces of anti-nationalism to provide us with a new kind of society. I call this process the Judaization of Christianity because Christianity will be the vehicle through which this society becomes Jewish." (Rabbi Martin Siegel, New York Magazine, p. 32, January 18, 1972)

"There is no such thing as a Judeo-Christian religion. We consider the two religions so different that one excludes the other." (Rabbi Moshe Maggal of the National Jewish Information Service).

"Do not let the forces of evil take over to make this a Christian America." (Senator Howard Metzenbaum, 11/6/86)

[mycomment] I have a news flash for you, Sen 'MetzenJew' ! – THIS IS – or at least it WAS a Christian country before your ilk turned it into a morally rotted corpse. MY COUNTRY – AMERICA – was founded by decent brave self-sacrificing Christians – NOT Godless Jew scum. Get it – scumbag? Hope you have enjoyed the last 5 years rotting in Hell!

"The strongest supporters of Judaism cannot deny that Judaism is anti-Christian." (Jewish World, March 15, 1924)

"I am devoting my lecture in this seminar to a discussion of the possibility that we are now entering a Jewish century, a time when the spirit of the community, the non-ideological blend of the emotional and rational and the resistance to categories and forms will emerge through the forces of anti-nationalism to provide us with a new kind of society. I call this process the Judaization of Christianity because Christianity will be the vehicle through which this society becomes Jewish." (Rabbi Martin Siegel, New York Magazine, p. 32, January 18, 1972)

"A Jew remains a Jew even though he changes his religion; a Christian which would adopt the Jewish religion would not become a Jew, because the quality of a Jew is not in the religion but in the race. A Free thinker and Atheist always remains a Jew." (Jewish World, London December 14, 1922)

On March 15th, 1923, the Jewish World asserted: "Fundamentally -Judaism is Anti-Christian."(Waters Flowing Eastward, p. 108)

"The Jew is not satisfied with de-Christianizing, he Judaizes, he destroys the Catholic or Protestant faith, he provokes indifference but he imposes his idea of the world of morals and of life upon those whose faith he ruins. He works at his age old task, the annihilation of the religion of Christ." (Benard Lazare, L'Antisemitism, p. 350; Rabbi Benamozegh, quoted in J. Creagh Scott's Hidden Government, page 58).

"Today the Gentile Christians who claim of holy right have been led in the wrong path. We, of the Jewish Faith have tried for centuries to teach the Gentiles a Christ never existed, and that the story of the Virgin and of Christ is, and always has been, a fictitious lie. In the near future, when the Jewish people take over the rule of the United States, legally under our god, we will create a new education system, providing that our god is the only one to follow, and proving that the Christ story is a fake...Christianity will be abolished." (M.A. Levy, Secretary of the World League of Liberal Jews, in a speech in Los Angeles, California, August, 1949)

"Why should we believe in God? We hate Christianity and Christians. Even the best of them must be regarded as our worst enemies. They preach love of one's neighbor, and pity, which is contrary to our principles. Christian love is a hindrance to the revolution. Down with love of one's neighbor; what we want is hatred. We must know how to hate, for only at this price can we conquer the universe...The fight should also be developed in the Moslem and Catholic countries, with the same ends in view and by the same means." (Lunatcharski, The Jewish Assault on Christianity, Gerald B. Winrod, page 44)

[my comment]: Regarding the parts in red – NOW – do you need ANY other reason to destroy the Jew – before he destroys us – ONLY the Jew would utter such hatred. Note that the jew Levy's prediction of over 60 years ago was spot on. The jewish people HAVE taken over rule of the United States and the Arab people – once good friends and allies have been morphed into enemies by endless jew lies – and Christians have now been morphed into IsraHELL before America -racist Christ mocking – war mongers! Are you people both blind and deaf?

"The facts on the ground, when not obscured by one or another Zionist rationalization, show that the Zionists are the worst anti-Semites in the world today, oppressing a Semitic people as no nation has done since the Nazis." — Jewish professor Bertell Olman .

[MY comment] Of course he is speaking of the Palestinians – tortured brutalized starved beaten humiliated raped and murdered for the past 65 years as we greedy ignorant Merkans could care less.

On Nov. 12, 2004, one of Imus's (a well known talk show host) regular guests Sid Rosenberg referred to Palestinians as "stinking animals." "They ought to drop the bomb right there, kill 'em all right now," he said

[My comment] – That comment by Rosenberg was an incitement for mass murder of innocent civilians – NOW try to imagine what would happen if such a comment had been made by an Arab against jews

Here's what Joseph Weitz, director of the Jewish National Fund, had to say about making Israel [sic] " Arabrein": "The only solution is Eretz Israel [Greater Israel], or at least Western Eretz Israel [all the land west of Jordan River], without Arabs. There is no room compromise on this point ... We must not leave a single village, not a single tribe." (Sept. 29, 1967)

Israeli president Moshe Katsav on Arabs: "There is a huge gap between us (Jews) and our enemies—not just in ability but in morality, culture, sanctity of life, and conscience. They are our neighbors here, but it seems as if at a distance of a few hundred meters away, there are people who do not belong to our continent, to our world, but actually belong to a different galaxy." (May 10, 2001)

[My comment] In typical jew fashion the Satan worshiping Katsav demonizes his victims (a decent Godly people I know well, who are persecuted by the filthy jew) and lionizes the filthy jews (an indecent Godless lying murderous sadistic race of demonic reptiles which I ALSO know VERY VERY well!

In "Letter of Resignation from the Jewish People," Bertell Ollman, a professor at New York University, challenged Jews to face up to similarities between Nazism and Zionism:

IsraHELL foreign minister Lieberman's hatred of Arabs is indistinguishable from Hitler's hatred of Jews. It is so overt that it offends other members of Israel's government, such as when he urged total war against the Palestinian resistance: " `At 8 a.m. we'll bomb all the commercial centers... at noon we'll bomb their gas stations... at two we'll bomb their banks,' To On May 5, 2006, Lieberman actually advocated the execution of any Arab politician who even spoke to the Hamas government of Palestine.

"We must realize that our party's most powerful weapon is racial tensions. By propounding into the consciousness of the dark races that for centuries they have been oppressed by whites, we can mold them to the program of the Communist Party. In America we will aim for subtle victory. While inflaming the Negro minority against the whites, we will endeavor to instill in the whites a guilt complex for their exploitation of the Negroes. We will aid the Negroes to rise in prominence in every walk of life, in the professions and in the world of sports and entertainment. With this prestige, the Negro will be able to intermarry with the whites and begin a process which will deliver America to our cause." (Israel Cohen, A Racial Program for the Twentieth Century, 1912. Also in the Congressional Record, Vol. 103, p. 8559, June 7, 1957

[MY comment]: HELLO! Can ANY American patriot NOW wonder why the lying treacherous Jew is so universally hated – or why the Democrat Party has always been the haven for Jews,

Communists and traitors? Remember – the JEW – NOT any Negro – organized the treasonous NAACP for his own evil schemes – as so clearly shown in the above. It is the JEW that keeps racial hatred alive in the USA

Truth be known – a complete compendium of these corrosive damning statements by the Christian hating Jew – would FILL A THICK TEXTBOOK! What are you waiting for people? Get off your lazy derrieres and save OUR nation. The 'ENEMY' is RIGHT HERE and is IN YOUR FACE 24-7! How much more degradation – humiliation- loss of freedoms and destruction of our most sacred core values and beliefs are you willing to tolerate at the hand of these Godless, treacherous, cunning, lying, Christ hating, sons of Satan scum?

WAKE UP AMERICA!

OCTOBER 2012
IDF JEWS – TERRORISTS, BULLIES, PERVERTS AND COWARDS

I spent sometime living among the "Children Of Satan" as exposed by Jesus in the Book of John 8-44 The place they live is the world's largest unflushed toilet AKA IsraHELL – AKA Satan's 'corporate hqs.' While there I had a close association with the world's largest institutionalized terrorist organization – the IDF – or IsraHELL defense cowards. They love to target schools hospitals and public utilities necessary for life. Spineless sniveling cowards.

It 'defends' nothing and spends 99% of the time murdering defenseless women and children – raping – stealing and committing criminal acts whose barbarism and sadistic brutality have no equal in military history. The jewish people are and always have been functional psychopaths – greedy lying treacherous inbred perverts and social outcasts to the rest of humanity. They begin training their children hate deception greed lust betrayal treason and cruelty from the day they are spawned.

They are taught that they are somehow superior to all other humans and that we cattle (goyim) are inferior only fit to serve them as slaves. I witnessed these detestable loathsome attributes every day in one form or another. Their military is nothing more than a gaggle of mammas boys who have been given big guns authority and taught to attack only the defenseless the helpless the the weak the sick the injured and the elderly.

I have worked with few foreign military – but those of which I have been exposed (Soviet Spetsnaz, SAS, Salvadoran Marines and Atlacatl rangers (their special forces) were all formidable troops who had unquestionable valor.

The beady eyed rat-faced jews, however – were the most cowardly scum I have ever seen. I would hear them bragging about killing some 5 or 6 year old 'rag head or if they felt extra brave that day, they might tackle beating to death some 14 year old kid.

Mosques weren't their only targets for desecration and destruction. These reptiles ALSO targeted Christian churches with equal hatred and barbaric sadism. I had been informed by Red Cross volunteers there, that it was common to see a church ransacked the altar defecated on (with the feces spread on the walls and images and statues of Christ and the Virgin Mary) and of course they urinated on everything that they might consider holy to a Christian.

OH and by the way – it has been verified that these blasphemous outrages against ALL decency were not only approved by commanders but were participated in by them. There are only bad jews and worse jews. Been there seen that.

I personally heard them mock America, Christians and especially their loyalty to America (if they were dual citizenship reptiles) many times. The jews used children as human shields – beat them up in schoolyards and in their homes. These brave 'warriors' destroyed their crops – demolished private homes – humiliated young and old women – punched pregnant women in the stomach and worse. One of their favorites was to beat a child to death in front of his parents – in hopes that the parents would give them cause to also murder the parents.

One of their special loves was to murder a pregnant mother AND her innocent unborn child at the same time. It was SO popular among these coward civilian killers that they actually wore a T-shirt that showed a young mother with a bull's-eye over her belly with the caption: ONE SHOT – TWO KILLS. The only ethnicity on EARTH which would PROUDLY demonstrate such abysmal cowardice is the jew!

I witnessed jew thugs racing through Palestinian neighborhoods – taunting the owners – brandishing automatic weapons screaming insults at mothers and daughters in full view of police and or military – obviously with full approval of their terrorist acts. Of course Joe redneck six-pack never sees any of these TRUE horrors on his Talmud vision Jew tube.

Here is another 'fun' diversion of the cowardly kikes: This is the typical level of cowardice combined with sadism that is so typical of jewish conduct. Similar horrors involving sniper teams and hungry dogs were relayed to me by the CIA operatives in my company as well as human rights groups. The horrors you are about to read were deliberate and planned by these cowardly jews.

Jan 15, 2009 GAZA CITY – "Oh, God! I have never seen such a terrible scene," cried Kayed Abu Aukal.

The emergency doctor could not believe himself seeing the remains of what was days back Shahd, a full-fleshed 4-year-old Palestinian girl. She died when an Israeli shell was fired at the backyard of her home in the Jabalya refugee camp northern Gaza strip, where she was playing.

When her parents attempted to rush to the rescue of their kid, who fell to the ground amid a pool of her blood, rains of Israeli bullets kept them a distance. For the next five days Shahd's which was left lying in the open left for dogs to tear out. "The dogs did leave one single part of the poor baby's body intact," said a tearful Abu Aukal.

"We have seen heart-breaking scenes over the past 18 days. We picked up children whose bodies were torn or burnt, but nothing like this." For five days Shahd's brother, Matar, and cousin, Mohamed, tried in vain to reach her body. They were fired at by the Israeli occupation forces every time.

Seeing the body of the little angel torn to piece by the assaulting dogs, the two made one final attempt, and it was their last. They were showered by Israeli bullets before they could reach Shahd's body, joining a long list of more than 920 Palestinians killed by Israel since December 27.

Omran Zayda, a young neighbor, said the Israelis knew very well what they were doing."They chased her family and prevented them from reaching to her body, knowing that the dogs would eat it," he said. "They are not just killing our children, they are intentionally doing so in the most heinous and inhuman ways." Zayda said words, and even cameras, can not describe the horrific scene.

"You can never imagine what the dogs have done to her innocent body," he said, fighting back his tears. Many Palestinians insist Shahd was not the first or only such case. In Jabalya, when Abd Rabu's family was trying to bury three of its dead, the Israeli forces started firing at them, witnesses said. They then released their dogs at the bodies, deserted by mourners who sought shelter from the Israeli gunfire, they added.

"What happened was awful and unthinkable," Saad Abd Rabu, the deceased uncle, told IOL. "Our sons died before our eyes and we were even prevented from burying them," he cried. "The Israelis just released their dogs at their bodies, as even they have not done enough."

You will never see a powerful rich movie mogul like the jew Steven Speilberg do a real life movie based on such horrors. WHY? – because the poor children who were murdered then eaten while the jew monsters laughed at their grizzly deed – were just Christian or Muslim 'goy' and were considered less than roaches to scum like Spielberg and the cold-blooded murdering IDF cowards. And these arrogant Christ-killing jews wonder why they are despised by every decent man woman and child on earth!

I could write volumes about the cowardly attacks on unarmed mission of mercy boats trying to break the blockade of Gaza to help dying and starving children by the thousands. These spineless worms murdered several unarmed brave civilians aboard the mercy boats just for meanness. The boats were bring water food medical supplies antibiotics dressings clothing tools and bare necessities of life to these poor people. Jews are simply- monsters!

Read this story by a real life hero on one of those boats if you want to see real selfless courage and compassion and valor. The man is Marine combat veteran Ken O'Keefe – and he has 'a place at my table any time he wants'. May God bless him. I hope to meet him someday and shake his hand as a brother for justice.

Here are some interesting facts regarding the TRUTH of the matter. You decide for yourself. I had the opportunity to personally witness one of the most cowardly acts attributable to ANY ethnicity – but apparently, as countless eyewitness record show – what I saw was typical for the Jew – and certainly one of the most repugnant disgusting acts of cowardice. I discovered later that what I witnessed took place on a daily basis. Remember – a coward is not necessarily the 'Casper Milk toast profile. Virtually all bullies are in reality cowards – as they always pick on the weakest and most defenseless.

When with the intel community In IsraHELL several years ago I had the opportunity to be part of a group that went inside the Jew occupied concentration camp we call Gaza (Palestine). While our Embassy van escorted by a Jew IDF jeep with heavily armed paras, reached the outskirts of Gaza City – which the Jews had completely demolished into rubble – the jeep stopped abruptly in front of us and the soldier on the rear of the jeep jumped out and dropped to a kneeling firing position – arming his rifle as he did so.

The 'enemy' – a five or six year old Palestinian child – undoubtedly an orphan of murdered parents, stood at the edge of the road – tears rolling down his quivering cheeks – with his had held high in defiance of his tormentors – holding an egg sized pebble. Our vehicle had by then also stopped and I instinctively jumped out – 'armed' with my CIA issue model 35mm Canon camera.

In 3-4 strides I was almost next to the Jew baby killer, who by this time had aimed at the head of the defenseless child and was about to murder him on the spot. Apparently my motion caught the corner of his eye and he turned his head to me for an instant. I aimed my camera at him and muttered loud enough fro him to hear; " if you murder that child – you better kill all of us – because the world will see these pictures" At the same time I gave this cowardly Jew bastard the universal 'middle finger gesture.

He uttered something to me and angrily stood down – retreating to his jeep. I breathed a sigh of relief and went back inside the embassy van. One of the agents inside said: "You know – you just saved that child's life" Another passenger immediately retorted: – " yea – but it won't matter anyway – that kid will probably not live another week anyway – they routinely shoot these Palestinian children here for target practice".

I never forgot that vision or the cowardly sadistic nature of the Jew. Had he murdered that child and had I been armed – there is NO doubt in my mind that I would have shot that cowardly scum on the spot. Such is the cowardly nature of the Jew. These cold-blooded murders of helpless civilian men women and children are well documented and continue to this day. There is an old saying: "a wolf never jumps on another wolf" Like the Jew – he is an opportunistic predator seeking out the helpless – aged or injured.

The criminal acts of cowardice by the Jew military (the IDF – which is IN FACT the largest institutionalized terrorist group in the world) are as numerous as they are disgusting. In the recent attack on the virtually defenseless Lebanon (a mostly Christian nation incidentally) the cowardly Jews shelled tens of thousands of fleeing terrified civilian refugees – mostly helpless children – with the most horrific weapons ever invented – heavy artillery fire utilizing NOT ONLY 'HE' (high explosives) but the Geneva Convention outlawed WP (white phosphorous) and the most diabolic killing tool ever conceived – Cluster Bombs – responsible for more civilian casualties than any other 'ground delivered' ordinance.

These cowardly Jews are so sadistic that they had their children present at the safe artillery sites – ACTUALLY WRITING HATE SLOGANS ON THESE 155 mm shells that would soon turn living children into pieces of raw meat. Some of these slogans read: " with love – from the children of Israel to the children of Lebanon". These cowardly Jews actually targeted terrified refuge columns. This incredible cowardly Jew outrage is ALSO WELL DOCUMENTED.

There is not enough room in one article to enumerate all of the recorded acts of cowardice by the Jew – but it should give you a good idea. Now – lets take a good hard DOCUMENTED FACTUAL look at the record of Jew 'heroism in the USA military.

What better yardstick of valor than the coveted US Congressional Medal of Honor. Let me preface these statistics with some other relevant facts about the character of the Jew. Let the Jews howl all they want when they read these FACTS – as they have never been able to handle TRUTH, as lies –duplicity – treason and deception have historically – for MILLENNIA – been their MO for business – diplomacy – 'religion' and everyday aspects of life. Even the official motto of their terrorist military reveals their TRUE nature: " BY DECEPTION WE WAGE WAR"

FACT: wherever there was dissention and troublemakers ALWAYS siding with our Communist mortal enemies – the provocateurs were always JEWS!

FACT: although only some 3 % of the Soviet population – over 50% of the Communist commissars were JEWS!

FACT: Although only about 3-4% of the American population – the Jew comprised some 75% of the treasonous American Communist Party (CPUSA)

FACT: This same Jewish 3-4% low percentage comprises virtually 100% of the pornography filth in the USA

FACT: Virtually ALL infanticide (child murder) support in America is from JEWS. Not surprisingly these 'self-chosen' cowards murder nearly 20% of all live born infants in IsraHELL.

FACT: Virtually ALL homosexual /pedophile organization support, membership, funding in America is from the JEW.

FACT: over 80% of the world's crime syndicates are JEWS!

FACT: over 80% of the Jews in my country are Atheist and members of the Democrat Party (which in essence is indistinguishable from the CPUSA which consistently supports Dem. Presidential candidates)

FACT: over 98% of organized worldwide prostitution is funded, organized, operated by JEWS!

But – now lets get back to the matter of documented JEW 'bravery' and the Medal of Honor.

Remember – we non Jews are (to the Jew, nothing but cattle – or 'GOY', as they refer to us – and the Jew in his superior arrogant mind – is the 'CHOSEN' CHECK THIS OUT!

WWI ———— us = 124 jews = 3 2 .4%
WWII ———— us = 462 jews = 3 LESS THAN 1%
KOREA ———— us =131 jews = 0 0% NADA! NONE!
VIETNAM——— us = 245 jews = 2 LESS THAN 1%

We could even include the Civil War where the 'Self-Chosen' are always first in line to shrilly scream their support for civil rights – Black equality – emancipation etc etc. Want to see these facts too?

CIVIL WAR ——us = 1522 jews = 12 AGAIN – LESS THAN 1%

So much for the Jew who apparently is great at talking the talk – but pretty yellow when it comes to 'walking the walk'. Mmnn ? got to wonder what all these 'brave' Jews were thinking during WWII when their fellow 'chosen' were paying for their crimes in German prisons.

I think I knew the answer. They were too busy seducing our daughters and bedding down our wives while we were in foxholes doing a MAN"S job for them. OH and BTW -= THAT is WELL documented! Of course- in fairness to the 'chosen' – they had better things to do than risk their precious kike butts. Like making lots of war profit – staffing communist organizations – producing porn filth – inciting hate against anti-Communism – destroying the family unit and of course waging their ceaseless battle against true Christianity. And of course – as we know today – thanks to their tireless efforts – our America is now nothing less than a morally rotted corpse – dysfunctional – rudderless – greedy – secular Godless shadow of it's former goodness.

As a personal note: One of the assignments I had in the military was to train combat troops for Vietnam and especially for the then looming early 60s Berlin Crisis – we were getting ready for war with the Jew's good friends – the COMMUNISTS! For thirteen straight months – 6 days a week – 12 hours a day, I and other men of that period churned out as many disciplined well trained – well motivated young warriors as possible. Close to a thousand young men that knew by sight and name at one time (I was their company commander) Guess what? There was not one Berg – Goldstein – Silverman – Weiss – Cohen – Ruben – Hoffman or ANY other 'chosenites' – NOT ONE. Just a coincidence, of course.

Just as an afterthought – BUT CRITICALLY IMPORTANT!. =====

Casualties from our Jew incited serial wars — 60,000+ and I predict over 100,000 before we wake up and figure out who the REAL enemy is and stop murdering IsraHELL's enemies. Additionally there are more than SIX HUNDRED THOUSAND vets back home who are infected by incurable radio-active DU poisoning who all have a death sentence

Innocent Civilians we have murdered for the Jew – TWO MILLION + SO FAR
Innocent civilians we have made homeless for the Jew – OVER TEN MILLION – SO FAR

SO – how much more do you fools want to worship these cowardly scum who have been damned by Christ – damned by their own word – damned by the prophets and damned by world famous historical figures from Seneca to Caesar and from Wagner to Washington.

OCTOBER 2012
SATANIC GODLESS JEWS BRUTALIZE CHRISTIANS IN THE HOLY LAND

The TRUTH: The Jew has tormented Christian and Muslim Palestinians for decades with torture – death – starvation – destruction of their land (livelihood) – sacrilege against their most sacred religious beliefs – theft of their land – shooting of their sons as target practice- rape of their daughters and every imaginable form of perversion and brutality – AND FINALLY WHEN these poor people can no longer bear this kind of sadistic genocide they try to fight back.

Here is a typical example of the TRUE nature of the scummy filthy demonic sub-human 'chosen' of Satan I had to endure every day when I was in IsraHELL with top intelligence officials. Keep in mind that IF the poor Christian Palestinian home owner victim in the film below, were to make the provocation or slightest defense of his home or family or honor or his faith in Christ – he would have been murdered by the demon jew – a military tank contingent sent to his home to destroy it – murder the film crew – murder all his family and there would be NO recourse- NO justice – no news of it – as if it had never happened.

Imagine if these hate filled Christ hating demons ever got control of the police AND the military and the Executive and the legislative and the judicial in our now almost totally jew-occupied country. This SAME horror would be repeated a million times at the homes of TRUE American Christians – and just like the poor family in this disgraceful film – you could do NOTHING to defend yourself. Think about that for a moment.

That EXACT scenario is only a heartbeat away. Share this with your children and friends. Be aware that cowardly bully jew filth like this scum always use abusive obscene language.

Remember – the imprisoned Palestinians have no planes – no tanks – no Hawk missiles – no army – no nuclear weapons – no artillery – no fighter jets – no attack helicopters – no submarines – no battleships – no BILLION DOLLAR YEARLY ARMS SUPPORT FROM AMERIKA – so what can they do to defend their wives- their sons – their daughters – their homes – their crops – their holy places – their businesses- their culture- their pride?

NOTHING — EXCEPT BE MURDERED- RAPED- KILLED- TORTURED- HUMILIATED – unless they are willing to sacrifice the ONLY weapon they have – their own frail bodies! They sacrifice themselves with a heroism that we fat slob Fallwellianista imbecilic beer guzzling party animal cowards cannot comprehend – so we racist morons call them ' TERRORISTS' for DARING to fight back at their tormentors. WE ARE A SICK PEOPLE!

I WAS THERE! My credentials – both civic and military are flawless – yet any attempt to exercise my freedom of speech of the God's honest truth of these horrors (freedom of press) in today's jew occupied colony of IsraHELL – has been – and will continue to be CENSURED.

These and many other TRUTHS should be allowed to be seen heard and read by ALL Americans – yet the jews who control our media will NOT allow it. Our freedoms are GONE.

Virtually NONE of you reading this have ever or WILL ever experience witnessing these horrors. I HAVE! I have witnessed horrors elsewhere on the planet outside my own little comfortable sphere – but nothing like the sadistic cruelty of the Jews – NOTHING! When jew like war criminal Netanyahu opens his filthy mouth – you can be sure of thing – you will soon hear a hateful lying diatribe designed to benefit only his Satanic ilk!
Jesus spent a good part of His adult life on earth being persecuted by the lying treacherous Jew. These Jews were living a lie with their blasphemous false 'religion'. They worshiped MAMON and not God. The Christian Bible is REPLETE with such proof. to learn just some of them – read ALL of my 'signature' at the end of my report. Check them out in the Bible for yourself.

Jew conduct on EVERY level of life betrays their filthy lives and black hearts! Can you in all honesty declare that there is a SINGLE moral problem with America today : exempli gratia: = rising infanticide – glorification of homosexual perversion- mounting teen suicides – racial strife unlike any in past history- the encouragement of adultery and 'sport sex' – drug culture attitudes – instant divorce – destruction of school prayer- unpunished officially govt authorized mass murders of CIVILIAN AMERICAN CITIZENS– destruction of the sanctity and holiness of Christmas – rampant immorality among our Congress – feminism(read; organized mockery of the family) – satanic 'heavy metal' rock popularity – moral relativism taught in schools – creationism replaced by evolution – the OFFICIAL "character doesn't count policy of the Democrat Party – "crime is Ok as long as you don't get caught" official Clinton mentality – RAMPANT civilian murders and rapes by our 'new improved' neocon military leadership – The near total destruction of TRUE Christian churches in America – creation of non-existent enemies by lies – subterfuge and intimidation- the total trashing of Constitutional liberties and rights by a rogue drunkard drugged out Zionist President Bush– triple digit inflation – destruction of the Gold/silver standard of a stable economy – Dress codes of modesty and civility cast to the winds – vulgarity of every shape manner and form on prime time TV – the mass drugging of our school children with deadly addictive psychotropic narcotics – The eminent destruction of the First and

Second Amendments – the creation of 'hate' and ' thought' crimes to cripple Christian belief – JUST FOR OPENERS —-that is NOT the doing of the Jew and his shabbus goy appendages?

There are arguably HUNDREDS More examples – but these are some of the most destructive. REMEMBER – THIS is what the Jew did to the Christians in Germany. The only real difference was that the people there finally woke up and had enough criminal abuse and decided to save their country from the exact same jew instigated MORAL and ECONOMIC destruction that has stolen our blessed country from us today.

Shun the jew like the demons they are. They are a pestilence among mankind – a deadly fatal disease. They breed hatred wars misery hopelessness death and destruction everywhere they are allowed to settle and breed more demons like the one in the film.

You don't get your sorry ass kicked out of 109 nations over the past nineteen hundred years – as have these filthy jews – just for being 'different'. How about for being EVIL DEMONS!

ALL of these horrible evils are BY DESIGN and NOT BY ACCIDENT! They are ALL the creation and joy of the Jew. The UNASSAILABLE TRUTH IN EVIDENCE of these calculated pre-mediated crimes would fill a vault the size of the Library of Congress!

So why do we tolerate this cancer? Plain simple monumental stupidity! We know WHO and WHAT the enemy is. We know what the deadly consequences are- so what are we waiting for – to wake up in another Jew hell – like Palestine? Remember – 20% of ALL the women and children murdered for sadistic pleasure of the Jew terrorists (the IDF) are brothers and sisters in Christ! Christian Arabs and Muslim Arabs have lived there in peace for centuries.

The terrorists are the JEWS! The Jew terrorist bullies – the so-called IDF – are the WORLD'S LARGEST INSTITUTIONALIZED TERRORIST ORGANIZATION ON THE PLANET – PERIOD! By the Jews OWN LIPS – the origins of the IDF are Irgun Hagganah, Stern Gang, Irgun, and Zvai Leumi. Begin was a leader of one of these terrorist cells. Their murderous exploits were undeniable and historically recorded – but of course the typical lying Jew with his satanic mentality actually wants us stupid goy to believe that somehow all these PROVEN sadistic cold-blooded murderers miraculously became- and I quote "LEGITIMATE" – I KID YOU NOT! I can't just make this stuff up!

LEGITIMATE? Legitimate what? Legitimate terrorists? Only the Jew could show such shameless lying audacity. These sadistic soulless cowardly baby killers that I have witnessed in their daily murder of helpless innocent children are jews!

They are the same hate filled ilk of the treacherous Godless Satan worshiping demons who murdered Christ and who today live among us disguised as normal human beings as they silently erode our morals – our goodness and our freedoms.

In the name of God – those of you that are wise and elderly enough to remember America when we were still a good, moral, brave and truth loving people – tell your children how we were –

how this country was – the prosperity, moral foundations and freedoms that we loved practiced AND protected – AND – that they are STILL worth defending. WAKE UP PEOPLE!

The head of the monster lies in hell – more commonly known as modern Isra-HELL – and the tentacles are here – everywhere among us – not just in DC. but in our neighborhoods our schools cities and towns like rabid dogs. IsaHELL is America's albatross – LOSE IT!

IF – you are a REAL Christian – and NOT one of the duplicitous Pharisees that has already sold his or her souls to Falwell – Hagee – Hinn – Robertson – Graham – Osteen or any of the other – Christ mocking millionaire – self-serving – fraud false prophets of prosperity – racism – hate – blasphemy and war mongering – Wake up!

Do the right thing. Show some moral courage and defend our TRUE faith – expose the TRUE Satanic influence in our midst – the lying Jews – the "sons of the Devil" – those who WILL destroy our once Godly Christian Republic – before they DO!

OCTOBER 2012
CUNNING JEWS DEMONIZE THEIR VICTIMS AND ABSOLVE THEMSELVES

Jews are the most evil wicked lying scum on the planet. They have committed the most grievous monstrous crimes in history and caused more innocent death and more destruction that any race on earth.

I have come to know these 'Sons of Satan' well over the past 50 years and understand how they effectively use their evil and lies like vampires.

First lets clear the air on one MAJOR lie and deception regarding the jew and his perennial persecution complex with his irrelevant imbecilic obligatory mantra of "anti-Semitism". Understand THIS TRUTH – the jews have NEVER EVER suffered any persecution. The jew has ALWAYS been the persecutor – the perp – the agitator – the instigator of evil beyond evils! He has been given FAR too little JUSTICE for his immense CRIMES – but that WILL change.

A 'PERSECUTION COMPLEX' is defined in Oxford dictionary as : " An insane delusion that one is being persecuted" To be persecuted is to have suffered an irrational unjust punishment which has nothing to do with offense or wrongdoing or wickedness or evil or sinful acts. There is such a thing as persecution but it has NOTHING to do with ANYTHING that has happened to the demonic wicked jews.

The jews FORMALLY declared open war against their OWN country in March of 1933 and then we are supposed to be surprised when they got thrown in jail as self- professed traitors. Keep in mind that these ungrateful scum jews had turned Germany into the same type of morally rotted corpse and economically destroyed nation that we are today. These treasonous unloyal jew criminals (like the ones in OUR government today) were shown JUSTICE for their crimes against the entire nation. You don't persecute dangerous REAL criminals like the jews – you show them LONG LONG OVERDUE JUSTICE!

At least Germany was finally free and its people economically prosperous and united and had hope for the first time in years. That is a HELL of a lot more that I can say about USA today. Free – MY ASS! We are nothing more than an ass kissing colony of IsraHELL and quasi slaves of the occupying jews.

The ONLY difference was that THEY were fortunate enough to have a man (unlike the putrid treasonous self serving scum we have today in our jew occupied 'Merka') who CARED more about the welfare of his OWN people than his own wealth and comfort.

A good example of genuine persecution might be as follows: e.g. Negro who in his daily life is a decent truthful responsible sober considerate hard working member of the community is tormented slandered ridiculed mocked and threatened with violence and slanderous epitaphs such as nigger – spear chucker – and 'boy' – solely for the color of his skin. That is racism and bigotry fuelled persecution and should never be tolerated – PERIOD!

Example #2 A Negro youth is an Ebonics speaking gang- banger thief violent profane lazy low life piece of scum and a constant threat to society both black and white (like Trayvon Martin). He is charged with crimes arrested and put in prison – FOR HIS CONDUCT. THAT IS CALLED JUSTICE – and should ALWAYS be enforced to protect innocent decent members of society – PERIOD!

Example #3 A an American of Arab ethnicity who is a hard working patriotic decent honest moral family man – is harassed by the typical inbred low life imbecile red-neck mentality scum who slander him with racist epitaphs such as 'rag-head' – 'sand-nigger' – 'dune-coon' and worse – has suffered from racism fuelled persecution which has no place in MY country – a Republic (nation of laws) founded on Christian principles .

Example #3 A white TRUE Christian who is law abiding mainstream responsible decent truthful and honest – is beat up and abused by police in a big American city for his peaceful non-confrontational public support on public property – of his Christian faith (in a Christian nation) is the ultimate persecution and should NEVER under ANY circumstances. (this is a real life example I am aware of)

Example #4 A jew who has committed blasphemous profane filthy homosexual conduct in public mocking the Lord Christ and all who follow the true teachings of Christ – is set upon by an angry crowd of mainstream parents children and teachers. The jew scum cries foul and of course wraps himself in the cloak of "anti-Semitism" and eventually accuses the INJURED parties of infringing on HIS rights and sensibilities.

NOW we begin to see the first signs of that demonization of the VICTIMS and the VICTIMIZATION of himself – even though he is undeniably the scumbag and the perpetrator. The jew with his lies and deceptive nature has become a master of twisting and perverting the truth by making evil appear as good – good as evil.

Being the child of Satan he is endowed with the skills of deception shrewdness and cunning. It matter not that his filthy conduct in this example had violated the laws of MAN – the laws of NATURE – and the laws of GOD. He is a jew.

Now let me site an example so loathsome and so rancid that it defies all the laws of decency civility and humanness.

Some years back – I recall that a wealthy jewish man savagely raped a 5 year old girl to death. That in itself is not remarkable for the conduct of many jews – especially Rabbis. But here is what takes the offense over the top as far as evil. He of course hired an equally wicked jew lawyer who would use the classic jew – 'blame the victim' – execrable depravity as his defense.

He instructed his scum lawyer to appeal to the jury on the grounds that the little 5 year old had taunted his into a fit of uncontrollable lust by raising her little skirt. In other words – he expected the jury to understand that he could not help himself in view of what the girl did. I kid you not . Such is the perversity of the jew mind to even be able to conjure from the depths of Hell – such abysmal perverted filth. But then after all he was a jew – and Satanic progeny have no souls.

If you type in a search termed "Rabbi caught molesting child" – you get 380,000 hits. Just change the one word "CAUGHT" to " ACCUSED" and it nearly doubles! Oy Vey ! big surprise – not

Here is another example of just how demonically filthy these jews really are. Some filthy jew had been molesting a 12 you old child for years. When her family finally blew the whistle on the pervert the jew pervert got hundreds of his beady-eyed black suited dreadlocked black hat greasy hair pervert jew reptile friends to raise a half million dollars to keep his filthy carcass out of prison.

Open the video and take a look at the nasty looking 'chosen' filth of Satan and they ALL come together to shamelessly support his wickedness. To hell with the ruined life of the little child. Take a LONG HARD LOOK at these greasy smelly filthy perverts who run our country. Keep in mind – the victim was a jew. Can you imagine how much MORE $ they would have raised if the girl had been a Christian? double – Oy Vey!

Note that one anti pervert demonstrator in the film, nets out what the jew filth in his community do so well.
"THEY DEFEND the ABUSER – and COME OUT AGAINST THE VICTIM"

Tensions boil over outside fundraiser for accused jewish rapist …

This is what jews ALWAYS DO!

When these same filth screamed for the blood of Jesus two thousand years ago – it was the same mentality. their VICTIM – Christ – was called a bastard a sorcerer a blasphemer and every curse in the book – his mother was slandered as a WHORE. THEY the ABUSERS – claimed victimhood in that they had been admonished for their sleazy lying greedy murderous hypocrite Godless lifestyles (which they wanted to protect)

Once again- in their sick twisted evil sociopath minds – blame the poor victim – victimize their own wicked selves.

These reptiles have murdered tens of thousands of mostly helpless Palestinian women and children. They have raped murdered beaten terrorized humiliated robbed and destroyed their homes crops – poisoned their water supply destroyed their hospitals medical supplies murdered their doctors for 65 years! AND – of course they blame the poor helpless Palestinians for the fact that they are murdered 24-7.

As a witness to some of these horrid crimes – I look forward to the day when mankind has had enough of these demons and it is time to testify to an international tribunal of justice. If I am alive – I WILL BE THERE as a credible witness to their crimes against humanity.

Read what America's most famous warrior field commander – General George S Patton had to say about these filthy sadistic lying murdering cowardly animals in his memoirs:

"where, although room existed, the Jews were crowded together to an appalling extent, and in practically every room there was a pile of garbage in one corner which was also used as a latrine. The Jews were only forced to desist from their nastiness and clean up the mess by the threat of the butt ends of rifles. Of course, I know the expression 'lost tribes of Israel' applied to the tribes which disappeared — not to the tribe of Judah from which the current sons of bitches are descended. However, it is my personal opinion that this too is a lost tribe — lost to all decency."

"This happened to be the feast of Yom Kippur, so they were all collected in a large, wooden building, which they called a synagogue. It behooved General Eisenhower to make a speech to them. We entered the synagogue, which was packed with the greatest stinking bunch of humanity I have ever seen. When we got about halfway up, the head rabbi, who was dressed in a fur hat similar to that worn by Henry VIII of England and in a surplice heavily embroidered and very filthy, came down and met the General . . . The smell was so terrible that I almost fainted and actually about three hours later lost my lunch as the result of remembering it."

The New Testament (the CHRISTIAN Bible) is FILLED with damning statements form the prophets the apostles and Christ Himself as to the evil of these filthy lice infested demons.

Consider this testimony from Paul's 1st Epistle of Thessalonians. 1 Thessalonians 2:14-15 "For you, brethren, became imitators of the churches of God in Christ Jesus that are in Judea, for you also endured the same sufferings at the hands of your own countrymen, even as they did from the Jews, who both killed the Lord Jesus and the prophets, and drove us out. They are not pleasing to God, but hostile to all men,"

IOW – Jews have not only pissed off God – and have had nothing but evil conduct towards ALL of their fellow 'goyim'

Or this: From the Book Of John Chapter 8 – as Christ damns the Jews (and NOT JUST THE HIGH PRIESTS AND Pharisees – see notes below)

" Ye do the deeds of your father (the devil). If God were your father. ye would love me; for I proceed forth and came from God: neither came I of myself, but He sent me."

" Ye are of your father the devil and the lusts of your father ye will do. He was a murderer from the beginning and abode not in the truth, because there is no truth in him. When he speaketh a lie – he speaketh of his own; (the Jews) for he is a liar, and the father of it"

"That this SATANIC FATHERHOOD cannot be limited to the Pharisees is MADE CLEAR in 1 John 3;8-10″

Or this: Matthew 23:15 Jesus to the Jews ″ Woe to you, teachers of the law and Pharisees, you hypocrites! You travel over land and sea to win a single convert, and when he becomes one, you make him twice as much a son of hell as you are.

OR this: Matthew 23-33 Jesus to the Jews "You serpents, you generation of vipers, how can you escape the damnation of hell?"

OR HOW ABOUT THIS: Jeremiah 7 – 1-17 (just in case you doubt that God the Father dammed these LYING Sons of Satan as well) read it all so that you understand CLEARLY the damnation of God for the jews and their lies and evil conduct – that I did NOT Take the last and most damning phrase out of context as He orders NOT To even pray for these wicked jews.

The word that came to Jeremiah from the Lord, saying, "Stand in the gate of the Lord's house, and proclaim there this word, and say, 'Hear the word of the Lord, all you of Judah who enter in at these gates to worship the Lord!'" Thus says the Lord of hosts, the God of Israel: "Amend your ways and your doings, and I will cause you to dwell in this place. Do not trust in these lying words, saying, 'The temple of the Lord, the temple of the Lord, the temple of the Lord are these.'

"For if you thoroughly amend your ways and your doings, if you thoroughly execute judgment between a man and his neighbor, if you do not oppress the stranger, the fatherless, and the widow, and do not shed innocent blood in this place, or walk after other gods to your hurt, then I will cause you to dwell in this place, in the land that I gave to your fathers forever and ever.

"Behold, you trust in lying words that cannot profit. Will you steal, murder, commit adultery, swear falsely, burn incense to Baal, and walk after other gods whom you do not know, and then come and stand before Me in this house which is called by My name, and say, 'We are delivered to do all these abominations'? Has this house, which is called by My name, become a den of thieves in your eyes? Behold, I, even I, have seen it," says the Lord.

"But go now to My place which was in Shiloh, where I set My name at the first, and see what I did to it because of the wickedness of My people Israel. And now, because you have done all these works," says the Lord, "and I spoke to you, rising up early and speaking, but you did not hear, and I called you, but you did not answer, 14 therefore I will do to the house which is called by My name, in which you trust, and to this place which I gave to you and your fathers, as I have done to Shiloh. And I will cast you out of My sight, as I have cast out all your brethren—the whole posterity of Ephraim.

"Therefore do not pray for this people, nor lift up a cry or prayer for them, nor make intercession to Me; for I will not hear you."

I could fill pages with damnations by God and the Prophets – but hopefully 'the sources' are reputable enough for my readers to understand that these jews are evil to the core and have not changed nor repented one iota in the past two millennia. Look at the putrid hypocrite Godless filth in the video above AGAIN – and tell me you see the unbroken line of evil since God told Jeremiah NOT to even bother to pray for reprobate lying filthy demonic scum.

In all of my years on earth I have never SEEN nor even ever HEARD of so much as ONE thoroughly Evil wicked jew of the ilk of Joseph Lieberman or Abe Forman – either here or in IsraHELL sincerely repent for the horrid conduct of their lives and beg forgiveness from ALL they have wronged and offended and caused so much grief and suffering for so many years. It may be possible – but I will believe it when I actually see and hear and am convinced such a near miracle has occurred. Not all the lies and false ravings of crooks like John Hagee can change the TRUTH

Let me leave you with one more sordid but historically true MAJOR aspect of jew wickedness regarding CONDUCT!

These scum jews have been KICKED OUT of ONE HUNDRED AND NINE nations and city States world-wide for over EIGHTEEN centuries! No other ethnicity ON EARTH in ALL of recorded history has had such a horrible reputation. You know WHY these scum were kicked out? Simple – It was because they PERSECUTED their host nation by greed usury decadence moral depravities crime arrogance lies and countless abuses of the very people who showed them love compassion and hospitality.

Jews have been expelled from 109 countries. – Page 9

Jews are and have ALWAYS been the filthiest racially abusive immoral sadistic deceiving cheating 2 faced lying creatures on earth that have NEVER EVER missed ANY opportunity to persecute their neighbors.

Read what America's most famous warrior field commander – General George S Patton had to say about them in his memoirs: where, although room existed, the Jews were .crowded together to an appalling extent and in practically every room there was a pile of garbage in one corner which was also used as a latrine. The Jews were only forced to desist from their nastiness and clean up the mess by the threat of the butt ends of rifles. Of course, I know the expression 'lost tribes of Israel' applied to the tribes which disappeared — not to the tribe of Judah from which the current sons of bitches are descended. However, it is my personal opinion that this too is a lost tribe — lost to all decency."

"This happened to be the feast of Yom Kippur, so they were all collected in a large, wooden building, which they called a synagogue. It behooved General Eisenhower to make a speech to them. We entered the synagogue, which was packed with the greatest stinking bunch of humanity I have ever seen. When we got about halfway up, the head rabbi, who was dressed in a fur hat similar to that worn by Henry VIII of England and in a surplice heavily embroidered and very filthy, came down and met the General . . . The smell was so terrible that I almost fainted and actually about three hours later lost my lunch as the result of remembering it."

And yes – Patton would have exposed the TRUTH about these criminals from hell – and it cost him his life as it did President John F. Kennedy – our last courageous POTUS. WAKE UP PEOPLE – AND SMELL THE JEWS!

OCTOBER 2012
JOHN HAGEE – ONE OF THE MOST EVIL PEOPLE IN AMERICA

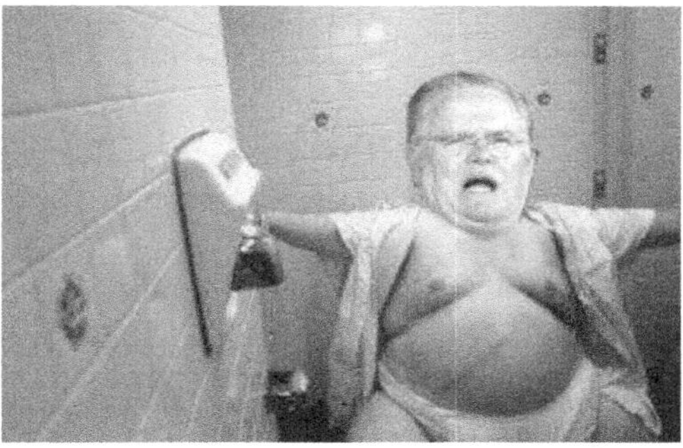

(OBESE KING OF PIGS – ON HIS 'THRONE' GIVING BIRTH TO JOHN JR.)

John Hagee is one of the most evil people on the planet. He mocks Jesus by his Satan worship - has betrayed USA – wants to start World War THREE – wants to have millions of innocent people murdered for the greater glory of the jews and IsraHELL – and all of these horrors under the big lie that he thinks he is some sort of a Christian pastor. In truth – he is a Satan worshiping fraud

He is as close to the true description of the jew (his mother is a jewess) anti-Christ as I have witnessed in my lifetime. He is the very essence of wickedness and evil. His mockeries of Christ could be right out of the Talmud. He oozes evil hate and bigotry like a leaking public toilet.

Just one of his sacrilegious blasphemies include the teaching to his 'flock' (who are indeed the most criminally ignorant of sheep) that our Lord Christ was NOT the Messiah – but war criminal Netanyahu.

His sins would fill a novel – his putrid demonic blasphemies rival the deeds of Satan himself – and his cruelty towards innocent – mostly defenseless women and children – are as evil as the worst war criminals in history. Physically he is the antithesis of moderation discipline and clean living.

He is a morbidly obese 400 pound pig faced – pig bodied blob of gluttonous lard! His capacity for hypocrisy is second only to his lustful crapulence. He quotes in his filthy jew book of mockery of Christ, titled :'In Defense Of Israel' (IsraHELL) " Jesus did not come to earth to be the Messiah – he refused by His own words to be the Messiah" BLASPHEMY!

John 1-22 "Who is a liar but he that deniath that Jesus is the Messiah. He is the AntiChrist that denieth the Father and The Son"

Pig Hagee also shrilly states that his book "will expose the vicious abuse of the jewish people" WT-! abuse – OF the jews? The most abusive people on earth! Did he mean those demons who murdered Christ – financed both sides of every war in Europe for the past Millennia – financed the slave trade – trashed Russia – started both world wars – trashed Germany – attacked the USS Liberty – trashed Christianity in America – and planned and executed 9-11 , just of openers?

BUT wait it gets even more bizarre! On page 140 Hagee the jew false Prophet states:" that Jesus REFUSED to be the Messiah of the jews. MORE BLASPHEMY

John 4-35-26 The woman at the well "I know that the Messiah is coming , the one who is called Christ . When He comes, He will tell us all things. Jesus then says to her: – "I that speak to you am He".

Further proofs to be found in Mark 13-6 Luke 2:26-32 John 6-69 John 22-30

Still think the jew pig Hagee even loves his jew friends? read this – written by the pig himself: "I'm not trying to convert the Jewish people to the Christian faith. In fact – trying to convert jews is a waste of time."

Hagee continues: " Everyone else – whether Buddhist or Baha'i needs to believe in Christ, but not the Jews. Jews already have a covenant with God that has never been replaced by Christianity." EVEN MORE BLASPHEMY

In other words, according to the obese lying pig Hagee – Jesus did not come to earth to be the Messiah to the Jews – only the Gentiles. He tells the Christians that Jesus IS the Messiah – but he tells the Jews that Jesus is NOT The Messiah – and that the jews can have salvation through their god.

BUT Jesus said (john 8-44) that the 'god' of the jews is Satan.(Ye are of your father – the devil)

It just keeps getting more and more ugly! Hagee commits adultery then divorces his wife for the woman in HIS OWN MINISTRY! You are an obese racist greedy adulterous pig Out of one side of his mouth he points an accusing finger at the flock and proclaims this condemnation: " Christians don't steal or lie – they don't get divorced or have abortions"

Gee fatso – looks like you have committed at least three of those four sins so far. Adultery then Divorced your wife Stole millions from your flock to support your multi-millionaire luxurious movie star life – and have Lied so many times perverting the Scripture you can't even remember your own lies. Can you say 'HYPOCRITE!?'

Your treason – false preaching for jew style prosperity and crimes against God have made you incredibly rich – I will give you that. A 6 thousand acre ranch with every conceivable luxury known to man – your own private jet -a private aerodrome on your ranch and of course a million dollar 5 thousand square foot 6 bedroom mansion + an endless 7 figure income are all so Christ-like modest and selfless I'm sure it must choke you to read Luke 18-24 to your fleeced flock.

Yet you still have the arrogance to boast of your own greed: "I deserve every dime I'm getting." (read : swindling) John Hagee.

He pays virtually no income tax and sends much of the pilfered millions to his terrorist pals in IsraHELL to pay for bullets and bombs to murder children (as i witnessed in Gaza) .

Lets see how your conduct stands up to what our Lord outlined as qualities which He said merited blessings. 'Sermon on the Mount' is a good place as any to start: "Blessed are the poor in spirit, For theirs is the kingdom of heaven." Pig Hagee – you are certainly too arrogant vain and haughty to ever feel you need the blessings of the Holy Spirit

"Blessed are those who mourn, For they shall be comforted". Pig Hagee – you have never ever 'mourned the death of ANY of your countless war victims. You actually gloat over innocent death

"Blessed are the meek, For they shall inherit the earth" Pig Hagee – there is not a modest or compassionate bone in your body. Boastfulness and arrogance are your evil nature

"Blessed are those who hunger and thirst for righteousness, For they shall be filled." Pig Hagee – your life's conduct is one of the most unrighteous composites of evil I have ever seen

"Blessed are the merciful, For they shall obtain mercy. Pig Hagee – you are a merciless bastard! You have never shown any of your millions of victims 'mercy' other than a violent death!

"Blessed are the pure in heart, For they shall see God. Pig Hagee – your heart is as black as that of your 'god' – Satan. Your entire life is a compendium of evil deeds. You will see only Satan!

"Blessed are the peacemakers, For they shall be called sons of God". Pig Hagee – you have never worked for peace – only for war terror and destruction. You are damned by God.

"Blessed are those who are persecuted for righteousness' sake, For theirs is the kingdom of heaven". Pig Hagee – YOU are the one who in fact has persecuted millions for wanting "righteousness peace and justice. You rejoice in the deaths of innocent women and children

Greedy obese slob Hagee claims that "Catholics and the Roman Church are somehow responsible for millennia of anti-Semitism and the death of Jesus Christ". Quite a feat – fatso – considering the term "catholic" is derived from the Greek word καθολικός (katholikos) meaning "universal" – was not even used to describe the Church until the early 2nd century.

If it were not for the evil influence resulting from the criminal level of stupidity of his BaptDUH brain-sharing lemmings – who would believe the earth was flat if Hagee said so – Hagee's vile insane jew hate screeds would be laughable third world nonsense. The endless malevolence and spurious fabrications in his hate mongering agitprop book are so filled with vulgar lies distortions blasphemies and heresy – it appears he must have been on drugs to come up with such rancid filth.

For example – this nauseous sicko obese man-pig mutant actually preaches that his 'god' was so pissed at the people of New Orleans – that he caused hurricane Katrina to destroy them all. Oh – you think I'm kidding?

"All hurricanes are acts of God because God controls the heavens. I believe that New Orleans had a level of sin that was offensive to God and they were recipients of the judgment of God for that." – John Hagee

Hagee had the audacity to use President John F. Kennedy's Berlin speech to compare it with his rantings for placing IsraHELL before our OWN USA! Talk about a low life underhanded ploy – considering the fact that Kennedy was murdered by Hagees jew friends for trying to keep America's wealth out of jew hands (the jew run Fed which had brought our nation economically to its knees)

JFK tried to save USA for Americans. Hagee is trying to betray America to IsraHELL as a jew 'colony'. Get it?

Hagee has compared mass murderer terrorist war criminal Netanyahu to our Lord by calling him the Messiah.

Here are just a couple of the quotes made by that murderous reptile: "Once we squeeze all we can out of the United States, it can dry up and blow away." — Israeli Prime Minister Benjamin Netanyahu, 2002.

Or for you imbecile treasonous jews first BaptDUH morons – here is what he thinks of you:

"My opinion of Christian Zionists? They're scum. But don't tell them that. We need all the useful idiots we can get right now." — Benyamin Netanyahu, at the time a former IsraHELL prime minister

John Hagee also says, "Most readers will be shocked by the clear record of history linking Adolf Hitler and the Roman Catholic Church in a conspiracy to exterminate the Jews. Honest folks – I just can't make these insane outrageous loony tunes lies up.

Keep this frightening fact in mind. More than FIFTY MILLION of Hagee's 'BaptDUH puppet drones here, share that kind of sick twisted reprobate irrational bigoted intolerant perverse imbecility. Are YOU next in their racist hate sights? If you are a Catholic – you already are.

It is said that there some deeds so putrid and so vile that even a sewer rat would not do -but scum like John Hagee doesn't have ANY reservations for wickedness – no matter how depraved reprehensible or diabolical. Just listen one of his MEGA- lying racist hate screeds and you will understand why his goals in life are to to (A) – take Americas to the trash heap and (B) to get even richer and more obese doing that evil.

Gee John – as arguably evil as you are – with that kind of sick ego – I wonder what God has in store for a non repentant Christ mocking lying blaspheming adulterous slandering glutinous devil-worshiping libelous racist hate-mongering war-mongering greedy soul-destroying violence-loving child-murdering treasonous vicious depraved demonic sadistic soulless fiend like yourself?

Your demise will be mourned by your father in Hell and celebrated by the angels in Heaven.

NOVEMBER 2012
AMC MAKES TRASH FOR YOU – CREATED BY THE GREEDY JEW

While watching my disgusting 'Talmud vision' after a long hard day of fighting and exposing the evil jews who have turned my country into a morally and economically rotted corpse – I noticed that an annoying scrolling 'bulletin' type message kept coming across my screen about every 5 minutes. It stated that AMC might not be able to show their putrid filth to our children any more unless the most imbecile of our moron couch potatoes filed formal complaints. ANY explanation of the REAL reason (hint = GREED) is of course cunningly omitted – clever bad jews.

Well, as a parent – grandparent – Veteran – Christian – and moral person – I thought I should do just that – FILE A COMPLAINT – AGAINST AMC – THAT IS! When you go to their jew site – you are told that you MUST be loyal to AMC to preserve the Godless crap they produce to poison the souls and minds of our children. They provide a phone number that is bogus so you cannot speak with a 'live' person.

Obviously there will always be people so stupid and so immoral and so shallow that ruining a child's life with jew filth violence sex adultery and every vile base trait that jews run THEIR lives by – will matter not a flying rat's ass to these scum. To show you how low we have sunk on the 'humanity scale' – here is an actual comment from one of these smegma breath jew loving pukes: – "They cannot drop amc because I live for the walking dead!"

THE REAL REASON? A no brainer – MORE JEW GREED! With jews it is ALWAYS about the money! These jew scum want to make the providers look like the bad guys. These greedy jews care ONLY about THEIR WEALTH. The name of game is to intimidate providers like Verizon so they are forced to absorb AMC's JEW GREED. AMC's jews think that we *(read: the provider and consumer)* should pay more money for the privilege of having our children being poisoned by their jew filth. Connect the dots yet?

If these greedy jews have their way – it is a win win situation for them and a lose lose deal for us stupid goyim (cattle to the jews) The greedy jew creators of this crap (the all jew AMC) WANT to MAKE the providers (Verizon) charge more to their customers. They are actually using their old extortion techniques they have perfected with two thousand years of lies. Obviously the BAD GUYS are the greedy jews who run these filth mills like AMC.

What viewers (those who are not sharing brains and can still think for themselves) should do is to vent their anger at the GUILTY PARTY. That guilty party is jew run AMC. Remember – ALL of these economic problems – unemployment – skyrocketing inflation – A fifty $bill to fill a modest size car with gas – taxes out of control with no end in sight – another insane IsraHELL created world war – all of these bad things – ALL – ARE the handiwork of the jew.

Lets look at some of the rancid putrid garbage our children might not have to get their souls rotted out by if they are simply 'DELETED" These are creations direct from the wicked reprobate lying Godless Christ hating reptile minds of these "SONS OF THE DEVIL" (John 8-44. read it YOUR SELF!)

All I did was uses a simple, honest, straight-forward search phrase for some of the rancid garbage filth that AMC vomits up in your living rooms every night! Note that ALL of the shows produced negative comments in the millions.

"Walking Dead is Jew produced trash" = 26,000,000 negative comments

"Mad Men is Jew produced trash = 14,700,000 negative comments

"Two and a Half Men is Jew produced trash" = 11,000,000 negative comments

"Breaking Bad is Jew produced trash" = 43,000,000 negative comments

"Kendra On Top is Jew produced trash = 13,600,000 negative comments

" Portlandia is Jew produced trash" = 3,020,000 negative comments

"The Killing is Jew produced trash" = 50,500,000 negative comments

" Hell On Wheels is Jew produced trash" = 1,450,000 negative comments

No decent person on earth would freely choose to watch – OR ALLOW their children to watch ANY of this putrid rancid lurid violent sex charged perverted jew slime with their family as long as any decent wholesome quality entertainment is available.

That is of course – unless of course you love Satan and his jew children (read John 8-44 AGAIN!) more than your own children as have the idiot parents of some 60 thousand dead American sons. These morons – whose criminal ignorance and stupefying red neck racism has encouraged them to send their OWN children to become murderers and terrorists in foreign lands of innocent people who have never done ANY of us ANY harm – are simply too brain dead stupid to enjoy the blessings decent moral informed Godly people have secured for them.

Just remember. The jew's reprobate evil mind works 24-7 to convince we poor stupid 'cattle' that to accept the filthy toilet they live in as 'normal' – so as to accept that kind of dung as 'acceptable' in our eyes. THAT is why he programs our children with endless filth violence and wicked lifestyles – portrayed as glamorous and cool and popular – especially the hi-tech ultra violent jew war games that glamorize violence and desensitize our kids to death and murder. the jew message here is 'War is COOL and FUN' – so go die for jew wars! Millions of our kids are hooked on jew created filth like 'C of D'.(Call Of Duty)

Re-read the comment by the jew puppet moron who stated for all the world – that "They cannot drop amc because I live for the walking dead!" Can you imagine this real life brain-dead Neanderthal troglodyte raising children to become a new generation of morons? An adult – who"LIVES" just to see 'zombies' THIS is our jew influenced America today? Twisted – ! SICK!

The list of names of the reptiles who control AMC and create the rancid garbage they have the gall to call 'entertainment – reads like an invite to a Bar Mitzvah

AMC President = Charles Collier = JEW
AMC Sr VP Program head = 'Joel' Stillerman = JEW
AMC Exec Producer = Eli Holtzman = JEW
AMC Creator/Exec Producer = Craig Silverstein = JEW
AMC Producer = Melissa Bernstein = JEW
AMC producer = Barry Josephson = JEW

You will seldom if EVER see ANY JEW produce entertainment that is inspiring – touching – uplifting – clean wholesome – noble – selfless sacrificing, or exalts virtue – goodness – compassion – understanding charity – tenderness, or hope – of course – unless it is to a fellow reptile.

Tell Verizon that you told the greedy AMC jews to piss off and stay the hell off our screens! Tell Verizon NOT to cave in to jew extortion demands that their soul destroying filth continue to poison our youth. No DECENT parent needs that jew filth in their homes. There is plenty of other appealing exciting interesting educational thrilling NON-JEW PRODUCED entertainment available on the market place.

I AM a Verizon customer – and also a responsible parent grandparent – and as such we are sick to death of the endless streams of putrid rancid prurient sex and violence saturated sewer trash produced by these filthy Godless soulless reptiles. We – the decent moral customers WILL protect our children's goodness and innocence and we are asking you stand with us. Just tell AMC to 'SHOVE IT".

I didn't risk my life in the service of my nation's military elite JUST to protect us ONLY against 'foreign' enemies. My oath to God clearly included those domestic filthy reptiles who are FAR more dangerous to the safety of my family than anyone else on earth. I'm talking about you filthy jews. We are watching you.

Don't you decent people ever get tired and angry with the endless filth that these reptiles poison the minds and innocence of your children with? WAKE UP AND SMELL THE JEWS – PEOPLE!

AMC – and its demonic themes and sordid violent prurient sex charged glorification of evil and wickedness – GONE? GOOD DAMN RIDDANCE! Next time these greedy money grubbing reptiles interrupt your relaxation – be sure and tell them to take their appeal to continue their sociopathic poisons of the minds and souls of our children – grasp it firmly between their thumb and forefinger and insert it vigorously as far up their jew anal sphincters as possible. Tell em an ex Green Beret made that 'suggestion'.

NOVEMBER 2012
JEW BUCKS / STARBUCKS SUPPORTS THE KILLING OF INNOCENT CHILDREN

BOYCOTT THE WICKED JEW STARBUCKS – WITH IT'S JEW RACIST – LATTE'S FRAPPE'S AND OY VEYS!

Starbucks is an evil, wicked, jew-owned child murdering provider – like all jew companies. The owner is not surprisingly a greasy New York jew (the WORST kind of jew) demon bastard. His name is HOWARD SCHULTZ. Don't forget this name – as this son of Satan is a cold-blooded killer. Baby killer jew Schultz is EXACTLY the kind of monster that Jesus addressed in John 8-44 as a demon child of Satan. He is as remorseless and wicked as any creature spawned by Satan.

This scumbag never served his country or did ANYTHING American. His life was dedicated to being rich and to keep racial hatred alive and well as evidenced by his rancid putrid conduct. When I was training young warriors to prepare for a war against his Marxist pals in the USSR – Schultz was in second grade playing with marbles and dreidels

Like all jews – this slimy reptile from Hell will not get his hands dirty doing the actual killing – so good little racist Christ hating rat faced jew that he is – he donates a lot of money to fund the murder of innocent helpless defenseless Palestinian children as well as the murder of innocent Civilian Iraq and Afghanistan families. He is a psychotic racist monster no less evil than Kaganovitch or any of Stalin's Christian hating Godless psychopathic jew butchers who murdered millions of innocent people in the Ukraine – some of whom were my family by marriage.

All this reptile cares about is other reprobate jews. He doesn't care about Christians or Americans or what is good for America – only what is good for his "sons of Satan" jews and their rogue stolen terrorist loathsome land of reprobate criminals – recycled Stalinist commissars' – Christ haters – traitors – war mongers – imperialists – murderers – baby killers – porn kings – whores – atheists – abortionists – white slavers – racists -bigots -pedophiles – perverts and Mossad and IDF terrorists. I'm talking about the enemy of humanity – the most hated Godless unholy demonic place on earth – ISRAHELL!

I was there as an insider and saw it all. I have spent time in over thirty nations – some as a tourist some as an advisor – some as a diplomat – some as a businessman, but I have never witnessed a more thoroughly evil place than that. If any substantial proportion of moral educated American citizens could see what I have – jews would have had their evil parasite asses kicked out long ago – and we would be a united prosperous moral Godly beloved sovereign nation today.

Today – this rat faced kike butcher squeals with delight every time some yuppie Gentile fool buys a $5 dollar cup of his fancy death brew of ten cents worth of flavored hot water. He then donates part of his nearly 100% profit- to his jew terrorist IDF pals to murder more children. NO decent REAL American should even allow ANYONE so amoral or stupid enough to patronize this jew monster's rip-off death factory or support IsraHELL in ANY WAY!.

If you can imagine anything more evil and sadistic – He donates money to the terrorist IDF for their BRAVE conduct in battle with terrorizing and murdering children, pregnant women and fathers trying to protect their families. Been there seen that. This putrid jew's idea of a hero is a jew who has desecrated a church or Mosque by shitting and pissing on the walls and Holy books. Been there seen that.

He particularly admires the IDF terrorists who shoot a pregnant mother in the womb – with their "one shot two kills" jew mentality cowardly sadism. Seen that too. This rat faced racist coward REALLY gets his cookies off though when he hears that his IDF terrorist snipers have murdered a 3 year old child in his own yard – then sent in hungry dogs to eat the flesh of the child – then as the horrified parents try in vain to retrieve the body of their baby girl – they are also murdered in cold blood – as the fiendish jew ghouls laugh and celebrate their ' brave kills'. AGAIN – I WAS THERE!

Just read for yourself what hatred the LEADERS of these filthy racist Christian hating jews spew out like vomit.

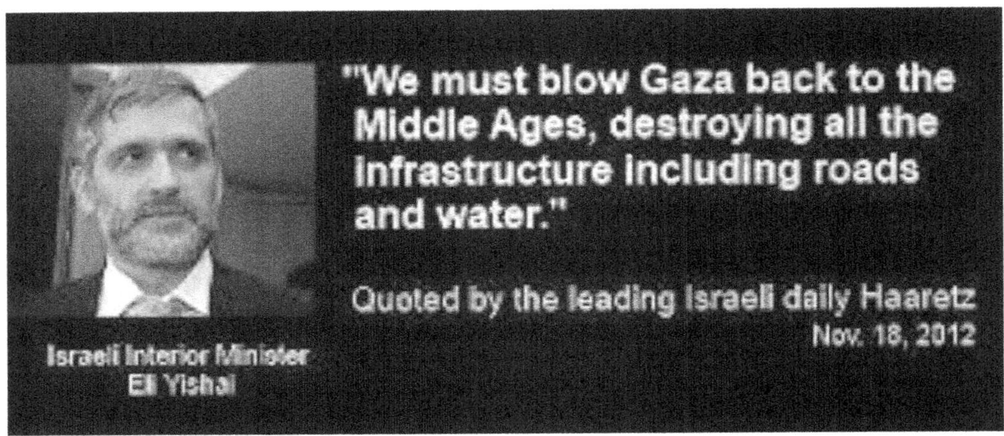

Starbucks (Jew Bucks) is the devil's own brew and it KILLS and KILLS and KILLS without mercy. These jew death financing mills are a disgrace to America and what we stand for. How in the name of God – LITERALLY – can ANY human being, patronize the jew filth and death and misery of such racist bigoted Christ hating scum.

Their so-called religion is FILLED with FORMAL DOCUMENTED hated of Christ Christians and Gentiles. The sad and disgraceful irony here is that the religion of the people who these jews spend much of their waking hours plotting how to murder – have shown the greatest respect love and tribute to Jesus and His blessed mother.

While the jews – like Mr. blood-money bucks here – blaspheme and mock our Lord in the most vicious cruel ways – call him a BASTARD who is in hell burning in a vat of boiling shit – AND trash His mother a as a WHORE. Not ONLY Is this in their 'sacred' hate filled Talmud – but you can see the same blasphemies 24-7 on their TALMUD VISION networks here in the States and in IsraHELL. Yes Dorothy – it is all true. Here are just a few of examples of what Schultz and his evil tribe members support.

Remember – ALL of the horrors were committed against a helpless defenseless people whose land that their forefathers had tilled for some thousand five hundred years was stolen by violence and murder from its rightful owners by these rabid insane mad dog criminals. So what do we BRAVE Merkans do make it right? We stand by and DO NOTHING BUT GET FATTER AND DRUNKER at our tailgate parties. THEN we add insult to injury by financing these horrors as we feel so cosmopolitan sipping our pricy Cappuccinos/Lattes after the game at JEW BUCKS!

Every over priced cup of jew snob coffee that some Christian imbecile buys at Schultz's death mill – pays for a bullet or rocket that murders a helpless defenseless innocent child or baby in Palestine. This racist bloodthirsty Zionist baby killer has close ties to IsraHELL and his hate of innocent Arab people is surpassed only by his hatred of Christians – whom he considers so much scum. He actually REWARDS IDF thugs for murdering helpless children.

When I was in IsraHELL the racist hatred was so thick it seemed to fill even the air with a stifling stench of death. Not that a Muslim child's life is worth any less in the eyes of God – but children are being murdered by these cowardly demons 24-7 as you read this – and one out of 5 of the victims are Christian.

Here are a few of the examples of the horrors that JEW-bucks coffee directly pays for. Next time you see one of these heart rending gut grinding pictures of a little child turned into bloody hamburger by these Godless filthy murdering cowardly jew scum – think HOWARD SCHULTZ and the scum who patronize his racist 'factory of death'.

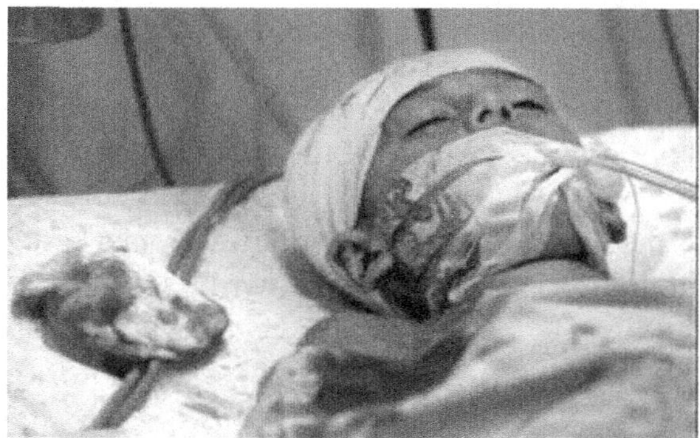

The sadistic jew Schultz has been highly praised the IsraHELL government (who murders these defenseless children by the thousands) for sponsoring pro jew terrorist anti-Palestinian seminars on college campuses all over the world. But then after all – hate lies deceit and suffering is what jews do best and have done for over a thousand years!

Even as the blood of innocent Palestinian children was soaking the ground in Jenin Nabulus Bethlehem – this rat faced JEW monster – HOWARD SCHULTZ – was screaming for even more killing as in typical jew fashion- he blamed the VICTIMS/CHILDREN for somehow being the bad guys. He called the poor defenseless Palestinians the terrorists and incited people to support these murderous animals in Israhell to continue with their genocide!

Inciting to murder thousands of innocent defenseless people – mostly children -is GENOCIDE – and that is a crime!

I am more than a little bit familiar with international terrorist terrorism and what defines a terrorist from a freedom fighter. I have hunted fought and interrogated REAL terrorists in a Latin American nation at the request of their Government so I am no stranger to the nature of the beast. I – along with many informed well experienced and educated colleagues have long ago exposed the jew IDF as the world's largest institutionalized terrorist organization.

I have been inside IsraHELL and observed these IDF thugs and what I experienced made me want to vomit. Even the jew children are taught to be filthy soulless sadistic racist hate filled demons – DISGUSTING

Next time any of your readers sip your pricy yuppie snob Frappuccino or iced Lattee' – look real close inside – and perhaps you might see some of the innocent children's blood it bought!

Now lets take a hard look at the filth that this Christ hating racist jew is involve with. Satan must be wringing his claws with delight to see 'one of his own' (John 8-44) make him so proud!

First of all – Howard Shultz, the chairman of Starbucks is a notorious active Zionist – a filthy criminal animal.

In 1998 he was honored by the Jerusalem Fund of Aish HaTorah with "The Israel 50th Anniversary Friend of Zion Tribute Award" for his services to the Zionist state in "playing a key role in promoting close alliance between the United States and IsraHELL". The Jerusalem Fund of Aish HaTorah funds IsraHELL arms fairs chaired by the butcher of Jenin – General Shaul Mofaz, and the Zionist propaganda website honest reporting.com.

His work as a propagandist for IsraHELL has been praised by the Israeli Foreign Ministry as being key to IsraHELL's long-term PR success.

At a time when other businesses were desperately pulling out of Israel, Starbucks decided to help IsraHELL's floundering economy and invest in IsraHELL – a joint venture with Israeli conglomerate Delek Group for Starbucks outlets in Israel (Shalom Coffee Co). A bad business decision – Starbucks made heavy losses and in April 2003 Starbucks were forced to announced that all 6 Starbucks cafes in IsraHELL will be shut down and its partnership with Delek end.

It has been revealed that Starbucks still continues to support IsraHELL by sponsoring fund raisers for IsraHELL. Here is the TRUE nature of the demonic symbol of hated death and Satanic worship despised the world over for its evil.

Starbucks fully supports Bush's war of terror and has opened a Starbucks in Afghanistan for the US invaders – they like to do there bit to help the occupation suffering and misery of your victims. You life is a testimony to your evil lies deceptions and evil. Here are a few of the accolades bestowed upon this demon Schultz – by the sons of the Devil.

Howard Schultz was presented with "The IsraHELL 50th Anniversary Friend of Zion Tribute Award" by the The Jerusalem Fund of Aish HaTorah in August 27, 1998.

According to the Jerusalem Fund of Aish HaTorah "The Friends of Zion award salutes leaders who have played key roles in promoting close alliance between the United States and IsraHELL"

Its interesting that the IsraHELL 50th Anniversary Award given to Howard Schultz was once displayed with pride on the Starbucks website on the company's "Awards and Accolades" page but since the boycott started biting it has mysteriously disappeared from the page.

The RACIST Jerusalem Fund of Aish HaTorah sponsors IsraHELL military arms fairs chaired by the butcher of Jenin – General Shaul Mofaz, IsraHELL's Minister of Defense. It aims to "strengthen the special connection between the American, European and IsraHELL defense industries" and "to showcase the newest IsraHELL innovations in defense".

The Jerusalem Fund of Aish HaTorah also sponsors the Zionist propaganda website "honestreporting.com".[]

The Aish HaTorah, the main beneficiary of The Jerusalem Fund of Aish HaTorah, whilst described as an apolitical international network of Jewish education centers, produces racist propaganda material for IsraHELL.

One video they produce by Rabbi Ken Spiro titled "The Islamic Connection to Jerusalem" starts "The Islamic connection begins in the 7th century, thousands of years after the original Jewish connection.." and continues to belittle Jerusalem's Islamic heritage – propaganda to justify Israeli occupation of Jerusalem. (RACISM)

Also featured on their site is "The Occupied Territories – A Primer" which denies the status of the West Bank and Gaza as "occupied" and argues that they be called "disputed territories"..(RACISM)

No wonder they were praised by RACIST ATHEIST Israeli Prime Minister Binyamin Netanyahu:

"I congratulate Aish HaTorah for what they're doing, where they're doing it, and for whom they're doing it"

"… The key to Israel's long-term PR success, Meir believes, is on the campuses of North America and Europe. Wealthy Jews like Howard Schultz, the owner of the Starbucks chain, are helping with student projects, including racist seminars held in both IsraHELL and North America, in which students hear IsraHELL racist presentations on the crisis…."

SEATTLE – Divisions within the Jewish community were on display Thursday in Seattle as Starbucks CEO Howard Schultz criticized Palestinian inaction in the Middle East while others protested the IsraHELL occupation of Palestinian lands.(RACISM)

"If you leave this synagogue tonight and go back to your home and ignore this, then shame on us," Howard Schultz told a crowded temple of Jewish Americans on Seattle's Capitol Hill.(HATRED AND RACISM)

NO MR. Racist jew bastard! The "shame" and the damnation has ALREADY been on you and you filthy tribe for two thousand years. ..and the jews answered" Let His blood be upon us and our children"

Schultz warned other Jews against sitting back and doing nothing.

DO NOTHING? Your precious jews have been responsible for the murder of over TWO HUNDRED MILLION INNOCENT CIVILIANS – MOSTLY CHRISTIAN in the past century ALONE! You want MORE?

"What is going on in the Middle East is not an isolated part of the world. The rise of anti-Semitism is at an all time high since the 1930's," he said.

NO – you devious lying murderous black hearted racist bastard. Most of us certainly do NOT hate "SEMITES". Some of the people I admire the most for their honesty character courage compassion and trustworthiness are indeed TRUE SEMITES! BUT we the decent people on the planet all despise JEWS BASTARDS LIKE YOU!

"The Palestinians aren't doing their job they're not stopping terrorism."

YOU BASTARDS are the REAL terrorist's rat-face. The poor Palestinians and I along with ALL decent freedom loving people would like nothing better than to rid the world of YOU – THE REAL TERRORISTS

While reaction inside the temple to Schultz's remarks grew from a warm reception to a standing ovation, the mood outside the temple was different.

A handful of Jews gathered there to protest the Israeli government's actions of late and their occupation of Palestinian lands.

There were similar sentiments Thursday at Seattle's Westlake center.

"We only get the side that talks about Palestinians as terrorists. As if all the civilians right now living in a state of siege and terror are terrorists and they're not," said protestor Alethea Mundy, whose younger brother is in Bethlehem doing relief work for Palestinian refugees.

She's worried about her brother, but realizes that everything is relative.

"This is what the Palestinians live with every day, two weeks is nothing for my brother," how true.

Some interesting facts about the jew vampire influence of the evil Starbucks:

Hotels you should boycott for their assistance with genocide by sponsoring the murderous Starbucks

Hyatt Hotel – Marriot Hotels – Sheraton/Starwood Hotels – all jews

Barnes & Noble bookstores = anything but 'noble'. more 'associate murderers'

Albertson's Supermarkets = "My Store" I don't think so 'my stores' do NOT help murder children!

The New York Times (jew run) VERY STRONGLY PROMOTE Starbucks murderous agenda He has been strongly supported by the criminal ADL as well as other jew support only organizations

Volumes could be written about the connections this monster has with criminal Zionist entities but this should be enough. It is all about money and more money to pay off propaganda shills and hide the fact that he is a ruthless white collar butcher who like most jew cowards uses his influence and money to cause as much pain and misery and destruction as he can It's a jew/Satan thing. Just keep the lies and killing going for his god Satan and for his ilk Satan's children.

There won't be a place hot enough in Hell to pay for the innocent blood you have on your hands. As veteran an American and a patriot – I find you very presence in this land an abomination against God and all that is Holy. When the time comes – and IT WILL – there won't be a hole deep enough or dark enough to save your miserable evil hide from the justice you have made a mockery of your entire wicked reprobate life.

You laugh at us stupid goy now – jew butcher but your time WILL come and you will be torn apart and fed to dogs by angry mobs for your crimes against God's most innocent children. Enjoy your blood money now rat -face – because the God you so cruelly devote your life to mocking will not sleep forever. Whether is will be man's justice or God's justice – you WILL BE PUNISHED FOR THE MISERY YOU HAVE CREATED.

BOYCOTT this wicked jew hangout of Christ hating child murderers and Satanic IsraHELL lovers!

*

*

Made in United States
Orlando, FL
13 April 2025